'The Palestinian refugee problem wa
Jewish or Arab. It was largely a by-p
and of the protracted, bitter fighting ᴛʜᴀᴛ ᴄʜᴀʀᴀᴄᴛᴇʀɪsᴇᴅ ᴛʜᴇ ꜰɪʀsᴛ
Israeli–Arab war; in smaller part, it was the deliberate creation of
Jewish and Arab military commanders and politicians.'

From Benny Morris's Conclusion

This book is the first full-length historical study of the birth of the
Palestinian refugee problem. Based on recently declassified Israeli,
British and American state and party political papers and on
collections of hitherto untapped private papers, it traces the stages
of the 1947–9 exodus against the backdrop of the first Arab–Israeli
war and analyses the varied causes of the flight. The Jewish and
Arab decision-making involved, on national and local levels,
military and political, is described and explained, as is the
crystallisation of Israel's decision to bar a refugee repatriation. The
exodus from Haifa and Jaffa (April–May 1948) and the expulsion
from Lydda and Ramle (July 1948), as well as the flight of the rural
communities of Upper Galilee and the northern Negev approaches
(October–November 1948) and the Israeli border-clearing
operations of November 1948 to July 1949, are described in detail.
The subsequent fate of the abandoned Arab villages, lands and
urban neighbourhoods – destruction or resettlement by Jewish
immigrants – is examined. The study looks at the international
context of the first Israeli–Arab war and the struggle, in
Washington, London and the UN, over efforts to repatriate or
resettle the refugees, ending with the talks at Lausanne which
effectively sealed the refugees' fate.

Throughout, the book attempts to describe what happened,
rather than what successive generations of Israeli and Arab
propagandists have said happened, and to analyse, on the basis of
documentation, the motives of the protagonists.

BENNY MORRIS was born and educated in Israel and received his doctorate from the University of Cambridge. He is diplomatic correspondent for *The Jerusalem Post*.

Illustration: Palestinian refugees making their way to Lebanon from Galilee in October–November 1948. (Photograph by Fred Csasznik)

Cambridge Middle East Library

The birth of the Palestinian refugee problem, 1947–1949

Cambridge Middle East Library

Also in this series

The birth of the Palestinian refugee problem, 1947–1949

BENNY MORRIS

CAMBRIDGE
UNIVERSITY PRESS

PUBLISHED BY THE PRESS SYNDICATE OF THE UNIVERSITY OF CAMBRIDGE
The Pitt Building, Trumpington Street, Cambridge CB2 1RP, United Kingdom

CAMBRIDGE UNIVERSITY PRESS
The Edinburgh Building, Cambridge CB2 2RU, UK http://www.cup.cam.ac.uk
40 West 20th Street, New York, NY 10011–4211, USA http://www.cup.org
10 Stamford Road, Oakleigh, Melbourne 3166, Australia

First published 1987
Reprinted 1988
First paperback edition 1989
Reprinted 1989, 1991, 1994, 1996, 1997, 1998

Printed in the United Kingdom at the University Press, Cambridge

British Library cataloguing in publication data
Morris, Benny
The birth of the Palestinian refugee
problem, 1947–1949.—(Cambridge Middle East
Library).
1. Palestinian Arabs—Middle East—
History—20th century   2. Refugees, Arab
—Middle East—History—20th century
I. Title
325′.21′095694   DS113.7

Library of Congress cataloging in publication data
Morris, Benny, *1948–*
The birth of the Palestinian refugee problem, 1947—
1949.
(Cambridge Middle East Library)
Bibliography.
Includes index.
1. Refugees, Arab.   2. Palestinian Arabs.
3. Israel–Arab War, 1948–1949—Refugees.   4. Jewish–Arab
relations–1917–1949.   I. Title.   II. Title: Palestinian
refugee problem, 1947–1949.   III. Series.
HV640.5.A6M67   1987   362.8′7′0899275694   87–14295

ISBN 0 521 33889 1 paperback

To the memory of my mother, Sadie, from whom I may
have inherited a way of thinking, and to my father,
Ya'akov

Contents

Acknowledgements

In writing this book, which I began in 1982, I was helped financially only by the British Council. Their grant enabled me to carry out research in British archives and, later, to give a lecture at a seminar on refugees in Oxford. I thank them. I would also like to thank Dr Roger Owen, of St Antony's College, Oxford, and Professor Yehoshua Porath, of the Hebrew University of Jerusalem, for their solicitude and help in seeing this work through. I owe them both a large debt. The Senior Associate Membership I held in St Antony's College, for which I thank the fellows and college officers, facilitated my research. I have frequently bothered with questions Ya'acov Shimoni, formerly of the Israel Foreign Ministry, and he deserves special thanks for his patience and help.

I would like to thank the staffs of the Israel State Archives (especially Yehoshua Freundlich, Yemima Rosenthal and Professor Avraham Alsberg), the Central Zionist Archives, the Hashomer Hatzair Archives, the Kibbutz Meuhad Archives, the Labour Party (Beit Berl) Archives, the Labour (Histadrut) Archives, the Jabotinsky Institute, the Ben-Gurion Archives, the Haifa Municipal Archives, the Tiberias Municipal Archives, the Mishmar Ha'emek Archive, the Kibbutz Ma'anit Archive, all in Israel; of the Public Record Office in London and St Antony's College Middle East Centre Archives in Oxford; and of the National Archives in Washington DC.

My biggest debt is to my family – my wife, Leah, and my children, Erel, Yagi and Orian – for holding up under the strain of my years' long commitment to completing this book and its entailed price in time and attention.

Abbreviations

AHC	Arab Higher Committee
ALA	Arab Liberation Army
BG, DBG	David Ben-Gurion
CP	Sir Alan Cunningham Papers, Middle East Centre Archives, St Antony's College, Oxford
CZA	Central Zionist Archives
DBG-YH	David Ben-Gurion's *Yoman Hamilhama, 1948–49* (The War Diary)
HHA	Hashomer Hatzair Archives (Mapam, Kibbutz Artzi Papers)
HHA-ACP	Hashomer Hatzair Archives, Aharon Cohen Papers
HMA	Haifa Municipal Archives
IDF	Israel Defence Forces
ISA	Israel State Archives
AM	Agriculture Ministry Papers
FM	Foreign Ministry Papers
JM	Justice Ministry Papers
MAM	Minority Affairs Ministry Papers
PMO	Prime Minister's Office Papers
IZL	*Irgun Zva'i Leumi* (National Military Organisation) or the Irgun
JEM	Jerusalem and East Mission Papers, Middle East Centre Archives, St Antony's College, Oxford
JI	Jabotinsky Institute (IZL and LHI Papers)
JNF	Jewish National Fund
KMA	Kibbutz Meuhad Archives
KMA-AZP	Kibbutz Meuhad Archives, Aharon Zisling Papers
KMA-PA	Kibbutz Meuhad Archives, Palmah Papers
LA	Labour Archives (Histadrut)
LHI	*Lohamei Herut Yisrael* (Freedom Fighters of Israel) or Stern Gang
LPA	Labour Party Archives (Mapai)

Map 1 The United Nations Partition Plan, November 1947
(Based on Martin Gilbert, *The Arab–Israeli Conflict, its History in Maps*, new edn, London, Weidenfeld & Nicolson, 1976)

Map 2 Arab settlements abandoned in 1948–9 and date and main causes of abandonment
(*Note*: The map omits a dozen or so very small or satellite villages and small bedouin tribes or sub-tribes)
(Based on *Carta's Historical Atlas of Israel, The First Years 1948–61*, ed. by Jehuda Wallach and Moshe Lissak, Jerusalem, Carta, 1978, p. 139)

Map 3 Jewish settlements established in 1948–9
(*Note*: Several of the settlements established in 1948–9 were either dismantled or collapsed. Some changed their names. Others subsequently moved from the original sites to nearby sites)
(Based on The Survey of Palestine 1946 Map with additions by the Survey Department of the State of Israel, made available by the kind permission of the Hebrew University of Jerusalem's Geography Department and Map Collection)

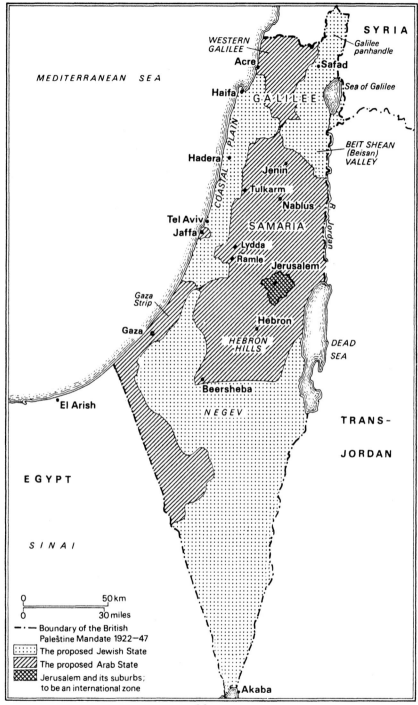

MEDITERRANEAN SEA

SYRIA

WESTERN
GALILEE

Galilee
panhandle

Acre

Safad

Haifa

GALILEE

Sea of Galilee

BEIT SHEAN
(Beisan)
VALLEY

Hadera

Jenin

Tulkarm

Nablus

Tel Aviv

SAMARIA

Jaffa

R. Jordan

Lydda

Ramle

Jerusalem

Gaza
Strip

Hebron

HEBRON
HILLS

DEAD
SEA

Gaza

Beersheba

El Arish

NEGEV

TRANS-

JORDAN

EGYPT

SINAI

0   50 km
0   30 miles

— · — Boundary of the British
        Paleštine Mandate 1922–47

The proposed Jewish State

The proposed Arab State

Jerusalem and its suburbs:
to be an international zone

Akaba

Map 1

ix

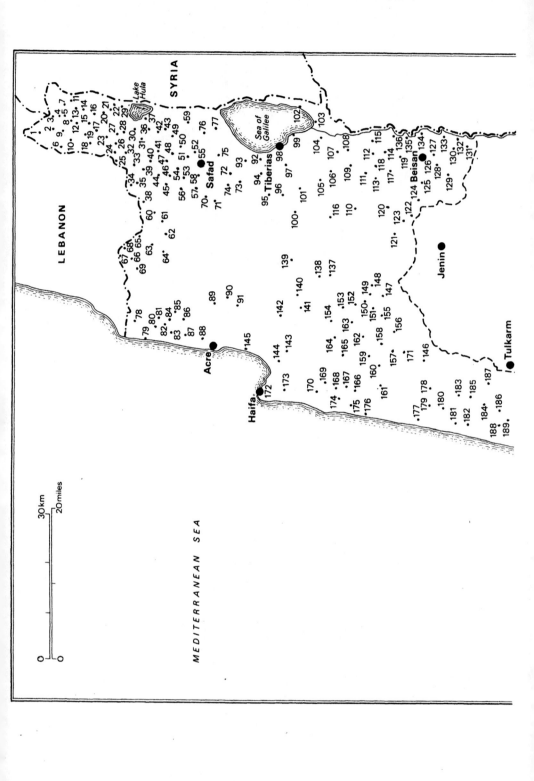

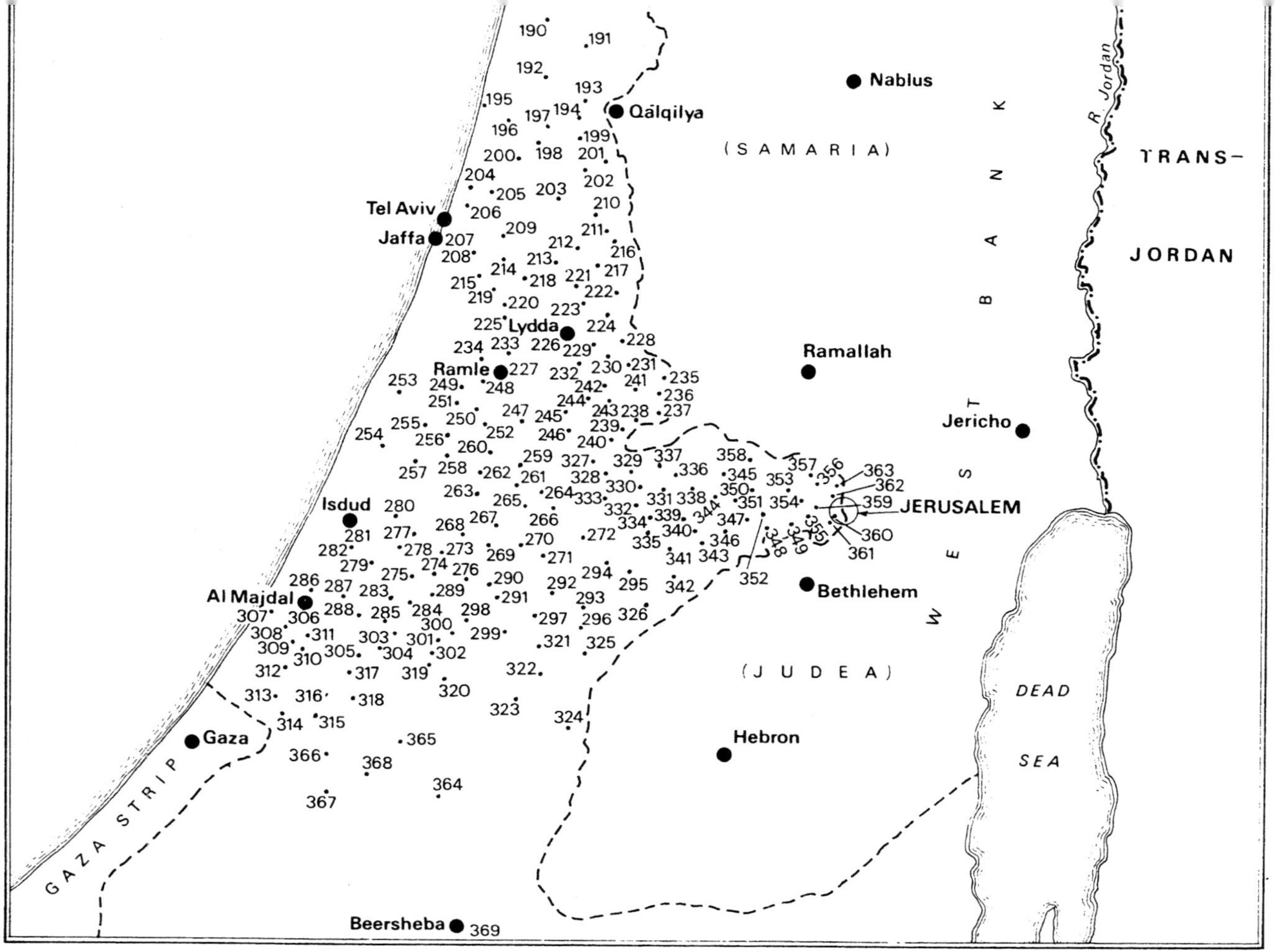
Nablus
Qalqilya
(SAMARIA)
WEST BANK
R. Jordan
TRANS-
JORDAN
Tel Aviv
Jaffa
Lydda
Ramle
Ramallah
Jericho
JERUSALEM
Bethlehem
Isdud
Al Majdal
(JUDEA)
Hebron
DEAD
SEA
Gaza
GAZA STRIP
Beersheba

Map 2

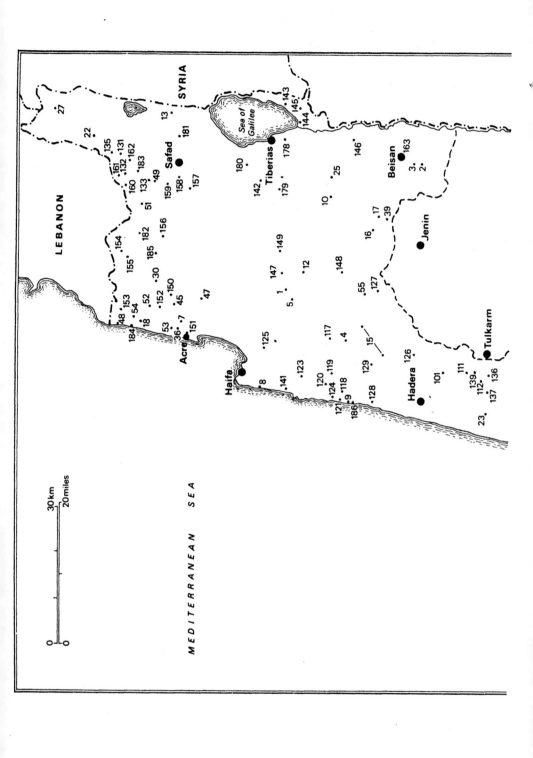

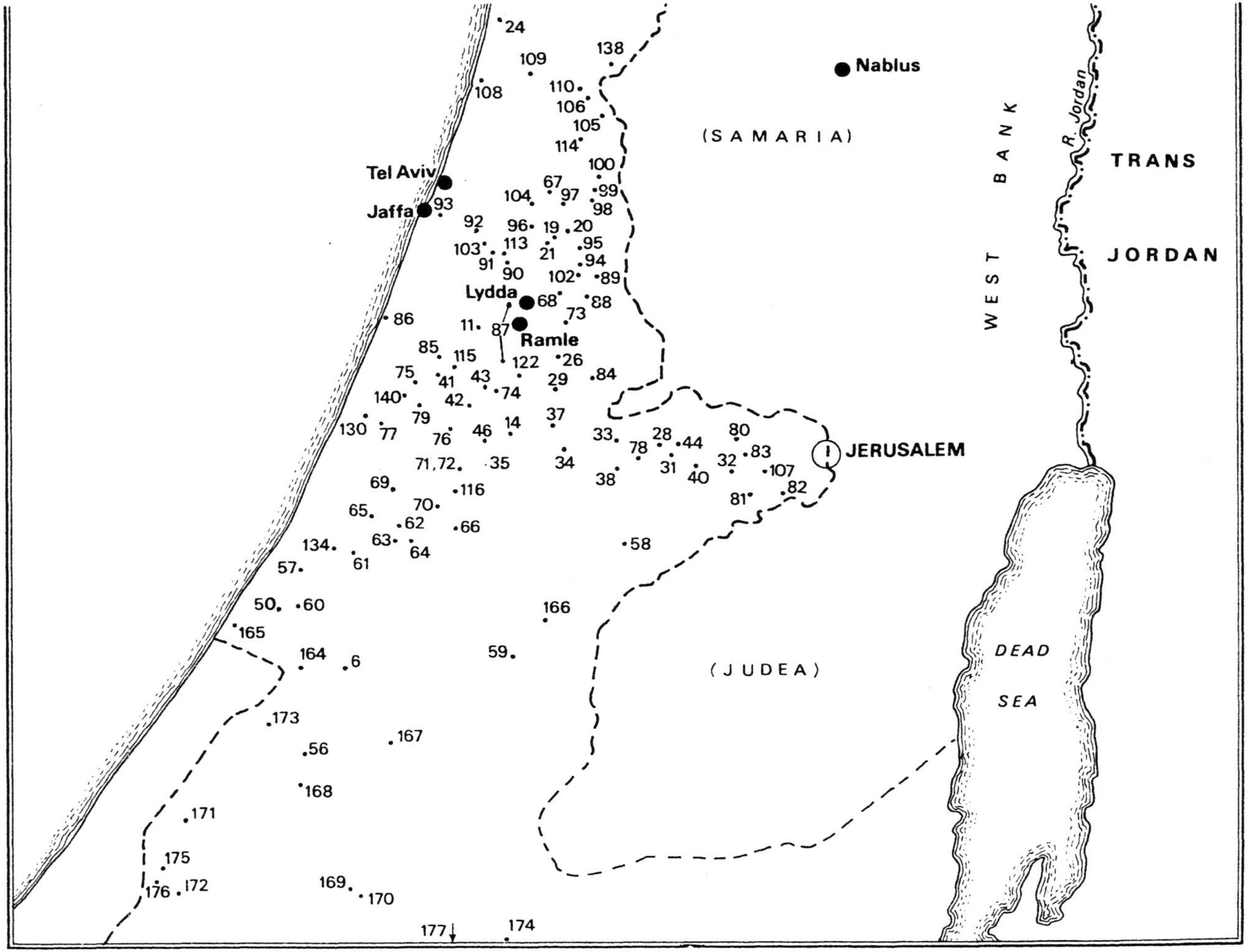

Map 3

Key to Map 2

In the Key, the following codes are used for decisive causes of abandonment:
E   Expulsion by Jewish forces
A   Abandonment on Arab orders
F   Fear of Jewish attack or of being caught up in the fighting
M   Military assault on the settlement by Jewish troops
W   Haganah/IDF "whispering" campaigns (i.e., psychological warfare geared to obtaining an Arab evacuation)
C   Influence of fall of, or exodus from, neighbouring town

The lines between C, F and M are somewhat blurred. It is often difficult to distinguish between the flight of villagers because of reports of the fall of or flight from neighbouring settlements, flight because of fears of being "next" or flight due to the approach of a Haganah/IDF column. I have generally ascribed the flight of inhabitants on the path of an Israeli military advance to M even though some of the villagers may have already taken to their heels upon hearing of the fall of a neighbouring village (which could go under C or F).

Similarly, the line between M and E is occasionally blurred.

Galilee panhandle

1 Abil al Qamh – F, C, 10 May 1948
2 Zuq al Fauqani – W, M, 21 May 1948
3 Shauqa at Tahta – F, 14 May 1948
4 As Sanbariya – May 1948 (?)
5 Khisas – W, C, 25 May 1948
6 Hunin – F, 3 May 1948
7 Al Mansura – W, 25 May 1948
8 Lazzaza – W, 21 May 1948
9 Zuq at Tahtani – C, 11 May 1948
10 Al Khalisa – C, W, 11 May 1948
11 Al Madahil – F, 30 April 1948
12 Qeitiya – W, 19 May 1948
13 Al 'Abisiya – C, 25 May 1948
14 Dawwara – W, 25 May 1948
15 As Salihiya – F, W, 25 May 1948
16 Al Muftakhira – F, 16 May 1948
17 Az Zawiya – M, 24 May 1948
18 Al Buweiziya – C, 11 May 1948
19 An Na'ima – C, 14 May 1948
20 Al Hamra – F, M, 1 May 1948
21 Ghuraba – F, 28 May 1948
22 Khirbet Khiyam al Walid – F, 1 May 1948
23 Jahula – May 1948 (?)
24 Qadas – C, 28 May 1948
25 Al Malikiya – M, 28 May 1948
26 Nabi Yusha – M, 16 May 1948
27 Beisamun – W, 25 May 1948
28 Mallaha – W, 25 May 1948
29 Ad Darbashiya – May 1948 (?)

Upper Galilee

30 Al 'Ulmaniya – M, 20 April 1948
31 'Arab Zubeid – F, 20 April 1948
32 Deishum – M, 30 October 1948
33 'Alma – M, 30 October 1948
34 Saliha – M, 30 October 1948
35 Fara – M, 30 October 1948
36 Al Huseiniya – C, 21 April 1948
37 Tuleil – late April 1948 (?)
38 Kafr Bir'im – E, early November 1948
39 Ras al Ahmar – M, 30 October 1948
40 Dallata – not known
41 Marus – C, 26 May 1948 and M, 30 October 1948
42 Kirad al Ghannama – C, 22 April 1948 (later resettled and abandoned)
43 Kirad al Baqqara – C, 22 April 1948 (later resettled and abandoned)
44 Teitaba – May 1948 (?)
45 Safsaf – M/E, 29 October 1948
46 Qaddita – C, 11 May 1948
47 Ammuqa – M, 24 May 1948
48 Qabba'a – M, 26 May 1948
49 Weiziya – May 1948 (?)
50 Mughr al Kheit – M, 2 May 1948
51 Fir'im – M, 26 May 1948
52 Ja'una – C, 9 May 1948
53 'Ein az Zeitun – M, 2 May 1948
54 Biriya – M, 2 May 1948
55 (Arab) Safad – M, 10–11 May 1948
56 Meirun – (?) C, (?) 10–12 May 1948

57 Sammu'i – C, 12 May 1948
58 Dhahiriya Tahta – C, 10 May 1948
59 Mansurat al Kheit – M, 18 January
1948
60 Sa'sa – M/E, 30 October 1948
61 Ghabbatiya – (?), 30 October 1948
62 Sabalan – (?), 30 October 1948
63 Deir al Qasi – M, 30 October 1948
64 Suhmata – M, 30 October 1948
65 Al Mansura – E, early November
1948
66 Tarbikha – E, early November 1948
67 Suruh – E, early November 1948
68 Nabi Rubin – E, early November
1948
69 Iqrit – E, early November 1948
70 Farradiya – E, February 1949
71 Kafr I'nan – E, February 1949
72 Ash Shuna – Not known
73 Yaquq – May 1948 (?)
74 Al Qudeiriya – M/E, 4 May 1948
75 'Arab as Suyyad – (?) M/E, 4 May
1948
76 Zanghariya – M/E, 4 May 1948
77 'Arab ash Shamalina – M/E, 4 May
1948

Western Galilee

78 Al Bassa – M/E, 14 May 1948
79 Az Zib – M, 14 May 1948
80 At Tell – M, 21 May 1948
81 Al Kabri – F, M, 5, 21 May 1948
82 An Nahr – M, 21 May 1948
83 Umm al Faraj – M, 21 May 1948
84 Al Ghabisiya – E, May 1948; E, 1949
85 Amqa – M, 10–11 July 1948
86 Kuweikat – M, 10 July 1948
87 As Sumeiriya – M, 14 May 1948
88 Manshiya – M, 14 May 1948
89 Al Birwa – M, 11 June 1948 (?)
90 Ad Damun – M, 15–16 July 1948
91 Ar Ruweis – M, 15–16 July 1948

*Lower Galilee, Jordan, Jezreel and Beit
Shean valleys*

92 Majdal – M, C, 22 April 1948
93 Ghuweir Abu Shusha – C, 21 and 28
April 1948
94 Hittin – F, M, 16–17 July 1948
95 Nimrin – (?) F, M, 16–17 July 1948
96 Lubiya – F, M, 16–17 July 1948

97 Khirbet Nasir ad Din – M, C, F, 12
and 23 April 1948
98 (Arab) Tiberias – M, 18 April 1948
99 Khirbet al Manara – M, early March
1948
100 Ash Shajara – M, 6 May 1948
101 Kafr Sabt – C, 22 April 1948
102 As Samra – C, 21 April 1948
103 Samakh – M, 28 April 1948
104 Al 'Ubeidiya – F, 5 March 1948
105 Ma'dhar – A, 6 April 1948
106 Hadatha – A, 6 April 1948
107 'Ulam – A, 6 April 1948
108 Sirin – A, 6 April 1948
109 At Tira – W, 15 April 1948
110 Indur – C, M, 24 May 1948
111 Danna – E, 28 May 1948
112 Al Bira – C, 16 May 1948
113 Yubla – C, 16 May 1948
114 Jabbul – C/F, 18 May 1948
115 Kaukab al Hawa – M, 16 May 1948
116 'Arab as Subeih – C, 19 April 1948
117 Al Murassas – C, 16 May 1948
118 Kafra – C, 16 May 1948
119 Al Hamidiya – C, 12 May 1948
120 Qumiya – F, 26 March 1948
121 Zir'in – M, 28 May 1948
122 Al Mazar – M, 30 May 1948
123 Nuris – M/E, 29–30 May 1948
124 Khirbet al Jaufa – (?) C, 12 May 1948
125 Tall ash Shauk – (?) C, 12 May 1948
126 Beisan – M, C, 12 May 1948
127 Al Ashrafiya – (?) C, 12 May 1948
128 Farwana – M, 11 May 1948
129 As Samiriya – M, 27 May 1948
130 Al 'Arida – C, 20 May 1948
131 'Arab al Khuneizir – C, 20 May 1948
132 'Arab al Safa – C, 20 May 1948
133 'Arab az Zarra'a – (?) C, 20 May 1948
134 'Arab al Ghazawiya – (?) C, 20 May
1948
135 'Arab al Bawati – (?) C, 16 or 20 May
1948
136 'Arab al Bashatwi – C, 16 May 1948
137 Al Mujeidil – M, 15 July 1948
138 Ma'lul – M, 15 July 1948
139 Saffuriya – M, 16 July 1948
140 Beit Lahm – M, April 1948
141 Waldheim (Umm al 'Amad) – M,
April 1948
142 Khirbet Ras 'Ali – Not known
143 Yajur – M, C, 25 April 1948
144 Balad ash Sheikh – M, C, 25 April
1948
145 'Arab Ghawarina – (?) W, M, mid-
April 1948

*Hills of Ephraim (Ramot Menashe) and
Mishmar Ha'emek area*

146 Wadi 'Ara – F, 27 February 1948
147 Lajjun – M, 30 May 1948 (?)
148 Al Mansi ('Arab Baniha) – M, 12–13
   April 1948
149 An Naghnaghiya – M, 12–13 April
   1948
150 Ghubaiya al Fauqa – M, 8–9 April
   1948
151 Ghubaiya al Tahta – M, 8–9 April
   1948
152 Abu Shusha – M, 9–10 April 1948
153 Abu Zureiq – M, 12–13 April 1948
154 Qira wa Qamun – W, (?) late March
   1948
155 Al Kafrin – M, 12–13 April 1948
156 Al Buteimat – F, (?) May 1948
157 Umm ash Shauf – M, 12–14 May
   1948
158 Khubbeiza – M, 12–14 May 1948
159 Sabbarin – M, 12–14 May 1948
160 As Sindiyana – M, 12–14 May 1948
161 Bureika – C, 5 May 1948
162 Daliyat ar Ruha – W/M, late March
   1948
163 Ar Rihaniya – Not known
164 Umm az Zinat – Not known
165 Khirbet Qumbaza – May 1948 (?)
166 'Ein Ghazal – M, 24–26 July 1948
167 Ijzim – M, 24–26 July 1948
168 Jaba – M, 24–26 July 1948
169 Al Mazar – c.15 July 1948
170 'Ein Haud – c.15 July 1948
171 Qannir – C, F, 25 April 1948

Northern Coastal Plain

172 (Arab) Haifa – M, A, 21 April–1 May
   1948
173 At Tira – M, 16 July 1948
174 As Sarafand – M, c.16 July 1948
175 Kafr Lam – M, c.16 July 1948
176 Tantura – M/E, 21 May 1948
177 Qisariya – E, 15 February 1948
178 Khirbet as Sarkas – E, 15 April 1948
179 Ad Dumeira – E, 10 April 1948
180 'Arab al Fuqara – E, 10 April 1948
181 'Arab an Nufeiat – E, 10 April 1948
182 Wadi al Hawarith – M, F, 15 March
   1948
183 Raml Zeita – Not known

184 Khirbet Manshiya – F, 15 April 1948
185 Khirbet Zalafa – F, 15 April 1948
186 Wadi Qabbani – Not known
187 Qaqun – M, 5 June 1948
188 Umm Khalid – Not known
189 Khirbet Beit Lid – F, 5 April 1948
190 Birket Ramadan – Not known
191 Miska – E, 15 April 1948
192 Tabsar (Khirbet 'Azzun) – F, E, 3
   April 1948
193 Kafr Saba – M, 15 May 1948
194 Biyar 'Adas – M, 12 April 1948
195 Al Haram (Sidna 'Ali) – F, 3
   February 1948
196 Jalil – F, 3 April 1948
197 'Arab Abu Kishk – F, C, 30 March
   1948
198 'Arab as Sawalima – F, C, 30 March
   1948
199 Al Mirr – F, February 1948
200 Sheikh Muwannis – M/F, 30 March
   1948
201 Ras al 'Ein – M, 13 July 1948
202 Majdal Yaba – M, 13 July 1948
203 Fajja – W, 15 May 1948
204 Jammasin – F, 17 March 1948
205 Al Mas'udiya (Summeil) – F, 25
   December 1947
206 Sarona – Not known
207 Jaffa – M, late April–early May 1948

*Lower Coastal Plain and northern Negev
approaches*

208 Salama – M, 25 April 1948
209 Al Kheiriya – M, 25 April 1948
210 Al Muzeiri'a – Not known
211 Qula – M, 10 July 1948
212 Rantiya – M, 28 April 1948; M, 10
   July 1948
213 Al Yahudiya – M, 4 May 1948
214 Saqiya – M, 25 April 1948
215 Yazur – C, M, 1 May 1948
216 At Tira – M, 10 July 1948
217 Wilhelma – M, 10 July 1948
218 Kafr 'Ana – M, 25 April 1948
219 Beit Dajan – C, 25 April 1948
220 As Safiriya – Not known
221 Deir Tarif – M, 10 July 1948
222 Beit Nabala – A, 13 May 1948
223 Jindas – Not known
224 Al Haditha – M, 12 July 1948
225 Sarafand al 'Amar – Not known

325 Deir Nakh-khas – M, 29 October
1948
326 Khirbet Umm Burj – Not known

Jerusalem corridor

327 Deir Muheisin – M, 6 April 1948
328 Beit Jiz – M, 20 April 1948
329 Beit Susin – M, 20 April 1948
330 'Islin – M, 18 July 1948
331 Ishwa – M, 18 July 1948
332 Sar'a – M, 18 July 1948
333 Deir Rafat – M, 18 July 1948
334 'Artuf – M, 18 July 1948
335 Deiraban – M, 19–20 October 1948
336 Beit Mahsir – M, 10–11 May 1948
337 Deir Ayub – M, April 1948
338 Kasla – M, 17–18 July 1948
339 Deir al Hawa – M, 19–20 October
1948
340 Sufla – M, 19–20 October 1948
341 Jarash – M, 21 October 1948
342 Beit Nattif – M, 21 October 1948
343 Beit 'Itab – M, 21 October 1948
344 Beit Umm al Meis – (?) M, 21
October 1948
345 Saris – M, 16–17 April 1948
346 Allar – M, 22 October 1948
347 Ras Abu 'Ammar – M, 21 October
1948

348 Al Qabu – M, 22–23 October 1948
349 Al Walaja – M, 21 October 1948
350 Khirbet al 'Umur – (?) M, 21
October 1948
351 Deir ash Sheikh – (?) M, 21 October
1948
352 'Aqqur – M, 13–14 July 1948
353 Suba – M, 13 July 1948
354 Sataf – M, 13–14 July 1948
355 Al Jura – Not known
356 Al Qastal – M, 3 April 1948
357 Beit Naqquba – M, early April 1948
358 Beit Thul – Not known
359 Qaluniya – M, 3 April 1948
360 'Ein Karim – C, 10 and 21 April
1948; M, 16 July 1948
361 Al Maliha – C, 21 April 1948; M, 15
July 1948
362 Deir Yassin – M/E, 9–10 April 1948
363 Lifta – M, January 1948

Negev

364 Jammama – M, 22 May 1948
365 'Arab al Jubarat – Not known
366 Huj – E, 31 May 1948
367 Al Muharraqa – M, 25 May 1948
368 Kaufakha – M, 25 May 1948
369 Beersheba – M/E, 21 October 1948

Key to Map 3

The Hebrew name of the settlement is given first, followed by the former Arab name of
the site or nearest site and the date of the settlement's establishment.

1 Beith Lehem Hag'lilit – Beit Lahm –
April 1948
2 Sheluhot – Al Ashrafiya – June 1948
3 Reshafim – Al Ashrafiya – June 1948
4 Ramot-Menashe – Daliyat ar Ruha –
July 1948
5 Bama'avak (Ma'avak, Alonei Abba) –
Waldheim – May 1948
6 Brur Hayil – Bureir – May 1948
7 Shomrat – south of As Sumeiriya –
May 1948
8 Hahotrim – north of At Tira – June
1948

9 Nahsholim – Tantura – June 1948
10 Ein Dor – Kafr Misr – June 1948
11 Netzer (Sereni) – Bir Salim – June
1948
12 Timurim (Shimron) – Ma'lul – June
1948
13 Habonim (Kfar Hanassi) – Mansurat
al Kheit – July 1948
14 Yesodot – Umm Khalka – July 1948
15 Regavim – Buteimat (July 1948),
moved to Qannir – 1949
16 Yizra'el – Zir'in – August 1948
17 Gilbo'a – Zir'in – July 1948

96 Yehud – Al Yahudiya – 1948
97 Rantiya – Rantiya – 1949
98 Mazor – Al Muzeiri'a – 1949
99 Nahshonim – Majdal Yaba – 1949
100 Migdal-Yaffo – Majdal Yaba – 1949
101 Lehavot Haviva – west of Jatt – 1949
102 Kfar Truman – west Beit Nabala – 1949
103 Mishmar Hashiv'a – Beit Dajan – 1949
104 Magshimim – west of Rantiya – 1949
105 Yarhiv – east of Jaljuliya – 1949
106 Hak'ramim – Kafr Saba – 1949
107 Ein Kerem – 'Ein Karim – 1949
108 Reshef – Al Haram (Sidna Ali) – 1949
109 Tabsar (Khirbet Azzun) – 1949
110 Neve-Yamin – south of Kafr Saba – 1949
111 Ometz – Qaqun – 1949
112 Olesh – south of Qaqun – 1949
113 Sharir – As Safiriya – 1949
114 Hagor – south of Jaljuliya – 1949
115 Zarnuqa – Zarnuqa – 1949
116 Talmei Yehiel – Masmiya al Kabira/ Qastina – 1949
117 Elyakim – Umm az Zinat – 1949
118 Ein Ayala – 'Ein Ghazal – 1949
119 Kerem Maharal – Ijzim – 1949
120 Geva-Carmel – Jaba – 1949
121 Habonim – Kafr Lam – 1949
122 Ramot Meir – west of Na'ana – 1949
123 Ein Hod – 'Ein Haud – 1949
124 Tsrufa – As Sarafand – 1949
125 Tel Hanan – Balad ash Sheikh – 1949
126 Barka'i – Wadi 'Ara – 1949
127 Giv'at Oz – Zalafa – 1949
128 Ma'agan Micha'el – Kabara – 1949
129 Alona (Amikam) – As Sindiyana – 1949–50
130 Nir Galim – 'Arab Sukreir – 1949
131 Dishon – Deishum – date uncertain but possibly 1949 (re-established 1953)
132 Porat – Fara – 1949
133 Shahar – near Safsaf – 1949
134 Nir Yisrael – west of Julis – 1949
135 Malkiya – Al Malikiya – 1949
136 Be'erotayim – Khirbet Burin – 1949
137 Burgta – Khirbet al Burj – 1949
138 Eyal – Khirbet Hanuta – 1949
139 Gan Yoshiya – south of Qaqun – 1949
140 Beit Gamliel – southeast of Yibna – 1949
141 Megadim – Bir Badawiya – 1949

142 Lavi – Lubiya – 1949
143 Ha'on – As Samra – 1949
144 Ma'agan – Samakh – 1949
145 Beit Katzir (Tel Katzir) – east of Samakh – 1949
146 Bashatwa (Neve-Ur) – Al Bashatiwa – 1949
147 Hasolelim – west of Saffuriya – 1949
148 Hayogev – Khirbet Beit Lid al Awadim – 1949
149 Tsipori – Saffuriya – 1949
150 Amqa – 'Amqa – 1949
151 Hayotzrim – Manshiya – 1949
152 Ben-Ami – An Nahr – 1949
153 Betset (Shlomi) – Al Bassa – 1949–50
154 Shomera – Tarbikha – 1949
155 Yoqrat – Iqrit – 1949
156 Hossen – Sukhmata – 1949
157 Farod – Farradiya – 1949
158 Kfar Shamai – Sammu'i – 1949
159 Meiron – Meirun – 1949
160 Bar'am – Kafr Bir'im – 1949
161 Nir-On (Yiron) – Saliha – 1949–50
162 Alma – Alma – 1949
163 Beit She'an – Beisan – 1948
164 Erez – Dimra/Najd – 1949
165 Zikkim – Hirbiya – 1949
166 Beit Guvrin – Beit Jibrin – 1949
167 Beit Kama – southeast of Jammama – 1949
168 Beit Hagadi – south of Al Muharraqa – 1949
169 Gilat – 'Arab al Qudeirat – 1949
170 Tifrah – northeast of Khirbet Umm al Khrum – 1949
171 Beit Re'im – 'Arab al Hanajira – 1949
172 Magen – Sheikh Nuran – 1949
173 Mefalsim – southeast of Beit Hanun – 1949
174 Omer – east of Khirbet 'Amra – 1949
175 Ein Hash'losha – east of Khan Yunis – 1949
176 Nirim – east of Khan Yunis – 1949
177 Mash'a'bei Sadeh – east of Bir Asluj – 1949
178 Poriya – south of Tiberias – 1949
179 Sdeh Ilan – Kafr Sabt – 1949
180 Arbel – Khirbet Irbid – 1949
181 Elifelet – 'Arab Zanghariya – 1949
182 Alkosh – Deir al Qasi – 1949
183 Kerem Ben-Zimra – Ras al Ahmar – 1949
184 Tzahal – north of Az Zib – 1949
185 Me'una – Tarshiha – 1949
186 Doar – Tantura – 1949

Introduction

This study sets out to describe the birth of the Palestinian refugee problem which, along with the establishment of the State of Israel, was the major political consequence of the 1948 war. It will examine how and why, over December 1947 to September 1949, some 600,000–760,000 Palestinian Arabs became refugees and why they remained refugees in the immediate post-war period.

The Palestinian refugee problem and its consequences have shaken the Middle East and acutely troubled the world for the past four decades. The question of what caused the refugees to become refugees has been a fundamental propaganda issue between Israel and the Arab states for just as long. The general Arab claim, that the Jews expelled Palestine's Arabs, with predetermination and preplanning, as part of a grand political–military design, has served to underline the Arab portrayal of Israel as a vicious, immoral robber state. The Israeli official version, that the Arabs fled voluntarily (not under Jewish compulsion) and/or that they were asked/ordered to do so by their Palestinian and Arab states' leaders, helped leave intact the new state's untarnished image as the haven of a much-persecuted people, a body politic more just, moral and deserving of the West's sympathy and help than the surrounding sea of reactionary, semi-feudal, dictatorial Arab societies.

The recent declassification and opening of most Israeli state and private political papers from 1947 to 1949 and the concurrent opening of state papers in Britain (which governed Palestine until May 1948) and in the United States (which from the summer of 1948 became increasingly involved in the refugee problem) has made possible the writing of a history of what happened on the basis of a large body of primary, contemporary source material.

The continued unavailability of Arab state papers from 1947 to 1949 necessarily leaves the historian burdened by a major problem. The Palestinian Arabs, who were highly disorganised and failed to put together a state apparatus, produced no state papers to speak of. The Arab states have always refused to open their papers on the 1948 war – which they regarded as a humiliating catastrophe – to historians, either Arab or non-Arab. I have done my best to reduce the "area of darkness" thus created by integrating the Arab "side" through culling heavily from Jewish and Israeli intelligence reports and from British and American diplomatic dispatches dealing with the Arab world and, specifically, with aspects of the evolving refugee problem. The intelligence and diplomatic reports, as shall be seen, go a long way towards filling out the picture of what was happening in the field, in the Arab towns and villages in Palestine, during 1948. They are less enlightening, with important exceptions, about policy-making in the Arab capitals and military headquarters. But, as shall be seen, this relative paucity of information is not as important as it might have been, because the disarray, confusion and general absence of clear policy in the Arab capitals concerning the emerging refugee problem over the crucial period between December 1947 and June 1948 meant that in any case there was very little connection between what was happening in the field and what was discussed and even decided by the Arab leaders.

Where necessary, however, I have used some contemporary Arab memoirs and diaries, and some books based on interviews with contemporaries, to round out the picture. The reader will have to judge whether the ultimate product takes sufficient account of the Arab perspectives, and whether the result, taken as a whole, is comprehensive, credible and convincing.

After careful and long thought, I decided to refrain almost completely from using interviews, with Jews or Arabs, as sources of information. I was brought up believing in the value of documents. While contemporary documents may misinform, distort, omit or lie, they do so, in my experience, far more rarely than interviewees recalling highly controversial events some 40 years ago. My limited experience with such interviews revealed enormous gaps of memory, the ravages of aging and time, and terrible distortions or selectivity, the ravages of accepted wisdom, prejudice and political beliefs and interests. I have found interviews of use in obtaining "colour" and a picture of the prevailing conditions. Only very, very rarely have I relied on oral history to establish facts.

The Arab exodus from the Jewish-held parts of Palestine occurred over a space of 20 months, from December 1947 to July 1949, and in the course of a war marked by radically shifting circumstances and conditions in the various areas of the country. The exodus of the rich from Jaffa and Haifa over December 1947 to January 1948 was vastly different from the mass flight of the inhabitants of Haifa and Jaffa in April and early May 1948; the flight from Haifa was markedly different from that from Jaffa; and both had little in common with the expulsion and flight from Lydda and Ramle in July or from Eilabun, Ad Dawayima and Kafr Bir'im in October–November 1948. To describe and explain the exodus I have had to describe and explain events and circumstances during the war's various stages and in the different areas. Where necessary, I have gone into considerable detail.

The study generally proceeds chronologically, from the United Nations General Assembly Partition resolution of 29 November 1947 to the collapse of the Lausanne conference in September 1949 and, in examining the exodus from various areas, is, in parts, constructed geographically. But the chronological–geographical narrative and flow is interrupted by horizontal chapters dealing with specific subjects through the 1947–9 period.

It cannot be stressed too strongly that, while this is not a military history, the events it describes – cumulatively amounting to the Palestinian Arab exodus – occurred in wartime and were a product, direct and indirect, of that war. Throughout, when examining what happened in each area at different points in the war, the reader must recall the nature of the backdrop – the continuing clash of arms between Palestinian militiamen and, later, regular Arab armies and the Yishuv (the collective term for the Jewish community in Palestine before and during 1948); the intention of the Palestinian leadership and irregulars and, later, of most of the Arab states' leaders and armies in launching the hostilities in November–December 1947 and the May 1948 invasion to destroy the Jewish state and possibly also the Yishuv; the fears of the Yishuv that the Palestinians and the Arab states, if given the chance, intended to re-enact a Middle Eastern version of the Holocaust (a bare three years after the horrendous European version had ended); and the extremely small dimensions (geographical and numerical) of the Yishuv in comparison with the Palestine Arab community and the infinitely larger surrounding Arab hinterland. At the same time, it is well to recall that, from July 1948, it was clear to the Yishuv (and to the Arab leaders) that Israel had won its war for survival, at least in the short term, and that the subsequent Israel Defence Forces' offensives were geared to securing the political–military future of the Jewish state in what continued to be a hostile geopolitical environment and to rounding out its borders.

Chapter 1

Background

A brief history

Modern Zionism began with the prophetic–programmatic writings of Moses Hess, Judah Alkalai, Zvi Hirsch Kalischer and Theodore Herzl and the immigration from Russia to Ottoman-ruled Palestine in the 1880s of Jews dedicated to rebuilding a national home for the Jewish people on their ancient land. The immigrants were impelled both by the positive ideal and by the negative experience of oppression in Eastern Europe.

In the first years of the twentieth century, with the spread of the spirit of nationalism to the colonial world, Syrian, Lebanese and Palestinian Arab intellectuals began to propound the idea of liberation from the Ottoman yoke and the establishment of an independent Arab state. At the same time, with the spread of Jewish settlement in Palestine, friction developed in various localities between neighbouring Arab and Jewish communities. The highly conservative Arab villagers resented the advent of foreign elements and may have begun to fear trespass, encroachment and perhaps even displacement.

World War I radically changed Palestinian history. The idea of national self-determination, trumpeted by the victors, fired the imagination of the educated throughout the colonial world; Britain, in 1917, committed itself in the Balfour Declaration to helping establish a "National Home for the Jewish People" in Palestine while promising to safeguard "the civil and religious rights" of the existing Arab inhabitants, and conquered Palestine from the Turks. In the post-war years Britain accepted a Mandate from the League of Nations to rule Palestine while preparing its inhabitants for self-government.

Post-war troubles in Eastern Europe and the attractions of good British administration prompted new waves of Jewish immigration to Palestine. The contradiction between Britain's dual commitment to fostering Jewish self-determination and to safeguarding Arab rights soon became apparent, and the inevitability of the clash between Jewish and Arab national aspirations became manifest.

The Palestinian Arab nationalist "awakening" was slow but steady. Two political camps emerged over the 1920s and 1930s. One, headed by the Husayni family, posited the end of the Mandate and the establishment of an Arab state in all of Palestine, with civil and religious rights for the Jews already in the country and a cessation of immigration in the future. A more moderate camp, usually called the Opposition and led by the Nashashibi family, was agreeable, at least in the 1930s, to a compromise, even one based on Partition. But the Husaynis generally set the tone of Palestinian Arab attitudes and in the mid-1930s won the struggle for the Arab masses.[1]

In the Yishuv the moderate, Labour camp, led by David Ben-Gurion and his Mapai party (*Mifleget Poalei Eretz Yisrael*, the Land of Israel workers party), dominated the political arena, with the right-wing Revisionists (who sought Jewish sovereignty over all of Palestine *and* Transjordan) never capturing more than a minority of Yishuv votes. Ben-Gurion, a pragmatist, was generally willing to accept Partition and the establishment of a Jewish state in part of the country, although throughout he remained committed to a vision of Jewish sovereignty over all of Palestine as the ultimate goal of Zionism.

Anti-Jewish Arab riots and pogroms in the towns of Palestine in 1920–1 and 1929 demonstrated the growing hatred of the Palestinian masses – egged on by a mixture of real and imagined religious and nationalist grievances, and preaching – for the Zionist presence. Arab fears of displacement, heightened by the mass Jewish immigration from Europe of the mid-1930s (sparked by the rise of Nazism) and the Jewish land purchases for new settlement, and a sense that violence would turn the British around, led to the 1936 general strike and the 1936–9 Arab revolt.

The strike and revolt, directed in the first instance against the British and, secondly, against what were seen as their Zionist wards, spread from the towns to the countryside, and won for the Husaynis and their allies the unchallenged leadership of the national movement. In the course of the revolt, which was eventually firmly suppressed by the British military, the Opposition, which in 1938–9 had collaborated with the British in crushing the revolt, expired as a major political force.

The revolt, though crushed, persuaded Whitehall, beset as it was by the imminent prospect of multi-front world war against Germany, Japan and Italy, of the advisability of maintaining tranquillity in the Middle East. The British therefore dispatched to Palestine the Peel Commission, which in 1937 proposed the partition of the country into two states, one Jewish (comprising the Galilee and the Coastal Plain), and the other Arab, with a strip comprising Jerusalem and Jaffa to remain British. The Yishuv was divided, but the Arab Higher Committee (AHC) opposed the plan. The

5

British abandoned the proposal. Quiet was to be had through appeasing the Arabs. The 1939 White Paper severely curbed Jewish immigration, blocking off a major escape route for Europe's Jews, who were about to fall victim to the Nazi extermination machine, and almost stopped altogether Jewish land purchases in the country. But Hitler's continuing destruction of European Jewry added urgency, momentum and political thrust to the Zionist aim of immediate Jewish statehood. For the first time, the movement forthrightly declared that nothing less than full, independent Jewish statehood was its goal (the Biltmore Programme, May 1942).

With the Arab nationalists weakened by the abortive revolt and their leaders in exile or in jail, the war years served as a pause in which both communities rested and readied for the battle which all thought imminent. The Yishuv prepared efficiently; Palestine's Arabs preferred to trust in salvation by the Arab states.

The trauma of the revolt and Arab terrorism, the upsurge of anti-British Jewish terrorism by the *Irgun Zvai Leumi* (IZL) and *Lohamei Herut Yisrael* (LHI), the morally and politically embarrassing efforts by Britain to bar illegal Jewish immigration and the moral-political pressure exercised by the Holocaust and by the growing, pro-Zionist American involvement, persuaded Whitehall that withdrawal from Palestine was the better part of valour, and dumped the matter in the lap of the United Nations.

The United Nations' Special Committee on Palestine (UNSCOP) recommended a solution based on Partition and, on 29 November 1947, the United Nations General Assembly, by a vote of 33 to 13 (10 members abstaining), endorsed the recommendation to partition Palestine into two states, with Jerusalem and Bethlehem constituting a neutral international enclave. The Yishuv greeted the resolution with joy and immediately announced the acceptance of its terms; the Palestinian Arab leaders, headed by the exiled AHC chief and Grand Mufti of Jerusalem, Hajj Amin al Husayni, rejected Partition and launched a three-day general strike, accompanied by a wave of anti-Jewish terrorism in the cities and on the roads. Within weeks it became clear that the country was sliding into full-scale war. The British, generally adopting a neutral stand of non-interference between the belligerents, announced that they would terminate the Mandate and withdraw by 15 May 1948. While initially at least intending an orderly transfer of power, their actions over December 1947 to May 1948 remained primarily geared to assuring that their withdrawal would run as smoothly and as costlessly as possible. Inevitably, both Jews and Arabs accused them, in successive episodes, of partiality toward the other side.

Between December 1947 and mid-May 1948 the Palestine conflict was an admixture of civil and guerrilla warfare between the two highly intermingled communities. There were mixed neighbourhoods (in Jerusalem); there were patchworks of Arab and Jewish neighbourhoods (in Jerusalem and Haifa); and in each rural district and along almost every road there was an interspersing of Arab and Jewish villages. Each side could with ease cut off and besiege the other's towns, villages and outposts. In January–March 1948 the Arabs were reinforced by small contingents of volunteers from the neighbouring Arab states; the Jews received financial and political support, and a handful of volunteers, from the Diaspora.

The Yishuv was militarily and administratively vastly superior to the Palestinian Arabs. General Jewish restraint over December 1947 to January 1948 marked by an effective "draw" on the battlefield gave way, .in February and March, to major Jewish setbacks in the battle for the roads. During April and May, bringing its military and organisational superiority to bear, the Haganah (the Defence), the main Jewish militia, switched to the offensive, driven by a sense of imminent logistical asphyxiation, and by the prospect of the imminent British withdrawal and the expected invasion of Palestine by the armies of the Arab states. The Palestinian militias were roundly defeated; the Palestinian masses in each successive area conquered fled from their towns and villages. On 14 May, the Yishuv's leaders declared the establishment of the State of Israel. On 15 May, the armies of Transjordan, Syria, Lebanon, Egypt and Iraq invaded Palestine. The war became a conventional multi-front, multi-army confrontation. After blocking the initial Arab offensives, a series of Israeli campaigns in July and October 1948 and December 1948–January 1949 secured a decision and assured the existence of the State of Israel.

Palestine Arab society in 1947

Arab Palestine in 1947 was essentially a peasant society, but with a large, important urban component. During the Mandate years, partly through British influence and under the impact of the burgeoning, neighbouring Jewish society, the transformation which in the last decades of Ottoman rule had begun to shift the economic, social and political centres of gravity from the countryside to the towns and cities, gained momentum. These towns and cities, for centuries stagnant, during the first decades of the twentieth century began to grow as a flow of landless or poor *fellahin* moved to them from the villages. The relative prosperity and order of Mandate Palestine also drew thousands of Arab immigrants from the neighbouring countries to Haifa, Jaffa, Jerusalem and the outlying smaller towns.

7

Political consciousness, focusing on an Arab and, eventually, a Palestinian Arab nationalism, gradually emerged. The particular conditions in Palestine – with the neighbouring Arab states of Transjordan, Egypt, Syria and Lebanon steadily moving towards complete independence, with the British government in Palestine specifically, if controversially, mandated to prepare the local inhabitants for self-rule, and with the neighbouring, thrusting Jewish national movement offering a constant model, challenge and threat – afforded special stimuli to the birth of an uncompromising nationalism. While it was among the mainly urban elite and middle classes that the Palestinian Arab national movement at first took root, over the years of British rule the national idea filtered down to the urban and peasant masses.

In Palestine by 1947 there were between 1.2 and 1.3 million Arabs (about 1.1 million Muslims and 150,000 Christians), 65–70% of them living in some 800–850 villages. The remaining 30–35% lived in cities and towns. Some 70,000 were bedouin, mostly concentrated in the northern Negev; their number was steadily decreasing as they became settled villagers or moved into towns. Of the approximately 370,000 town and city dwellers, some 260,000 were Muslims and 110,000 Christians. Between 60 and 62% of the Palestine Arab labour force were village-dwelling *fellahin*. There were also many town and city-dwellers who worked in agriculture.[2]

The countryside

While the rural majority and its agricultural economy remained largely primitive and inefficient, there were the beginnings, under British prompting and under the influence of the neighbouring models of the Jewish settlements, of innovation and modernisation, especially in the Coastal Plain. In 1922 there were some 22,000 dunams of Arab land producing citrus crops; in 1940 there were 140,000, mostly destined for export. In 1931 there were 332,000 dunams under orchards (apples, olives); in 1942, 832,000. By and large, however, in Arab Palestine agriculture remained geared to local consumption. The *fellahin* in 1947 had almost no tractors and used a primitive plough, a simple crop cycle and almost no irrigation or fertilisers. Jewish political leaders and settlement executives through the 1930s and 1940s spoke, with varying degrees of sincerity, of helping to reform Arab agriculture to increase its output which, in turn, would allow both the Arab population (increasing through a high birth rate) and the Jewish population (multiplying through immigration) to coexist peacefully while living on a constant, relatively small piece of shared land. By the 1940s about half the Arab land in

Palestine was owned by small proprietors and much of the rest was held by big, absentee land-owners (often living in Lebanon, Egypt or Syria).

Arab rural society was based on the village rather than the district or the country. The *fellah* was by and large apolitical; his interests and loyalty revolved around the village and *hamulah* (clan). Most villages had two or three clans, headed by notables, usually on the basis of wealth. The village headman (*mukhtar*) was often the head of the village's main clan or his appointee. Clan power was largely determined by property holding (land). In many villages, land was owned collectively by the community. Many clans had a regional dispersion and influence, with groups of members scattered in a number of neighbouring villages. In some areas, there were blocs or alliances of villages, based on extended clans inhabiting more than one village, or marital and other alliances between clans (as in the 'Ein Ghazal-Jaba-Ijzim triangle south of Haifa and the Bani Hassan around Jerusalem).

The villages tended to be socially and politically self-centred and self-contained; economically, they were largely self-sufficient. The villager rarely visited the "big city" (Haifa, Jaffa, Jerusalem) or his local town (Lydda, Ramle, Acre, Nazareth, Safad, Majdal) and seldom saw newspapers. Very few villagers could read and write,[3] and most villages had only one radio, usually in the *mukhtar*'s house or in the village coffee shop, where the males would gather in the afternoons and evenings to play backgammon and to talk. Generally the villagers were politically ignorant. The fact of British rule and administration from 1917 to 1948, and the almost complete absence of local, district and national Palestinian political and administrative institutions, and the lack of democratic structures in the few that existed, meant that Palestinian rural society, beyond the village structure, was largely apolitical and uninvolved in national affairs, and that it was unrepresented. Limited exceptions to this were the villages of the Samaria and Judea areas, whose leaders took part in the Palestinian congresses of the first years of the Mandate,[4] and many of whose young men participated in the rebellion of 1936–9. The villages of the Coastal Plain, and Jezreel and Jordan valleys were not represented at these congresses and were largely uninvolved in the rebellion. In general, rural Arab Palestinian interests were represented by the elite urban families, some of whom originated in the countryside, who owned much of the arable land. The large land-owners exercised a great deal of influence and power over the *fellahin*.

Each village tended to act as a collective and to act alone: the village resisted the British or fought the Haganah or agreed to and maintained non-belligerency with the Jews. The solidarity of the village was both its strength and a major weakness. Flight, like resistance, come 1948, usually occurred *en masse*. Moreover, the villages tended to decide on a course and act alone. Villages in 1948 often fought – and fell – alone; the Haganah was able to pick them off one at a time in many districts. In many areas, there was not even defensive co-operation between neighbouring villages, since relations between them, as often as not, were clouded by clan or family feuds and rivalry over land. In a few areas, however, such as the 'Ein Ghazal-Jaba-Ijzim triangle, and on the western edge of Jerusalem (Al Maliha, 'Ein Karim, etc.), regional village blocks and alliances existed, which resulted in the adoption of regional political positions, even if real military co-operation remained largely elusive.

The village mentality, which included a great deal of fatalism, was essentially defensive. The offensive, which required stocks of arms and ammunition, logistics, organisation and effective military leadership and doctrine, was alien to the Palestinian Arab *fellahin*. Bands of villagers could briefly attack a Jewish settlement, herd or convoy, but they were not able to mount a sustained, planned, co-ordinated assault. The exceptions to this were the two main bands of Arab irregulars in the central area (Hassan Salama's and 'Abd al Qadir al Husayni's), which were largely rural in composition, and the *faz'a*, a more or less spontaneous mobilisation of armed villagers to take care of a specific problem (as against the Yehiam convoy in March 1948 and at Gush Etzion in May).

The villages, though often sited on hilltops or high ground and, in the main, consisting of stone-faced houses, lacked trench systems, bunkers and shelters. Their inhabitants were not psychologically "built" for attack, which in 1948 often included mortar barrages and, occasionally, light air raids.

By contrast, the Jewish settlements, most of them collectives (kibbutzim), were inhabited by the most politically advanced and committed elements of the Jewish population. They supplied much of the Yishuv's military and political leadership. Characterised by a pioneering and frontier spirit, demarcating the perimeters of the Yishuv, and having experienced Arab attacks over the decades, the kibbutzim were built with defence in mind – often on high ground, with trenches, bunkers and shelters. Only a handful of kibbutzim fell to Arab attack in 1948; almost none were abandoned by their inhabitants.

In general, Palestinian society was marked by a vast gulf and hostility between town and country, with the deeply conservative *fellahin* suspicious of "city ways" and innovations and resentful of the city's economic and political power over them. Many city dwellers regarded the *fellahin* with contempt.

The towns and cities

Roughly a third of Palestine's Arabs lived in towns. There were 17 wholly Arab towns – Beersheba, Khan Yunis, Gaza, Majdal (Ashkelon), Ramle, Lydda, Hebron, Bethlehem, Beit Jala, Ramallah, Tulkarm, Nablus (Shechem), Jenin, Shafa 'Amr (Shfar'am), Acre, Beisan (Beit Shean) and Nazareth. Some of these, such as Tulkarm, Jenin, Beisan, Shafa 'Amr, were little more than overgrown villages serving as marketing centres and service stations for the surrounding rural communities. In addition, there were five cities and towns with a mixed population of Arabs and Jews – Jerusalem, Haifa and Tiberias, with Jewish majorities, and, predominantly Arab, Safad and Jaffa.

Some 30–35% of the urban Arabs were employed in light industry, crafts and construction, 15–17% in transportation, 20–23% in commerce, 5–8% in professions, 5–7% in public service and 6–9% in other services. While Palestinian society in general was in the throes of urbanisation, urban society was largely still unaffected by industrialisation (though World War II had triggered a measure of industrialisation). There were no modern industrial plants in Arab Palestine (except perhaps for a cigarette factory and a few small clothing plants). There were some 1,500 industrial workshops employing altogether some 9,000 workers with an average work-force of 5 to 6 employees per workshop. By contrast there were 1,900 industrial workshops and plants in Jewish Palestine, employing 38,000 workers, an average of 19–21 workers per plant. Other Arabs worked in Jewish-owned plants and in British-run plants and industrial services. Altogether, the Arab proletariat numbered some 35,000. The Palestine Arab industries produced soap, olive oil, clothes, cigarettes, shoes and bread.

Society and politics

Palestinian Arab society was led by an elite of several dozen, city-based families – the Nusseibehs, Al Khatibs, Al Khalidis, Nashashibis and the Husaynis in Jerusalem, the 'Amrs, al Tamimis and Al Ja'baris in Hebron, the Sa'ids, Al Bitars and Dajanis in Jaffa, the Shawas and the Husaynis in Gaza, the Taji al Faruqis and Al Ghusayns in Ramle, the Tawqans, 'Abd al Hadis, Al Nabulsis, Al Shak'ahs and Al Tamimis in Nablus, the 'Abd al Hadis and 'Abushis in Jenin, the Khalils, Shukris, Tahas, Al Khayats and Al Mahdis in Haifa, the Shuqayris and Khalifas in Acre, the Al Fahums, the Dahirs and the Zu'bis in Nazareth, the Tabaris in Tiberias and Al Khadras in Safad.[5] The families provided Arab Palestine's big land-owners, politicians, judges, merchants, mayors, high civil servants, religious leaders, doctors, lawyers and intellectuals. Each family usually covered most or all fields, one member being a judge or a mayor; others were merchants, professionals and civil servants. Their power, influence and connections were usually local rather than national; their obligations were to family, dependents, city and district, in that order. It was a highly regional, oligarchic structure. While the elite families exercised power over much of the rural and urban populations through direct and indirect economic and religious levers, they maintained a vital distance from the *fellah* and the urban worker; the vast socio-economic gulf was marked by resentment and mutual suspicion.

During the Mandate years, a small middle class emerged – of professionals, officials and shopkeepers. But, while aspiring to merge with the elite families socially, and occasionally moving or marrying into them, the middle class remained too small and the traditional elitist structure too powerful to allow the bourgeoisie effectively to wield political and economic power.

In the late 1940s, 28 of the 32 members of the AHC were from these elite families, and the remaining four were bourgeoisie. None were peasants or proletarians. Some 24 were of urban extraction, and only four or five were originally from the countryside. There was, and remained through 1948, a wide gulf of suspicion and estrangement between urban and rural Arab Palestine, which was to underlie the lack of co-ordination between the towns and their rural hinterland during the hostilities. The elite families by and large had no tradition of, or propensity for, national service and their members did not do military service with the Turks, the British or neighbouring Arab armies. Few of the military leaders of the 1936–8 rebellion were from the ruling families. It was mainly a peasant rebellion, with the town-dwellers restricting themselves largely to civil protest (demonstrations, riots and a general strike) and, at a later stage, to inter-factional terrorism.[6]

From 1919–20, the political families of Arab Palestine divided into two main camps, the *Majlisiyyun* and the *Mu'aridun* – that is, those supporting the Husaynis, the Supreme Muslim Council, of which Hajj Amin al Husayni was president, and the Arab Executive Committee, which the Husaynis controlled, and those opposed to the Husaynis, led by the Nashashibis. The Arab communities were split not so much along ideological lines as along lines of family and local loyalty. The struggle between the Husaynis and their opponents was mainly over power and its economic spoils; the political–ideological differences were secondary, though the Nashashibis, with their rural allies in the Hebron, Nablus and Nazareth areas, tended to take a more moderate line towards Zionism and the Mandate. The Nashashibis often secretly met Jewish representatives and, in private, frequently adopted a conciliatory tone. At various times in the 1920s and 1930s, the Opposition factions received Zionist financing. This split between the Husaynis and their opponents was to characterise Arab politics down to 1948 and the friction between the two camps was to dissipate Palestinian strength at crucial junctures, including 1936–9, when the Husaynis assassinated many of their opponents, and 1947–8.

During the 1930s, the elite families set up formal political parties. In 1935 the Husaynis established the Palestine Arab Party (*Al Hizb al Arabi al Falastini*), which became Arab Palestine's main political organisation. Earlier, in 1934, the Nashashibis had set up the National Defence Party (*Hizb al Difa al Watani*). In 1932 Awni 'Abd al Hadi of Samaria set up the Istiqlal Party, which was pan-Arab in ideology, and in 1935, Jerusalem mayor Dr Husayn Khalidi set up the Reform Party (*Hizb al Islah*). The early 1930s also saw the establishment by Ya'qub Ghusayn of the Youth Congress Party and the Nablus-based National Bloc Party (*Al Kutla al Wataniya*). The proliferation of parties tended to dissipate the strength of the Opposition.

All the parties opposed Zionism and, in varying degrees, British rule, and aimed at Arab statehood in all of Palestine (though the Istiqlal did not espouse separate Palestinian statehood). The parties had no internal elections or western-style institutions, and no dues, and were based on family and local affiliations and loyalties. Families, clans and villages rather than individuals were party members, with semi-feudal links of dependence and loyalty determining attachment. The elite families usually identified with either the Husayni or the Nashashibi camp; a few prominent families managed to remain unattached.[7]

The parties, including the Husaynis and Nashashibis, initially made common cause in 1936 in supporting and leading the troubles. Differences were set aside and party activity was stopped. Representatives of the six parties constituted the Arab Higher Committee (AHC) on 25 April 1936 to co-ordinate the struggle nationally. On the local level, the parties set up National Committees in each town and city to run the strike and other political activities, but as the general strike gave way to widespread rebellion, the traditional enmities re-surfaced, with the Nashashibis and their allies re-emerging as the Opposition. The Nashashibis came to represent and lead those Palestine Arabs – the traditional anti-Husayni groups, much of the aristocracy and middle class, and much of the countryside – who came to regard the strike and revolt as fruitless. Assassination and intimidation by the Husaynis decimated the Opposition ranks; terrorism, extortion, rapine and brigandage against villagers and town-dwellers by the armed bands and the inevitable search and destroy operations against the rebels by the British military alienated much of the population. Rebel bands often fought among themselves. By 1938–9, the rural population had grown tired of the fight. Villages turned against the rebels and anti-rebel "peace bands" were formed.[8]

The outcome of the rebellion, apart from the political gains embodied in the 1939 White Paper, was that thousands of Arabs – rebels and bystanders – were killed or gaoled, thousands of rebel and Opposition members fled the country and much of the Palestinian elite and middle class was driven or withdrew in disgust from the political arena. Implacable blood feuds were born, with telling effect for the denouement of 1946–8; Husayni–Nashashibi alliance or compromise became inconceivable.

In suppressing the rebellion, the British outlawed the AHC, arresting or exiling its members, some of whom (including Hajj Amin al Husayni) went to Europe and served the Axis during World War II. The country remained politically inactive during the war years, with several of the parties officially reconstituting themselves only in 1944–5. The AHC also re-emerged, with the Husaynis holding a majority but with the other parties also represented. In early 1946 the rifts reappeared and in March 1946 the Arab League stepped in and appointed a new AHC composed only of Husaynis and their allies. Its members were Hajj Amin al Husayni (president), Jamal Husayni (deputy president), Dr Husayn Khalidi (secretary), and Ahmad Hilmi Pasha and Emil Ghawri. The Opposition was left out in the cold.

The end-result of the rebellion, its suppression and the following six years of world war was the political and military neutering of the Palestinian Arabs. The Arab states increasingly represented Palestinian demands and interests, with the Husaynis usually determining what was acceptable. The Nashashibis, decimated by Husayni's assassins, and tarnished with the brush of collaboration with the British in the last stages of the rebellion, disbanded politically. The Arab League's clear support for the Husaynis in 1945–6 ended hopes of a Nashashibi revival. Zionist efforts through 1942 to 1947 to revive the moderate camp – which the Jewish Agency always believed represented majority Palestinian opinion – were to no avail. Even as late as January–February 1948 senior Jewish Agency Political Department and Haganah Intelligence Service figures, such as Gad Machnes, Ezra Danin and Elias Sasson, hoped that the Opposition would reassert itself, restrain Arab militancy and wrest control of the Palestinian masses away from the Husaynis. The Yishuv's Arab experts generally asserted that this was unlikely unless the Husaynis suffered major military defeat and Transjordan's King Abdullah supported the Opposition politically and with arms and money.[9]

The divide between the Husaynis and the Opposition had relatively clear geographical as well as familial-clan demarcations, both reflecting and intensifying the regionalism that had characterised Palestinian society and politics for centuries. Husayni strength was based on Jerusalem and its surrounding villages, rural Samaria and Gaza; the Opposition was strong in Hebron, the Galilee, Tiberias and Beisan, Nablus, Jenin and Haifa.

This regionalism, one element of which was the perennial resistance in Haifa, Nablus and Hebron to the supremacy of Jerusalem in Palestinian life and another, the contempt of the highland inhabitants in Samaria and Judea for the Coastal Plain Arabs, was to constitute a major source of Palestinian weakness during the battles of December 1947–May 1948. As the Haganah was able to pick off village after village without each coming to the other's assistance, so it was able, because of the Arab regional animosities, to fight and overrun one area after another of Palestine without having to face a co-ordinated multi-regional defence. The situation in early 1948 reflected in great measure the regionalism, disunity and lack of co-ordination between the armed bands in 1936–9. Regionalism, reflecting and bolstering the fissures between the Husayni and Opposition constituencies, in the 1947–8 battles, despite efforts to present a united front, was partially to underlie the denial of assistance in arms, reinforcements or diversionary attacks by the Husaynis and their allies to traditional Opposition strongholds (as happened, for example, at Haifa between January and April 1948).

A further divisive element built into Palestinian society was the Muslim–Christian rift. The Christians, concentrated in the towns and cities, were generally wealthier and better-educated than the Muslims. They prospered under the Mandate. The Muslims throughout the Mandate feared that the Christians would "sell out" to the British (fellow Christians) and/or make common cause with the Jews (a fellow minority). Indeed, Christians took almost no part in the 1936–9 rebellion. The Christian leaders repeatedly went out of their way to express devotion to the Palestinian national cause; a coterie of Christian notables was prominent in the Husayni camp. In 1948, as some Muslims had anticipated, the Christian Arab community leaders, notably in Haifa and Jaffa, by and large were far less belligerent than their Muslim counterparts. Zionist leaders repeatedly tried to exploit this rift but at the last moment the Christians almost always shied away from advancing from conciliatory private assurances to moderate public commitment and action.

But what was to prove the fatal weakness of Palestinian Arab society stemmed not from the perennial Husayni–Opposition conflict nor from the regional patriotism with which it overlapped nor from the Muslim–Christian divide but from that society's fundamental lack of self-governing institutions, norms and traditions. The British Mandate of 1920–48 can be seen as a nursery in which two societies competed and raced to achieve self-government. The Yishuv won the race outright. Its "National Institutions" almost from the first were built with an eye to conversion into institutions of state. By May 1948, it had a shadow government, with almost all the institutions (and, in some fields, such as agriculture and settlement, an excess of institutions) of state in place and ready to take over. The Jewish Agency, with its various departments (political, finance, settlement, immigration, etc.), became the government, the departments smoothly converting into ministries; the Haganah became the Israel Defence Forces (IDF); the Jewish Agency Executive and, subsequently, the "People's Administration" (*minhelet ha'am*) became the Cabinet; and so on. The Yishuv taxed itself, its various institutions obtaining funds for the diverse national services and goals; the Histadrut (the trade union federation) taxed its members to provide health services and unemployment allowances; the Jewish National Fund (JNF) levied taxes for afforestation and settlement; special taxes were instituted to purchase arms for the Haganah and to cover the absorption of new immigrants. At the same time, the Yishuv received continuous financial aid from the Jewish communities of the Diaspora, with large emergency funding during 1947–9.

The Arabs of Palestine, on the other hand, despite continuous efforts, enjoyed no such steady, reliable aid from the hinterland of neighbouring Arab states and the Muslim world. Indeed, the rejection by the Arab governments and armies of local and national Palestinian pleas for money, arms and reinforcements in late 1947 and early 1948 was merely a continuation of what had gone before. Cumulatively, it engendered among the Palestinians a strong feeling of abandonment by their brother Arabs, to some degree accounting for the Palestinians' sense of despair in 1948. All told, some 5,000 Arab volunteers reached Palestine by March 1948. Most of them were from the urban slums of Iraq, Syria and Lebanon, organised as the Arab Liberation Army (ALA) under Fawzi al Qawuqji. Militarily they were fairly useless, and throughout they were at loggerheads with the local Palestinian militiamen and population.

During the Mandate, the National Council and the Jewish Agency, coupled with Jewish municipalities and local councils and the Histadrut, provided the Yishuv with most essential services (health, education, social welfare, industrial development, settlement) in co-ordination with the Mandate government's own departments. By 1948, the Yishuv – a tightly-knit, centrally organised community of some 650,000 Jews (of whom 80–

90% were of European birth or extraction) – was an almost completely self-governing society with the tools in hand to convert to independent, fully-fledged statehood within days or weeks. Moreover, the years of practical self-rule and preparation for statehood, while involving the usual struggles for power between and within parties, had thrust to the fore an exceptionally talented, self-sacrificing and committed leadership in the fields of politics, the economy, settlement and defence. The quality of the national leadership was echoed lower down on the level of municipal and local government, in the kibbutzim and *moshavim* and in the Haganah.

The Yishuv was a community with an exceptionally high level of political consciousness and commitment. The bulk and dominant elements of the Yishuv were, to one degree or another, socialist, their socialism in singular fashion bolstering rather than detracting from the nationalist aspirations. By the end of 1947, the Yishuv was united around a single national purpose – statehood, come what may, and quickly, against all odds. This goal was imbued with messianic character; it was viewed against the backdrop of the Holocaust (1939–45) which had just ended, and the 2,000 years of persecution of Diaspora Jews that had gone before it. The Yishuv saw itself as a community without choice – it was statehood or bust, and bust, given the depth of Arab enmity for Zionism, meant a possible repetition, on a smaller scale, of the Holocaust.

By contrast, the Palestinian Arabs were backward, disunited and often apathetic, a community only just entering the modern age politically and administratively. In many fields the Palestinian leaders consciously tried to copy Zionist models, but the vast differences in the character of the two populations and levels of consciousness, commitment, ability and education meant that the Arabs qualitatively were radically outclassed. The moment the Yishuv quantitatively reached what proved a critical mass, the outcome was ineluctable.

By 1947 much of the Palestine Arab population had only an indistinct, if any, idea of national purpose and statehood. There was clarity about one thing only – the Jews aimed to displace them and therefore they had to be driven out. The Arabs were probably less enthusiastic or clear about wanting to be rid of the British. Indeed, one may assume that many of the Christian Arabs probably preferred the continuation of the Mandate to either Muslim Arab or Jewish rule. But on the whole, save for the numerically small circle of the elite, the Palestinians were unready for the national message or for the demands that the national idea was to make upon the community, both in 1936–8 and, far more severely, over 1947–8. Commitment and readiness to pay the price for national self-fulfilment presumed a clear concept of the nation and of national belonging, which

Palestine's Arabs, still caught up in a village-centred (or at best a regional) political outlook, by and large completely lacked. Most Palestine Arabs had no sense of separate national or cultural identity to distinguish them from, say, the Arabs of Syria, Lebanon or Egypt. Over the Mandate years, with the spread of education, literacy, newspapers and radios, and reinforced by the thrusting presence of burgeoning Zionism, that sense of separate identity and purpose gradually matured. But the process proved too slow; it failed to keep pace with the realities and demands of a swiftly changing historical situation. For decades the Arab elite families may have vied for power in the rarified arena of newly defined Palestinian nationalist politics, even to the point of killing each other, but for the mass of the country's Arabs, the struggle to establish a state was largely a remote affair.

Administratively, things were not much better. For a variety of reasons, including lack of educated personnel and political consciousness, Palestine's Arabs never established state or pre-state structures akin to those of the Yishuv; in the main, they lacked all self-governing and administrative machinery by 1948. Only on the municipal level and in the sphere of religious life did Palestine's Arabs garner experience and establish patterns of very limited self-rule during the Mandate.

The municipalities, the only important Arab or semi-Arab institutions for which there were popular elections (albeit irregularly held, in 1926, 1934 and 1946, and with very limited, propertied suffrage), carried out few of the functions of the same institutions in the Yishuv, and, by British accounts, carried them out poorly. The budgets of the municipalities give an idea of the limited scope of their operations. Ramle, with a population of over 20,000 in 1941, had an annual budget of Palestine pounds (P£) 6,317. Jenin, a far smaller town, had a budget of P£2,320, Bethlehem, with a population of over 10,000, P£3,245, Nablus, with a population in 1942 of about 30,000, P£17,223 and Jaffa, with a largely Arab population of about 80,000 in 1942, P£90,967. By comparison, all-Jewish Petah-Tikvah, with a population of 30,000, had a budget of P£39,463 in 1941; Tel Aviv, with a population of some 200,000, in 1942 had a budget of P£779,589.[10]

The only Palestinian Arab national administrative institution during the Mandate was the Supreme Muslim Council (SMC) (*Al Majlis al Islami al A'la*), which until 1937 was presided over by Hajj Amin al Husayni. The SMC was the institutional power base from which Husayni during the late 1920s and 1930s won the supreme leadership of the Palestine Arab community, and, apart from a hiatus over 1937–45, the SMC was to remain under the sway of the Husaynis until 1948. The SMC managed the *awkaf* (the Muslim trusts responsible for holy sites and properties) and the Islamic courts (*shar'i*), maintained the mosques and appointed religious officials (imams, preachers, etc.), and ran a number of limited educational and social services (schools, orphanages, etc.). The SMC members were appointed by the Mandate authorities. During the 1920s and 1930s the Husaynis used the financial weight of the SMC to mobilise and retain support for their faction against the Nashashibis; at the same time, SMC funds were withheld from Opposition centres such as Hebron. The SMC became politically marginal in the mid-1930s after the AHC was set up and after Husayni was dismissed from its presidency.

During the Mandate, Arab leaders, usually for factional or party political reasons, tried to set up trade unions and a national trade union federation, but these efforts were marked by almost complete failure. The main reason for this was probably the primitive nature of the Arab economy; it lacked industry and had spawned only a small class-conscious proletariat. Moreover, the unionisation efforts were marked by, and regarded by all as part of, the Husayni–Opposition struggle. By 1947, only some 30,000 Palestine Arab workers were unionised, and the unions – unlike the Histadrut in the Jewish sector, which, given its functioning as the umbrella organisation of the Haganah, the Hapoel sports association and the main health service (*Kupat Holim Clalit shel ha' Histadrut*), served as a national rather than merely a workers' organisation – were insignificant organisations. A high level of unionisation was achieved by the Arabs only in the relatively small Palestine railways and the postal services.

In general, in complete contrast to the Yishuv, Palestine's Arab community failed completely to organise itself for statehood. It remained throughout dependent on the British Mandate administrative machinery and bureaucracies. Consequently, when these withdrew in the spring of 1948, Arab Palestine – and especially the towns and cities – slid into chaos, with confusion or even anarchy characterising the distribution and sale of food, public transport and communications, law and order (uncontrolled armed bands took over neighbourhoods and villages as most policemen deserted their posts, taking their rifles with them), etc. The spread of Arab-Jewish hostilities over December 1947 to May 1948 exacerbated the situation. Palestine Arab society fell apart. The Yishuv, suffering from the same conditions of warfare and siege, and with far less manpower and no hinterland of friendly states, proved able to cope.

Nowhere was this pre-1948 organisational disparity between the two communities greater than in the military field. The Palestine Arabs began preparing for hostilities against the Yishuv (and the British) in the early 1930s. But the results were inconsiderable and their worth was diminished by partisan political affiliation and loyalties.

Three small *jihadiyya* (fighting societies) were established: *al Kaff al*

Khadra (the Green Palm) in the Hebron area, *al Jihad al Muqaddas* (the holy war), led by Amin al Husayni's nephew, 'Abd al Qadir al Husayni, in the Jerusalem area, and *al Shabab al Tha'ir* (the rebellious youth) in the Tulkarm–Qalqilya area. All three planned and/or carried out anti-British attacks, albeit in a small way. More dramatic were the brief activities of Sheikh 'Izz al Din al Qassam around Haifa and in northern Samaria towards the end of 1935. After killing several Jewish settlers and a policeman, the band was cornered and al Qassam was killed by the British.

More important in the process of the militarisation of the Palestine Arab youth was the establishment by the Husaynis of the *Futuwwah* (youth companies), in which party-affiliated youngsters were trained in military drill and the use of weapons. The movement, modelled after the Nazi youth organisations,[11] never amounted to much though it supplied some of the political cadres who organised the general strike of 1936 and the terrorism of the later part of the rebellion. The *Futuwwah* were re-established after World War II but never numbered more than several hundred youths under arms.

A larger organisation was the *Najjada* (auxiliary corps), set up in the post-war period, largely at Opposition initiative, with its centre in Jaffa. In summer 1946 it had 2,000–3,000 members and was led by Mohammad Nimr al Hawari; its officers were mainly Palestinians who had served in the British Army. In the run-up to the 1948 war, the Husaynis tried to gain control of the *Najjada* companies, with varying degrees of success.[12] The *Najjada*, too, lacked arms. Neither the *Najjada* nor the *Futuwwah* had branches in the countryside.

The bulk of the arms, which amounted to several thousand rifles, of varying ages, in Palestinian hands at the end of 1947 were dispersed in the villages around the country, the private property of each family and clan. The armed, able-bodied villagers formed a loose, untrained militia at each locality. They were equipped neither psychologically nor physically, in terms of logistics, organisation and weaponry, for sustained action outside their village or in concert with other armed groups. Many armed villagers intermittently joined or assisted the volunteer units that moved into Palestine at the beginning of the war, but, in general, they and their weapons remained rooted in each village and, with the possible exception of the persistent attacks in early 1948 on the Tel Aviv–Jerusalem convoys, were never centrally organised or mobilised for effective battle against the Yishuv.

The Palestine Arabs had no arms production capacity (except for primitive bombs). Exact figures about numbers and stocks of arms of the Palestinian Arab para-military organisations do not exist, but an idea of

Palestine Arab military strength can be gained from figures relating to individual villages. Ghuweir Abu Shusha, by the Sea of Galilee, with a population of 1,240, in April 1948 had some 48 militiamen with 35–40 assorted rifles, and 20–50 rounds of ammunition per man. 'Ein az Zeitun near Safad, with a population of 820, had 50–60 militiamen with 40–50 assorted rifles and one or two machineguns, with 25–35 rounds of ammunition per rifle. Safad, with about 9,500 Arabs, had 200–250 local armed militiamen with 35–50 rounds per rifle. Al Khalisa, in the Galilee panhandle, with a population of 1,840, had 35–40 armed militiamen, with 50–70 rounds per rifle.[13] In the main towns, where the *Futuwwa* and the *Najjada* had branches, the situation was proportionately no better. Despite the arrival of small irregular units as reinforcements in early 1948, matters did not greatly improve during the first months of the war. An Arab intelligence report from Damascus in late March 1948 stated that the urban militias had "no more than a few old rifles and a very small number of machineguns and grenades. Were it not for the occasional intervention of the British Army . . . the ability of these forces to hold off the Jews, who are superior in number and equipment, must be in doubt."[14] In general, the Palestine Arabs by the end of 1947 had a healthy and demoralising respect for the Yishuv's military power. A Jewish intelligence source in October 1947 described the situation in the countryside thus: "the *fellah* is afraid of the Jewish terrorists . . . who might bomb his village and destroy his property . . . The town-dweller admits that his strength is insufficient to fight the Jewish force and hopes for salvation from outside [i.e., by the Arab states]." At the same time, the "moderate majority" of Palestine's Arabs, "are confused, frightened . . . They are stockpiling provisions . . . and are being coerced and pressured by extremists . . . [But] all they want is peace, quiet."[15] If it came to battle, the Palestine Arabs expected to lose but, conceiving of the struggle as lasting for decades or centuries, believed that the Jews, like the Medieval Crusader kingdoms, would ultimately be overcome by the surrounding Muslim world.[16]

By contrast, following the Arab riots and pogroms of 1920–1 and 1929, the Yishuv fashioned a highly organised, effective underground self-defence organisation in the Haganah. After a massive, covert arms acquisition campaign in the West following Ben-Gurion's assumption in 1946 of political direction of the organisation, and on the basis of his perception that the Yishuv had to make ready to defend itself both against a guerrilla campaign by Palestine's Arabs and a conventional attack by the surrounding Arab states, the Haganah, by September 1947, possessed 10,489 rifles, 702 light machineguns, 2,666 sub-machineguns, 186 medium machineguns, 672 2-inch mortars and 92 3-inch mortars. (The

Haganah had no tanks or artillery at the start of the 1948 war.) Thousands more weapons were purchased, or stolen from the withdrawing British, during the first months of the war. Moreover, the Yishuv had a relatively advanced arms producing capacity. Between October 1947 and July 1948, for example, the Haganah's arms factories produced 3 million 9mm bullets, 150,000 mills grenades, 16,000 sub-machineguns (Stens) and 210 3-inch mortars.[17]

In May 1947, the Haganah's total adult membership, both male and female, numbered 35,000, with another 9,500 members in its para-military Gadna (*g'dudei no'ar*, youth battalions) corps. Of the 35,000 some 2,200 were the permanently mobilised members of the Palmah (*p'lugot mahatz*, shock companies).[18] By May 1948, the Haganah had mobilised and deployed in standing military formations 35,780 troops – some 5,500 more than the combined strength of the regular Arab armies who invaded Palestine on 15 May (though the invaders were far better equipped and, theoretically, better trained).[19] The Haganah's successor from the beginning of June, the Israel Defence Forces (IDF), in July 1948 had 63,000 men under arms.[20]

But, perhaps even more important than the numbers, which meant that one person in ten in the Yishuv was mobilised by July 1948, was the Haganah's organisation, from its highly talented, centralised General Staff, with logistical, intelligence and operational branches, down to its brigade and battalion territorial and mobile formations. Apart from the Palmah battalions, few of the units had been well trained by December 1947, but the organisation had a relatively large pool of veterans of the British Army and a highly committed, internally trained officer corps. Before 1948, the Haganah had been an underground army. In the course of that year, it emerged and efficiently functioned as a large conventional force, beating first the Palestinian Arab militias and then the combined irregular and regular armies of the Arab states. By April–May 1948, it was conducting brigade-size offensives, by July, multi-brigade operations; and by October, divisional, multi-front offensives.

It was in the realm of the organisation and control of armed forces, especially in the towns and cities, that the Palestine Arabs were at the greatest disadvantage, as was to emerge starkly during the first months of the war. The Husayni domination of the AHC and of the political arena assured, at least on the surface, a unity of sorts at the start of the hostilities. Husayni–Opposition differences were buried and coalition National Committees (on the 1936 model) were set up in December 1947 and January 1948 by the leaders of the communities in each town and city, and in many villages. But the different political outlooks of the parties and the divergent political and economic interests quickly began to tell. In some areas, Husayni domination of the population (around Jerusalem) meant an aggressive, offensive strategy by armed bands of irregulars and militiamen. In other areas, where the Husaynis were weak, and where upper and middle class business interests came to the fore, as in Jaffa and Haifa, the Husayni supporters were unable to unleash attacks and struggled against the moderate elements to adopt a more militant posture. For months there was lack of co-ordination and co-operation between the AHC and the National Committees in Opposition-led Jaffa and Haifa. The Mufti and the AHC tried to assert control through direct contacts with their supporters (imams, municipal officials, local militia leaders), bypassing the National Committees.[21]

The militias in each area and town, sometimes cutting across the Husayni–Opposition divide, in large measure operated independently of political control or interest. This was especially the case in towns where there were large contingents of non-local irregulars, such as Jaffa. Militia units in Jaffa, Haifa and Jerusalem continually and blatantly ignored instructions from National Committees and, occasionally, from the AHC or the Defence Committee in Damascus. In late January 1948, Jerusalem National Committee leader and AHC member Husayn Khalidi complained to the Grand Mufti in Cairo that 'Abd al Qadir al Husayni's irregulars were generally ignoring the local National Committees and did what they liked without any co-ordination: "indescribable confusion is being created," said Khalidi.[22] The British authorities believed that, in general, the National Committees and the AHC managed to exercise only "comparatively feeble authority" over the militias in the towns.[23] The general picture of lack of arms and trained manpower, and disorganisation and confusion reflected the lack of adequate preparation for the war by Palestine's Arabs in the pre-1948 period.

The notion of transfer in Yishuv thinking

Throughout the 1930s and 1940s, Palestine's Arabs, or at least the politically aware sectors of the community, believed that the Yishuv was bent on expansion and, ultimately, partial or complete displacement of the country's Arab inhabitants. The rise of Jewish political and military power, and especially the enormous influx of Jewish immigrants fleeing persecution in Europe in the mid-1930s, was seen as proof that such a process was taking place, whether or not it stemmed from an overall plan. Jerusalem lawyer Fa'iz Haddad, it was reported, "does not fear us at present and he believes that for the moment we don't have ambitions to dominate Palestine's Arabs and the Arab world. But the Jews, he says, are talented and ambitious, and he fears that the future generations will display expansionist tendencies."[24] The Jews were insufficiently aware of the real fear in the Arab world of a Jewish State, should it be established, thought Za'far Dajani, chairman of the Jaffa Chamber of Commerce.[25]

British observers in Cairo, reporting on the conference of Arab prime ministers in December 1947, summarised the Arab view of Zionist ambitions thus: the ultimate aim of all the Zionists was "the acquisition of all of Palestine, all Transjordan and possibly some tracts in Southern Lebanon and Southern Syria." The Zionist "politicians", after taking control of the country, would at first treat the Arabs "nicely." But then, once feeling "strong enough," they would begin "squeezing the Arab population off their lands . . . [and] if necessary out of the State." Later, they would expand the Jewish state at the expense of the Palestine Arab state.

However, the more militant Haganah commanders wished to move more quickly, believed the Arab leaders, according to the British. Exploiting the weakness and disorganisation of the Arabs, they would first render them – especially in Jaffa and Haifa – "completely powerless" and then frighten or force them into leaving, "their places being taken by Jewish immigrants." The Arab leaders, according to the British observers, thought that there existed a still more extreme Jewish plan, of the Revisionists, calling for more immediate expansion.[26]

Such Arab prognoses were to be in the nature of self-fulfilling prophecies. In 1948, Arabs were to be "squeezed" out of Jaffa and Haifa, and the Jews were to behave, at least in part, as the Arab leaders expected and said they would behave.

However, these prognoses also had a basis in mainstream Jewish thinking, if not actual planning, from the late 1930s and 1940s. Ben-Gurion put it clearly at a meeting of the Jewish Agency Executive in June 1938: "The starting point for a solution of the Arab problem in the Jewish state" was the conclusion of an agreement with the Arab states that would pave the way for a transfer of the Arabs out of the Jewish State to the Arab countries. Ben-Gurion supported the establishment of a Jewish State on a small part of Palestine "not because he is satisfied with part of the country, but on the basis of the assumption that after we constitute a large force following the establishment of the state – we will cancel the partition of the country [between Jews and Arabs] and we will expand throughout the Land of Israel." When one of the participants asked him whether he contemplated such a population transfer and expansion "by force," Ben-Gurion said: "[No]. Through mutual understanding and Jewish–Arab agreement . . . [But] the state is only a stage in the realization of Zionism and it must prepare the ground for our expansion throughout the whole country through a Jewish–Arab agreement."[27]

The idea of a "voluntary" or "compulsory" transfer of all or the bulk of the Arabs inhabiting the Jewish State areas had been in the air since the mid-1930s. All schemes for establishing a Jewish State in Palestine, including the Peel Commission recommendations of July 1937, came up against the major problem of the existence of a large Arab minority: any way in which the land could possibly be partitioned would still leave a sizeable Arab minority in the Jewish State area. And while the Yishuv looked to massive Jewish immigration to fill up the state, it was clear that if a large Arab minority was left *in situ*, their far higher birthrate would mean that they would constitute a perpetual threat to the Jewish majority and, given their active or potential hostility, to the body politic itself. The idea of transferring the Arabs out of the Jewish State area to the Arab state area or to other Arab states was seen as the chief means of assuring the stability and "Jewishness" of the proposed Jewish State.

In proposing Partition, with the Jews to get a mini-state consisting of much of the Coastal Plain and the Galilee, and the Arabs to get, for their state, Samaria, the bulk of Judea, the southern Coastal Plain and the Negev, the Peel Commission recommended the transfer, with British assistance and by force, if necessary, of many or all of the some 225,000 Arabs living within the proposed Jewish state area.

During World War I, Ben-Gurion had written that the Jews had not come to Palestine to "dominate and exploit" the Arabs: "We do not intend to push the Arabs aside, to take their land, or to disinherit them."[28] But the following years, which saw the Balfour Declaration and the Arab eruptions of 1920–1, 1929 and 1936–9, transformed his outlook. He posited the Peel Commission recommendation, writing: "The compulsory transfer of the Arabs from the valleys of the proposed Jewish state could give us something which we never had, even when we stood on our own during the days of the First and Second Temples," a Galilee without Arabs. "We are being given an opportunity which we never dared to dream of in our wildest imaginings. This is more than a state, government and sovereignty – this is national consolidation in a free homeland."[29] Ben-Gurion understood that few, if any, of the Arabs would uproot themselves voluntarily; the compulsory provision would have to be put into effect. "We must expel Arabs and take their places . . . and if we have to use force – not to dispossess the Arabs of the Negev and Transjordan, but to guarantee our own right to settle in those places – then we have force at our disposal," he wrote to his son, Amos, contemplating the implementation of the transfer recommendation of the Peel Commission report.[30]

The Jewish Agency Executive, the "government" of the Yishuv, in June 1938, against the backdrop of the Woodhead Commission's review of possible solutions to the conflict, debated at length various aspects of the transfer idea. Ben-Gurion proposed "Lines of Action" for the Jewish State-to-be: "The Jewish state will discuss with the neighbouring Arab states the matter of voluntarily transferring Arab tenant-farmers, labourers and *fellahin* from the Jewish state to the neighbouring states." Such a transfer and the concomitant encouragement of Jewish immigration to the state "were not tantamount to discrimination," he said.[31]

The executive meetings were held in the shadow of events in Europe, where minority problems, especially involving Germans, were visibly and dramatically undermining the stability of a cluster of states in the heart of the continent. Ben-Gurion read out a letter from General Zionist Party leader Fischel Rottenstreich, a member of the executive away due to illness, which said that in view of events in Poland and Czechoslovakia, the Yishuv must look with concern to its minority problem: "We must . . . stand by the Peel Commission proposal, which sees in transfer the only solution to this problem." But the transfer idea was always regarded, at least by Ben-Gurion, as a matter to be carried out in an agreed and orderly fashion between the Arab states and the Yishuv, with compensation and planned resettlement for those transferred.[32] Other members of the executive spoke of Eastern Europe, and especially of the Sudeten German problem; there was a consensus in favour of implementing the proposed transfer, though an argument raged about its scale and about whether it was to be accomplished with or without Britain, and voluntarily or compulsorily.

The issue took up almost the whole of the day-long executive meeting of 12 June, which was also attended by members of the Political Committee of the Zionist Actions Committee. Shmuel Zuchovitzky (Zakif), of Magdiel, a major Yishuv agricultural sector figure, thought that the British should carry out the transfer. Werner David Senator, an executive member, said that the Yishuv must aim for a "maximal transfer." Yehoshua Supersky, of the Zionist Actions Committee, said that the Yishuv must make sure that "a new Czechoslovakia is not created here [and that this could be assured] through the gradual emigration of part of the Arabs." Avraham Menahem Ussishkin, the head of the Jewish National Fund (JNF), thought that there was nothing immoral about transferring 60,000 Arab families: "It is the most moral [thing to do]," he said. "We will not be able to begin our political life in a state in which Arabs will constitute 45% [of the population]." But Ussishkin did not believe that the Yishuv could or should carry out the transfer by force; the world would oppose and stop it. Only the British could do it, he argued. Berl Katznelson, the most important of the Labour Zionist leaders who opposed accepting Partition, said that the Yishuv could not carry out the transfer alone: it would have to be in, and after, agreement with Britain and Arab states. "But the principle should be that there must be a large agreed transfer," he said. The Jewish Agency's Treasurer, Eliezer Kaplan, thought that perhaps, with proper financial inducement and if left impoverished in the nascent Jewish State, the Arabs might agree to a "voluntary" transfer. Eliahu Berlin, a leader of the Knesset Yisrael religious party, suggested that "taxes should be increased so that the Arabs will flee because of the taxes." Ben-Gurion referred to the Peel Commission's transfer recommendation, calling it an incomparable "achievement in terms of Jewish settlement. With compulsory transfer we [would] have a vast area . . . I support compulsory transfer. I don't see in it anything immoral." He too thought that it must be carried out by Britain rather than by the Jews.[33]

The transfer solution to the Arab minority problem, while deliberately aired little in public, fired the imagination of many Yishuv executives. Yosef Weitz, the director of the JNF's key Lands Department and a major settlement executive, wrote in his diary on 20 December 1940:

it must be clear that there is no room in the country for both peoples . . . If the Arabs leave it, the country will become wide and spacious for us . . . The only solution [after the end of World War II] is a Land of Israel, at least a western Land of Israel [i.e., Palestine], without Arabs. There is no room here for compromises . . . There is no way but to transfer the Arabs from here to the neighbouring countries, to transfer all of them, save perhaps for [the Arabs of] Bethlehem, Nazareth and old Jerusalem. Not one village must be left, not one [bedouin] tribe. The transfer must be directed at Iraq, Syria and even Transjordan. For this goal funds will be found . . . And only after this transfer will the country be able to absorb millions of our brothers and the Jewish problem will cease to exist. There is no other solution.[34]

As the solution to the seemingly insoluble Arab minority problem of the future Jewish State, the transfer idea continued to preoccupy Weitz and other Yishuv leaders for years. In 1942 Weitz noted that Kaplan "absolutely" suppported a transfer but thought that the matter must be approached "with great care." A number of Yishuv committees (one of them including Kaplan, Jewish Agency Political Department director Moshe Shertok (Sharett) and Dov Yosef) between 1938 and 1942 looked into various aspects of the transfer proposal, such as how to implement it, the absorptive capacity of the neighbouring states, financing the implementation, and so on. The proposal remained on a back-burner so long as the prospect of the establishment of the Jewish State remained remote, but the idea continued to command attention and, with some figures, like Weitz, to grip the imagination as the only clear solution to the prospective Jewish State's major problem.[35]

During the post-World War II years the transfer idea, always prickly, was avoided in public discussions. In the run-up to the UN General Assembly Partition Resolution of November 1947, the Yishuv leaders usually ignored the subject. The British had made it clear that they opposed a transfer and certainly would not implement it on behalf of the Jews, and the various United Nations bodies dealing with Palestine between 1945 and 1947 similarly showed no inclination to adopt a transfer solution. The Yishuv leaders understood that the new Jewish State would have to cope with its Arab minority as best it may. Talk of transfer would only torpedo the passage of the Partition resolution. Hence Ben-Gurion, testifying before UNSCOP on 8 July 1947, went out of his way to reject the 1945 British Labour Party platform "International Post-war Settlement" which supported the encouragement of the movement of the Palestine Arabs to the neighbouring countries to make room for Jews. "We did not accept it then," Ben-Gurion said of the Labour Party proposal. "We do not claim that any Arab ought to be moved," he told the United Nations Commission.[36]

In early November 1947, the Jewish Agency Executive discussed various proposals for giving the prospective Jewish State's Arab minority citizenship in the neighbouring prospective Palestine Arab State. The consensus was for giving as many of the Arab minority in the Jewish State citizenship of Arab Palestine rather than Jewish State citizenship. In the event of war between the two Palestine states, said Ben-Gurion, the Arab minority in the Jewish State would be "a Fifth Column." Hence, it was best that they be citizens of the Palestine Arab State so that, if hostile, they "could be expelled" to the Palestine Arab State. But if they were citizens of the Jewish State, "it would only be possible to imprison them, and it would be better to expel them than to imprison them." There was no explicit mention of the collective transfer idea.[37]

However, there was perhaps a hint of the idea in Ben-Gurion's speech to Mapai's supporters four days after the UN Partition resolution, just as Arab–Jewish hostilities were getting under way. Ben-Gurion starkly outlined the emergent Jewish State's main problem – its prospective population of 520,000 Jews and 350,000 Arabs. Including Jerusalem, the state would have a population of about one million, 40% of which would be non-Jews. "This fact must be viewed in all its clarity and sharpness. With such a [population] composition, there cannot even be complete certainty that the government will be held by a Jewish majority ... There can be no stable and strong Jewish state so long as it has a Jewish majority of only 60%." The Yishuv's situation and fate, he went on, compelled the adoption of "a new approach ... [new] habits of mind" to "suit our new future. We must think like a state."[38]

Chapter 2

The first wave: the Arab exodus, December 1947 – March 1948

The United Nations General Assembly vote of 29 November 1947, which supported the partition of Palestine into two states, one Jewish and one Arab, prompted Arab attacks and sniping against Jewish passers-by in the big towns, and on Jewish traffic on the roads, the following day. The AHC, which completely rejected Partition, declared a three-day general strike, beginning on 1 December, thus releasing the Arab urban masses for action. On 2 December an Arab mob, unobstructed by British security forces, stormed though the Jewish commercial centre of Jerusalem, looting and burning shops and attacking Jews. Arab and Jewish snipers exchanged fire in Haifa and attacks were launched on the neighbourhoods in Tel Aviv which adjoined Jaffa and its suburbs. Parts of Palestine were gripped by chaos; the escalation towards full-scale war had begun. As in 1936, National Committees were set up in the Arab towns to direct the struggle in each locality.

December was marked by a spiral of violence between the militias of the neighbouring urban communities, which included sniping, bomb attacks and several main assaults. Traffic to and from the Jewish neighbourhoods and towns was often interdicted, prompting Jewish retaliatory strikes.

In January 1948, in line with Arab League resolutions in December 1947 supporting indirect intervention, Arab volunteers (some of them ex-soldiers), spearheaded by the battalions of the Arab Liberation Army (ALA), began to move into the country. The first full-scale Arab attacks on Jewish settlements were launched with the aim of destruction and conquest – on Kfar Szold (9–10 January), Kfar Uriah (11 January) and the Etzion Bloc (14 January).

During February and March, as the British stepped up their preparations for withdrawal and increasingly relinquished the reins of government, the battle, especially along the roads, intensified. Given the geographically intermixed populations, the presence of British force˜ ˙ nd the militia-cum-underground nature of the opposing Arab and Jewish forces, the hostilities during December 1947 – March 1948 combined elements of a guerrilla, civil and conventional war. Large bombs and continuous sniping caused death and destruction both in the centres of the Arab and Jewish towns and in their border neighbourhoods. In the countryside, the Arabs gained the upper hand in their efforts to block the roads between the main Jewish population centres: the introduction by the Haganah in January–February of escorted convoys was matched in March by improved Arab tactics and increased firepower, which, in a series of major ambushes of the Khulda, Nabi Daniel and Yehiam convoys, managed to destroy most of the Yishuv's armoured truck fleet.

The defeats of March and the prospect of invasion of the emergent Jewish State by regular Arab armies prompted the Haganah's switch in April to the strategic offensive. By then, the Arab exodus from Palestine had begun. By February–March 1948, some 75,000 Arabs, mostly from the urban upper and middle classes of Jaffa, Haifa and Jerusalem, and from villages around Jerusalem and in the Coastal Plain, had fled to Arab centres to the east, such as Nazareth and Nablus, or out of the country.

Ben-Gurion's Arab affairs advisers had already informed the Yishuv's leader on 11 December 1947 that "Arabs were fleeing from Jaffa [and] from Haifa. Beduins are fleeing from the Sharon [i.e., the Coastal Plain]." Yehoshua (Josh) Palmon and Ezra Danin, senior Haganah Intelligence Service (*Shai*) officers, told Ben-Gurion that Arabs were fleeing their villages to live with relatives elsewhere; ex-villagers resident in towns tended to flee back to their native villages. Urban families were fleeing to Nazareth and Nablus. Palmon thought that Haifa and Jaffa would be evacuated "for lack of food." Danin favoured strangling the urban Arabs economically by destroying their buses, trucks and cars, cutting off the roads into Palestine and blocking Palestine's Arab ports.[1] Ben-Gurion was persuaded that the inhabitants of Jaffa and Haifa, "islands in Jewish territory," were at the Yishuv's mercy and could be starved out.[2]

By 11 January 1948, according to Elias (Eliahu) Sasson, the director of the Arab division of the Jewish Agency's Political Department, Arab morale was low in all the main towns and in their rural hinterlands. Sasson wrote to Transjordan's King Abdullah:

Hunger, high prices, and poverty are rampant in a frightening degree. There is fear and terror everywhere. The flight is painful, from house to house, from neighbourhood to neighbourhood, from city to city, from village to village, and from Palestine to the neighbouring countries. The number of these displaced persons is estimated in the thousands.[3]

Haganah policy, December 1947 – March 1948

The outbreak of Arab violence in various parts of Palestine in the immediate wake of the United Nations Partition resolution was viewed initially by the Yishuv and the Haganah leadership as a possibly ephemeral new bout of troubles akin to the outbreaks of 1920–1, 1929 and 1936–9, and not necessarily as the start of a war.

After the first day of Arab attacks, Ben-Gurion, on 1 December 1947, called in Sasson, and Golda Myerson (Meir) and Reuven Zaslani (Shiloah), both top officials of the Jewish Agency Political Department. Shiloah proposed Jewish restraint, arguing that the Mufti, Hajj Amin al Husayni, was interested in a "sharp" Jewish reaction which he could use to stir up the Arab masses, and he opposed a one-to-one policy of retaliation.[4]

In meetings of the Defence Committee (*va'ad habitahon*), which was composed of 12 representatives of major bodies and groups in the Yishuv, including the Haganah National Command, the Jewish Agency, the Histadrut and the National Council (*ha'va'ad haleumi*), and of the Haganah General Staff during the first week of hostilities, it was agreed that

the outbreaks should not yet be seen as the start of planned, systematic and organised Arab aggression . . . The Arab population does not want a disruption of peace and security and there still is not a decision [by the Arab leadership to go to war]. We evaluated these outbreaks as of a local character . . . [We decided] that we were not interested by our behaviour to aid the AHC and the Mufti to suck into this circle [of violence] wider strata of the Arab population.

The Defence Committee, which exercised parliamentary political control over the Haganah, and the Haganah commanders decided against "widening the circle of violence."[5]

The Haganah at first adopted a purely defensive strategy. But this changed after the first month of hostilities as Arab attacks spread to new areas and as Jewish casualties increased, and as the feeling grew that the Husaynis were gaining control of the Arab masses. Already in mid-December, pressure began to mount for a switch to a more aggressive strategy. In his speech on 10 December to the Histadrut Executive Committee, Israel Galili, the head of the Haganah National Command, spoke of the spread of the violence, which "also necessitates changes in our behaviour." These changes were needed, Galili felt, because of the erosion of the Yishuv's military self-confidence. The Arabs were interpreting the Jews' purely defensive strategy as a sign of weakness, Galili told the Defence Committee on 11 December. He proposed that the Haganah adopt a strategy of "active defence," hitting back when Jewish targets were attacked and initiating attacks against Arab targets. Specifically he posited attacks on "Arab transport . . . hitting the property of those responsible, inciters and organisers [of attacks on Jews]" and against bases of Arab irregulars. At the meeting, Galili found wide support for a change of strategy. Ya'acov Hazan, a leader of the socialist Mapam (*Mifleget Poalim Meuhedet*, united workers party), proposed an even "more severe" Haganah strategy.[6]

Two senior Haganah figures, Yohanan Retner and Fritz Eisenstadt (Shalom Eshet), on 19 December called for an "aggressive defence," meaning: "In each [Arab] attack [we should] be prepared to reply with a decisive blow, destruction of the place or chasing out the inhabitants and taking their place."[7]

At the meeting of the Defence Committee the day before, two leading Yishuv figures called, for the first time, for the levelling of offending Arab villages. Eliahu Elyashar, the leader of Jerusalem's Sephardi community, urged the "uprooting" of Abu Kabir, outside Jaffa, "as a lesson to the rural communities"; and Binyamin Mintz, the leader of the orthodox Poalei Agudat Yisrael Party, said with respect to a village in the Negev: "If the possibility arises of evicting all its inhabitants and destroying it, this must be done." (But Yosef Sapir, the mayor of Petah Tikva and a major orange-grove owner, argued against destroying whole villages, "even small [ones] . . . This recalls Lidice – [and] here is food for thought.")[8]

The first operational proposal by the Haganah to level a village was made on 11 January 1948, in an intelligence report on the murder on 9 January of 11 Haganah scouts outside Gan-Yavne by militiamen from 'Arab Sukreir. The report, written apparently by the Haganah Intelligence Service, recommends: "The village should be destroyed completely and some males from the same village should be murdered."[9]

The gradual shift in strategy during December 1947 in practice meant a limited implementation of *Tochnit Mai* ("Plan May"), which, produced in May 1946, was the Haganah master plan for the defence of the Yishuv in the event of the outbreak of new troubles similar to those of 1936–9. The plan included provision, *in extremis*, for "destroying the Arab transport" in Palestine, and blowing up houses used by Arab terrorists and expelling their inhabitants.[10]

The British quickly – indeed, somewhat prematurely – noted the Haganah's change of strategy, and claimed that "spontaneous and unorganised" Arab rioting might well have subsided had the Jews not resorted to retaliation with firearms. "The Haganah's policy was initially of defence and restraint, which quickly gave place to counter-operations," wrote the High Commissioner, Alan Cunningham. He believed that the AHC was not initially interested in "serious outbreaks" but that the Jewish response had forced the AHC to organise and raise the level of violence. Cunningham deemed some of the Jewish reprisals – such as the attack on the Arab Haifa bus on 12 December 1947 – "an offence to civilization." Cunningham preferred not to differentiate between the Haganah's operations and those of the IZL and LHI.[11]

But if there was a shift to more forceful retaliatory responses in many areas, Haganah national strategy remained – and was to remain until March 1948 – one which would restrict as far as possible the scope of the conflagration and which would not strike in areas so far free of hostilities. Initially, the motive was to avoid an all-out war between the Jewish and Arab populations. Deliberately provoking violence in hitherto quiet areas could bring the Yishuv into conflict with the British – the last thing Ben-Gurion wanted as he contemplated the countdown to statehood and probable war with the Arab states. Moreover, the Haganah, in February–March 1948, felt stretched enough without adding new areas of hostilities. Palmon, at the meeting of Ben-Gurion with his Arab affairs advisers and Haganah chiefs on 1 January 1948, put it this way: "Do we want the Arab people to be united against us, or do we want to benefit from . . . their not being united? Do we want to force all the . . . Arabs to act against us, or do we want to give them the opportunity not to act against us?" Palmah OC Yigal Allon agreed. "There are still untroubled places in the country. There is no need to hit an area which has been quiet for a long time . . . we must concentrate on areas where in effect we are at war."

During December 1947, however, and occasionally thereafter, remote Haganah units, without General Staff direction, carried out a number of unauthorised or poorly conceived operations, which tended to widen rather than curtail the area of hostilities. These operations subsequently came in for severe criticism in the Yishuv's political and intelligence institutions, and, occasionally, in the General Staff itself.

Summarising the first month of fighting, the heads of the Arab Division of the Jewish Agency's Political Department on 1–2 January, in a meeting with Ben-Gurion and the Haganah commanders, severely criticised Haganah attacks in December on Romema and Silwan in Jerusalem, in the Negev, near Kfar Yavetz, and at Khisas, in the Galilee panhandle. Danin and Gad Machnes, another Arab affairs expert, charged that the Khisas attack – in which about a dozen civilians, including four children, had been killed – had unnecessarily spread the fighting to a hitherto quiet area. They had hoped that Jewish restraint would enable the Arab Opposition leaders to re-emerge and frustrate the Husayni-inspired Arab militancy. However the Haganah commanders, including the relatively junior Moshe Dayan, attending as an Arab affairs expert, rejoined that whether or not the Khisas attack had been misconceived, it had prompted the local Arab inhabitants to seek a peace agreement with the Yishuv. Apparently, it had also prompted neighbouring villages to ask non-local Arab irregular bands to leave the area. The implication was that, however unpleasant, the use of force, even if occasionally excessive, was in the long run fruitful. Ben-Gurion, however, in a cable to Shertok, then in New York, said that the Khisas attack had been unauthorised and that the Haganah had apologised for the death of the civilians. A major upshot of the mistaken attacks on Khisas and in Jerusalem was the appointment of Arab affairs advisers – drawn mainly from the Haganah Intelligence Service – to some Haganah district, brigade and battalion headquarters. Throughout the war, these advisers complained that their advice was often ignored or rejected.[12]

As to the Negev, Ben-Gurion, at a meeting of the Mapai Centre (or central committee) on 8 January 1948, said that the Haganah had been largely responsible for "spreading the fire" there; a Palmah unit had "mistakenly" entered an Arab village, provoking Arab fear and attack.[13]

However, these incidents were the exception rather than the rule. Haganah operations were usually authorised and effectively controlled by the General Staff. Moreover, notwithstanding the British view of Haganah operations, the General Staff, through December 1947 – March 1948, attempted to keep its units' fighting as "clean" as possible. While coming to accept the general premise that retaliatory strikes against Arab traffic and villages would inevitably involve the death and injury of innocent people, general orders were repeatedly sent out to all Haganah units to avoid killing women, children and old people. In its specific orders for each operation, the General Staff almost always included instructions not to harm non-combatants, as happened, for example, in an attack on the village of Salama, outside Jaffa, in early January, when Galili specifically forbade the use of mortars because they might cause casualties among non-combatants.[14]

Through January and February the Haganah continued outwardly to accuse the Mufti of waging an organised, aggressive war against the Yishuv. However, the Palestinian war effort was a disorganised, sporadic affair. "The Arabs were not ready [for war] ... There was no guiding hand ... The National Committees and the AHC were trying to gain control of the situation – but things were happening of their own momentum," Machnes told Ben-Gurion and the Haganah commanders on 1 January 1948, and added that most of the Arab population had not wanted hostilities. The Mufti had wanted (and had incited) "troubles" but not of such scope and dimension, said Sasson (who disputed that the outbreaks had been generally spontaneous and unorganised).[15]

After the first weeks of hostilities, the Mufti apparently became perturbed about the situation in Jaffa and Haifa, the main Arab towns, probably in part because of the spectacle of Arab flight. In late December 1947 and in January 1948, Yishuv intelligence sources reported that the

Mufti had decided to shift the focus of Arab military activity from the towns to the countryside in order to relieve the pressure on the towns, but said that the villagers "were not rushing to start operations." However, the Mufti's favourite military commander, 'Abd al Qadir al Husayni, met with other irregulars' commanders, and it was decided to send contingents to the villages, from which they would mount "hit and run" attacks on the Jews. Arab irregulars moved into several villages. Jewish intelligence sources were not optimistic about the villagers' ability to expel the irregulars.

Here, too, there were exceptions. The Mufti apparently was not interested in inciting violence everywhere. In late January, according to Haganah intelligence, he told a delegation from the village of Masmiya al Kabira in the south "to keep quiet and not to clash with the Jews, unless attacked. Similarly, Hajj Amin [al Husayni] added: 'so long as help from the Arab States is not assured, one should avoid battle with the Jews.'"

The change in Arab strategy, moving the focus of violence from the towns to the countryside, had come about, Sasson explained to Ben-Gurion, because of pressure on the Mufti from the townspeople. Sasson advised that the Haganah should keep up or step up its pressure on the towns so that the urban leaders would press for a cease-fire. Attacks on villages, Sasson felt, would lead nowhere as the Mufti would be indifferent to "the death of *fellahin*."[16] During late January, February and March, the Haganah, mainly through a partial siege, maintained the pressure on the main Arab towns.

On 8 January, Ben-Gurion said that so far, only the Arabs of the three big cities (Haifa, Jaffa and Jerusalem) had been sucked into the hostilities; the countryside, despite efforts by the Husaynis to incite it, had remained largely quiescent and non-belligerent. It was in the Yishuv's interest that the countryside remain quiet, and this depended in large measure on the Yishuv's own actions. "We [must avoid] mistakes which would make it easier for the Mufti" to stir up the villages, he said.[17]

Regarding the countryside, the Haganah's policy throughout February and March was "not to extend the fire to areas where we have not yet been attacked" while at the same time vigorously attacking known bases of Arab attacks on Jews and, in various areas, attacking Arab traffic.[18] This policy also applied to the Negev. Yosef Weitz, the chairman of the Negev Committee (the Yishuv's civilian district governor) and director of the Jewish National Fund's Lands Department, put it this way: "As to the Arabs, a policy has been determined: We extend our hand to peace. Every beduin who wants peace, will be satisfied. But if anyone dares to act contrariwise – his end will be bitter."[19] A few weeks earlier, on 13 February, the Palmah's commander in the Negev, Nahum Sarig, instructed his officers on Haganah policy in the south: "(A) Our job is to appear before the Arabs as a ruling force which functions forcefully but with justice and fairness. (B) We must encourage the Arabs to carry on life as usual. (C) We must avoid harm to women and children. (D) We must avoid harm to friendly Arabs." In praxis, this meant, according to the Negev OC, that "Arabs should be allowed to graze their sheep in their fields. If [he] grazes in a Jewish field, [you] must open fire, but avoid hitting the shepherd or confiscating the herd." Searches in Arab settlements should be conducted "politely but firmly . . . If the search is a result of an attempt to hit our forces, you are permitted to execute any man found in possession of a weapon."

The Haganah's difficulty during January–March 1948 was that while it sought to maintain quiet and to pacify as much of the country as possible, its reprisals, sometimes misdirected, sometimes excessive, tended to suck in more and more Arabs into the circle of violence. Only strong, massive, retaliatory action, it was felt, would overawe the Arabs and silence them. But the retaliatory strikes often hit the innocent as well as the guilty, bred anger and vengefulness and made more and more Arab communities susceptible to Husayni's militant–nationalist appeals, despite great initial reluctance to enter the fray.[20]

By and large, however, until the end of March, the Haganah's operations conformed to the general principle of limiting the conflagration, at least in terms of geography, as much as possible. At the same time, Haganah reprisals tended to increase in ferocity as the months passed, as the Haganah units grew accustomed to operations in increasingly larger formations and became more efficient, as Jewish casualties increased and as the Yishuv realised that the life and death struggle had only just begun. But from December 1947 through March 1948 the organisation's policy remained constant: to defend against Arab attack and to retaliate in so far as possible against the guilty, while seeking to limit the scope and dimensions of the conflict.[21] In part, this policy stemmed from Haganah weakness; in large measure, it was due to the belief, at least until the end of March, that the Haganah must hold its fire and horses as the British would not allow a radical change in the Jewish/Arab military balance before their withdrawal from Palestine.

Jewish and Arab peace-making efforts through December 1947 to March 1948

Side by side with the Haganah's policy during the early months of the conflict of trying to restrict the scope of the violence, various Jewish bodies – including the Arab Division of the Jewish Agency Political

Department, the Histadrut's Arab Worker's Department, Mapam and local Jewish authorities – and local Arab leaders, both in towns and villages, tried to make peace, or at least maintain a cease-fire, in many areas of the country.

Good neighbourly relations between Jewish and Arab communities were most long-lasting in the Hefer Valley, around Hadera, in the northern half of the Coastal Plain, and in the area to the east, along northern Samaria's western foothills. Strenuous efforts were also made during the first months of the conflict by Jewish officials, led by Danin and Palmon, to keep peace between the Yishuv and several Arab villages and bedouin tribes in the Coastal Plain north of Tel Aviv, and by Histadrut officials in the Jerusalem area.

In September 1947, as the clouds of war gathered over Palestine, some of the Arab villages in the Samaria foothills initiated a large, "peace meeting" with their Jewish neighbours. The meeting was attended by about 70 Arab local leaders – including the *mukhtar*s of Wadi 'Ara, Ar'ara and the Turkeman tribe near Kibbutz Mishmarot – and 40 Jewish local leaders. The leaders of the largest Arab village in the area, Baqa al Gharbiya, refused to attend. The Arab and Jewish leaders appointed a standing committee to settle disputes between the communities, should they arise.[22]

In the Hefer Valley proper, the newly initiated Arab–Jewish contacts led, on 22 October, to a visit by 60 children from the Kibbutz Ein Shemer school to the school in Khirbet as Sarkas, "where they were received very well." The visit reciprocated one by a class from Khirbet as Sarkas to Ein Shemer and Kibbutz Gan Shmuel earlier that month.[23]

From the local Jewish leadership's point of view, the start of hostilities elsewhere in the country made the strengthening of contacts with their Arab neighbours in the Hefer Valley imperative. "The order of the day is to strive for good neighbourly relations," the local Jewish authorities announced.[24] Earlier, on 12 December 1947, the Jewish and Arab leaders in the Hefer Valley had held a peace celebration in the Emek Hefer Regional Council building, called on the initiative of the *mukhtar* of the 'Arab al Shimali tribe. The Arab leaders said they wanted peace and a continuation of their good relations with their Jewish neighbours. They asked for a promise that the Jews would not harm them and for "the protection of the [regional] council." Announcing the meeting, the Hefer Valley Jewish authorities said the meeting took place despite attempts by emissaries from Tulkarm to "incite" these Arabs against the Jews. The Jews would maintain the peace so long as the Arabs did not break it, said the council. Officials of the Jewish Agency Political Department's Arab Division helped set up the meeting.[25] The Jewish local leaders also made arrangements to provide some of the neighbouring Arab villages with supplies, especially flour, in the event that these should be cut off. Arab families living in Hadera had fled but Arab workers continued to come into the town to work.[26]

Soon after the start of the hostilities, the somewhat inactive Arab Worker's Department of the Histadrut initiated contacts with Arabs in order to promote peace or truces between neighbouring communities in various areas. The fraternity of workers of all nations lay at the core of the trade union federation's ideology. The Histadrut, on 21 January 1948, issued a poster to all Arab "workers" to live in peace with the Jews and to turn their backs on their leaders, "who are leading you to destruction."[27]

The founder of the Arab Worker's Department, who was also its senior official in Jerusalem, Aharon Haim Cohen (no relation of Mapam's Aharon Cohen), was instrumental during January and February in concluding peace agreements between Jewish Jerusalem and its outlying Arab villages of Al Qastal, Sur Bahir and Al Maliha. In early February he reported to the department from Jerusalem that two additional villages, 'Ein Karim and Beit Safafa, had also sent out feelers, saying they were interested in concluding a formal peace. Cohen suspected a Husayni trick, but he noted that 'Ein Karim and Al Maliha that week had "not welcomed" a band of irregulars led by 'Abd al Qadir al Husayni who had asked permission to bivouac in these villages.[28] Several other villages in the Jerusalem area, including Deir Yassin, had already concluded non-belligerency agreements with Jewish Jerusalem.[29]

The following month, 'Abd al Qadir al Husayni's irregulars were again poorly received by the villagers around Jerusalem (in "Qaluniya, Abu Ghosh, Suba, Al Qastal and Sataf"), were not allowed to stay and had to return to their original base at Beit Surik, northwest of the city.[30] A fortnight before, 'Abd al Qadir had tried to incite the inhabitants of Shu'fat, north of Jerusalem, to attack neighbouring Neve Ya'acov. The villagers had demurred, reportedly arguing that if they raided the Jewish settlement, the Jews would retaliate and destroy their village. They were willing to attack Neve Ya'acov, according to the Haganah intelligence report, only if the aim was "real [i.e., permanent] conquest."[31]

The other major irregulars' leader in the centre of the country, Hassan Salama, of Qula, proved equally unsuccessful in stirring up the locals to attack the Jews. The Ramle National Committee told him that they would not attack neighbouring Jewish settlements unless they were themselves attacked. Lydda's National Committee took the same line.[32] Similar resistance to the presence and/or incitement of the militants was displayed in the villages between Tel Aviv and Herzliya (Sheikh Muwannis, Al Mas'udiya (Summeil) and Jammasin). In December 1947 or January

1948, the leaders of these villages, and the *mukhtars* of 'Arab Abu Kishk and Jalil, met with Haganah representatives in the house of Avraham Schapira in Petah Tikva and expressed a desire for peace. They said that if they could not withstand the irregulars unaided, they would call on the Haganah for help. These overtures were apparently matched on the Jewish side in January and February by visits by Palmon and Danin to several villages, including Sheikh Muwannis and 'Arab Abu Kishk, where they asked the inhabitants to remain where they were and to accept Jewish protection and rule.[33] Even as late as early May peace overtures of a sort were reportedly made by several Arab villages. Haganah intelligence reported that As Sindiyana, Sabbarin and Al Fureidis, south and southeast of Haifa, were all interested in "surrendering to the Haganah" but none of them was willing to be "the first." The villagers of Al Kheiriya, east of Tel Aviv, who had evacuated the village weeks before, were reported to be interested in returning and "accepting Jewish authority."[34]

The AHC strongly opposed such local peace initiatives and agreements. The Mufti may at times have wanted a reduction of the scale of the conflict, but he was opposed to anything that resembled peace with or implicit recognition of the Yishuv. The AHC stymied a number of local peace efforts. In mid-January, for example, the British Galilee District Commissioner reported that the Arab leaders of the town of Beisan and the Jewish settlements in the surrounding valley were interested in reaching "an informal agreement of mutual restraint" but the AHC had vetoed the idea. In the Nazareth area and in Acre, the Arab local leaders, the District Commissioner reported, were also interested in some form of cease-fire or curtailment of hostilities.[35]

By and large, however, as the fighting spread, suspicion and antagonism between neighbouring, and in some cases traditionally friendly, settlements grew and the possibility of concluding or maintaining local Arab–Jewish cease-fires or peace agreements receded. This was especially true in the centre of the country, where much of the fighting was concentrated. In the south and north, some neighbouring settlements maintained effective cease-fires for months, primarily because of the mutual need to protect and carry out the summer harvest of their fields. A similar state of non-belligerency, based on tacit or explicit understandings, prevailed with regard to the harvest of the citrus crop in the southern Coastal Plain during the first months of 1948.

The general sense of despair at restoring any form of Jewish–Arab amity and of containing the war emerged in meetings at the end of March of the officials of Histadrut Arab Worker's Department, whose fraternal activities through the first months of the war had largely been limited to distributing peace-promoting leaflets and circulars. One of the Arab Worker's Department officials, Avraham Ben-Zur, on 26 March said that the Arab villages along the border between the prospective Jewish and Arab Palestine states could serve as "bridgeheads" of peace and co-operation between the two emerging entities. He cited a teacher in Khirbet as Sarkas as one possible vehicle for such peaceful endeavour. Eliahu Agassi, the department director, spoke of the leaflets being distributed in the Hefer Valley–Samaria foothills area and of the joint Arab–Jewish supplies committee operating in the Hefer Valley. However, the general tenor of the meeting was not hopeful. At a second meeting, on 30 March, the Department's officials spoke rather unrealistically of possible Jewish–Arab cooperation in the railways, radio station and oil refinery, although they understood that Arab–Jewish coexistence in the countryside had broken down. They focused their attention on one of the last districts in which Arabs were still living in the Jewish state area – in and around Hadera – and planned to visit the town the following week. Agassi said: "Perhaps our visit could stop the exodus of the Arabs from the area." Whether the visit took place is unclear.[36] What is clear is that within a fortnight the Haganah, for strategic reasons, decided that no Arabs should remain in the Hadera area and those still there were expelled (see chapter 3).

By the end of March, there was an impasse. The Husaynis, as in 1936–9, had managed to still the moderate voices in the Arab camp and had gained a firm hold over almost all of Arab Palestine. Most of the country was engulfed in warfare. The Haganah, especially on the roads, was sorely pressed and on the defensive. While some local truces remained in force between neighbouring communities, most Arab villages were now dominated by elements hostile to the Yishuv and many harboured active irregular units. And where the Husaynis were not in control, the locals, fearing the Mufti's wrath, preferred to have no truck with the Jews. They were caught between the hammer and the anvil. Palmon told a meeting of the executives of the Political Department held on 25 March that contacts with the Arabs had been almost completely severed and that "in general, the Arabs could be defined as united [behind the Husaynis] . . . Today, there is almost no area of the country where we can talk with the Arabs, even on local matters, to pacify and calm things down."

Both Palmon and Danin thought that in large measure the situation was a product of ill-conceived Jewish military actions and over-reactions, and that by and large, the Arab affairs experts on the national level and in each locality had been, or were being, ignored by the Yishuv military commanders. The situation, Palmon said, was such that in future the Yishuv might find it difficult "to prove that we weren't the aggressors" –

apart from the Jerusalem area, where the violence was clearly a product of Arab initiative. Danin added that "as a result of several superfluous [Haganah] operations, which mainly hurt 'good' Arabs who were in contact with us . . . the [Arab] mass exodus from all places was continuing. The Arabs have simply lost their faith [in our goodwill?]."

The situation had caused general demoralisation in the Political Department's Arab Division, whose ambivalent functions included both peace-making contacts with Arabs and intelligence-gathering. Danin said that if things continued as they were, the Division "should be closed down." Ya'acov Shimoni, a senior Division official, said that the Haganah Commanders argued that "war was war and that there was no possibility of distinguishing between good and bad Arabs."[37]

The first stage of the exodus: December 1947 – March 1948

The hostilities of December 1947 to March 1948 triggered the start of the exodus of Palestine's Arabs. We shall first examine what happened in the cities, then in the countryside.

The cities

Haifa The exodus from Haifa, which had a population of about 70,000 Arabs and a similar number of Jews, began in early December 1947, a few days after the start of Arab–Jewish hostilities. A British intelligence unit reported that both Jews and Arabs were evacuating the border areas between the two communities and moving to safer districts. The unit commander, stressing, curiously, the movement of Jews rather than Arabs, commented that these initial shifts of population "lead one to speculate on the eventual magnitude that this problem will present during the implementation of partition." The first reported evacuation was of 250 Arab families from the Halissa quarter on 4 December.[38] Abandoning one's home, and thus breaking a major psychological barrier, paved the way for eventual abandonment of village or town and, ultimately, of country. Danin and Palmon on 11 December noted the start of the emigration out of Haifa. Most of the Arab movement out of Haifa's border areas was due to the fighting – sniping, bombings and demolitions – and fears of fighting that marked life on the peripheries of each community. Some Arab families who lived inside or on the edges of Jewish districts on Mount Carmel were intimidated, possibly at IZL or LHI instruction, into leaving their homes.[39]

The intermittent shooting of December culminated in an IZL bombing at the gates of the Haifa oil refinery, the vengeful Arab massacre of Jewish refinery workers and the Haganah reprisal of 31 December at Balad ash Sheikh, a large satellite village southeast of Haifa. The British, for whom Haifa was pivotal to their plans for organised withdrawal from Palestine, increased their patrols and presence in the city and things calmed down. However the attacks on Balad ash Sheikh and neighbouring Hawassa, and several Jewish retaliatory strikes inside the Arab downtown districts, had severely shaken local morale; the Arabs sorely felt the topographical advantage held by the Jews through their command of the Mount Carmel high ground, and the Jews' superiority in organisation, arms and equipment.[40] "The Haifa Arab public began to feel the weakness of its position and there were residents who began to emigrate from the city. Of course, this had a dampening effect on those who remained in the town," later recalled Haifa National Committee member Hajj Mohammad Nimr al Khatib.[41]

Mandate Government sources, according to Ben-Gurion, estimated that by mid-December "15,000–20,000" Arabs had fled from Haifa, but this is probably an exaggeration. The evacuees included Haifa residents who hailed originally from Egypt and Syria, and some of the city's wealthier families. Businesses were closing down, and Arab shopkeepers were selling their stock to Jews at 25% reductions in order to close up quickly.[42] By 22 January, according to Haganah intelligence, some 20,000 Arabs had left Haifa; Arab sources put the figure at 25,000.[43] It is likely that, over the following weeks, a small number of the early evacuees returned to the city, only to leave again in April.

The meeting of the Haifa National Committee of 19 January was dominated by talk of Arab suffering and emigration from the city.[44] The National Committee, largely a reflection of Haifa's Arab business community, "believes that Haifa needs quiet, or at least not to jump to the head of the [Arab] war [effort]" or that "it is in their interest to maintain peace in Haifa as long as possible."[45]

The committee members, led by chairman Rashid al Hajj Ibrahim, wanted an end to the fighting but proved unable to completely restrain the bands of local and foreign irregulars in the city. In mid-January, Ibrahim travelled to Damascus and Beirut to obtain an AHC or Arab League order to curb the militias but he was unsuccessful. On 21 January, the National Committee sent a delegation, headed by the city's Greek Catholic archbishop, George Hakim, and by Sheikh Abd al Rahman Murad, a leading Muslim clergyman, to plead directly with the Mufti, in Heliopolis, Egypt (where Amin al Husayni lived during the war). According to Haganah intelligence, the delegation intended to demand the removal of the non-local irregulars from the city; otherwise, the National Committee would resign and "Haifa would be evacuated."[46]

What the delegation actually told the Mufti is unclear, though presumably it was nothing that could lay them open to charges of betraying the Palestinian war effort. The delegation returned, for all practical purposes, empty-handed. The Mufti had refused to sanction a cease-fire. According to one Haganah informant, the Mufti had said the problem was a national, not a local one, and had reportedly ended the meeting on an ominous note: he had suggested that the Arab struggle against the Jews and the British "could [end by] destroying half the Arabs in Palestine" and had advised the delegates "to remove the women and children from the danger areas in order to reduce the number of casualties."[47]

The British view of the outcome of the Heliopolis meeting was somewhat different: the British thought that the Mufti had agreed that all the irregulars in Haifa be placed under the authority of the local National Committee.[48] If, indeed, this was the agreement, it was never put into practice. The irregulars remained unruly, initiating attacks on Jewish targets and drawing down Haganah retaliation, which, in turn, generated further flight from the Arab neighbourhoods. National Committee members, such as Victor Khayyat, Farid Sa'ad and Judge Ahmad Bey Khalil, told Jewish contacts that they were trying to pacify the town but that the non-local irregulars were being uncooperative and were initiating outbreaks of fighting.[49]

However, the strong British presence, the Haganah's disinclination to launch a major attack and the continued resistance of the moderates in the National Committee to aggressive initiatives by the irregulars combined to contain the situation in the town. Indeed, the moderates repeatedly sought to conclude a truce, lasting at least until 15 May, with the Haganah. And by March even the extremists, according to local Haganah intelligence, sought a truce, probably driven, at least in part, by the spectacle of the steady exodus of the middle classes, which further fighting would only increase.

The Haganah repeatedly brushed aside these Arab overtures believing that a formal truce would not be obeyed by the irregulars and that it would be used by the Arabs to stockpile weaponry. On 30 March, the two Haifa Mapai leaders, Abba Khoushi and Yosef Almogi, brought Ben-Gurion yet another Haifa Arab peace proposal, this one conveyed by Archbishop Hakim to Haifa mayor Shabtai Levy. The Hakim initiative may have been prompted by the 17 March Haganah ambush north of Haifa, in which a large Arab arms shipment headed for the city was destroyed and the commander of the town's irregulars, Mohammad bin Hammad al Huneiti, was killed. The blow severely undermined Haifa Arab morale. Ben-Gurion apparently dismissed the overture. The Haganah city commander, Ya'akov Lubliani, opposed a truce. Taking account of

Lubliani's views Ben-Gurion on 10 March jotted down in his diary: "The Arabs are still leaving Haifa" – seemingly linking in his mind Lubliani's opposition to a truce with the idea that a truce might halt the Arab exodus.[50]

The food shortages and the sense of military vulnerability and isolation caused by the presence of Jewish settlements on the city's access roads certainly contributed to the demoralisation which underlay the exodus; so did the concomitant breakdown of law and order. The irregulars robbed and intimidated the local population, terrorizing the Arab inhabitants they had been sent to protect, in the words of Nimr al Khatib. He blamed equally the irregulars, the British, for doing nothing, and the civilians who had fled, leaving behind houses that invited despolation.[51] "Bands of robbers organised themselves . . . In March . . . waves of robbery and theft became frequent in Arab Haifa . . . From day to day, the feeling grew that Arab Haifa was on the verge of collapse. Anarchy and disorder prevailed in everything." The situation was aggravated that month by the wholesale desertion and flight of the city's Arab constables, who usually took with them their rifles and ammunition.[52]

The exodus from Arab Haifa was fairly closely linked to Haganah retaliatory strikes, Arab attacks and Arab fears of subsequent Jewish retaliation, but for the better educated, especially the civil servants and professionals, there were also several, constant long-term considerations. Ephraim Krischer, a Mapam activist in the town, identified a general fear of future "great disorder" as the main reason for this early stage of the exodus, adding more specifically, that Arab municipal and Mandate employees feared that "in the Jewish State they wouldn't have any chance of advancement in their careers because precedence would be given to Jews." This feeling was reinforced by the fact that most Arab officials lacked fluent Hebrew.[53]

Mapam's Arab Department, probably in part on the basis of Krischer's report, in March analysed the Arab flight from Haifa. The department noted the Arabs' "fears . . . for their future," both in the transitional pre-State period and under Jewish rule, and pointed out that it was mainly "Christians, professionals, officials" who were leaving. By 1 March, the mainly Christian districts of "Old Carmel" and Wadi Nisnas were "almost completely" empty. "The flight is less marked in the eastern parts of town, where the poorer classes, who are under the influence of the extremists, are concentrated," stated the Department. According to this analysis, the Christians were mainly worried about the transitional period, between the end of effective Mandate government and the start of effective Jewish government. They felt that they would then be "between the hammer and the anvil, the Arab terrorist operations and Jewish reactions." Arab public servants feared that their advancement would be blocked by their "lack of Hebrew." Arab railway workers worried about the fate of the railway under Jewish rule.[54]

While the Arab National Committee was clearly worried by the exodus, its efforts to stem it through most of the December 1947 – April 1948 period appear to have been half-hearted and muted. In only one of the 12 communiqués issued by the Committee over the period did it urge the Arab community to remain in the city. On 12 December 1947 the Committee warned against "Fifth Columnists" spreading defeatism and influencing people "to leave their properties and houses, which have become easy prey to the enemy who has seized and occupied them ... Stay in your places," the Committee urged. In none of the communiqués, however, did the Committee explicitly order the population not to leave Haifa and only in Communiqué No. 5, of 16 December 1947, was the call to "stay in your houses" reiterated. Over January–March 1948, the communiqués failed altogether to order or urge the populace to stay at home or in the city. Several, however, urged Arabs to "stay at your posts" – referring, apparently, to militiamen and public servants.[55]

The National Committee's failure to act strenuously to halt the exodus is easily understood. The Committee lacked legal powers to curb the emigration. More important, the pre-April 1948 exodus encompassed mostly the middle and upper classes – precisely the social strata from which the Committee members were drawn. It was their relatives and friends, first and foremost, who were leaving the embattled city. Indeed, many of the Committee members were among the evacuees. By 28 March, according to the Haganah, 11 of the Committee's 15 members had left the town; efforts by chairman Rashid Hajj Ibrahim to lure them back had failed.[56] Those members who had remained behind were hardly in a position to vilify, condemn or punish would-be evacuees, however disruptive the exodus was understood to be to the Arab cause and prospects. This mass flight of the community leaders was to culminate, with telling effect, during the battle for the city on 21–22 April 1948.

Jaffa The exodus from Jaffa, with a pre-war Arab population of some 60,000–70,000, was triggered by the start of hostilities between the town's militiamen and the militia forces of neighbouring Tel Aviv, to the north. No doubt, many of the inhabitants foresaw that the situation would deteriorate as the date of the British evacuation approached. There were strong, constant fears of Jewish retaliatory strikes.[57]

The exodus began in Jaffa's border suburbs. Haganah intelligence on 2 December had already reported an exodus from the Manshiya and Abu Kabir districts: "Empty carts are seen entering and, afterwards, carts loaded with belongings are seen leaving." Loaded trucks were also seen leaving Jaffa itself. Jewish intelligence agents monitored conversations among Jaffa Arabs about leaving. No doubt, the defeatism and exodus of the border districts spread as a result of the influx of their refugees into Jaffa proper.[58]

Six weeks of hostilities and frequently interdicted traffic had left Jaffa on the verge of chaos, according to Yishuv intelligence sources. The LHI's destruction of the Jaffa municipality (*saraya*) with a powerful car-bomb on 4 January 1948 had an especially devastating effect on local morale. Utilities and municipal services broke down, and there were major food shortages. With the flight of middle and upper class families, businesses closed and unemployment became rife.[59] Because of the hostilities, Jewish employers stopped using Arab labour, aggravating the unemployment in the town. The local leaders grew resigned and depressed.

Their defeatism is well illustrated in telephone conversations from Jaffa, which were intercepted and recorded by IZL intelligence (known as the "Delek"). Jaffa lawyer Sa'id Zain ad Din related to a friend or relative in Khan Yunis what had happened on the day when the *saraya* was blown up. Two of the lawyer's relatives had been injured and a whole street had been badly damaged. "Why not move here?" asked the man from Khan Yunis. "We will come soon," said Zain ad Din.

Two days later, on 6 January, the following conversation took place between Abdul Latif Qaddumi, an officer from the contingent of Nablus irregulars in Jaffa, and "Abu Ahmad," from Nablus:

Abdul Latif Qaddumi: "Where is Abu Fiad Qaddumi?"
"Abu Ahmad": "He went to Nazareth."
Abdul Latif Qaddumi: "I think I will soon return to Nablus."
"Abu Ahmad": "If your people in Jaffa don't know how to operate and allow the Jews to do to them as they wish, then leave them and come [back] here."
Abdul Latif Qaddumi: "Indeed, they don't know how to operate here . . . I *will* leave them, let them do as they wish, and [I will] return to Nablus."

In a third conversation, also recorded on 6 January, Rafiq Tamimi, the AHC leader in Jaffa, complained to militia officer Mohammad Khuri that when he had visited the Jibalya and Manshiya districts, the militiamen there had said that they lacked food and were unwilling to do guard duty. Khuri replied that he supplied them with *pita* (Arab bread) and cheese for breakfast, tangerines or oranges and *pita* for lunch and white cheese, *pita* and olives for supper. "That's not enough," said Tamimi, and recommended that occasionally they should also be given meat. Khuri replied "I have no meat." Throughout, the tapped conversations reveal an oppressive fear of the Jews and a fear that other local Arab officials were about to abandon their posts and flee, leaving behind administrative chaos.[60]

By 18 January, the situation in Jaffa was such that an Arab informant told Sasson: "there is no work. Whoever could leave, has left, there is fear everywhere, and there is no safety. Robbery and theft are common," and the National Committee had lost its authority and was expected to resign.[61]

The local notables who constituted the Jaffa National Committee were generally against initiating hostilities with Tel Aviv, fearing Jewish retaliation. Jaffa mayor Yussuf Haykal probably flew to Cairo in early December 1947 to obtain Arab League permission to conclude a cease-fire,[62] but the Husayni activists in the town were busy provoking incidents with the Haganah, and undermining the National Committee. At the same time, the local militia were very poorly armed.[63]

Through January, and perhaps also early February 1948, some Jaffa notables, if not the bulk of the National Committee, sought to conclude a truce agreement with the Haganah. However, the Haganah, as in Haifa, was reluctant – apparently because they felt that Jaffa, like Haifa, was at the Yishuv's mercy and would be beaten to its knees. In February, Ben-Gurion wrote to Shertok saying that Jaffa mayor Haykal, through a British intermediary, was trying to secure a peace agreement with Tel Aviv but that the new, non-local Arab irregulars' commander, Abdul Wahab Ali Shihaini, had blocked him. The mayor had said "that without agreement, Jaffa [would] be entirely destroyed." According to Ben-Gurion, Shihaini had answered: "I do not mind [the] destruction [of] Jaffa if we secure [the] destruction [of] Tel Aviv."[64]

However, to judge from the meeting of the Yishuv political and military leaders held on 1–2 January, Ben-Gurion and the Haganah commander were as opposed to a truce between Tel Aviv and Jaffa as Shihaini. The Haganah, as with Haifa, had the upper hand *vis-à-vis* Jaffa and had no intention of letting Jaffa live in peace and be reinforced so long as the Arabs in other places – principally in Jerusalem – did not allow the Jews to live in peace. Moreover, the Haganah leaders believed, probably with justification, that concluding a truce with Jaffa's civil leaders would not necessarily lead to a cessation of fire by the irregulars.[65]

As in Haifa, the irregulars in Jaffa intimidated the local population, echoing the experience of 1936–9. "Most of the people who stayed with their commander, Adel Nijam ad Din, behaved towards the inhabitants like conquerors. They confiscated their weapons and sold them, imposed fines and stole, and confiscated cars and sold them . . . The inhabitants were more afraid of their defenders/saviours than of the Jews their enemies," wrote Nimr al Khatib. Relations between the various, non-local irregular contingents and the National Committee generally remained poor.[66]

A major reason for the Jaffa National Committee's reluctance to initiate hostilities around the town and against Tel Aviv was fears for the citrus crop, which was then being harvested. The town's economy in large measure was based on the citrus industry – especially on orange exports to Europe through Jaffa port – and the grove-owners and exporters feared that the Jews would block the movement of the crop.[67]

The fears of the Jaffa citrus merchants closely mirrored those of their neighbouring Jewish citrus owners and exporters in the Coastal Plain and were largely responsible for the British-mediated gentleman's agreement of December that the two sides should not hit each other's citrus groves, citrus-carrying trucks and citrus-exporting facilities.[68] That agreement, acquiesced in by the local Tel Aviv Haganah chiefs under pressure from the local Jewish farmers and businessmen, was opposed by the Haganah National Staff and became a major subject of debate in the meeting of 1–2 January 1948 between Ben-Gurion and his top defence and Arab affairs experts. The representatives of the Arab Division, led by Machnes, who was himself a Coastal Plain orange-grove owner, successfully opposed a complete blockade of Jaffa – as demanded by several General Staff members, including Yigael Yadin and Moshe Sneh. The debate on Jaffa ended with Ben-Gurion concluding that there was general agreement on the need to "blockade Jaffa" but that the Arab orange cultivators and Arab orange shipments should be left alone.[69]

The Jewish orange-growers, represented by Yosef Ya'akobson, through January continued to press for a formal cease-fire agreement with the Arabs of the citrus-growing areas (around Jaffa, Rehovot, Nes-Ziona and east and north of Tel Aviv), but to no avail. Ya'akobson charged that Haganah troops in the area were intimidating and terrorising Arab orange cultivators and looting Arab property. Moshe Dayan opposed an agreement, because this was an area in which the Haganah was stronger and also because the Arab irregulars could be supplied elsewhere in the country with food from this area, were it quiescent. Ben-Gurion's aide, Levy Shkolnik (Eshkol), argued that the Yishuv needed quiet in the area during the three months of the orange harvest, but Haganah chiefs Galili and Yadin said that such a truce would benefit the Arabs more than the Jews as "Jaffa and Haifa were Arab weak points." An agreement covering the Coastal Plain would free the Mufti of the pro-peace pressures emanating from the two towns. Ben-Gurion said that while in general he was for limiting the area of hostilities, "I . . . do not believe in the maintenance of [such a] ceasefire as it will be disrupted."[70]

However, a complete blockade was not imposed on Jaffa, and the bilateral orange-picking and exporting continued largely unhampered. In general, the Haganah knew that the British, for political reasons, would crush a Jewish attempt to take the Arab town. Between January and mid-April, the Haganah restricted its activities on the Jaffa front to a partial siege, limited retaliatory strikes and occasional harassment but refrained – except in the case of the Abu Kabir district on 12 March – from major operations.

At the same time, Jaffa's Arab irregulars, because of lack of weapons, trained personnel and good commanders, restricted themselves to sniping, attacking from Abu Kabir Jewish traffic and defensive operations, but the very meagre assistance in additional manpower and material provided by the AHC and the Arab states to the town's defenders over the weeks and months of semi-siege, punctuated by the occasional bomb, sniper's bullet and mortar round, and the knowledge that the Jews could at any time completely cut off the town, wore down the morale of the inhabitants. The middle and upper classes, seeing only a bleak future ahead, continued to leave, further undermining the confidence of the urban masses.

Jerusalem According to the United Nations Partition resolution, Jerusalem, with about 100,000 Jews and 50,000 Arabs, was to be an international zone, albeit one lodged in the middle of the Palestine Arab state. Its hinterland and the access roads to it were dominated by clusters of Arab villages. When the hostilities erupted, the Jewish neighbourhoods, mostly in the western part of the town, came under sniping attacks from the Arab quarters and the community was gradually strangled by the Arab blockade of the main road westwards, to Tel Aviv. By the end of March, despite the convoy system and occasional British military assistance, the city's Jewish districts were under almost complete siege. However, the Haganah and the smaller IZL and LHI units in the town were relatively well-armed and organised, and in the fighting which erupted, the Arab neighbourhoods along the "seam" between the two communities and the semi-isolated Arab quarters in mostly Jewish western Jerusalem were repeatedly hit.

The depopulation of the Arab neighbourhoods in western Jerusalem began with the suburb village of Lifta, and the adjacent districts of Romema and Sheikh Badr, which dominated the beginning of the Jerusalem–Tel Aviv road. Hostilities there were triggered when the

Haganah killed the owner, who came from the nearby Arab village of Qaluniya, of a petrol station in the mixed neighbourhood of Romema; they had suspected him of informing Arab irregulars about the departure of Jewish convoys to Tel Aviv. The following day, Qaluniya villagers avenged the attack by throwing a grenade at a Jewish bus. From then on, Jewish and Arab militiamen around Romema and Lifta exchanged fire daily and the Haganah, IZL and LHI repeatedly raided the two suburbs. The raids, as was their intention, caused the evacuation of the Arabs of Lifta and Romema during December 1947 and January 1948.

A British intelligence report described what happened in neighbouring Sheikh Badr: after a day of Arab sniping, the Haganah, on 11 January, "took the matter into their own hands and blew up the house of Hajj Sulayman Hamini, the village *mukhtar*." A second raid followed on 13 January, with some 20 houses being damaged, and the suburb, after receiving a Haganah order, was evacuated. On 16 January, Sheikh Badr was looted by a Jewish crowd.[71]

The Arabs living in the prosperous western Jerusalem district of Qatamon began evacuating their homes after the Haganah bombing of the Semiramis Hotel on the night of 4–5 January 1948. The Haganah suspected, mistakenly, that the hotel served as the headquarters of the local irregulars. Several Arab families, and the Spanish consul in the city, died in the explosion, and a sharp dispute broke out inside the Haganah and with the British authorities. The action was carried out without Haganah General Staff instruction or consent; Golda Myerson (Meir), the director of the Jewish Agency Political Department in Jerusalem, complained that it had been carried out without her knowledge.[72] High Commissioner Cunningham took Ben-Gurion personally to task for the attack. Cunningham described the Yishuv leader as "clearly upset by this event" and Ben-Gurion, calling the attack "entirely wrong," dissociated himself from it. On 8 January, he informed Cunningham that the Haganah officer responsible, Mishael Schechter (Shaham), the deputy commander in Jerusalem, had been removed from his command.[73] The bombing caused major panic in Qatamon. "Many flats were evacuated, but . . . only by women, the old and children. The young men stayed," stated a Jewish Agency intelligence report of 8 January.[74]

Other retaliatory strikes hit Arab border districts, principally Sheikh Jarrah, at the northern end of town. The cumulative effect of the hostilities on the whole of the city's Arab population, not just in the western parts of the town, was illustrated by a telephone conversation, tapped by Haganah intelligence, between Dr Husayn Khalidi, the AHC member, and an Arab merchant identified as Abu Zaki. Khalidi told Abu

Zaki on 10 January: "Everyone is leaving me. Six [AHC members] are in Cairo, 2 are in Damascus – I won't be able to hold on much longer . . . Jerusalem is lost. No one is left in Qatamon, Sheikh Jarrah has emptied, people are even leaving the Old City. Everyone who has a cheque or a little money – is off to Egypt, off to Lebanon, off to Damascus."[75]

The diary of Palestinian teacher and writer Khalil Sakakini, a resident of Qatamon, provides an insight into the level of fear and mentality of the middle class, urban Palestinian at this time. On 30 March he recorded:

The Jews launched a heavy attack on our neighbourhood . . . last night . . . There were explosions the likes of which were never seen. [Lord] Kitchener, in all his battles, did not hear what we heard tonight . . . The constant whistle of bullets and thunder of shells . . . was unlike anything heard in previous wars . . . No wonder this situation has made residents consider moving to another neighbourhood or town . . . What was most distressing and nerve-wracking was the anxiety which has overcome the women and children . . . Many residents of our neighbourhood have left for the Old City or Beit Jala, Amman or Egypt.

By 13 April, shortly before he and his family fled from Palestine, Sakakini was writing: "Day and night, the heavy artillery shelling and firing of machineguns has been continuous, as if we were on a battlefield . . . Night falls and we cannot get any sleep, and we say that when the morning comes we shall leave our neighbourhood of Qatamon for somewhere else, or leave the country altogether."[76]

It seems that a contributory factor in the flight of the Jerusalem upper and middle classes was the fear of internecine Arab strife as a by-product of the Arab–Jewish hostilities. All remembered the events of 1936–9, when, after the collapse of initial Arab unity, Husayni gunmen assassinated the moderate Nashashibis and their supporters, and remembered the terrorisation of the Arab urban rich and villagers by bands of irregulars.[77]

On 20 January, Israel Zablodovsky (Amir), the Haganah commander in Jerusalem, reported to Ben-Gurion on the demographic movement in the city. The officer related that the Haganah had decided in which mixed Jewish–Arab districts the Jews would stay and ordered them to remain there. In Romema, which had had an Arab majority, the Jews had intended to leave "but the Haganah had not let them," and the Arabs had left. "The eviction of Arab Romema had eased [the Jewish] traffic situation," he reported. The Arabs had also evacuated Kerem as Sila, Sheikh Badr and, in large part, Lifta. "Talbiyeh is also increasingly becoming Jewish, though a few Arabs remain." Sheikh Jarrah's inhabitants had also decamped.[78]

Ben-Gurion summarised what had happened in Jerusalem at a meeting of Mapai leaders on 7 February.

From your entry into Jerusalem through Lifta-Romema, through Mahane Yehuda, King George Street and Mea Shearim – there are no strangers [i.e., Arabs]. One hundred per cent Jews. Since Jerusalem's destruction in the days of the Romans – it hasn't been so Jewish as it is now. In many Arab districts in the west – one sees not one Arab. I do not assume that this will change.

Ben-Gurion added that

what had happened in Jerusalem . . . could well happen in great parts of the country – if we [the Yishuv] hold on . . . And if we hold on, it is very possible that in the coming six or eight or ten months of the war there will take place great changes . . . and not all of them to our detriment. Certainly there will be great changes in the composition of the population of the country.[79]

Ben-Gurion's view of what was happening and what would and should happen nationwide was embodied in his instructions to David Shaltiel, the new Haganah OC in Jerusalem. On 5 February, Ben-Gurion ordered the new OC to conquer Arab districts and to settle Jews in the abandoned and conquered Arab districts.[80] On 12 February, after a Jewish woman had been shot in Talbiyeh, a Haganah loudspeaker van toured the neighbourhood ordering the remaining Arab residents to leave or else "they and their property would be blown up. The van and its occupants were arrested," states a British report, but "the Arabs did evacuate."[81]

During January, many Arab families evacuated the "seam" districts of Musrara and Schneller and the suburban districts or villages of Beit Safafa, Abu Dis, Al 'Eizariya (Bethany) and Beit Sahur. Over the following weeks, more Arab families moved out of Qatamon, the "seam" neighbourhoods and various rural suburbs of Jerusalem. Western Jerusalem became completely Jewish and the eastern Arab parts of the city were partially evacuated.

The beginning of the exodus of the Arab rural population, December 1947 – March 1948

The Arab flight from the countryside began, with a trickle, from a handful of villages, in December 1947, and became a steady, though still small-scale, emigration over January–February 1948. In March, in certain parts of the country, the rural emigration turned into an exodus. In general, the emigration was a direct result of, and response to, specific Haganah (and, in small measure, IZL) attacks and retaliatory strikes and to fears of such attacks, and it was confined to the areas hit by hostilities and/or adjacent to Jewish centres of population. Several communities were attacked or surrounded and expelled by Haganah units and several others were deliberately intimidated into flight by IZL operations. A small number of sites were abandoned or partially abandoned as a result of pressure or commands by Arab irregulars.

The Coastal Plain The flight from the countryside during this period was most pronounced in the Coastal Plain (the Sharon), between Tel Aviv and Hadera, where the Jews were in the majority and which, according to the United Nations Partition resolution, was to be the core of the Jewish State.

The first village to be largely abandoned was Khirbet 'Azzun (Tabsar), just north of Ra'anana, on 21 December 1947, apparently out of fear of Jewish attack. The next to follow were Al Mas'udiya (Summeil), a few hundred yards north of Tel Aviv, on 25 December, which was completely evacuated, and neighbouring Jammasin, on 7 January 1948, which was partially evacuated. The flight from the two was apparently also due to fear. It is worth noting that the inhabitants of Al Mas'udiya fled in the first instance to Jammasin, probably infecting the host villagers with "flight fever"; the guests brought with them a contagious fear and a model of how to respond to the situation – a pattern of temporary refugees precipitating flight by their host communities, to be repeated throughout the country in the following months.

Further to the north, the first weeks of war were marked by the flight eastwards, out of Jewish-dominated areas, of several bedouin tribes or sub-tribes – the 'Arab Balauna on 31 December 1947, the 'Arab Abu Razk on 31 January 1948, the 'Arab an Nuseirat on 3 February and the 'Arab Shudkhi on 11 February. Most of these bedouins evacuated because of fear of Jewish attack. The 'Arab an Nuseirat fled after an actual Haganah attack and the 'Arab Shudkhi after an attack on their encampment by the IZL.

In the following days, the Sharon was evacuated by other tribes and sub-tribes, including the 'Arab ar Rumeilat and the 'Arab Hawitat, both on 15 February, the 'Arab Hijazi on 25 February, the Wadi al Hawarith on 15 March, the 'Arab al Kuz on 23 March, the 'Arab Abu Kishk and the 'Arab as Sawalima, both on 30 March, and the 'Arab Amarir, the 'Arab al Huk and the 'Arab al Falk, all on 3 April. According to Haganah intelligence, the flight was largely motivated by fear of Jewish attack. The 'Arab ar Rumeilat encampments (near Netanya, Kibbutz Hama'apil and Kadima) were evacuated after Haganah intelligence mounted a psychological warfare operation geared to obtaining their departure. The Wadi al Hawarith were attacked and apparently also advised to leave by Haganah intelligence (though earlier, it seems that friendly Jewish local leaders had asked the Wadi al Hawarith to remain). Fear prompted the departure of the 'Arab as Sawalima after the IZL operation at Sheikh Muwannis (see chapter 3). One encampment of 'Arab Abu Kishk was attacked and expelled by an IZL force.[82]

Like the bedouins, the villagers of the Sharon decamped over December 1947 – March 1948 mainly because of Haganah or IZL attacks or fear of such attacks.

The inhabitants of Arab Caesarea, who lived on leased Jewish (PICA) lands, began to evacuate out of fear on 12 January, and others followed on 9 February. On 15 February the village was captured and most of its remaining inhabitants fled or were ordered to leave. Some 20 villagers stayed behind but were expelled on 20 February, after a Palmah unit surrounded the village and destroyed the Arabs' houses. The Haganah perhaps feared that the British army would occupy the village and use it as a base to stop Jewish illegal immigration into Palestine.

This operation was preceded by a Haganah General Staff decision, apparently taken in the first days of February, which was reported to Mapam's Political Committee by Galili on 5 February. The decision to destroy the houses, which were mostly Jewish property, was opposed by Yitzhak Rabin, the Palmah's OC Operations, but he was overruled. Thirty houses were demolished; six were left intact for lack of explosives. The Caesarea Arabs, according to Mapam's Aharon Cohen, had "done all in their power to keep the peace in their village and around it . . . The villagers supplied agricultural produce to the Jewish market in Haifa and Hadera." Caesarea was the first pre-planned, organised expulsion of an Arab community by the Haganah in 1948.[83]

However, the majority of the Sharon's Arab villages were evacuated because their inhabitants feared the Yishuv and felt isolated from the Arab centres of population and highly vulnerable. Al Mirr, northeast of Petah Tikva, was abandoned on 3 February out of "general fear," according to the IDF Intelligence Department. Al Haram (Sidna Ali), west of Herzliya, was abandoned on the same day because of "fear of hostilities." Fajja, adjacent to Petah Tikva, was partially abandoned on 17 February after an IZL attack. Jammasin was left by its last inhabitants on 17 March out of "general fear." Umm Khalid, east of Netanya, was evacuated on 20 March for similar reasons. Jaramla, whose inhabitants began to leave on 8 February after being instructed to do so by Arab irregulars, was finally abandoned on 1 April out of "general fear."[84] In addition, the commanders of Arab irregulars in the Sharon ordered women and children to be evacuated eastwards, "to safety," from a number of villages in late February and early March.[85] In other places, the departure or retreat of garrisons of irregulars affected the local inhabitants, who also took flight.[86]

Flight from other rural communities, December 1947–March 1948 "There is a tendency among our neighbours . . . to leave their villages," the director of the Jewish National Fund's Lands Department, Yosef Weitz, wrote on 31 March 1948 to the JNF's chairman, Avraham Granovsky (Granott). Weitz, writing after a visit to the North, cited the organised departure, in British army trucks, of the inhabitants of Qumiya in the Jezreel Valley on 26 March.[87]

This "tendency" was being promoted and expanded in part by Weitz himself, who was responsible for the Yishuv's land acquisition and, in great measure, for the establishment of new settlements. Soon after the start of hostilities, Weitz realised that the circumstances were ripe for the "Judaization" of tracts of land bought and owned by Jewish institutions (the JNF, PICA) on which Arab tenant farmer communities continued to squat. Under the British, the Yishuv had generally been unable to remove these inhabitants from the land, despite offering generous compensatory payments. Indeed, on occasion, Arab tenant-farmers accepted Jewish compensation and then reneged on their promises to decamp.

The conditions of war and anarchy of early 1948, Weitz understood, at last enabled the Yishuv to physically take possession of these tracts of land. There was also pressure by local Jewish settlers to take over these areas and to remove the tenant farmers. Weitz related on 31 March that Jewish farmers from Nahalal, the Beit Shean (Beisan) Valley and Kfar Yehezkeel had come to him in Haifa to discuss "the problem of our lands in those places with regard to our possession and their liberation from the hands of tenant farmers. We agreed on certain lines of action in certain conditions . . ."[88]

However, Weitz was not, as he sometimes liked to make out in contacts with Granovsky, the mere voice of the Jewish settlements; he was an executive, an initiator of thinking and policy. Already in early January 1948, Weitz's perception of how to solve the Arab tenant farmer problem was beginning to crystallise. After meeting with JNF officials in the North about the tenant farmers in Yoqne'am and Daliyat ar Ruha, Weitz wrote in his diary: "Is not now the time to be rid of them? Why continue to keep in our midst these thorns at a time when they pose a danger to us? Our people are weighing up [solutions]."[89] On 20 February Weitz noted that bedouins in the largely Jewish-owned Beisan Valley, some of whom were living on Jewish-owned lands, were beginning to cross over to the Transjordan. "It is possible that now is the time to implement our original plan: To transfer them there."[90]

The following month, Weitz, on his own initiative, began to implement his solution to the problem of tenant farmers. First he tried, and failed, to obtain a Haganah General Staff decision in principle to evict the tenant farmers. Then, using his personal contacts in the settlements and local Haganah units, and Haganah Intelligence Service officers, he organised several evictions. At Yoqne'am, southeast of Haifa, he persuaded intelligence officer Yehuda Burstein to "advise" the local tenant farmers and those in neighbouring Qira wa Qamun to leave, which they did. Weitz and his JNF colleagues in the North then decided to raze the tenant farmers' houses and to destroy their crops, and to pay the evicted Arabs compensation.[91] At the same time, he organised with the settlers of Kibbutz Kfar Masaryk the eviction of the Ghawarina bedouins in Haifa Bay, who were also squatters on Jewish land, and the eviction of small tenant farmer communities from Daliyat ar Ruha and Al Buteimat, southeast of Haifa.[92]

Towards the end of March, Weitz began pressing the military–political leadership – Galili, Ben-Gurion and Shkolnik (Eshkol) – for a decision at national level to expel the Arabs from the Jewish State area defined by the Partition plan, but his continuous representations and lobbying met with resistance or deflection; the leaders either rejected, or were unwilling to commit themselves to, a general policy or strategy of expulsion.[93] Weitz, at this stage, was therefore forced to privately promote local eviction and expulsion operations. On 26 March, for example, at a meeting with JNF officials, he called for the expulsion of the inhabitants of Qumiya and At Tira, to the northeast, arguing that the inhabitants of the two villages were "not taking upon themselves the responsibility of preventing the infiltration of irregulars . . . They must be forced to leave their villages until peace comes."[94]

While in general the Haganah rejected a policy of expulsion, its strategy of forceful retaliation in the first months of the conflict resulted in the flight of a number of rural communities. The semi-bedouin settlement of Mansurat al Kheit, on the Jordan, was temporarily evacuated during a Haganah retaliatory strike on 18 January. Nearby Al Huseiniya was completely evacuated, as were neighbouring Al 'Ulmaniya and, temporarily, Kirad al Ghannama, near Lake Hula, in mid-March following a Palmah strike on Al Huseiniya which left dozens of dead. The strike followed an Arab landmine attack on Jewish traffic near Yesud Hama'ala on 10 March.[95]

Elsewhere in the north, several Arab villages were completely or partly abandoned during the early months of the conflict out of a feeling of isolation and a sense of vulnerability to Jewish attack. The inhabitants of Al 'Ubeidiya, south of the Sea of Galilee, left for the Nazareth area on 3

March. Many of the inhabitants, especially the rich, of nearby Samakh, left during the first months of the war for similar reasons, and the village was completely evacuated at the end of April.

In the south, the hostilities around the Yishuv's water pipeline to its isolated Negev settlements resulted in March in the flight of bedouin and semi-bedouin communities from their encampments as Arab irregulars blew up the pipeline and Palmah units retaliated by attacking nearby Arab encampments.[96]

Arab attitudes to the exodus, December 1947 – March 1948

The Arab reactions to the start of the Palestinian exodus over December 1947 to March 1948 was confused and uncoordinated – mirroring the confusion and lack of co-operation between the Arab states, between the states and the AHC, between the states, the AHC and the National Committees, the AHC and the foreign Arab volunteer contingents, and between the National Committees and local leaders and the bands of irregulars and militiamen in each locality during the first months of the war.

The exodus at first appeared merely to reproduce what had happened in 1936–9, when approximately 40,000 Palestinians had temporarily fled from the country.[97] As then, the evacuees who reached the Arab states during the first months of the war were mainly middle and upper class families, whose arrival was barely felt and was certainly not burdensome to the host countries. The rural evacuees from the Coastal Plain and north mainly headed, at least initially, for Arab centres of population and villages to the east, inside Palestine (the Jenin–Tulkarm–Nablus triangle). It seems likely that most of the evacuees regarded their dislocation as temporary.

Hence, until the end of March, the exodus had slight impact in the Arab states and troubled their leaders little, if at all. During this period the Arab states did nothing to precipitate flight from Palestine, but, feeling obliged to accept fellow Arab refugees from a holy war with the Jews, they did nothing initially to bar the refugees from entry. Indeed, even before the war, in September 1947, the Arab League Political Committee expected, and theoretically made provision for, an influx of "women, old people and children" from Palestine into their countries. The AHC seems to have opposed this and argued against giving visas to refugees from Palestine.[98]

On a national level, however, Syria and Lebanon had begun to sense by December 1947 that a problem might develop along their borders. On 21 December the Syrian newspaper *Al Ayyam* reported that Damascus and Beirut had asked the AHC to influence the Palestinians along their borders not to flee to Syria and Lebanon but to stay put and fight.[99] Yet, by and large, until May 1948 the Arab states put no physical or legal obstacles to entry in the path of emigrating Palestinians.

By late January, the AHC was itself worried by the phenomenon, according to British military intelligence. Those who had left, the British reported, had been ordered by the Mufti to return to their homes "and, if they refuse, their homes will be occupied by other [foreign] Arabs sent to reinforce [Arab defences in] the areas."[100] Elias Koussa, an Arab lawyer from Haifa, years later recalled that the Mufti in 1948 had had a "stay in Palestine" or "return home" attitude.[101] The Mufti had apparently been especially concerned about the flight from Palestine of army-age males.

However, at this time the Mufti and the AHC did not mount a clear, consistent and forceful campaign against the flight from Palestine. Perhaps they were not overly perturbed by the phenomenon which was still relatively small-scale. Perhaps, also, the Husaynis were not altogether unhappy with the departure from Palestine of many of the middle and upper class families who were traditionally identified with the Opposition. Moreover, the exodus of December 1947 – March 1948 included families and members of families affiliated to the Husaynis themselves, including many AHC members: to condemn them too strongly for fleeing might prompt dissension and backbiting within the Husayni camp. In general, the Palestinian leaders were quicker to condemn flight from the villages than to condemn the exodus of their urban relatives. In addition, the Mufti and the AHC had only an infirm grip on events and developments in the localities around Palestine. The fact that Amin al Husayni disapproved of flight was no assurance that local National Committees or irregular contingents would do much to stop it. As we have seen, the local leaderships and militias had their own set of concerns and priorities. In various parts of the country, especially in the cities, National Committees were hampered in halting the exodus by the fact that many of the evacuees were from among their own kith and kin. Indeed, National Committee members were prominent among the evacuees. By and large, the local leaderships and militia commanders, whether in obedience to the AHC or independently, discouraged flight, even to the extent of issuing formal threats and imposing penalties, but it all proved of little avail.

Haganah intelligence noted the continuing Arab exodus and the local Arab leaders' efforts to stem it: "The Arab institutions are barring [the flight] of those wishing to settle abroad. [But] they are still not preventing the departure of those [claiming to] leave for other reasons, despite [the fact that] many of these are [in fact, would-be refugees], apparently because of a lack of an appropriate apparatus to check these cases."[102]

Another reason for the failure of the Arab institutions at this time to stem the exodus was the caveat endorsed by the Arab states, the Mufti and some of the National Committees themselves, regarding women, the old and children. Amin al Husayni at times explicitly permitted and even encouraged the evacuation of women, children and old people from combat zones or prospective combat zones in order to reduce the possibility of Arab civilian casualties. He may also have believed, mistakenly, that the departure of dependents would heighten the males' fighting motivation. On 8 March, the AHC issued a circular advising the National Committees to move out "women, children and the old" from combat or potential combat zones,[103] but the flight of the dependents seems, in the end, to have weakened rather than strengthened the resolve of the menfolk to stay and fight.

In general, the National Committee members who had remained in Palestine regarded the exodus negatively. Their approach was perhaps embodied in an article in *As Sarikh*, an Iraqi-financed Jaffa paper, on 30 March:

The inhabitants of the large village of Sheikh Muwannis and of several other Arab villages in the neighbourhood of Tel Aviv have brought a terrible disgrace upon all of us by quitting their villages bag and baggage. We cannot help comparing this disgraceful exodus with the firm stand of the Haganah in all localities in Arab territory . . . Everyone knows that the Haganah gladly enters the battle while we always flee from it.[104]

The period between December 1947 and March 1948 saw the start of the exodus of Palestine's Arabs from the areas earmarked for Jewish statehood and areas adjacent to them. The spiral of violence precipitated mass flight by the Arab middle and upper classes from the big towns, especially Haifa, Jaffa and Jerusalem, and their satellite rural communities. It also prompted the piecemeal, but almost complete, evacuation of the Arab rural population from what was to be the heartland of the Jewish State – the Coastal Plain between Tel Aviv and Hadera – and a small-scale, partial evacuation of other rural areas hit by hostilities and containing large Jewish concentrations, namely the Jezreel and Jordan valleys.

The Arab evacuees from the towns and villages left largely because of Jewish – Haganah, IZL or LHI – attacks or fear of impending attack, and from a sense of vulnerability to such attack. The feeling that the Arabs were weak and the Jews very strong was widespread and there was a steadily increasing erosion of the Arabs' confidence in Arab military power. Most of the evacuees, especially the prosperous urban families, never thought in terms of permanent refugeedom and exile; they contemplated an absence from Palestine or its combat zones similar to that of 1936–9, lasting only until the hostilities were over and, they hoped, the Yishuv vanquished. They expected the intervention, and possibly victory, of the Arab states.

Only an extremely small, almost insignificant number of the refugees of this early period left because of Haganah or IZL or LHI expulsion orders or forceful "advice" to that effect, or, from the other side, such orders from Arab military and political leaders. In various areas, in Jerusalem and in some villages, Arab women and children were evacuated on orders or advice from Arab leaders out of fear for their safety rather than as part of any general policy or strategy of evacuation.

Neither the Yishuv, the Palestine Arab leadership nor the Arab states during these months had a policy of removing or moving the Arabs out of Palestine or the Jewish-dominated parts of Palestine. With the exception of the tenant farmers, the few expulsions that occurred in these first months were dictated by Haganah strategic considerations; the few cases where Arab local commanders ordered a village to be evacuated or partially evacuated occurred for similar reasons.

In general, during the first months of war until April 1948, the Palestinian leadership struggled, if not very manfully, against the exodus. "The AHC decided . . . to adopt measures to weaken the exodus by imposing restrictions, penalties, threats, propaganda in the press [and] on the radio . . . The AHC tried to obtain the help of neighbouring countries in this context . . . [The AHC] especially tried to prevent the flight of army-age young males," according to IDF intelligence.[105] But there was no stopping the exodus.

Chapter 3

The second wave: the mass exodus, April–June 1948

The Yishuv looked to the end of March with grim foreboding: it was a community with its back to the wall in almost every sense. Politically, the United States appeared to be withdrawing from its earlier commitment to Partition and a Jewish State, and was pressing for "trusteeship" – an extension of Great Power rule – in Palestine beyond 15 May. Militarily, the Arab campaign along the roads, which was interdicting Jewish traffic, was slowly strangling the Jewish towns and threatening the existence of the outlying, rural settlements. Most Jewish settlements had Arab neighbours; Arab villages and towns sat astride the roads between the Jewish settlements. Some clusters of Jewish settlements were in particular jeopardy. The Galilee panhandle settlements could be reached only via the Jordan Valley road and the Nahariya–Upper Galilee road, both of which were dominated by Arab villages. Nahariya and the kibbutzim of Western Galilee were cut off from Jewish Haifa by Acre and a string of Arab villages. Haifa itself could not be reached from Tel Aviv via the main coastal highway since At Tira, Ijzim, Jaba and 'Ein Ghazal dominated the northern sector. The veteran Mapam kibbutz, Mishmar Ha'emek, which dominated the potential major route of advance for an Arab army from the Jenin–Nablus–Tulkarm triangle (henceforward referred to as the Triangle) to Haifa, was surrounded by Arab villages. To the south, the 100,000 Jews of Jerusalem were almost completely besieged and running low on ammunition and food. In the Hebron Hills, the four kibbutzim of the Etzion Bloc were under siege, and the cluster of 15 or so Jewish settlements in the Negev were each under intermittent siege, with their vital water pipeline continuously sabotaged by marauding bedouin. Three major Jewish convoys, the Yehiam convoy, the Nabi Daniyal convoy and the Khulda convoy, were ambushed and destroyed during the last week of March, with the loss of more than 100 Haganah troops and the bulk of the Haganah's armoured truck fleet. The British evacuation, which would remove the last vestige of law and order in the cities and on the roads, was only weeks away, and the neighbouring Arab states were openly threatening to intervene and invade Palestine. The Yishuv was struggling for its life; an invasion by the Arab states, including the British-officered Arab Legion, could deliver the *coup de grâce*.

It was with this situation and prospect in mind that the Haganah chiefs, in early March, produced "*Tochnit Dalet*" (Plan D), a blueprint for securing the emergent Jewish State and the clusters of Jewish settlements outside the State's territory against the expected Arab invasion on or after 15 May. The battle against the local and foreign irregulars had to be won first if there was to be a chance of defeating the invading regular Arab armies. To win the battle of the roads, the Haganah had to pacify the Arab villages and towns that dominated them: pacification perforce meant either the surrender of the villages or their depopulation and destruction. The essence of the plan was the clearing of hostile and potentially hostile forces out of the interior of the prospective territory of the Jewish State, establishing territorial continuity between the major concentrations of Jewish population and securing the Jewish State's future borders before, and in anticipation of, the Arab invasion. As the Arab irregulars were based and quartered in the villages, and as the militias of many villages were participating in the anti-Yishuv hostilities, the Haganah regarded most of the villages as actively or potentially hostile.

Plan D's architects, headed by Haganah OC Operations Yigael Yadin, did not know whether the British would withdraw piecemeal and gradually from various areas of the country during the months and weeks before 15 May or whether they would pull out *en masse* on or just before that date. In any case, Yadin and the officers envisaged activating the plan on or about 15 May, with preparations for its implementation beginning on 7 May. However, the military realities of clogged Jewish lines of communication, of besieged and slowly asphyxiated settlements, and of gradual and early British withdrawal from various areas forced the Haganah General Staff to bring forward its timetable. The implementation over April–May followed hard on the heels of the successive British military withdrawals from each district. The Haganah offensives generally followed the geographical, strategic and tactical guidelines set down in the plan; but, in part, they were also dictated by the specific requirements of situation and Jewish peril in the various districts. The plan augured a quick end to the civil and guerrilla war that was raging between the thoroughly intermixed Arab and Jewish populations and a switch to straightforward or almost straightforward conventional warfare after the expected Arab invasion on or after 15 May.

Plan D was not a political blueprint for the expulsion of Palestine's Arabs: it was governed by military considerations and was geared to achieving military ends. But, given the nature of the war and the admixture of the two populations, securing the interior of the Jewish State for the impending battle along its borders in practice meant the depopulation and destruction of villages that hosted hostile local militia and irregular forces.

The plan called for "operations against enemy settlements which are in the rear of, within or near our defence lines, with the aim of preventing their use as bases for an active armed force." For the first time in Haganah strategy during the war, Plan D provided for the conquest and permanent occupation, or levelling, of Arab villages and towns. It instructed that the Arab villages should be surrounded and searched for weapons and irregulars. In the event of resistance, the armed forces in the village should be destroyed and the inhabitants should be expelled from the State. In the event of non-resistance, the village should be disarmed and garrisoned. Some hostile villages (the report does not specify which ones) were to be destroyed "([by] burning, demolition and mining of the ruins) – especially . . . villages that we are unable to permanently control." The Haganah wanted to preclude the renewed use of such villages as anti-Yishuv bases.[1]

The plan, which reached all brigade OCs and district commanders, and probably also many battalion-level commanders, was neither used nor regarded by the Haganah senior field officers as a blanket instruction for the expulsion of the country's civilian inhabitants. But, in providing for the expulsion of communities and/or destruction of villages that had resisted the Haganah, it constituted a strategic–ideological anchor and basis for expulsions by front, district, brigade and battalion commanders (who in each case argued military necessity) and it gave commanders, post facto, a formal, persuasive covering note to explain their actions.

However, during April–June relatively few Haganah commanders faced the dilemma of whether or not to carry out the expulsion clauses of Plan D. The Arab townspeople and villagers usually fled from their homes before or during battle; the Haganah commanders had rarely to decide about, or issue, expulsion orders (though they usually prevented inhabitants who had initially fled from returning home after the dust of battle had settled).

Plan D aside, there is no trace of any decision-making by the Yishuv's or Haganah's supreme bodies in March or early April in favour of a blanket, national policy of driving out the Arabs. Had such a decision in principle been taken by the People's Administration, the Jewish Agency Executive, the Defence Committee or the Haganah General Staff, it would have left traces in the sources. Nor – perhaps surprisingly in retrospect – is there evidence, with the exception of one or two important but isolated statements by Ben-Gurion, of any general expectation in the Yishuv of a mass exodus of the Arab population from the Jewish or any other part of Palestine. Such an exodus may have been regarded by most Yishuv leaders as desirable; but in late March and early April, it was not regarded as necessarily likely or imminent. When it occurred, it surprised even the most optimistic and hardline Yishuv executives, including the leading advocate of the transfer policy, Yosef Weitz. On 22 April 1948 he visited Haifa, witnessed the start of the mass exodus and wondered about "the reason . . . Eating away at my innards are fears . . . that perhaps a plot is being hatched [between the British and the Arabs] against us . . . Maybe the evacuation will facilitate the war against us." The following day he wrote: "Something in my unconscious is frightened by this flight."[2]

However, from the beginning of April, there are clear traces of an expulsion policy on both national and local levels with respect to certain key strategic districts and localities. Sometime during 7–9 April Ben-Gurion and the Haganah General Staff, under the impact of the dire condition of Jewish Jerusalem and the ALA attack on Mishmar Ha'emek, and under pressure from local Jewish settlements and Haganah commanders, decided, in conformity with the general guidelines of Plan D, to clear out and destroy the clusters of hostile or potentially hostile Arab villages dominating vital axes. A policy of clearing out Arab communities sitting astride vital routes was instituted. Sometime during 8–10 April orders went out from the General Staff to the Haganah units involved to clear away and, if necessary, expel most of the remaining Arab rural communities along the Tel Aviv–Hadera axis, the Jenin–Haifa road (around Mishmar Ha'emek) and along the Jerusalem–Tel Aviv road. Exceptions were made only of Al Fureidis and the 'Arab al Ghawarina (Khirbet Jisr az Zarqa) on the Tel Aviv–Haifa road and Abu Ghosh on the Tel Aviv–Jerusalem road.

Reinforcement of this policy and an insight into Ben-Gurion's views in the matter were provided at a meeting between Ben-Gurion and two of his Arab affairs advisers on 6 May. The three agreed, regarding "troublesome [Arab] villages [*kfarim mafri'im*]," that, concerning "an Arab village that hinders the Yishuv's plans or is provocative, the Arab Affairs Department has permission to decide on its removal [*siluko*]."[3]

Military action "in the spirit of" Plan D began at the start of April with Operation Nahshon, in which the Haganah, temporarily lifting the siege of Jewish Jerusalem, for the first time permanently took and occupied an Arab village (Al Qastal, 2–9 April) and levelled other villages (Qaluniya, 11 April; Khulda, 20 April). At the same time, in the battles for Mishmar Ha'emek (4–15 April) and Ramat Yohanan (15–17 April), the Haganah underlined the radical shift in strategy, in accordance with the precepts of Plan D, by taking, permanently occupying and/or levelling a cluster of Arab villages. The formal, premature implementation of Plan D began a few days later with the conquest of Arab Tiberias (16–18 April) and Arab Haifa (21–22 April).

The society against which the offensives of Plan D were to be unleashed, had, as we have seen already undergone months of strain and
corrosion. Palestinian arms, supplemented by a steady stream of foreign
volunteers, had partially succeeded in wearing down the Haganah and had
severely curbed Jewish use of the roads, but while many Jewish
settlements remained under semi-permanent siege, the Arab forces had
failed to capture any of them, although not for lack of effort. Worse,
Jewish ambushes and road-blocks had in turn isolated many Arab
settlements and a feeling of siege was apparent in the two main Arab
centres, Haifa and Jaffa. The flight of the middle and upper classes from
these towns and from Jerusalem during the previous months had severely
undermined general morale; so had the gradual breakdown of law and
order in the Arab neighbourhoods, which stemmed from the influx of the
armed foreign volunteers and the concomitant devolution, and expectations of the imminent devolution, of British government.[4]

The process of disintegration accelerated in April. Policemen ran off
with their weapons; increasing numbers of officials failed to arrive for
work. The volunteers stole property, molested women and in general
intimidated the townspeople, and at the same time did not carry out their
martial duties with particular effectiveness or in a manner likely to
maintain the communities' confidence in their ability to beat off, let alone
defeat, the Haganah.[5] In addition, the Palestinian Arabs' "national" sense
of isolation from the surrounding Arab world was continually reinforced
by the repeated rejections by the Arab States, the AHC and the Defence
Committee in Damascus of requests for arms from this or that village or
town. Furthermore, in the towns there were intermittent food shortages,
sharp price rises and widespread unemployment.

By and large the situation in the villages was better than that in the
cities; the villages were more or less economically autarkic and not all areas
of the country were engulfed or seriously affected by the conflagration.
However, most of the villages, in one way or another, were affected by
what happened in the cities, to which they looked for leadership,
information and support. In the area around Tel Aviv and Jaffa, in the
Jerusalem corridor, in eastern Galilee and in the Negev, the villagers were
also directly caught up in the fighting, sustaining losses and Haganah
attacks. The general slide into lawlessness, fears about the harvest of
summer crops and about whether the Jews would interfere and burn
fields, fear of the Haganah and of the IZL, and concern about what would
happen when the British left, in varying degrees all affected the villagers.

The Haganah's offensives in April caught the Arab states and the AHC
by surprise; so did the mass exodus which they precipitated. For several
weeks, the Arab world failed to react to the evacuation – until the exodus
from Haifa (22–30 April). Given the poor communications, it probably

took some days for them to learn of, and understand, what was happening, especially regarding the exodus from the countryside. Perhaps some of the leaders feared to make too much of the exodus lest they stoke up public pressure in their own countries to invade Palestine even before the British withdrawal. In terms of propaganda value, and as a priori justification for their contemplated invasion of Palestine, nothing suited better than the exodus, which could be – and was – presented to the world as a deliberate, mass expulsion of the Arabs by Jews. And, alternatively, if there were uncoerced evacuations, surely they demonstrated – again to the benefit of Arab propaganda – that Arabs were unwilling to live under Jewish rule, making nonsense of the minority provisions in the Partition resolution. In any case, no one regarded the exodus as permanent; surely the refugees would within weeks return to their homes, in the wake of the Arab invaders?

Whatever the reasoning and attitudes of the Arab states' leaders, I have found no contemporary evidence to show that either the leaders of the Arab states or the Mufti ordered or directly encouraged the mass exodus during April. It may be worth noting that for decades the policy of the Palestinian Arab leaders had been to hold fast to the soil of Palestine and to resist the eviction and displacement of Arab communities.

Two qualifications are necessary, one relating to the continued promotion of the evacuation of women, children and the old from front line or potential front line areas, and the other to the compulsory evacuation of specific villages by order of Arab military or political leaders for mainly military reasons.

During April, the irregulars and at least some of the National Committees, apparently at the behest of the AHC, continued to promote, either out of inertia or in line with reiterated policy, the departure from combat and potential combat zones of women, children and the old. Ben-Gurion at the start of the month speculated with regard to this partial evacuation from the Coastal Plain villages: "Possibly it is being done because of pressure from the gangs' [i.e., irregulars'] commanders out of Arab strategic needs: Women and children are moved out and fighting gangs are moved in."[6] His remarks were based on Haganah intelligence reports. On 22 April the National Committee in Jerusalem, citing the AHC circular of 8 March, ordered its local branches around Jerusalem (Sheikh Jarrah, Wadi Joz, Musrara, Qatamon, etc.) to move out their women, children and old people "to places more distant, away from the dangers." The National Committee warned that resistance to this order by the local branches would be seen as "an obstacle to the Holy War [*Jihad*] and in the way of the fighters, and would hamper their actions in these neighbourhoods."[7] On 24 April, the ALA ordered the inhabitants of

Al Fureidis, south of Haifa, to evacuate their women and children from the village, "and make ready to evacuate [the village] completely."[8] A few days later, the Arabs around Rosh Pinna, in the Eastern Galilee, were ordered to evacuate their women and children, the men staying "to guard the settlements."[9] Even units of the Arab Legion, until 14 May nominally a part of the British Army, in early May ordered the evacuation of women and children from Beisan in order to better defend it against Jewish attack.[10]

During April–May, more than 20 Arab villages were largely or completely evacuated because of orders by local Arab commanders, by Arab governments or by the AHC, mostly for pre-invasion military reasons. On 13 May the villages of Shu'fat, Beit Hanina, Al Jib, Judeira, Beit Nabala and Rafat were evacuated at the command of the Arab Legion. Issawiya, also in the Jerusalem area, was evacuated at AHC command on 30 March. On 20 May the villagers of Ad Dahi, Nein, Tamra, Kafr Misr, At Tira, Taiyiba and Na'ura, all in the Mount Gilboa district, were ordered to leave by Arab irregular forces (who apparently feared that the villagers intended to throw in their lot with the Yishuv), and on 6 April, the AHC, probably for similar reasons, ordered the evacuation of the Lower Galilee villages of Sirin, 'Ulam, Hadatha and Ma'dhar.[11]

Until the last week of April, the AHC and the Arab governments, at least publicly, did not seem to be unduly perturbed by the exodus. Azzam Pasha (Secretary General of the Arab League), to be sure, in April used the flight and the massacre at Deir Yassin (see below) to drive home anti-Zionist propaganda points, but there seems to have been no feeling that something momentous was happening. The Arab states did nothing: they acted neither to aggravate the exodus nor to stem it.[12]

The AHC was probably driven by a set of contradictory interests. On the one hand, its members – almost to a man out of Palestine by the end of April – were unhappy at the sight of the steady dissolution of Palestinian society and the uprooting of the villages. The exodus dashed their hopes of a successful Palestinian resistance against the Yishuv. On the other hand, led by the Mufti, they understood by late April that the Palestinian–Yishuv battle was lost, and that now, all depended on intervention by the Arab states. Amin al Husayni well knew the essential fickleness of the Arab leaders, and understood that Egypt's King Farouk, Transjordan's King Abdullah and Lebanon's Prime Minister Riad Solh and the rest were not overly eager to do battle with the Haganah on the Palestinians' behalf. The bigger the tragedy in Palestine, the greater would be the pressure – by public opinion at home, by the other states and by the demands of Arab "honour" – on these leaders to abide by their commitment to intervene. Nothing would bind them to their word like a great tragedy. Moreover, the AHC was unhappy at the prospect of Arab communities surrendering to Jewish arms and agreeing to live in peace under Jewish rule. Probably pulled hither and thither by these contradictory considerations, the AHC members seem to have preferred to do and say nothing. During April, Amin al Husayni and the AHC remained silent about the unfolding exodus.

Given the lack of clear direction from the Arab states and from the AHC, the burden of decision-making fell mainly on the shoulders of local Palestinian leaders, both civil and military. It is largely to the local leadership, therefore, that one must look for decision-making concerning staying or leaving by this or that Arab community during April 1948. Local leaders may have been motivated in part by what they thought the AHC would want them to decide, as in Haifa on 22 April, but in general, they were left to their own devices. Thus in cases where it was the Arab decision-making element, rather than Jewish attack, that was important, the pattern of behaviour was haphazard and idiosyncratic. The National Committee in Jerusalem, for example, preferred to hold on and sit tight; it repeatedly ordered the Arab population, on pain of punishments, to stay put. On the other hand, in Jaffa, most of the National Committee members fled during the fighting and none apparently acted to stem the exodus.[13]

However, the fall of Arab Haifa on 21–22 April and the subsequent mass exodus of its inhabitants, the previous evacuation of Arab Tiberias, and the start of the exodus from Jaffa, at last sounded the alarm in the Arab capitals. The exodus was becoming massive, and the Arab states would be burdened with a giant problem if the tide was not turned. Already in late April Haganah officers noted that Abdullah was pressing the refugee bedouin of the Beit Shean (Beisan) Valley to cross the Jordan and go back to their homes.[14]

In early May, the Arab states neighbouring Palestine, spearheaded by Transjordan and the ALA, launched a public campaign to stem the outflow of refugees from Palestine and to induce those who had fled to return. Again, the policy was uncoordinated and the communications poor and often inconsistent, but its thrust was clear. Orders went out to the local irregulars' commanders and *mukhtars* to bar flight. In Kafr Saba, the locals, under threat of Haganah attack, wanted to leave, but were ordered to stay by the ALA garrison.[15] According to Haganah sources, the ALA, with the population of Ramallah about to take flight, blocked all roads into the Triangle: "The Arab military leaders are trying to stem the flood of refugees and are taking stern and ruthless measures against them." Arab radio broadcasts, picked up by the Haganah, conveyed orders from the ALA to all Arabs who had left their homes to "return within three days. The commander of Ramallah assembled the *mukhtar*s from the area" and demanded that they strengthen morale in their villages. The local ALA commanders turned back trucks which were coming to take families out of Ramallah.[16] Qawuqji threatened that the homes of villagers who left would be blown up and their lands would be confiscated. Haganah intelligence on 6 May reported that "Radio Jerusalem in its Arabic broadcast (14:00 hours, 5 May) and Damascus [Radio] (19:45 hours, 5 May) announced in the name of the Supreme Headquarters: 'Every Arab must defend his home and property . . . Those who leave their places will be punished and their homes will be destroyed.' The announcement was signed [by] Qawukji."[17] Haganah Radio related that "in an endeavour to put a stop to the flight of Arabs from towns and villages, the Arab command has issued a statement warning all Arabs that from now on they are expected to guard their own houses and property . . . Any Arab leaving his place of residence will be severely punished."[18] In the south, some of the inhabitants of Beit Daras, fleeing their homes after a Haganah attack, were sent back by the Arab military command in Majdal.[19]

Over 5–15 May, Abdullah, the AHC, the National Committees and Azzam Pasha in semi-coordinated fashion issued a series of announcements designed to halt the flight and to induce the refugees to return to their homes. A special appeal to return home, which was also promoted by the British Mandate authorities, was directed at the refugees from Haifa. The various National Committees issued bans on flight. The Ramle National Committee set up pickets at the exits to the town to prevent Arabs departing. The inhabitants of the villages east of Majdal (Beit Daras, the Sawafirs, etc.) were warned not to abandon their homes and the pickets in Majdal and Gaza were warned not to allow them in with their belongings. On 15 May, Faiz Idrisi, the AHC's "inspector for public safety," issued orders to Palestinian militiamen to help the invading Arab armies and to fight against "the Fifth Column and the rumour-mongers, who are causing the flight of the Arab population." On 10–11 May, the AHC called on officials, doctors and engineers who had left the country to return and on 14–15 May, repeating the call, warned that officials who did not return would lose their "moral right to hold these administrative jobs in the future." Arab governments began to bar entry to the refugees – as happened, for example, on the Lebanese border in the middle of May.[20] By the end of May, with the Arab armies fully committed, the Arab states and the AHC put pressure on the refugee communities encamped along Palestine's frontiers to go home. According to monitored Arab broadcasts, the AHC was arguing that "most of the [abandoned] villages had been made safe thanks to Arab victories." Jamal Husayni, a key AHC member, pressed for the return of the refugees.[21]

However, the sudden pan-Arab concern in the first half of May that the Arabs remain in Palestine or, if in exile, return to their homes, came too late and perhaps was not expressed forcefully enough. Concern was not translated into effective policy nor given executive teeth. Having failed to halt the mass exodus *ab initio*, the Arab states proved powerless to neutralise its momentum, let alone reverse the process in the following weeks. In any case, the refugee flood of late May and early June was relatively unimportant for the Arab leaders, who were preoccupied instead with the generally poor performance of their armies in Palestine, with inter-Arab political feuding and with the anti-Zionist diplomatic struggle at the United Nations, in London and in Washington. By mid-June, when the First Truce took effect, and the Arab states were able to turn attention to the refugee problem, conditions in the field had radically changed. The borders had become continuous front lines with free-fire zones separating the opposing armies, and the victorious Yishuv was resolved to bar a return. Thus, the pressure by some of the Arab countries to push the refugees back across the borders, reported by IDF intelligence in early June, had little effect.[22]

To understand what happened over April–May 1948, when the major wave of the Palestinian exodus took place, it is necessary to examine in detail what occurred in the field. To describe and analyse what happened in every operation and area would be repetitive and, ultimately, confusing. I shall therefore focus on the cities and main towns and on key areas of the countryside.

The cities

Tiberias The first Arab urban community to fall was that of Tiberias, the mixed Jewish–Arab town on the western shore of the Sea of Galilee, which sat astride the north–south road linking the Jewish settlements in the Galilee panhandle with those in the lower Jordan Valley.

Intermittent sniping started in early February, souring the traditionally peaceful relations between the city's 6,000 Jews and 4,000 Arabs, who were concentrated in the downtown Old City area. Arabs began sending their families to safer areas, and Jews began to leave the Old City for the larger Jewish districts.[23] At the beginning of March, a Haganah raid precipitated the evacuation of the Arab village of Al Manara, two-and-a-half kilometres south of Tiberias.[24] A few days later, Arab–Jewish sniping was renewed. It ended in a local agreement between Jewish and Arab notables, which received the blessing of Haganah chief Israel Galili: "It's good that you've done this," he told the Tiberias Jewish notables who came to him, "because we have plenty of fronts and we would rather not spread ourselves [too thin]."[25]

The shooting in and around the Old City was renewed on 8 April. The large British force in the town tried to make peace but failed. On 12 April, a Haganah force captured the village of Khirbet Nasir ad Din and the Sheikh Qaddumi hilltop above it, overlooking Tiberias, cutting the city off from Lubiya, the major Arab centre to the west. Some non-combatants were apparently killed and some houses destroyed. Most of the population fled to Lubiya or to Tiberias, from where British troops evacuated them to Lubiya. Several dozen villagers remained *in situ*. The arrival of the Khirbet Nasir ad Din refugees probably helped to undermine the morale of the Arabs of Tiberias.[26]

The Haganah decided to pacify Arab Tiberias. On the night of 16–17 April, units of the Golani Brigade and the Palmah's 3rd Battalion attacked the Old City, using mortars and dynamite, and blowing up eight houses. The attack caused "great panic" among the Arab inhabitants. Arab notables apparently sued for a truce but the Haganah commanders refused to negotiate; they wanted a surrender.[27] The Arabs then appealed to the British to lift the Haganah siege on the Old City and to extend their protection to the Arab areas. At the same time, they asked the ALA contingent to withdraw from the town.[28] The British, however, said they intended to evacuate the city within a few days and hence could offer no protection to the Arabs beyond 22 April. The Arab notables then decided, perhaps with British prompting, to evacuate the city with British help. The British governor subsequently called in the Jewish representatives and informed them that they would be leaving in a few days, that they were unwilling to guarantee the Arabs' safety after their departure and that "in order to assure the Arabs' safety, it had been decided to evacuate the Arabs from the town."[29] According to the ranking Jewish representative, Moshe Tzahar, the news of the Arab evacuation came to him as a "shock." He was unable to consult with the Haganah in Tel Aviv as the telephone lines were down. According to his recollection, he protested to the military governor against the evacuation but the British "did not relent." Tzahar then asked that the governor summon the Arab leaders so that he could argue with them against the decision. The governor answered: "There are no longer leaders [here]. They have fled. There is a population without leadership." A truce was instituted. The British then brought up buses and trucks, the Arabs got on and the buses, under British escort, took them to Nazareth and Transjordan. "There is a chance," reported the 3rd Battalion on 18 April, "that Tiberias tomorrow will be empty of Arabs." The Golani and 3rd Battalion troops had not been ordered to expel the inhabitants of

Tiberias, nor had they done so. Indeed, they had not expected the civilian population to evacuate the town. At the same time, once the decision to evacuate had been taken and once the evacuation was in progress, at no point did the Haganah act to stop it, or in any way indicate dissatisfaction with, or opposition to, the Arab departure.[30]

During the night of 18–19 April, Tzahar and the heads of the Tiberias Jewish community printed a proclamation explaining what had happened. They wrote that the Arabs had started the fighting on 8 April, the Haganah had responded, the Arabs had decided to leave, and "We did not deprive the Arab inhabitants of their homes." The leaflet enjoined the Tiberias Jews not to lay hands on Arab property and houses as "the day will come when the Arab inhabitants will return to their homes and property in the town."[31]

Three days later Jamal Husayni informed the United Nations that the Jews had "compelled the Arab population to leave Tiberias." A few years later, the OC of the Golani Brigade seemed to concur with this judgement when writing that the brigade's conquest of the key Arab military position in the town had "forced the Arab inhabitants to evacuate [the city]."[32] Both protagonists apparently meant that, given the Haganah's unwillingness to agree to a truce short of complete victory and takeover of control in Tiberias, the local Arabs had felt that they had had no choice but to leave; they had apparently been unwilling to resign themselves to Jewish rule.

However, to judge from the evidence, the decision to evacuate Tiberias was taken jointly by the local Arab leaders and the British military authorities; it is more than possible that the idea of the evacuation, under British protection, was first suggested by British officers. Elias Koussa a year later charged that "the British authorities forcibly transported the Arab inhabitants [of Tiberias] en masse to Transjordan." Instead of forcefully restoring order in the town, as was their "duty," they "compelled the Arabs to abandon their homes and belongings and seek refuge in the contiguous Arab territory."[33]

Two possible precipitating factors in the Arab decision to evacuate Tiberias were the prior evacuation of Al Manara and the Jewish conquest of Khirbet Nasir ad Din, which left the Tiberias Arabs isolated and cut off from the south and west, and the British unwillingness to offer long-term protection as well as the announcement of the impending British withdrawal from the city. The flight, at the start of the battle, of leading Tiberias notables, including the Sudki al Tabari family, was probably a major factor in the exodus of the remaining Arab inhabitants.[34] The "atrocity factor" should probably also be considered here as a contributing factor since the Arabs of Tiberias were no doubt still under the impress of the massacre the week before at Deir Yassin and, more recently, of the alleged or actual killing of non-combatants at nearby Khirbet Nasir ad Din.

Haifa The exodus of the Arabs of Haifa was one of the major events of the war. The departure of the city's Arab population, which before the war had been 70,000, alone accounted for some 10% of the total of Palestine Arab refugees. The fall of, and exodus from, Arab Haifa, given the city's pivotal political, administrative and economic role, especially in the north, was a major direct precipitant and indirect cause of the subsequent flight of Arabs from the Haifa sub-district and other areas of the country, including Jaffa, Acre and Safad.

The exodus of 22–30 April must be seen against the backdrop of the gradual evacuation of the city by some 20,000–30,000 Arabs, including most of the middle and upper classes, over the period between December 1947 and early April 1948. This, and the months of skirmishing, bombings, food shortages and the sense of vulnerability and isolation from the Arab hinterland, had combined to steadily unnerve the 40,000–50,000 remaining Arabs. When the Haganah launched its onslaught on 21–22 April, the remaining Arab population was in great measure psychologically already prepared for evacuation.

According to the British GOC North Sector, Major General Hugh C. Stockwell, the final battle was triggered by the town's Arab irregular units, who in mid-April "went over to the offensive in many quarters . . . with the object tactically to push forward from two salients, Wadi Nisnas and Wadi Salib, to get astride Herzl Street, the main Jewish thoroughfare in Hadar Hacarmel, and from the morale point of view to strengthen the personal positions of both Amin Bey Azzadin and Yunis Nafa'a," the Arab militia's two commanders.[35]

The British reading in the days after 21–22 April of the precipitation of the Haganah offensive was only partially accurate. Sir Henry Gurney, who believed that the Arabs had played into the Haganah's hands, had it more right than he knew. The Arab provocations of mid-April had dovetailed with Haganah national planning. However, the Haganah had intended to leave Haifa till last, in view of the continued and large British presence in the city and of the British view that the city was crucial to their orderly evacuation from Palestine: the Haganah was far from eager to provoke the British or to tangle with the withdrawing, though still powerful, British Army. However, the Arab pressure in mid-April, which culminated in the abrupt British withdrawal of forces from the "seam" between the two communities in the city on the night of 20–21 April, forced the Haganah's hand. It implemented the provisions concerning Haifa of Plan D.

Plan D called for the consolidation of the Jewish hold on the mixed cities by "gaining control of all government property and services, the expulsion of the Arabs from the mixed districts and even from certain [all-Arab] neighbourhoods that endanger our lines of communication in these cities or that serve as staging grounds for attack [upon us]. Also [Plan D called for] the sealing off of the Arab population – in a part of the city that will be surrounded by our forces." The plan assigned the neutralisation of Arab Haifa to the Carmeli Brigade, which was specifically instructed "to conquer and take control of Elijah's Cave, the Old City, the German Colony, Jaffa Street, the old and new commercial districts, Nazareth Street, Wadi Rushmiya, the 'shacks neighbourhood [i.e., Ard al Ghamal]' and [the village of] Balad ash Sheikh."[36]

Throughout the crisis, Stockwell was primarily motivated by the desire to assure the safety of his troops and to guarantee that the British withdrawal from Palestine – much of it taking place through Haifa port – should not be impeded. He was also interested in pacifying the city for which he was responsible. In mid-April, Stockwell visited the Jewish and Arab militia liaison officers and urged them to step down their attacks. Both sides gave him "vague and useless promises."

On the afternoon of 19 April, Abba Khoushi (Schneller), the Histadrut and Mapai leader in Haifa, went to Stockwell and sounded him out on the British attitude to a possible major Haganah offensive against the Arab militia in Haifa. According to Stockwell, Khoushi said that the Jewish position was "no longer tolerable" and that Hadar Hacarmel was "being threatened by the Arab offensive." Stockwell responded that a major Jewish offensive would be "most unwise." Khoushi reported this back to Tel Aviv and the idea of a Haganah push in Haifa – if it was being contemplated – was temporarily dropped.

Stockwell, however, perhaps partly on the basis of the conversation with Khoushi, was convinced that a "major clash" was imminent. He believed that with the "slender forces" at his command in the city, he would be unable to stop the fighting and that his troops would suffer casualties. He decided that of the three courses open to him – "To maintain my present dispositions in Haifa and Eastern Galilee," "To concentrate the Eastern Galilee force in Haifa," and "To retain my present dispositions in Eastern Galilee and to redeploy my forces in Haifa, whereby I could secure certain routes and areas vital to me and safeguard as far as possible my troops" – the third course was the most attractive.

He ordered his troops, the 1st Guards Brigade and auxiliary units, to redeploy "by first light on 21 April" and to move out of their positions in the city centre and along the "seam" between the Jewish and Arab districts. The redeployment was effected by 06:00 hours, 21 April. Firefights between Jews and Arabs for possession of buildings evacuated by the British spontaneously erupted along the front lines.[37]

According to Nimr al Khatib (the Haifa Muslim preacher, member of the AHC and the Haifa National Committee in 1948), in "the early morning" of 21 April a pro-Arab British officer telephoned the head of the Haifa Arab National Committee, Rashid al Hajj Ibrahim, and informally told him of the "impending" British redeployment.[38] Similar informal notice may have been given to the Haganah by pro-Jewish British officials.

Stockwell, for his part, at 10:00 hours summoned Jewish and, subsequently, Arab leaders and handed them a prepared statement announcing the redeployment, by that time already completed. He asked both sets of leaders to end the hostilities and vaguely promised British assistance in maintaining peace and order. At the same time, he said that the British security forces henceforward would refrain from involvement "in any way" in the clashes.[39]

The sudden British redeployment triggered a hurried consultation in Carmeli Brigade headquarters where, during the morning and early afternoon of 21 April, a hastily-conceived plan, called *Mivtza Bi'ur Hametz* (Operation Passover Cleaning), was formulated. It was in part based on a plan conceived in late March, *Pe'ulat Misparayim* (Operation Scissors), which had provided for a multi-pronged assault on Arab militia positions and the neutralisation of the irregulars' power to disrupt Jewish traffic and life in the Jewish neighbourhoods. The objective of *Pe'ulat Misparayim* was to damage and shock rather than to conquer. The aim of *Mivtza Bi'ur Hametz* was to "break the enemy" by simultaneous assault from various directions, "to open communications to the Lower City [i.e., the downtown area and the port] and to gain control of Wadi Rushmiya in order to safeguard the link between Haifa and the north of the country."[40] The planning did not call for, or anticipate, the conquest of most of the Arab parts of the city; the Carmeli Brigade commanders, led by brigade OC Moshe Carmel, on 21 April deemed such an objective over-ambitious and probably unattainable, both because of Arab strength and because of expected British intervention.

Before the planning of *Bi'ur Hametz* was completed, a Haganah platoon was dispatched, at around 13:00 hours, 21 April, to take the Building of the Committee of the Arab Eastern Districts, known as Najjada House, which dominated the Rushmiya Bridge and the eastern approach to Haifa. Arab efforts to recapture the house and the desperate Jewish attempts through the day and the following night to reinforce the remnants of the besieged platoon inside turned into a general battle for the Halissa and Wadi Rushmiya districts, the ultimate Jewish victory assuring an open link between Jewish Haifa and the Jewish settlements to the east and north. It was the hardest and longest-fought engagement in the battle for the city and, in retrospect, can be seen as having been decisive, sealing the fate of Arab Haifa.

As the Jewish relief column, supported by mortar barrages, fought its way to Najjada House, the Arab force in Halissa broke and fled, and the bulk of the population of Halissa and Wadi Rushmiya fled in its wake northwestwards, towards Wadi Salib and the downtown area. The arrival of the latter, panic-stricken and battered, during the night of 21–22 April could not have failed to instil in the inhabitants of the central Arab neighbourhoods similar feelings of panic and dread while offering them a precedent and model of flight as a means of escaping the encroaching ravages of war.

The relieving Jewish column reached Najjada House at 09:00 hours, 22 April. While that company had been on the move, three other Haganah companies, one of them Palmah, and an independent platoon, had launched a simultaneous assault at 01:00 hours on the main Arab defensive positions in the downtown area. The attacks, on the Railway Offices Building (Khuri House) in Wadi Nisnas, the telephone exchange and the Arab City Militia headquarters building between Wadi Nisnas and Wadi Salib, overlooking the Old Marketplace, by the early afternoon broke the back of Arab resistance.

Throughout the battle, the Haganah made effective use of loudspeaker vans and Arabic broadcasts. The vans announced that the Haganah had gained control of all approaches to the city and no reinforcements could reach the Arab districts. The announcers called on the Arabs to lay down their arms and urged the irregulars "from Syria, Transjordan and Iraq" to "return to [their] families." *Kol Hahaganah* (the *Voice of the Haganah*) broadcasts announced that "the day of judgement has arrived . . . We say to the inhabitants of Haifa: He who wants to fight us, let him do so. But for God's sake, it is best that you first remove from the Arab districts the women and children . . . [to safer] areas." The news of the flight in mid-battle of the Haifa Arab community leaders (see below) was also broadcast.[41]

Jewish tactics in the battle were designed to stun and quickly overpower opposition. Demoralisation of the enemy was a primary aim; it was seen to be as important to the outcome of the battle as the physical destruction of the armed Arab units. The mortar barrages and the psychological warfare broadcasts and announcements, and the tactics employed by the Haganah infantry companies, advancing from house to house, were all geared to this goal. The 22nd Battalion (Carmeli Brigade) orders to its troops were "to kill every [adult male] Arab encountered" and to set alight with firebombs "all objectives that can be set alight. I am sending you posters in Arabic; disperse on route."[42]

The British estimated that in the battle for Haifa some "2,000" Arab militiamen were set against "400 trained Jews backed by an indeterminate number of reserves." The estimate of the number of "trained Jews" – a somewhat vague phrase – was on the low side, the estimate of Arab militiamen probably somewhat high. But the key factor in the battle was not numbers or firepower but organisation, control and morale (which was strongly affected by the element of surprise). Haifa's Arabs entered the battle largely demoralised and psychologically unprepared. The Arab population, stated one British intelligence report from just before the battle, "freely admit that the Jews are too strong for them at present." The Haifa Arab militiamen were poorly trained and armed. The repeated requests over the previous months for reinforcements and arms from Damascus had been mostly ignored or turned down. According to British Military Intelligence, "the hurried departure of Ahmad Bey Khalil, [the city's] Chief Magistrate and only remaining AHC representative in Haifa, for the Lebanon by sea on 21 April is a very significant illustration of the opinion of the local Arabs as to the outcome of any extensive Jewish operations at present."[43]

Stockwell's post facto report concurred with this judgement: "I think local Arab opinion felt that the Jews would gain control if in fact they launched their offensive." He, too, remarked on the fact that Damascus had ignored the Haifa Arabs' requests for reinforcements, thus underlining their sense of isolation and vulnerability.[44]

The flight of Ahmad Bey Khalil early on 21 April was not merely an illustration of low Arab morale; taken together with the flight that day and the next of many of the city's other Arab leaders, it was one of its main causes. Bey's departure was apparently followed in the early afternoon of 21 April by that of Amin Bey Azzadin, the Lebanese Druse commander of the city's militia and irregulars. Azzadin's deputy, Yunis Nafa'a, a former Haifa sanitation inspector, fled from the city on 22 April. The departure of these two men was probably known almost immediately to the whole militia officer corps, to many of the militia rank and file and, probably within hours, to the whole of Haifa's Arab community.[45]

Towards the end of April, British Military Intelligence assessed that "the hasty flight of Amin Bey Azzadin . . . [was] probably the greatest single factor" in the demoralisation of the Haifa Arab community.[46] This was also the judgement of the High Commissioner. On 26 April Cunningham devoted a whole telegram to Secretary of State for the Colonies, Creech-Jones, on the flight of the Arab leaders from Haifa and Jaffa.[47] The British view was succinctly expressed by British Military

Headquarters Palestine in its intelligence assessment of 6 May: "The desertion of their leaders and the sight of so much cowardice in high places completely unnerved the [Arab] inhabitants [of Haifa]."[48]

Like the British, American diplomats on the scene were equally convinced that the departure of the Arab military and other leaders just before and during the battle severely affected Arab morale in the city. American Vice-consul Lippincott reported on 23 April that "the Arab Higher Command all [reportedly] left Haifa some hours before the battle took place." Lippincott was comprehensively contemptuous of the Arab performance: "the Haifa Arab, particularly the Christian Arab, . . . generally speaking . . . is a coward and he is not the least bit interested in going out to fight his country's battles."[49]

The Haganah drive through Halissa and Wadi Rushmiya and the simultaneous push down the Mount Carmel slope into Wadi Nisnas and Wadi Salib and up from the New Commercial District caused panic and flight among the Arab militiamen and civilians throughout the downtown area. In the early hours of the morning of 22 April, members of the National Committee asked to see Stockwell with "a view to my [Stockwell] obtaining a truce with the Jews." Stockwell contacted lawyer Ya'acov Salomon, the Haganah liaison, and asked to know the Jewish "terms [for an Arab] surrender." Brigade OC Moshe Carmel was astounded since the Arabs, though strongly pressed, did not appear to him on the verge of collapse. He also thought that the local Arab forces could rely on assistance from Arab forces outside the city. The situation did not seem to warrant an Arab surrender "and the idea of our complete conquest of all of Haifa still appeared so fantastic as to be incomprehensible." Nonetheless, Carmel, after a brief consultation with his staff, jotted down surrender terms and sent them to Stockwell, "who . . . said that he thought they were fair conditions, and the Arabs would accept them after their defeat in battle."[50]

The Arab appeal to Stockwell apparently followed a gathering during the night of 21–22 April of community leaders in the house of Farid Sa'ad, a banker and National Committee member. The meeting drafted a document stating that the Arabs held Stockwell responsible for the situation in the town and appealed to the British commander "to stop the massacre of Arabs" by intervening on the ground or, alternatively to allow Arab reinforcements to enter the city.[51]

There are two versions of what transpired at the subsequent meeting, held at around 10:00 hours on 22 April between Stockwell, flanked by Cyril Marriott, the new British Consul-General-designate to Haifa, and the Arab delegation, consisting of Sa'ad, Victor Khayyat (a businessman and Spain's honorary consul in the city), lawyer Elias Koussa, Anis Nasr (a judge of the Haifa District Court) and National Committee member and lawyer George Mu'ammar. The subsequent Arab version is that the delegation straightforwardly asked Stockwell to intervene against the Haganah or to allow in Arab reinforcements. Stockwell refused, saying that the Arabs must accept "the principle of the truce" (i.e., surrender). The Arabs demanded that Stockwell put this in writing. Stockwell and the "Arab Emergency Committee" members then signed a statement saying that the GOC North Sector Palestine had replied to an Arab appeal to intervene by saying that he was "not prepared to clash with either of the two contesting parties and that he would not allow the Arab armed forces to enter the town to help its Arab inhabitants. He was only prepared to act as a peace intermediary if the Arabs accepted in principle the condition of the truce." The Arabs then asked to hear the Haganah truce conditions.[52]

The contemporary British descriptions of the proceedings are somewhat different, laying stress not on the Arab appeals to Stockwell to intervene or allow in reinforcements, but on the Arab readiness for a truce based on the implicit recognition that the battle was already lost. In their reports, neither Stockwell nor Marriott mentioned that Stockwell had signed any document. According to the British reports, the Arabs sought Stockwell's help in obtaining a cease-fire with the Haganah, but the delegation feared that this would be interpreted by at least some in their community as a surrender and betrayal. Hence, they wanted the onus for their appeal for a truce to fall on the British. Stockwell had to be manoeuvred into a position from which it would be clear to all that the delegation had been "forced" to accept a truce. The Arabs would ask the British to fight the Haganah or allow in outside reinforcements; Stockwell predictably would refuse; and the Arab Emergency Committee, bowing to *force majeure*, would then be able to accede to the truce terms.

This, at least, is how Stockwell viewed the meeting. "They felt that they in no way were empowered to ask for a truce, but that if they were covered by me, they might go ahead," Stockwell reported. Stockwell recorded that the Arabs "wanted [him] to say" that he would not intervene against the Haganah or allow in Arab reinforcements. Stockwell did as he was asked: he said that he could not intervene in the fighting and that allowing Arab reinforcements would result in renewed major fighting and "very considerable loss of life." He then issued orders to bar Arab reinforcements from the city.[53]

From Stockwell's and Marriott's reports it emerges that the interests and views of the British and the Arab community leaders in Haifa intermeshed on the morning of 22 April. Both feared, and opposed, a renewal of major fighting; both understood that the Haganah had won; both feared that the arrival of Arab reinforcements would not tip the scales but would cause only unnecessary Arab bloodshed; both wanted a truce. Stockwell, to achieve it, was willing to "play the game" according to the Arab delegation's rules.

The Arabs then asked to see the Haganah truce terms. Stockwell presented them and the delegation "left to discuss the matter." Apparently, the Arabs felt that immediate acceptance of the terms would leave them vulnerable to criticism if not to charges of betrayal. Through the Syrian consul in Haifa, Thabet al Aris, they proceeded to attempt to contact the Defence Committee in Damascus for instructions, but despite repeated reminders by al Aris, Damascus through the afternoon failed to respond.[54]

Meanwhile, Stockwell examined the Haganah terms, was "not entirely satisfied," and sent for the Jewish leaders. Harry Beilin, the Jewish Agency Political Department representative in Haifa, Ya'acov Salomon, and Mordechai Makleff, OC Operations of the Carmeli Brigade, duly arrived and, after a brief discussion, agreed to Stockwell's proposed amendments.

The truce terms called for the disarming of the Arab community (with the arms, in the amended, final version, going to the British authorities who only on 15 May would transfer them to the Haganah); the deportation of all foreign Arab males of military age; the removal of all Arab road-blocks; the arrest of European Nazis found in Arab ranks; a 24-hour curfew in the Arab neighbourhoods to assure "complete disarming;" freedom for "each person in Haifa . . . to carry on with his business and way of life. Arabs will carry on their work as equal and free citizens of Haifa and will enjoy all services along with the other members of the community."[55]

Stockwell then summoned Jewish and Arab community leaders to a meeting at the Haifa Town Hall at 16:00 hours on 22 April. The British were represented by Stockwell, Marriott, District Commissioner Law, Brigadier General G. F. Johnson (OC 1st Guards Brigade) and other officers; the Jews by Haifa mayor Shabtai Levy, Beilin, Salomon, Almogi (Khoushi having broken a leg earlier in the day), "Major" (as the British designated him) Makleff, and others; and the Arabs, who arrived in British armoured cars, by Khayyat, Sa'ad, Koussa, Anis Nasr, Mu'ammar, Ahmad Abu Zeid (a businessman) and Sheikh Abdul Rahman Murad, the Muslim religious leader. Outside, during the afternoon, the Haganah slowly pushed its units into the main, downtown Arab districts while maintaining a sporadic mortar barrage, "to keep up the pressure" on both the Arab militiamen and on the negotiators assembling or about to assemble in the Town Hall.[56]

At that first meeting, according to Stockwell and Marriott, both delegations "unanimously agreed" to a truce, which in the circumstances amounted to an Arab surrender.

Haifa mayor Shabtai Levy opened the meeting by expressing a wish that "members of both communities in Haifa should live in peace and friendship together." Stockwell then read out the Haganah terms. The Arabs criticised some points and a discussion ensued, focusing on the question of arms: the Arabs wished to be allowed to retain possession of licensed arms and wanted the curfew and house-to-house searches to be conducted by the British rather than by the Haganah. At the same time, while having no objection to handing over their arms to the British and not minding what the British did with the arms after 15 May, "they objected most strongly . . . to the fact that the arms were eventually to be handed over to the Haganah being recorded on paper. This was evidently to protect themselves against the displeasure of the AHE [i.e., AHC]."[57] The Jews, however, insisted that the clause remain, as formulated in the amended truce terms.

In general, Stockwell found the Jewish representatives "conciliatory." Marriott, who was soon to turn fiercely anti-Israeli, was even more emphatic. "The Jewish delegation," he wrote, "made a good impression by their magnanimity in victory, the moderation of their truce terms, and their readiness to accede to the modifications demanded by General Stockwell." Marriott, who arrived in Haifa just days before the battle, described Levy as a man of "courage and character . . . warm-hearted and friendly," whose "main concern is the peace and prosperity of Haifa." Marriott thought Salomon "not without personality and a sense of humour – at least when he is on the winning side." As to P. Woolfe-Rebuck, the Jewish liaison officer with the British, he "speaks with what is known as an Oxford accent but is not devoid of brains."

On the other hand, the Arab delegation "made a lamentable impression" on Marriott. The force of this judgement was underlined by Marriott's description of himself as one whose "experiences of Jews was gained in Rumania (where one knew that if there were a dirty house in a village it was the Jew's); in New York (where they were rarely met in decent society but were regarded in business circles as kikes and shysters); and in South America (where many of the leading families, though now Catholics, trace their descent from escapers from the Holy Inquisition)." The Arab, for Marriott, newly arrived in the Middle East, "was a romantic figure living in the open air and spending much of his life on camel-back or riding blood-horses."

The Arabs at the Town Hall meeting thoroughly failed to meet up to Marriott's expectations, save for Murad, the Muslim preacher, whom Marriott described as "a simple man . . . who, I am sure, in the absence of a Jihad, desires peace." Khayyat was "obviously, not to say ostentatiously, wealthy and is said still to own a shop in Fifth Avenue, New York, where objets d'art are dealt in." Sa'ad struck the British consul as "a hard business man" with an obvious dislike for the British. "The only word to describe Mr. Elias Koussa is revolting," wrote Marriott. "He suffers from having an artificial eye which fits so poorly that, in his moments of excitement, it rolls up, leaving but the thinnest rim of brown iris showing. He is a lawyer and I would neither employ him nor wish to see him representing the other side." Marriott did not take kindly to Koussa's declaration that while the Arabs had lost one round of fighting, there would be others.[58]

The afternoon meeting recessed at about 17:30 hours, the Arabs asking for 24 hours in which to consider the truce terms. The Jews demurred. At the GOC's insistence, it was agreed that the Arabs would have an hour to consult and that the meeting would reconvene at 19:00 hours at the latest. The delegates reassembled at 19:15, with the Arabs stating "that they were not in a position to sign a truce, as they had no control over the Arab military elements in the town and that, in all sincerity, they could not fulfill the terms of the truce, even if they were to sign. They then said as an alternative that the Arab population wished to evacuate Haifa . . . man, woman and child."[59]

The Jewish and British officials were surprised, even shocked, by the Arab announcement. Mayor Levy immediately appealed to the Arabs "very passionately . . . and begged them to reconsider." He said that they should not leave the city "where they had lived for hundreds of years, where their forefathers were buried and where, for so long, they had lived in peace and brotherhood with the Jews." But the Arabs responded that they "had no choice."[60] According to Carmel, who was briefed on the meeting by Makleff, Stockwell "went pale" when he heard the Arabs' decision, and also appealed to them to reconsider and not to make "such a grave mistake." He urged them to accept the Jews' terms: "Don't destroy your lives needlessly," Carmel quotes the British general as saying. Stockwell then turned to Makleff, the Haganah representative, and asked: "What have you to say?" Makleff replied: "It's up to them [i.e., the Arabs] to decide."[61] Salomon, in his recollection of events, wrote that he also appealed to the Arabs to reconsider, but to no avail.[62]

Carmel and other Israeli chroniclers of these events subsequently asserted that the Haifa Arab leadership on 22 April had been ordered by the AHC to evacuate the city. Carmel wrote that sometime after 22 April "we learned that during the intermission [in the Town Hall meeting] they had contacted the AHC and asked for instructions. The Mufti's orders had been to leave the city and not to accept conditions of surrender from the Jews, as the invasion by the Arab armies was close and the whole country would fall into [Arab] hands."[63]

The Jewish authorities, flustered by the exodus from Haifa, at the time sincerely believed that it was part of a comprehensive Arab plot, which also accounted for the mass flight from other parts of Palestine in late April. On 23 April Sasson cabled Shertok, who was in New York:

Mass flight of Arabs now witnessed here there Palestine, as Tiberias, Haifa, elsewhere, is apparently not consequence of mere fear and weakness. Flight is organised by followers of Husseinites and outcarried cooperation foreign 'fighters' with object: (1) Vilifying Jews and describing them as expellants who are out outdrive Arabs from territory Jew[ish] State. (2) Compelling Arab States intervene by sending regular armies. (3) Create in Arab world and world opinion in general impression that such invasion undertaken for rescue persecuted Pal[estinians].

Sasson asserted that the flight of the Arab commanders at the start of each battle was part of the Husayni plot to "spread chaos, panic" among the Arabs, leading to flight.[64]

However, if Sasson meant that the exodus was conceived and orchestrated by the AHC leaders from outside Palestine, the weight of the evidence suggests that this explanation, as applying to the decision of the Haifa Arab Emergency Committee on 22 April, is probably incorrect. That day the Haifa Arab leaders indeed tried to obtain instructions from the Defence Committee or the AHC representatives in Damascus, but to no avail. No word came, and for obvious reasons. What could the Defence Committee, the AHC or the Syrian Government, for that matter, have done for the hard-pressed Arabs of Haifa? Invade the Galilee thus precipitating war with Britain? Advise the Haifa Arabs to surrender and implicitly recognise Jewish sovereignty? Openly order the community to go into exile and thus, in advance, clear the Jews of the charge of expulsion? Damascus and the AHC preferred silence: Haifa's Arabs were left to decide on their own.[65]

A persuasive explanation of how the members of the Haifa Emergency Committee reached their decision in the late afternoon of 22 April – probably taken during the recess between 17:30 and 19:15 hours – was provided by Salomon in his recollection of the events a year later. A key to what happened was provided by the absence of Sheikh Murad (who had been present at the first session in the Town hall) from the reconvened meeting in the evening.[66] Salomon recalled that on the evening of 23 April he had driven home several members of the Arab Emergency Committee, following a meeting with Jewish and British officials in which the mechanics of the Arab evacuation were hammered out. "On the way," recalled Salomon, "they told me that they had instructions not to sign the truce [document] and that they could not sign the truce on any terms as this would mean certain death at the hands of their own people, particularly the Moslem leaders, guided by the Mufti [i.e., Husayni]; that the Moslem representative . . ., namely Sheikh Murad, who originally headed the truce delegation, had left during the intermission; and that it was quite clear that no Christian could do anything that might displease the Moslems."[67]

The shadow of the Husayni terrorism of 1936–9 apparently loomed over the decision of 22 April by the Haifa Arab notables to evacuate the city. The Muslim "instructions" to the Christian Arab notables who constituted the Arab delegation to the second half of the Town Hall meeting had been against signing any truce agreement. Perhaps these "instructions" had also explicitly included, if no acceptable alternative presented itself, the announcement of a mass Arab evacuation of the city. Thus, the Christian Arab delegates, unwilling to agree to a truce, because that implied acceptance of the Jewish victory and sovereignty, and unwilling to reject a truce, because that would trigger further, useless bloodshed in the city, and with an eye to the welfare of the Arab community and to their own personal safety, opted for evacuation. Perhaps the Arab delegates thought that their announcement would shock Stockwell into acting against the Haganah, but there is no evidence for this, and Stockwell did not take any such action. He asked the Arabs to reconsider, and after this failed, acceded to the Arab request to provide British transport for the exodus.

But if the initial order to the city's Arabs to evacuate had come not from outside Palestine but from the local Haifa Arab leadership (pressed by their Muslim, pro-Husayni wing), the AHC endorsed it ex post facto during the following days. The AHC made no gesture or effort to halt the exodus, which lasted a full eight or nine days; indeed, its local activists and supporters did their best, by all accounts, to egg it on. The United States' representative in the city, Lippincott, on 25 April reported: "Local Mufti dominated Arab leaders urge all Arabs leave city," and added the following day: "Reportedly AHC ordering all Arabs leave."[68]

British observers concurred. Cunningham on 25 April reported to Creech-Jones: "British authorities at Haifa have formed the impression that total evacuation is being urged on the Haifa Arabs from higher Arab quarters and that the townsfolk themselves are against it." The 6th Airborne Division was more explicit: "Probable reason for Arab Higher Executive [i.e., AHC] ordering Arabs to evacuate Haifa is to avoid possibility of Haifa Arabs being used as hostages in future operations after May 15. Arabs have also threatened to bomb Haifa from the air." The division was unable to evaluate the information about the possible targeting of Haifa for Arab aerial attack, and concluded: "It is possibly a rumour put about to encourage Arab population to evacuate town." The British Middle East headquarters similarly referred to "the evacuation of

Haifa by the AHC ... who ... have encouraged the population to evacuate ... greatly embarrass[ing] the Jews."[69]

The idea of a mass Arab evacuation of Haifa was not a bolt from the blue. Haifa's Arab community leaders had the very fresh model of Tiberias (evacuated on 18–19 April) before their eyes. By the evening of 22 April, when the leaders announced their decision, many thousands of Haifa Arabs had already voted with their feet for evacuation, by fleeing the embattled neighbourhoods in a panicky rush which had begun on the previous evening. Thus, they had already shown their leaders the way out of the straits bounded by the Scylla of betrayal of the Arab cause and the Charybdis of renewed full-scale fighting.

During the night of 21–22 April, the inhabitants of the city's eastern districts, Halissa and Wadi Rushmiya, had fled their homes moving into the downtown, central districts (and no doubt carrying with them the contagion of panic and flight). From the morning of 22 April, under sporadic Haganah mortar fire, and under threat from the steadily advancing Haganah infantry, thousands of panic-stricken Arabs from the downtown districts rushed towards the British-held port area. According to Nimr al Khatib, some of the Haganah mortar bombs hit Arab homes, which collapsed on top of their inhabitants.

Suddenly a rumour spread that the British army in the port area had declared its readiness to safeguard the life of anyone who reached the port and left the city. A mad rush to the port gates began. Man trampled on fellow man and woman [trampled on] her children. The boats in the harbour quickly filled up and there is no doubt that that was the cause of the capsizing of many of them.[70]

The Haganah mortar attacks on 22 April were primarily designed to break Arab morale in order to bring about a swift collapse of resistance; the Carmeli brigade commanders also hoped that they would pressure the Arab leaders into a speedy surrender on Haganah terms. There is no evidence that the architects of, and commanders involved in, the offensive of 21–22 April hoped that it would lead to an Arab evacuation of Haifa.

But clearly that offensive, and especially the mortaring which took place during the morning of 22 April, precipitated the mass exodus. The 3-inch mortars "opened up on the market square [where there was] a great crowd ... a great panic took hold. The multitude burst into the port, pushed aside the policemen, charged the boats and began fleeing the town."[71] British observers noted that

during the morning they [i.e., the Haganah] were continually shooting down on all Arabs who moved both in Wadi Nisnas and the Old City. This included completely indiscriminate and revolting machinegun fire and sniping on women and children ... attempting to get out of Haifa through the gates into the docks ...

There was considerable congestion outside the East Gate [of the port] of hysterical and terrified Arab women and children and old people on whom the Jews opened up mercilessly with fire.[72]

Clearly the Haganah was not averse to seeing the Arabs evacuate the city, as is illustrated by Makleff's "no comment" to Stockwell's question about the Haganah's attitude to the Arabs' evacuation announcement on the evening of 22 April. The Carmeli Brigade commanders no doubt realised that an Arab exodus would solve the brigade's main problem – how to secure Jewish Haifa with very limited forces against attack by Arab forces from outside the town while having to deploy a large number of troops inside the town to guard against insurrection or attack by a large, potentially hostile Arab population.[73]

Some 15,000 Arabs evacuated Haifa during 21–22 April in the initial flight from the embattled city. Most of these left via the port on boats to Acre and Lebanon, well before the Emergency Committee had concluded its meeting with the British and Jewish representatives in the Town Hall and before it had announced the decision to evacuate the city. The frightened populace, as it were, showed their frightened, remaining leaders the way.

By nightfall on 22 April, there were still some 30,000–45,000 Arabs in the city. Stockwell had agreed to assist their evacuation. From 23 April, four Royal Navy Z-Craft, which had been withdrawn from their pre-arranged duties of moving British stores from shore to waiting vessels as part of the general British withdrawal from Palestine, and a small fleet of lorries and armoured car escorts, began to ferry the refugees to Acre by sea and land. The Z-Craft, operating until 28 April, shuttled across Haifa Bay while the lorries, in convoys, went up the coast road through successive Haganah, British and Arab checkpoints. Dozens of Egyptian families left Haifa for Alexandria on a chartered schooner and Syrian nationals sailed to Beirut on another boat. At the same time, the Arab Emergency Committee and Arab entrepreneurs each day organised private convoys of Arab lorries, escorted by British armoured cars, which took out hundreds of Arab families to Acre, Nazareth, Jenin and Nablus.[74]

It was clear to the British troops involved in the evacuation, and to British and American officials, that the Arabs who departed after 22 April were urged to take this course by most of their remaining leaders. (The local leaders may have assured the evacuees that they would soon be returning to their homes in the wake of victorious Arab armies; but I have found no evidence of this.) The Arab leaders' urgings were in the form of threats, warnings and horrific rumours. The cumulative effect of these rumours in inducing flight among the Haifa Arabs cannot be exaggerated. "Most widespread was a rumour that Arabs remaining in Haifa would be taken as hostages by the Jews in the event of future attacks on other Jewish areas. And an effective piece of propaganda with its implied threat of Arab retribution when the Arabs recapture the town, is that people remaining in Haifa acknowledged tacitly that they believe in the principle of the Jewish State. It is alleged that Victor Khayyat is responsible for these reports," wrote one British intelligence unit. But for these "rumours and propaganda spread by the National Committee members remaining in the town," many of the Arabs "would not have evacuated Haifa" over 22–28 April, according to 257 and 317 Field Security Section.[75]

As late as 29 April, National Committee members were reported to be "for the most part" encouraging the Arabs to leave. An exception may have been Farid Sa'ad, who himself left at the end of the month. He told Lippincott that the National Committee members were telling the population "to use their own judgement as to whether they should stay or leave."[76]

On 23 April the Arab leaders even appealed to the Jewish authorities for help in organising the Arab departure as the British, they complained, were not supplying enough transport. Beilin responded enthusiastically: "I said that we would be more than happy to give them all the assistance they require."[77] However, Beilin, at this stage, was unrepresentative of the local Jewish political leadership which, for the most part, was clearly embarrassed by the mass Arab exodus. One Haifa Jewish figure, Ya'acov Lishansky, later recalled that "there was a feeling of discomfort . . . As soon as we capture a city . . . the Arabs leave it. What will the world say? No doubt they will say – 'such are the Jews, Arabs cannot live under their rule'." Lishansky recalled that he and several Arabic-speaking colleagues went down to the Arab areas to try to persuade the inhabitants to stay put.[78]

According to Lippincott, quoting Farid Sa'ad, the Haifa Jewish leaders had "organized a large propaganda campaign to persuade Arabs to return" to the city. But, Sa'ad said, the Arabs no longer trusted the Jews. *The Times* correspondent in the city on 25 April noticed the same thing: "The Jews wish the Arabs to settle down again to normal routine but the evacuation continues . . . Most of the Arabs seem to feel there is nothing to stay for now."[79]

British military intelligence offered a similar assessment of the situation. "The Arab evacuation is now almost complete," wrote 257 and 317 Field Security Section on 5 May. "The Jews have been making extensive efforts to prevent wholesale evacuation, but their propaganda appears to have had very little effect." The unit noted that, in trying to check the Arab exodus, the Haganah "in several cases [had resorted] to actual intervention . . . Appeals have been made on the [Jewish] radio and in the press, urging Arabs to remain in the town; the Haganah issued a pamphlet along these lines and the Histadrut, in a similar publication, appealed to those Arabs previously members of their organisation [*sic*], to return. On the whole, [however] Arabs remain indifferent to this propaganda."

The British, including Cunningham, believed that the Jews of Haifa for economic reasons wanted the Arabs to stay put. The Jews feared "for the economic future of the town" once its Arab working class had departed, reported the High Commissioner. This judgement was probably based on prejudice as well as reports from British units in the field, which noted that work had stopped in various plants due to the absence of Arab labourers or, in another version, to the absence of "cheap" Arab labour.[80]

According to all British observers, during the more than week-long Arab evacuation of Haifa the Jews were interested in the Arabs staying and the local Arab leadership was bent on a complete exodus. The only exception noted by the British was the IZL, which moved into part of downtown Haifa on 23 April. IZL policy, wrote 1st Battalion Coldstream guards, "was to promote a further rush of armed forces into the Suq and other places where Arabs were still living in order to force the issue by creating more refugees and a new wave of terror. Looting by IZL took place."[81]

But the situation in Haifa between 23 April and 1 May was extremely confused and complex. The British, restricted to semi-isolated enclaves and bent on only one thing – to get out and get out safely – failed to note the full spectrum of events.

Initial Jewish attitudes towards the Arab decision to evacuate changed within days; and what Jewish liaison officers told their British contacts did not always conform with the realities on the ground or with those quickly changing attitudes. The local Jewish civilian leadership initially sincerely wanted the Arabs to stay (and of course, made a point of letting the British see this). But the Haganah offensive of 21–22 April had delivered the Arab districts into Haganah hands, relegating the civil leaders to the sidelines and for almost a fortnight rendering them relatively ineffectual in all that concerned the treatment of the Arab population. At the same time, the attitude of some of these local leaders radically changed as they took stock of the historic opportunity afforded by the Arab exodus – to turn Haifa permanently into a Jewish city. As one knowledgeable Jewish observer put it a month later, "a different wind [began to] blow. It was good without Arabs, it was easier. Everything changed within a week."[82]

At the same time, the local Haganah command's attitude from the start was ambivalent – as exemplified by Makleff's "no comment" stance on the evening of 22 April on the Haganah's attitude to the Arab exodus. Militarily, it was clear that an Arab evacuation of the town would greatly ease the Carmeli Brigade's strategic situation and work-load.

The British withdrawal from downtown Haifa on 21 April and the Haganah's victory left the Haganah in control of the Arab areas until 3 May. During this time the Carmeli Brigade's relatively meagre forces, still worried about the possible intervention of Arab forces from outside the town, had to conduct a complex security operation in conditions of extreme disorder: to sift through tens of thousands of frightened Arabs, to search among the abandoned or semi-abandoned Arab districts for ex-combatants and arms, and to clear the area of unexploded projectiles and mines. All this had to be done, and done quickly, while thousands of refugees were on the move out of the city, in order to free the battalions for defensive or offensive operations. At the same time, the Haganah, in conjunction with the civil authorities, had to provide food and restore basic services for the Arabs, whose commercial system and services had completely broken down on 21–22 April. The provision of bread and water became a major problem.

The Haganah security operation in the downtown areas – involving searches, shifting about population, interrogations and the incarceration of many young adult males – took about a week and perforce included a great deal of arbitrary behaviour and unpleasantness towards the Arabs. The situation also lent itself to unauthorised, individual excesses – looting, intimidation, beatings. The British – and the Haganah – generally preferred, with only partial justification, to attribute these excesses wholly to the IZL.

What was happening was well-described at the meeting of Jewish and Arab local leaders which took place on 25 April. The meeting was called to find ways to ease the situation of the city's Arabs and to assist those who wanted to leave. The sense of the meeting, and of the statements of the Jewish participants, was against the Arab exodus, but none of the Jewish participants, who included Levy, Salomon, Beilin and Dayan, explicitly renewed the appeal to the Arabs to stay.

That morning, the Haganah had firmly driven the IZL units out of the downtown areas, and one or two IZL members had been shot. The condition of the Arab population, according to George Mu'ammar, had remained "catastrophic" and was "getting worse." The Haganah troops, he complained, had not allowed him to take a sack of flour to the market-place to distribute among the thousands of Arabs temporarily encamped there. (The Arab bakeries had all closed down on 21–22 April.) Looting and robbery, he said, were rampant. He had appealed to the Haganah and had been told that they had "a list of shops that they must search." Once the shops' shutters were prised open, however, they became prey to Jewish and Arab looters. "Houses in Wadi Nisnas had been completely looted. Was that the Jews' intention in Haifa?" asked Mu'ammar. He added that one Arab notable, Sulayman Qataran, had been beaten up that morning; moreover, Arabs had been robbed during Haganah identity checks. "If our people had [previously] considered staying in the city, that thinking has been severely undermined," concluded Mu'ammar.

Another Arab participant, George Tawil, recalled that at the previous Jewish–Arab local leaders' meeting, on 23 April, he had said that "if there were suitable conditions," the Arabs should stay in Haifa. Tawil added that after that meeting he had "tried to persuade our people to stay. But I must sadly say that the Haganah command has been harsh, if not to use a stronger word." He told the participants about a Haganah search of his house and said: "I have reached the conclusion that I will leave the city if I am to live [here] a life of humiliation."[83]

Without perhaps fully understanding what was happening, the Arab participants at the meeting on 25 April were describing what amounted to a divorce or temporary rupture between the local Jewish civil and military authorities, which reflected, and was part of, the similar, larger rupture between these authorities that characterised much of the Yishuv's policy-making and actions through the 1948 war. In Haifa, the civilian authorities were saying one thing and the Haganah was doing something else altogether. Moreover, Haganah units in the field acted inconsistently and in a manner often unintelligible to the Arab population.

Haganah martial rule in Haifa was formally decreed by Carmel on 23 April; it subordinated all civil authority to the military. It was lifted on 3 May, when the Haganah command announced that the stabilisation of the situation in the city enabled the units to return to regular military duties.[84] The Haifa Arab community leaders had grown accustomed to the reality and workings of Jewish civil leadership over decades of joint management of municipal life, and during the period 22 April – 1 May continued to regard the Jewish civil leaders as effectual. The Jewish civil authorities' essential powerlessness in the new circumstances was not properly grasped by the Arab leaders, and this lack of comprehension underlies much of the dialogue at the 25 April meeting.

At the meeting it was Victor Khayyat who voiced the major Arab complaint that the Arabs were being prevented from returning to their homes, which were being searched. He charged that this was contrary to the promises given by the Jewish civil leaders at the meeting held on 23 April. At that earlier meeting, Salomon had assured the Arabs that "orders have already been issued by the Haganah command that the old, women and children could that very evening return to their homes."

(Young Arab males were still being held for interrogation.)[85] Nevertheless the Arabs were still being barred from their homes. Khayyat described the situation as "shameful and opprobrious to the Jewish community."

Pinhas Margolin, a municipal councillor, put his finger on the problem when he conceded that the Jewish civil authorities had "for three days been unable to take control of the situation." He assured the Arabs that matters would "soon" be put right. But Nasr commented: "By the time you take control of the situation, there won't be one Arab left in Haifa."

Tuvia Arazi, a Haganah Intelligence Service officer and official of the Jewish Agency Political Department (Arab Affairs Division), assured the participants in the name of the Haganah, that "we are making a supreme effort to bring things back to normal . . . Bad things have happened," he conceded, but "the Haganah command has issued sharp orders [against robbery] and it is possible that robbers will be shot . . . Women, the old and children should return home . . . [but] they cannot return to all places at once, because first of all the city must be cleared of Arab bombs. And this is for the good of the Arabs themselves."[86]

Unknown to the Jewish leaders, the Arab Emergency Committee on that same day, 25 April, had renewed its appeal to the British to intervene. They asked Stockwell to reimpose British rule in downtown Haifa to assure "peace and order . . . in conformity with the declared policy of HMG." Above all, the Committee sought "the removal of members of Jewish armed forces from Arab quarters." This, they argued, would restore Arab confidence, "minimizing the number of Arab evacuees [a curious phrase, given the fact that at least some of the committee members had promoted and were promoting the exodus]."[87] Stockwell rejected the appeal.

By 27–28 April, there had been a slight improvement in conditions in the Arab areas of Haifa. Most of the Arabs still in the city had been allowed to return to their homes, although martial law remained in force. Arabs needed special travel passes, obtainable only after a long wait in a queue and close questioning, to move from neighbourhood to neighbourhood. There was no electricity in most Arab areas (and, hence, Arabs could not hear radio), no Arabic newspapers, no buses, and Arabs were not allowed to drive cars – the Haganah arguing that the IZL might confiscate them. Arrests and house searches were common. Aharon Cohen on 28 April assessed that whether the Arab population of Haifa increased, remained stable or decreased depended in large measure on "the policy of the Jewish institutions," despite what he described as the continuing appeals of the local Arab leaders to complete the evacuation of the city.[88]

A fortnight later, however, after the resumption of civilian rule in the city, the situation apparently was not much better. The Israel Communist

Party, in a report presented to Agriculture Minister Aharon Zisling (who on 20 May submitted it to the Cabinet), charged that Haifa's remaining "4,000" Arabs for the most part lacked running water and electricity; garbage had not been collected and had piled up on sidewalks, the looting of Arab property continued, many shops remained closed, employment exchanges had not opened, and, with the tight curbs on freedom of movement, the city's Arab inhabitants lived in "a prison regime."[89]

Conditions in the Arab districts of Haifa during the week following the Haganah offensive of 21–22 April had more or less reflected the normal dislocations and stringencies of war, but they were exacerbated by the general military and political situation in Palestine and by the particular circumstances in Haifa – the continuing mass evacuation of the Arab inhabitants, the continued British control of parts of the city, the presence of Arab Legion units in camps around the city, the continuing possibility of Arab attack on the city from without and the breakdown of municipal services and government.

After 22 April, the Haganah's actions to consolidate its hold on Arab Haifa – by disarming the Arab community, weeding out hostile elements and, in general, keeping the remaining inhabitants under tight rein – were characterised by the natural arbitrariness and harshness of military rule, and certainly contributed to the steady Arab exodus by helping, to an indeterminable extent, the undecided to make up their minds to leave.

But were Haganah actions, over 23 April – 1 May, motivated by a calculated aim of promoting the Arab evacuation?

At the level of Carmeli Brigade headquarters, no orders were ever issued to the troops dispersed in the Arab districts to act in a manner that would precipitate flight. Rather the contrary is the case. Strict, if somewhat belated, orders were issued forbidding looting, and leaflets calling on the Arabs to remain calm and return to work – if not explicitly to stay in the city – were distributed around the city.[90]

But if this was the official, mainstream Haganah policy, there was certainly also an undercurrent of more militant thinking, akin to the IZL approach. At the company and platoon levels, officers and men cannot but have been struck by the thought that the steady Arab exodus was "good for the Jews" and must be encouraged to assure the security of "Jewish" Haifa. A trace of such thinking in Carmeli Brigade headquarters can be discerned in the diary entries of Yosef Weitz for 22–24 April, which the JNF executive spent in Haifa. "I think that this [flight-prone] state of mind [among the Arabs] should be exploited, and [we should] press the other inhabitants not to surrender [but to leave]. We must establish our state," he jotted down on 22 April. On 24 April, Weitz went to see Carmel's adjutant, who informed Weitz that the nearby Arab villages of

Balad ash Sheikh and Yajur were being evacuated by their inhabitants and that Acre had been "shaken." "I was happy to hear from him that this line was being adopted by the [Haganah] command, [that is] to frighten the Arabs so long as flight-inducing fear was upon them."[91] There was a dovetailing here of Jewish interests, as perceived by Weitz and likeminded Yishuv figures, with the wishes of the local Arab Haifa leaders and, apparently, the AHC, who believed that the exodus from the city would serve the Palestinian cause (or, at least, that the non-departure of the inhabitants would serve the Zionist cause). Weitz, it appears, had found a responsive echo in Carmeli Brigade headquarters. It made simple military as well as political sense: Haifa without Arabs was a more easily defensible, less problematic city for the Haganah than Haifa with a large Arab minority.

In the days following the offensive of 21–22 April, the Haganah set its mind and forces to safeguarding the Jewish hold on Haifa by securing the approaches to the city and by opening up the routes to the clusters of Jewish settlements to the south, north and east of the city. The exit to the north and east was dominated by Balad ash Sheikh, Yajur and Hawassa; the southern exit was dominated by At Tira, whose population was considerably bolstered during 21–24 April by refugees from Haifa.

The Haganah attacked Balad ash Sheikh, which had had a pre-war population of some 5,000, on 24 April and At Tira during the following two days. It is not completely clear that the Haganah intended to cause the evacuation of the inhabitants of the two villages as well as to conquer them, but the method of attack on Balad ash Sheikh and the subsequent Jewish–Arab–British negotiation seem to have been designed to achieve both goals. This, at least, was the understanding of the British observers involved.

Balad ash Sheikh (and neighbouring Hawassa) had been partially evacuated on 7 January 1948, following the Haganah's retaliatory strike on the night of 31 December 1947 – 1 January 1948, which was triggered by the massacre by Arabs of the 70 Jewish oil refinery workers on 30 December 1947. The fall of Arab Haifa on 22 April sparked a further evacuation of the village's women and children: the villagers expected to come under immediate Haganah attack, reported British observers.[92]

During the early morning hours of 24 April, Haganah units surrounded the village and demanded that the villagers surrender their arms. The Arabs handed over "22 old rifles" and asked for a truce. The Haganah responded by threatening to attack if the villagers did not give up the rest of their weapons. The villagers appealed for British intervention. At 05:00 hours the Haganah opened up with 3-inch mortars and machineguns.

93

Many of the villagers fled, "leaving women and children behind." There was "virtually no reply" from the village to the Haganah fire, reported a British unit which reached the scene at 06:00 hours. The firing then ceased and, after a brief negotiation, the British, Haganah and Arabs agreed that the Arabs would evacuate the village under British escort. There can be no doubt that the fall of Arab Haifa and the news of the exodus of its inhabitants had thoroughly unnerved the villagers of Balad ash Sheikh and served as a model for their behaviour on 24 April, and that the inhabitants of Hawassa and Yajur were similarly influenced. They decided not to wait to be attacked in turn, and also evacuated their homes.[93]

The following day Haganah units attacked At Tira, the large village south of Haifa that for months had blocked Jewish traffic on the coast road. Here there was no prior negotiation. Starting at 01:40 hours, Haganah units began to mortar and machinegun the village. The firing stopped with the arrival on the scene of a British unit. The villagers, under British protection, then evacuated some of their women and children. The Haganah renewed their attack on 26 April but once again the assault was called off as a British unit arrived. The British arranged a further orderly evacuation of women and children, and on 5 May conveyed some 600 inhabitants to Jenin and Nablus.[94] Hundreds of the menfolk stayed on, however, successfully defending the village until July.

Meanwhile, Haifa IZL units turned their attention to Acre, and on 26 April mounted a short mortar and machinegun attack on the outskirts of the town. The attack was broken off when British armoured cars arrived on the scene. A second mortar attack was mounted against Acre on 28–29 April, apparently by the Haganah.[95]

The general assessment of 1st Battalion Coldstream Guards, whose officers consistently showed pro-Arab sympathies in their reports, was that the Jews wanted to open up the approach roads to Haifa. The officers thought it "likely that the Haganah will continue mortaring and shelling around Haifa to create an evacuation of the [Arab] population."[96]

By the beginning of May, only some 3,000–4,000 Arabs were left in Haifa; the largest and, in terms of influence on the departure of other communities, perhaps the most significant exodus of the war was over. Haifa had become a Jewish city.

Ben-Gurion drew a major political conclusion from the Arab exodus from Haifa and other places in April. Speaking to the People's Council (*mo'etzet ha'am*, the pre-state Yishuv parliament), he pointed out that no Jewish settlement to date had been abandoned in the war – in contrast with "some 100 Arab settlements." The Arabs had abandoned "cities . . . with great ease, after the first defeat, even though no danger of destruction or massacre . . . confronted them. Indeed, it was revealed with overwhelming clarity which people is bound with strong bonds to this land.''[97]

Jaffa During the early morning hours of 25 April, the IZL launched what was to be its major offensive of the war – the assault on Jaffa, the largest Arab city in Palestine. According to Gurney, the Arabs "attach[ed] more value to Jaffa on historical and sentimental grounds than to any other Palestine town except Jerusalem."[98] Jaffa was earmarked in the 1947 United Nations Partition Plan as an Arab enclave in the Jewish-dominated Coastal Plain; as we have seen, its situation during the first months of the hostilities was in great measure determined by this location. About 50,000–60,000 of its pre-war population of 70,000–80,000 was *in situ* at the start of the final battle.

Through the war the Haganah believed that there was no need to frontally assault Jaffa. While firing from it occasionally disturbed Tel Aviv, especially along the Arab–Jewish "seam" between the two cities, Jaffa posed no strategic threat to the Jewish capital. It was felt that the inhabitants' sense of isolation and the Haganah siege would eventually bring the town to its knees; it would fall like a ripe plum when the British withdrew.

Plan D did not call for the conquest of Jaffa but rather for the conquest of its suburbs of Manshiya, Abu Kabir and Tel ar Rish, while penning up the city's population.[99] The idea was blockade and military quarantine rather than conquest and occupation. The Haganah planners failed completely to anticipate, let alone plan for, the exodus of the population of Jaffa.

But the Haganah was not to have the decisive say. Since the start of April, when the Haganah went over to the offensive, the IZL leaders had been looking around for a major objective to conquer, partly to demonstrate that the Haganah was not the only effective military force in the Yishuv. Begin had considered Jerusalem, the Jenin–Nablus–Tulkarm triangle, Jaffa, and the Hills of Ephraim (also called the Hills of Menashe, southeast of Haifa). The IZL leadership on 23–24 April decided on Jaffa, which they regarded as a "cancer" in the Jewish body-politic and as the scourge of Tel Aviv (which was the IZL's powerbase).

The equivalent of six infantry companies were assembled on 24 April and, of overwhelming importance, as we shall see, two 3-inch mortars – stolen from the British in 1946 – were taken out of hiding, along with some 20 tons of bombs. In the early morning hours of 25 April the IZL struck, attacking the Manshiya quarter at the northern end of Jaffa; the aim was to drive through the quarter's southern end to the sea, severing it from Jaffa.

If all went well, Jaffa itself was then to be attacked. At the same time, the mortars were to lay down an unceasing barrage on Manshiya and on downtown Jaffa.

The IZL forces encountered strong resistance and proved inadequate and poorly trained, yet, after initially being repulsed, the units broke through and reached the sea on 27 April, the third day of the offensive, having suffered some 40 dead. The inhabitants of Manshiya, under constant ground and mortar attack, fled southwards to the Ajami and Jibalya districts.

But what was to be of even greater consequence was the ceaseless, three-day mortaring of the Ajami and other central Jaffa areas. The fall of Arab Haifa and the continuing exodus of its inhabitants had already severely jolted morale in Jaffa. According to Nimr al Khatib, Jaffa's Arabs felt that "now their turn had come."[100] The attack on Manshiya and the mortaring of the downtown districts broke the back of the town's civilian morale and military resistance.

Begin, writing a few days or weeks after the battle for Jaffa, said that the mortarmen were ordered to avoid hitting "hospitals, religious sites" and consulates.[101] But as the IZL's fire control and ranging were at best highly amateur and inaccurate, even if such restrictions had been imposed, they would have been meaningless. In any case, the objectives of the mortar barrage, which went on without respite for three days, with nine tons of explosives being delivered on day two of the attack, were clear, as described by IZL OC operations, Amihai Paglin, in his pre-battle briefing to his troops: "To prevent constant military traffic in the city, to break the spirit of the enemy troops, [and] to cause chaos among the civilian population in order to create a mass flight." The mortars were aimed roughly at "the port area, the Clock Square, the prison, King George Boulevard and [the] Ajami [quarter]."[102] Cunningham wrote a few days after the attack: "It should be made clear that IZL attack with mortars was indiscriminate and designed to create panic among the civilian inhabitants."[103]

Jacques De Reynier, the Red Cross representative in Palestine, described the panic that took hold of Jaffa's medical staff during the mortaring: "soon the flight started. In the hospital, the drivers of cars and ambulances took their vehicles, collected their families and fled without the slightest regard to their duty. Many of the . . . nurses and even doctors left the hospital [only] with the clothes they had on and ran to the countryside."[104]

An IZL intelligence report from 28 April, based on interrogations of Arab POWs captured in Jaffa, states:

Our shells . . . fell on many central sites near the post office, near the municipality . . . and near the port. A coffee shop in the vegetable market was hit and tens of gang members [i.e., irregulars] were killed and injured. The prisoners who fell into our hands know of more than 200 hit in the barrage . . . The barrage stopped the movement of buses to Jaffa and in it and paralysed completely the supply of food to the city and in it. Hotels turned into hospitals. The shelling caused great panic. The port filled up with masses of refugees and the boarding of boats took place in confusion.

The Manshiya police force, added the report, fled their station and abandoned the population during the battle.[105]

It is possible that some of the Jaffa inhabitants at some point in the battle learned that it was the IZL, rather than the Haganah, attacking them and that this knowledge was a contributing factor to the exodus. Deir Yassin, known to be an IZL operation, had taken place a fortnight before and was certainly fresh in people's minds. Begin and other IZL spokesmen subsequently asserted that this knowledge was a major factor in the Jaffa inhabitants' precipitate exodus, but it is impossible to determine how many inhabitants knew that the attack was by the IZL or at what point they became aware of it.[106]

According to British observers, one of the major causes of the mass exodus from Jaffa, as from Haifa and Tiberias, was the flight of the city leaders before and during the battle. Even before the battle, Jaffa, far more than the other Arab cities in Palestine, was characterised by disunity of command. There were in April seven distinct, different and in part rival power centres in the town, which had overlapping responsibilities: the municipality, the National Committee, Rafiq Tamimi (the Mufti's representative), the Najjada, the local militia and its command, the various non-local irregular units and the separate commander appointed by the Arab League Defence Committee. The IZL attack encountered disunity and triggered dissolution, and the leaders fled. "It is pathetic to see how the [Jaffa] Arabs have been deserted by their leaders," recorded Gurney.[107] Cunningham, pointing directly to the leaders' flight as a precipitant of the mass flight, reported on 26 April that the mayor of Jaffa, Haykal, had gone on "four days' leave" 12 days before and had not yet returned, and that half the members of the city's National Committee had left.[108] The War Office, not completely accurately, informed senior British Cabinet ministers on 29 April that "all [Jaffa] Arab Leaders have left and town appears dead."[109]

Shertok, the Yishuv's *de facto* foreign minister, on or about 27 April, in an address to the United Nations General Assembly charged that both in Tiberias and Jaffa "the mass evacuation had been dictated by Arab commanders as a political and military demonstration . . . The Arab command ordered the people to leave." With regard to Jaffa, there is little evidence for this assertion;[110] rather, an obverse process seems to have occurred. The shelling "had produced results beyond expectation." It had "caused dread and fear among the inhabitants of the city," precipitating flight.[111] The flight of the inhabitants had led in turn to a collapse in the morale of the irregulars, who then also took to their heels.[112]

The IZL assault on Jaffa, following hard upon the fall of Arab Haifa, had placed the British in a difficult position, eventually sparking a minor crisis in Whitehall.

The Arab leaders in Palestine and the neighbouring states blamed the British on various counts for what had happened in Haifa: they claimed that Stockwell had conspired with the Haganah, or at least had played into the Haganah's hands, by his sudden redeployment of troops out of the city centre on 21 April; that he had prevented Arab reinforcements from reaching the city during the battle; that he had failed to step in and halt the Haganah offensive, which, the Arabs alleged (wrongly), had included massacres of Arab inhabitants; and that he had promoted the truce, which was effectively an Arab surrender. In general, the Arabs argued that Britain was officially and legally in control of Palestine until 15 May and should have acted as the responsible power. Syria, which always projected a protective attitude towards the Arabs of the Galilee and Haifa, had even threatened to send its army across the border to intervene.[113]

Cunningham, Stockwell and the War Office rejected the Arab charges. As the War Office succinctly put it: "After defeat at Haifa[,] in order to excuse their own ineptitude, Arab leaders accused us of helping Jews and hindering Arabs although it was actually due to inefficient and cowardly behaviour of Arab Military Leaders and their refusal to follow our advice and to restrain themselves. Consequently[,] Anglo-Arab relations have considerably deteriorated."[114]

This deterioration, which took place against the backdrop of the impending final British withdrawal from Palestine, was acutely felt in Whitehall, and led directly to a clash between Foreign Secretary Ernest Bevin and the Army chiefs and to British military intervention in the battle for Jaffa. The Foreign Office felt that the Haifa episode had undermined Britain's position throughout the Arab world. On the evening of 22 April, the Chief of the Imperial General Staff (CIGS), Field Marshal Montgomery, was summoned to 10 Downing Street, where he was apparently forced to admit that he had not been kept posted by his generals in Palestine about the state of play in Haifa. Bevin "became very worked up; he said 23,000 Arabs had been killed and the situation was catastrophic." Montgomery said he would try to ascertain what was happening.[115]

The Prime Minister, Clement Attlee, Bevin and Montgomery reconvened the following morning at 10 Downing Street, with Bevin, according to the Field Marshal, "even more agitated." Bevin thought the Army should have stopped the Haganah; "the massacre of the Arabs had put him in an impossible position with all the Arab states." Bevin concluded his attack by saying that "he had been let down by the Army."[116] Montgomery, according to his own account, demanded that Bevin retract the insult, formally complained to Defence Minister A. B. Alexander, and attacked Bevin's handling of the Palestine crisis, saying that the Foreign Secretary was "now . . . trying to make the Army the scapegoat." Montgomery, according to his account, threatened to resign and make disclosures in the House of Lords. "This fairly put the cat among the piegons," he recalled, and Alexander and Attlee were forced to summon a further meeting at 10 Downing Street on 7 May.

As things turned out, Montgomery got little joy out of it. Attlee thought that Montgomery was making a major issue out of "a phrase in the course of . . . a discussion" and criticised the Army's lack of up-to-date information. Bevin "still felt" that the Army should "not have lost control over the perimeter of Haifa and allowed so many Arabs to be driven out of the city." According to Montgomery, the meeting ended on a light note, with everyone present "laughing . . . Attlee handled the situation beautifully; and it was impossible to be angry with Ernie Bevin for long." But Montgomery received no apology, and both Stockwell and Marriott (the latter for supporting Stockwell) were long to remain the butts of Foreign Office criticism.[117]

Whitehall squabbling aside, the chief upshot of the Haifa episode was to be forceful British military intervention against the IZL attack on Jaffa. Its aim was to "compensate" for Britain's alleged role in Haifa and to restore the prestige and goodwill lost by Britain in the Arab world. When the first news of the IZL attack reached London, Bevin "got very excited . . . and [instructed] the CIGS . . . to . . . see to it that the Jews did not manage to occupy Jaffa or, if they did, were immediately turned out." Such was Bevin's fear of a re-enactment of Haifa that he had bypassed normal channels (the Defence Minister and High Commissioner) in trying to get the Army in Palestine to act.[118] On 27 April, the British military – who had no direct lines to the IZL – informed the mayor of Tel Aviv, Yisrael Rokah, that they intended to "save Jaffa for the Arabs at all costs, especially in the light of the fact that the Jews had conquered Haifa."[119] On 28 April, the British went into action: some 4,500 troops, with tanks, were moved into the city; Spitfires swooped overhead and fired some bursts; warships anchored in Jaffa harbour; and British mortars shelled IZL positions and the IZL headquarters at Neve Shalom. A tripartite negotiation began between Britain, the Haganah and the IZL, the British demanding the IZL's withdrawal from Manshiya. On 30 April, agreement was reached, the IZL withdrew – after blowing up the district police fort – and British troops were left in control of Jaffa.

The British troops, or at least some of them, initially tried to stem the Arab exodus, but to no avail. "The British tried to calm the terrified inhabitants of Jaffa. Only in Jaffa did the British try to prevent the flight of the Arabs . . . and so they repeatedly announced that they would defend Jaffa with all their military strength. But all their soothing efforts came to nought . . . Nothing could have prevented the complete evacuation of the town," Begin wrote at the time.[120]

Part of the reason why the British were unsuccessful over 28–30 April in persuading the Jaffa Arabs to stay put was *Mivtza Hametz* (Operation Hametz), the Haganah's attack during the same days on the Arab villages east of Jaffa. The Haganah took Yazur, Salama, Al Kheiriya and Saqiya – all without a fight. The inhabitants began fleeing in panic the moment the Haganah columns approached or rounds began to hit the villages. Salama was evacuated "at the first onslaught," Haganah radio announced. When Ben-Gurion visited the village on 30 April he found there "only one old blind woman."[121] The swift collapse of Arab resistance in Jaffa's rural hinterland and the flight of these villages' inhabitants was in large measure attributed by the IZL and the Haganah to the IZL conquest of Manshiya and the demoralisation and exodus of Jaffa's own inhabitants.[122] In turn, however, the fall of these satellite villages further undermined the morale of the 15,000–25,000 inhabitants still left in Jaffa on 30 April; the city was completely cut off from all centres of Arab population and from any possibility of military relief, and its rural hinterland, which had supplied much of the city's food, had vanished.[123]

The remaining Jaffa municipal leaders on 30 April or 1 May asked the British commanders to arrange the evacuation of some of the city's remaining Arabs "by sea . . . to Beirut." Others apparently sought British help in leaving by land through Haganah lines. Alexandroni Brigade OC Dan Even agreed, but on condition that the Haganah would search the departees for arms. This was agreed and thousands more left the city.[124]

Another reason why the British were unable to persuade the Jaffa inhabitants to stay was clearly formulated by Cunningham on 3 May: "We are in a weak position in attempting to discourage evacuation because whatever counter-operation we might take against the Jews we cannot guarantee safety of Arabs in a fortnight's time [that is, after the end of the Mandate]." The Jews made things easier by undertaking not to attack Jaffa again if the foreign irregulars in the town withdrew.[125]

The chaos that reigned in the semi-abandoned city also contributed to the Arabs' flight. Some municipal services were apparently restored with the return to town on or about 28 April of Mayor Haykal, but broken waterpipes and telephone lines, demolished houses, looting by Arabs and Jews, murder, robbery and rape by the undisciplined Arab irregulars and the general sense of dread about the future after the British departure all caused despair among the remaining inhabitants. Nimr al Khatib described the last days of Arab Jaffa thus: the ALA contingent, headed by Michel al Issa, which reached the city at the end of April, "acted as if the town was theirs, and began to rob people and loot their houses. People's lives became worthless and women's honour was defiled. This prompted many inhabitants to leave under the protection of the British tanks."[126] By 5 May, the situation had become catastrophic. Cunningham reported that "municipal services have completely broken down and remnants of Liberation Army are looting. Nearly all councillors and members of National Committee have fled." The mayor, too, had gone, "without even saying goodbye," Gurney complained. Those remaining had apparently asked that the Jews be allowed to take over and restore law and order.[127]

On 13 May, with the final British evacuation, the Jaffa Arab Emergency Committee, representing the 4,000–5,000 remaining inhabitants, signed a formal surrender agreement with the Haganah.[128] On 18 May Ben-Gurion visited the conquered city for the first time and commented: "I couldn't understand: Why did the inhabitants of Jaffa leave?"[129]

The main towns

On 16 April the British evacuated Safad and on 28 April, the Rosh Pinna area. On 21 April Palmah OC Allon flew to Eastern Galilee to review the military situation. He returned to Tel Aviv the following day, reported to Yadin and Galili, and recommended launching a series of operations, in line with Plan D, that would brace the Yishuv in the area for the expected Arab invasion. Among his recommendations were: "the harassment of Beit Shean in order to increase the flight from it . . . [and] the harassment of Arab Safad in order to speed up its evacuation." Both were sensitive border towns – Safad 12 kilometres from the frontier with Syria and Beisan 5 kilometres from the frontier with Transjordan – and Allon clearly did not want to leave any Arab population centres immediately behind what would be the front lines.[130]

Safad Immediately after presenting his recommendations, Allon was appointed OC of the campaign to conquer Eastern Galilee, later named *Mivtza Yiftah* (Operation Jephtah or Yiftah). The conquest of Arab Safad, the area's main town, was the linchpin of the campaign. Safad, with a population of 10,000–12,000 Arabs and 1,500 Jews, was Eastern Galilee's major ALA base and centre of anti-Yishuv activity.[131]

The attack on Arab Safad began on 1 May, with the conquest by the Palmah's 3rd Battalion of 'Ein az Zeitun and Biriya, two Arab villages one kilometre north of Safad. The local and foreign irregulars in Safad, numbering 700–800, did nothing to help the two villages during the battle.

'Ein az Zeitun had for months served as an irregulars' base from which attacks were launched on Jewish traffic and on the nearby kibbutz, Ein Zeitim. The attack on 'Ein az Zeitun began at 03:00 hours with a barrage by a Davidka mortar (a locally produced, primitive Haganah weapon), two 3-inch mortars and eight 2-inch mortars, followed by a ground assault by two platoons. At the same time, an independent squad took Biriya. While most of 'Ein az Zeitun's young adult males fled as the Palmah troops approached, some of the village women, children and old men stayed put. These apparently were rounded up by the Palmah troops and expelled, with shots fired over their heads to speed them on their way.[132] Some 37 of the young men caught in the village were detained. They were probably among the 70 or so Arab prisoners massacred by two Palmah 3rd Battalion soldiers, on battalion OC Moshe Kelman's orders, on 3 or 4 May in the gully between 'Ein az Zeitun and Safad.[133] Several villagers tried to return to 'Ein az Zeitun on 2 or 3 May but were fired upon and fled; one of them apparently was killed.[134] On 2 and 3 May, Palmah sapper units blew up and burned houses in the village with the dual aim, according to one participant, Gavriel (Gabbi) Cohen, of "destroying an enemy base and of undermining the morale of the Arab inhabitants of Safad," who could see the levelling of the village from nearby hills.[135]

The conquest of 'Ein az Zeitun and Biriya, which opened the route for Palmah reinforcement of the Jewish garrison in Safad, sparked the start of the evacuation of Arab Safad. The city's inhabitants were already perturbed by the news of the fall of Arab Tiberias and Haifa, and by the evacuation of the inhabitants of Ja'una, to the east of the city, and Ghuweir Abu Shusha, to the southeast. On 2 May, "panic took hold of the Safad inhabitants, and long columns of Arabs began to leave the town in the direction of Meirun."[136] That day Haganah radio announced, somewhat prematurely, that "Safad is being evacuated by its Arab population." The Palmah informed the Haganah General Staff on 3 May that, following a brief Davidka shelling of Arab Safad on 2 May, "many Arabs were seen making their way from Safad down the path . . . in the direction of the Jordan [River]." British military intelligence also noted the start of the Arab evacuation of the city, attributing it to the general demoralisation precipitated by the fall of Arab Tiberias and Arab Haifa.[137]

The first Palmah ground attack on Arab Safad took place on 6 May. The attacking battalion failed to take the main objective, the citadel, which dominated the Arab quarters. According to the Palmah analysis, the failure was due in part to the sparse and inaccurate preliminary mortar bombardment. Nonetheless it succeeded in "terrifying" the Arab population sufficiently to prompt further flight, urgent calls for outside Arab help and an effort to obtain a truce with the Haganah. Allon turned down the Arab overture.[138]

The plight of Arab Safad triggered a wave of protests from the Arab world to Britain. Azzam Pasha, the Arab League Secretary General, rather accurately described the aim of Plan D, of which Operation Yiftah was a part, when he said: the "Jews were following a perfectly clear and ruthless plan . . . They were now drawing [driving?] out the inhabitants of Arab villages along the Syrian and Lebanese frontiers, particularly places on the roads by which Arab regular forces could enter the country. In particular, Acre and Safad were in very great danger of Jewish occupation. It was obvious that if this continued, the Arab armies would have great difficulty in even entering Palestine after May 15."[139] The British Minister in Damascus, Philip M. Broadmead, was then informed by the Syrian government of the attack on Safad and was warned that the "situation at Safad was desperate and that unless there was immediate [British] intervention there would be second Deir Yassin . . . If massacre took place, Syria would be blamed throughout the Arab world for not having intervened [the Syrians argued]."[140]

Broadmead's cable elicited from London the desired response. Colonial Secretary Creech-Jones, presumably after consulting with Bevin, authorised Cunningham to intervene militarily to prevent a Jewish victory in Safad: "The Arab States are clearly most concerned at the possibility of an Arab disaster [in Safad] and it is of the greatest importance to our relations with them to avoid anything of this kind. Such a disaster would almost certainly involve the entry of forces of Arab states into Palestine before the end of the Mandate. If you would in your judgement warrant it[,] you and the G.O.C. are authorised to use all practical means including air action to restore the situation."[141] However, the Haganah attack of 6 May failed.

But the British did not intervene in any way in the second attack, which began on 9–10 May. On 9 May, units of the Palmah's 1st Battalion attacked the village of Akbara, two-and-a-half kilometres south of the town. The aim of the attack was threefold: "A) The village served as a way station for Syrian spies who infiltrated to help Safad. B) To create among the Arabs of Safad a feeling that they were about to be surrounded and would be unable to flee. C) To destroy a base from which Jewish traffic between Tiberias and Rosh Pinna was attacked." Many of the villagers – old men, women and children – had already fled to the neighbouring villages of Farradiya and Sammu'i, after hearing of the fall of 'Ein az Zeitun. The remaining villagers fled during the 9 May attack after putting up "moderate" resistance. The occupying units blew up some of the village houses.[142] The fall of Akbara further undermined the morale of the inhabitants of Safad.

The attack on Safad proper began at 21:30 hours on 10 May with a massive, concentrated barrage by 3rd Battalion's mortars, reinforced by several home-made anti-tank guns. The Davidka mortar bombs, which made a tremendous noise on impact, accounted for a great deal of the panic that followed. Some of the inhabitants apparently believed that the Davidka bombs were atom bombs, both because of their noise and their great flash on explosion.[143] The Palmah troops fought from house to house to reach the citadel, Beit Shalva and the police fort between the Arab and Jewish quarters, the town's three dominant buildings. The Arab irregulars, who were supported throughout the battle by ALA artillery pieces based at Meirun, began to flee; the civilian inhabitants fled in their wake. The Palmah "intentionally left open the exit routes for the population to 'facilitate' their exodus . . . The 12,000 refugees (some estimate 15,000) . . . were a heavy burden on the Arab war effort," recalled Allon.[144] On 11 May, the Palmah troops moved into and secured the empty Arab quarters of Safad.

A major cause of the collapse of Arab resistance in Safad and the exodus was the absence of the town's military commanders during the battle. Between 2 and 8 May, Amin (or Imil) Jmai'an, the Transjordanian deputy town commander, was away in Damascus and Amman. On 9 May the town commander, Sari Fnaish, resigned his post and left Safad for Damascus, apparently on orders from King Abdullah. Jmai'an, upon returning from Amman on 8 May, apparently told the townspeople that he had been ordered to pull out the Transjordanian volunteer unit from the town as Safad was in the Lebanese–Syrian area of control. Jmai'an ordered his troops to withdraw at 01:00 hours on 10 May, hours before the start of the final Palmah offensive. Moreover, Adib Shishaqli, the ALA regional battalion commander, was not in the town during the battle; nor was Ihsan Kamlamaz, a leading figure in the local militia.[145]

The crucial Transjordanian pull-out from Safad was apparently linked to the rumoured intention by the Mufti, then reportedly in Tyre, to declare the establishment of a provisional Palestinian government in the Galilee, with Safad as its capital. That event was to have been linked to the ALA conquest of Jewish Safad, which was to have started on 11 or 12 May. The Jewish attack, according to this explanation, pre-empted the ALA offensive. But King Abdullah, the Mufti's chief enemy in the Arab world, wanted to frustrate Husayni's plans for a Palestinian government, and sought to avert an ALA victory in Safad; hence, the pre-emptive Transjordanian pull-out from the city.[146]

The Palmah troops scouring the abandoned Arab quarters found in the houses about 100 Muslims, "with an average age of 80," according to Safad's military governor, Avraham Hanuki, of Kibbutz Ayelet Hashahar. These inhabitants were rounded up and expelled to Lebanon apparently in late May or early June.[147] All that remained in Arab Safad were 34–6 mostly elderly Christian Arabs. On 13 June, this last remnant of the town's Arab community was removed by lorry to Haifa and put in the care of two convents – Les Filles de la Charité Sacré Cœur and Les Dames de Nazareth – with the Arab Affairs Committee of Haifa providing some of the maintenance costs. The matter caused a rather bitter wrangle within the Israeli bureaucracy, with the Foreign Ministry demanding that the IDF allow the three dozen Christians back to Safad "in order to improve our relations with our minorities." Perhaps the Ministry was also worried about the effect that the eviction might have on relations with the Christian churches. The army refused. Shertok, angry, took up the matter personally. Shertok's stand, as conveyed by his military aide-de-camp Yehoshafat Harkabi, was that while Israel absolutely refused "to accept back Arab refugees from outside Israel, we must behave towards the Arabs inside the country with greater moderation. Through this will be tested our ability to govern the Arab minority." Shertok, supported by the Minority Affairs Ministry, demanded that at least some of the Christians be allowed back to Safad.[148] But, against the backdrop of the start of the settlement of new Jewish immigrants in the abandoned Arab quarters of Safad, the army rejected the request. The Safad Christian group remained in Haifa, social cases maintained by the Haifa municipality, local Arabs and the Haifa convents. By spring 1949, three of the party – of whom three had been over 80 years of age and six over 70 – had died, five were hospitalised and "2 women have become demented," according to Marriott.[149] None ever returned to Safad.

Beisan (Beit Shean) The Beit Shean (Beisan) Valley, with the all-Arab town of Beisan (population 6,000) at its centre, was viewed by the Haganah General Staff as a major probable entry route for

Transjordanian forces in the expected invasion of Palestine. Allon's recommendation of 22 April, that the town had to be conquered and its population harassed into flight, reflected general Haganah thinking on the eve of the expected Arab invasion and conformed with the general guidelines of Plan D. There was also strong pressure from the area's Jewish settlements on the local Haganah command to push out the Arabs still left in the town and its rural hinterland. A delegation of Jewish settlers from the Beit Shean and neighbouring Jezreel valleys journeyed to Tel Aviv on 4 May to persuade the Yishuv leaders to move against the Arabs in Beit Shean. At one of their meetings, with Yosef Weitz, the delegation warned that Arab Legion troops had moved into the town and were fortifying it. The settlers urged Weitz to press the Haganah to attack. Weitz, agreeing, responded: "The evacuation [of the Arabs] from the Valley is the order of the day." That night Weitz talked to Ben-Gurion's deputy, Shkolnik, who agreed that the Haganah had to move.[150]

At the end of April Golani Brigade units placed Beisan under intermittent siege, instilling fear among the townspeople. The fall of Arab Tiberias a fortnight before had already affected morale, and the well-to-do families – 'Ali Abu Rabahs, the Shakshirs and the Jamus – began to leave for Transjordan.[151]

On the night of 10–11 May, Golani units attacked and captured Beisan's two main satellite villages, Farwana and Al Ashrafiya, the inhabitants fleeing to Transjordan as the troops approached. Haganah sappers began to blow up the village houses. The following night, Golani units mortared the town and stormed Tall al Husn, a hill dominating Beisan from the north. During the battle, Avraham Yoffe, the commander of the Golani battalion, telephoned the Beisan municipal elders and threatened that if the town did not surrender, the Haganah would level it. He offered safe passage to all inhabitants who wanted to leave. The elders agreed to negotiate, a truce was declared and on 12 May Haganah representatives met with the elders in the Beisan train station. The Haganah demanded that the town surrender its arms and all foreign irregulars. The elders asked for time to consult with Arab leaders in Jenin. Later that day, as the ALA contingents and most of the town's inhabitants fled, mainly across the river to Transjordan and some towards Jenin, the elders – mayor Rashid Darwish Ahmad and Father Yuhanna al Nimri – formally announced the town's surrender.[152]

Some 700–1,500 Arabs initially remained in the town, to Weitz's chagrin.[153] Martial law and a curfew were imposed, and a committee of Jewish settlers from the area was appointed to oversee property and life in the town. An Arab "militia" or police force was appointed. However, the presence of this large Arab concentration just behind the front lines and the constant coming and going of Beisan residents and former residents during the nights troubled the local Haganah commanders. They almost immediately sought and obtained authority, probably from Haganah General Staff in Tel Aviv, to expel the remaining inhabitants. "There was a danger that the inhabitants would revolt in the rear, when they felt a change in the military situation in favour of the [Arab] invaders, [so within days] an order was given to evict the inhabitants from the city." Most were apparently expelled on 14 or 15 May across the Jordan,[154] but about 250–300 inhabitants, apparently mainly Christians, were left in place until 28 May, when they were given the choice of going to Transjordan or to Nazareth. The majority preferred Nazareth, to which the IDF trucked them the same day.[155] The town of Beisan had become Beit Shean.

Under the influence of the exodus from the town of Beisan and under pressure from the Haganah, the remaining Arabs, mostly bedouin and semi-bedouin, of the Beit Shean Valley crossed over to Transjordan or to the Jenin area. The inhabitants of the villages of Al Hamidiya, north of the town, and As Samiriya, to the south, also fled the country, on 12 May. What Weitz and the Jewish settlements in the area had wanted had come to pass. "For the first time . . . the Beit Shean Valley had become a purely Jewish valley," wrote David Yizhar, one of the contributors to the official history of the Golani Brigade's 1948 campaigns.[156]

Acre The exodus from Arab Haifa at the end of April 1948 had turned Acre, with a pre-war population of 12,000–15,000, into a major refugee way-station and absorption centre. The town was not built for it. According to the British, Acre's population by 5 May had swollen to 40,000. Haganah intelligence noted and described the appalling conditions in Acre, with people sleeping "in the streets and in the coffee shops."[157] As the refugees poured into the town, by sea and land, from the south, the town's wealthier inhabitants, on or about 25 April, began to flee northwards, to Lebanon. The fall of Arab Haifa and the influx of the refugees severely shook morale. The influx, according to an Arab agent working for the Haganah, Sheikh Salah Kaniffas of Shafa 'Amr, had sowed "feelings of defeatism and bitterness" among Acre's inhabitants.[158]

This first wave of departures from Acre was triggered specifically by Jewish mortar harassment of the town in the last week of April, which produced the feeling that Acre was next on the list. The Haganah also cut off electricity and generally tightened the noose around the town. There were "unemployment, fear, filth and hunger," according to Carmel. One inhabitant of Acre on 26 April 1948 described the harassing attacks in a letter to his son, Munir Effendi Nur, in Nablus: they had "caused panic among the inhabitants and many intend to leave . . . Possibly we shall go to Beirut. The urge to flee Acre has hit all classes, the rich, the middle [class] and the poor – all are preparing to leave and are selling everything possible . . . A terrible tension prevails in the town . . . and taxi fares have risen to imaginary heights." The panic also took hold of the refugees in the town from Haifa and Balad ash Sheikh.[159]

The fall of Haifa and its repercussions prompted the British to seek to prevent the fall of Acre, as of Jaffa, to Jewish forces before their scheduled withdrawal from the country. At the end of April, British troops repeatedly intervened – at least once with artillery fire – to frustrate Jewish attacks on the town. But the exodus to Lebanon continued. During the first days of May, the British withdrew their troops from the camps around Acre as part of the general pull-back into the Haifa enclave, prior to the final withdrawal from Palestine; this further undermined Acre morale.

At the start of May, a further precipitant to flight was added in the form of an outbreak of typhoid. At the end of April, British observers had predicted an outbreak of disease in overcrowded Acre.[160] By 5 May, typhoid had indeed broken out, affecting also British troops stationed nearby. Cunningham feared "a very large number of cases." Indeed, conditions in the town were such that many of the refugees now wanted to return to Haifa, but were being prevented from doing so, according to the British, by "strong [anti-return Arab] propaganda". In any case, Cunningham, the Haganah and the Jewish authorities in Haifa at the time thought such a return "inadvisable" precisely because of fear of the spread of the epidemic. A Red Cross team was sent to the town to investigate.[161] However, the severity of the Acre typhoid epidemic is unclear. IDF intelligence estimated that more important than the epidemic itself in generating flight was "the panic that arose following the rumours of the spread of the epidemic."[162]

To these reasons for flight were added the fear of impending Jewish attack and conquest, and the collapse and departure of Acre's military and political leadership prior to the Haganah assault of 16–17 May. According to an Arab source, the town's mayor fled to Lebanon on 11 May, the local militia commander announced his withdrawal from the town the same day or just after it, and on 14 May, two further members of the town's National Committee fled to Beirut.[163]

The Haganah offensive in Western Galilee, called *Mivtza Ben-Ami* (Operation Ben-Ami), began on 13 May and ended with the conquest of Acre on 17 May. In the first two days of the Operation, ground columns and amphibious units of the Haganah bypassed Acre and captured all the Arab villages and positions, including Napoleon Hill, immediately east of

Acre and northwards up to the Lebanese border. The successful push completely cut the town off from its rural hinterland and dealt a mortal blow to local hopes of relief by the Arab states.

The attack on Acre began on the night of 16–17 May with a mortar barrage from positions on Napoleon Hill, which dominated the town from the east. As the Carmeli Brigade units advanced into the town, an armoured car mounting a loud-speaker, in a psychological warfare ploy broadcast the imminent fall of the town and declared that the choice before the inhabitants was either surrender or suicide. At the same time, in a lull in the fighting on 17 May, Carmel sent an Arab POW into the town with a message to the town elders saying that large Haganah forces had surrounded the town. He demanded the town's surrender, declaring that "we will destroy you to the last man" if the fight was continued.

Towards evening, Haganah troops renewed the assault and took the strategic police fort on the northern edge of town. Haganah boats machine-gunned the town from the sea. "Panic took hold in the town and terrible shrieks were heard coming from it," relates Carmel; resistance collapsed. During the night of 17–18 May, a priest, holding a white flag, emerged from Acre's Old City, asked to see Carmel and requested surrender terms. These, which included the handover of all arms and foreign irregulars, acceptance of Haganah rule and Haganah protection of those who remained, were taken back to the remaining elders in the town. Later that night the priest returned to the Haganah headquarters and announced acceptance of the terms. Early on the morning of 19 May, Haganah units, unopposed, moved slowly into the heart of Acre, collected weapons and detained foreign irregulars. It is unclear how many of the town's original population and refugees were in Acre on 17–18 May. More townspeople left for Lebanon and central Galilee in the days following the Haganah conquest. The Carmeli Brigade immediately set up a military administration in the town, headed by Major Rehav'am Amir, and looting and abuse of the inhabitants were kept to a minimum. No expulsion orders were issued and no pressure was exercised on the townspeople to leave. About 5,000–6,000, most of whom were from among the original inhabitants, remained.[164]

Following the depopulation of Haifa and Jaffa, Acre emerged as the biggest Arab town in the Jewish State, remaining so until the conquest in July of Nazareth. The front line between the Haganah/IDF and the ALA stretched along a line 7–10 kilometres to the east of the town.

Towards the end of the First Truce (11 June – 9 July), IDF Northern Front sought to evict the inhabitants of Acre, intending to move them either to Jaffa or to expel them across the border. The IDF did not want such a large Arab civilian concentration just behind its front lines and had difficulty sparing the manpower needed to oversee and provide for the inhabitants of the semi-abandoned town. However it encountered opposition from various civilian government offices.

During the first week of July the acting director of the Foreign Ministry's Middle East Affairs Department, Ya'acov Shimoni, was asked by the IDF for the ministry's opinion in the matter. Shimoni asked Shertok. Shertok, according to Shimoni, "had no objection in principle to the transfer of [Acre's] Arab inhabitants to another place (Jaffa), in order to free our soldiers tied down in guarding them." But there would be a problem of maintenance. Shimoni asked Minority Affairs Minister Bechor Shitrit for his opinion.[165]

Shitrit was upset: he had heard nothing from the IDF about the eviction plan concerning inhabitants who, after all, were part of his "constituency" as the minister responsible for the Arab minority. Indeed, he informed Shimoni on 19 July, there was a standing IDF General Staff order (from 6 July) that no inhabitants "were to be uprooted from their places without a written order from the Defence Minister [i.e., Ben-Gurion]." In my opinion, wrote Shitrit, "so long as the Defence Minister has not . . . issued a written command, the local [Acre] army authorities must not evacuate a complete town and cause suffering, wandering and upset to women, children and the old." The Acre population could not be evicted. He added, on a general note, that Jaffa could not serve as the absorption centre "for the ingathering of Arab exiles (*kibbutz galuyot shel Aravim*)"; nor could the Minority Affairs Ministry care for their maintenance. Lastly, the empty houses in Jaffa were, in any case, needed for the resettlement of Jews.[166] To be on the safe side, Shitrit sought and obtained the support of Finance Minister Eliezer Kaplan against the planned eviction; Kaplan thought the proposal to move Acre's population to Jaffa "strange."[167]

The idea of transferring Acre's population was dropped. Shitrit's stand meant that to expel them across the border or to transfer them to Jaffa would have required a written order from Ben-Gurion – and Ben-Gurion through 1948 carefully avoided issuing such written orders. In addition the absorption and maintenance in Jaffa of another 5,000–6,000 Arabs would have been difficult.

The countryside

Yosef Weitz, in the middle of the exodus from Palestine's countryside, visited the area around Kibbutz Mishmar Ha'emek, on the western edge of the Jezreel Valley. He found the Arab villages "in ruins. No one has remained. The houses and huts are completely destroyed . . . Among the ruins echoed the cries of an abandoned chicken, and a miserable and orphaned ass strayed along the village paths." Why did the Arabs leave? "Out of a psychosis of fear . . . Village after village was abandoned in a panic that cannot be explained . . . The villages of the Coastal Plain are steadily emptying. Between Tel Aviv and Hadera, you won't find today a single Arab. During the past days multitudes left the large villages around Tel Aviv." Weitz reasoned that "the very presence of many refugees among the Arabs weakens their position and brings nearer our victory."[168]

Like the exodus from the towns and cities, the Arab evacuation of the countryside in April–May closely followed, and was largely precipitated by, Jewish offensives that were part of the implementation of Plan D. The Arab exodus almost completely followed the sequence of Jewish attacks in each area, but it was Arab military pressures in several key areas that forced the Haganah prematurely to launch these offensives, which, in retrospect, were to be regarded as the beginning of the implementation of Plan D, and which involved for the first time the conquest and permanent occupation of continuous swathes of territory and the clearing of these areas of Arab population.

Operation Nahshon During the first months of 1948, irregulars and militiamen from the Arab villages dominating the eastern half of the Tel Aviv–Jerusalem road – Deir Muheisin, Beit Mahsir, Suba, Al Qastal, Qaluniya, etc. – had intermittently attacked Jewish traffic to and from Jerusalem; by late March, Jewish Jerusalem, despite occasional British intervention, was under siege, its 100,000 inhabitants sorely pressed for food and munitions.

On the night of 31 March – 1 April, Ben-Gurion and the Haganah General Staff decided that the Yishuv's first priority was to relieve the pressure on Jerusalem. At Ben-Gurion's insistence, a force of 1,500 Palmah and regular Haganah troops – some three battalions – were mobilised for the largest Jewish offensive to date. Givati Brigade OC Shimon Avidan was appointed Operation Nahshon commander. His operational orders, of 3 or 4 April, stated that "all the Arab villages along the [Khulda–Jerusalem] axis were to be treated as enemy assembly or jump-off bases." Plan D had specified that such villages, if offering resistance, should be destroyed and their inhabitants expelled. As a first stage, the orders called for the conquest of the three Arab villages at the western entrance to the Jerusalem corridor – Deir Muheisin, Khulda and Seidun.[169]

Galili, head of the Haganah National Staff, on 2 April defined the radical strategic change which was about to occur as a shift from a diffuse defence to a concentrated offence, with the Haganah embarking on "operations of conquest and occupation."[170] The following day, the Palmah's 4th Battalion, unopposed, captured the village of Al Qastal, just west of Jerusalem; its inhabitants and irregulars had already fled. It was the first Arab village during the 1948 war to be taken by the Haganah with the aim of permanent conquest and occupation. And, in accordance with the guidelines of Plan D, the operational instructions were that if there was no opposition, "the village's houses should not be blown up."

In his report on the action, the commander of the unit that had taken the village appealed against this order, saying that leaving the village's houses intact had made "the defence of the site difficult."[171] The Palmah local company commander, Uri Ben-Ari, in a second report on the action, defined the non-demolition of the village houses as "a decisive mistake."[172] The village was retaken by Arab irregulars in a bitter fight on 8 April. The "mistake" was rectified on 9 April, after the hilltop village fell to a renewed Palmah attack: "The blowing up of all the houses not needed for defence of the site was immediately begun," reported the commander.[173] The lesson of Al Qastal was quickly extended to other sites. Palmah units spent 10 and 11 April blowing up the houses of neighbouring Qaluniya, which had already been abandoned by most of its inhabitants on 2 April.[174]

On 6 April – the official start of Operation Nahshon, which ended on 15 April – the villages of Khulda and Deir Muheisin fell to Haganah forces; and on 16 April, Saris. The villages of Biddu and Beit Suriq were raided and in part demolished on 19–20 April. In all cases, the inhabitants had fled their homes either before or during the Haganah attacks; there had been no need to issue expulsion orders. Khulda was levelled by Jewish bulldozers on 20 April.

Operation Nahshon had been a watershed, characterised by an intention and effort to clear a whole area, permanently, of Arab villages and hostile or potentially hostile villagers. The destruction of the corridor villages both symbolised and finalised the change in the Haganah's strategy. This change was epitomised in the successive orders regarding Al Qastal. The 2 April order, issued by the Haganah's Jerusalem (Etzioni Brigade) headquarters, instructed the attacking unit if unopposed not to destroy the village's houses; the 9–11 April orders directed the conquering units to level Al Qastal and Qaluniya. When it came to the praxis, the Plan D provision to leave intact non-resisting villages was superseded by the decision to destroy villages in strategic areas or along crucial routes regardless of whether or not they were resisting Haganah conquest. The Al Qastal episode had powerfully and expensively demonstrated why the harsher course had to be taken. Intact villages could quickly revert to becoming Arab bases.

If at the start of the war the Yishuv had been reluctantly willing to countenance a Jewish State with a large, peaceful Arab minority, by April the military commanders' thinking had radically changed: the toll on Jewish life and security in the battle of the roads and the dire prospect of the invasion of Palestine by Arab armies had left the Haganah with very narrow margins of safety. The Yishuv could not leave pockets of actively or potentially hostile Arabs or ready-made bases for them behind its geographically unnatural front lines. This was certainly true with regard to strategically vital roads, and areas such as the Jerusalem corridor.

No comprehensive expulsion directive – beyong the preamble of Plan D – was ever issued; no hard and fast orders went out to front, brigade and battalion commanders to expel Arab villagers *en masse* or to level villages. But the doctrinal underpinning of Plan D was taken for granted by the majority of the Haganah commanders at this crucial juncture of the war, when the Yishuv faced, and knew it faced, a life and death struggle. The gloves had to be, and were, taken off.

Operation Nahshon was partially successful; it briefly opened the Tel Aviv–Jerusalem road and enabled the Haganah to push through three large convoys, loaded with supplies, to the besieged city. It was followed, in the second half of April and in May, by operations Harel, Yevussi and Maccabi, which all aimed at re-securing and widening the Jewish-held corridor through the Judean Hills to Jerusalem and at wresting from Arab control further areas in and around Jerusalem. The Haganah units involved were ordered to raid and/or occupy and destroy clusters of Arab villages, including An Nabi Samwil, Beit Iksa, Shu'fat, Beit Hanina and Beit Mahsir.

But, ironically, it was not a Haganah but a joint IZL–LHI operation, undertaken with the reluctant, qualified consent of the Haganah commander in Jerusalem, which probably had the most lasting effect of any single event of the war in precipitating the flight of Arab villagers from Palestine. On 9 April, IZL and LHI units, for part of the battle supported by Haganah mortars, attacked and took Deir Yassin, a generally non-belligerent village on the western outskirts of Jerusalem. The attack loosely meshed with the objective of Operation Nahshon, which was to secure the western approaches to Jerusalem. After a prolonged firefight, in which Arab family after family were slaughtered, the dissidents rounded up many of the remaining villagers, who included militiamen and unarmed civilians of both sexes, and children, and murdered dozens of them. Altogether some 250 Arabs, mostly non-combatants, were murdered; there were also cases of mutilation and rape. The surviving inhabitants were expelled to Arab-held East Jerusalem. The weight of the evidence suggests that the dissident troop did not go in with the intention of committing a massacre but lost their heads during the battle, which they had found unexpectedly tough-going. It is probable, however, that the IZL and LHI commanders from the first had intended to expel the village's inhabitants. The massacre was roundly condemned by the mainstream Jewish authorities, including the Haganah, the Jewish Agency and the Chief Rabbinate, and Ben-Gurion sent a message to King Abdullah, condemning it.[175]

News of what had happened quickly reached the Arab world, and the British, through the survivors who reached Arab Jerusalem and through British and Red Cross officials. The Arab media in Palestine and the surrounding states focused on the episode and for days and weeks thereafter broadcast the tale of horrors and atrocity as a means of rallying Arab public opinion and governments against the Zionists. Cunningham on 17 April wrote that "the bitterness resulting from the Deir Yassin massacre has produced an atmosphere in which local Arabs are little inclined to call off hostilities." The massacre and the way it was trumpeted by the Arab media added a great deal of pressure on the leaders of the Arab states to come to the aid of the embattled Palestinians and hardened their resolve eventually to intervene in Palestine. The news aroused great public indignation in the Arab capitals – which the leaders could not ignore.[176]

However, the most important immediate effect of the massacre and of the Arab media atrocity campaign that followed was to trigger and promote fear and further panic flight from the villages and towns. In trying to justify their actions, the IZL immediately lighted upon this side-effect of the "conquest of Deir Yassin." It promoted "terror and dread among the Arabs in all the villages around, in Al Maliha, Qaluniya and Beit Iksa a panic flight began that facilitates the renewal of road communications . . . between the capital [Jerusalem] and the rest of the country," declared the IZL on or about 12 April. An IZL radio broadcast on 14 April repeated the message: the surrounding villages had all been evacuated because of Deir Yassin. "In one blow we changed the strategic situation of our capital," boasted the organisation.[177] The IZL commander, Begin, who denied that civilians had been massacred, later recalled that the "Arab propaganda" campaign had spread fear of the Irgun soldiery among the Arabs and "the legend was worth half a dozen battalions to the forces of Israel . . . Panic overwhelmed the Arabs of Eretz Yisrael . . . [It] helped us in particular in . . . Tiberias and the conquest of Haifa."[178]

The IZL may have had an interest in exaggerating the panic-generating effects of Deir Yassin on the Arabs of Palestine, but they were not far off the mark. In the Jerusalem corridor area, its effect was certainly immediate and profound. Haganah intelligence reported on 14 April that the episode was "the talk of the Old City." The horrors, sufficiently gruesome in themselves, were being amplified and exaggerated in the Arab retelling.[179] The British noted that the Haganah, whether or not involved in the episode, had "profited from it. The violence used so impressed Arabs all over the country that an attack by Haganah on Saris [in the Jerusalem corridor] met with no opposition whatsoever."[180]

Less directly, the news of the massacre also affected Arab communities farther afield. Ben-Gurion on 1 May reported that some Muslims had fled Haifa because of fear of a "Deir Yassin" befalling them.[181] Mapam's leaders, more generally, assessed in May and June that the massacre had been one of the two pivotal dates (the other being the fall of Arab Haifa) in the exodus of Palestine's Arabs.[182] This, more or less, was also the judgement of IDF intelligence, which, in its report on the causes and nature of the Arab exodus, defined Deir Yassin as a "decisive accelerating factor" (*gorem mezarez machri'a*) in the general evacuation up to June 1948. "Deir Yassin especially [from among IZL and LHI operations] greatly influenced the thinking of the Arab," with particular effect in the central and southern areas of the country.[183]

The battle of Mishmar Ha'emek The battle of Mishmar Ha'emek, over 4–15 April, was initiated by Qawuqji's irregulars and took place before Plan D formally was put into operation. It began as a desperate Jewish defence and turned into a Haganah offensive conforming to Plan D guidelines. The available evidence seems to indicate that for the first time Ben-Gurion explicitly sanctioned the expulsion of Arabs from a whole area of Palestine (though, as we shall see, the expulsion was largely pre-empted by a mass Arab flight from the area because of, and during, the fighting).

The battle began on 4 April when the ALA shelled and attempted to take Mishmar Ha'emek, the Mapam (Hashomer Hatzair) kibbutz which sat astride the Jenin–Haifa road, which the Haganah commanders regarded as one of the main likely routes for a major Arab attack on the Yishuv on or after 15 May. Local Haganah militiamen, backed by Palmah reinforcements, beat off the attack. The shelling was stopped by a British unit that arrived on the scene. The ALA attack, especially after its failure, was viewed with trepidation and distaste by at least some of the local Arab inhabitants, according to the British. The locals were also "getting very fed up with the Liberation Army but they are frightened of them and do what they are told. The officers of the ALA treat the locals like dirt," reported one British officer.[184]

On 7 April, the ALA units agreed to cease the attack, which had clearly failed, on condition that the Jews promised "not to take reprisals on local villages."[185] The Mishmar Ha'emek commanders opposed the offer but told the British commander that they had to get instructions from Tel Aviv.[186] Probably on 8 or 9 April, a delegation of Mishmar Ha'emek leaders came to Ben-Gurion and, according to Ben-Gurion, "said that it was imperative to expel the Arabs [in the area] and to burn the villages. For me, the matter was very difficult. [But] they said that they were not sure [the kibbutz could continue to exist] if the villages remained intact and [if] the Arab inhabitants were not expelled, for they [i.e., the Arab villagers] would [later] attack them [i.e., Mishmar Ha'emek]."

Ben-Gurion, speaking in July to the Mapai Centre, related the Mishmar Ha'emek episode within the context of his argument with Mapam, which was accusing him of implementing a policy of expulsion towards the Palestinian Arabs. He charged the Mapam leaders with hypocrisy, saying that at Mishmar Ha'emek they had come to realise that ideology (i.e., Jewish–Arab brotherhood) was one thing and strategic necessity another. "They faced a cruel reality . . . [and] saw that there was [only] one way and that was to expel the Arab villagers and burn the villages. And they did this. And they were the first to do this."[187]

This point was made repeatedly, if rather quietly in view of its sensitive nature, ("dirty laundry"), in the continuing debate between Mapam and Mapai over policy towards the Arabs. For example, a publication of the Mapai-affiliated Gordonia–Maccabi Hatzair kibbutz movement on 17 September was to charge: "Mishmar Ha'emek was the first to demand the destruction of the Arab villages around it." Gordonia leader Pinhas Lubianker (Lavon) told the meeting of the Zionist Actions Committee on 23 August 1948 that "When the Arab inhabitants around [his kibbutz] Hulda and around Mishmar Ha'emek were ejected for security reasons, neither the inhabitants of Mishmar Ha'emek nor of Hulda objected to it. Because Mishmar Ha'emek knew and Hulda knew that if they [were allowed to] stay during wartime, surrounded by three–four Arab villages, then they would not be safe."[188]

Ben-Gurion and the Haganah commanders decided to reject the ALA cease-fire proposal, to counter-attack extensively, to clear the ALA and the local Arab inhabitants out of the area, and to level the villages in order to permanently remove the threat to Mishmar Ha'emek. During the following days, Haganah and Palmah units counter-attacked all the villages around the kibbutz. The bulk of the Arab inhabitants fled before or during each attack. The villages were then razed and the remaining inhabitants expelled southwards, towards Jenin.

Ghubaiya at Tahta, Ghubaiya al Fauqa and Khirbet Beit Ras were attacked and captured on 8–9 April and blown up piecemeal during the following days. On 10 April, Haganah units took Abu Shusha, north of Mishmar Ha'emek; most of the villagers had already fled. Those who had remained behind were expelled. The village was destroyed that night. On 12 April Palmah units took Al Kafrin, which was found empty, and Abu Zureiq, where some 15 adult males and some 200 women and children were taken captive. The women and children were sent towards Jenin. Some 30 of Al Kafrin's houses were blown up that day and some of Abu Zureiq's houses were blown up that night. Abu Zureiq was completely demolished by 15 April. During the night of 12–13 April Palmah units also attacked Al Mansi and An Naghnaghiya, southeast of Mishmar Ha'emek. The villages' houses were blown up during the following days. On 19 April, a Palmah unit used Al Kafrin to train for fighting in built-up areas. At the end of the exercise the village was levelled.[189]

During the following days, under the impact of the ALA defeat and the fall and evacuation of the villages around Mishmar Ha'emek, the inhabitants of Al Buteimat, three kilometres southwest of Al Kafrin, also evacuated their village.[190]

Weitz rather accurately described what was happening:

Our army is steadily conquering Arab villages and their inhabitants are afraid and flee like mice. You have no idea what happened in the Arab villages. It is enough that during the night several shells will whistle over them and they flee for their lives. Villages are steadily emptying, and if we continue on this course – and we shall certainly do so as our strength increases – then villages will empty of their inhabitants.[191]

An epilogue to the battle of Mishmar Ha'emek was provided by the IZL, whose units from Zikhron Ya'acov, Hadera, Binyamina and Netanya on 12 May attacked and cleared the last Arab villages in the Hills of Menashe, overlooking Mishmar Ha'emek from the west. The dissidents attacked the villages of Sabbarin, As Sindiyana, Bureika, Khubbeiza and Umm ash Shauf. Most of the inhabitants fled as the Jewish forces approached and laid down mortar fire. At As Sindiyana, the *mukhtar* and his family and some 300 inhabitants stayed put and raised a white flag. They apparently were expelled eastwards. At Sabbarin, where the IZL met resistance, the villagers fled after 20 died in the firefight, and an IZL armoured car fired at the fleeing villagers. "More than one hundred" old people, women and children, who had not fled from Sabbarin and the other villages, were held for a few days behind barbed wire at an assembly point in Sabbarin, after which they were expelled to Umm al Fahm, a village in Arab-held territory to the southeast. The Jewish troops combed the villages to ascertain that they were empty and to make sure they stayed empty. An IZL officer at Umm al Shauf later recalled searching a column of refugees and finding a pistol and rifle among their possessions. The troops detained seven young adult males and sent the rest of the column on its way to Umm al Fahm. The troops then demanded to know who the weapons belonged to. When the seven Arabs refused to own up, the IZL men threatened to kill them. When no one owned up, the IZL officers held "a field court martial . . . which sentenced the seven to death." The seven were then executed.[192]

The Coastal Plain

Most of the Arab population of the Coastal Plain from Tel Aviv northwards had evacuated their homes and villages during the preceding months. April and early May witnessed the completion of that exodus, save for the isolated villages of At Tira, Ein Ghazal, Jaba and Ijzim, south of Haifa. The April–May evacuations were prompted by IZL actions, a growing feeling of isolation, Haganah attacks, pressure and overt expulsion orders, and pressure on the local inhabitants by Arab irregular formations.

The final evacuation of the area just north of Tel Aviv was prompted in large measure by a series of IZL actions, the most important of which was the kidnapping at the end of March of five notables from the large village of Sheikh Muwannis, which until then had resisted the entry of Arab irregulars and loosely co-operated with the Haganah. According to the IDF intelligence assessment made less than three months later, the kidnapping triggered flight because "the Arab learned that it was not sufficient to reach an agreement with the Haganah and that there were 'other Jews' [i.e., the dissidents] of whom one had to beware and perhaps of whom to beware of more than of the Haganah, which had no control over them." The kidnappings immediately triggered the evacuation of Sheikh Muwannis itself, on 30 March, and several satellite bedouin encampments. The Arabs still remaining in Khirbet 'Azzun (Tabsar), bordering on Ra'anana, also evacuated their homes on 3 April, by order of the Haganah.[193]

The Arabs of Khirbet Beit Lid, east of Netanya, evacuated out of fear and isolation, on 5 April. A few days later, the Haganah completed the clearing of the Coastal Plain area south of Zikhron Ya'acov by issuing a series of expulsion orders to the remaining Arab communities. The Haganah General Staff had concluded that the area between Tel Aviv and Zikhron Ya'acov, the core of the emergent Jewish State, had to be secured. The bedouin communities around Hadera – the 'Arab al Fuqara, 'Arab an Nufei'at and Ad Dumeira – were all ordered to leave on 10 April. A similar order was issued by the Haganah to the inhabitants of Khirbet as Sarkas, a friendly Circassian community east of Hadera, on 15 April. On or about the same day, the inhabitants of Khirbet Zalafa and Khirbet Manshiya, south of Hadera, evacuated eastwards, apparently after reaching an agreement with Haganah representatives that the Jewish settlements would safeguard their property and allow them to return to their homes after the war. It seems that in the case of Khirbet Manshiya, the local Haganah intelligence officer, Aharon Braverman, of Kibbutz Ein Hahoresh, pleaded with the villagers to stay put and accept Haganah protection, but to no avail. On the other hand, the inhabitants of Khirbet Zalafa, who for years had been in conflict with the local Jewish settlements, were not asked to stay put and may have been pressured to leave. The inhabitants of the large village of Miska, northeast of Qalqiliya, were expelled on 20–1 April after it had been conquered by units of the Alexandroni Brigade. Miska's militiamen and irregulars had for weeks sniped at, and skirmished with, the Jewish settlement of Ramat Hakovesh. The Alexandroni commanders "did not make do with the expulsion of the Arabs of Miska but demanded immediate action against [the neighbouring village of] At Tira," recorded the Alexandroni Brigade's official historian. Apparently, the Haganah, on 15 April, had already ordered the Miska villagers to evacuate but the order was not heeded. Jewish military activity around Biyar Adas, southeast of Qalqiliya, had led to the evacuation of that village on 12 April. At the end of April and in early May, the Haganah, assisted by the local Jewish settlements, systematically destroyed the houses and huts at Khirbet as Sarkas, Khirbet Manshiya and Khirbet Zalafa, and of Ad Dumeira, Wadi al Hawarith and 'Arab an Nufei'at, thereby making a return all but impossible.[194]

By the beginning of May, there were very few Arab inhabitants left in the Coastal Plain. A meeting of local Haganah Intelligence Service officers and national Arab affairs experts – including Danin – was called for 9 May to decide what to do. At the end of their meeting in Netanya, the experts decided to advise the Haganah to "expel or subdue" Kafr Saba, At Tira, Qaqun, Qalansuwa and Tantura (the first four along the eastern frontier of the emergent Jewish State), as well as to expel the remaining inhabitants of Fajja, the Arab village adjoining Petah Tikva.[195]

Alexandroni units attacked and took Kafr Saba on 13 May, which prompted a mass evacuation. According to the Alexandroni Brigade's official history, the Syrian irregulars in the village stopped each would-be refugee and demanded P£5 as a "departure tax"; most paid. The attack and the arrival of the Kafr Saba refugees triggered widespread panic and flight from Qalqiliya and its satellite villages. "Everyone who could . . . fled," reported Haganah intelligence. Due to this panic-bearing influx and to Israeli harassing attacks, Qalqiliya was completely, although temporarily, abandoned on 19 May.[196]

The 33rd Battalion, Alexandroni Brigade, attacked Tantura, a large village south of Haifa on the Mediterranean coast, on the night of 22–23 May. The attack was preceded by a Haganah effort to obtain the village's surrender without a battle; the village elders refused, rejecting the Haganah's terms, which included the hand-over of all arms and non-local irregulars. "It was [then] decided to capture the village and to clear the sea coast of enemy forces," writes the Alexandroni Brigade historian. The village fell after a brief fight. It is unclear whether the villagers were ordered to leave or more subtly pressured into leaving. At all events, it is clear that the Alexandroni commanders wanted the village emptied of its inhabitants and that at least some of them were expelled.[197]

Some of the Tantura villagers went to Arab-held territory in the Triangle. Many others, numbering 500–1,200, moved or were evicted to Al Fureidis, an Arab village to the east that had earlier surrendered to the Haganah. On 31 May, Minority Affairs Minister Shitrit asked Ben-Gurion whether to expel the Tantura women and children in Al Fureidis, since maintaining them there was a problem.[198] Whether or what Ben-Gurion replied is unknown, but two weeks later, some 1,200 Tantura refugees were still in Al Fureidis. A meeting of local Mapam Haganah and Arab affairs officers on 17 June discussed whether to expel them to Arab-held Tulkarm, to leave them in place or to put the problem in the hands of the Red Cross. The meeting was indecisive but most of the Tantura refugees were moved out of Jewish-held territory that summer. Some 200 women and children, however, probably with menfolk still in Israeli detention, stayed on in Al Fureidis. The government did not maintain them. They slept out in the open and were short of clothes. Israeli officials worried about what would happen to them come winter.[199]

Before 1948 Fajja had served as a base for attacks on neighbouring Petah Tikva and had been hit repeatedly by Haganah and IZL attacks in the first months of the war. Some of its population had fled on or about 17 February after an IZL strike, others left subsequently. But as the 15 May "deadline" approached and despite a Haganah expulsion decision, several dozen inhabitants stayed put. The intelligence officers' meeting in Netanya on 9 May decided that these last inhabitants, "who were a bothersome element," also had to go, and in addition resolved to "demand" that the Haganah expel the inhabitants of nearby Nabi Thari. The last inhabitants of Fajja left on 15 May, according to IDF intelligence because of "pressure by us – a whispering operation."[200]

Operation Yiftah During the second half of April and the first half of May, as part of Plan D, the Haganah devoted a great deal of energy and blood to securing the Eastern Galilee border, from Metulla down to the Sea of Galilee, a border along which Syrian forces were expected to invade the new State. The campaign, eventually dubbed *Mivtza Yiftah*, began with two failed Palmah assaults, on 15 and 20 April, on the Nabi Yusha police fort at the southern end of the Galilee panhandle.

The General Staff then sent Palmah OC Allon to look over the situation and, upon his return to Tel Aviv, appointed him commander of the operation. He had very limited forces (equivalent to two battalions) and few arms, and faced an area with dozens of Arab villages, the town of Safad and a more or less open, and proximate Syrian border. To judge from his report of 22 April and from his subsequent actions, Allon concluded that clearing the area completely of all Arab forces and inhabitants was the simplest and best way of securing the frontier.[201]

However, the planned offensive had to wait for the British evacuation of the area. The British, partly on the whim of local commanders, transferred most of the Eastern Galilee police forts and army camps to the Arabs, but on 28 April a local commander handed over the police fort of Rosh Pinna and the Philon camp to local Haganah and Palmah units, facilitating the start of the attack on Arab Safad.

In order to clear his lines of communications, Allon decided first to drive out the Arabs, who for months had harassed Jewish traffic, from the area east of the Tabigha–Rosh Pinna road, north of the Sea of Galilee. In his report to the General Staff of 22 April, Allon had already recommended, among other things, "an attempt to clear out the beduins encamped between the Jordan [River], and Jubb Yusuf and the Sea of Galilee." With the conquest of Safad on the agenda, such a sub-operation became imperative.[202]

At the same time, the Arabs north and east of Rosh Pinna were apparently ordered by Syrian officers or Arab irregulars' commanders, including the Emir Fa'ur, to evacuate their villages, at least of women and children, in order to make room to quarter the irregulars. On 30 April Palmah troops had already noticed a major movement of villagers out of the area between the Sea of Galilee and Lake Hula. The menfolk mostly stayed on to protect their homes.[203]

On the night of 2 May, Palmah units sporadically mortared the villages of Fir'im, Mughr al Kheit and Qabba'a, just north of Rosh Pinna, "in order that in the end the Arabs would flee from them."[204]

Following this, on 4 May Operation Yiftah headquarters launched Operation Broom (*Mivtza Matate*), a sub-operation designed to clear out the Arab population from the Jordan Valley area south of Rosh Pinna between the north–south road and the Jordan River. The bedouins of the area – Al Qudeiriya, 'Arab as Samakiya, 'Arab as Suyyad, 'Arab ash Shamalina and the Zanghariya – had for months harassed and blocked Jewish traffic to and from Rosh Pinna. Operation Yiftah headquarters defined the objectives of Operation Broom as "(a) the destruction of bases of the enemy, who sabotages and harasses our traffic in the Galilee, (b) to destroy points of assembly for invading forces from the east [and] (c) to join the lower and upper Galilee with a relatively wide and safe strip" of continuous, Jewish territory. The order to the company commanders involved stated that the Arab villages at Zanghariya and Tabigha, and the area of 'Arab ash Shamalina should be attacked, "their inhabitants expelled and the[ir] houses blown up." Friendly Arabs "should on no account be harmed," concluded the operational order. The assault was preceded by mortaring and the Arabs in the area fled eastwards, into Syria, with the approach of the Palmah columns.[205] The following day, Palmah sappers methodically blew up more than 50 houses in Zanghariya and other villages in the area. The Syrian authorities told the British that the Palmah thrust had created a further 2,000 refugees.[206]

According to Allon, Operation Broom had a "tremendous psychological impact" on the Arabs of Safad and of the Hula Valley to the north, and paved the way for the conquest of the town and the valley and for the flight of their inhabitants.[207]

The conquest of Safad on 9–10 May was the linchpin of Operation Yiftah. In turn, it helped the Palmah precipitate the evacuation of the Arab villages of the Galilee panhandle to the north, which was to be the Haganah's biggest psychological warfare operation of the war. Allon described it in *Sefer Hapalmah*:

The echo of the fall of Arab Safad carried far . . . The confidence of thousands of Arabs of the Hula [Valley] was shaken . . . We had only five days left . . . until 15 May. We regarded it as imperative to cleanse [of Arabs] the interior of the Galilee and create Jewish territorial continuity in the whole of Upper Galilee. The protracted battles reduced our forces, and we faced major tasks in blocking the [prospective Syrian and Lebanese] invasion routes. We, therefore, looked for a means that would not oblige us to use force to drive out the tens of thousands of hostile Arabs left in the Galilee and who, in the event of an invasion, could strike at us from behind. We tried to utilize a stratagem that exploited the [Arab] defeats in Safad and in the area cleared by [Operation] Broom – a stratagem that worked wonderfully.

I gathered the Jewish *mukhtar*s, who had ties with the different [local] Arab villages, and I asked them to whisper in the ears of several Arabs that giant Jewish reinforcements had reached the Galilee and were about to clean out the villages of the Hula, [and] to advise them, as friends, to flee while they could. And the rumour spread throughout the Hula that the time had come to flee. The flight encompassed tens of thousands. The stratagem fully achieved its objective . . . and we were able to deploy ourselves in face of the [prospective] invaders along the borders, without fear for our rear.[208]

Semi-ironically, one Palmah commander in Eastern Galilee, perhaps

Allon himself, just after Operation Yiftah summarised what had occurred in the Galilee panhandle by saying: "The only joint operation between the Jews and the Arabs was the evacuation by the Arabs of the Hula area. Orders from abroad [i.e., apparently Syria] for the evacuation of the whole area by the Arabs were buttressed by a whispering campaign by our intelligence services."[209]

IDF intelligence on 30 June estimated that only 18% of the Arab exodus from the Galilee panhandle was due to the Palmah whispering campaign. It attributed the flight from Qeitiya (19 May), Lazzaza (21 May), Zuq al Fauqani (21 May), Al Manshiya (24 May), Khisas (25 May), Al Mansura (25 May), Dawwara (25 May), Al 'Abisiya (25 May), Beisamun (25 May) and Mallaha (25 May), at least in part, to that campaign; some of these villages are reported to have left because of the whispering campaign and one or more other factors, such as the effect of the fall of Safad or Haganah mortaring.[210]

Several villages in the panhandle were abandoned for more complex reasons than fear-instilling Jewish rumours or advice but they may also have been targets of the psychological warfare operation. According to IDF intelligence, the inhabitants of Al Khalisa evacuated the area on 11 May after their request for an "agreement" was turned down by the Haganah. The fall of Arab Safad the day before undoubtedly also had a strong effect on the villagers. The inhabitants of Al Buweiziya, five kilometres to the south, evacuated the same day under the influence of the flight from Al Khalisa. The inhabitants of As Salihiya left on 25 May, according to IDF intelligence, for a reason similar to that of the inhabitants of Al Khalisa: "They wanted negotiations [with us]. We did not show up. [They became] afraid." The village traditionally was "friendly" towards the Yishuv.

From the IDF intelligence breakdown it appears that even more important than the deliberate Palmah whispering campaign in the evacuation by the Arabs of the Galilee panhandle were the traumatic effect of the fall of their "capital," Safad, Jewish attacks and a general fear of becoming victims in a clash between Jewish and Arab armies. The report says that Ja'una (9 May), Dhahiriya Tahta (10 May), Ibl al Kamah (10 May), Qaddita (11 May), Zuq at Tahtani (11 May), Al Khalisa (11 May), Sammu'i (12 May) and possibly also An Na'ima (14 May) were evacuated in some measure because of the fall of Safad.

Jewish attacks – mortaring or ground assaults – and fear of Jewish revenge or of becoming embroiled in others' battles led directly and indirectly to the flight in late April and in May, according to IDF intelligence, of the inhabitants of Al 'Ulmaniya (20 April), Al Huseiniya (21 April), Kirad al Baqqara (22 April), Kirad al Ghannama (22 April), Al

Madahil (30 April), Al Hamra, Khirbet Khiyam al Walid, Khirbet al 'Azaziyat and Ghuraba (all on 1 May), Al Muftakhira (1 and 16 May), Hunin (3 May), Az Zawiya (24 May), 'Ammuqa (24 May), Fir'im (26 May) and Marus (28 May), and Al Malikiya (28 May). Some of the villagers specifically feared being in harm's way during the expected Syrian invasion. This factor is cited in the evacuations from Kirad al Baqqara and Kirad al Ghannama (22 April) and Ibl al Kamah (10 May).

The picture that emerges from the IDF Intelligence Department analysis in June 1948 of the Arab evacuation of the Galilee panhandle is far more complex than Allon's subsequent recollection – that the exodus was in the main due to the deliberate, organised whispering campaign. Allon certainly wanted and acted to achieve the exodus, and was happy to claim credit. But the Eastern Galilee exodus was the result of a mixed, complex pattern of causes, varying from locality to locality, starting with some orders to evacuate by Arab irregulars (and, possibly, by Syria as well), and proceeding through Jewish harassment and assaults, fear of Jewish attack, the whispering campaign, and a general fear of being caught up in a battle between two regular armies.[211]

Operation Ben-Ami (Mivtza Ben-Ami) The last major Haganah operation before the termination of the Mandate, in line with Plan D's provision for the securing of blocks of Jewish settlement even outside the Partition plan borders, was the Carmeli Brigade's thrust up Western Galilee to the Lebanese border. Called Operation Ben-Ami, the offensive, carried out over 13–14 May, saw the brigade capture all the Arab villages along the coast road and a few to the east of it, and the flight of almost all their inhabitants. The brigade was not ordered by Haganah General Staff or its commander to drive out the civilian population but it is probable that Moshe Carmel wanted the operation to end in both the conquest and evacuation by the Arabs of the area.

The attacking forces took As Sumeiriya on the morning of 14 May. Carmel attacked from the northwest and the south, leaving the village's eastern side wide open to allow the Arabs to escape – which the villagers did as the units mortared the site and closed in. Apparently, many of the villagers had already left, either on 13 May or before; they were demoralised by the news of the fall of Arab Haifa and Arab Safad, and by the lack of assistance from the ALA.[212] The next major village was Az Zib, with which the Haganah had a long account. The villagers under mortar barrage and fearful of Jewish retribution for their past anti-Yishuv activities, fled during the battle.[213] The last major village to fall was Al Bassa. The women and children had already been evacuated to Lebanon, and only several hundred old people and armed militiamen remained, most of whom fled during the assault. Several families who remained were ordered or "advised" to go northwards, to Lebanon. Another 100 persons, mostly old and/or Christians, were within days transferred to Al Mazra'a, the only coastal Western Galilee village not evacuated by all its inhabitants. A few people from Az Zib were also moved to Al Mazra'a, which became the collection point for all the Arab "remainders" of Western Galilee.[214]

In the second stage of Operation Ben-Ami, on 20–21 May, Carmeli Brigade troops attacked the villages of Umm al Faraj, Al Kabri, At Tell and An Nahr, east of Nahariya. The aim of the action was mainly to push through and finally open the route to Kibbutz Yehiam, an isolated Jewish settlement in the hills to the east. Carmel's operational order of 19 May to his battalion commanders read: "To attack in order to conquer, to kill among the men, to destroy and burn the villages of Al Kabri, Umm al Faraj and An Nahr."[215] Al Kabri had long been a centre of anti-Yishuv forces. In early May, most of its inhabitants fled following a Haganah retaliatory action, in which a number of villagers were killed.[216]

The last village to fall in the second stage of Operation Ben-Ami was Al Ghabisiya, south of Al Kabri. The village apparently formally surrendered. Some of its population remained briefly *in situ* before being expelled sometime during the following days or weeks.[217]

In the days following the capture of Western Galilee, on Carmel's orders, most of the villages were razed by Haganah sappers; Carmel wanted both to punish the villagers, especially of Az Zib and Al Kabri, for past acts against the Yishuv, and to make sure the villagers could and would never return.[218]

The south, April–June 1948 The Haganah and, later, the IDF remained on the strategic defensive in the south throughout the period. No major offensives were undertaken and, from the Egyptian invasion of 15 May, the Negev and Givati brigades had their hands more or less full averting a Jewish collapse. However, both brigades during this period mounted sporadic, local attacks on the peripheries of their zones, usually with a specific tactical or strategic reason (to gain room for manoeuvre and depth), which were designed primarily to facilitate defence against the expected or continuing Egyptian invasion. These attacks, especially those east of Majdal (Ashkelon) and Isdud by Givati, caused the flight of tens of thousands of local Arab inhabitants.

Plan D's guidelines to the Givati Brigade gave brigade OC Shimon Avidan wide discretion. In order to stabilise his defensive lines, the plan stated "you will determine alone, in consultation with your Arab affairs advisers and Intelligence Service officers, [which] villages in your zone should be occupied, cleaned up or destroyed."[219] With the expected Egyptian invasion only days away, Avidan moved to expand his area of control westwards and southwards.

The large village of 'Aqir, south of Rehovot, was surrounded by Givati troops on 4 May. On the Haganah's demand that the villagers surrender and give up their weapons, some 100 rifles, Stens and pistols were handed over. But Givati's intelligence officers believed that the villagers were holding back, and Givati troops therefore took eight 'Aqir Arabs hostages, promising to release them when the remaining weapons were surrendered. Meanwhile, a British unit arrived on the scene and the Givati troops withdrew. In further contacts that day, it was agreed that the villagers would hand over the weapons the following day. But on 5 May, the great majority of the villagers fled the village towards Yibna and Al Mughar. Givati troops moved into the village. Within weeks, the 30-odd villagers who had remained behind were expelled – an act that sparked a flurry of protests in Mapam, which over the years had had contacts with a small group of leftists in the village who were willing to live in peace with the Yishuv.[220]

Next was Qatra, four kilometres west of 'Aqir, where the same pattern was repeated. In talks between the Haganah and the village *mukhtar*, it was agreed that the villagers would hand over their weapons on 6 May. Givati troops surrounded Qatra that morning "to make sure that the Qatra Arabs carried out" the agreement. Several dozen armed men tried to break out of the village and were stopped. The villagers then handed over several dozen rifles and the Givati troops moved in. One of them, while looting, was shot dead by a villager. Givati, looking for foreign irregulars, arrested some of the villagers and, within a few days, either intimidated the rest of the villagers into leaving or ordered them to leave.[221]

On 9 May, the clearing of the southern end of Givati's zone of control in anticipation of the Egyptian invasion began in earnest with the launching of Operation Lightning (*Mivtza Barak*). The objective of the operation was: "To deny the enemy a base . . . creating general panic and breaking his morale . . . It can be assumed that delivering a blow to one or more of these centres [i.e., Majdal, Isdud or Yibna] will cause the wandering [i.e., exodus] of the inhabitants of the smaller settlements in the area. This outcome is possible especially in view of the wave of panic that recently swept over [the Arabs of] the country."[222]

Givati's attacks created the desired wave of panic and flight in the satellite villages. Mortaring almost invariably preceded each ground assault. The attack on Beit Daras on 10 May prompted the flight of its inhabitants and affected neighbouring villages. The village houses were blown up.[223] Bash-shit, to the north, which fell next, was evacuated by its inhabitants at the start of the attack, as were nearby Batani Sharqi and Barqa. Abu Shusha, southeast of Ramle, was mortared on the night of 13–14 May; its population fled. Some of the houses were then blown up. The same day, the nearby village of Na'ana was surrounded and given an ultimatum to hand over its arms; as at 'Aqir, hostages were taken pending a hand-over of arms. Arms were handed over and the village was then occupied. Many villagers stayed on, apparently, until 10 June, when they were probably ordered to leave or intimidated into leaving.[224]

During the second stage of Operation Lightning, Givati troops captured Al Mughar (15 May), Sawafir ash Sharqiya and Batani Gharbi (18 May) and Al Qubeiba (27 May). Most of the inhabitants of these villages had fled either before or during the attack; a few were probably expelled.

On the day of the fall of Al Qubeiba, Givati troops also occupied the large, semi-abandoned village of Zarnuqa. Some of the villagers had remained since the village had traditionally been friendly to the Yishuv. But Avidan apparently wanted only empty villages. A graphic description of what happened in Zarnuqa on 27–28 May was given a few days later in a letter to the Mapam daily, *Al Hamishmar*, by a party member who was briefed by a Haganah soldier who had participated in the conquest: the village had not resisted the Haganah take-over.

The soldier told me how one of the soldiers opened a door and fired a Sten at an old man, an old woman and a child in one burst, how they took the Arabs . . . out of all the houses and stood [them] in the sun all day – in thirst and hunger until they surrendered 40 rifles . . . The Arabs had claimed that they hadn't [weapons, and] in the end they were expelled from the village towards Yibna.

The Arabs protested that they were being driven towards their enemies, anti-Zionist Arabs whom they, in Zarnuqa, had not allowed into their village, "but this did not help, and, screaming and crying, they left the village." The following day the Zarnuqa inhabitants came back relating that the Yibnaites had driven them off as "unredeemable traitors who were unworthy of hospitality." These returnees watched the Jewish troops and farmers from neighbouring settlements ransack their homes. Then, for the second time, they were ordered to leave. Zarnuqa's houses were demolished during June. In August, Kvutzat (kibbutz) Schiller, a nearby settlement, asked the Jewish settlement authorities to lease Zarnuqa's lands.[225]

In the following days, the Givati Brigade captured several more villages on the southern edge of its zone of control, chief of which was Yibna. After mortaring and a brief fight, the units entered the village, which they found deserted "save for some old Arab men and women," who were sent packing.[226]

In co-ordination with Givati's local pushes southwards, the besieged Palmah Negev Brigade during May carried out a number of small pushes northwards and eastwards. The large village of Bureir, northeast of Gaza, was taken on 12–13 May, its inhabitants fleeing to Gaza. The same day the inhabitants of neighbouring Sumsum and Najd, to the west, were expelled. The inhabitants of Huleiqat and Kaukaba, to the north, fled westwards under the impact of the fall of Bureir.[227] A fortnight later, on the night of 27–28 May, Negev Brigade units raided the villages of Al Muharraqa and Kaufakha, 11 kilometres south of Bureir, driving out their inhabitants. The villagers of Kaufakha had earlier repeatedly asked to surrender, accept Jewish rule and be allowed to stay, all to no avail. The Haganah always regarded such requests as either insincere or unreliable; with the Egyptian army nearby, it was felt that there was no room to take a chance.[228]

Three days later, the brigade ordered the villagers of nearby Huj to leave. Huj had traditionally been friendly towards the Yishuv – in 1946, its inhabitants had hidden Haganah men from a British dragnet. In mid-December 1947, while on a visit to Gaza, the *mukhtar* of Huj and his brother were shot dead by a mob that accused them of "collaboration with Jews." On 31 May 1948, however, the Negev Brigade, fearing that Huj, near the front with the Egyptian army, was unreliable, expelled the inhabitants westward and looted and blew up their houses.[229]

Conclusion

From the foregoing, it emerges that the main wave of the Arab exodus, encompassing 200,000–300,000 refugees, was not the result of a general, predetermined Yishuv policy. The Arab exodus of April–May caught the Yishuv leadership, including the authors of Plan D, by surprise, though it was immediately seen as a phenomenon to be exploited. As Galili put it on 11 May: "Up to 15 May and after 15 May we must continue to implement the plan of military operations [i.e., Plan D] prepared a while ago, which did not take into account the collapse and flight of Arab settlements following the route in Haifa ... [But] this collapse facilitates our tasks."[230]

A major shift in attitudes towards Arab civilian communities can be discerned in the Haganah and among Yishuv civilian executives during March–April, when, reeling from the blows of the battle for the roads, the Yishuv braced itself for the expected Arab invasion. The guidelines of Plan D, formulated in early March, to a certain degree already embodied this new orientation. Their essence was that the rear areas of the Jewish State's territory and its main roads had to be completely secured, and that this was best done by driving out hostile or potentially hostile Arab communities and destroying the villages. During the first half of April, Ben-Gurion and the Haganah General Staff approved a series of offensives (which were in nature counter-attacks) embodying these guidelines. During the following weeks, Haganah and IZL offensives in Haifa, Jaffa, Eastern Galilee and Western Galilee precipitated the mass exodus.

During its first months, the exodus was regarded by the Arab states and the AHC as a passing phenomenon of no particular consequence. Local Palestinian Arab leaders and commanders tried to fight it, unsuccessfully. The transformation of the exodus in April into a massive demographic upheaval caught the AHC and the Arab states largely unawares and was a cause of grave embarrassment: it highlighted the AHC's (and the Palestinians') defeat and the Arab states' inability, so long as the Mandate lasted, to intervene. At the same time, it propelled the states closer to the brink of an invasion about which they were largely unenthusiastic. There is no evidence to show that the Arab states and the AHC wanted a mass exodus or issued blanket orders or appeals to the Palestinians to flee their homes (though in certain areas the inhabitants of specific villages were ordered by Arab commanders or the AHC to leave, mainly for strategic reasons). The behaviour of the different Arab communities was in great measure dictated by local circumstances and, where relevant, by decision-making on the local level, by National Committee members and local military leaders.

The picture that emerges is complex and varied, differing widely from place to place and week to week. In trying to elucidate patterns, it is necessary to distinguish between the cities and towns, and the countryside.

The evacuation of the towns and cities over April–May must be seen as the culmination of a series of events and against the backdrop of the basic weaknesses of Palestinian Arab society rather than in isolation: the Arab inhabitants of Haifa, Jaffa, Tiberias and, to a lesser extent, of Safad, Beisan and Acre had for months suffered from a collapse of administration and law and order, difficulties of communications and supplies, isolation, siege, skirmishing and intermittent harassment at the hands of the Haganah and the dissident Jewish organisations. In the case of Jaffa, Haifa and Jerusalem, the steady exodus of the middle and upper classes over December 1947 to March 1948 considerably demoralised the remaining inhabitants and provided a model for their own departure once conditions became intolerable. The urban masses (and the *fellahin*) had traditionally looked to the urban upper and middle classes for leadership.

A major factor in the exodus from each town was the fall of and exodus from the previous town. The exodus from Arab Tiberias four days before the fall of Arab Haifa served as a pointer and model for Haifa's Arab leaders on the eve of their decision to evacuate the town. It also undermined morale in Safad. Even more telling were the fall and exodus of Arab Haifa: these strongly affected the inhabitants of Jaffa, and also radiated defeatism throughout the north, affecting Safad, Beisan and Acre, and many villages. If mighty Haifa could fall and be uprooted, how could relatively unarmed, poor and small communities hope to hold out against the Haganah? The fall of Tiberias, earlier, had resulted in panic and exodus from a series of Sea of Galilee area villages (Ghuweir Abu Shusha, Tabigha, etc.), and the collapse of, and flight from, Jaffa had a similar effect on Arab Jerusalem and on Jaffa's hinterland villages (Salama, Yazur, etc.).

In turn, the defeat of, and exodus from, hinterland villages served to undermine morale in the towns. The townspeople felt, and were, cut off. The fall of Al Manara and Khirbet Nasir ad Din undermined morale in Arab Tiberias; the fall of Salama and other satellite villages contributed to the exodus from Jaffa; the fall of Biriya and 'Ein az Zeitun triggered the start of the exodus from Safad; the fall of villages around Beisan contributed to demoralisation in Beisan; and the fall of the villages of Western Galilee precipitated the collapse of Acre.

The "atrocity factor" certainly counted for something in the process of demoralisation. What happened, or allegedly happened, at Nasser ad Din undoubtedly affected the Arabs of Tiberias during their last days in the town, and in a more general way, the massacre at Deir Yassin, descriptions of which were luridly and repeatedly broadcast by Arab radio stations for weeks, undermined Arab morale throughout Palestine, though far more in the countryside – especially around Jerusalem – than in the cities. Probably more potent still were Arab fears of Jewish atrocities than knowledge of either real or alleged past Jewish misdeeds.

Another major factor in the exodus from the cities was the dissolution and flight of the local civil and military leadership just before and during the final battles. The flight of the al Tabaris just before or during the battle for Tiberias; the flight of the civil and military commanders of Arab Haifa just before and during the battle for Haifa; the flight of Jaffa's leaders during and after the IZL assault on Manshiya; and the departure from Safad and Beisan of prominent local families and military commanders before and during the Haganah attacks all contributed to the mass exodus from each town.

In the villages, there was normally no flight of leaders before or during attack. Except for those evacuated earlier by women and children, villages were by and large abandoned at one go; the *mukhtar*, the *mukhtar*'s family and the militia commanders all left together with the population.

Undoubtedly, as was perceived by IDF intelligence during June, the most important single factor in the exodus of April–June from both the cities and from the villages, was the Haganah/dissident military attack on each site. This is demonstrated clearly by the fact that each exodus occurred during and in the immediate wake of each military assault. No town was abandoned by the bulk of its population *before* Jewish attack.

In the countryside, while many of the villages were abandoned during Haganah/IZL attacks and because of them, other villages were evacuated as a result of Jewish attacks on neighbouring villages or on towns in the area. The underlying fear was that they would be next.

In general, operational orders in Haganah attacks on both urban and rural targets did not call for the expulsion or eviction of the Arab civilian populations, but the phenomenon of spontaneous, panicky, mass Arab flight may have served to whet the appetite of local Haganah commanders and, perhaps, the General Staff as well. They, like Ben-Gurion, realised that a transfer of the prospective Arab minority out of the emergent Jewish State had begun and that with very little extra effort and nudging on the part of the Jewish forces, it could be expanded. The temptation proved very strong, for obvious military and political reasons.

By and large, when it came to ejecting Arab communities, the Haganah commanders exercised greater independence and forcefulness in the countryside than in the towns. This was due partly to the greater distance from major Haganah headquarters, where senior officers, as exemplified by Ben-Gurion, were reluctant to openly issue or endorse expulsion orders, and partly, to the guidelines set down in Plan D, which enabled local commanders to expel and level villages for strategic reasons but contained no provision for wholesale expulsion from towns and cities.

There was also an obvious time factor which influenced the Haganah's behaviour towards Arab communities between the end of March and mid-May. The closer drew the 15 May British withdrawal deadline and the prospect of invasion by the Arab states, the readier became Haganah commanders to resort to clearing operations and expulsions to rid their rear areas and main roads of hostile and potentially hostile civilian concentrations. After 15 May, the threat and presence of the Arab regular armies near the Yishuv's centres of population dictated a play-safe policy of taking no chances with Arab communities to the rear of the front lines; hence, the Givati Brigade's expulsions in May in the northern Negev approaches. In general, however, the swift collapse under Haganah attack of almost all the Palestinian and foreign irregular formations and of civilian morale, and the spontaneous panic and flight of most Arab communities meant that Jewish commanders almost invariably were not faced with the dilemma of issuing expulsion orders in overrun villages: most of the villages were completely or almost completely empty by the time they were occupied.

Chapter 4

Deciding against a return of the refugees, April–December 1948

The Arab mass exodus confronted the Yishuv with a major political problem: whether or not to allow those who had fled or been expelled to return.

During the spring, refugees in various localities had already begun pressing to return to their homes and villages. Local Haganah and civil leaders had to decide, without having national guidelines, whether to allow such a return – and they almost invariably ruled against it.[1] The Arab states, led by Transjordan, in May began clamouring for a refugee return. From early summer the Yishuv's national political–military leadership was subjected to intense international pressures – spearheaded first by Count Folke Bernadotte, the United Nations Mediator for Palestine, and, later, by the United States – in favour of mass repatriation of the refugees. During June, the Israeli government confronted the issue and decided to bar a return; it was one of the most important decisions taken by the new State in 1948.

The decision, taken against the backdrop of the invasion of the newborn State by the Arab armies and the intensification of the fighting, crystallised over May–June. Hard thinking in the Yishuv about the exodus in general and about a possible refugee return in particular had already been precipitated by the fall of Haifa and Jaffa and the Arab evacuation of these towns.

Golda Myerson (Meir) visited Arab Haifa a few days after its conquest. She reported to the Jewish Agency Executive on 6 May: "It is a dreadful thing to see the dead city. I found next to the port [Arab] children, women, the old, waiting for a way to leave. I entered the houses, there were houses where the coffee and *pitot* were left on the table, and I could not avoid [thinking] that this, indeed, had been the picture in many Jewish towns [i.e., in Europe, during World War II]." The situation, she said, "raised many questions." Should the Jews "make an effort to bring the Arabs back to Haifa, or not [?] Meanwhile, so long as it is not decided differently, we have decided on a number of rules, and these include: We won't go to Acre or Nazareth to bring back the Arabs [of Haifa]. But, at the same time, our behaviour should be such that if, because of it, they come back – [then] let them come back. We shouldn't behave badly with the Arabs [who remained in Haifa] so that others [who fled] won't return."[2]

Myerson spoke about the question of a return within the wider context of general policy towards Palestine's Arabs during the meeting of the Mapai Centre a few days later. She suggested that the Yishuv could not treat the inhabitants of villages who had fled because they did not want to fight against the Yishuv, "such as Sheikh Muwannis," in the same way as hostile villagers. But while implying that she thought "friendly" villagers should be allowed back, Myerson avoided taking a stand. Rather, she asked: "What are we to do with the villages . . . abandoned by friends . . . Are we prepared to preserve these villages in order that their inhabitants might return, or do we want to wipe out every trace that there had been a village on the site?" She then turned to the subject of Haifa and said: "I am not among those extremists – and there are such, and I applaud them – who want to do everything that can be done in order to bring back the Arabs. I say I am not willing to make extraordinary arrangements to bring back Arabs." But the question was whether the Yishuv should behave well or poorly towards the Arabs who had remained, either encouraging or discouraging a refugee return. Ill-treatment, of course, might also prompt those who had remained to pack up and leave, "and we would be rid of the lot of them." She concluded by saying that the party and, by implication, the Yishuv, had entered the war unprepared and without a clear policy on the treatment of Palestine's Arabs. She called on the Mapai Centre to hold a comprehensive discussion on the Arab problem.[3] The call went unheeded.

Myerson's line was an amplification of the policy laid down by Ben-Gurion during a visit to Haifa on 1 May: the Jews should treat the remaining Arabs "with civil and human equality" but "it is not our job to worry about the return of the Arabs [who had fled]." Clearly, neither he nor Myerson was interested in the return of the refugees (though Myerson, it seemed, was willing to make an exception of "friendly" Arabs). Ben-Gurion had already said as much back in early February, specifically with regard to the depopulation of the Arab districts of west Jerusalem.[4]

The crystallisation of the policy against a return was heralded on 25 April – as the Haifa Arab exodus was under way – in a cable from Moshe Shertok (Sharett), the new State's foreign minister-to-be, in New York, to his officials in Tel Aviv: "Suggest consider issue warning Arabs now evacuating [that they] cannot be assured of return."[5]

Pressure for a return began to build up in early May as, for their part, the Arab leaders began to contemplate the enormous political, economic, and military implications of the mass exodus from Palestine. At a meeting in Amman on 2 May, Arab officials and notables from the exiled Haifa Arab community agreed that "the Arabs should return to Haifa." There was, apparently, co-ordination with the British as the following day the British Army removed several Haganah road-blocks in Haifa and took up positions in the abandoned Arab neighbourhoods. During the following days both Azzam Pasha and Abdullah issued well-publicised calls to the Palestinian refugees to return to their homes, while on 6 May the Mandate Government proclaimed in Jerusalem: "In the view of the Government the Arabs can feel completely safe in Haifa." On 5 May Abdullah had called on "every man of strength and wisdom, every young person of power and faith [from Palestine], who has left the country, let him return to the dear spot. No one should remain outside the country except the rich and the old." Abdullah went on to thank "those of you . . . who have remained where they are in spite of the tyranny now prevailing" and went out of his way to cite the Jewish Agency condemnation of the massacre at Deir Yassin.[6]

This joint Arab–British effort, aimed at the repatriation not only of the Haifa refugees, but also of all Palestine refugees, came to nought. The Haganah was not allowing Arabs to return and, given the continued fighting and confusion on the ground, the call to return may not have generated much enthusiasm among the refugees themselves. In Haifa itself, where initially the local Jewish civilian leadership had not been averse to an Arab return, a major change of thinking had taken place in the course of May. By 6 June, the drift of a meeting in the Haifa town hall was, in the words of one participant: "There are no sentiments in war . . . Better to cause them injustice than that [we suffer] a disaster . . . We have no interest in their returning."[7]

The talk and diplomatic movement in May surrounding a possible return helped trigger the consolidation of an effective, if loosely co-ordinated, lobby in the Yishuv against repatriation of the refugees. The lobby consisted of various local authorities, the kibbutz movements, the settlement and land departments of the National Institutions, many of the Haganah commanders and a number of powerful Yishuv executives, including Weitz and Danin.

Weitz regarded the Arab exodus, which he had helped to promote in a number of places, as an implementation, albeit unplanned and largely spontaneous, of the transfer schemes of the late 1930s, which had envisaged the movement of the Arab minority out of the future Jewish State so that it would become demographically homogeneous, politically stable and secure against subversion from within. In Weitz's view, the mass Arab exodus of the first months of the war had amounted to such a transfer. He and his colleagues realised that, for Israel's sake, the exodus must be expanded by nudging or propelling more Arab communities into flight and the post-exodus status quo consolidated and safeguarded. A return would vitiate this major political–military gain of the war, endangering the future Jewish State. Weitz considered that the matter was vital and serious enough to merit the establishment of a separate, powerful state authority to supervise what he defined as the "retroactive transfer." During March and April, Weitz desperately sought political backing and help to implement the transfer. From May, Weitz pressed Ben-Gurion and Shertok to set up a "Transfer Committee," preferably with himself at its head, to oversee "transfer policy," which in the main was to focus on measures assuring that there could be and would be no return. More guardedly, the Transfer Committee was also to advise the political leadership and the Haganah commanders on expulsions of further Arab communities.

The first unofficial Transfer Committee – composed of Weitz, Danin and Sasson, now head of the new Middle East Affairs Department of the Foreign Ministry – came into being at the end of May, following Danin's agreement to come in on the scheme in mid-May and Shertok's unofficial sanction of the Committee's existence and goals on 28 May.

In mid-May, Danin resigned from the Yishuv's Committee for Abandoned Arab Property, whose task had been to protect such property from looting and to channel it or profits from it to the Yishuv's treasury. Danin, on 18 May, wrote Weitz that what was needed was "an institution whose role will be . . . to seek ways to carry out the transfer of the Arab population at this opportunity when it has left its normal place of residence." Danin thought that Christian groups could be found, acting under the banner of helping the refugees, who would help in the permanent resettlement of the refugees in the Arab countries. "Let us not waste the fact that a large Arab population has moved from its home, and achieving such a thing would be very difficult in normal times," he wrote Weitz. Concretely, Danin said that "if we do not seek to encourage the return of the Arabs . . . then they must be confronted with *faits accomplis.*" Among the *faits accomplis* he proposed were the destruction of Arab houses, "settling Jews in all the area evacuated" and expropriating Arab property.[8]

On 28 May, Weitz went to Shertok and proposed that the Cabinet appoint himself, Sasson and Danin as a Transfer Committee "to hammer out a plan of action designed [to achieve] the goal of transfer." Shertok, according to Weitz, congratulated him on his initiative and agreed that the "momentum [of Arab flight] must be exploited and turned into an accomplished fact."[9] On 30 May, Weitz met Finance Minister Kaplan (number three in the Mapai hierarchy) and, according to Weitz, received the Minister's blessing for the implementation of the transfer policy.[10] That day, the Transfer Committee met for its first working session, and Weitz began preparing a draft proposal for its activities.

But official authorisation and appointment of the Committee by either Ben-Gurion or the Cabinet continued to elude him. Nonetheless, from the beginning of June, with funds from the JNF, the Committee began organising and overseeing the destruction of Arab villages in various areas of the country. On 5 June, Weitz, armed with a three-page memorandum, signed by himself, Danin and Sasson, entitled "Retroactive Transfer, A Scheme for the Solution of the Arab Question in the State of Israel," saw Ben-Gurion.

The memorandum stated that the war had unexpectedly brought about "the uprooting of masses [of Arabs] from their towns and villages and their flight out of the area of Israel . . . This process may continue as the war continues and our army advances." The war and the exodus had so deepened Arab enmity "as perhaps to make impossible the existence of hundreds of thousands of Arabs in the State of Israel and the existence of the state with hundreds of thousands of inhabitants who bear that hatred." Israel, therefore, "must be inhabited largely by Jews, so that there will be in it very few non-Jews" and that "the uprooting of the Arabs should be seen as a solution to the Arab question in the State of Israel and, in line with this, it must from now on be directed according to a calculated plan geared towards the goal of 'retroactive transfer'."

To consolidate and amplify the transfer, the Committee proposed the following actions:

(1) Preventing the Arabs from returning to their places.
(2) [Extending] help to the Arabs to be absorbed in other places.

Regarding the first guideline, the Committee proposed:

(1) Destruction of villages as much as possible during military operations.
(2) Prevention of any cultivation of land by them, including reaping, collection [of crops], picking [olives] and so on, also during times of ceasefire.
(3) Settlement of Jews in a number of villages and towns so that no "vacuum" is created.
(4) Enacting legislation [geared to barring a return].
(5) [Making] propaganda [aimed at non-return].

The Committee proposed that it oversee the destruction of Arab villages and the renovation of other sites for Jewish settlement, negotiate the purchase of Arab land, prepare legislation for expropriation and negotiate the resettlement of the Arabs in Arab countries.

How did Ben-Gurion react? According to Weitz, "he agreed to the whole line" but thought that the Yishuv should first take care of the destruction of the Arab villages, establish Jewish settlements and prevent Arab cultivation and only later worry about plans for the organised resettlement of the refugees in the Arab countries. Ben-Gurion agreed to the idea of a supervisory committee but was opposed to Weitz's "temporary committee." At the same time, he approved the Committee's start of organised destruction of the Arab villages, about which Weitz had informed him.

According to Ben-Gurion's account of the meeting, Ben-Gurion approved the establishment of a committee to oversee "the cleaning up [*nikui*] of the Arab settlements, cultivation of [Arab fields] and their settlement [by Jews], and the creation of labour battalions to carry out this work." Nowhere did he refer clearly to the destruction of Arab villages or the active prevention of an Arab refugee return.[11]

The following day, 6 June, Weitz wrote Ben-Gurion: "I . . . take the liberty of setting down your answer [of yesterday 5 June] to the scheme-proposal I submitted to you, that: A) You will call a meeting immediately to discuss [the scheme] and to appoint a committee . . .; B) You agree that the actions marked in clauses 1, 2 . . . begin immediately [i.e., referring to the destruction of Arab villages and the prevention of Arab cultivation]." Weitz continued: "In line with this, I have given an order to begin [these operations] in different parts of the Galilee, in the Beit Shean Valley, in the Hills of Ephraim and in Samaria [meaning east of Hadera]."[12] Weitz, of course, was covering himself. He knew that on this sensitive subject, Ben-Gurion preferred never to commit anything to writing, and he did not want to leave himself open to charges that he had acted without political authorisation. He also wanted to prod Ben-Gurion at long last to set up the Committee, and he may even have hoped to get a written response from Ben-Gurion. He did not.

In any event, using his JNF apparatus and network of land-purchasing agents and intelligence operatives, Weitz immediately set in motion the levelling of Arab villages (Al Mughar, near Gedera, Fajja, near Petah Tikva, Biyar Adas, near Magdiel, Beit Dajan, east of Tel Aviv, Miska, near Ramat Hakovesh, As Sumeiriya, near Acre, Al Buteimat and Sabbarin, southeast of Haifa). His agents toured the abandoned countryside to determine which villages should be destroyed and which should be preserved as suitable for Jewish settlement. He remained hopeful that, eventually, Cabinet-level authorisation of his actions would be forthcoming and that the Transfer Committee would at last receive an official letter of appointment. He was unaware of the fact that his semi-covert activities had been noted by Mapam and that Mapam, together with Shitrit, had launched a strong counter-campaign in the Cabinet and elsewhere in the government bureaucracy against the continuing destruction of the Arab villages and the general policy of transfer of which the destruction was a major component. At the start of July, still not having received official sanction, Weitz suspended the destruction operations, effectively terminating the activities of the first, unofficial, "self-appointed" Transfer Committee.

As to the political decision-making concerning a return, it was Shertok who heralded the adoption of the formulation that was to emerge. Against the backdrop of dissonant *Kol Yisrael* (Voice of Israel) radio broadcasts on 29 May proclaiming that Israel would allow a refugee return, he minuted Foreign Ministry Director General Walter Eytan on 6 June: "We must avoid unequivocal statements on this matter. For the moment, only [use] a negative formulation. That is, so long as the war continues, there should be no talk of allowing a return. [But don't let it appear] from our statements that at the war's end, they will be allowed back. Let us keep open every option."[13]

It was Weitz who had sounded the alarm about the *Kol Yisrael* broadcasts. But the other lobbyists and interest groups were also hard at work during the crucial days before and during the First Truce (11 June – 8 July 1948) making sure that the Cabinet did not succumb to international or Mapam pressure and open the doors to refugee repatriation. From around the country, local Jewish leaders, some journeying to Tel Aviv, demanded that the government bar a return. The more distant or isolated the settlement from Jewish centres of population, the stronger was the clamour against a return.

In the first days of June, the notables of the 1,700-strong Jewish community of Safad (whose 10,000 Arab population had fled in May) attempted to appeal directly to the Cabinet. They got as far as Shlomo Kaddar, the Principal Assistant at the Cabinet Secretariat. He reported that the Safad notables had demanded that the government bar a return, set up a ring of new Jewish settlements around the town and settle Jews in the town's abandoned Arab houses. "The Jewish community will not be able to withstand the pressure of the returning Arabs, especially in view [of the fact] that most of the Arab property in Safad has been stolen and plundered since the Arabs left," said the Safad Jewish notables. If the Arabs were allowed to return, the Jewish community would leave, they warned. The same message was conveyed by Safad's Jewish leaders to a visiting delegation of Yishuv officials on 5 July. If Jewish settlers were not brought to Safad, then it were best that "the Arab houses . . . be destroyed and blown up lest the Arabs have somewhere to return to."[14] If the Jews did not quickly fill the abandoned Arab villages, they would be "filled with returning Arabs with hatred in their hearts," Weitz concluded after a visit to Safad.[15]

A similar note was struck by Ephraim Vizhensky, Secretary of the Western Galilee Settlements Block Committee and a member of Kibbutz Evron, in a letter to Agriculture Minister Zisling. Western Galilee "no longer [has] an Arab population." There was a need "to exploit the situation which [has] arisen . . . [and] immediately to establish [new Jewish] settlements" in the area to assure its "Judaization."

At the same time, a delegation of local Jewish Western Galilee leaders arrived in Tel Aviv seeking audience with ministers. Shertok refused to see them. They told the Cabinet Secretariat "that a return to the status quo ante and a return of the Arabs were unthinkable. If the Arabs returned, they [i.e., the Jews] would leave [the area] . . . If they stay put, then it is on condition that the Arabs do not return and that the area [earmarked in the Partition resolution for the Palestine Arab state] be incorporated in the Jewish state."[16]

Similar letters and demands arrived from other parts of the country. For example, on 2 June, Shmuel Zagorsky, the inspector of Arab property and a major local figure in the Gilboa area, urged Avraham Hartzfeld, the head of the Agricultural Centre, to see to the establishment of new Jewish settlements in the Beit Shean Valley as a means of preventing an Arab refugee return. "I am fearful that the Arabs of the area will return to these areas and that we will lose the immediate opportunity to set up new settlements. For my part, I have done all in my power to close the way back to the Arabs, but pressure by them to return is already being felt," he warned.[17]

The input of the military lobby may have weighed even more heavily. IDF intelligence regarded the prospect of a mass refugee return as a major threat to the Yishuv's war effort. On 16 June, the Director of the IDF Intelligence Department wrote to Shiloah, the Director of the Foreign Ministry's Political Division: "There is a growing movement by the Palestinian villagers who fled to the neighbouring countries [to] return now, during the days of the [First Truce]. There is a serious danger [that returning Arab villagers] will fortify themselves in their villages behind our front lines, and with the resumption of warfare, will constitute at least a [potential] fifth Column, if not active hostile concentrations."

If nothing was done about the return of refugees, there was a danger that at the end of the Truce, the IDF would have "to set aside considerable forces again to clean up the rear and the lines of communication."[18] The military's opposition to a return remained firm and consistent through the summer. On 14 August, IDF OC Operations (and acting chief of staff) Yadin wrote to Shertok: "Because of the spread of diseases among the Arab refugees, I propose that [we] declare a quarantine on all our conquered areas. We will thus be able to more strongly oppose the demand for the return of the Arab refugees and all infiltration by Arabs

[back] into the abandoned villages – in addition to our opposition [to a return] on understandable military and political grounds."[19]

At the start of the First Truce, the Foreign Ministry's Middle East Department noted the Arab leaders' calls for the return to Palestine of "the 300,000 refugees." It also noted the trickle of refugees infiltrating back to their villages. The Department conjectured that a major reason for this return of Arabs was their desire "to harvest the [summer] crops . . . The Arabs in their places of wandering are suffering from real hunger." But this harvest-geared return, the department warned, could "in time bring in its wake [Arab] [re-]settlement in the villages, something which might seriously endanger many of the achievements we accomplished during the first six months of the war. It is not for nothing that Arab spokesmen are . . . demanding the return . . . [of the refugees], because this would not only ease their burden but would weigh us down considerably."[20]

On 1 June, a group of senior ministers and officials, including Shertok, Shitrit, Cabinet Secretary Sharef, the Director General of the Minority Affairs Ministry Gad Machnes, and Sasson discussed the issue in Tel Aviv and, in Ben-Gurion's diary phrase, concluded that the Arabs "were not to be helped to return" and that the IDF commanders "were to be issued with the appropriate orders."[21] Orders to bar a return were duly issued to the military units.[22]

Shertok, who through the summer was the main Cabinet patron of the Transfer Committee, in a letter to the chairman of the World Jewish Congress, Nahum Goldmann, explained the primary political consideration behind the Yishuv's crystallising hardline against a refugee return: "The opportunities which the present position open up for a lasting and radical solution of the most vexing problem of the Jewish State [i.e., the Arab minority problem] are so far-reaching as to take one's breath away. Even if a certain backwash is unavoidable, we must make the most of the momentous chance with which history has presented us so swiftly and so unexpectedly."[23]

Matters came to a head in mid-June. The institution of the First Truce had for the first time during the war stilled the guns along the front lines, seemingly presenting the physical possibility of a refugee return. A trickle of refugees began making their way back to villages and towns. At the same time, the Truce enabled the Arab states to take note and stock of the enormous burden that they had unexpectedly incurred. Solving the refugee problem became a major Arab policy goal. Similarly, as the dust of battle temporarily settled, the world community at last took note of the birth of the problem. Public opinion in the West began to mobilise and refugee relief drives were inaugurated. The newly-appointed United Nations Mediator for Palestine, Bernadotte, who in World War II had worked on refugee assistance, made clear his intention to focus his peace-making efforts, in the first instance, on solving the refugee problem. He was due in Tel Aviv on 17 June.

The Cabinet met on 16 June. In a forceful speech, Ben-Gurion set out his views, which were to serve as the basis of the consensus that emerged. "I do not accept the version [i.e., policy] that [we] should encourage their return," he said, in an obvious response to Mapam's decision of the previous days to support the return of "peace-minded" refugees at the war's end. "I believe," said Ben-Gurion, "we should prevent their return . . . We must settle Jaffa, Jaffa will become a Jewish city . . . The return of the Arabs to Jaffa [would be] not just foolish." If the Arabs were allowed to return, to Jaffa and elsewhere, "and the war is renewed, our chances of ending the war as we wish to end it will be reduced . . . Meanwhile, we must prevent at all costs their return," he said, and, leaving no doubt in the ministers' minds about his views on the ultimate fate of the refugees, he added: "I will be for them not returning after the war."[24]

Shertok spoke with equal force against a return. "Can we imagine a return to the status quo ante?" he asked. It was inconceivable. Rather, the government should now persuade the Yishuv of "the enormous importance of this [demographic] change in terms of [possibilities of Jewish] settlement and security, and in terms of the solidity of the state structure and [of] the solution of crucial social and political problems." Israel should be ready to pay compensation for the abandoned land but "they will not return. [That] is our policy. They are not returning," he said.[25]

No formal vote was taken at the 16 June Cabinet meeting. But the line advocated by Ben-Gurion and Shertok – that the refugees should not be allowed back – had now become official Israeli policy.

Outwardly, at least, this policy was given a somewhat less definitive, more flexible countenance. At their meeting on 17 June, Bernadotte asked Shertok whether Israel would allow back "the 300,000" refugees "and would their proprietary rights be respected?" Shertok responded that "the question could not be discussed while the war was going on" and said that "the government had not yet fixed its policy about the ultimate settlement of the matter." He added that "proprietary rights would certainly be respected."[26]

Shertok, while rejecting any consideration of the matter while the hostilities lasted, had appeared to leave open the possibility that after the war Israel might allow back the refugees. This implied flexibility clearly eased the task of Israeli officials in their talks with United Nations and American representatives. But it seems to have been the product less of diplomatic expediency than of the exigencies of Israeli coalition politics and the need to maintain national unity in wartime.

The nettle in the coalition garden was Mapam, Mapai's chief partner in the 1948 coalition. Mapam opposed the transfer policy and endorsed the right of the refugees to return after the war. Had Ben-Gurion definitively closed the door to the possibility of a return, Mapam would probably have been forced to bolt from the coalition, causing a breakdown of national unity and the isolation of Mapai in the Cabinet, where Ben-Gurion's party would have been left, embarrassingly, with only non-socialist and religious parties as partners. Moreover, the top echelons of both the military and, to a lesser degree, the civil bureaucracies of the new State in 1948 were heavily manned by Mapam's cadres.

After weeks of debate on the Arab question, Mapam's Political Committee in mid-June had set down the party's policy in a document entitled "Our Policy Toward the Arabs During the War," which was distributed to all party workers. The party declared its opposition to "the tendency [*megama*] to expel the Arabs from the areas of the emerging Jewish State." The Committee proposed that the Cabinet issue a call to peace-minded Arabs "to stay in their places." As to the Arabs already in exile, the party declared: "The cabinet . . . should [announce] that with the return of peace they should return to a life of peace, honour and productivity . . . The property of the returnees . . . will be restored to them."[27]

Thus, while Mapam – as its co-leader Meir Ya'ari said at the time – was agreeable to deferring a refugee return until the termination of hostilities,[28] Mapai could not have forced through a definitive cabinet decision to bar a return without causing a major government crisis.

On 27 June, Bernadotte demanded that Israel recognise "the right of the residents of Palestine who, because of conditions created by the conflict there, have left their normal places of abode, to return to their homes without restriction and to regain possession of their property."[29] The Israeli reply of 5 July was negative, dismissing Bernadotte's suggestions to curtail Jewish immigration, to hand over Jerusalem to Arab rule and to reach an imposed solution through mediation rather than through direct Israeli–Arab negotiations. The Israeli reply did not refer directly to the demand that Israel recognise the "right of return," but suggested generally that Bernadotte reconsider his "whole approach to the [Palestine] problem."[30]

Diplomacy was suspended when the First Truce collapsed. During the fighting of 9–18 July, the IDF conquered large areas in the centre of the country (Lydda–Ramle) and in the Galilee (Nazareth). The fighting increased the number of refugees by about 100,000.

The start of the Second Truce, on 18 July, saw a major resurgence of international concern about the refugees. In an interview in *The New York Herald Tribune* of 21 June, Sasson had said that there would be no return of refugees except as part of a peace agreement with the Arab states; restitution for confiscated Arab property would be linked to compensation for Jewish property confiscated in Arab countries; and any return would be selective. This was a new formulation of Israel's position, and Israel's delegation at the United Nations, prodded by the Americans, sought clarification from Tel Aviv.[31]

Shertok replied on 22 July:

Our policy: 1) Arab exodus direct result folly aggression organized by Arab states . . . 2) No question allowing Arabs return while state of war continuing, as would mean introduction Fifth Column, provision bases for enemies from outside and dislocation law and order inside. Exceptions only in favour special deserving cases compassionate grounds, subject security screening . . . 4) Question Arab return can be decided only as part peace settlement with Arab State[s] and in context its terms, when question confiscation property Jews neighbouring countries and their future will also be raised.[32]

The Cabinet consensus of mid-June had thus undergone a significant reshaping. The Cabinet had formally resolved against a return during the hostilities, leaving open the possibility of a reconsideration of the matter at the war's end. Shertok, however, was saying that there would be no return during the war and reconsideration and a solution of the problem only within the framework of talks aimed at a general peace settlement. A link was thus established between a full-fledged peace and Israeli willingness to consider a return, making the refugees a bargaining counter in Israel's quest for recognition and peace in the region; and a second link vaguely connected the fate of the Palestinian refugees with that of the Jews in the Arab countries.

Dr Leo Kohn, Shertok's veteran Political Adviser, may have been alluding to this shift in policy when he wrote to the Foreign Minister on 22 July that "as far as I know, our attitude on this question has hardened in recent months." Kohn anticipated that Bernadotte would continue to press the refugee issue,[33] and he was to be proved right. Bernadotte raised the problem again with Shertok in Tel Aviv on 26 July, Shertok replying that there could be no return during hostilities and that the matter could be reconsidered thereafter "in the context of a general peace settlement."[34]

Meanwhile, as Bernadotte prodded the Israelis on repatriation, the spokesmen of the Arab minority within Israel began to press for some measure of repatriation, with special pleading with regard to the particular localities of Haifa and Jaffa and to Christians. This sparked repeated debates within the Israeli military and civil bureaucracies.

On 26–27 June the Greek Catholic Archbishop of Haifa, George Hakim, just returned from Beirut, met with Haifa lawyer Ya'acov

Salomon and then with Shitrit, Machnes and Sasson. He pleaded that Israel allow back at least Haifa's Christian refugees. "We were frank with him," Shitrit reported, "and we asked him if the return of Christian Arabs to Haifa, without Muslims, would not damage Muslim–Christian unity." The Archbishop, according to Shitrit, said that he was not troubled by this question and, in any case, would not publicly appear as seeking only a return of Christian Arabs. But both on the local and national levels, Hakim met with only negative responses.[35]

Appeals on behalf of the refugees from Jaffa began to reach the Israeli authorities in June, less than two months after the town's population had fled. The petitions, presented by the leaders of the remaining Arab population, were based on the surrender agreement signed between the city's Arab notables and the Haganah on 13 May. Those wishing to leave, stated that agreement, were free to do so. "Likewise, any male Arab who left Jaffa and wishes to return to Jaffa may apply for a permit to do so. Permits will be granted after their bona fides has been proven, provided that the [city] commander of the Haganah is convinced that the applicants will not . . . constitute a threat to peace and security."[36]

Citing this agreement, the remaining Jaffa notables on 26 June appealed to the IDF to allow back exiled relatives of Arabs still in Jaffa.[37] The following day, Yitzhak Chisik, the IDF military governor of Jaffa, wrote to Shitrit, appending the text of the Jaffa Arab appeal: "You will certainly recall," wrote Chisik to the Minority Affairs Minister, "that in Clause 8 of the surrender agreement it states that every Arab who left Jaffa and wishes to come back, can do so by submitting a request, on condition, of course, that their presence here [in Jaffa] will not constitute a security risk."[38]

Chisik's letter sparked a wide-ranging debate in the upper echelons of the government. Shitrit wrote to Ben-Gurion and Shertok that similar appeals were reaching him from Haifa. Apparently, he did not feel that the 16 June Cabinet consensus covered such specific requests.[39] Replying for Ben-Gurion, Shlomo Kaddar, on 5 July, wrote: "I have been asked to tell you that the prime minister is opposed to the return of the Arab inhabitants to their places so long as the war continues and so long as the enemy stands at our gates. Only the full Cabinet, the prime minister believes, can decide on a change of approach."[40]

Shertok passed on Shitrit's letter for comment to Yehoshua Palmon. Palmon's response was something of a surprise: "I think that we should adopt a public posture that we do not oppose the return of the Arab inhabitants of Jaffa, and even to announce this in a [radio] broadcast to the Arabs – but, in practice, their return should be contingent on certain conditions and restrictions." Palmon thought that the returnees should be asked to sign a loyalty oath and fill out detailed questionnaires. This, he argued, "would leave in our hands complete supervision of their actual return. We shall have the ability to let back mainly [non-Moslem Arabs] . . . something that could be of use [to us] in the future."[41]

Palmon's letter drew a sharp rejoinder from Ya'acov Shimoni, the acting director of the Foreign Ministry's Middle East Affairs Department. Shimoni was prepared to allow exceptions in special cases of hardship, but in general he supported the "no return during the war" line.[42] Shertok himself came down solidly behind Shimoni, adding: "I fear a loosening of the reins . . . Permission [to return] should be forthcoming only in a limited number of special cases."[43]

At the start of the Second Truce, individual Arabs and families tried to infiltrate back into the country. The IDF again instructed its units to prevent the return of refugees, "also with fire."[44]

But Israel's main problem was not the uncoordinated, individual or communal Arab attempts to return or requests to return but the increasing international pressure, spearheaded by Bernadotte, for a mass return which was renewed with the start of the Second Truce. The Mediator was dissatisfied with Shertok's position at their meeting of 26 July. On 28 July he submitted to Tel Aviv a strongly-worded "Note," suggesting that Israel accept the principle that "from among those who may desire to do so, a limited number . . . and especially those formerly living in Jaffa and Haifa, be permitted to return to their homes." Bernadotte accepted Israel's differentiation, on security grounds, between army-age would-be returnees and "others."[45] Bernadotte wanted to wedge open the door, however slightly.

He was unsuccessful. Kohn drafted a proposal for a response: "Present Arab outcry for return of refugees is move in warfare. Purposes are not, or not merely, humanitarian but desire to get rid of incubus, saddle Israel with it, introduce explosive element into Israel, eliminate sources of menacing bitterness from their own midst, show some tangible success to their disaffected following, etc." And Kohn divined the chink in Bernadotte's argument, the special pleading for the Jaffa and Haifa exiles. He asked: "Is suffering of those from other towns or from villages less acute, or are they less deserving?"[46] Kohn's view was that the existence of the refugee problem, on balance, benefited Israel. For the Arab states, the refugees were "the greatest inconvenience"; for Israel "at the present moment [they are] our most valuable bargaining asset." But the Foreign Minister's Political Adviser realised that they were also a strong card in the hands of the Arab governments "in the councils of the UN and among world opinion generally."[47]

Shertok replied to Bernadotte's "Note" on 1 August. Israel, he wrote, was "not unmindful of the plight of the Arabs . . . Our own people has suffered too much from similar tribulations for us to be indifferent to their hardships." But Israel could not agree to readmission: it would "prejudice Israel's rights and positions." Shertok then took up Kohn's line, asking why Bernadotte had seen fit to plead for special treatment for the exiles of Jaffa and Haifa. The Foreign Minister concluded by saying that while Israel might reconsider the issue at war's end, it was not now in a position "to readmit the Arabs who fled . . . on any substantial scale."[48]

From Israel's point of view, Shertok's use of the phrase "on any substantial scale" was to prove an embarrassing mistake. The Mediator referred to it in his talks with the Foreign Minister in Tel Aviv four days later. If Israel was unwilling to contemplate a "substantial" return at present, how about an insubstantial one, Bernadotte asked, and immediately suggested several categories of refugees who might be allowed back immediately – "refugees [from] territory controlled by Israeli forces" but lying outside the Jewish State as defined in the United Nations Partition resolution, "citrus farmers . . . communities . . . whose villages . . . are intact . . . [those] for whom employment is available . . . [and] special cases on humanitarian grounds."

Shertok quickly explained that "only in exceptional cases would we allow people to come back . . . We are against whole categories of people returning while the war is on."[49]

Kohn identified Israel's main potential problem – American involvement in the refugee question. He surmised that the growing American concern was a result of pressure by American ambassadors in Muslim countries, who were arguing that the "pauperized, embittered" exiles were a seedbed for "communist revolution" in the host countries, and that it was best that the refugees be returned to Palestine.[50] The chief Israeli fear was that the United States would soon openly back the Mediator's position on a refugee return. American diplomats were already bluntly describing – even to Israelis – Israel's stated positions as "rigid and uncompromising."[51]

The Americans had begun to sense that Israel was never going to allow a refugee return. "There is little if any possibility of Arabs returning to their homes in Israel or Jewish-occupied Palestine," wrote the American Consul General in Jerusalem, John MacDonald. He described the conditions of those camped out near Jericho and Ramallah as "not yet desperate" but predicted that they would be "completely destitute" and highly vulnerable to the elements when winter arrived.[52] Jefferson Patterson, the American chargé d'affaires in Cairo, at the same time reported that the International Committee of the Red Cross had supplied information "indicating that there may be little prospect for the several hundred thousand Arab refugees from Palestine to return to their former homes."[53]

Israel's position appeared rigid. Indeed, the resolve of both its leaders and public opinion against a return hardened daily. But the leaders realised that while this resolve itself would be a major factor in shaping the outcome, to some degree at least the ultimate issue would depend on external factors – especially on the amount and character of international, particularly American, pressure to allow the refugees back. As Ben-Gurion put it: "we do not know if this [i.e., the outcome] will depend on us." Matters had to be left fluid, Ben-Gurion said.[54]

John Reedman, the special representative in Palestine of the United Nations Secretary General, gave Israeli officials an idea of how things stood with pro-Israeli international opinion. He said he understood Israel's opposition to a mass return of refugees but suggested that "a trickle" could be allowed back. Alternatively, Israel could at least announce its intention "to solve the refugee problem after a final peace settlement."[55] Bernadotte, frustrated, spoke more bluntly. He told Shertok at their meeting in Jerusalem on 10 August that Israel was "driving too hard a bargain" and that Israel's "stock was dropping." Shertok, who may have regarded the use of these images from the business world as veiled anti-Semitism, countered by informing Bernadotte of the "vast potentialities" of Syria and Iraq as absorption sites for the refugees. "In the long run," Shertok said, "it was in the interests of all concerned that the Arab minority in the State of Israel be a small . . . one."[56]

Bernadotte thought Israel was showing "every sign of having a swelled head." It opposed a return on security grounds and because it needed "space" for Jewish immigrants. "It seemed to [Bernadotte] an anomaly that the Israeli Government should advance as an argument for the establishment of their state the plight of Jewish refugees and to demand the immediate immigration of [Jewish] diplaced persons [in Europe] at the same time that they refused to recognize the existence of the Arab refugees which they had created." The abandoned Arab property – "loot" – was being distributed among the new Jewish immigrants, according to one American report.[57]

Only one voice of dissent emerged from within the higher reaches of the Israeli bureaucracy, that of Sasson, the peripatetic Director of the Foreign Ministry's Middle East Affairs Department and former member of Weitz's self-appointed Transfer Committee. Sasson, an Arabist with a liberal outlook, wrote to Shertok: "I would advise reconsidering the refugee problem . . . I do not by this advice mean, heaven forbid, the return of all the refugees. No, and again no. My meaning is to the return of a small part of them, forty to fifty thousand, over a long period . . . [starting] immediately, to silence a lot of people in the next meeting of the UN [General Assembly]."[58] Sasson was to remain a consistent (and isolated) advocate of this position – prompted both by a desire to brighten

Israel's image in the West and to facilitate peace talks with the Arabs – through the rest of 1948 and early 1949.[59]

Just how isolated Sasson was became clear at a meeting called by Ben-Gurion on 18 August to review Israeli policy on the issue. The review was prompted by problems arising out of the need to cultivate and expropriate Arab lands, pressure by Bernadotte and the impending arrival of the first United States Representative to Tel Aviv, James McDonald.

The meeting was attended by the country's senior political leaders (though none from Mapam were invited) and senior political and Arab affairs officials. The participants included Ben-Gurion, Shertok, Shitrit, Kaplan, David Horowitz, Machnes, Weitz, Danin and Zalman Lifshitz, the cartographer and land expert who was to replace Sasson on Weitz's "transfer" team, Palmon, Shimoni and Shiloah, General Elimelech Avner, the head of the Military Government in the Conquered Territories, and Kaddar. The meeting was to be a milestone in the finalisation of Israeli policy on a possible return of the refugees. Shimoni summed it up the following day: "The view of the participants was unanimous, and the will to do everything possible to prevent the return of the refugees was shared by all."[60]

According to Weitz, Shertok opened the discussion with introductory remarks, posing the problem "with clarity." Ben-Gurion then spoke, confusing the issue, according to Weitz, by straying into the question of the fate of the abandoned Arab lands. David Hacohen, a senior IDF intelligence officer and Mapai leader in Haifa, proposed that Jews settle on the abandoned lands. Horowitz agreed, but proposed the sale of Arab property to private individuals ("one can sell [it] to Jews in America"), with the proceeds going to the original owners as compensation. "The solution [should not be] the prevention [of an Arab return] by force but through a commercial transaction," said Horowitz. Kaplan objected to the destruction of the abandoned Arab villages, and said that Jewish settlement on Arab lands presented a serious problem of principle "if [we] are speaking of more than [temporary] cultivation."[61]

Shimoni the following day was to write about the Finance Ministry's representatives that while all at the meeting were agreed that it was best that the refugees not be allowed to return, "Kaplan and [Horowitz] were more conservative and careful regarding [the means] that could be used immediately and principally regarding the fate of Arab property."[62]

Weitz then managed to steer the talk back to what he regarded as the cardinal issue: should the Arabs be allowed to return?

If the policy we want is that they should not be allowed to return, [then] there is no need to cultivate land beyond what is needed for our existence. It is possible that Jews should be settled in some [abandoned] villages and that there are villages that should be destroyed so that they do not attract their refugees to return. What can be bought [from Arabs] should be bought . . . [But] first we must set policy: Arabs who abandoned [their homes] should not [be allowed to] return.

He also recommended that plans be developed for the resettlement of the refugees in the Arab countries. Hacohen agreed with Weitz. Israel should "reap, plough, settle on [Arab] land – until it enters their heads that they will not be allowed to return."

Ben-Gurion's own thinking was clear. "We must start out," he said, "from an assumption, of how to help those who will not return, whatever their number (and we want them to be as numerous as possible), to resettle abroad."[63] According to Danin's recollection a month later, during the discussion Ben-Gurion had not allowed "any alternate" thinking – such as discussion about allowing the return of "20,000 or 50,000 or 100,000 refugees" – to be broached.[64]

Weitz (once again) proposed the appointment of a non-governmental authority to formulate a "plan. for the transfer of the Arabs and their resettlement."[65] Although no formal decision was taken at the meeting, a committee – the second and official Transfer Committee – with far narrower terms of reference than Weitz had been seeking since May, was at last appointed by Ben-Gurion at the end of August.[66]

The 18 August gathering at the Prime Minister's Office had been defined as a "consultative" meeting. But given the functions of the participants, the decisions reached and the consensus that emerged on the main issues, it carried the weight and finality of a Cabinet meeting. Indeed, the following day renewed orders went out to all IDF units to prevent the return of refugees. The participants had been united on the need to bar a return and there was general, if not complete, agreement as to the means to be used to attain this end – destruction of villages, settlement of other villages and on abandoned lands, cultivation of Arab fields, purchase and expropriation of Arab lands, and the use of propaganda to persuade the refugees that they would not be allowed back.

Shertok explained Israel's stand to Zionism's elder statesman and the president of the Provisional Council of State, Chaim Weizmann, four days later:

With regard to the refugees, we are determined to be adamant while the war lasts. Once the return tide starts, it will be impossible to stem it, and it will prove our undoing. As for the future, we are equally determined – without, for the time being, formally closing the door to any eventuality – to explore all possibilities of getting rid, once and for all, of the huge Arab minority which originally threatened us. What can be achieved in this period of storm and stress will be quite unattainable once conditions get stabilized. A group of people from among our senior officers [i.e., the Transfer Committee] has already started working on the study of resettlement possibilities [for the refugees] in other lands . . . What such permanent resettlement of 'Israeli' Arabs in the neighbouring territories will mean in terms of making land available in Israel for the settlement of our own people requires no emphasis.[67]

Serious American pressure on Israel over the plight of the refugees began to be felt only in August. Israel's representative in Washington, Eliahu Epstein (later Elath), reported: "American public opinion gradually being undermined . . . All hostile forces unite in publicising and shedding crocodile tears regarding plight Arab refugees."[68] America's representative, James McDonald, met Ben-Gurion for the first time on 20 August and warned the Prime Minister that the United States was contemplating measures on the refugee question that would prove unpalatable to Israel, and that Washington might even be prepared to impose sanctions to enforce its will. Ben-Gurion replied that Israel would not compromise on its "security and independence." Returning the refugees "so long as an invading army" was on Israeli soil was hazardous. "We could not allow back one who hates [us], even if sanctions were imposed on us," he concluded.[69]

A specific American initiative was launched in early September, with the submission to Tel Aviv of "suggestions" to facilitate the peace process. The United States suggested the exchange of Western Galilee (in Israeli hands since mid-May but originally allotted to the Palestine Arab state) for the Negev (still largely in Egyptian hands but allotted in the Partition Plan to the Jewish State) and a solution to the problem of Jerusalem based on "internationalisation." Moreover, Washington said it "would like the Israeli government to consider some constructive measures for the alleviation of Arab refugee distress."[70]

Ben-Gurion, Shertok and James McDonald met two days later to discuss the American "suggestions." Ben-Gurion left it to Shertok to deliver the Israeli response. "[Shertok] said that we were [willing] to consider the return of individual refugees now, and the return of part of the refugees after the war, on condition that most of the refugees would be settled in Arab countries with our help." This marked a substantial softening of Israel's public position, but McDonald failed to realise this. He asked whether "the door is shut" to a return and Ben-Gurion responded: "In my opinion, the door is not shut – if we discuss the arrangement of a solid, stable peace with the Arabs. As part of such an arrangement, one can discuss anything."[71]

But if in private Ben-Gurion and Shertok were exhibiting or appeared to be exhibiting a real measure of flexibility with the Americans, Israel's official and public policy continued to conform with the 16 June Cabinet consensus. On 12 September the Cabinet approved Shertok's draft instructions to the Israel delegation to the meeting of the United Nations General Assembly. The proposed instructions stated: "No return before the end of the war save for individual cases; a final solution to the refugee problem as part of a general settlement when peace comes. In informal conversations, the delegation will explain that it were better that the problem be solved by settling the refugees in the neighbouring countries." No mention was made of possible Israeli readiness to allow back a proportion of the refugees.[72]

The first round of the diplomatic battle over the return of the refugees climaxed on 20 September, with the publication of Bernadotte's report on his mediation efforts. The report had been completed on 16 September, the day before the Mediator's assassination at the hands of LHI (Stern Gang) terrorists in Jerusalem. In the report, Bernadotte strongly supported the right of the refugees to return to their homes "at the earliest practical date." No "just and complete" settlement was possible, the Mediator wrote, if the right of return was not recognised. "It would be an offence against the principles of elemental justice if these innocent victims of the conflict were denied the right to return to their homes while Jewish immigrants flow into Palestine and, indeed, at least offer the threat of permanent replacement of the Arab refugees," he wrote. At the same time, however, Bernadotte was fully aware that the radically changed and changing circumstances in Israel (including the immigrant influx) strongly militated against a future mass return of refugees. "It must not be supposed," he wrote, "that the establishment of the right of refugees to return . . . provides solution of the problem. The vast majority of the refugees may no longer have homes to return to and their re-establishment in the State of Israel presents an economic and social problem of special complexity."[73]

The Israeli response to the Bernadotte report, which embodied a plan for solving the major issues in the conflict, was tailored to suit the highly embarrassing and vulnerable diplomatic position in which Tel Aviv found itself. The Mediator had been murdered by – albeit dissident – Israelis and his report included proposals, such as handing over the Negev to the Arabs, which were anathema to Tel Aviv. The circumstances required contrition and caution but without saying anything that could later be construed as concrete concessions by Israel. In its response on 23 September, Tel Aviv, on the refugee issue, simply ignored the Mediator's call for recognition of the right of return.[74]

Meanwhile, a new wave of *ad hoc* appeals from various exiled Arab communities to be allowed back reached Shitrit. Shitrit generally referred them to Ben-Gurion, the IDF and Shertok for a ruling. By nature and politically a softliner, Shitrit, by the end of August, had more or less come around to Ben-Gurion's and Shertok's view of things. Allowing any Arabs back might serve as a precedent and might constitute a security problem. As his Ministry Director General put it: "over time views have changed, and now the Minority Affairs Ministry is doing all in its power to prevent the Arabs who have gone from returning to the country."[75]

A major debate, in which the various arguments of the decision-makers surfaced, took place concerning the refugees of Huj, near the Gaza Strip. Its inhabitants had been expelled eastwards, to Dimra, on 31 May (see chapter 3). Nothing demonstrated so convincingly the inflexibility of the Israeli resolve against a return as the case of Huj.

In September, the exiled inhabitants, noting that the Truce was holding and that the area around their village was quiet, appealed to Israel to allow them back. The appeal, as usual, made the rounds of the bureaucracies – the IDF, the Military Government, the Middle East Affairs Department of the Foreign Ministry and the Minority Affairs Ministry. Shimoni was advised that the Huj appeal deserved "special treatment" because the inhabitants had been "loyal collaborators" with the Yishuv, "because they had not fled but had been expelled," and because they had not wandered far afield and were still living near their village. His department, therefore, in view of "the commonly held opinion that an injustice had been done," would be willing to recommend that the IDF permit the villagers to return to Israeli territory, albeit not necessarily to Huj itself but rather to another "abandoned village."

But, Shimoni added: "The problem of precedents arises. If we allow these [to return], hundreds and thousands of others may perhaps come, each with his own good reasons [for asking to be allowed back]." So he concluded his qualified recommendation by writing that "if the Defence Ministry found a way" to prevent the Huj case from becoming a precedent, "then we withdraw our opposition [to a return] in this particular case."[76]

Shitrit found Shimoni's reservations irksome. He wrote that he did "not believe that allowing some . . . to return would [necessarily] serve as a precedent." After all, there was a firm Cabinet decision that so long as the war continued, "there could be no speaking of a return of Arabs to the State of Israel." So if the Middle East Affairs Department supported allowing the inhabitants of Huj to return, "there will be no opposition on our part," wrote Shitrit. But he too thought that the villagers would have to be resettled "inside" Israel rather than in their home village, which was near the front lines.[77]

However, these rather hesitant recommendations by two civilian bodies proved unavailing. The defence authorities overruled Shitrit and Shimoni, and the inhabitants of Huj, whether because of arguments of security or precedent, were never allowed back. The flare-up of hostilities between Israel and Egypt a few weeks after these interdepartmental exchanges probably sealed the fate of the Huj villagers.

The post-Bernadotte months were dominated by the reverberations of the report or "plan" he had left behind, and by the growing awareness, abroad as well as among the Israeli public, of the solidity and inflexibility of Israel's resolve to bar the return of the refugees.[78] In this respect, Bernadotte's passing from the scene worked to Israel's advantage: he had made the solution of the refugee problem, including the principle of the right of return, a personal issue and goal. His successor as Mediator, Ralph Bunche, displayed far less resolve and ardour in pursuing a solution based on a return.

On 27 September, a senior Israeli diplomat, Michael Comay, apprised the Israel Delegation to the United Nations General Assembly meeting in Paris of his meetings on 23–24 September in Haifa with Bunche and two of his aides, Reedman and Paul Mohn. While the United Nations' officials had reiterated Bernadotte's commitment to securing recognition of the refugees' right of return, "they were all of the opinion that for the most part the Arabs did not want to go back and live under Jewish domination." The middle-class exiles were definitely unenthusiastic about returning, and some of the villagers who wanted to return would, once back, no doubt "drift off again when they saw some of the things that were alleged to be going on in Israel, such as destruction of villages and taking over of land." Comay reported that, according to Reedman, Bernadotte had first thought in terms of a general return of refugees "but had retreated from this position when he came to realize the deep-rooted and permanent complications." Thereafter, Bernadotte had sought only a partial return, for political and humanitarian reasons, agreeing that the main solution must be found through organised resettlement in the Arab countries.[79]

Henceforward, while lip-service was still occasionally paid to the concept of "the right of return," the international community was to focus more and more on the necessity or desirability and on the possibility of a partial repatriation coupled with the re-settlement of the bulk of the refugees in Arab lands. Israel, it would later be seen, had successfully rebuffed the pressures for a mass return.

Within Israel, the continued state of war had been decisive in the crystallisation of the decision to bar a return. The hostilities facilitated the task of those like Ben-Gurion, Weitz and Shertok, who, from early on, realised and argued that to be established securely and remain secure, the new-found Jewish State had to have as small as possible an Arab minority. The political argument against having a 40% Arab minority in the "Jewish" State intermeshed with the strategic argument against retaining or bringing back hundreds of thousands of Arabs who would or might constitute a perpetual Fifth Column. The fighting provided both the opportunity and the reason for creating or at least keeping an Arab-free country.

A mass return of refugees would have created grave problems for all the Israeli agencies prospectively involved in their repatriation – the IDF, the police, the civilian bureaucracies and the Jewish settlements – at a time when their energies and resources were being strained to capacity by the war and by the influx of masses of Jewish immigrants.

To this, as the weeks and months passed, were added the "positive" arguments of the Yishuv's settlement and immigration absorption bodies. To expand (and it had to expand to meet the needs of the burgeoning Jewish population), Jewish agriculture had to have the abandoned Arab lands. Jewish settlements, in general, needed more land. And the new immigrants (and the many more potential immigrants) required land and houses.

The political decision to bar a return matured over April–June and was reaffirmed on 18 August. It was reaffirmed, repeatedly, at various levels of government over the following months as successive communities of exiles asked to be allowed back. But, out of consideration for national unity and because of the exigencies of international diplomacy, the decision was not at the time translated into a formal, binding Cabinet resolution.

However, during the second half of 1948 and the first half of 1949, developments on the ground worked to harden the status quo and certify the refugeedom of Palestine's Arabs.

Chapter 5

Blocking a return

In the course of 1948 and the first half of 1949, a number of processes definitively changed the physical and demographic face of Palestine. Taken collectively, they steadily rendered the possibility of an Arab refugee return more and more remote until, by mid-1949, it became virtually inconceivable. These processes were the gradual destruction of the abandoned Arab villages, the cultivation and/or destruction of Arab fields and the share-out of the Arab lands to Jewish settlements, the establishment of new settlements on abandoned lands and sites and the settlement of Jewish immigrants in empty Arab housing in the country-side and in urban neighbourhoods. Taken together, they assured that the refugees would have nowhere, and nothing, to return to.

These processes occurred naturally and were integral, major elements in the overall consolidation of the State of Israel in wartime. They were not, at least initially, geared or primarily geared to blocking the possible return of the refugees. They began in order to meet certain basic needs of the new State. Some of the processes, such as the destruction of the villages and the establishment of new settlements along the borders, were dictated in large part by immediate military needs. Others were due to basic economic requirements – the kibbutzim's need for more land, the Yishuv's growing need for more agricultural produce, the new immigrants' need for housing. But, taken together, these processes substantially contributed, and were understood by the Yishuv's leaders to contribute, to definitively barring a refugee return.

The destruction of the Arab villages

About 350 Arab villages and towns were depopulated in the course of the 1948–9 war and during its immediate aftermath. By mid-1949, the majority of these sites were either completely or partly in ruins and uninhabitable.

Some of the desolation was caused during abandonment and, later, by the ravages of time and the elements. Some of the destruction was the result of warfare – villages were mortared, shelled and, occasionally, bombed from the air, and houses were often destroyed to clear fields of fire immediately after conquest. In general, however, the Jewish forces, who were short of artillery and bombers, especially before July 1948, caused little destruction during the actual fighting. Most of the destruction in the 350 villages was due to vandalism and looting, and to deliberate demolition, with explosives, bulldozers and, occasionally, handtools, by Haganah and IDF units or neighbouring Jewish settlements in the days, weeks and months after their conquest. We shall try to trace this destruction in the following pages.

The destruction of the villages can be said to have begun with, and stemmed naturally from, pre-war Haganah retaliatory policy and British Mandate anti-terrorist policy. In punishing Arab terrorists and irregulars during the 1936–9 rebellion and in the countdown to 30 November 1947, both the British and the Haganah destroyed Arab houses, in towns and in villages. Destroying the house of a terrorist or his accomplice was regarded as just punishment and as a deterrent. The British meted out the punishment in an open and orderly fashion; the Haganah, usually in night-time raids. On 20 May 1947, for example, a Palmah unit blew up a coffee house in Fajja after the murder of two Jews in neighbouring Petah Tikva. In August, a Haganah unit blew up a house, suspected of being an Arab terrorist headquarters, in the Abu Laban orchard, outside Tel Aviv.[1]

After the start of general hostilities in December 1947, the dynamiting of Arab houses and parts of villages became a major component of most Haganah retaliatory strikes. Several houses were blown up at Khisas on 18 December; several dozen were destroyed at Balad ash Sheikh on 31 December in the revenge attack following the Arab massacre of Jewish workers at the Haifa oil refinery. The theoretical underpinning of the destruction of indivual Arab houses in retaliatory strikes was formulated in a Haganah General Staff directive of 18 January 1948. Operations Branch targeted for destruction "houses serving as concentration points, supply depots and training sites" as well as certain public buildings.[2]

As the fighting gained in intensity, so did the efficiency and destructiveness of the Haganah raids. Through January, February and March 1948, the raiders destroyed houses and parts of villages that harboured or were suspected of harbouring hostile Arab militiamen and irregulars. While the main aim of the raids was cautionary and punitive, they inevitably led to the evacuation of families from the raided villages. The destruction of houses had a major demoralising effect in each village attacked.

In January and February, Palmah raiders destroyed houses in Yazur and Salama, east of Jaffa. The operational orders for the attack on Salama were typical. They stated: "The villagers do not express opposition to the actions of the gangs [i.e., the irregulars] and a great many of the [village] youth even provide [the irregulars with] active cooperation . . . The aim is . . . to attack the northern part of the village of Salama . . . to cause deaths, to blow up houses and to burn everything possible." A qualification stated: "Efforts should be made to avoid harming women and children."[3]

In March, the Palmah's 3rd Battalion twice raided the village of Al Huseiniya, near the Hula Lake in Upper Galilee. In the first raid, on 12 March, the battalion blew up five houses. In the second raid, on 16–17 March, "more than 30 Arab adults (excluding women and children) were killed . . . The village was abandoned by all its inhabitants," who "fled across the border."[4]

In the first months of the war the Arab leadership in Palestine took note of the Haganah's policy of destroying houses, but, according to Ezra Danin, the Mufti's men were dismissive, saying "that the Jews don't know how to fight – therefore [instead] they destroy houses."[5]

The Haganah strategy of aggressive defence, consisting mainly of retaliatory strikes, gave way in April to an offensive strategy, in line with Plan D, of conquest and permanent occupation of Arab sites. In the section on "consolidating defence systems and obstacles" of its preamble, Plan D provided for the "destruction of villages (burning, blowing up and mining the ruins)" that the Haganah was incapable of permanently controlling and that might be used as bases for Arab forces.[6]

As the Haganah Operations Branch 18 January directive had provided the theoretical foundation for the destruction of individual houses in retaliatory strikes, so Plan D supplied the theoretical underpinning for the post-March levelling of whole Arab villages and districts. The passage from the January directive to the March plan paralleled the growing scale of the war as well as its increased brutality. The directive had sought to pinpoint "guilty," individual targets; Plan D, on the other hand, consigned to collective destruction whole hostile and potentially hostile villages. However, the degree to which Plan D's provision for destroying Arab villages was implemented in different sectors over March–May 1948 depended largely on the local military situation (i.e., Arab resistance and topography) and on the availability to the Haganah units of dynamite, bulldozers and manpower.

During the Haganah offensives of April and May, swathes of Arab villages were partly or completely destroyed – in the Jerusalem corridor, around Mishmar Ha'emek, and in Eastern and Western Galilee. The destruction of most of the sites was governed at this time by the cogent military consideration that, should they be left intact, Arab irregulars or, come the invasion, Arab regular troops, would reoccupy them and use them as bases for future attacks on the Yishuv. An almost instant example of this problem was provided at Al Qastal in early April (see chapter 3). The Haganah lacked the manpower to strongly garrison each abandoned village.

During the April–May fighting in the Jerusalem corridor, Palmah units more or less systematically levelled the villages of Al Qastal, Qaluniya and Khulda, and largely or partly destroyed Beit Surik, Biddu, Shu'fat, Beit Iksa, Beit Mahsir and Sheik Jarrah (a Jerusalem neighbourhood).[7]

The destruction of these villages reflected the changed military situation and the resultant change of mood, perception and policy among the Yishuv's leaders. During the first months of hostilities the Haganah, while battling the Arab irregulars for control of, or freedom of passage along, the roads, determined its strategy, operations and, to a degree, tactics in line with the political framework and constraints of the 1947 Partition resolution – that is, a Jewish State within Partition Plan borders and with a substantial Arab minority. But the lack of a quick and favourable resolution to the battle of the roads in February–March, and the increasingly certain and ominous prospect of an invasion of Palestine by the armies of the Arab states by the beginning of April radically altered the military situation. Bases – i.e., villages – which were filled with irregulars, or had harboured irregulars, or which might do so in the immediate future, could no longer be tolerated in strategic areas (such as the Jerusalem corridor, the lifeline to Jerusalem's besieged 100,000 Jews).

The operational order for Operation Nahshon in the Jerusalem corridor had included no blanket instruction to the units to destroy each village captured. But sometime during the second week of April, as a component of the decision (discussed in chapter 3) to expel the Arab inhabitants of strategically vital areas, Ben-Gurion and the Haganah General Staff, prompted by the battle at Mishmar Ha'emek, agreed to, or ordered, the destruction of the conquered villages in these areas to assure that they would not again constitute a threat to the Yishuv.

In the days following Qawuqji's abortive assault on Mishmar Ha'emek, Haganah – mainly Palmah – units, after counter-attacking, systematically destroyed the surrounding Arab villages with the assistance of local Jewish settlers. Ghubaiya at Tahta, the village closest to Mishmar Ha'emek, was blown up first. Its sister village, Ghubaiya al Fauqa, nearby Khirbet Beit Ras, and Abu Shusha, a few hundred yards north of the kibbutz, were destroyed on 8 April and during the following days. The large village of Al Kafrin, southwest of the kibbutz, was attacked and partly destroyed on 12 April. Abu Zureiq, three kilometres north of the kibbutz, was levelled that night and during the following days. Al Mansi and An Naghnaghiya, to the southeast, were also levelled.[8] One of the empty villages was destroyed as part of a Haganah training exercise. Palmah headquarters informed the Haganah General Staff on 19 April: "Yesterday company exercises in fighting in built-up areas took place south and east of Mishmar Ha'emek. At the end of the exercises, the village of Al Kafrin was blown up completely."[9]

The destruction of the Arab villages around Mishmar Ha'emek and in the Jerusalem corridor were the first regional razing operations of the war, born of local military imperatives admixed with a measure of vengefulness.

A policy of destroying Arab villages as part and parcel of operations was to characterise Haganah attacks in April in other areas. For example, on 19 April Palmah headquarters ordered 1st Battalion OC Dan Lanner "to destroy enemy bases in Al Mazar, Nuris and Zir'in [in the Jezreel Valley] . . . Comment: With the capture of Zir'in, most of the village's houses must be destroyed while [some houses] should be left intact for accommodation and defence."[10] In the northern Negev, on 4 April, Haim Bar-Lev, a company commander, reported to OC Negev Brigade Nahum Sarig on an Arab mine attack on a Jewish patrol and on the Jewish retaliation in the Shahut area that followed. A Palmah unit in two armoured cars destroyed "nine bedouin lay-bys and . . . one mudhut . . . The mudhut was destroyed by a blow from an armoured car going backwards. It is worth noting that this seems very efficient and one blow completely demolished the mudhut."

Operation Yiftah in May was characterised by similar demolition of the conquered Arab villages. The Yiftah Logbook entry for 4 May reads: "The operation is going according to plan and at 9.00 o'clock [a.m.?] the units reached their objectives as, on the way, they blow up all the houses and burn all the bedouin tents."[11]

The destruction of the Arab villages went to the heart of the political dilemma faced by Yishuv left-wingers, who believed in the possibility of Jewish–Arab coexistence. Was the destruction dictated by military imperatives or was it, at least in part, politically motivated, with all the political implications that this entailed? Already in early May, Mapam's Aharon Cohen wrote that "a policy of eviction" was being implemented. The Yishuv had insufficient troops to garrison every village it occupied, so a policy had been adopted of "blowing up villages so that [Arabs] would not return."[12]

On 10 May, Cohen completed a six-page memorandum entitled "Our Arab Policy in the Midst of the War," which he circulated among the

Mapam Political Committee members in advance of the Committee's debate on the party's Arab policy. He attacked what he saw as an emergent policy of transfer. He added: "The complete destruction of captured villages is not always carried out only because of 'lack of sufficient forces to maintain a garrison' or only so 'that the gangs [that is, irregulars] will not be able to return there so long as the war continues'."[13]

However, the assessment of Marxist Mapamniks, that the destruction of the villages was a main component of a politically motivated, systematic policy of transfer being implemented by the Haganah–Mapai leaders, was probably a few weeks premature.

Until May, what was perceived as strategic necessity underlay the Haganah's destruction of the empty Arab villages. There may have been local, isolated cases of destruction – in the Beit Shean Valley, in the northern Negev approaches and in the Sharon – where other reasons obtruded or were dominant: the desire to settle a score with an Arab neighbour or a wish to appropriate lands belonging to an Arab village or a politically-based desire to see as few as possible Arabs in the emergent Jewish State. Such considerations certainly guided some of the activities of Yosef Weitz over March–May 1948.[14] But primarily, until May, the destruction of the villages was carried out by the Haganah with clear military motives – to deny bases and refuge to hostile irregulars and militiamen, to prevent a return of irregulars to strategic sites and to avoid the emergence of a Fifth Column in areas already cleared of hostile or potentially hostile Arabs.

The mass Arab exodus of April and early May 1948 focused Jewish minds wonderfully. During May, ideas about how to consolidate and give permanence to the Palestinian exile began to crystallise, and the destruction of the villages was immediately perceived as a primary means of achieving this aim. The destruction of the villages became a major political enterprise. Henceforward, while on the local level the military continued to destroy villages for military reasons, major figures in the Yishuv sought the destruction of the villages with a primarily political rather than military objective in mind.

The guidelines of the programme which was to mature in the Transfer Committee's deliberations in late May and June 1948, which included the destruction of Arab houses to bar a refugee return, were augured in Danin's letter of 18 May to Weitz.[15]

On 4 June, the three members of the "self-appointed" Transfer Committee – Weitz, Danin and Sasson – discussed the "miracle" of the Arab exodus. The question was "how to make it permanent." The answer, according to the Committee, was to prevent an Arab return by destroying Arab villages and settling Jews in other villages. Weitz agreed to allocate Israeli pounds (I£) 5,000 from JNF funds "to begin destruction and renovation activities in the Beit Shean Valley, near Ein Hashofet [the Ramot Menashe area, southeast of Haifa] and in the Sharon [that is, the Coastal Plain]."[16]

The next day, 5 June, Weitz, armed with the Transfer Committee's proposal, "Retroactive Transfer, a Scheme for the Solution of the Arab Question in the State of Israel," saw Ben-Gurion. One of its major recommendations was the destruction of the abandoned Arab villages.[17] According to Weitz, Ben-Gurion agreed to the whole proposed policy, including the destruction of villages, the settlement of abandoned sites and the prevention of Arab cultivation of fields though he did not agree to Weitz's "temporary committee." Weitz, nevertheless, informed the Prime Minister that he had "already given orders to begin here and there destroying villages and [Ben-Gurion] approved this. I left it at that," Weitz recorded.[18]

The following day, 6 June, Weitz sent Ben-Gurion a list of the abandoned villages and towns, and a covering note stating that at their meeting, Ben-Gurion had agreed to the start of the Transfer Committee's destruction of villages: "In line with this, I have given an order to begin [these operations] in different parts of the Galilee, in the Beit Shean Valley, in the Hills of Ephraim and in Samaria [that is, the Hefer Valley and Ramot Menashe areas]."[19]

There was no reply from Ben-Gurion. But, at this stage, Weitz was not deterred by the lack of formal authorisation. On 7 June, Weitz and Danin discussed the enterprise, and Weitz recorded: "Preparations are under way for action in the villages. We have brought in [Yoav] Zuckerman, who will act in his area [i.e., around Gedera, southeast of Tel Aviv]. The questions are many: The town of Beit Shean, to leave it alone completely, or part of it . . . and Acre and Jaffa? And Qaqun?"[20]

With most able-bodied men in the Yishuv conscripted, with most equipment, such as tractors and tracked vehicles, in use by the army and in agriculture, and with dynamite always in short supply, Weitz had a problem organising what amounted to a giant demolition project. But he had his "personal" JNF apparatus at hand; the network of regional JNF offices and workers, and a web of land-purchasing agents and intelligence and settlement contacts around the country.

On 10 June, Weitz sent two officials, Asher Bobritzky and Moshe Berger, to tour the Coastal Plain to determine which empty Arab villages should be destroyed and which settled with Jews. The same day, Zuckerman informed him that he had made arrangements for the destruction of the large village of Al Mughar, near Gedera, which was to begin the next day.[21]

On 13 June, Weitz travelled north, to the Jezreel and Beit Shean valleys, where he met with local leaders and IDF officers. He recorded that he found there agreement to his programme of "destruction, renovation and settlement" by Jews. It can be assumed that he advised or ordered those he talked with to go ahead in their areas.[22] On 14 June Danin informed Weitz of the progress in the destruction of Fajja and Zuckerman gave a progress report on the destruction of Al Mughar.[23] On 15 June, Weitz went to look for himself. At Al Mughar, he recorded: "Three tractors are completing its destruction. I was surprised that nothing moved in me at the sight . . . Not regret and not hatred, as [if] this is the way of the world . . . The dwellers of these mud-houses did not want us to exist here."[24]

Almost certainly on the basis of a progress report from Weitz, Ben-Gurion, on 16 June, partially summarised the destruction of Arab villages to date: "[Al] Mughar, Fajja, Biyar Adas [near Magdiel] have been destroyed. [Destruction is proceeding in] Miska [near Ramat Hakovesh], Beit Dajan (east of Tel Aviv), in [the] Hula [Valley], [in] Hawassa near Haifa, As Sumeiriya near Acre and Ja'tun [perhaps Khirbet Ja'tun] near Nahariya, Manshiya . . . near Acre. Daliyat ar Ruha has been destroyed and work is about to begin at [Al] Buteimat and Sabbarin [both in the Ramot Menashe area, southeast of Haifa]."[25]

Through June, Weitz pressed the national leadership to formally adopt his transfer policy and appoint the Transfer Committee. But Ben-Gurion prevaricated. He was happy that the work was being done but could not, for a variety of reasons, bring himself to openly support the policy or Weitz's activities in the field. Weitz grew frustrated and wary.

By the end of June, the momentum of the self-appointed Committee had collapsed. "There are no tools and no materials" with which to continue the work of demolition, Weitz recorded.[26]

But it went deeper. How could Weitz and his Committee take upon themselves such politically momentous actions without clear-cut endorsement from the political leadership? Weitz had nothing in writing. He got cold feet. Angry and frustrated, he at last gave instructions to cease work.[27]

Unknown to Weitz, word of his Committee's activities had quickly spread in the Yishuv, generating anger and dissent on the Left. At the same time, the army's separate but complementary demolition activities in the Arab villages were also noted. Opposition to the destruction of the villages quickly crystallised in Mapam and in the Cabinet. The item "destruction of Arab villages" – for discussion or response – appears on the Cabinet agendas for its meetings on 16, 20, 23, 27 and 30 June.[28]

Agriculture Minister Zisling spoke at length about the destruction of the villages at the Cabinet meeting of 16 June. Zisling differentiated between "destruction during battle" – citing al Qastal – and destruction afterwards – citing the destruction of the Arab town of Beisan. Destruction of a site during battle "is one thing. But [if a site is destroyed] a month later, in cold blood, out of political calculation . . . that is another thing altogether . . . This course [of destroying villages] will not reduce the number of Arabs who will return to the Land of Israel. It will [only] increase the number of [our] enemies." Zisling said that Ben-Gurion was "responsible."[29]

Four days later, Minority Affairs Minister Shitrit specifically raised the question of the "destruction of Al Qubeiba and Zarnuqa." Ben-Gurion promised to investigate.[30]

The destruction of the villages also encountered "economic" opposition: it made no sense in terms of the country's economic needs, officials began to complain. Yitzhak Gvirtz, a former Haganah intelligence officer, a member of Kibbutz Shefayim and the director of the Absentee Property Department in the Office of the Custodian of Abandoned Property (part of the Finance Ministry) wrote Shitrit: "[I am] ready to accept the premise that we do not want the return of the Arabs to these villages." But why the wanton destruction? Why not first extract some benefit (doors, frames, tiles, etc.)?[31]

Zisling returned to this theme in the Cabinet meeting of 4 July. "The army had received orders to destroy houses in the Arab villages in my area [i.e., the Jezreel Valley]." Zisling said that he did not know who was the source of the order and asked the Prime Minister to instruct all units that villages should not be destroyed in future without express orders from Ben-Gurion himself.[32]

Weitz was openly criticised by his boss, JNF chairman Avraham Granovsky (later Granott). Granovsky on 1 July spoke "at length of the negative and dangerous phenomenon of the destruction of the villages."[33]

This cumulative pressure against a policy of expulsion and against the destruction of the villages, including the activities of Weitz and his colleagues, resulted in the IDF General Staff's general order, almost certainly at Ben-Gurion's instruction, of 6 July, stating: "Outside of the actual time of combat, it is forbidden to destroy, burn and demolish Arab towns and villages [and] to expel Arab inhabitants from the villages . . . without special permission or an explicit instruction from the minister of defence in each case."[34]

By then, Weitz had already suspended his destructive operations. He and his colleagues had accounted directly for only a handful of villages, and perhaps for a dozen more through "advice" and "instructions" dispensed in tours around the country. But Weitz's continuous lobbying, arguments and activities in the field had constituted a major factor in the crystallisation among the Yishuv's leaders of a policy against an Arab refugee return, with a focus on the necessity of immediately destroying the empty villages (or alternatively filling them with Jewish settlers). Weitz, arguing clearly and acting with speed and determination, had shown the way.

Paradoxically, it is possible that his activities had also contributed to Ben-Gurion's difficulties in implementing the Transfer Committee programme. The destruction of Arab villages during or after conquest by the IDF could always be explained away on grounds of military necessity. Civilian critics, however august their positions, had difficulty in assailing the army's actions let alone criticising its motives. Who was Zisling to say whether the local IDF commander's decision to destroy Beisan lacked military merit or motivation? But the simultaneous and similar activities of a shadowy, apparently unauthorised civilian group – clearly motivated by political considerations – cast a shadow on the motives of the military when doing the same things.

However, the IDF continued to raze villages, apparently with Ben-Gurion's tacit approval. Mapam leaders kept up a barrage of criticism and parliamentary and Cabinet questions,[35] which Ben-Gurion usually parried by claiming ignorance or asking the critics to supply more "facts." Zisling, at the Cabinet of 14 July, said: "I will not make do with the answer that you [Ben-Gurion] don't know who destroyed [several villages named]." Ben-Gurion responded that he could not be expected "to send out men to look for destroyed villages."[36]

The continued pressure of the dissident Cabinet ministers bore fruit at the 21 July Cabinet meeting. It was resolved that jurisdiction over the abandoned villages henceforward would reside with the Ministerial Committee for Abandoned Property, which had been set up in early July. But the Ministerial Committee was to prove almost completely ineffectual in halting the private vandalisation and organised destruction by IDF units of the empty villages. As Kaplan told his colleagues on the Committee on 26 July: "In practice, [the Finance Ministry and the Custodian for Abandoned Property] have no control over the situation, and the army does as it sees fit." Kaplan charged that his ministry's representative "was not even allowed [by the IDF] to enter occupied territory [so] how can he be responsible for property in such a situation?"[37]

IDF units, during and immediately after battle, continued to destroy villages in various parts of the country, even after the start on 19 July of the Second Truce. But it had become increasingly difficult. A Ministerial Committee was now, at least formally, responsible for the villages. Moreover, when the guns were silent, as they were from mid-July until mid-October, the argument of "military necessity" as the reason for the destruction inevitably lost some of its persuasiveness. Lastly, the influx of Jewish immigrants had begun to focus attention on housing needs and possibilities. The contradiction between destroying villages and preserving them for Jewish use quickly pushed itself to the fore.

Hence, the IDF now occasionally felt compelled to apply to the Ministerial Committee for permission to destroy this or that village. Thus, for example, Ben-Gurion on 13 September asked his colleagues on the Committee for permission to destroy a cluster of villages in the central area. As was his wont in these matters, the Prime Minister carefully made the request not in his own name but in that of OC Central Front, General Zvi Ayalon. Ayalon, wrote Ben-Gurion, had written to him that "because of a lack of manpower to occupy the area [in depth] . . . there was a need to partially destroy the following villages: 1. As Safiriya, 2. Al Haditha, 3.'Innaba, 4. Daniyal, 5. Jimzu, 6. Kafr 'Ana, 7. Al Yahudiya, 8. Barfiliya, 9. Al Barriya, 10. Al Qubab, 11. Beit Nabala, 12. Deir Sharif [should be Deir Tarif], 13. At Tira, 14. Qula."

Ben-Gurion in a strategem designed to neutralise opposition to the request, said that he wanted not a meeting of the Committee but individual answers in writing to the request from each minister. He added: "I will wait for your answer for three days . . . Lack of response will be regarded as consent."

Zisling was upset. He said the Committee should be convened to discuss the request. It is not clear whether, in the end, the Committee discussed the matter or whether the army went ahead without Cabinet authorisation and levelled the villages.[38]

Ben-Gurion consistently distanced himself in public from the destruction of the Arab villages as, more generally, from any linkage to expulsion of Arabs. He was probably driven more by concern for his place in history and the image of himself and of the new State he wished to project for posterity than by fears for coalition unity and of possible rebellion by Mapam. In his diary, Ben-Gurion occasionally seems to have deliberately tried to put future historians off the scent. Thus on 27 October – a day filled with important happenings and meetings – he found time to insert the following: "Tonight our army entered Beit Jubrin . . . Yigal [Allon, OC Southern Front] asked [permission] to blow up some of the houses. I responded negatively."[39] Usually, however, he chose the path of omission. For example, his lengthy diary entry on the 18 August meeting in the Prime Minister's Office on policy against a refugee return, in which several participants expatiated on the need to destroy the Arab villages, completely omits any mention of the subject.[40]

But Ben-Gurion's role was understood by the Mapam leaders. "The method of destruction *vis-à-vis* the abandoned Arab village is continuing

... It is difficult to be free of the impression that there is a guiding hand, for whom the possibility that the Arabs will have nowhere to return to, or for what, is unproblematic," stated a circular of the Mapam-affiliated Kibbutz Artzi kibbutz movement to its members serving in the IDF.[41] "Ben-Gurion," according to Mapam Political Committee member Aharon Cohen, "orders the destruction of villages without strategic need ... In the ruling [i.e., Mapai] circles there is an inclination to erase more than one hundred Arab villages ... Will our state be built on the destruction of Arab settlements?" he asked. Zvi Lurie called for legislation to prevent the destruction of the villages. "There is a group of people in the Defence Ministry who are busy 'improving the landscape,'" he charged.[42]

Through the second half of 1948, the IDF, under Ben-Gurion's tutelage, continued to haphazardly destroy conquered Arab villages, usually during or just after battle, occasionally, weeks and months after. The destruction stemmed from both immediate military needs, as in Operation Dani, and from long-term political motives.

Over 10–13 July, Dani Operation units, on orders from the operation headquarters, systematically blew up parts of or whole villages upon conquest. On 10 July, for example, the headquarters ordered the Yiftah and 8th Brigades to blow up most of the villages of 'Innaba and At Tira, while leaving a few houses intact to accommodate a small garrison.[43] That day, Yiftah Brigade reported that its units had conquered the villages of Kharruba and Khirbet al Kumeisa (perhaps Al Kunaiyisa). "After blowing up the houses and cleaning up the village [*sic*] – our troops occupied strongpoints overlooking the village," reported the brigade.[44] On 11 July, Dani headquarters ordered Yiftah's units "to dig in in every place captured and to destroy every house not intended for occupation [by IDF troops]."[45]

During the three months of the Second Truce, from 19 July until mid-October, the army continued to destroy abandoned villages in piecemeal fashion, usually for reasons which were described as military. In the centre of the country, for example, most of the village and the old monastery of Deir Rafat were blown up in September. In the Negev and northern Negev approaches, where the IDF and the Egyptian army were strung out in an uneasy truce, with a handful of Jewish settlements more or less besieged behind Egyptian lines, the raiding war continued through October. Villagers were expelled and villages were blown up or burned, as happened to Al Muharraqa on 16 August,[46] and to the small bedouin villages and encampments east of the line Al Imara–Ze'elim in the last days of September and the first days of October.[47]

The demolition of the villages occasionally encountered local opposition, usually from Hashomer Hatzair kibbutzim. Sha'ar Ha'amakim,

Aharon Cohen's kibbutz, for example, objected to and campaigned against the Golani Brigade's intention to blow up neighbouring 'Arab Zubeidat, a traditionally friendly village.[48] Mapam's Labour Minister Mordechai Bentov even raised the matter in Cabinet. Ben-Gurion denied all: "No permission was given [by me] to any commander to destroy houses." He promised to investigate.[49] The commotion stirred up by Sha'ar Ha'amakim and Mapam about Zubeidat stayed the advance of the bulldozers for several months. However, it was not sufficient to pry permission out of the authorities for the return of the villagers, and, in the absence of such a return, the village was doomed.[50]

In the south, several kibbutzim took up the cause of the friendly village of Huj, protesting against the vandalisation of its houses.[51] Yitzhak Avira, an old-time Haganah Intelligence Service officer and member of Kibbutz Ashdot Yaakov, in the Jordan Valley, registered a protest against the continuing destruction of the villages and against policy towards the Arabs in general. He wrote to Danin that "recently a view has come to prevail among us that the Arabs are nothing. 'Every Arab is a murderer,' 'all of them should be slaughtered,' 'all the villages that are conquered should be burned' . . . I . . . see a danger in the prevalence of an attitude that everything of theirs should be murdered, destroyed and made to vanish." Danin answered: "War is complicated and lacking in sentimentality. If the commanders believe that by destruction, murder and human suffering they will reach their goal more quickly – I would not stand in their way. If we do not hurry up and do [things] – our enemies will do these things to us."[52]

Some Mapam members in government service also tried to stem the tide of destruction. Moshe Erem, a member of Mapam's Political Committee and an assistant to Minority Affairs Minister Shitrit, tried to halt the destruction of some of the villages – 'Innaba, Al Barriya and Barfiliya – listed in September for demolition by OC Central Front, General Zvi Ayalon. Erem said he understood the army's desire to level the sites in order "to prevent infiltration," but he regarded as "simplistic" the assumption that "demolished villages would not attract refugees and would, therefore, reduce the influx [into Israel] of [Arab] refugees . . . It is the land rather than the buildings which attract [the refugees]."[53]

These dissident kibbutzim and bureaucrats were the exceptions, however. The great majority of the Jewish settlements and officials supported the destruction. Benny Marshak, of Kibbutz Givat Hashlosha and the "Education Officer" of the Palmah, was representative. He frequently spoke in favour of the destruction of (usually hostile) clusters of abandoned Arab villages, including those in the Jerusalem Corridor.[54]

Other kibbutzniks demanded – and often themselves carried out – the destruction of neighbouring villages for local (and selfish) reasons. On 27 July, Alexander Prag of Kibbutz Beit Zera complained of the destruction of villages and take-over of Arab lands in the Jordan Valley, south of the Sea of Galilee, by the local Settlements Block Committee, led by Ben-Zion Israeli.[55] Prag's complaint reached Ya'acov Peterzil, a Mapam activist, who wrote to Zisling, Bentov and Erem saying: "Once again, proof is given that behind the government's back, action is taken aimed at destroying Arab villages and expropriating their lands."[56]

To the south, in the Beisan (Beit Shean) Valley in September, pressure built up in the kibbutzim to level a cluster of neighbouring Arab villages. In a letter which was probably addressed to Aharon Cohen, a local leader (possibly named Salem Horowitz), appealed for support and permission to destroy Al Hamidiya, Kaukab al Hawa, Jabbul and Al Bira, on the heights north of the Beit Shean Valley. At the same time, he criticised the continuing destruction of a cluster of less proximate villages – Na'ura, At Taiyiba, Danna, Al Murassas, Yubla and Kafra – which, he thought, would be willing to co-operate with the Yishuv and to "allocate part of their lands for our settlement [purposes]."[57]

In the north, the hand of Weitz and his Transfer Committee can be traced in the work of destruction. The following complaint reached Mapam's leaders in August:

The destruction of the Arab villages has been going on for some months now. We are on the Syrian border and there is a danger that the Arabs will use [the abandoned villages] for military operations if they get a chance. But I spoke to a number of members from [Kibbutz] Ma'ayan Baruch and nearby kibbutzim and I got the impression that there exists the possibility that there is a desire to destroy the villages and [the Arabs'] houses so that it will be impossible for the Arabs to return to them. A week ago a representative of the JNF [possibly Yosef Nahmani, director of the JNF's Galilee district office and Weitz's agent in the area] came to visit. He saw that in the [abandoned Arab] village of As Sanbariya, which is a kilometre from Ma'ayan Baruch, several houses are still standing, albeit without roofs. He told the secretariat of the kibbutz to destroy the houses immediately and he said openly that this will enable us to take the village's lands, because the Arabs won't be able to return there. I am sorry to say the kibbutz agreed immediately without thinking about what they were doing.[58]

Through the summer and autumn of 1948 Weitz and his associates were active in dispensing this type of advice or instruction, indirectly carrying out the executive task they had abandoned at the end of June.

Over September–October, however, a gradual but important shift occurred in the thinking of Yishuv executives charged with the fate of the abandoned Arab sites. They began to think more in terms of their renovation and settlement with Jews than of destruction. Two major factors contributed to this. The first, clearly, was the growing awareness that the threat of an Arab refugee return lacked substance. The First and Second Truces saw the IDF in control of the front lines and in most areas able to bar any significant infiltration of refugees back to their homes. Politically, the Yishuv had successfully staved off international and Arab pressures to allow a return. Secondly, the legal immigration of Jews into Israel, renewed with the lifting of the British naval blockade in May, began to assume mass proportions. By the autumn of 1948, it became clear that the country faced a major housing problem. It was necessary to save rather than destroy Arab houses.

Hence, by October–November, important officials began to battle openly against any further demolitions by the IDF and other bodies. In late November, Weitz records, two of his officials, one of them Yosef Nahmani, complained that "the army continues to destroy villages in the Galilee, which we are interested in [settling]."[59] Weitz himself, the following month, during a visit to Az Zib, in Western Galilee, voiced apparent regret at some of the destruction. The village had been "completely levelled and I now wonder if it was good that it was destroyed and would it not have been a greater revenge had we now settled Jews in the village houses." Weitz reflected that the empty houses in the villages were "good for the settlement of [our Jewish] brothers, who have wandered for generation upon generation, refugees . . . steeped in suffering and sorrow, as they, at last, find a roof over their heads . . . This was [the reason for] our war."[60] In early November, Finance Minister Kaplan complained about the rumoured destruction of Arab villages in the wake of the IDF conquest of upper central Galilee. "Every possibility of accommodating [immigrants] must be exploited and a general order must be issued to the army not to destroy houses without a reason." Some 20,000 immigrants were already living in tent camps, Kaplan said.[61]

During the rest of 1948, and through 1949 and the early 1950s, the destruction of abandoned Arab sites, usually already half-destroyed, continued. By then, the threat of an Arab return had disappeared and the destruction was part of the process of clearing areas for Jewish habitation or cultivation rather than an act directed against would-be returnees. Quantification of the destruction in the course of 1948 and early 1949 is impossible: how many of the 350-odd villages were completely destroyed, how many largely destroyed and how many only partially destroyed is unclear. Nor is it possible accurately to quantify and distinguish between the amounts of destruction for strictly military reasons, or through political motives or for economic reasons, especially as much of the destruction stemmed from a combination of motives.[62]

The take-over and allocation of the abandoned lands, 1948–9

A question related to, but distinct from, the problem of destroying or renovating the villages was the fate of the abandoned Arab lands. Ben-Gurion provided an early clue to his attitude in an address to the Mapai Council on 7 February. He spoke of the necessity of a Jewish presence in the hills of the Jerusalem corridor. Someone interjected: "We have no land there [i.e., no Jewish-owned land]." Ben-Gurion: "The war will give us the land. The concepts of 'ours' and 'not ours' are only concepts for peacetime, and during war they lose all their meaning."[63]

In a similar vein, he asked Weitz whether the JNF was ready to buy "from him" land at P£ 25 a dunam. Weitz replied: "If the land is Arab [owned] and we will receive the deed of property and possession – then we will buy. Then he [i.e., Ben-Gurion] laughed and said: Deed of property – no, possession – yes." The next day, Weitz and Granovsky lunched with Ben-Gurion, who re-stated his "plan . . . Our army will conquer the Negev, will take the land into its hands and will sell it to the JNF at P£ 20–25 per dunam. And there is a source . . . of millions [of pounds]. Granovsky responded jokingly that we are not living in the Middle Ages and the army does not steal land. After the war the beduins [of the Negev] will return to their place – if they leave at all – and will get [back] their land."[64] A week later, Ben-Gurion suggested to Weitz that he divest himself of "conventional notions . . . In the Negev we will not buy land. We will conquer it. You are forgetting that we are at war."[65]

Of course, Ben-Gurion was thinking ahead – and not only about the Negev. The White Paper of 1939 had almost completely blocked Jewish land purchases, asphyxiating the kibbutzim and blocking Jewish regional development. In 1947, Jews (i.e., the JNF, the PICA and private landholders) owned some 7% (i.e., 1.775 million dunams) of Palestine's total of 26.4 million dunams of land. The Partition resolution had earmarked some 60% of Palestine for the Jewish State; most of it was not Jewish-owned land. But war was war and, if won, as Ben-Gurion saw things, it would at last solve the Jewish State's land problem.

.The Jewish take-over of the Arab lands in Palestine began with the *ad hoc*, more or less spontaneous reaping of crops in abandoned Arab lands by Jewish settlements in the spring of 1948. The summer crop ripened first in the Negev, and it was here that Jewish reaping of Arab fields began. On 21 March, in the first documented incident of its kind, kibbutzniks from Kfar Darom, near the Gaza Strip, reportedly began reaping Arab wheat adjacent to their own fields. Arab militiamen retaliated by firing on the Jewish settlement and British troops intervened, ordering the Arabs to cease firing and the Jews "to stop cutting the grass."[66]

Weitz, as chairman of the Negev Committee, the *de facto* Jewish governor of the Negev, linked Jewish harvesting of Arab fields to Jewish claims for war damages. He wrote to Sarig, OC Negev Brigade, which guarded the Jewish Negev settlements and the roads and water pipeline between them, that "until a [national level] decision was taken regarding the Arab wheat crop in the area – the committee believes that our settlements in the Negev, whose fields were destroyed by their Arab neighbours, will receive compensation by [way of] reaping the fields of the saboteurs to the [same] extent that their own fields were damaged."[67] Sarig thought otherwise. On 8 May he informed the kibbutzim in his jurisdiction that "all the crops reaped by the settlements will remain the property of the [Brigade] HQ and the settlements have no right to use them."

As the summer crop ripened and as the Arab evacuation gained momentum, Jewish harvesting of Arab fields spread to other parts of the country. During late April and early May, as requests from settlements and regional councils to harvest abandoned fields poured into the Committee for Abandoned (Arab) Property, headed by Gad Machnes, the Committee's Yitzhak Gvirtz began to organise the cultivation. In co-ordination with the Settlements Block Committees, he allocated the fields to the settlements. The Committee for Abandoned Property – which soon became the Arab Property Department and then the Villages Department in the Office of the Custodian for Abandoned Property – regarded the abandoned crop as Jewish state-property and sold the right to reap it to Jewish farmers and settlements. The emerging, embattled state needed the money as well as the extra grain. The reaping was "crucial to the war effort," wrote Gvirtz.[68]

The mechanics of the harvest were described at a meeting between local Jewish leaders in the Galilee panhandle and Machnes and Gvirtz on 5 June. Immanuel (Mano) Friedman (of Rosh Pina), Binyamin Schapira (of Kibbutz Amir), Moshe Aliovich (of Kibbutz Kfar Gil'adi), Shaul Sofer (of Kibbutz Dafna) and Yehuda Greenstein (of Rosh Pina) reported:

When the Arabs left their villages they took all their moveable possessions . . . All the villages from Metulla to the Sea of Galilee . . . were evacuated. The urgent problem now was the reaping . . . We [i.e., the Committee for Abandoned Property] demanded that the settlements institute mutual help . . . Now they are completing [the reaping of] the Jewish fields and in a few days' time [they] will turn to the Arabs' fields . . . Apart from the Nabi Yusha–Al Malikiya–Kadesh Naftali area, there are about 12,000 dunams of wheat and 3,000 dunams of barley. It was agreed that the buyer of the seeds would be the purchasing organisation of the Upper Galilee settlements. The question arose of the [war-]damaged settlements who demanded that they be given compensation from among Arab fields. They were told to ask for compensation from the minister of finance.[69]

Not everywhere were things so well organised. Many settlements, without institutional authorisation or permission, took the initiative and harvested abandoned fields – and avoided payment to the government. In June and July, Gvirtz sent out a spate of angry notes to settlements, demanding that they reach formal agreements with his Department. "I heard with bewilderment and sorrow," he wrote to Kibbutz Ma'ayan Zvi, "that [your] members . . . are stealing vegetables in the eastern fields of Tantura. Don't your members have a more honourable way to spend their time in these days?"[70] Gvirtz regarded such unauthorised harvesting as part of the widespread, private looting of Arab property. Several disputes broke out between neighbouring Jewish settlements over the right to cultivate the abandoned fields.[71]

By the beginning of July, the reaping of the summer crop in the abandoned fields was nearing completion. Several objectives were achieved, according to Gvirtz: "(A) We added 6–7,000 tons of grain to the Yishuv's economy. (B) We denied them to those fighting against us. (C) We earned more than IL 100,000 for the Treasury."[72]

During May, the organised reaping of the abandoned Arab fields by the Yishuv dovetailed with the emergent Haganah strategy of preventing Arab farmers from reaping and destroying Arab fields which, for military or logistical reasons, could not be harvested by Jewish farmers. While before May, burning Arab crops was mainly a Haganah means of retaliation for Arab attacks on Jewish fields, traffic and settlements, during May–June the destruction of the fields hardened into a set policy designed to demoralise the villagers, hurt them economically and, perhaps, precipitate their exodus. Certainly, it served to sever the *fellah* physically and psychologically from his land. During June, the prevention of Arab harvesting, especially near the military front lines, was seen by the Yishuv's political and military leadership as a means of preventing a return of the Arab refugees (just as infiltration by Arab farmers through Jewish lines to reap their fields was seen as the start of a process of return). The IDF General Staff repeatedly ordered its brigades through the summer of 1948 to prevent Arab reaping with light arms fire. The burning of Arab fields inaccessible to Jewish cultivation and the prevention of Arab harvesting continued around the country through 1948.[73]

Meanwhile, the cultivation by the Jewish settlements of the abandoned Arab lands gave rise to possessive urges. For decades the Mandatory authorities and Arab nationalists had blocked Jewish acquisition of Arab lands. The settlements had felt choked for land. Suddenly, the mass Arab exodus seemed to hold out a solution. The Jewish settlements were being asked to temporarily cultivate the abandoned fields; it was but a short step to thinking in terms of permanent possession. Such thinking began to surface from late April.

The concept of "compensation" for war damage offered a morally "soft" entry point. Kibbutz Mishmar Hasharon, in the Coastal Plain, wrote twice to Machnes's Abandoned Property Committee listing the war damage it had suffered at Arab hands (3,400 dunams of wheat and barley burned) and requesting compensation. The kibbutz pointedly referred in this connection to 400 dunams of Arab land between Kfar Yona and Ge'ulim and another 80 dunams near Shuweiqa, implying a desire for more than temporary possession.[74]

The line between requesting the right of temporary cultivation and requesting possession or permanent leasehold of a tract of abandoned land was almost imperceptibly crossed by the settlements and the land-allocating institutions during May. A request from one settlement rapidly triggered requests from neighbouring settlements, prompted perhaps by a natural instinct to follow suit or fear that they would be ignored by the land-dispensing institutions. Thus, for example, Kibbutz Sdeh Nehemia (Huliot), in the Hula Valley, objecting to a land-allocation proposal they had seen, wrote to Hartzfeld asking, somewhat shamefacedly, for 1,700 dunams of the lands of Al 'Abisiya.[75]

While some settlements in the spring of 1948 were already inching towards the idea of permanent acquisition of the abandoned lands of Arab neighbours, the thrust of individual requests and institutional activity in the Yishuv over April–June was *ad hoc* and hand to mouth – to reap the largely abandoned summer crop so that it would not go to waste. This done, the settlements and agricultural institutions turned to the question of the future of the Arab lands. The question was inexorably linked to the wider, political one – that of a refugee return. A decision against a return would enable permanent possession and distribution of the lands among the settlements.

The cultivation of the abandoned tracts over the summer built up and reinforced resistance in the Yishuv to a return. The farmers grew attached to "their" new lands. The settlements delighted in the newly-won expanses for economic reasons and relished the sense of security entailed by the permanent departure of the neighbouring Arab communities. They emerged as a powerful interest group in the battle against a refugee return.

By late July, settlements formally applied for permanent possession. The Tel Mond Settlements Block Committee wrote the Agricultural Centre that it was interested in "receiving in perpetuity" two tracts of Arab land (near Tulkarm and At Taiyiba). Kibbutz Neve-Yam on the Mediterranean asked for the lands of neighbouring As Sarafand; the Arab departure had "opened up the possibility of radical solution which once and for all could give us sufficient land for the development of [our] settlement." Mishmeret, in the Coastal Plain, asked for permanent possession of lands of At Tira. Kibbutz Ein Harod asked for the lands of neighbouring Qumiya. Kvutzat (Kibbutz) Schiller applied to the Agricultural Centre for the lands of Zarnuqa and Al Mughar, southeast of Rehovot – "to be transferred into our hands in perpetuity as a supplement to our land allocation." Kibbutz Genossar, on the northwest shores of the Sea of Galilee, asked the Agricultural Centre for a permanent "supplement" to their land allocation from neighbouring fields, arguing war damages. The Mapam-affiliated kibbutz pointed out that, in any case, the lands they coveted were not owned by *fellahin* but by effendis. The veteran *moshava* Nahalal, in the western Jezreel Valley, asked for some 700 dunams of land belonging to the village of 'Ilut. There was a danger, wrote Nahalal, that an Arab village would at some point be established on this land: "It seems to us that the time is now ripe to transfer this land to permanent Jewish possession."[76]

From June, the national institutions – the Agriculture Ministry, the Agricultural Centre, the Arab Property Department – began to receive requests from the settlements for the formal leasehold of abandoned lands. But, as Gvirtz pointed out, there was as yet no legal basis for such leases.[77]

On 30 June, the provisional government had issued Emergency Regulations (Cultivation of Abandoned Lands) empowering itself to declare any depopulated conquered Arab area an "abandoned area." The government could then impose any "existing law" on the area or "regulate regulations as [it] sees fit, " including "confiscation of property."[78] But the ordinance, according to legal experts, while covering "confiscation" of property, failed to relate to leasing of lands. During the following months, the Ministerial Committee for Abandoned Property and the Justice and Agriculture ministries hammered out the appropriate legal measure, opting in the end for a government administrative order rather than legislation. The "Emergency Regulations Relating to Absentees Property" were published by the government on 12 December, giving the Agriculture Ministry control or possession (*khazaka*) of the lands.[79] The insufficiency of the Regulations, and the possible illegality of some of the operations being carried out with respect to the lands in their name, drew strong criticism, culminating in the detailed analysis of 18 March 1949 by the Prime Minister's Adviser on Land Matters, Zalman Lifshitz.[80] The deliberations dragged on until the passage in 1950 of the Absentees Property Law.

But in the summer of 1948, a major quarrel over the fate of the abandoned lands developed between the government and the JNF, which hitherto had been the official purchaser, proprietor and dispenser of almost all the land in the Yishuv. It was the JNF which leased agricultural lands to the settlements. The impending "annexation" of vast tracts of Arab land and its dispensation to settlements by the government promised a radical, indeed revolutionary, change and threatened the JNF's *raison d'être*.

By mid-May, Weitz was certain that the refugees "would not return" and that this would lead to "a complete territorial revolution . . . the state was destined to expropriate . . . their land."[81] But Weitz felt threatened on two fronts: within the JNF directorate, there was serious opposition in principle to the expropriation of the Arab lands. And that expropriation, under whatever legal cover, threatened to leave the JNF, and Weitz, out in the cold. Weitz therefore campaigned to persuade the government to transfer to JNF custodianship or sell outright to the JNF over 300,000 dunams of arable abandoned lands that the Yishuv had long sought to purchase. After months of negotiation, the government agreed to JNF control of the fate of these 300,000 dunams, according the JNF the right to lease the lands to the settlements or, at least, to exercise control over the Agriculture Ministry's leasing of them.[82]

Meanwhile, against the backdrop of the hardening government resolve never to allow back the refugees, the Agriculture Ministry, in early August set up an inter-departmental committee – the Committee for the Cultivation of the Abandoned Lands – to oversee and co-ordinate the leasing of the lands to the Jewish settlements. The Ministerial Committee for Abandoned Property had decided to put the cultivation of the abandoned lands on a formal, orderly and relatively long-term basis. The Committee for Cultivation usually dealt with the regional councils and Settlements Block Committees; occasionally, it dealt directly with the settlements.[83]

From early August, the Agriculture Ministry and the JNF began formally leasing the abandoned fields to the settlements, for periods of six months to a year. The initiative often came from the agricultural and settlement institutions; more often, from below, from the settlements themselves. Word of the establishment of the inter-departmental Committee itself generated many leasing requests. Some of the settlements needed, and requested, government funding to cover the purchase of seeds for the sowing of the winter crop.

The regional Settlement Block Committees drew up proposals for the distribution of the local abandoned fields among their settlements. Inevitably, some settlements regarded the proposals as inequitable or illogical. Kibbutz Mishmar Ha'emek, for example, remonstrated with the Jezreel Valley Committee, demanding "several hundred additional dunams of sorghum," arguing war damages.[84] But generally government officials during the summer of 1948 rejected the argument of compensation for war damage to justify claims to Arab lands.[85]

Through August–September, the Agriculture Ministry, the JNF and the Agricultural Centre were flooded with leasing requests from the settlements. Given the novelty of the enterprise, the settlements often did not know which was the right body to turn to; on occasion, neither did the institutions involved.[86]

The *ad hoc*, often spontaneous harvesting of the abandoned Arab crops of the spring and early summer of 1948 had within weeks led to a feeling – on both the national and local levels – of acquisitiveness. Land long-coveted before the war had become land temporarily cultivated. Temporary cultivation had led to a wish for permanent possession. The agricultural cycle itself had reinforced the drift of political and demographic change. The harvesting of the summer crop had left the fields ready for the sowing of the winter crop, but this meant large-scale investment of funds and workdays – which made sense only if harvesting of the winter crop was assured. Such assurance – to the extent that there can be any certainties in wartime – could be vouchsafed only by long-term leasing. (Almost all agricultural land in the pre-1948 Yishuv was owned by the JNF, which leased it to the settlements for 49 or 99 years.) The one-year leases of autumn 1948 were a way-station on the road to such long-term leases and to the "equalisation" of the status of the abandoned Arab lands with the original JNF lands.

During September and October, the land administration authorities leased tens of thousands of dunams of abandoned Arab lands to Israeli settlements and farmers. The leasing arrangements were co-ordinated with the Office of the Custodian for Abandoned (Absentees) Property. The leases were for no more than one year because of the political situation and because of the authorities' desire to retain full powers to carry out a definitive distribution of the lands, should they remain in Jewish hands, at a later date. Moreover, the government and the JNF had to consider both the equitability of distribution between existing settlements and the need to leave land aside for the establishment of new settlements.

By 10 October, the Agriculture Ministry had formally leased or approved the leasing for cultivation of 320,000 dunams of abandoned land, and Ministry Secretary Avraham Hanuki expected that another 80,000 would soon be approved for Jewish cultivation. However, he told Zisling, not all the leased tracts would in fact be cultivated as the Jewish settlements lacked manpower and equipment (much of both were still mobilised by the IDF).[87]

For the most part, the leasing of the abandoned lands, despite the rush, proceeded smoothly, and their cultivation – usually meaning the sowing of the winter crop – began immediately. But in various places, the hasty distribution, coupled with the duplication of functions engendered by the involvement of three leasing bodies (Agriculture Ministry, Custodian and JNF), their local representatives and a myriad of lobbying bodies with semi-official status, such as the Agricultural Centre, the local Settlement Block Committees, regional councils, farmers' associations, etc., led to inequities and complaints.

A major subject of complaints by private (*moshava, moshav*) farmers was alleged discrimination in favour of the kibbutzim. For example, Menahem Berger, a farmer from Pardes Hanna, complained that he had signed a leasing agreement with a local inspector for abandoned property (attached to the Custodian's office) for 250 dunams of abandoned land belonging to Baqa al Gharbiya. "After the kibbutzim in the area found out about this, they activated all the factors [i.e., bodies concerned] to dispossess me of these lands and, under pressure from the Agricultural Centre, the Ministry of Agriculture decided" to deprive Berger of half the allocation, which was transferred to the kibbutzim Ein Shemer, Gan Hashomron and Ma'anit. Berger, according to the complaint, was left with 125 dunams "in a remote corner."[88] In the north, the *moshava* (private farmers' settlement) of Migdal, on the northwest shore of the Sea of Galilee, complained that while "we have suffered from an acute lack of land for years . . . we know that [the nearby kibbutzim] Genossar, Hukok and Hahoshlim have received large tracts" of neighbouring abandoned lands, and "only we have been discriminated against, and have not received one extra foot of land." After investigation, the Ministry agreed to lease the settlement one tract (of unspecified size). In the second round of leasing, in the summer–autumn of 1949, Migdal shared with Kibbutz Genossar the substantial lands of Ghuweir Abu Shusha.[89]

A similar problem arose a few kilometres to the southwest between the *moshava* Ilaniya (Sejera) and Moshav Sharona. Ilaniya had been besieged and devastated in the early months of the war. The *moshava* had demanded compensation and had been allocated 350 dunams of the lands of Kafr Sabt, "our destroyers." But the farmers of Sharona, "off their own bat, had ploughed and sowed this land . . . displaying very saddening covetousness . . . [and] taking over the land by force." Ilaniya demanded that the ministry intervene. The authorities duly ordered the Sharona farmers off the land.[90]

Better off than either Migdal and Sejera was Kibbutz Tel-Yitzhak, in the Coastal Plain, which had a powerful political backer in the person of Interior Minister Yitzhak Gruenbaum. Gruenbaum was the leader of the General Zionists Party and Kibbutz Tel-Yitzhak was founded by the party's labour organisation, Ha'oved Hatzioni. The Tel Mond Settlements Block Committee had allocated Wakf lands, south of Moshav Even-Yehuda, to a number of local *moshavim* to the ire of Tel-Yitzhak. The kibbutzniks had appealed to Gruenbaum, who, on 9 November, warned the Agriculture Ministry that a "land dispute" was in the offing, which might disturb "the public peace," a matter which fell within his jurisdiction as Minister of Interior. The kibbutz was not left dissatisfied, receiving part of the lands of Birket Ramadan.[91]

There were also disputes over abandoned lands between kibbutzim, though they usually managed to solve these between themselves, without having to appeal to the national institutions. The kibbutzim by and large did well. For example, the kibbutzim of the Hefer Valley, around Hadera, had received by December 1948 about 15,000 dunams out of the 21,000 dunams of abandoned lands in the area (though kibbutzim constituted only a quarter of the 22 settlements among which this land was distributed).[92]

By the start of 1949, the first wave of leasing was over. By mid-March, some 680,000 dunams of abandoned lands had been leased to Jewish settlements and farmers in the Galilee, Jezreel Valley, Samaria, Judea and the northern Negev approaches, of which about 280,000 dunams had been sown with winter crops.[93]

However, the leasing mechanism was cumbersome and, possibly, legally and politically problematic. The December 1948 Absentees Property Regulations cleared away the obstacles to a more efficient arrangement, one which had been on Ben-Gurion's mind since February. Why should the State not sell the land to the JNF, which would lease it out to the settlements? The State would thus earn a large sum of money and be divested of the complex and politically irksome management of the abandoned lands.

In late December, Ben-Gurion broached the idea over lunch with Granovsky, Kaplan, Eshkol (Sholnik) and Weitz: the JNF would buy from the state one million dunams of abandoned land, paying I£ 10 per dunam on account. If Israel ended up paying the owners more than this in compensation, the JNF would then pay the state another I£ 20 per dunam. There was agreement in principle.[94] The terms of the purchase were concluded the next month and, on 28 January 1949, a signed letter from Ben-Gurion and Kaplan informed Weitz of the implementation of the sale. During the following months, the JNF leased out much of the land, mostly to new settlements.[95]

In the spring and early summer of 1949, most of the leases signed between the Agriculture Ministry and the settlements in the autumn of 1948 expired. A renewed leasing campaign began, adding one million dunams to Jewish agriculture. The Ministry pressed the settlements to cultivate more and more land, an expansion made possible by the demobilisation and the influx of new immigrants. The Ministry anticipated leasing a further one million dunams during the second half of 1949.[96]

Weitz well conveyed the Yishuv's sense of the giant agrarian revolution transforming the country: during the Mandate years, the JNF had purchased land "crumb by crumb." "But now, a great change has taken place before our eyes. The spirit of Israel, in a giant thrust, has burst through the obstacles, and has conquered the keys to the land, and the road to fulfillment has been freed from its bonds and its guardian-enemies. Now, only now, the hour has come for planning considered [regional] plans . . . The abandoned lands will never return to their absentee owners.[97]

The leases of summer 1949 were generally for one year. The political–geographical status quo had not yet formally frozen. The authorities wanted to retain full control of the lands until their ultimate disposition was planned and agreed upon (and until the abandoned lands were politically and legally "ripe" for leasing for 49 or 99 years). Regional planning and the need to leave aside land for settlements yet to be established were paramount considerations. The leasing correspondence was characterised by fears among the officials that the settlements were becoming overly attached to the lands they were already cultivating.[98]

The establishment of new settlements, 1948–9

There were 279 Jewish settlements in Palestine on 29 November 1947. Between the start of Arab–Jewish hostilities the following day and the beginning of March 1949, 53 new Jewish settlements were established, followed by about 80 more by the end of August 1949. Almost all these settlements were established on Arab-owned lands and dozens of them were established on territory earmarked in the 1947 United Nations Partition resolution for the Palestine Arab state.[99]

The establishment of new, mainly agricultural settlements lay at the core of Zionist ideology and the Zionist enterprise: the settlements embodied the drive to free the new Jew from the coils of mercantilism and lower middle class existence by once again, as 2,000 years ago, mating him to the soil. Working the land was at once the symbol and the fulfilment of nationalist Jewish aspirations. But agricultural settlement was not only a matter of ideology. The settlements, mostly kibbutzim, had expanded and deepened the Jewish hold on parts of Palestine, gradually making more of the country "Jewish," or at least not *Judenrein*. In the successive partition plans, the presence of clusters of Jewish settlements in this or that part of the country determined what would constitute the areas of Jewish statehood. Settlements ultimately meant sovereignty. Each new settlement or cluster of settlements staked out the Jewish claim to a new area. Linked to this was their military–strategic value and staying power. The settlements over the decades successfully stymied Arab marauders and irregulars.

Nothing demonstrated the political import and the military viability and significance of the settlements more than the United Nations Partition resolution of November 1947 and the subsequent months of hostilities. The Partition Plan largely followed the pattern of settlement/population distribution around Palestine. Areas with no, or practically no, Jewish settlements (except for the Negev) were automatically assigned to Arab sovereignty. In the first months of the fighting, the areas of Jewish strength and control by and large overlapped the areas with concentrated Jewish settlement.

The Partition resolution, only reluctantly accepted by the Yishuv's leaders, left outside the Jewish state-to-be several clusters of Jewish settlements – the Etzion Bloc, the settlements in Western and Upper Galilee and several settlements north and east of Jerusalem – and forbade, at least for a transition period, Jewish settlement in the areas earmarked for the Palestine Arab state.

But as the hostilities turned into full-scale war, attitudes in the Yishuv to the Partition resolution and to settlement changed. The Partition Plan was a peacetime solution to Palestine's problems; the war undermined its "sanctity." Already in early February 1948, Ben-Gurion spoke of the need, in order to secure the road to Jerusalem, to establish Jewish settlements in the Jerusalem corridor (an Arab-owned area earmarked in the Partition Plan for the Palestine Arab state).[100] Establishing settlements was a tool in the struggle. Security needs, he said in March, dictated setting up "a string of points [i.e., settlements]" in the Negev, the Beit Shean (Beisan) Valley and in the Galilee.

Of course, there were problems: lack of funds and manpower, and not everyone – according to Ben-Gurion – understood the importance of setting up new settlements in the middle of the war.[101] But he did. On the brink of the Haganah offensives of April, and to consolidate the expected victories, Ben-Gurion said: "We shall enter the empty villages and settle in them. The war will also bring with it favourable internal changes in the internal constitution of the Yishuv; tens of thousands will move to less populated centres [i.e., districts] – to the Negev, to the Galilee and to the area of Jerusalem. We shall cure the Jewish body. In peacetime we would not have been able to do this." Ben-Gurion had outlined two major characteristics of the settlement drive of the following months: settlement of the abandoned Arab villages and settlement in areas thinly populated by Jews (Western Galilee, Upper Galilee, the Jerusalem corridor).[102] Two days later, he added: "We will not be able to win the war if we do not, during the war, populate Upper and Lower, Eastern and Western Galilee, the Negev and the Jerusalem area, even if only in an artificial way, in a military way . . . I believe the war will also bring in its wake a great change in the distribution of the Arab population."[103]

Preliminary discussions about the organisation of new settlement ventures took place at the end of March.[104] On 13 April, Galili, the Haganah chief, wrote Weitz: "We regard as important to security new settlements being established in the following places . . . .: Beit Mahsir, Saris, Khirbet ad Duweir, Kafr Misr, Khirbet Manshiya, Tantura, Bureir, Mis [?]." Galili asked that the establishment of the settlements at these sites be carried out "as soon as possible."[105]

At a meeting on 22 April between Weitz and the Haganah commanders, including Yadin, the Haganah agreed to provide manpower and equipment to set up six new settlements, all on Jewish-owned (or non-Arab) land – at Bureir, Khirbet ad Duweir, Kafr Misr, Ma'lul (west of Nazareth), Al Ashrafiya (in the Beit Shean Valley) and Daliyat ar Ruha (in the Hills of Menashe, southeast of Haifa). Already on 18 April a group of Jewish settlers had moved into Beit Lahm (Galileean Bethlehem), one of the German colonies in Palestine, making it the first Jewish settlement established during the war. The German colonists were evicted and their Arab workers fled when the Haganah had captured the site a few days before.[106]

In March, Weitz had already started pressing the Haganah and local Jewish settlements to set up new settlements in place of the Arab tenant-farmer communities southeast of Haifa, such as Daliyat ar Ruha. At the same time, at a meeting with Weitz and Hartzfeld, local kibbutz leaders from the Beit Shean Valley had demanded the establishment of a settlement in their area "as a means of freeing our land [from Arab farmers] and of preventing the return of beduins [from the area] who had fled to Transjordan." This is the first linkage in the documents between the proposed setting up of a settlement and the prevention of the return of refugees.[107]

Once the Haganah and the settlement bodies (the JNF, the Agricultural Centre, and the Jewish Agency Settlement Department) had agreed in principle on the establishment of new settlements, the kibbutz and *moshav* movements were approached to supply the requisite manpower. The movements began to jockey for the best sites, and established kibbutzim became worried by the prospect of good neighbouring tracts of land going to new settlements.[108]

Weitz and Hartzfeld were depressed by the slowness in the settlement process. Weitz felt that those with the power – such as Jewish Agency Treasurer Kaplan – were shirking a decision. A great opportunity was being missed.[109] Weitz himself was under pressure from local lobbyists, like the two Jordan Valley representatives, who on 3 May told him that their area had emptied of Arabs – "Samakh, Al 'Ubeidiya, As Samra [on the southern shore of the Sea of Galilee]. Now was the time to act in setting up settlements. They demanded the establishment of settlements at Khirbet ad Duweir and As Samra."[110]

The settlement enterprise began to pick up steam. Weitz and Hartzfeld met Ben-Gurion and Shkolnik on 7 May and, again, on 9 May, the second meeting attended by Yadin. The focus remained on settlement on Jewish-owned land and within the Jewish State Partition borders. The upshot, according to Hartzfeld, was: "There are now 24 sites [all inside the Partition borders] for settlement that we can actually settle tomorrow . . . Apart from the settlement value [of such new settlements], there are also security . . . [considerations] pushing and motivating us." Another 18 sites, said Hartzfeld, were being considered for settlement for security reasons – eight of them (in the Corridor and in Western Galilee, on Arab-owned lands) outside the Partition borders.[111]

In planning the imminent settlement ventures, some officials were already thinking in terms of the absorption of the expected mass influx of Jewish immigrants. As Haim Gvati, of the Agricultural Centre, put it: "the establishment of the state and the opening of the gates to large immigration in the not distant future obliges us to plan for agricultural settlement with momentum and with scope which we never anticipated until now."[112]

As with expulsions and the destruction of villages, criticism of the planned mass settlement drive surfaced in Mapam. Hazan warned against settling on lands owned by *fellahin* (though agreed to settling on effendi-owned land). Other Mapam leaders were more critical. "Should we use this moment of opportunity when the Arabs have fled in order to create settlement facts?" asked party stalwart Ya'acov Amit.[113]

The advent of the First Truce in June considerably galvanised the pro-settlement lobbyists and executives: the cease-fire raised the prospect of Arab infiltration back to fields and villages; the establishment of settlements on the abandoned sites would help neutralise this danger. (As we have seen in chapter 4, this was the line used by Weitz with Ben-Gurion, and by the Safad Jewish community notables, Ephraim Vizhensky and other local leaders with anyone who would listen to them.)

Matters may not have moved as fast as Weitz and Hartzfeld would have liked, but they were moving. Four new settlements had been set up in May

– at Beit Lahm, Waldheim and Shomrat in the Galilee and in Bureir (Brur Hayil) in the south. Twice as many new settlements were founded in June – Hahotrim (near At Tira, south of Haifa, on 7 June), Reshafim and Sheluhot (on the lands of Al Ashrafiya, in the Beit Shean Valley, on 10 June), Nahsholim (on the lands of Tantura, on 14 June), Ein Dor (on the lands of Kafr Misr, in the Galilee, on 14 June), Netzer-Sereni (at Bir Salim, east of Ramle, on 20 June), Timurim (on the lands of Ma'lul, in the Galilee, on 21 June) and at Kfar Yavetz (a Coastal Plain *moshav* that was abandoned at the start of the war and resettled on 29 June).[114] Most of these settlements were established on Jewish-owned land but, from the start, their fields comprehended abandoned Arab lands. Three of the settlements – at Beit Lahm, Bir Salim and Waldheim – were set up on German-owned lands. Five of the new settlements of June (and one of those of May) were settled by Mapam groups.

Five new settlements went up in July, all on Jewish-owned lands and within the Jewish State Partition borders.[115] But pressure was building up for settlement on Arab-owned lands within and beyond the Partition borders. The IDF victories in mid-July contributed to this by adding territory outside the Jewish State borders that, to be retained, would have to be settled with Jews. On 21 July, Shkolnik called for the establishment "within one or two days" of four new settlements in the Jerusalem corridor (before the arrival of United Nations truce inspectors, who might view new settlements as a truce violation). Weitz and Hartzfeld agreed, but JNF chairman Granovsky "doubted the legality of settlement on Arab land." Weitz also anticipated opposition from Mapam's Zisling and Bentov.[116]

Two days later, Weitz, at a meeting with Ben-Gurion, asked for decisions in principle on whether the Yishuv should establish settlements beyond the Jewish State Partition borders, whether settlements should be set up on Arab-owned lands and, if so, should differentiation be made between the various types of Arab-owned lands (land owned by foreigners, effendi-owned land and *fellahin*-owned land). Ben-Gurion evaded direct response on the principles but advocated the immediate establishment of "10–12" new settlements in the Jerusalem corridor and in the Lydda–Ramle area (all outside the Partition borders). He agreed with Weitz that "military victories [should be] translated into political achievement."[117]

On 28 July, Weitz, Hartzfeld and Yehuda Horin (Director of the Jewish Agency Settlement Department) presented to Ben-Gurion the first comprehensive wartime settlement plan, calling for the establishment of 21 settlements on mostly Arab-owned lands in the Jerusalem corridor, the Lydda–Ramle area and Western Galilee.[118]

Weitz explained the plan to the JNF directorate on 16 August. Granovsky supported it, pointing to the plan's "strategic-political" importance. Granovsky stressed that the Yishuv would only expropriate some of the land of the Arab sites. The rest of the lands, "with their houses and trees," would be left untouched and set aside for the *fellahin* and tenant farmers "for when they return." Then the Yishuv would pay the returnees for the expropriated lands and help the Arabs modernise their cultivation from "extensive" to "intensive" agriculture so that less land would produce more crops (Mapam's "surplus lands" formula).[119]

Mapam's leaders had worked out the "surplus lands" formula during July. In mid-July, Zisling had spoken of the need for "development" schemes that would enable the Arabs to return. Haim Kafri, a Mapam leader in the Hefer Valley area, a fortnight later explained that through "agrarian reform" and "intensification" of cultivation, it was possible both to set lands aside ("surplus lands") for the Arabs to return to and to embark on a "giant" Jewish settlement drive at the same time.[120]

The "21 settlements" plan forced Mapam to face the ideological problem of Jewish settlement on Arab-owned lands and on land earmarked for Arab sovereignty. The party supported continued Jewish–Arab coexistence and the return of the refugees. But the kibbutzim, of both the Hashomer Hatzair and Ahdut Ha'avodah wings of the party, favoured the establishment of new settlements and the expansion of Jewish agriculture. On both local and national levels, the establishment of new settlements, both inside and outside the Partition borders, was seen as serving security and strategic interests. The "surplus lands" formula seemed to point the way to both having one's cake and eating it: strategic and agricultural–territorial interests could be safeguarded while at the same time lands could be set aside for a possible return of the refugees. In any case, the Arabs were to be compensated for the lands expropriated. Hence, it was to be "development for the benefit of both peoples," as Hazan described it; or, "we must fight for development and against eviction," said party co-leader Ya'ari. Mapam had found a formula that seemed to marry strategic and economic expediency with principle.[121]

Mapam successfully imposed the "surplus lands" formula on Weitz and the other settlement executives. On 20 August, the executives submitted a revised plan, calling for 32 new settlements on JNF, State and Arab-owned lands. They stressed that settlement on Arab land would be only on sites where there would be sufficient surplus land to accommodate and maintain the original inhabitants, should they return. The 32 were: Khulda (Kibbutz Mishmar-David), Khirbet Beit Far (Tal-Shahar), Beit Jiz (Kibbutz Harel), Beit Susin (Taoz), Sar'a (Kibbutz Tzor'a), Beit

Mahsir/Saris (Beit Meir and Shoresh), Kasla (Kesalon) and Khirbet Deir 'Amr (Giv'at Yearim/Eitanim) – in the Jerusalem corridor; three new settlements on the lands of Wilhelma (Bnei Atarot, Mahane Yisrael and Be'erot Yitzhak), Al Haditha (Beit Nehemia), Khirbet Zakariya/Jimzu (Gimzo) and Al Kunaisiya/Al Qubab (Mishmar-Ayalon and Kfar Bin-Nun) – in the Lydda–Ramle area; two setttlements on the lands of Qazaza-Amuriya (Tirosh), Al Kheima (Kibbutz Revadim), Barqusiya-Summeil (Segula and Nahala), Zeita (Kibbutz Gal-on), Hatta (Revaha), Karatiya (Otzem or Komemiut), Jaladiya (Zerah'ya/Shafir) and Bash-shit (Meishar/Asoret/Zekher-Dov/Shdeima/Kfar Mordechai) – in the northern Negev approaches, along the "corridor" tenuously linking the heart of the Yishuv in the Coastal Plain to the semi-besieged, cut-off kibbutzim in the Negev; Al Birwa (Ahihud/Kibbutz Yas'ur), Kafr Yasif/Amqa/Abu Sinan (Amqa), Khirbet Shifiya (Ein Ya'akov/Kibbutz Ga'aton), Khirbet Jalil (Goren), I'ribbin (on the Lebanese border, north of Kibbutz Eilon), Al Bassa (Shlomi) and As Sumeiriya (Kibutz Lohamei Hagetaot/Regba) – in the upper Western Galilee; Nimrin (northwest of Kibbutz Lavi) and Eilabun – in eastern Galilee.

Several of the proposed sites, such as Eilabun, had not yet been conquered. Almost all were aptly described as strategic sites as almost all were along the front lines established in the late summer of 1948 opposite the Transjordanian, Egyptian and Lebanese armies. All but five of the proposed sites lay outside the Partition borders. The settlements were to be on 120,000 dunams of land, of which only 23,000 were Jewish owned; most was Arab private land (58,000 dunams) and Wakf lands. The settlements were mainly designed to safeguard the road to Jerusalem and to bolster Israel's military–political hold on Western Galilee, according to Kaplan. Shitrit thought the plan involved no "wrongdoing" as the original landowners were to be compensated. Zisling supported the plan for "security" reasons and reiterated the "surplus lands" formula.[122]

The political shift from the new settlement ventures of June–July to those planned in August is clear: the mid-summer settlements had been established mainly on Jewish-owned lands and within the Jewish State Partition Plan borders; those established in August (Kibbutz Sa'ar, north of Nahariya, on 6 August; Be'erot Yitzhak, Bnei Atarot and Mahane Yisrael, on the lands of Wilhclma, on 7–9 August; Kibbutz Yiftah, on the lands of Blida, in the Galilee panhandle, on 18 August; Nordiya, at Khirbet Beit Lid in the Coastal Plain, on 15 August; Kibbutz Yizra'el, next to Zir'in, in the Jezreel Valley, on 20 August; and Udim, in Wadi Faliq south of Netanya, on 29 August) were mostly on non-Jewish owned lands but inside the Partition State borders; and those planned in August for the following weeks and months were almost all outside the Partition borders of the Jewish State and almost completely based on the expropriation of Arab and German-owned lands.

But in the autumn of 1948 the Yishuv lacked the resources to immediately implement the 32-settlement plan in full. As the IDF General Staff Settlement Officer put it: "The weak link in the establishment of new settlements on a very wide scale remains the question of manpower ... [Moreover] the difficulties in building fortifications for the new settlements are still not small, especially in [the lack of] heavy equipment."[123]

During the following months attitudes against a return, both within Mapam and nationally, hardened. The "surplus lands" concept provided a smokescreen behind which those who opposed a return – Ben-Gurion, Sharett, Weitz and many in Mapam – were able, without disturbing the national consensus, to implement a settlement policy whose effect (and, in part, purpose) was to bar any possibility of a return. This was understood in Mapam, where Meir Ya'ari acknowledged that, if the implementation was in the hands of the anti-return majority, then the "surplus lands" concept was all so much hot air. "They want to sweep under the carpet the problem of the return of the refugees by [espousing] theories of planning and development," he said.[124] Mapam's posture remained clear: theoretically it was troubled and divided; in practice, it was as forward as any in participating in the settlement drive, on Arab-owned lands and outside the Partition State borders. As Kibbutz Artzi member Shlomo Rosen put it: "We have no choice; we must contribute our share towards the defensive settlement along the borders, despite our doubts about the intentions of those at the helm of government."[125]

Settlement policy was a barometer of general attitudes towards a return. In early December, Weitz recorded the traditionally softline Shitrit agreeing to the establishment of settlements on the actual sites of abandoned Arab villages, rather than merely on their lands. Kaplan that month also agreed to "free use of the villages."[126] On 18 December, Weitz asked Ben-Gurion whether, in planning settlements, "surplus land" should still be set aside for a possible refugee return. Ben-Gurion replied: "Not along the borders, and in each village we will take everything, as per our settlement needs. We will not allow the Arabs back."[127]

In the course of September–December 1948 and January 1949, the bulk of the 32-settlement plan approved in August was carried out (though there were delays in October and December because of the renewed hostilities). During September 1948, five new settlements were established – Kibbutz Gazit (Kibbutz Artzi, 10 September) at At Tira, in Eastern Galilee; Barriya Bet (Hapoel Hamizrahi, 21 September) at Al

Barriya, southeast of Ramle; Kibbutz Hagoshrim (Kibbutz Me'uhad, 26 September) at the site of the former Jewish settlement of Nehalim in the Galilee panhandle, next to the abandoned village of Khisas; Beit Meir (then called Lehagshama, Hano'ar Hatzioni, 27 September) at Beit Mahsir, in the Jerusalem corridor; and Ameilim (Hever Hakvutzot, 30 September) at Abu Shusha, southeast of Ramle. Another five were established in October – Kibbutz Ga'aton (Kibbutz Artzi, 8 October) at Khirbet Shifiya, in Western Galilee; Kesalon (Herut, 11 October) at Kasla, in the Jerusalem corridor; Ameilim (later called Kibbutz Tzova) (Kibbutz Me'uhad, 19 October) at Suba, in the Jerusalem corridor; Kibbutz Eretz-Yisrael Yod-Gimel, Gizo (Kibbutz Artzi, 27 October) at Beit Susin, in the Jerusalem corridor; and Tal-Boqer (later Tal-Shahar) (the Moshav Movement, 27 October), at Khirbet Beit Far, at the western end of the Jerusalem corridor.

Only one new settlement was added in November, Kibbutz Revadim (Kibbutz Artzi, 20 November) at Al Kheima, at the western end of the Jerusalem corridor.

In December, three new settlements were established – Bustan Hagalil (1 December) on the lands of As Sumeiriya, in Western Galilee; Kibbutz Misgav-David (later changed to Mishmar-David, Hever Hakvutzot, 7 December) at Khulda, at the western end of the Jerusalem corridor; and Kibbutz Tzor'a (Kibbutz Me'uhad, 7 December) at Sar'a, in the Jerusalem corridor.

In January 1949, 11 new settlements were established – Habonim (later called Beit Ha'emek, Kibbutz Me'uhad, 4 January) at Kuweikat, in Western Galilee; Netiva (Poalei Agudat Yisrael, 4 January) at Al Mukheizin, south of Rehovot; Kibbutz Yas'ur (Kibbutz Artzi, 6 January) at Al Birwa, northeast of Haifa; Kfar Rosh Hanikra (Hever Hakvutzot, 6 January) near al Bassa, in Western Galilee; Hashahar (later called Sifsufa, Hapoel Hamizrahi, 11 January) at Safsaf, northwest of Safad; Mavki'im (Haoved Hatzioni, 12 January) at Barbara, just south of Al Majdal (Ashkelon), north of the Gaza Strip; Kibbutz Sasa (Kibbutz Artzi, 13 January) at Sa'sa in Upper Galilee; Kibbutz Kabri (Hever Hakvutzot, 18 January) at Al Kabri in Western Galilee; Kibbutz Lohamei Hageta'ot (Kibbutz Me'uhad, 27 January) on the lands of As Sumeiriya in Western Galilee; Beit Ha'arava (later Kibbutz Gesher Haziv, 27 January) at Az-Zib in Western Galilee; and Yosef Kaplan (later Kibbutz Meggido, Kibbutz Artzi, 27 January) at Lajjun, at the western edge of the Jezreel Valley.

In the latter months of 1948, as the 32-settlement plan was being implemented, thinking about a "second series" began to mature. The 32 settlements were designed mainly to fortify Israel's new borders and to stake out the State's claims to the new areas – such as Western Galilee, the Jerusalem corridor and the Lydda–Ramle district – conquered by Jewish arms. But this chain of new settlements would not solve the problem of the vast "vacuum" in the rear created by the Arab exodus.

Ra'anan Weitz, Secretary of the Jewish Agency's Settlement Department (and son of Yosef Weitz), set the ball rolling on 30 November, when he submitted his plan for a 96-settlement "second series" to the Ministerial Committee for Abandoned Property – 40 in newly-conquered Upper Galilee, 8 more in the Jerusalem corridor, 18 in the northern Negev and the Negev approaches, 8 along the Mediterranean coast and 22 in the central Negev. Weitz stated: "Wherever conditions make it necessary, the new settlement should be established [on the site of] the existing [Arab] village" – a practice avoided almost completely in the first series.[128]

The plan, in a much-reduced version of 41 new settlements, was endorsed by the JNF directorate on 7 December, with the stipulation that lands be set aside for returning Arabs. At the meetings of the Committee of Directorates of the National Institutions on 3 and 10 December, Kaplan and, apparently, Zisling opposed the plan's call for establishing settlements on the actual sites of Arab villages (some of which were still inhabited), and Kaplan reiterated the need to set aside a "territorial reserve" for the Arabs. Weitz commented: "Many of the ministers were worrying more about [re]settling the Arabs than settling the Jews." Weitz feared that, if there was delay in implementation, "many Arab will manage to infiltrate back [from exile] to their villages." But the 41-settlement plan, "with reservations," was approved by the Committee and, subsequently, by the Cabinet, and the majority of the sites were among the more than 100 settled in 1949.[129]

The absorption and settlement of the new immigrants, 1948 – early 1949

Almost all the settlements established during 1948 were founded by pioneering youth groups (*halutzim*) drawn from the socialist youth movements of Palestine or their affiliates in the Diaspora; many, such as the Palmah kibbutzim in the Jerusalem corridor and Kibbutz Yiftah in the Galilee, were settled by settlement groups (*gar'inim*) on active duty as part of, or at the end of, their military service. Almost all were founded as – and remained – kibbutzim. Almost invariably, they settled outside the perimeter of actual abandoned Arab villages (though often on Arab-owned lands).

Most of the settlements established in 1949 were something else altogether. To be sure, several dozen new kibbutzim were founded. But the old Yishuv's human resources for further pioneering settlement had been almost exhausted by the settlement efforts of 1948, war losses and the needs of the state bureaucracies for high-calibre personnel. The bulk of the new settlers of 1949 were new *olim* (immigrants), who were pouring into the country in increasing numbers from May 1948. (Between 14 May 1948 and 9 February 1949, 143,000 *olim* arrived in Israel.)[130] There was mutuality and reciprocity in the process: the State needed to fill the empty villages for political reasons and, for political and security reasons, to line its new borders with settlements; the immigrants needed a roof over their heads and work – with agriculture, for which not all were qualified, requiring the least investment and offering the most immediately promising prospects. And, of course, agriculture had to be expanded to make up for the ravages of the war and to feed the rapidly growing population. The bulk of the sites in the 41-settlement plan, like the vast majority of all the sites settled in 1949, were filled with new immigrants – from the Middle East, North Africa and Europe, survivors of Hitler's death camps.

To settle the new immigrants – mostly indigent and without Hebrew, and often without skills – either directly or after a sojourn in transit camps (*ma'abarot*) into the abandoned villages and urban neighbourhoods seemed natural and appropriate. Few of the new *olim* were suited to the ideologically inspired but materially rigorous demands of the collective life-style of the kibbutzim; almost all were settled in co-operative or semi-private farming villages (*moshavim*) or in towns. Unlike the new settlements of 1948, many of the new settlements of 1949 were founded on the actual sites of abandoned Arab villages and towns. In part, this was because renovation of existing villages was quicker and cheaper than building new settlements from scratch.

The immigration absorption authorities in February 1948 anticipated that in the first wave of immigration to the new Jewish State, some 150,000 would arrive by September–October 1949. They believed that this would necessitate "the construction of more than 60,000 rooms"; they were thinking, at this time, of "construction" rather than take-over and occupation of Arab districts and housing.[131] But the projections of February 1948 fell short of the reality: by autumn 1949, more than 200,000 immigrants had arrived. Moreover, the Yishuv's mobilisation of resources and energies for the war effort of 1948–9 and the destruction in the war of Jewish settlements and housing further curtailed the authorities' ability properly to accommodate the immigrant influx. One upshot was the establishment of the transit camps, which housed (usually in squalor) tens of thousands of immigrants, most of whom were Jews from Muslim countries until the mid-1950s. The other was the abrupt settlement of new immigrants in (often derelict) abandoned Arab villages and towns.

The accommodation of new immigrants in abandoned Arab housing began in 1948, in the towns rather than in the countryside. It began almost immediately with the flight of Arab families from mixed Jewish–Arab and Arab districts in the mixed cities. Perhaps a first trace of the policy can be found in Ben-Gurion's instructions to the newly-appointed Haganah commander in Jerusalem, David Shaltiel, at the end of January 1948. Some Arab districts in western Jerusalem had already been abandoned, and Ben-Gurion ordered Shaltiel "to settle Jews in every house in abandoned, half-Arab neighbourhood[s], such as Romema."[132]

It was the Transfer Committee that first proposed that the government adopt, as part of a coherent and multi-faceted programme to bar a return of the refugees, the settlement of new immigrants in abandoned Arab housing. In his letter of 18 May to Weitz, Danin recommended "settling Jews in all the abandoned area."[133] The Transfer Committee's proposals to Ben-Gurion in early June included "the settlement of Jews in a number of villages and cities to prevent a 'vacuum',"" to which, according to Weitz, Ben-Gurion agreed.[134] That month, during his tours around the country, Weitz instructed or advised local leaders to settle new immigrants at various outlying abandoned sites, and pressed the government to do so.[135]

The first mass settlement of new immigrants in Arab housing occurred in the centre of the country, in Jaffa and Haifa, where the largest – and most modern – concentrations of abandoned Arab houses were to be found. The settlement of new *olim* in the abandoned parts of these cities was facilitated by their proximity to existing Jewish municipal services and infrastructure. The process began in late May or June. First to be settled in the abandoned Arab districts were several hundred Yishuv families displaced by the war and Arab conquest. Then, with their influx into the country, came the *olim*. "We want to make it easier for ourselves by exploiting the housing possibilities that have opened up as a result of the development of the war. We want now to introduce another 2,000 families to Haifa and 1,000 families to Jaffa," Kaplan said at the beginning of July.[136] The concentration of Haifa's remaining 3,000 Arabs in the Wadi Nisnas district and on Abbas Street in the beginning of July, and the similar concentration in August of Jaffa's remaining Arabs in a small area of the town, facilitated the settlement of the new *olim* in the empty neighbourhoods.[137]

By 1 August 1948, according to Kaplan, 51,000 new *olim* had entered the country since the start of the year. The hostilities had "greatly facilitated" their absorption, said the Finance Minister, as "because of the war, thousands of flats had come into our hands. Into Haifa alone had moved since [the city's] liberation 12,000 people, and some say 13,000 . . . Haifa [authorities] demand another 20,000 . . . We tried to send hundreds to Tiberias and Safad."[138]

A variety of problems – mainly of poor infrastructure and the continued dispersal of the remaining Arab population of Jaffa around the town – through July prevented the start of settlement of *olim* in the former Arab city. On 25 July, Yitzhak Chizik, the military governor of Jaffa, resigned. Since May, he had been battling IDF units, various Jewish bodies, vandals and private looters to protect the property of Jaffa's refugees. He may have opposed the settlement of *olim* in the Arab houses, which all understood would spell the end to any hope of a refugee return. Ben-Gurion appointed lawyer Meir Laniado in his stead, and a few days later the concentration of Jaffa's Arabs was carried out. The orders were "to evict the Arabs from the places where Jews were to be settled." Many of the Arab families were happy with the transfer as they ended up with better housing, wrote Laniado. *Olim* began to move into the houses at the start of September.[139]

In Haifa and Jaffa, the start of organised settlement by *olim* in Arab houses was characterised by a great deal of confusion, which in the latter city bordered on anarchy. Lack of resources meant that many houses were not properly renovated. Impatient *olim*, uncomfortably quartered in schools and other public buildings, "invaded" the empty Arab districts and seized houses without waiting for official allocation. Jaffa was settled by "invasions and counter-invasions," wrote the Custodian for Absentees Property in disgust. Occasionally, the "invaders" roughly evicted Arabs still living in houses. Some houses were allotted to veteran citizens with "connections."[140]

In the towns as in the countryside, settlement followed relatively hard on the heels of IDF conquest. Less than six weeks after the capture of Ramle the OC Military Government, General Elimelech Avner, asked Ben-Gurion about settling new immigrants in the town. He complained that Shertok and Kaplan opposed this for political reasons.[141] The ministers' objections prevailed for a time, bolstered apparently by the IDF's reluctance to have masses of *olim* settle close to the front.

But the needs of the new State, inundated with *olim*, were inexorable. Giora Yoseftal, Director of the Immigration Absorption Department of the Jewish Agency, two months later predicted a housing crisis. He asked that the IDF "free" Arab housing. He estimated there was accommodation for 2,000 families in Ramle and Lydda.[142] On 5 November the Ministerial Committee for Abandoned Property at last discussed the possibility of settling *olim* in Ramle, as "the country is in a bad way in connection with the continuing arrival of new immigrants. Every possibility of accommodation should be exploited and the army should be given a general instruction not to destroy houses without cause. . . . There are 20,000 [*olim*] in transit camps [in Israel]," said Kaplan.[143] By 16 November, some 100 immigrant families had moved into Ramle, with another 500–600 families due in the following months.[144] In December, Ben-Gurion removed the ban on Jewish settlement in Lydda, and *olim* began to move in at the end of the month or the following month.[145]

Acre was settled with Jews in September. At first, the local military commander – who was worried about Arab–Jewish relations in the town – blocked the move, and Shitrit, wary of a repetition in Acre (where some 5,000 Arabs had remained) of what had happened in Jaffa, counselled that it would be prudent to hold off.[146] But the law and order problem was apparently sorted out and on 18 September Shitrit, General Avner, the Custodian for Absentees Property and Ben-Gurion decided to go ahead with the settlement of Acre. By 22 November, Acre had 2,000 Jewish settlers.[147]

On 5 December, the Ministerial Committee for Abandoned Property approved the settlement of Beersheba, conquered on 21 October, but the army resisted.[148] Ben-Gurion intervened, ordering Southern Front headquarters to free "half the town for civilian purposes." However, infrastructure problems delayed implementation. The first 17 immigrant families settled in the town only on 23 February 1949. Plans provided for some 3,000 Jewish settlers by the end of the year.[149]

The settlement of *olim* in the abandoned, former Arab districts of Jerusalem began somewhat later than in the other formerly Arab or mixed towns, probably because of political considerations. The city was split roughly in half, with the IDF holding the western side and Transjordanian (and some Egyptian troops, on the southern edge of the city) holding the eastern districts. Jerusalem had been designated an international enclave in the Partition Plan and for various reasons, some of them religious, there was acute sensitivity among the western powers and in the Muslim world to what was happening in the city. But from mid-1948 veteran Jewish Jerusalemites and Jews displaced from front-line areas in and around the embattled Jewish parts of the city began to move into, and occupy, houses in the abandoned Arab and mixed Arab–Jewish districts of western Jerusalem – Qatamon, Romema, Sheikh Badr, Talbiye, Bak'a and Al Maliha (a small Arab village on the southwestern edge of the city, now part of municipal Jerusalem, renamed Manahat). Mass movement of *olim* to Jerusalem began at the end of December 1948 with the settlement of some 150 families in 'Ein Karim, an Arab village to the west of the city (now part of municipal Jerusalem, renamed Ein Karem).[150]

Boundary demarcation considerations apparently also played a role in the decision-making concerning settlement of Jews in Jerusalem's neighbourhoods. In mid-March 1949 the military governor of Jewish Jerusalem, Colonel Moshe Dayan, demanded that "civilians" be immediately settled in the southern neighbourhoods of Talpiyot, Ramat Rachel (a war-ravaged kibbutz, on the southern edge of the city) and Abu Tor because if a United Nations-chaired mixed armistice commission team visited the neighbourhoods "and finds [them] empty of civilians, there will be United Nations pressure [on us] to evacuate the area."[151] It is unclear if this demand was acted upon.

By the end of May, it appears that all of western Jerusalem's former Arab districts (save for Abu Tor) had been settled, at least to some extent, by Jews, most of them *olim*. An Interior Ministry official reported that the Musrara (later Morasha) neighbourhood was being settled with new *olim* from Muslim countries, and that Abu Tor also had to be settled if Israel wanted to hold onto it.[152]

During the summer of 1949, several hundred new *olim* from Eastern Europe were settled in Deir Yassin, despite a protest to Ben-Gurion by several of the Yishuv's leading intellectuals, including Martin Buber and Akiva Ernst Simon. They wrote that while aware of the suffering of the new *olim* and of their need for housing, they did not think that Deir Yassin was "the appropriate place ... The Deir Yassin episode is a black stain on the honour of the Jewish people ... It is better for the time being to leave the land of Deir Yassin uncultivated and the houses of Deir Yassin unoccupied, rather than to carry out an action whose symbolic importance vastly outweighs its practical benefit. The settlement of Deir Yassin, if carried out a mere year after the crime, and within the regular settlement framework, will constitute something like . . . approbation of the slaughter." The intellectuals asked that the village be left empty and desolate, as "a terrible and tragic symbol . . . and a warning sign to our people that no practical or military necessity will ever justify such terrible murders from which the nation does not want to benefit." Ben-Gurion did not reply, despite repeated reminders, and "Givat Shaul Bet" was duly established on the site, with several Cabinet ministers, the two chief rabbis and Jerusalem's mayor attending the dedication ceremony.[153]

The settlement of *olim* in the abandoned Arab villages began in the last months of 1948, as the momentum of settlement by pioneers began to run out and after most of the housing potential of the towns was exhausted. An initial recommendation to settle *olim* in abandoned villages (usually in the existing Arab houses) was submitted to the Military Government Committee on 23 September 1948. OC Military Government General

Avner named as suitable the villages of 'Aqir, Sarafand al Kharab, Beit Dajan, Al Yahudiya, Zarnuqa, Kafr 'Ana and houses in Abu Kishk (all in the Tel Aviv–Rehovot–Ramle triangle).[154]

No less pressing than the new immigrants' need for housing was the State's need to settle and fill out the newly-conquered territories, lest the absence of a civilian population undermine Israel's territorial claims when negotiations began regarding the borders. Ben-Gurion thought that *olim* as well as veteran pioneers should be used to fill up the Galilee.[155] Weitz's thinking ran along similar lines in his proposal to immediately settle in 36 abandoned Galilee sites. "This emptiness, besides leaving a stamp of desolation [which can be attributed to] the Israeli army, serves as a weak point for the return of the Arab refugees ... by way of infiltration [of the exiles back to their villages]." On the one hand, natural erosion was quickly destroying the villages while on the other, Israel faced the problem of accommodating tens of thousands of new *olim*.[156] On 23 December, Ben-Gurion instructed immigration absorption chief Yoseftal to send "ten thousand *olim*" to the Galilee villages.[157]

But the plan prompted political opposition. Mapam's views were expressed clearly by Pinhas Ger, a member of Kibbutz Ma'anit: "As Zionists, we never thought of settling a Jewish *oleh* in the house of the expelled Arab. It is the right of the Arabs who were expelled or fled to return to the Land of Israel. And the [problem of] Jewish *aliya* should not be solved at the expense of Arab housing."[158] When General Avner proposed that *olim* be settled in the Lebanese border villages of Al Bassa, Deir al Qasi and Tarshiha (where some 700 Arabs still lived), Zisling asked that the decision be postponed. The militarily useful settlement of pioneers, who knew how to use weapons, was one thing; putting in *olim* was quite another.[159] General Avner complained to Ben-Gurion about Zisling's stand and tactics and the Prime Minister brought the matter for decision to the Cabinet on 9 January 1949. A majority, supporting Ben-Gurion, voted "to encourage introducing *olim* into all the abandoned villages in the Galilee."[160]

Zisling's objection to the settlement of *olim* in the abandoned Arab villages in the Galilee may not have been motivated solely by political considerations. It was perhaps also an expression of the growing antagonism of the two Mapam kibbutz movements to the settlement of *olim* in the countryside. The kibbutzim had no problem with the settlement of *olim* in the cities or with absorbing a small proportion of them in the kibbutzim themselves. But massive settlement of the *olim* on the land in *moshavim* augured a threat to the kibbutz movements' domination of agriculture and to the collectives' general status in the

Yishuv. The enormous growth of *moshavim* could not but proportionally reduce the national and political influence of the kibbutzim and might well – if the *moshavim* proved successful – threaten the kibbutzim ideologically as well. Furthermore, land allocated to *moshavim* in the end meant less land for kibbutzim.

Weitz, who emerged as a powerful proponent of the rural settlement of *olim*, marvelled at the kibbutzniks' inability to see that sending the *olim* to the abandoned villages "is the basic way to turn them into farmers." The kibbutzniks, felt Weitz, feared that the *olim* would adopt the *moshav* form of settlement. "But is collectivism [*kibbutziut*] the goal or the means [to consolidate] the state [of Israel]?" he asked. He suggested that the kibbutzim also opposed the new *olim* settlements out of fear that kibbutzniks would leave their collectives and move to *moshavim*. In any case, there was no other way to quickly fill the abandoned villages, he believed.[161]

The usually subterranean antagonism between kibbutzim and the *olim* settlements occasionally surfaced in open violence – usually over land. Kibbutz Ameilim-Gezer, at the western end of the Jerusalem corridor, for example, in July 1949 complained that the new settlers at Al Qubab were preventing them from ploughing lands they had received from the Agriculture Ministry.[162]

A further problem arose out of some *olim*'s lack of motivation. Unskilled in agriculture and preferring the seeming comforts of town, some *olim* simply abandoned newly-settled sites, as occurred at Al Barriya (settled in September 1948), near Ramle.[163] In general, however, the *olim* settlements took root, if only because life in a transit camp was the only alternative for most of the immigrants.

In April 1949, Yoseftal reported that of 190,000 *olim* who had arrived since the establishment of the State, 110,000 had been settled in abandoned Arab houses. Most had been settled in the Arab districts of Jaffa and the mixed towns (Jerusalem, Haifa, Safad); some 16,000 had been settled in Arab towns (Ramle, Lydda, Acre); and 18,800 in the abandoned villages.[164] By May, the number of *olim* settled in abandoned villages had risen to 25,000.[165] By 27 May, new *olim* had been settled in 21 abandoned villages – Masmiya al Kabira, Tall al Batikh (Sitriya), 'Aqir, Zarnuqa, Yibna, As Safiriya (Shafrir and Kfar Habad), Al Qubeiba, Qastina, Qatra, and Majdal-Gad, in the south; Ijzim (Kerem Maharal) and 'Ein Haud, in the Coastal Plain; Tarshiha, Safsaf (Sifsufa), Al Bassa (Shlomi), Tarbikha (Shomera), Deir al Qasi, Meirun (Meiron) and Sammu'i (Kfar Shamai) in Western and Upper Galilee; and Deir Tarif (Beit Arif) and Umm Zeira, near Lydda. Another six villages were to be settled by new *olim* in the following days – At Tira (Bareket and Tirat-Yehuda), Al Maliha (Manahat), Deir Yassin, Rantiya, Ras al Ahmar (Kerem Ben Zimra) and Suhmata (Tzuriel).[166]

Over the following months, with the towns saturated, dozens more abandoned villages were similarly filled with new *olim* as the new State fought an increasingly desperate fight to properly house the influx of immigrants.

Chapter 6

The third wave: the Ten Days (9–18 July 1948) and the Second Truce (18 July – 15 October)

The First Truce ended on 8 July, with the IDF shifting to the strategic offensive on the three fronts. In the north, in Operation Dekel (Operation Palm Tree), the IDF conquered parts of Western Galilee and the Lower Galilee, including the towns of Shafa 'Amr and Nazareth. In the south, the IDF failed to secure a corridor to the besieged Negev settlements but widened its hold on the northern Negev approaches by capturing the villages of Masmiya al Kabira, At Tina, Qazaza, Tall as Safi, Qastina, Jaladiya, Juseir and Hatta, critically narrowing the Egyptian army's corridor from the Gaza Strip to the Hebron Hills. The main thrust was in the centre of the country, where Operation Dani was designed to fully open and secure the vital Tel Aviv–Jerusalem road and to push back the Arab Legion from the vicinity of Tel Aviv by conquering the towns of Lydda and Ramle and, in the second stage, Latrun and Ramallah, which dominated the highway. Operation Dani attained only its first objectives, with the IDF overrunning the Lydda–Ramle plain, which included Lydda Airport.

The long-planned IDF operations of 9–18 July, triggered by the Arab states' unwillingness to prolong the 28-day truce and, in the south, by local pre-emptive attacks on 8 July, created a major new wave of refugees, who fled primarily to Transjordanian-held eastern Palestine, and to Upper Galilee, Lebanon and the Egyptian-held Gaza Strip.

IDF policy towards the Arab civilian population on all three fronts was not guided by any Cabinet directives. Indeed, in the week before the offensives, the Cabinet was preoccupied with an internal crisis revolving around Ben-Gurion's status as supreme warlord and with responding to the latest set of Bernadotte proposals.

Under continuous pressure from his Cabinet colleagues, Ben-Gurion, on 6 July, just before the start of the "Ten Days," had instructed the IDF to issue a general order to all units concerning behaviour towards Arab civilians. The order, signed by General Ayalon "in the name of the Chief of Staff," stated: "Outside the actual time of fighting, it is forbidden to destroy, burn or demolish Arab cities and villages, to expel Arab inhabitants from villages, neighbourhoods and cities, and to uproot inhabitants from their places without special permission or explicit order from the Defence Minister in each specific case. Anyone violating this order will be put on trial."[1] This order was a grudging, political response to political pressure, and, at least in the higher echelons of the IDF, may have been understood to be such, rather than necessarily a reflection of Ben-Gurion's or the Chief of Staff's real wishes in the matter. However, it probably reached all large formations and headquarters, and must have been seen at least as a formal obstacle to the deliberate precipitation of mass civilian flight (and to the destruction of villages) without authorisation from Ben-Gurion.

During the "Ten Days," Ben-Gurion and the IDF were largely left on their own to decide and execute policy towards conquered Arab communities, without interference or instruction by the Cabinet or the ministries. That policy, as shall be seen, was inconsistent, circumstantial and haphazard. The upshot – different results in different places – was determined by a combination of factors, chief of which were the religious–ethnic identity of the conquered populations, specific local strategic and tactical considerations and circumstances, Ben-Gurion's views on the cases brought, or of interest, to him, the amount and quality of resistance offered in each area to the IDF advance or occupation, and the character and proclivities of the IDF commanders in each area. The result was that the Ramle–Lydda and Tall as Safi areas during the "Ten Days" emptied almost completely of their Arab populations while in Western and Lower Galilee the bulk of the Christian and Druse inhabitants – about half the total population – as well as many Muslims stayed put.

The north

The first stage of Operation Dekel, over 8–14 July, saw the 7th Brigade and the 21st Battalion of the Carmeli Brigade advance eastwards from the Acre–Nahariya area into the western Galilee's hill-country, capturing the villages of Amqa (Druse), Kuweikat (Muslim), Kafr Yasif (Muslim and Christian), Abu Sinan (Druse and Christian), Julis (Druse) and Al Makr (Christian and Muslim) and then, further to the south, I'billin (Christian and Muslim) and Shafa 'Amr (Muslim, Christian and Druse).

The majority of the villages' Druse and Christians stayed put, remaining in Israeli-held territory; the bulk of the Muslims fled. Apparently, this was what the IDF commanders involved wanted. Dov Yirmiya, a company commander in the 21st Battalion, recalled the attack on Kuweikat thus: "I don't know whether the artillery softening up of the village caused casualties but the psychological effect was achieved and the village's non-combatant inhabitants fled before we began the assault." A few of the village's inhabitants had participated in the Yehiam Convoy battle and massacre of 28 March, and this, a fact known to the Israeli commanders involved, may have been a factor in unleashing a relatively strong artillery barrage on Kuweikat. Certainly the village's inhabitants feared retribution, which contributed to their panicky departure. Some of the villagers had already left in June, after an earlier, abortive IDF attack. ALA officers apparently told the villagers during the First Truce to prepare defences and not to send away their women, children and old; it was probably felt that leaving them in the village would bolster the militiamen's morale. On 9 July, the IDF asked the village to surrender, but the *mukhtar*, probably fearing a charge of treason by the ALA, refused. That night, the Carmeli Brigade let loose with artillery. One inhabitant later recalled: "We were awakened by the loudest noise we had ever heard, shells exploding . . . the whole village was in panic . . . women were screaming, children were crying . . . Most of the villagers began to flee with their pyjamas on. The wife of Qassim Ahmad Sa'id fled carrying a pillow in her arms instead of her child." The village militiamen quickly followed suit, some of them going to 'Amqa, whose inhabitants also subsequently fled following an IDF artillery barrage on the village. The handful of Kuweikat villagers – mostly old people – who had remained in the village when it fell were apparently expelled to neighbouring Abu Sinan. The Druse of Abu Sinan subsequently refused to give most of these refugees shelter and they moved on into Upper Galilee and Lebanon. 'Amqa, incidentally, was the only Druse village in Western Galilee so shelled and evacuated.[2]

In all the other villages, the IDF apparently refrained from serious use of artillery, and the Druse and Christian inhabitants stayed put, while many of the Muslim inhabitants fled. The Druse villagers, according to OC Northern Front Carmel, often helped the Israelis beforehand with intelligence and greeted the conquering IDF columns with song, dance and animal sacrifices.[3] It seems that most of the Muslims fled mainly out of fear of Israeli retaliation for having supported or assisted Qawuqji's troops.

At Shafa 'Amr, Israeli–Druse co-operation peaked, with IDF intelligence agents and Druse emissaries meeting on the night before the IDF assault and arranging a sham Druse resistance and Druse surrender. On 14 July, after a heavy artillery barrage on the Muslim quarter and military positions, the entering 7th Brigade columns found the town almost completely empty of Muslims. Most of them had fled to Saffuriya, to the east.[4]

During the second stage of Operation Dekel, on 15–18 July, units of the

7th Brigade captured Ar Ruweis (Muslim), Ad Damun (mostly Muslim), Kabul (Muslim), Sha'b (Muslim), Tamra (Muslim), Mi'ar (Muslim), Kaukab and Kafr Manda, while other units of the brigade, supported by battalions from the Golani and Carmeli Brigades, conquered Nazareth, the major Arab town in the Galilee, and the surrounding villages of Al Mujeidil (Muslim), Ma'lul (Christian and Muslim), Yafa (Muslim and Christian), 'Ilut, Saffuriya (Muslim), Ar Reina (Muslim and Christian), Kafr Kanna (Muslim and Christian), Rummana (Muslim), Uzeir, Tur'an (Muslim and Christian) and Bu'eina (mainly Muslim).

Events followed a pattern similar to that in the first stage of Operation Dekel. Either with the approach of the IDF columns or after the initial IDF artillery barrage or during the battle on the outskirts of each village, most of the Muslim inhabitants fled, eastwards and northwards. The earlier Arab losses of Acre and the villages to the east, and, later, Nazareth, Al Mujeidil and Saffuriya, severely undermined Muslim morale. Where there were substantial Christian communities, the IDF expected and encountered less resistance and, consequently, used less preliminary artillery fire – and the inhabitants by and large stayed put. Christian communities were not expelled. The inhabitants of several largely Muslim villages – such as Dabburiya and Iksal – who stayed put and offered no resistance were not molested when the IDF moved in.

The arrival of thousands of Shafa 'Amr refugees in Saffuriya on 14–15 July severely undermined local morale. IDF aircraft bombed the village on the night of 15 July, apparently killing a few inhabitants and causing panic; the villagers were not prepared for air attack. The village was also hit by artillery. The mass evacuation began, the villagers initially moving out of their houses to nearby gullys and orchards. Though sought, no help came from the ALA in Nazareth, and the local militiamen, despairing, by 16 July joined their families and fled northwards, mostly to Lebanon. A small number of inhabitants – about 100, mostly old people – stayed put,[5] and were only expelled from the site a few months later. Those remaining in Al Mujeidil were apparently driven out in the direction of Nazareth.[6] Of the villages captured in the second stage of Operation Dekel, only Al Mujeidil, Ma'lul, Ar Ruweis and Ad Damun were completely emptied of inhabitants and, later, along with Saffuriya, levelled. It is worth noting that four of these five villages were completely or overwhelmingly Muslim and that at least Saffuriya and Al Mujeidil had strongly supported Qawuqji's troops and had a history of anti-Yishuv behaviour (1936–9). Some of these villages, especially Saffuriya, put up strong resistance to the IDF advance. In all the other villages captured in the second phase of Operation Dekel and where the IDF had encountered no, or no serious, resistance, at least a core of inhabitants stayed put (usually by clan, some clans preferring to depart, some to stay), and these Arab villages exist today.

Most observers at the time believed that the IDF in Operation Dekel had roughly drawn a distinction between Muslims on the one hand and Druse and Christians on the other. Yitzhak Avira, an old-time Haganah Intelligence Service hand and something of an Arabist, wrote about this in somewhat critical terms to Danin. Avira noted the "cleansing [of the area] of Moslems and an easier attitude towards Christians . . . [and] Druse." He related that he had visited Shafa 'Amr and had seen "wanted" Christians and Druse who "not only walked about freely, but also had on their faces joy at the misfortune of the Moslems who had been expelled." While taking no pity on "Moslems who had been expelled," Avira warned of the "danger" of assuming that Christians and Druse were "kosher" while Muslims were "non-kosher." He conceded that the Muslims were "our serious enemies, especially the Husayni [supporters]," but added that some of the Druse and Christians were extremely dangerous and untrustworthy.[7]

Predominantly Christian Nazareth and its neighbouring satellite villages from the first were earmarked for special treatment because of the city's importance to the world's Christians. On 15 July, the day before the town's conquest, Ben-Gurion cabled Carmel to prepare a special administrative task force to take over and run the city smoothly and to issue severe orders against desecration of "monasteries and churches" and against looting. Israeli soldiers found looting should be fired upon, Ben-Gurion instructed.[8] The order – coming as it did only nine days after the general General Staff order of 6 July – was understood to imply a prohibition on the destruction of houses and expulsion of population as well. The letter and spirit of the order were transmitted down the ranks and were strictly obeyed. Carmeli Brigade instructed its battalions not to loot and not to damage churches in the city "holy to many millions." Similar orders were issued in the Golani Brigade. As the brigade's commander, Nahum Golan (Spiegel), later put it: "The conquest of Nazareth had a political importance . . . Because of its importance to the Christian world – the behaviour of the [Israeli] occupation forces in the city could serve as a factor in determining the prestige of the young state abroad."[9] Even the property of those who had fled the city was treated more diffidently in Nazareth than elsewhere.[10]

According to Ben-Gurion, Carmel on 17 July issued an order "to uproot all the inhabitants of Nazareth." Whether Carmel had indeed meant to expel the population or merely to temporarily clear the town of inhabitants to facilitate the search for Qawuqji soldiers and arms is unclear (though the passage seems to read in the sense of "expulsion").

However, according to Ben-Gurion, the 7th Brigade's OC "hesitated," Operation Dekel OC Haim Laskov asked the Defence Minister what to do and, before anything happened, Ben-Gurion intervened and cancelled the order.[11]

In the days following its conquest, Nazareth contained about 15,000 local inhabitants and something close to 20,000 refugees. During the following weeks, many of the refugees – from Shafa 'Amr, Kafr Kanna, Dabburiya, etc. – were allowed to return to their villages though those from Acre, Haifa, Beisan and Tiberias were not, or not immediately.

Why Nazareth's inhabitants, despite the battle around and in the city, had remained was explained – in part inadvertently – by Shitrit in his report on his visit to the city on 19 July. The city's inhabitants had "opposed the war" and Qawuqji's army had only entered the town on 9 July. It had apparently badly treated at least some of the Christian inhabitants and leaders. The city councillors had refused Qawuqji's appeal to help the ALA fight the Jews. The mayor, Yussuf Bek al Fahum, and possibly some of the councillors, as well, had stayed put, discounting fears of expected Jewish atrocities and retribution. Most of the city's 170 municipal policemen had stayed as had much, if not most, of the municipal bureaucracy. The occupying IDF troops had neither expelled nor harmed the local population nor looted or damaged property. A Minority Affairs Ministry official (Elisha Sulz) rather than a military man had quickly (on 18 July) been appointed military governor of the city, and had been advised by Chisik, former military governor of Jaffa, on how to act.

During his visit, Shitrit had also instructed Sulz on behaviour towards the population: to get the search for weapons over quickly and with the minimum of fuss, to get the shops open and to renew normal life as soon as possible. The Minister asked his fellow ministers to appoint a judge in the city, to reactivate the municipality and post office and to take measures against the spread of infection and epidemics. And Shitrit told the Cabinet that "the army must be given strict instructions to behave well and fairly towards the inhabitants of the city because of the great political importance of the city in the eyes of the world."

During 15–16 July some Nazareth inhabitants were apparently physically barred from fleeing by ALA troops, who probably feared that mass panic would undermine the city's defence. The hundreds or thousands who had nonetheless fled the city on the day of its conquest had done so, according to Shitrit, because they had believed "the spurious and counterfeit Arab propaganda." The Arabs had "disseminated information about atrocities by Jews, who cut off hands with axes, break legs and rape women, etc." The Jews were also said to act this way towards "submissive" inhabitants. Some 200 of the Fahum clan had fled to Lebanon, reported Shitrit, "mainly out of fear of rape of [their] women." Sulz later reported that most of those who had fled had been Qawuqji collaborators.[12]

The fall of Nazareth and its large satellite villages was a formidable blow to the morale of most Arabs in the Lower Galilee. It prompted, before the IDF attack, the almost complete flight on 16–17 July of the inhabitants of the large village of Lubiya and of Hittin, to the northeast.[13]

During the "Ten Days," some 20,000–30,000 new refugees were added to those already crowding Upper Galilee and southern Lebanon.

The centre

Operation Dani was the linchpin of the "Ten Days." The aim was to relieve the pressure on semi-besieged Jerusalem, secure the Tel Aviv–Jerusalem road and neutralise the potential threat to Tel Aviv itself from the Arab Legion, whose forward units, in Lydda and Ramle, were less than 20 kilometres from the Yishuv's capital city.

Before the First Truce the IDF General Staff and Ben-Gurion had already begun to think offensively about Ramle and Lydda, which for a long time had acted as bases for attacks on Jewish traffic and settlements. On 30 May the Defence Minister told his generals that the two towns "might serve as bases for attack on Tel Aviv" and other Jewish settlements. Their conquest by the IDF would gain new territory for the state, release forces tied up in the defence of Tel Aviv and the highway, and sever Arab transportation lines. While the Arab Legion had in fact only one, defensively-oriented company (about 120–150 soldiers) in Lydda and Ramle together, and a second-line company at Beit Nabala to the north, IDF intelligence and Operation Dani OC General Yigal Allon believed at the start of the offensive that they faced a far stronger Legion force and one whose deployment was potentially aggressive, posing a standing threat to Tel Aviv itself.[14]

Allon was appointed OC Operation Dani only on 7 July, some 48 hours before battle was joined. Neither his operational orders for Operation Dani, nor the operational orders for Operation Ludar and Operation LRLR, earlier plans upon which Dani was based, dealt with the prospective fate of the civilian population of the two towns and the surrounding villages. In July 1948 the two towns had a population of roughly 50,000–70,000 together, of whom 15,000 or so were refugees from Jaffa and its environs. The inhabitants' morale was relatively robust: the two towns lay outside the Partition Plan Jewish State's territory and the presence in them of the Arab Legion troops implied a solid commitment by Abdullah to their defence. (Conversely, the withdrawal of the Legion troops over 11–13 July was to have a devastating effect on morale in the towns.) Unlike Haifa or Jaffa (where the feeling of isolation and siege had been severe), the two towns were contiguous with the heavily populated Arab hinterland of the Triangle. And there had been the month of quiet during the First Truce (11 June – 9 July). "The civilian population has not left the cities, and they do not believe that we will succeed in conquering the two towns because they are well-fortified," an IDF intelligence officer concluded on 28 June.[15]

But there were serious demoralising factors. There had been two (unsuccessful) Jewish – mainly IZL – ground attacks on Ramle on the nights of 21–22 May and 24–25 May. The Haganah air arm had bombed Lydda on 25 May, flattening one house, killing three and wounding eight. Taken together, these attacks had certainly reminded the two towns' inhabitants that they were targeted. The presence in the towns over weeks and months of the thousands of refugees from areas already conquered by the Jewish forces must certainly have had a destabilising effect on the locals. The refugees were hungry and desperately short of money; braving possible IDF fire, they made foraging raids into the fields in no-man's land "to gather the stalks of wheat and vegetables." Moreover, the two towns had suffered from major unemployment since the start of the hostilities (many townspeople had been employed in Jewish settlements) and from occasional food shortages, which in turn had triggered sharp price increases. Some wealthy families had fled to the Triangle or Transjordan in the previous months.[16]

Operation Dani, which involved three to four IDF brigades and began on the night of 9–10 July, was swiftly to demoralise the inhabitants of Ramle and Lydda, and within days to result in the almost complete exodus of their inhabitants to Arab-held territory.

From the start, the operations against the two towns were designed to induce civilian panic and flight – as a means of precipitating military collapse and possibly also as an end itself. After the initial air attacks on the towns, Operation Dani headquarters at 11:30 hours on 10 July informed the General Staff: there was a "a general and considerable [civilian] flight from Ramle. There is great value in continuing the bombing." During the afternoon, the headquarters asked the General Staff for renewed bombing, and informed one of the brigades: "Flight from the town of Ramle of women, the old and children is to be facilitated. The [military age] males are to be detained."[17]

The bombings and shellings of 10 July were successful. The following day Yiftah Brigade's intelligence officer reported: "The bombing from the air and artillery [shelling] of Lydda and Ramle caused flight and panic among the civilians [and] a readiness to surrender." Operation Dani headquarters that day repeatedly asked for further bombings, "including [with] incendiaries."[18] Civilian morale (and the military will to resist) was further dented by the raid on 11 July of the 89th armoured Battalion (commanded by Lt Colonel Moshe Dayan) on Lydda and along the Lydda–Ramle road.

How many civilians fled Lydda and Ramle over 10–11 July, before the towns' capture, is unclear. But the flight gained momentum during the night of 11–12 July after the withdrawal from Ramle of the Arab Legion company based there. During the night, some of Ramle's fleeing notables were detained at an IDF checkpoint near Al Barriya. They were brought to Yiftah Brigade's headquarters at Kibbutz Na'an, where in the early hours of 12 July they signed a formal instrument of surrender, which went into force in Ramle at 10:00 hours. The instrument guaranteed the lives and safety of the inhabitants, the right to leave the town of persons of non-military age and the hand-over to the IDF of arms and non-local irregulars.[19] The Kiryati Brigade's 42nd Battalion entered the town during the morning and a curfew was imposed.

In Lydda, where no formal surrender instrument was signed, events proceeded differently. Elements of the Yiftah Brigade's 3rd Battalion entered the town on the evening of 11 July. Supported by a company from the brigade's 1st Battalion, the 3rd Battalion the following morning fanned out around the centre of the town. A small force of Arab Legionnaires and irregulars continued to hold out at the police fort. A curfew was imposed and the IDF began rounding up able-bodied males and placing them in temporary detention/identification centres in mosques and churches.

The calm in Lydda was shattered at 11:30 hours on 12 July when two or three Arab Legion armoured cars, either lost or on reconnaissance, entered the town. During the 30-minute firefight which ensued, apparently two 3rd Battalion soldiers were killed and twelve wounded. The scout cars withdrew, but the noise of the skirmish sparked sniping by armed Lydda townspeople against the occupying Israeli troops. Some of the townspeople probably believed that the Legion was counter-attacking and wished to assist it.

The 300–400 Israeli troops in the town, dispersed in semi-isolated pockets in the midst of tens of thousands of hostile townspeople, some still armed, felt threatened, vulnerable and angry: they believed that the town had surrendered. 3rd Battalion OC Moshe Kelman immediately ordered his troops to suppress the sniping – which Israeli historians and chroniclers were later to describe as an "uprising" – with the utmost severity. The troops were ordered to shoot at "any clear target" or, alternatively, at anyone "seen on the streets."[20]

Some townspeople, shut up in their houses under curfew, took fright at the sounds of shooting outside, perhaps believing that a massacre was in progress. They rushed into the streets – and were cut down by Israeli fire. Some of the soldiers also fired and lobbed grenades into houses from which snipers were suspected to be operating. In the confusion, dozens of unarmed detainees in the mosque and church compounds in the centre of the town were shot and killed. Perhaps some of these had attempted to escape, also fearing a massacre.[21]

By 14:00 hours it was all over. Yeruham Cohen, an intelligence officer at Operation Dani headquarters, later described the scene: "The inhabitants of the town became panic-stricken. They feared that . . . the IDF troops would take revenge on them. It was a horrible, earsplitting scene. Women wailed at the top of their voices and old men said prayers, as if they saw their own deaths before their eyes."[22]

The fire of the Yiftah Brigade's troops caused "some 250 dead . . . and many wounded."[23] Yiftah Brigade's casualties in the skirmish with the armoured cars and from the sniping in the town were between two and four dead and about a dozen wounded. The ratio of Arab to Israeli casualties was hardly consistent with the later Israeli (and Arab) descriptions of what had happened as an "uprising." In any event, the Israeli officers in charge were later to regard the suppression of the "uprising" (and the subsequent expulsion of the townspeople) as a dismal episode in Yiftah Brigade's history. 3rd Battalion was withdrawn from the line on the night of 13–14 July and spent 14 July in a collective "soul-searching assembly" in the near-by Ben-Shemen wood. "There is no doubt that the Lydda–Ramle affair and the flight of the inhabitants, the uprising and the expulsion [*geirush*] that followed cut deep grooves in all who underwent [these experiences]," Yiftah Brigade OC Mula Cohen was later to write.[24]

While some IDF officers began advising people in Lydda to leave the town during the morning of 12 July, before the shooting,[25] the mass exodus of the inhabitants of Ramle and Lydda, which began a few hours later, must be seen against the backdrop of that slaughter. The shooting in the centre of Lydda seems to have sealed the fate of the inhabitants of the two towns. The sniping had scared the 3rd Battalion; it had also apparently shaken Operation Dani headquarters, where, until then, it was believed that the two towns had been subdued and were securely in IDF hands. The unexpected outbreak of shooting highlighted the simultaneous threat of a Transjordanian counter-attack coupled with a mass uprising by a large Arab population behind Israeli lines, as Allon's brigades continued their push eastwards, towards the operation's second-stage objectives, Latrun and Ramallah.

The shooting focused minds at Operation Dani headquarters at Yazur. A strong desire to see the population of the two towns flee already existed: the shooting seemed to offer the justification and opportunity for what the bombings and artillery barrages, insubstantial by World War II standards, had in the main failed to achieve.

Ben-Gurion spent the early afternoon of 12 July at Yazur. According to the best account of the meeting, at which Generals Yadin, Ayalon and Allon, Israel Galilee and Lt Colonel Yitzhak Rabin (Chief of Operations Operation Dani) were present, someone, possibly Allon, after hearing of the start of the shooting in Lydda, proposed expelling the inhabitants of the two towns. Ben-Gurion said nothing, and no decision was taken. Then Ben-Gurion, Allon and Rabin left the room. Allon asked: "What shall we do with the Arabs?" Ben-Gurion made a dismissive, energetic gesture with his hand and said: "Expel them [*garesh otam*]."[26]

At 13:30 hours, 12 July, before the shooting had completely died down in Lydda, Operation Dani headquarters issued the following order to Yiftah Brigade headquarters: "1. The inhabitants of Lydda must be expelled quickly without attention to age. They should be directed towards Beit Nabala. Yiftah [Brigade headquarters] must determine the method and inform [Operation] Dani HQ and 8th Brigade HQ. 2. Implement immediately." The order was signed "Yitzhak R[abin]."[27] A similar order, concerning Ramle, was apparently communicated to Kiryati Brigade headquarters at the same time.

During the afternoon of 12 July Kiryati Brigade officers began organising transport to ferry Ramle's inhabitants towards Arab Legion lines. Local, confiscated Arab transport and the brigade's own vehicles proved insufficient. During the night of 12–13 July, Kiryati Brigade OC Michael Ben-Gal asked General Staff/Operations for more vehicles.[28] During the afternoon and evening of 12 July, thousands of Ramle's inhabitants streamed out of the town, on foot or in trucks and buses. In Lydda, with the troops recovering from the afternoon's shooting and burying the corpses, and the inhabitants under curfew shut away in their houses, the expulsion order was not immediately implemented. During the night of 12–13 July, two companies from Kiryati Brigade's 42nd Battalion arrived in Lydda to reinforce the 3rd Battalion.

Shitrit arrived in Ramle in the afternoon of 12 July – and almost halted the exodus in both towns before it was well under way. The Cabinet knew nothing of the expulsion orders. Shitrit, as was his wont, had come to look over his new "constituency"; he was responsible for the welfare of the

Arab minority. He was shocked by what he heard and saw; Kiryati's troops were in the midst of preparations to expel the inhabitants. Brigade commander Ben-Gal told him that "in line with an order from . . . Paicovitch [i.e., Allon] the IDF was about to take prisoner all males of military age, and the rest of the inhabitants – men, women and children – were to be taken beyond [*sic*] the border and left to their fate." The army "intends to deal in the same way" with the inhabitants of Lydda, Shitrit reported.[29] Upset and angry, Shitrit returned to Tel Aviv and that evening went to see Foreign Minister Shertok, reporting on what he had seen and heard. Later that night, Shertok went to see Ben-Gurion and the two men hammered out a set of policy guidelines for IDF behaviour towards the civilian population of Lydda and Ramle. Ben-Gurion apparently did not inform Shertok (or Shitrit) that he had been the source of the original expulsion orders.

The guidelines agreed between the two senior ministers, according to Shertok's letter to Shitrit of 13 July, were: "1. It should be publicly announced in the two towns that whoever wants to leave – will be allowed to do so. 2. A warning must be issued that anyone remaining behind does so on his own responsibility, and the Israeli authorities are not obliged to supply him with food. 3. Women, children, the old and the sick must on no account be forced to leave [the] town[s]. 4. The monasteries and churches must not be damaged." Shertok's letter ended with a caveat: "We all know how difficult it is to overcome [base] instincts during conquest. But I hope the aforementioned policy will be proof against malfunctions."[30]

These guidelines were passed on by Ben-Gurion to IDF General Staff/ Operations, which duly transmitted them to Operation Dani head-quarters at 23:30 hours, 12 July, in somewhat abridged form: "1) All are free to leave, apart from those who will be detained. 2) To warn that we are not responsible for feeding those who remain. 3) Not to force women, the sick, children and the old to go/walk [*lalechet* – an ambiguity, possibly deliberate, which left Operation Dani headquarters free to bus or truck out these categories of the populace]. 4) Not to touch monasteries and churches. 5) Searches without vandalism. 6) No robbery."[31]

Shitrit came away from his talk with Shertok on the night of 12 July and from his reading of Shertok's letter of 13 July believing that he had averted a wholesale expulsion from the two towns. He was wrong. The Arabs were being ordered and "encouraged" to leave. At the same time, by 13 July, the inhabitants – especially of Lydda – probably needed little such "encouragement." Within a 72-hour period, they had undergone the shock of battle and unexpected conquest by the Jews, abandonment by the Arab Legion, a slaughter (in Lydda), a continuous curfew with house-to-house searches, a round-up of able-bodied males and the separation of families, lack of food and medical attention, the flight of relatives, continuous isolation in their houses and general dread of the future. News of what had happened in Lydda in the afternoon of 12 July probably reached Ramle, three kilometres away, almost immediately, triggering fright. During the night of 12–13 July, most of the remaining inhabitants of the two towns probably decided that it would be best to leave and not to continue living under Jewish rule. The fall of the Lydda police fort on the moring of 13 July, may, for some, have clinched the issue.

Thus, at this point, there was dovetailing, as it were, of Jewish and Arab interests and wishes – an IDF bent on expelling the population and a population ready, perhaps even eager, to move to Arab-held territory. There remained, however, one problem: the detained able-bodied Ramle and Lydda menfolk, whom their parents, women and children were loth to abandon. The stage was set for the "deal" struck on the morning of 13 July and for the mass evacuation of the two towns that followed.

The "deal" was apparently struck that morning in "negotiations" between IDF intelligence officer Shmarya Guttman and other Palmah officers and some of the Lydda notables. The IDF said they wanted everyone to leave. The Arab notables said there could be no exodus so long as thousands of townspeople (many of them heads of families) were incarcerated in the detention centres. The officers agreed that the detainees would be freed and would leave the town with the rest of the population. Guttman then proceeded to the mosque, where his announcement that the detainees could leave was greeted with cries of joy. Town criers and IDF soldiers then went about the town telling the inhabitants they were leaving and where to muster.[32]

The bulk and end of the exodus from Ramle and Lydda took place on 13 July. Many of the inhabitants of Ramle were trucked and bussed out by Kiryati troops to Al Qubab, from where they made their way on foot to Arab Legion lines in Latrun and Salbit. Others walked all the way. All Lydda's inhabitants walked, making their way to Beit Nabala and Barfiliya.

To judge from the IDF signals traffic of 13 July, the commanders involved understood that the operation was an expulsion rather than a spontaneous exodus. Operation Dani headquarters informed General Staff/Operations around noon: "Lydda police fort has been captured. [The troops] are busy expelling the inhabitants [*oskim begeirush hatoshavim*]." At the same time, the headquarters informed Yiftah, Kiryati and 8th brigades that "enemy resistance in Ramle and Lydda has ended. The eviction/evacuation [*pinui*] of the inhabitants . . . has begun."[33] Operation Dani headquarters apparently expected the removal of Lydda's inhabitants to have been completed by the evening. At 18:15

hours, the headquarters asked Yiftah Brigade: "Has the removal of the population [*hotza'at ha'ochlosiah*] of Lydda been completed?"[34]

Through 12–14 July, some Yiftah and Kiryati soldiers remained unaware of the expulsion orders and believed that they were witnessing a spontaneous or semi-spontaneous exodus. The eagerness of some of the population in both towns to get out supported this. Moreover, IDF announcements to the populations were informative and instructive rather than imperative in tone: "You will assemble at such and such points," "you will walk towards Beit Nabala," and so on. Indeed, most of the soldiers involved probably had no need to say anything; the inhabitants understood what was expected of them. In Lydda, however, some Arab families were ordered to "get out" by soldiers who went from house to house.

All the Israelis who witnessed the events agreed that the exodus, under a hot July sun, was an extended episode of suffering for the refugees, especially from Lydda. Some were stripped by soldiers of their valuables as they left town or at checkpoints along the way.[35] Guttman subsequently described the trek of the Lydda refugees: "A multitude of inhabitants walked one after another. Women walked burdened with packages and sacks on their heads. Mothers dragged children after them . . . Occasionally, warning shots were heard . . . Occasionally, you encountered a piercing look from one of the youngsters . . . in the column, and the look said: 'We have not yet surrendered. We shall return to fight you.'" For Guttman, an archaeologist, the spectacle conjured up "the memory of the exile of Israel [at the end of the Second Commonwealth, at Roman hands]."[36]

One Israeli soldier (probably 3rd Battalion), from Kibbutz Ein Harod, a few weeks after the event recorded vivid impressions of the thirst and hunger of the refugees on the roads, and of how "children got lost" and of how a child fell into a well and drowned, ignored, as his fellow refugees fought each other to draw water.[37] Another soldier described the spoor left by the slow-shuffling columns, "to begin with [jettisoning] utensils and furniture and in the end, bodies of men, women and children, scattered along the way." Quite a few refugees died – from exhaustion, dehydration and disease – along the roads eastward, from Lydda and Ramle, before reaching temporary rest near and in Ramallah. Nimr al Khatib put the death toll among the Lydda refugees during the trek eastward at 335; Arab Legion commander John Glubb Pasha, more carefully wrote that "nobody will ever know how many children died."[38]

The creation of the refugee columns, which for days cluttered the roads eastwards, may have been one of the motives for the expulsion decision of 12 July by Ben-Gurion, Allon and Rabin. The military thinking was simple and cogent: the IDF had just taken its two primary objectives and had, for the moment, run out of offensive steam. The Arab Legion was expected to counter-attack (through Budrus, Jimzu, Nil'in and Latrun). Cluttering the main axes, deep into Transjordanian-held territory, with refugees would severely hamper such a counter-attack. And, inevitably, the large, new wave of refugees would sap Transjordanian resources at a crucial moment. A Palmah report, probably written by Allon soon after Operation Dani, stated that the exodus of the Lydda and Ramle inhabitants, beside relieving Tel Aviv of a potential, long-term threat, had "clogged the routes of advance of the Legion" and had foisted upon the Arab economy the problem of "maintaining another 45,000 souls . . . Moreover, the phenomenon of the flight of tens of thousands will no doubt cause demoralisation in every Arab area [the refugees] reach . . . This victory will yet have great effect on other sectors."[39]

Ben-Gurion, in his wonted oblique manner, had also referred to the strategic benefits that had sprung from setting loose the inhabitants of Lydda and Ramle on the roads east. "The Arab Legion cables that on the road from Lydda and Ramle some 30,000 refugees are on the move, who are angry with the Legion [because the Legion had lost the two towns]. They demand bread. They must be transferred to Transjordan. In Transjordan there are anti-government demonstrations," he recorded in his diary on 15 July.[40]

In the debate in Mapam on policy towards the Arabs in the following weeks and months, some criticism focused on Allon's use of tens of thousands of refugees to achieve strategic aims. Party co-leader, Meir Ya'ari, said: "Many of us are losing their [human] image . . . How easily they speak of how it is possible and permissible to take women, children and old men and to fill the roads with them because such is the imperative of strategy. And this we say, the members of Hashomer Hatzair, who remember who used this means against our people during the [Second World] war . . . I am appalled."[41]

After the dust of battle and flight settled, about 1,000 inhabitants remained in the two towns together, their number growing to some 2,000 by the beginning of 1949. Meanwhile, Lydda and Ramle were settled with new Jewish immigrants and became mainly Jewish towns.

Meanwhile, to the east, as part of Operation Dani, the Palmah's Harel Brigade and elements of the Jerusalem-based Etzioni Brigade launched a number of local attacks aimed at expanding the Jewish-held corridor to Jerusalem and at relieving the direct pressure on the city's western and southern neighbourhoods.

In the Jerusalem sector, Etzioni Brigade units on 15 July captured part of the village of Beit Safafa, which was abandoned (temporarily) by most of its inhabitants. Further to the east, on 14–15 July IZL and LHI units took the already semi-abandoned village of Al Maliha, held by irregulars. The large village of 'Ein Karim, some of whose population had fled in April following the attack on Deir Yassin two kilometres to the north, was completely abandoned on 11 July after Jewish forces captured the two dominating hilltops of Khirbet Beit Mazmil and Khirbet al Hamama and shelled the village.

Further to the east, Harel Brigade units expanded the corridor southwards, on 13–14 July taking the chain of small villages of Suba, Sataf, Khirbet al Lauz, Khirbet Deir 'Amr and 'Aqqur, and Sar'a (held by the Egyptians), and on 17–18 July taking Kasla, Ishwa, 'Islin, Deir Rafat and Artuf. Much of the population of these villages, which had been on the front line since April, had left the area previously. Most of the remaining population fled with the approach of the Harel columns and with the start of the mortar barrages. The handful of people who remained at each site when the Israelis entered were expelled.[42]

The south

During the "Ten Days," the IDF invested its main energies in the north and centre of the country. In the south, the Negev and Givati brigades tried – and failed – to establish a secure corridor between the isolated Negev Jewish settlements enclave and the Jewish-held areas of the Coastal Plain. But Givati succeeded in substantially expanding its area of control southwards and eastwards, conquering areas in the northern Negev approaches and in the western Hebron district foothills.

Givati Brigade OC Shimon Avidan clearly intended to precipitate the flight of the Arab population of the area, bounded by Qazaza, Jilya, Idhnibba and Mughallis in the east, Masmiya al Kabir and Qastina in the west, and Hatta and Beit 'Affa in the south. The Brigade headquarters on 5 July discussed and outlined its plans for the "Ten Days" and on 7 July Avidan issued operational instructions to his battalions. The 1st Battalion was ordered to take the Tall as Safi area and "to expel the refugees encamped in the area, in order to prevent enemy infiltration from the east to this important position." The nature of the written order and, presumably, the accompanying oral explanations, probably left little doubt in the battalion OC's mind that Avidan wanted the area completely cleared of inhabitants.

The area was overrun over 8–11 July, with most of the Arab population – estimated by the IDF at "more than 20,000" – fleeing before the Israeli columns reached each village. The IDF assessment was that the capture of Tall as Safi vitally undermined the morale of the inhabitants of the surrounding villages who, after its fall, felt cut off from the Egyptian and irregular Arab forces to the east and the south. The second stage of the Givati push, on 14–15 July, in which parts of Beit 'Affa, Hatta and Juseir fell under IDF control, further isolated the Tall as Safi-Masmiya al Kabir area to the north.

The Givati operations during the "Ten Days" precipitated the evacuation of the villages of Masmiya al Kabir, Masmiya as Saghira, At Tina, Al Kheima, Idhnibba, Mughallis, Jilya, Qazaza, Sajad, Tall at Turmus, Jaladiya, Summeil, Zeita, Bi'lin, Barqusiya and Tall as Safi, and a number of smaller villages and bedouin encampments. Most of the villagers fled to the Hebron Hills, with a small minority from the Masmiya area passing through Israeli-held territory to the Gaza Strip.[43]

Operations during the Second Truce, July–October 1948

During the three months between the start of the Second Truce on 18 July and the renewal of hostilities on 15 October, the IDF carried out a number of operations designed to clear its rear and front line areas of actively or potentially hostile concentrations of Arab population.

The major such operation during the Second Truce was the attack by units of the Alexandroni, Carmeli and Golani brigades on 24–26 July on the area then known as "the Little Triangle," comprising the three large villages of Jaba, Ijzim and 'Ein Ghazal, about 20 kilometres south of Haifa. The villages, which Israel believed hosted hostile irregular forces, overlooked the main Tel Aviv–Haifa coast road and by sniping had effectively blocked Jewish traffic on the road since the start of the war.

On 18 July, two Jewish car passengers were killed near Jaba. The inhabitants of the three villages were then warned by Israel to surrender or evacuate. They rejected both alternatives, apparently because of pressure by non-local irregulars. On 18–19 July, an initial IDF attack on the villages was repulsed. During the following days, the villages were intermittently shelled and bombed. Most of their inhabitants fled in the weeks and days before the final attack (called *mivtza shoter* (Operation Policeman), which began on 24 July. A major aerial and artillery onslaught on the three villages was carried out on the following day. (Foreign Minister Shertok lied to the United Nations Mediator when he wrote, on 28 September 1948, that "no planes were used" in the attack.) Small units of the Golani, Carmeli and Alexandroni brigades moved in and captured the three villages on 26 July, with almost all the remaining inhabitants being forced to leave or spontaneously fleeing eastwards, through Khirbet Qumbaza towards Wadi 'Ara, Jenin and the Druse villages on Mount Carmel, over 25–26 July. According to the accounts of several of the inhabitants, the fleeing refugees were repeatedly fired upon by Israeli soldiers and aircraft.[44]

Several dozen villagers, militiamen and resident refugees were killed in the successive attacks on the villages. The Secretary General of the Arab League, Azzam Pasha, complained to Count Bernadotte that the Israeli troops had committed atrocities during and after the attack, alleging that in one incident 28 persons were burned alive. Israel denied the allegations. The mass burning story, Israel said, may have originated in the burning of 25–30 bodies "in an advanced state of decomposition" found on or about 25 July near 'Ein Ghazal by the Israeli troops. For lack of timber, explained Walter Eytan, the bodies were only partially consumed, and captured villagers were assigned to bury them. Eytan did not explain where these 25–30 bodies had come from or how they had died; Azzam Pasha had alleged that most of the 28 "burned alive" had been refugees from At Tira (the large village south of Haifa, which fell to the IDF on 16 July, most of its inhabitants being expelled to the Jenin–Nablus–Tulkarm triangle or incarcerated in POW camps). On 28 July a United Nations observer visited the "Little Triangle" and, according to Count Bernadotte, found "no evidence to support claims of massacre."[45]

However, a United Nations investigation in August , based largely on interviews with refugees from the three villages encamped in the Jenin area, concluded that Israel's assault on the villages was "unjustified . . . especially in view of the offer of the Arab villagers to negotiate and the apparent Israeli failure fully to explore this offer." Bernadotte condemned Israel's subsequent "systematic" destruction of 'Ein Ghazal and Jaba and demanded that the inhabitants of all three villages be allowed to return, with Israel restoring their damaged or demolished houses. The United Nations investigators concluded that "with the completion of the attack . . . all the inhabitants of the three villages were forced to evacuate." The investigators found no evidence that the villagers, in the days before the IDF assault, had violated the Second Truce. The assault had been a violation of the truce.[46]

The Israeli Government was unhappy with the United Nations findings and recommendations. Shertok denied that the villagers had been expelled, stating that "when the action commenced on the 24th July, only few of the normal inhabitants were still in the villages." He rejected the Mediator's demand that the villagers be allowed to return. Acting United Nations Mediator Ralph Bunche replied that the inhabitants had been "forced to evacuate" and two of the villages had been "systematically destroyed."[47]

Elsewhere during the following months, the IDF mounted a number of "clearing" operations designed to rid areas behind or along the front lines of hostile or potentially hostile Arab communities. In the coastal area west of Yibna, the Givati Brigade mounted Operation Cleansing (*Mivtza Nikayon*) during 24–28 August. The 5th Battalion and the brigade's cavalry troop were sent to clear the area bounded by Yibna, An Nabi Rubin and Khirbet Sukreir, the camping grounds of the bedouin tribe of 'Arab Sukreir and the temporary resting place of refugees from Yibna, Al Qubeiba and Zarnuqa. The unit were ordered to destroy any armed force "and to expel all unarmed [persons] from [the area]." However, the units found few Arabs. A Givati intelligence officer explained, on 29 August, that the Arabs had already left as the harvest of their sorghum crop had ended. The units blew up stone houses and burned huts, and "ten Arabs who tried to escape were killed."[48]

Meanwhile, in the Negev, inside and on the peripheries of the Jewish settlements' enclave, the Negev Brigade during the Second Truce continued harassing the local Arab inhabitants and bedouin tribes. On 16 August the brigade carried out a full-scale clearing operation in the Kaufakha–Al Muharraqa area. "The villages' inhabitants and [bedouin] concentrations in the area were dispersed and expelled. A number of houses were blown up. Al Muharraqa and the houses of Sheikh Ukbi . . . were mined."[49]

Similar operations were conducted during the following months. At the end of September and in the first days of October, two clearing operations were launched by the Yiftah Brigade's 3rd Battalion and a unit of the 1st Battalion in the area between Kibbutz Tze'elim (south), Mishmar Hanegev (east) and Al 'Imara (north). The operations were mounted, according to Yiftah Brigade's Operations headquarters, because "enemy civilians . . . [in the area] had begun a partisan operation blowing up the water pipeline, mining the roads and hitting our people." "All the Arabs were expelled," their livestock was confiscated ("lest it fall into the enemy army's hands") and their wells blown up.[50]

The IDF's clearing operations in the Negev before the end of the Second Truce were criticised both by the Foreign Ministry and by some of the heads of local Jewish settlements. Shimoni described them as "contrary to the instructions of the Foreign Minister," who, for political reasons, was urging Israeli utilisation of the Negev bedouin. A few weeks earlier, the *mukhtar*s of the kibbutzim Dorot, Nir-Am and Ruhama had complained to Ben-Gurion that the army had "destroyed houses, robbed sheep, cattle and horses, and burned fields" belonging to local bedouins who had "throughout maintained a benign neutrality and helped us actively in our war by supplying [us with] information."[51]

While in general this pattern during the Second Truce of clearing rural Arabs out of rear areas along strategic routes or near the front lines in the south and centre of the country prevailed, exceptions were made of a handful of communities, such as Abu Ghosh, west of Jerusalem, and Al Fureidis and 'Arab al Ghawarina (Khirbet Jisr az Zarqa) in the Coastal Plain. In the north, while some bedouins (such as the 'Arab al Heib) were moved into the interior, Arab communities near or not far to the rear of the front lines generally were not moved or expelled during the Second Truce.

Altogether, the Israeli offensives of the "Ten Days" and the subsequent clearing operations probably sent something over 100,000 more Arabs into exile in Transjordanian-held eastern Palestine, the Gaza Strip, Lebanon and the Upper Galilee pocket held by Qawuqji's ALA.

Chapter 7

The fourth wave: the battles and exodus of October–November 1948

Bernadotte's report of 16 September, proposing the award of the Negev to the Arabs in exchange for Jewish sovereignty over Western Galilee, compelled the Israeli political and military leadership to focus attention on the south, where a surrounded, poorly supplied enclave of less than two dozen Jewish settlements was cut off from the rest of the Yishuv by Egyptian forces holding the Al Majdal–Faluja–Beit Jibrin–Hebron axis. Contrary to the truce terms, the Egyptians refused to allow Israeli supply of the enclave by land. The threat of an award of the Negev to the Arabs, the untenable geo-military situation and the plight of the besieged settlements made the breakdown of the truce, in the absence of a political settlement, inevitable. In late September, the Cabinet approved an Israeli offensive to link up with the Negev enclave and to rout the Egyptian army. The IDF deployed three-and-a-half brigades and, on 15 October, a supplies' convoy was sent in. The Egyptians, as expected, opened fire, providing a *casus belli*. The IDF launched Operation Ten Plagues, later renamed Operation Yoav, which lasted, with its appendages, until 9 November. During the three weeks of fighting, the IDF overran the southern Coastal strip, including the Arab towns of Isdud, Hamama and Al Majdal; Beersheba; Beit Jibrin, in the Hebron foothills; 'Ajjur, in the Judean Hills; and several dozen smaller villages, including Beit Tima, Kaukaba, Barbara, Hirbiya, Al Qubeiba and Ad Dawayima, between the Mediterranean and Hebron. The IDF conquests precipitated the exodus of tens of thousands of new and old refugees to the Gaza Strip and the Hebron Hills.

In a simultaneous, complementary attack, the Harel and Etzioni Brigades (Operations "Yekev" and "Ha'har", 19–22 October) captured from the Egyptians a string of Judean Hills' villages – Beit Nattif, Zakariya, Deiraban, Beit Jimal, etc. – in the southern half of the Jerusalem corridor. Thousands of local inhabitants fled to the Hebron Hills.

In the north, Qawuqji's ALA similarly provoked the Israeli conquest of the remainder of the Galilee when its units, on 22 October, stormed the Sheikh 'Abbad hilltop position, overlooking Kibbutz Manara, and opened fire on Israeli traffic. Four Israeli brigades, with auxiliary units, responded on 29 October, and within sixty hours, in Operation Hiram, conquered the Upper Galilee pocket bounded by the villages of Yanuh and Majd al Kurum in the west, Eilabun, Deir Hanna and Sakhnin in the south, Farradiya, Qaddita, Alma and Al Malikiya in the east, and the Lebanese border to the north. The pocket, according to Israeli estimates, contained about 50,000–60,000 Arabs, both local inhabitants and refugees from other areas.[1] Tens of thousands of villagers fled, mostly to Lebanon, during the offensive and its immediate aftermath.

Just after the start of the fighting in the south, and before the offensive in the Galilee, Ya'acov Riftin, Political co-Secretary of Mapam, asked Ben-Gurion what would be the fate of the Arab civilian population should the IDF overrun populated areas. "I was told that strict orders had been issued not to cause 'unhappy punctures' and that preparations had been made for [setting up] local administration[s]," Riftin related.[2] Ben-Gurion's answer had been vague and misleading. On 26 September he had told the Cabinet that, should the fighting be renewed in the north, the Galilee would become "clean" (*naki*) and "empty" (*reik*) of Arabs, and had implied that he had been assured of this by his generals. The Prime Minister had been responding to a statement/question by Shertok, who had implied that it were better that Israel should not take over the Galilee pocket as it was "filled with Arabs," including refugees from Western and Eastern Galilee bent on returning to their villages. On 21 October, when Ezra Danin discussed with Ben-Gurion the Foreign Ministry Arabists' project of setting up an Arab puppet state in the Triangle, Ben-Gurion had impatiently declared: "The Arabs of the Land of Israel [i.e., Palestine] have only one function left to them – to run away."[3] Ten days later, on a tour of the Galilee accompanied by General Carmel, Ben-Gurion described the Arab exodus from the area and commented (in his diary): "and many more still will flee." It was an assessment – and, perhaps, hope – shared also by Carmel.[4] It was also an attitude shared at the time by many key figures in the Israeli military and civil bureaucracies. Shimoni, of the Foreign Ministry, for example, that month informed a Tel Aviv travel agency that "we view favourably the migration of Arabs out of the country, and we would recommend assisting them to make it as easy for them as possible." Weitz, on hearing from Moshe Berger of the start of Operation Hiram on 29 October, wrote a note to General Yadin urging that the army expel the refugees from the newly-conquered areas.[5]

This attitude was not converted into or embodied in formal policy. Neither before, during nor immediately after Operations Yoav and Hiram did the Cabinet or any of its committees decide or instruct the IDF to drive out the Arab population from the areas it was about to conquer or had conquered. Nor, as far as the evidence shows, did the heads of the defence establishment – Ben-Gurion, IDF Chief of Staff Ya'acov Dori or Yadin – issue any general orders to the advancing brigades to expel or otherwise harm the civilian populations in their path. Nor, as far as can be ascertained, did any general orders issue from the headquarters of the two operations or from the headquarters of the six or seven brigades involved to their battalions and companies to this purpose. However, there were specific orders by the General Staff or the operations' headquarters or brigade-level commands, to expel this or that community for particular, local reasons during the fighting and in its immediate aftermath. Moreover, most IDF soldiers and officers at this stage in the war were happy – for military and political reasons – to see Arab civilians along their path of advance take flight. Arab flight vastly simplified things. IDF behaviour towards overrun Arab communities was largely governed by the political outlook and character of local commanders, the "collective outlook" of the units involved, circumstances of topography and battle, routes of advance and the religion and political or military affiliations of the Arab communities involved.

The south

Commanding Operation Yoav was OC Southern Front, Yigal Allon, who in all his previous campaigns had left no Arab civilian communities in his wake: so it had been in Operation Yiftah in the spring, so it had been in Operation Dani in July. He issued no formal, written orders at the start of, or during, Operation Yoav to drive out the Arab communities encountered, but it is quite possible that he indicated his wishes in pre-battle tête-à-têtes with his officers. And, perhaps, even without the OC saying anything, Allon's officers knew what he wanted.

The Arab population of the areas conquered in Operation Yoav was nervous and largely demoralised before the battle began. It was overwhelmingly Muslim. Towns like Isdud, Al Majdal and Hamama contained fairly large refugee populations who had fled from areas to the north in the spring and summer. They had been living under rather unfriendly Egyptian military rule since May. The Egyptians were often heavy-handed and were regarded by many locals as foreigner occupiers; they were perennially short of supplies and not generous with them with the locals, whose fields, in many cases, had been ravaged or rendered inaccessible by the hostilities. The local inhabitants, moveover, understood through the Second Truce that the stalemate would soon be broken, that they would be on the firing line, between hammer and anvil, and that the Egyptian army was weak. They feared the flail of renewed war and feared the Jews.

The IDF of October–November 1948 was radically different from the Israeli army of even three months before. It had – and deployed with telling effect – bombers and fighter bombers, battalions of field artillery and mortars, and tanks (in small numbers). Operation Yoav began on 15–16 October, with bombing and strafing attacks, on Beersheba, Gaza, Al Majdal, Hamama, Barbara, Isdud, Beit Hanun, Dimra, Hirbiya, Al Jura, Deir Suneid, Faluja and Beit Jibrin. While by World War II standards these attacks were minor and not particularly accurate, most of the affected communities had never experienced air attack and were not "built for it," either psychologically or in terms of shelters and ground defences. Artillery was also used far more extensively than in any previous IDF offensive, though mostly directed at Egyptian and Arab militia positions.

The aerial and artillery bombardment and the ground attacks of 15–20 October in the central area, where the IDF broke through the strong Egyptian defences and linked up with the besieged Negev enclave, caused "thousands of Arab refugees to flee from Iraq al Manshiya, Faluja and Beit Tima," according to Southern Front's operational logbook. There had also been flight from Huleiqat and Kaukaba, and from some of the coastal communities, especially Beit Hanun. There had been no expulsions; the locals had simply fled in face of the approaching hostilities.

The flight from the coastal communities increased following the Israeli navy's shelling of Gaza (on 17 October) and of Al Majdal (21 October), which were accompanied by a new wave of air attacks. It was another "first" for the local inhabitants, over whom "passed a wave of fear," according to IDF intelligence. Hundreds were reportedly hit in Gaza, near the train station. The naval and air attacks precipitated demonstrations in Al Majdal (and possibly elsewhere) of "the inhabitants against the [Egyptian] army" for its inability to defend them. There was flight from the northern end of the Egyptian-held coastal area (Isdud, Al Majdal, Al Jura, Hamama) towards Gaza and flight from Beit Hanun and Gaza to the dunes and orange-groves around the towns.

In the second wave of advances, over 19–24 October, the Harel Brigade captured Deiraban, Beit 'Itab, Sufla, Beit Jimal, Beit Nattif, Zakariya, Al Walaja and Bureij. Most of the population fled southwards, towards Bethlehem and the Hebron hills. At Beit Nattif – "the village of the murderers of the 35 [members of the Palmah relief column sent to the Etzion Bloc in January 1948], the attackers of the Etzion Bloc and the destroyers of [the] Jewish [village of] Har-Tuv" – the inhabitants "fled for their lives," as one Palmah report put it. A Palmah account, by a woman soldier, "Aviva R.," of a patrol in the Hebron Hills, near Al Jaba, in the wake of the Harel Brigade offensive, illustrates the immediate fate and condition of the refugees from these hilltop villages.

Scattered in the gulley, sitting in craters and caves . . . [were] dozens of refugees . . . We surprised them. A cry of fear cut through the air . . . They began to praise us and dispense compliments about the Jewish army, the State of Israel. With what obsequiousness! Old men bowing, genuflecting, kissing our feet and begging for mercy; young men standing with bowed heads and helpless . . . We tried to persuade them to flee towards Hebron. We fired several shots in the air – and the people [i.e., the refugees] were indifferent. 'Better that we die here than return [to Egyptian-held territory] to die at the hands of the Egyptians.' We fired again. No one moved. Tiredness and hunger deprived them of any will to live and of any human dignity. These are the Arabs of the Hebron Hills, and it is possible that this youngster, or that man, shed the blood of the 35 or looted the Etzion Bloc – but can one take revenge here? You can fight against people of your own worth, but against this 'human dust?' We turned back and returned [to our base] . . . That evening for the first time during the whole war I felt I was tired. My soul has grown weary of this war.[6]

The Givati Brigade, meanwhile, pushed northeastwards, conquering the villages of Kidna, Zikrin, Ra'na, Deir ad Dubban and 'Ajjur, in the Hebron and Judea foothills. Here too most of the population fled before the Israeli troops arrived in the villages, though those who remained were expelled eastwards.

On 21 October, the 8th Brigade's 89th Battalion, the (Palmah's) 7th Battalion and the Negev Brigade's 9th Battalion conquered Beersheba. Before, during and immediately after the conquest most of the town's population fled eastwards, towards the Hebron hills; a few went to Gaza. The wealthier inhabitants had left the town weeks and months before.[7]

A few days after the conquest, apparently on 25 October, the remaining population, consisting of hundreds of (mostly) women, children and the sick, were expelled to the Gaza Strip. About 100 able-bodied civilian males were left in the town to help in the clean-up and other work, before being transferred to a POW camp. According to General Avner, the women and children of Beersheba had asked to be sent to Gaza. The town was thoroughly looted by the occupying troops, much to the annoyance of Ben-Gurion and Shafrir, the Custodian of Absentees Property. On 30 October, Ben-Gurion visited the town. According to Galili, Allon asked the Prime Minister: "Why have you come?" Allon apparently added: "There are no longer minorities [i.e., Arabs] in Beersheba." Machnes, of the Minority Affairs Ministry, who accompanied the Prime Minister, then said, according to Galili: "We have come to expel the Arabs. Yigal, rely on me." But the Arabs, as Allon had pointed out, were already gone.[8]

In the third stage of Operation Yoav, during 28–29 October, the IDF captured Beit Jibrin, Al Qubeiba and Ad Dawayima in the Hebron foothills and Isdud and Hamama on the coast. These and the following days were marked by panic flight of the Arab civilian population and some expulsions.

In the east, there was panic flight from Beit Jibrin, which started after the IDF night raid of 24 October, and from Al Qubeiba. There was apparently also flight from Tarqumiya – which the IDF was expected to attack next – towards Hebron. In Hebron itself there was panic, and Abdullah issued assurances that, unlike Ramle and Lydda, he would firmly defend the town if it was attacked by the IDF. Sir Alec Kirkbride, the British minister to Transjordan, reported from Amman that the "principal" fear was that another wave of refugees, from Hebron, Bethlehem and the surrounding villages, would inundate Transjordan. Abdullah immediately sent Arab Legion units to Bethlehem and Hebron, where the Egyptian units were on the verge of collapse. Had he not done so, according to Kirkbride, "the majority of the local population . . . would have left their homes." Already, he commented, "the number of refugees . . . dependent on Transjordan is as disastrous as a military defeat." As it was, according to IDF intelligence, Hebron's rich were taking flight, lacking confidence in the Legion's ability to defend the town.[9]

Hundreds of the refugees who made their way up the hills towards Hebron were from Ad Dawayima, survivors of the massacre in the village on 29 October. Ben-Gurion, quoting General Avner, briefly referred in his war diary to the "rumours" that the army had "slaughtered 70–80 persons." What happened was described a few days later by an Israeli soldier-witness to a Mapam member, who transmitted the information to Eliezer Pra'i, the editor of the party daily *Al Hamishmar* and a member of the party's Political Committee. The party member, S. (possibly Shabtai) Kaplan, described the witness as "one of our people, an intellectual, 100 per cent reliable." The village, wrote Kaplan, had been held by Arab "irregulars" and was captured by the 89th Battalion (8th Brigade) without a fight. "The first [wave] of conquerors killed about 80 to 100 [male] Arabs, women and children. The children they killed by breaking their heads with sticks. There was not a house without dead," wrote Kaplan. Kaplan's informant, who arrived immediately afterwards in the second wave, reported that the Arab men and women who remained were then closed off in the houses "without food and water." Sappers arrived to blow up the houses. "One commander ordered a sapper to put two old women in a certain house . . . and to blow up the house with them. The sapper refused . . . The commander then ordered his men to put in the old women and the evil deed was done. One soldier boasted that he had raped a woman and then shot her. One woman, with a newborn baby in her arms, was employed to clean the courtyard where the soldiers ate. She worked a day or two. In the end they shot her and her baby." The soldier-witness, according to Kaplan, said that "cultured officers . . . had turned into base murderers and this not in the heat of battle . . . but out of a system of expulsion and destruction. The less Arabs remained – the better. This principle is the political motor for the expulsions and the atrocities."

Kaplan understood that Mapam in this respect was in a bind. The matter could not be publicised; it would harm the State and Mapam would be lambasted for it. But he demanded that the party "raise a shout" in internal debate, launch an investigation and establish disciplinary machinery in the army.[10]

Unbeknown to Kaplan, a number of parallel investigations were under way, the first being initiated by Allon himself. On 3 November, Allon cabled OC 8th Brigade, General Yitzhak Sadeh (the founder and first commander of the Palmah), to check the "rumours" that the 89th Battalion had "killed many tens of prisoners on the day of the conquest of Ad Dawayima," and to respond.[11] Meanwhile, Galili, after checking what had happened, said that the atrocity was committed by the 8th Brigade "but many there are [former members of] the LHI, Frenchmen, Moroccans, who tend to bad behaviour." Benny Marshak also blamed the LHI. Galili thought it "strange and contemptible" to blame Sadeh for what had happened.[12]

Word of the massacre, via the fugitives who reached the Hebron hills, was published by the Arab League in Paris a few days after the event – but as usual, with an element of error which made the story incredible. According to *The Times*, the raid, in which the IDF had "ruthlessly massacred Arab women, children and old people," had occurred in "Dawayma, in Upper Galilee."[13] In the Transjordanian-held areas, Arab sources claimed that "500 to 1,000" Arabs had been "lined up and killed by machinegun fire" after the capture of the village. United Nations observers reportedly confirmed the massacre but could not determine the number killed.[14] News of the massacre no doubt quickly reached the village communities in the western Hebron and Judean foothills, probably precipitating further flight.

To the west, on the Mediterranean coast, the bulk of the population of Isdud (Ashdod) fled along with the retreating Egyptian forces in advance of the Israeli conquest of the town on 28 October. Some 300 remained, and greeted the IDF with white flags. They were almost immediately expelled southwards.[15] The same day the IDF entered Hamama, which was reported "full of refugees" from Isdud and elsewhere.[16] The remaining Hamama population and the refugees in the town either fled southwards after the IDF conquest or were urged or ordered to do so by the troops.

The events in the Arab towns along the coast were summarised by the Intelligence Officer of the Yiftah Brigade on 2 November. The Israeli operations had caused "despair among the local inhabitants." The locals were certain that the Jews would win. There had been mass flight from Al Majdal towards the Gaza Strip towns. "Our air force had made a tremendous impact. It was a surprise for them to see squadrons of Jewish aircraft rule the skies." He reported that, initially, after the air raids, the townspeople of Gaza had fled the town to the dunes and beaches but had returned a few days later.[17]

Al Majdal (Ashkelon) was conquered by the IDF on 4 November. Much of the population, and the Egyptian garrison, had evacuated on 30 October, by boat and on foot. Indeed, the Egyptian divisional headquarters had left the town already on 19 October, and the steady Egyptian withdrawal southwards no doubt undermined civilian morale in the town and in the villages along the route of the Egyptian evacuation. The Egyptians apparently nowhere ordered the local inhabitants to stay put and, it may be surmised, may have encouraged at least some of the locals to withdraw with them. Nonetheless, something between 1,000 and 2,000 local inhabitants remained in Al Majdal when the Israelis marched in. The occupying units, according to Galili, were ordered, apparently by Southern Front headquarters, to expel the inhabitants but the order was disregarded or subsequently cancelled and the town was not looted.[18] The remaining population stayed put.

The upshot of the October–November battles in the south was that the Gaza Strip's refugee population had jumped from the pre-Operation Yoav figure of 100,000 to "230,000," according to an official of the United Nations Refugee Relief Project, F.G. Beard. Beard reported that the condition of these refugees "def[ies] description . . . Almost all of them are living in the open . . . [and are] receiving no regular rations of food . . . There are no sanitary facilities . . . and conditions of horrifying filth exist." Beard said the Egyptian Army and the Arab Higher Refugee Council had been "grossly negligent in their handling of the situation."[19]

The north

In the north, the 60-hour campaign, Operation Hiram, precipitated a major Arab civilian exodus from the Upper Galilee pocket held by Qawuqji's forces. Many fled from the approaching battle; some were expelled; many others, to be out of harm's way, initially left their villages for nearby gullys, orchards and caves. In many cases, Israeli units during the following days barred their return to their homes or encouraged them to move off to Lebanon. Some may have decided not to return to their villages to live under Israeli rule. Of the area's estimated 50,000–60,000 population (locals and refugees) before 29 October, something like half ended up in Lebanon. On 31 October Ben-Gurion recorded that roughly half the pocket's villagers had fled, but a few days later, the army estimated that only some 12,000–15,000 inhabitants had remained in the conquered pocket.[20]

The demographic upshot of the operation followed a clear, though by no means uniform or exact, religious–ethnic pattern: most of the Muslims in the pocket fled to Lebanon while most of the pocket's Christian population remained *in situ*.[21] Almost all the pocket's Druse and Circassian communities remained. Thus, despite the fact that no clear guidelines were issued to the commanders of the advancing IDF columns about how to treat each religious or ethnic group they encountered, what emerged roughly conformed to a pattern as if such "instinctive" guidelines had been followed by both the IDF and the different conquered communities.

At the same time, the demographic outcome generally corresponded to the circumstances of the military advance. Roughly, villages which had put up a fight or a stiff fight against the IDF units were depopulated: their inhabitants, fearing retribution for their martial ardour, or declining to live under Jewish rule, fled or, in some cases, were expelled. The inhabitants of villages that surrendered quietly generally stayed put and usually were not harmed or expelled by the IDF. They did not fear (or little feared) retribution. This apparently was the main reason why the inhabitants of the half-Muslim, half-Christian village of Fassuta decided to stay put: "The majority argued that the Jews had no reason to vent their wrath on Fassuta," which had not fought against the Haganah or the IDF. Only a few villagers fled to Lebanon.[22] The facts of resistance or peaceful surrender, moreover, roughly corresponded to the religious–ethnic character of the villages. In general, wholly or largely Muslim villages tended to put up a fight or to support units of Qawuqji's army which fought against the IDF, though there were Muslim villages that surrendered without a fight. Christian villagers tended to surrender without a fight or without assisting Qawuqji's units. In mixed villages where the IDF encountered resistance, such as Tarshiha and Jish, the Christians by and large stayed put while the Muslims fled or were forced to leave. Druse and Circassian villagers nowhere resisted the IDF advance.

A bald Minority Affairs Ministry list from this time of "Villages that Surrendered and [Villages that] were Conquered [after Resistance]

Outside the State of Israel [i.e., 1947 Partition boundaries]" underlines the connection between resistance and depopulation in Operation Hiram. The villages listed as "surrendering" are Al Bi'na (Muslim), Kaukab (Muslim), Kafr Manda (Muslim), Sakhnin (Muslim), Arraba (Muslim), Deir Hanna (Muslim), Maghar (Druse), Jish (Muslim–Christian), Rihaniya (Circassian–Muslim) and Alma (Muslim). Of these, only Alma was uprooted and expelled. Many of the inhabitants of the rest of the villages (mostly Muslims) fled northwards but the remaining population in each was left *in situ* and not uprooted by the advancing IDF units. The villages, except for Alma, exist to this day. The villages that resisted are listed as Eilabun (mostly Christian), Farradiya (Muslim), Meirun (Muslim), Sammu'i (Muslim), Safsaf (Muslim), and Al Malikiya (Muslim). All were depopulated – either by flight or by partial flight plus expulsion. None – except Eilabun, where the inhabitants were allowed back – exist as Arab villages today.[23]

Apart from these general patterns, the campaign was characterised by vagaries of time and place. Much depended on the circumstances surrounding the capture of a given village and on the character of local, middle-echelon IDF commanders. The history of each village, whether in the past "friendly" or hostile towards the Yishuv, also affected IDF behaviour.

Shimoni at the time accurately defined what had happened in the Galilee: "The attitude towards the Arab inhabitants of the Galilee and to the refugees [there] . . . was accidental/haphazard [*mikri*] and different from place to place in accordance with this or that commander's initiative or this or that official's . . .: Here [inhabitants] were expelled, there, left in place; here, the surrender of villages was accepted . . . there [the IDF] refused to accept surrender; here, [the IDF] discriminated in favour of the Christians, and there [the IDF] behaved towards the Christians and the Moslems in the same way . . .; here, refugees who fled in the first instance under shock of conquest were allowed back to their places, there, [they] were not allowed [back]."

The Foreign Ministry, prior to Operation Hiram, had advised the IDF "to try during conquest [to make sure] that no Arab inhabitants remain in the Galilee and certainly that no refugees from other places remain there. Truth to tell, concerning the attitude to the Christian [Arabs] and the problem of whether to discriminate in their favour and to leave them in their villages, clear instructions were not given [by us?] and we did not express an opinion." The Ministry, complained Shimoni, had simply not been informed that the Operation was about to be launched and, hence, had not had time to work out "an accurate plan."[24]

A few days later, in a general, plaintive report to Foreign Ministry

Director General Eytan, Shimoni was to write, after visiting the Galilee and talking to the Operation Hiram commanders: "From all the commanders we talked to we heard that during the operations in the Galilee . . . they had had no clear instructions, no clear line, concerning behaviour towards the Arabs in the conquered areas – expulsion of the inhabitants or leaving them in place; harsh or 'soft' behaviour; discrimination in favour of Christians or not; a special attitude towards Maronites; a special attitude towards Mattawalis [Shi'ites]." Shimoni added that he had no doubt that some of the atrocities committed would not have taken place "had the conquering army had a clear and positive line of behaviour." In general, Shimoni complained, the Ministry's opinion was not often elicited by the IDF, sometimes failed to reach the appropriate commanders and almost always was never taken into account during IDF operations.[25]

A few examples will illustrate the haphazardness of what happened. Ar Rama, a mainly Christian village with a substantial Druse minority, was taken without a fight by Golani units on 30 October. But the following day, another unit entered the village and expelled its almost 1,000 Christian inhabitants, on pain of death. The unit remained in the village until 5 November. The following day, the Christians, who had camped out in nearby caves and wadis, returned to their homes, apparently with IDF permission. The expulsion was probably ordered because one of the town's leading Christians, Father Yakub al Hanna, had loudly supported Qawuqji. There may also have been local Druse pressure on the IDF to expel the Christians.

Also among those in Ar Rama ordered to leave were some non-resident refugees, including a group from Ghuweir Abu Shusha, who had fled to Ar Rama at the end of April. One former Ghuweir resident, who was at Ar Rama on 31 October, decades later described what happened: "The people in Ar Rama were ordered to assemble at the centre of the village. A Jewish soldier stood on top of a rise and addressed us. He ordered the Druse present . . . to go back to their homes . . . Then he ordered the rest of us to leave to Lebanon . . . Although I was given permission to stay by my friend, Abu Musa [a local Jewish officer], I could not remain without the rest of my tribe who were forced to flee." Unlike the Ar Rama Christian community, these non-residents did not remain but moved off to Lebanon.[26]

In some villages, IDF units after the conquest almost immediately separated the local inhabitants from resident refugee families and clans, and expelled the refugees. This apparently happened at Al Bi'na. A refugee from Sha'b in Al Bi'na later recalled that at first "the Jews grouped us with the other villagers, separating us from our women. We

remained all day in the village courtyard . . . we were thirsty and hungry."
Two villagers, he recalled, were taken aside and shot, and the refugees
were robbed of their valuables. Some "200" men were selected and driven
off, presumably to a POW camp.

It was almost night . . . [The] Al Bi'na mukhtar asked the Jews to permit us to stay
overnight . . . rather than travel [northwards] at night with our old men, women
and children. The Jews rejected the mukhtar's request and gave us [i.e., the
refugees] half an hour to leave . . . When half an hour passed, the Jews began to
shoot in the air . . . they injured my nine-year-old son in the knee. We walked a few
hours until we reached Sajur . . . We were terrified, the road was full of people in
every direction you looked . . . all in a hurry to get to Lebanon.

A few days later, after a brief stay in the Druse village of Beit Jann, they
reached Lebanon.[27]

Some villages with an anti-Yishuv past, such as Majd al Kurum, were
not uprooted. Majd al Kurum was conquered on 30 October. About one-
third of its inhabitants left the night before the IDF arrived, after the ALA
garrison began to withdraw. The local ALA commander apparently
advised the young men and women of the village to leave with him.
According to one inhabitant's recollection, about 100–120 families left
that night: "We did not want to take any risks and decided to leave to
Lebanon." Those who stayed, according to Nazzal, did so "because they
were too old and were 'afraid of dying in a strange land' . . . [or feared] they
would starve" or out of general fatalism. Another inhabitant, who stayed
on for a few days after the conquest, recalled that another 60 families left in
the following days, after (he alleged) the conquering IDF troops picked
out 12 men and executed them in the village square, in front of the
remaining inhabitants.[28]

The haphazardness of what occurred in Operation Hiram is underlined
by the case of Mi'ilya, a Christian village whose militia had fought
alongside the ALA against the Oded Brigade troops. During the previous
months the villagers had decided not to allow any villagers to flee to
Lebanon. When the battle was lost, on 31 October, almost all the
inhabitants left the village, some crossing over to Lebanon. But during the
following days, the local IDF commanders allowed all those who had fled
to return to their homes, one of the few such cases during the 1948 war.[29]

At Tarshiha, the population had long feared Israeli retribution, in view
of their role in the massacre of the Yehiam Convoy on 28 March. The IDF
ground assault of 29 October was preceded by a short aerial bombardment
and a prolonged artillery barrage. Most of the villagers (Muslims) fled
with the ALA garrison that morning, before the Oded troops arrived. The
village's Christians by and large stayed and were not expelled.[30]

Christian villages, traditionally friendly or not unfriendly towards the Yishuv, were generally left in peace. An exception was Eilabun, a mainly Christian Maronite community, which fell to Golani units on 30 October after a battle with ALA units. The villagers hung out white flags and the Israeli troops entering the village were welcomed by four priests. The inhabitants huddled inside the churches while the priests formally surrendered the village. But the Israelis discovered in a house the severed heads of two missing IDF soldiers. What happened next is described in a letter from the village elders to Shitrit: the villagers were ordered to assemble in the village square. While assembling, one villager was killed and another wounded by IDF fire.

Then the commander selected 12 youngsters (*shabab*) and sent them to another place, then he ordered that the assembled inhabitants be led to Maghar and the priest asked him to leave the women and babies and to take only the men, but he refused, and led the assembled inhabitants – some 800 in number – to Maghar preceded by military vehicles . . . He himself stayed on with another two soldiers until they killed the 12 youngsters in the streets of the village and then they joined the army going to Maghar . . . He led them to Farradiya. When they reached Kafr 'Inan they were joined by an armoured car that fired upon them . . . killing one of the old men, Sam'an ash Shufani, 60 years old, and injuring three women . . . At Farradiya [the soldiers] robbed the inhabitants of IL 500 and the women of their jewelry, and took 42 youngsters and sent them to a detention camp, and the rest the next day were led to Meirun, and afterwards to the Lebanese border. During this whole time they were given food only once. Imagine then how the babies screamed and the cries of the pregnant and weaning mothers.

Subsequently, the army looted Eilabun.[31]

Not all the villagers were taken on the trek to Lebanon. Hundreds fled to nearby gullys, caves and villages, and during the following days and weeks infiltrated back to the village. The affair exercised the various Israeli bureaucracies for months, partly because the Eilabun case was taken up and pleaded persistently and ably by Israeli and Lebanon's Christian clergymen. The villagers asked to be allowed back, to repossess their property and to receive Israeli citizenship. They denied responsibility for the severing of the two soldiers' heads, blaming Fauzi al Mansur of Jenin, a sergeant in Qawuqji's army, for the killing.[32]

The Eilabun affair sparked a guilty conscience and sympathy within the Israeli establishment. Shitrit ruled that former inhabitants still living within Israeli-held territory must be allowed back to the village. But Major Sulz, the Military Governor of the Nazareth district, responded that the army would not allow the villagers back. He asserted that Eilabun had been "evacuated either voluntarily or with a measure of compulsion." A fortnight later, Sulz elaborated: "The village was captured after a fierce fight and its inhabitants had fled." The Foreign Ministry opined that even if an "injustice" was done, "injustices of war cannot be put right during the war itself."[33]

However, Shitrit, supported by Mapam and prompted by the priests, persisted. Zisling suggested that the matter be discussed in Cabinet. Shitrit requested that the villagers in Eilabun be granted citizenship (relieving them of the fear of deportation as illegal infiltrees), that the Eilabun detainees be released and that the villagers be supplied with provisions.[34] The inhabitants received citizenship and provisions, and the detainees were released. At the same time, Shitrit, as Minister of Police, persuaded Yadin, the new IDF Chief of Staff, to initiate an investigation of the massacre.[35]

In summer 1949, the combined pressure took effect. Eilabun exiles in Lebanon who wished to return were allowed to do so, as part of an agreement between Palmon, the newly appointed Arab Affairs Adviser at the Prime Minister's office, and Archbishop Hakim, concerning the return of several thousand Galilee Christians to their homes in exchange for the cleric's future goodwill towards the Jewish State. Hundreds returned to Eilabun.[36]

Eilabun was one of a series of atrocities committed by the IDF during Operation Hiram. All incidentally served to precipitate and enhance Arab flight. Some of the atrocities, as in Eilabun and Sa'sa, were bound up with, and were part of, expulsions. All the atrocities were initiatives of local commanders and troops; none were ordered, initiated or condoned by brigade, Operation Hiram or Northern Front headquarters. The perpetrators of at least some of the crimes were subsequently – if lightly – punished.

In his briefing of 11 November to the Political Committee of Mapam, Galili detailed some of the atrocities committed in the October fighting. He spoke of "52 men [in Safsaf] tied with a rope and dropped into a well and shot. 10 were killed. Women pleaded for mercy. [There were] 3 cases of rape . . . A girl aged 14 was raped. Another 4 were killed." At Jish, he said, "a woman and her baby were killed. Another 11 [were killed?]." At Sa'sa there were cases of "mass murder [though] a thousand [?] lifted white flags [and] a sacrifice was offered [to welcome] the army. The whole village was expelled." At Saliha, Galili said, "94 . . . were blown up with a house." The atrocities (apart from Eilabun) seem to have been committed mostly by the 7th Brigade, which Galili singled out for condemnation.[37]

These atrocities, mostly committed against Muslims, no doubt precipitated the flight of communities on the path of the IDF advance. A community already nervous at the prospect of IDF assault and probable Jewish conquest would doubtless have been driven to immediate panic by news, possibly embellished by the Arab penchant for exaggeration, of IDF atrocities in a neighbouring village. What happened at Safsaf and Jish no doubt reached the villagers of Ras al Ahmar, Alma, Deishum and Al Malikiya hours before the 7th Brigade's columns reached them. These villages, apart from Alma, seem to have been completely or largely empty when the IDF arrived. If the memory of a former inhabitant of Sa'sa is to be believed, the Safsaf atrocity, rather than the battle for Sa'sa, was what precipitated the exodus from Sa'sa.[38]

But the atrocities were limited in size, scope and time. Only in specific villages could they have had overwhelming effect; they could not have been known in most of the areas conquered by the Oded, Golani, and Carmeli brigades in time to have produced panic and flight. Atrocities did not occur in many of the villages captured in Operation Hiram. In most parts of the conquered Galilee pocket, the primary causes of the new wave of refugees were some of those that had precipitated the previous waves of flight: fear of being caught up and hurt in battle, fear of the conquerors and of revenge for past misdeeds or affiliations, a general fear of the future and of life under Jewish rule, and confusion and shock.

OC Northern Front Carmel a year later described the panic flight of some of the villagers.

They abandon the villages of their birth and that of their ancestors and go into exile . . . Women, children, babies, donkeys – everything moves, in silence and grief, northwards, without looking to right or left. Wife does not find her husband and child does not find his father . . . no one knows the goal of his trek. Many possessions are scattered by the paths; the more the refugees walk, the more tired they grow – and they throw away what they had tried to save on their way into exile. Suddenly, every object seems to them petty, superfluous, unimportant as against the chasing fear and the urge to save life and limb.

I saw a boy aged eight walking northwards pushing along two asses in front of him. His father and brother had died in the battle and his mother was lost. I saw a woman holding a two-week-old baby in her right arm and a baby two years old in her left arm and a four-year-old girl following in her wake, clutching at her dress.

Near Sa'sa, "I saw suddenly by the roadside a tall man, bent over, scraping with his fingernails in the hard, rocky soil. I stopped. I saw a small hollow in the ground, dug out by hand, with fingernails, under an olive tree. The man laid down the body of a baby who had died in the arms of his mother, and covered it with soil and small stones." Near Tarshiha, Carmel saw a 16-year-old youth "sitting by the roadside, naked as the day he was born and smiling at our passing car." Carmel described how some of the Israeli soldiers, regarding the refugee columns with astonishment and shock and "with great sadness," went down into the wadis and gave the refugees bread and tea. "I knew [of] a unit in which no soldier ate anything that day because all [the food] sent it by the company kitchen was taken down to the wadi," Carmel recalled.[39]

The atrocities of October prompted the war's first and only high-level, external investigation of IDF behaviour. Pressure for such a probe built up during the first week of November, as the news of what had happened filtered back to Tel Aviv and the kibbutzim from the battlefronts. Through the war, Ben-Gurion had consistently defended the men in uniform and their actions against all outside criticism and investigation; internal investigations and punishments for mistreatment of Arab civilians were kept to a minimum. The fate of the State had hung in the balance; the Haganah and IDF had had to be allowed to get on with the war.

But the danger to the State had passed and the October atrocities were too concentrated, widespread and severe to be ignored. The criticism, not limited to Mapam, was uncontainable: at the Cabinet meeting of 7 November the criticism of the soldiers' conduct was led off by Immigration and Health Minister Hayim Moshe Shapira (Hamizrahi–National Religious Party). He was followed by Interior Minister Yitzhak Gruenbaum (General Zionists) and Justice Minister Rosenblueth (Progressive Party). Labour and Construction Minister Bentov (Mapam) also spoke. Ben-Gurion bowed to the consensus. The Cabinet appointed a three-man (Bentov, Rosenblueth and Shapira) ministerial committee of inquiry to investigate "the army's deeds in the conquered territories." Bentov reported that only Ben-Gurion and Shertok appeared not to have been "shocked" by what had happened.[40]

The atrocities, and the start of the ministerial probe, were discussed in Mapam's executive bodies on 11 November. The party faced its usual problem: ideologically, it was motivated to lead the clamour; in practice, caution had to be exercised as its "own" generals, Sadeh and Carmel, were involved. Cohen, head of the party's Arab Department, demanded that the party set up its own, internal inquiry. Benny Marshak asked that the party executives refrain from using the phrase "Nazi actions" and said that the Palmah had already tried a number of soldiers for killing Arabs not during battle. Riftin asserted that there was "no connection" between the atrocities and the expulsion of Arabs. He called for death sentences for those guilty of committing atrocities. Galili warned against "rushing to attribute responsibility to our officer comrades" before investigation. But Bentov feared that the soldiers would decline to testify before the ministerial committee and that the ministers lacked an effective investigative apparatus. The Political Committee decided to hold formal "clarification" sessions with the Mapam officers involved and to urge its members to testify before the ministerial committee.[41]

The ministerial "Committee of Three" preoccupied the Cabinet and some of the political parties for weeks. Meanwhile, the IDF – Lt Colonel Haim Laskov, OC 7th Brigade during Operation Hiram – conducted and completed its own internal investigation of some of the atrocities. The "Committee of Three" encountered evasiveness, delays and silence from the army commanders. It asked Ben-Gurion for increased powers. The affair sparked a major Cabinet row on 14 November. Three days later, Zisling charged that for over half a year, Ben-Gurion had ignored the problem of Jewish behaviour towards the Arabs, had pleaded ignorance and had consistently deflected criticism of the army. Now Ben-Gurion was criticising the "Committee of Three" for "slowness." Zisling referred to a letter he had received about the atrocities – possibly Kaplan's on Dawayima – "and I couldn't sleep all night . . . This is something that determines the character of the nation . . . Jews too have committed Nazi acts." Zisling agreed that outwardly Israel, to preserve good name and image, must admit nothing, but the matter must be thoroughly investigated. Chief of Staff Dori, Zisling said, repeatedly postponed testifying, arguing that he did not yet have the information required, while a subordinate officer delayed appearing on the grounds that the Committee should first hear the Chief of Staff's testimony.

The Cabinet refused to increase the Committee's powers; Immigration and Health Minister Shapira resigned from the Committee. Ben-Gurion then proposed that the Committee be replaced by a one-man probe, and accompanied this with a statement apparently threatening, or implying a threat of, resignation from the Defence Ministry if he did not get his way. A majority then voted that "the Prime Minister investigate the charges concerning the army's behaviour towards the Arabs in the Galilee and in the South." Ben-Gurion then appointed Attorney-General Ya'acov Shimshon Schapira as investigator, assigning three officers to help him.[42] Ben-Gurion's letter of instruction to Schapira read: "You are requested herein . . . to investigate if there were attacks [*p'gi'ot*] by . . . the army on Arab inhabitants [i.e., civilians] in the Galilee and the South, not in conformity with the accepted rules of war . . . What were the attacks . . .? To what degree was the army command, low and high, responsible for these acts, and to what degree was the existing discipline in the army responsible for this and what should be done to rectify matters and to punish the guilty?" Ben-Gurion added that orders would be issued to the troops to provide all the necessary evidence and aid to the investigators.[43]

In a masterly political stroke Ben-Gurion then switched from an embarrassed defence to the offensive, outflanking Mapam on their own turf. On 21 November he wrote to the nation's leading poet, Natan Alterman, praising his poem *"Al Zot"* (On This). The poem, critical of the atrocities, had appeared in the Histadrut daily *Davar* two days before. Ben-Gurion requested the poet's permission for the Defence Ministry to reprint and distribute it in the IDF to all soldiers. The poem was duly reprinted and distributed, as was Ben-Gurion's letter to Alterman. Ben-Gurion later read out the poem at a meeting of the Provisional Council of State.

The poem describes a young, jeep-mounted Jewish soldier "trying out" his machinegun on an old Arab in a street in a conquered town. More generally, it castigates "the insensitivity [and lack of reaction] of the Jewish public" to the atrocities. Its publication in *Davar* was an "event."[44]

Ben-Gurion submitted Attorney-General Schapira's report to the Cabinet on 5 December and promised that the IDF was continuing its own investigation of the atrocities. The Cabinet set up a standing committee of five ministers to continue probing into past IDF misdeeds and to look into future ones, should these occur, and a second committee to formulate guidelines geared to preventing such atrocities in the future.[45]

The major outcome of the simultaneous Mapam, IDF and Schapira investigations into the October atrocities was the disciplining of some of the soldiers and officers involved – a few were cashiered from the army, others were gaoled for relatively short periods – and the publication in the IDF of strict rules on the treatment of Arab civilians. On 23 December, Ben-Gurion instructed General Avner to take severe measures to protect the inhabitants of the Gaza Strip – which the Prime Minister thought was about to fall into Israeli hands – and to avoid expulsions. General Allon on 17 December, just before the start of Operation Horev (in which the IDF reached El Arish and Abu Ageila and threatened to conquer the Strip) issued a detailed appendix to the operational orders setting out guidelines for the proper treatment of captured Arab soldiers and conquered civilian populations. The preamble referred to the "disgraceful incidents" that had occurred in the past. The appendix stated that the IDF should take prisoners where possible (rather than kill them); "unjustified killing of civilians will be regarded as murder . . . Torture of placid civilians will be dealt with sharply; Arab populations must not be expelled except with special permission from the Front Battle HQ." The appendix ordered commanders of brigades and districts to issue "special orders" to all units in this connection. All battalion commanders were instructed to sign a special form declaring that "they had received these orders and would abide by them." The brigade and district commanders were ordered to react to any infringement publicly and with extreme severity. Similar orders reached all large IDF formations during the winter.[46]

Conclusion

The primary aims of operations Yoav and Hiram were to destroy enemy formations – the Egyptian army in the south and Qawuqji's Yarmuk (ALA) brigades in the Galilee – and to conquer additional territory, giving the Jewish State greater strategic depth and pushing back hostile armies from the Jewish population centres. The operational orders, as in nearly all IDF offensives, did not refer to the Arab civilian populations. It was probably assumed by the colonels and generals, on both fronts, that once again there would be major, spontaneous Arab flight. No general orders were issued to drive out Arab populations on either front. But brigade, battalion and company commanders, by October 1948, generally shared the view that it was best that the Jewish State have as few Arabs as possible.

At the same time, the Arabs in both areas had for months lived with the fear of an Israeli onslaught and of the treatment they might receive at Israeli hands. Many, perhaps most, of the Arabs expected to be driven out, or worse.

Hence, when the offensives were unleashed, there was a "coalescence" of Jewish and Arab expectations, which led, especially in the south, to spontaneous flight by many of the locals and "nudging" if not direct expulsion orders by the advancing IDF columns.

However, there were major differences between the two fronts. In the south, the Front OC, General Allon, was known to want "Arab-clean" areas in the rear of his line of advance. Moreover, the nature of the battle in the area, involving two large armies and the use of relatively strong firepower (artillery and air bombings), affected civilian morale. The civilians in question were almost uniformly Muslim, had for months suffered serious material privations and had had a difficult, unhappy time under Egyptian rule. At the same time, the shock entailed by the Egyptian army's abrupt collapse and retreat was probably far greater than that experienced in the Galilee with the demise of the ALA (never regarded by anyone – Jew or Arab – as a serious military force). It is also possible that in some areas retreating Egyptian units urged local communities to retreat with them. Due to these factors, the exodus in the south to the Gaza Strip and the Hebron Hills during Operation Yoav was complete (save for 1,500 at Al Majdal).

In the Galilee, the picture was far more circumstantial and complex. There was no clear IDF policy. The various overrun communities and the various conquering units all acted differently. Druse and Christian villages by and large offered no or less resistance to the IDF and, hence, expected, and received, "better" treatment. Muslim villages often

235

resisted and expected, and received, worse treatment. In mixed villages, such as Tarshiha and Jish, Christians often remained while Muslims fled. Often, non-resisting Muslims stayed put and were left in peace (as happened, for example, in Arraba and Deir Hanna). Expulsions, where they occurred, were usually at the initiative of local commanders.

To the foregoing must be added the "atrocity factor," which played a major role in precipitating flight from several clusters of Galilee Muslim villages and from Ad Dawayima in the south over 29–31 October. The atrocities were largely limited to Muslim communities.

All this said, about 30–50% of the Galilee pocket's inhabitants stayed and were left in place during and immediately after Operation Hiram.

From the Arab side, there were several general factors which generated greater "staying power" in the Galilee than in the south. Firstly, the traditional "non-belligerency" towards the Yishuv of the Christians and Druse meant that they had less fear of Israeli conquest. Secondly, until October 1948 the war had not severely affected the lives of the inhabitants of the Upper Galilee pocket. There had been little Haganah/IDF harassment and no major food shortages.[47] And the presence of Qawuqji's troops may have been less irksome (except in the Christian villages) than, say, that of the Egyptians in the south. Lastly, during the battles of late October, the IDF had deployed far less firepower than in the South.

Together, Operations Hiram and Yoav had precipitated the flight of roughly 100,000–150,000 Arabs into refugeedom.

Chapter 8

Clearing the borders: expulsions and population transfers, November 1948 – July 1949

In the weeks and months after the termination of hostilities in the north, centre and south of the country, the Israeli military and political authorities adopted a policy of clearing the new borders of Arab villages and encampments. The policy, which matured *ad hoc* and haphazardly, was motivated mainly by military considerations: the country's borders were long and highly penetrable. In the newly-conquered areas, there were few, if any, Jewish settlements along the frontiers. Arab villages along the borders could serve as way-stations and bases for hostile irregulars, spies and illegal returnees. In the event of renewed war, such villages could serve as entry points for invading Arab armies. Some of the villages, such as Faluja and Iraq al Manshiya in the south, sat astride strategic routes. In general throughout this period, the political desire to have as few Arabs as possible in the Jewish State and the need for empty villages to house new Jewish immigrants meshed with the strategic desire to achieve "Arab-less" frontiers.

It was the IDF which set the policy in motion, with the civil and political authorities often giving approval after the fact.

The northern border

During the second week of November 1948, about 10 days after the completion of Operation Hiram, Carmel, with the General Staff's consent, decided to clear the Israeli side of the Israeli–Lebanese border of Arab villages to a depth of 5–15 kilometres. The IDF began with the villages closest to the border. The inhabitants of Nabi Rubin, Tarbikha, Suruh, Al Mansura, Iqrit, Kafr Bir'im and Jish were ordered to leave their villages. The villagers of Nabi Rubin and Tarbikha, Muslims, were ordered to cross into Lebanon. The villagers of Kafr Bir'im, Maronite Christians, were ordered to leave for Lebanon but the army allowed some of them to move to Arab villages deeper inside Israel. Some camped out for weeks in gullys and caves near the village, waiting to see whether the IDF would allow them back. The Bir'im and Iqrit villagers were told that their removal from their homes was temporary and that they would soon be allowed back. Some of the inhabitants of Iqrit and Al Mansura, also Christian villages, crossed into Lebanon but most were trucked by the IDF to Ar Rama, to the south.

In the case of Jish (Gush Halav), a large mainly Maronite village, the expulsion to Lebanon was never carried out. The villagers got Emmanuel (Mano) Friedman, the local Minority Affairs Ministry representative, to intercede with Mapai stalwart and Arabist Yitzhak Ben-Zvi, who got hold of Shitrit. Shitrit persuaded the military to cancel the order.[1]

Unusually, the military in the north sought the opinion of the Foreign Ministry's Arab affairs experts on the intended expulsions, deemed by the IDF "necessary for military–security reasons." But before the Ministry could supply a response, according to Shimoni, the IDF had gone ahead and carried out some of the evictions. Shimoni said that the Ministry would have advised, for instance, that the inhabitants of Al Mansura and Kafr Bir'im, because they were Maronites, be transferred deeper into Israel rather than be expelled to Lebanon.[2]

According to Ben-Gurion, on 16 November Carmel informed him that the army "had been forced for military reasons . . . to expel the villages on the border," mentioning Kafr Bir'im, Nabi Rubin, Tarbikha and Iqrit. Carmel, wrote Ben-Gurion, was now "ready to freeze the situation – not to expel more, and not to allow back" the villagers. Ben-Gurion agreed to this but proposed that the expelled Christians be told that Israel would consider allowing them to return "when the frontier was secured."[3]

Shitrit complained to Ben Gurion that the OC Military Government, General Avner, responsible for the Arab inhabitants in the conquered areas, had done nothing to stop the expulsions and that they had been carried out without his, Shitrit's, knowledge.[4] Shitrit then travelled north, to see what was going on. He was moved by the plight of the Bir'im villagers, who had always been "friendly." Several had been shot by Qawuqji's troops in Lebanon; seven Bir'im children, living out in the open, had reportedly died of exposure.[5] On 24 November, the Cabinet, post facto, endorsed the Lebanese border clearing operation. Ben-Gurion decided, probably in the interest of good Israeli–Maronite relations, to allow the Bir'im refugees in Lebanon to return to Israel, but not to their village.[6] Many of the Bir'im exiles and those encamped in the wadis near the village were then located by Friedman, and transported to Jish, where they were settled in abandoned Muslim houses. For lack of transport, according to Friedman, some of the Bir'im villagers were forced to remain at Rmaich, just across the border in Lebanon.[7]

For years thereafter, the refugees of Bir'im, Iqrit and Al Mansura pleaded unsuccessfully with the Israeli authorities to be permitted to return to their villages. The Bir'im villagers were supported by Shitrit and Ben-Zvi, president of Israel from 1952 to 1963. But the IDF and the intelligence services were consistently opposed to such a return. Within months, Bir'im's lands were distributed among Jewish settlements and, in the early 1950s, the village itself was levelled.

In February 1949, the Maronite church took up the Al Mansura case, appealing to the Foreign and Minority Affairs Ministries. However, the army's judgement was rigid and definitive: "For military reasons there is no possibility now to discuss the return of these villagers."[8]

The case of Bir'im, Iqrit and Al Mansura illustrates how deeply rooted was the IDF's determination from November 1948 onwards to create a northern border strip clear of Arabs. That determination quickly spread to the civilian institutions of state, particularly those concerned with the establishment of new settlements and the settlement of new *olim*. Weitz and other settlement executives immediately began planning new settlements along the border strip (5–15 kilometres deep) and exempted these from the surplus lands requirement. Kaplan and Zisling, while accepting the IDF's argument in favour of a strip, insisted that any Arabs evicted should be properly and comfortably resettled. Only the Minority Affairs Ministry Director General, Gad Machnes, opposed the principle of an Arab-less border strip.[9]

The expulsions and transfers of early November had only partially cleared the strip along the northern border. Shitrit's intervention, protests by Mapam and possibly "softness" on the part of some local IDF commanders, had left *in situ* villagers in about half a dozen sites. The IDF still wanted the strip cleared and, if possible, populated with Jews. Military attention focused on Tarshiha, the largest village in the area. Most of its original 4,000–5,000 population ($\frac{3}{4}$ Muslims) had fled during Operation Hiram. In December, the village had some 700 inhabitants, 600 of them Christians – a minority of them infiltrees (inhabitants who had fled and then infiltrated back to the village). The settlement authorities wanted the abandoned Muslim housing for Jewish immigrants; the military viewed settlement in the village as "very important," as only 12% of the Galilee's population at this time was Jewish.[10]

The military were clearly interested in clearing the villagers out of Tarshiha for the usual reasons of border security and to prevent a return to the village of those who had fled. The villagers lived in continuous fear of expulsion, and sent delegations to plead with Israeli officials. Shitrit interceded with Ben-Gurion, and the villagers were temporarily reassured.[11]

But the military periodically raided the full and half-empty Upper Galilee villages to weed out illegal "returnees" and infiltrators. The authorities did not recognise the legality of residence in the country of anyone not registered during the November 1948 census and issued with an identity card or military pass. Anyone who had left the country for any reason before the census, and was not registered and in possession of a card or pass was regarded as an "absentee." If he subsequently infiltrated back into the country (including to his home village), he was regarded as an "illegal" and could be summarily deported. The IDF repeatedly raided the villages, sorted out legal from illegal residents and, usually, expelled the "returnees."

The IDF raid on 16 January 1949 on Tarshiha and neighbouring Mi'ilya was typical: "The Israeli army formed a cordon around the village and imposed a curfew. All males over 16 years were gathered in the village square. Here they were questioned by a panel of 8 Israelis . . . In all, 33 heads of families and 101 family members . . . were arrested and deported." Apparently, one or more of the raiding party also informally told the legally resident inhabitants that it would be in their interest to leave as well. Representatives in Israel of the American Friends Service Committee (AFSC) (Quakers), Donald Peretz and Ray Hartsough, who visited Tarshiha soon after, believed that the "concerted" Israeli campaign against infiltrees and those who harboured them seemed to be directed at making "room for new Jewish immigrants. It is their belief that the Jews plan to make of Tarshiha a completely Jewish town." Some 300 Jewish immigrants moved into the village's abandoned houses over February and March and the dispersed Arab families were concentrated in one area.[12]

There was a consensus in the Israeli bureaucracies to move Tarshiha's Arabs. On 21 January, General Avner proposed that they be transferred to Mi'ilya, but political objections blocked a final decision. In March, Weitz lamented that it would be good, "if only it were possible," to empty the town so that "1,000 [Jewish] families" could be settled in it. But it was not possible: "The prime minister is against dealing with transfers at the moment, [and] this from an international [political] viewpoint," explained one of Ben-Gurion's aides, Zalman Lifshitz. He proposed "trying to persuade [the inhabitants] to move."[13]

After the settlement of the first Jewish families in Tarshiha, the pressure on the Arab inhabitants to move grew. On 5 June, Jewish officials met with the Tarshiha Arab leaders and, according to the AFSC representatives, said that the Arabs would have to move out. "The Arabs refused." The Jewish officials then said that the "115" illegal inhabitants (infiltrees) in the town would be expelled from the country – unless the infiltrees and the remaining "600" legal residents agreed to move to other Arab villages or Acre.[14] But the Tarshiha inhabitants stayed put.

A second series of evictions and expulsions took place at the start of 1949. These involved Muslim villages near strategic roads in which some of the population had stayed put and which were considered by the Israeli authorities economically unviable. Most of their breadwinners had fled, were incarcerated in POW camps or had been killed, and the remaining population was composed mainly of dependants. The chief problem was that these half-empty villages were attracting infiltrating returnees. Full villages could not absorb returnees in any quantity while completely empty ones could be destroyed or settled. The semi-abandoned villages were steadily filling with infiltrees, assuring a permanent increase of the country's Arab population. Some neighbouring Jewish settlements wanted the lands of the semi-abandoned villages.

During December 1948 and January 1949, pressure built up to evict the Arabs of Farradiya, near Safad, of neighbouring Kafr 'Inan, and the remaining inhabitants of Saffuriya, near Nazareth. Shitrit said that infiltration back to villages was increasing and that if the phenomenon was not halted, Israel would have to "conquer the Galilee anew." Major Sulz proposed that the 261 inhabitants of Farradiya and Kafr I'nan be moved to Tur'an while the 395 in Saffuriya be moved to neighbouring Ar Reina. The Committee for Transferring Arabs from Place to Place (*ha'va'adah le'ha'avarat Aravim mi'makom le'makom*) on 15 December endorsed Sulz's proposal but bureaucratic footdragging followed.[15]

Saffuriya, a large Muslim village with a history of anti-Yishuv activity, had almost completely emptied in July 1948. Some of the remaining inhabitants were expelled in September but over the following months hundreds infiltrated back. The Jewish authorities feared that if the infiltrees were left in place, the village would soon return to its pre-war population of 4,000. Besides, neighbouring Jewish settlements coveted Saffuriya lands. One senior official put it bluntly in November: "Next to Nazareth is a village . . . whose distant lands are needed for our settlements. Perhaps they can be given another place." In early January 1949, the remaining inhabitants were evicted and trucked to 'Ilut, Nazareth, Ar Reina and Kafr Kanna. The village lands were distributed in February: Kibbutz Sdeh Nahum was allotted 1,500 dunams and Kibbutz Heftzi-Bah 1,000 dunams. Later that year, Kibbutz Hasolelim received 3,795 dunams.[16]

The remaining inhabitants of Farradiya and Kafr I'nan, both Muslim villages, were evicted in February 1949, about half going to other villages in Israel and the rest across the border into the Triangle.[17] The Military Government said the evictions had been necessary to assure "security, law and order."[18] The remaining inhabitants of Al Ghabisiya, in Western Galilee, were also evicted at this time.

The last major wave of evictions in the Galilee, in mid-1949, aroused a spate of inter-departmental correspondence and, for the first time, a short public debate. The remaining inhabitants of Ja'una, east of Safad, and Khisas and Qeitiya, in the Galilee panhandle, were at midnight 5 June surrounded by IDF units, forced into trucks "with brutality ... with kicks, curses and maltreatment" (in the words of Mapam Knesset Member and *Al Hamishmar* editor Eliezer Pra'i), and dumped on a bare, sun-scorched hillside near the village of 'Aqbara, just south of Safad. The 55 Khisas villagers complained that they had been "forced with their hands to destroy their dwellings," had been treated like "cattle," and their wives and children were "wandering in the wilderness [near 'Aqbara] thirsty and hungry."[19]

Khisas and Qeitiya families had helped the Yishuv purchase Arab lands and had assisted the Haganah Intelligence Service since 1937. But in summer 1949 IDF intelligence learned that the Khisas villagers had become the target of a Syrian intelligence campaign. "We believe that the Syrians' objective is ... to use them against us," Sulz wrote. Hence, they had to be moved "away from the border."

The eviction of the remaining inhabitants of Khisas, Qeitiya and Ja'una sparked outrage in Mapam. Ben-Gurion responded that he found the military's reasons for the eviction "sufficient." The leading independent daily newpaper, *Ha'aretz*, in an editorial on 7 August, criticised Ben-Gurion's response as "not very convincing." The newspaper conceded the army's right to move Arabs out of "border areas," but such evictees must be adequately resettled, with land, houses and food. The editorial argued that this was sheer common sense as well as humanity, since to create a class of deprived and dispossessed Arabs would play into the hands of subversives bent on "undermining ... the state." The June evictions moved American chargé d'affaires Richard Ford to reflect pessimistically about the fate of Israel's Arab minority: "The unhappy spectacle presents itself of some scores of thousands of aimless people 'walking about in thistle fields' until they either decide to shake the ancestral dust of Israel from their heels or just merely die." Conditions at 'Aqbara, where "remainders" from various villages (Qaddita, Khisas, Ja'una, etc.) were clustered together, remained bad for years.[20]

The defence establishment had never definitively dropped the idea of achieving a completely Arab-free northern border strip. Towards the end of 1949, a new plan surfaced to expel the inhabitants of "Fassuta, Tarshiha, Mi'ilya, Jish (including the people of Bir'im living there), Hurfeish, Rihaniya" (as well as of Zakariya and Al Majdal in the south). But political objections by the Foreign Ministry (and perhaps others) blocked implementation.[21]

A last problem remained in the north; that of several clusters of villagers in the Demilitarised Zone (DMZ) along the Israeli–Syrian border whose presence was formally protected by the provisions of the Israeli–Syrian General Armistice Agreement (Article V) of 20 July 1949.[22] For military, economic and agricultural reasons, Israel wanted these Arabs – at Mansurat al Kheit, Kirad al Baqqara, Kirad al Ghannama, Nuqeib, As Samra, Tel Qasr and Al Hamma, numbering about 2,200 in all – to move, or move back, to Syria. The military suspected them of helping the Syrians, especially in trying to halt the Lake Hula swamp draining scheme. The DMZ inhabitants remained in the main loyal "Syrians" and refused to recognise the legitimacy of Israeli rule. Also, the villagers were suspected by local Jewish settlers of stealing cattle, trespassing and other criminal or troublesome behaviour.[23]

By a combination of stick and carrot – economic and police pressure and "petty persecution," and economic incentives – all of these small communities were induced to leave between 1949 and 1956. Most of them moved across the Jordan to Syria, although some transferred to Sha'b, near Acre.[24]

In the south

Within days of signing the Israel–Egypt General Armistice Agreement of 24 February 1949, Israel violated its terms by intimidating into flight some 2,000–3,000 villagers of Faluja and Iraq al Manshiya, the last Palestinian Arab communities in the northern Negev approaches.

At the beginning of 1949, there were some 3,140 Arab civilians trapped, alongside an Egyptian brigade, in the Faluja pocket, a surrounded Egyptian enclave north of Beersheba left after the December–January fighting. More than 2,000 of them were inhabitants of the villages of Faluja and Iraq al Manshiya and the rest, refugees from elsewhere in southern Palestine. The Egyptians had insisted that the armistice agreement explicitly guarantee the safety of the person, rights and property of these civilians.[25] Israel in an exchange of letters appended to the agreement agreed that "those of the civilian population who may wish to remain in Al Faluja and Iraq al Manshiya are to be permitted to do so . . . All of these civilians shall be fully secure in their persons, abodes, property and personal effects."[26]

A small number – perhaps a few hundred – of the civilians, mostly from among the refugees in the pocket, left the Faluja area with the departing Egyptian troops on, or a day or two after, 26 February. The great majority stayed on and were placed under Israeli Military Government rule, which included nightly curfews and restrictions on movement outside the villages.

Within days the status quo in the two villages was shattered by the local

Israeli garrison. Representatives of the AFSC called what happened "Jewish psychological warfare." The United Nations Mediator, Ralph Bunche, quoting United Nations observers on the spot, complained that "Arab civilians . . . at Al Faluja have been beaten and robbed by Israeli soldiers and . . . there have been some cases of attempted rape." The Israeli troops had been "firing promiscuously" and the 2,400 remaining Arab civilians, seeking protection, had "gathered around the UN observers." The civilians wanted to go to Transjordanian-held Hebron. The Quakers said that the Arabs now wanted to leave but that sincere reassurances by Israeli officials could still persuade the Arabs to stay. No such reassurances were issued.[27]

Yadin dismissed the United Nations complaints of Israeli intimidation as "exaggerated."[28] But Sharett, wary of the international repercussions and, especially, of the possible effect on Israeli–Egyptian relations, and angered by IDF action without Cabinet authorisation and behind his back, was not easily appeased. He let fly at IDF chief of staff, General Ya'acov Dori in most uncharacteristic language. The IDF's actions at Faluja threw into question "our sincerity as a party to an international agreement . . . One may assume that Egypt in this matter will display special sensitivity as her forces saw themselves as responsible for the fate of these civilian inhabitants. There is also room to fear that any attack by us on the people of these two villages may be reflected in the attitude of the Cairo Government to the Jews of Egypt." The Foreign Minister pointed out that Israel was encountering difficulties at the United Nations, where it was seeking membership, "over the question of our responsibility for the Arab refugee problem. We argue that we are not responsible . . . From this perspective, the sincerity of our professions is tested by our behaviour in these villages . . . Every intentional pressure aimed at uprooting [these Arabs] is tantamount to a planned act of eviction on our part." Sharett added that in addition to the overt violence displayed by the soldiers, the IDF was busy conducting covertly "a 'whispering propaganda' campaign among the Arabs, threatening them with attacks and acts of vengeance by the army, which the civilian authorities will be powerless to prevent. This whispering propaganda (*ta'amulat lahash*) is not being done of itself. There is no doubt that here there is a calculated action aimed at increasing the number of those going to the Hebron Hills as if of their own free will, and, if possible, to bring about the evacuation of the whole civilian population of [the pocket]." Sharett called the army's actions "an unauthorised initiative by the local command in a matter relating to Israeli government policy."[29]

The decision to intimidate into flight the inhabitants of Faluja and Iraq al Manshiya was probably taken by OC Southern Front General Allon after a meeting with Yosef Weitz on 28 February (and probably after getting agreement from Ben-Gurion). The two villages sat astride the strategically vital Gaza–Hebron axis and on good agricultural land. A few months before, Weitz and Ben-Gurion had agreed on the need to drive out by intimidation Arab communities along the Faluja-Majdal axis. Ben-Gurion may also have approved the action as Faluja had become a symbol of Egyptian military fortitude and courage.[30]

The fright inflicted on the pocket's civilians in the first days of March sufficed to persuade most of them to opt for the "Transjordanian solution," and most left for the Hebron Hills in the following weeks. The last batch left on 21 April.[31]

Subsequently, Israeli officials, sometimes feigning outrage, were not completely frank about what had happened. Foreign Ministry Director General Eytan, for instance, told the United States Ambassador, McDonald, that Israel had broadcast "repeated reassuring notices" to the Faluja and Iraq al Manshiya Arabs to stay put. However, the local inhabitants had acted "as if they smelled a rat" and abandoned their homes. Eytan described the Arabs, in this connection, as "primitive [and] rumour-ridden." Alternately, when admitting that intimidation had occurred, Israeli officials tended to put the blame on local initiatives and unruly local commanders.[32]

The other major border problem in the south, as seen from the Israeli perspective, was that of the Negev bedouin tribes. The Israeli leadership was split on the issue. One approach – initially voiced by the army – was that the bedouin were congenitally unreliable and unruly, had sided with the Arabs during the war and, given the chance, would do so again, and were incorrigible smugglers. It were best that the northern Negev, where they were concentrated, be cleared of them. A contrary attitude was taken by various Arabists, who differentiated between "good" bedouin and "bad" bedouins, and believed that bedouins naturally tended to accept, and display loyalty towards, those in power. These Arabists thought that the "good" bedouins could be harnessed to serve the Jewish State, particularly in the form of an *in situ* border guard.[33]

During Operation Yoav, in October, many of the bedouins had moved out of harm's way; those within a 10-kilometre radius of Beersheba were kicked out in the first week of November. The IDF was concerned about Arab infiltration into the town.

The conquest of the northern Negev wrought a change in the Foreign Ministry Arabists' thinking. Shertok reverted to his usual attitude towards Palestine's Arabs – the less of them in the country, the better. The bedouin chiefs wanted guarantees of safety and to be allowed to stay in exchange for loyalty. But Shertok, Shimoni and Danin now preferred that they leave the country; compensation would be offered.[34] The army, too, wanted "to push back the bedouin as much as possible from the [Beersheba] area, far into the desert." On 2 November Israeli officials and IDF officers met the bedouin chiefs and sought to engineer the voluntary departure of most of the tribes "far into the desert or into Transjordan." But the local Minority Affairs Ministry representative, Ya'acov Berdichevsky, thought the tribes could be usefully turned into a southern border guard.[35]

On 18 November, 16 chieftains formally presented a request to stay in Israel. Weitz feared that important settlement and agricultural interests were being sacrificed for short-term political gain. He wrote Ben-Gurion that it were best that the bedouins were not around. But, "if political requirements" compel leaving the bedouins, then it were best that they were "concentrated" in a specific limited area.[36]

Weitz's line of retreat was eventually adopted. On 25 November, Ben-Gurion met with his top Arab affairs and military advisers. Allon and the Negev Military Governor, Michael Hanegbi, favoured allowing the loyal bedouins to stay – but concentrated in a limited area east of Beersheba. Weitz and Shimoni were against. Ben-Gurion said that military rather than political or agricultural considerations should determine policy. The decision was left to the IDF.[37] Five days later, the Allon approach became official policy. In early 1949, thousands of bedouins living south and west of Beersheba were moved to the concentration area to the east of the city.[38]

But the paucity of Israeli forces, the relative vastness of the area and the migratory habits of the bedouin meant that Israel was left with a major and continuing problem in the Negev. Periodically, after smuggling or sabotage incidents, Israeli forces swept parts of the northern Negev for tribes and clans not in the concentration zone. A major expulsion of bedouins to Transjordan took place in early November 1949, with some 500 families being pushed across the border south of Hebron.[39] A similar expulsion occurred on 2 September 1950, when, according to the United Nations, some 4,000 bedouins were reportedly driven into Egyptian-held Sinai. Israel said the true figure was in "the hundreds" and that they had been "infiltrees."[40]

The last major concentration of Arabs in the south at the end of the war was at Al Majdal (Ashkelon). Some 1,400–1,600 had remained behind after conquest. In December 1948, the authorities approved the settlement of 3,000 Jews in the town; hundreds of families moved in during 1949. Outright eviction of the Arabs was ruled out (apparently for political reasons) but the settlement authorities wanted the houses.[41]

By February 1950, the Arab population had risen to 2,346, due to infiltration and births. There was smuggling across the Gaza Strip border and a security problem. The authorities began to apply subtle stick and carrot tactics to obtain an evacuation. Military government was burdensome; compensation was offered to leavers. The last of Al Majdal's Arabs left for the Strip early in 1951. Al Majdal had (again) become Ashkelon.[42]

Along the border with Transjordanian-held Palestine

Few Arab villagers were left on the Israeli side of the cease-fire lines separating the new Jewish State and the areas held by Transjordan and the Iraqi forces in the Triangle when the major hostilities ended in eastern Palestine in mid-1948. The empty villages were demolished by the IDF to render the sites less attractive to would-be returnees. Along the frontier, IDF units continuously harassed Arab cultivators and infiltrators; there was no telling who was a spy or potential saboteur and who a genuine civilian. The IDF played "safe."

The activities of the Palmah's 4th Battalion (Harel Brigade) in November 1948 were fairly representative of the period between the end of the hostilities and the signing, on 3 April 1949, of the Israeli–Jordanian General Armistice Agreement. The battalion held positions along the southern flank of the Jerusalem corridor, opposite the Arab Legion. On 5 November, B Company raided the area south of Beit Nattif and the border village of Al Jaba. At Khirbet Umm al Lauz, one platoon encountered dozens of refugees with flocks moving westwards. "The platoon . . . ordered them to get out [of Israeli-held territory]" and confiscated a flock of 65 goats, a camel and an ass. The following day, a platoon sent to "expel refugees" found some 150 at Khirbet Umm Burj, south of Beit Nattif. The unit expelled about 100, apparently injuring some of them. A raid on Al Jaba on the night of 5/6 November, in which some 15 houses were blown up, led to a temporary evacuation of the village.

Initially, 4th Battalion reported, the refugees were unresponsive to threats and refused to move eastwards. Some even asked "to live under 'Shertok's [*sic*] rule.'" But the raids ultimately proved persuasive, and the refugees encamped along the frontier south of Beit Nattif eventually moved off. Similar raiding, patrols and occasional sniping pushed eastwards refugees and local cultivators all along the line.

The Israeli–Jordanian armistice agreement of 3 April 1949 provided for minor frontier changes, with a few small areas (in the Beisan Valley and southwest of the Hebron Hills) going to Jordan, and some larger areas around and south of Baqa al Gharbiya and in Wadi 'Ara being ceded to Israel. In the secret negotiations with Abdullah and his emissaries, Israel had demanded that the Arabs cede territory to widen Israel's vulnerable Coastal Plain "waist" and almost openly threatened military action if

Transjordan and Iraq did not accede. Abdullah feared that a renewal of full-scale war would lose him the whole Triangle. The British chargé d'affaires in Amman, Pirie Gordon, compared Abdullah's cession of territory under military threat to Czech President Hacha's capitulation to Hitler in March 1939.[43]

Abdullah and the British feared that the cession, which involved handing over to Israeli rule 15–16 villages, would precipitate a new wave of refugees, 12,000–15,000 strong. It was to guard against this that Article VI, clause 6 of the armistice agreement explicitly protected the villagers against expulsion and confiscations.[44]

But the Americans, British and Transjordanians suspected that Israel, following the Arab withdrawal from the ceded areas in June, would engineer the departure of the villagers. The British Consul-General in Jerusalem Sir Hugh Dow, for instance, thought that the United Nations Relief for Palestine Refugees "would do well to prepare for a further 20,000 [refugees] . . . [they] will almost certainly be driven out on some pretext or other."[45] Secretary of State Dean Acheson instructed Mc-Donald to propose to the Israeli government to issue public reassurances to the villagers that they would be well-treated. At the same time, the Transjordanians took steps to allay the villagers' fears. Brigadier Ahmad Bey al Halil, the Transjordanian Military Governor of the Triangle, pleaded with Israeli representatives that Tel Aviv broadcast assurances "by wireless that [the civilians] would come to no harm should they remain in Israel . . . He . . . begged that no incidents occur that would discourage Arabs . . . to remain in Israel." IDF intelligence reported from mid-April that the Arabs "live in great fear of our 'barbarity' and it would take little inducement to persuade them to abandon their lands."

The Israelis reassured the United States that nothing would happen to the villagers. They did not want to jeopardise the implementation of the cession or damage relations with Washington. Eytan told McDonald that Tel Aviv was "keenly anxious" for the villagers to stay put as Israel did not wish to further aggravate the refugee situation and that if these villagers were to stay, it would serve as proof "to the world that mass exodus [from] other [previously] captured areas was more fault hysterical Arabs . . . than occupying forces." Eytan said that the troops who would take over the area were being thoroughly briefed about how to behave towards the inhabitants.[46] A fortnight later, McDonald conveyed Acheson's and Truman's concern directly to Sharett. The Ambassador asked that Israel reassure the inhabitants; harm to them might jeopardise the continuing Israeli–Jordanian peace negotiations. Sharett reassured McDonald that all would be well.[47] But Sharett's thinking in fact took another tack altogether: "We have inherited a number of important villages in the Sharon and Shomron and I imagine that the intention will be to be rid of them, as these sites are on the border. Security interest[s] dictate to be rid of them. [But] the matter [in light of the American diplomatic warnings] is very complicated."[48]

The cession in May passed smoothly. There was no expulsion and no IDF pressures on the locals. Political considerations – generated by the specific and repeated American warnings against the backdrop of the deadlocked Lausanne Conference – prevailed over the military's desire for Arab-less borders. There was apparently no "clean" way to pressure the Arabs into leaving. The inhabitants of Baqa al Gharbiya, At Taiyiba, Qaqun, Qalansuwa, Karf Qasim, At Tira and the Wadi 'Ara villages stayed put. As Sharett put it on 28 July: "This time . . . the Arabs learned the lesson; they are not running away. It is not possible in every place to arrange what some of our boys engineered in Faluja [where] they chased away the Arabs after we signed an . . . international commitment . . . There were warnings from the UN and the U.S. in this matter . . . [There were] at least 25–30,000 . . . whom we could not uproot."[49]

An exception was made of 1,200–1,500 refugees from elsewhere living in and around Baqa al Gharbiya. On the night of 27 June, they were "forcefully and brutally" (in Sharett's phrase)[50] evicted and pushed across the border into the Triangle.

The Israel–Jordan Mixed Armistice Commission, chaired by the United Nations, investigated the incident during the following two months. Israel argued that the armistice agreement protected only local inhabitants, not refugees temporarily resident in the ceded areas and that, in any case, it was the Baqa al Gharbiya *mukhtar* rather than the Israeli authorities who had ordered the refugees to leave. In September, the Commission – meaning its United Nations chairman – ruled in favour of Israel's interpretation (save for the case of 36 of the expellees, permanent inhabitants who had been driven out "illegally").

Not unnaturally, given the character of his relationship with the Israeli authorities, the *mukhtar* confirmed the Israeli arguments. He testified that "the village council decided for economic reasons [the village] could not maintain the many refugees in the village . . . and [therefore] told them to leave. No order to do this had been received from the Israeli military governor or from any other Israeli official. In certain cases, when refugees did not agree to leave, the *mukhtar* told them that this was an order from of the [Israeli] governor . . . (despite the fact that this order had not been issued by the governor)."[51]

One Israeli analysis explained that the refugees had left "under pressure from the local inhabitants" because they had been a burden, in terms of accommodation and employment, "they had stolen from the local inhabitants, they had stolen from the Jewish neighbours [in neighbouring settlements], [and they had] been engaged in smuggling." The refugees, as the Baqa al Gharbiya notables saw things, had also frustrated the development of good relations between the local inhabitants and the Israeli authorities.[52]

While the Commission's decision hung in the balance, Israel made it clear that, if forced to take the expellees back, they, the refugees, "would regret it" (in Dayan's phrase). General Riley, the United Nations chief of observers in Palestine, privately described this as "typical" of Israel's use of threats during negotiations.[53] At the same time, clandestinely, Israeli intelligence mounted a campaign to persuade the expellees now in the Triangle not to agree to return to Baqa al Gharbiya. "We are busy spreading rumours among the Arab refugees," Dayan wrote to Sharett, "that whoever is returned to Israel will not receive assistance from the Red Cross . . . would be returning against the wishes of the Israeli government [and] there is no chance that he would return one day to his [original] land. We therefore hope that . . . most of them will refuse to return." The rumour-mongering also included the idea that there would probably be a mass refugee repatriation in the future and that those Baqa expellees returning "prematurely" and against Israel's wishes would "suffer for it." The expellees duly told the United Nations' investigators that they were not eager to return. Arye Friedlander (Shalev), Dayan's deputy on the Mixed Armistice Commission, observed that "these rumours . . . are easily accepted by the Arabs . . ."[54]

The "pro-Israeli" vote at the Mixed Armistice Commission's meeting on 15–16 September was influenced at least in part by the Israeli threat of mistreatment of the refugees should they be returned to Israel.[55]

During late 1948 and early 1949, in a number of semi-intact sites along the border between Israel and Transjordanian-occupied Palestine, there was a small shifting population of uncertain, frightened Arabs who feared to stay and yet feared to go into permanent exile. All these villages were ultimately cleared of population and eventually levelled or settled with Jews. The longest-lasting of these communities was Zakariya, at the southwestern entrance to the Jerusalem corridor. In March 1949, pressing for the eviction of its remaining "145 or so" inhabitants, the Interior Ministry official in charge of the Jerusalem District pointed out that "in the village there are many good houses, and it is possible to accommodate in them several hundred new immigrants." In January 1950, Ben-Gurion, on vacation in Tiberias, met with Sharett, Weitz and other officials and decided to evict the Arabs of Zakariya (along with those of Al Majdal (Ashkelon) and several other sites) "[but] without coercion." Land-owners who wished to leave the country would be bought out. The health and food situation in Zakariya was appalling. Eventually, on 9 June 1950, the villagers were evicted, most being resettled in Ramle. Some may have moved to Jordan.[56]

The clearing of the borders of Arab communities in the wake of the hostilities was initiated by the IDF but, like the expulsions of the months before, was curbed by limitations imposed by the civilian leadership and was never carried out consistently or comprehensively.

Even the initial border clearing operation in the north in November 1948, which set as its goal an Arab-free strip about 10 kilometres deep, was carried out without consistency or political logic. Maronite communities such as Kafr Bir'im and Al Mansura were cleared out while some Muslims in Tarshiha and Fassuta were allowed to stay. Intervention by "soft-hearted" Israeli leaders, such as Shitrit and Ben-Zvi, succeeded in halting some evictions and expulsions. Consideration of future Jewish–Druse, Jewish–Circassian and Jewish–Christian relations, as well as fears for Israel's relations with the churches and its image abroad, played a decisive role in mobilising the various civilian bureaucracies against undifferentiating, wholesale expulsions and changed expulsion to Lebanon to eviction to sites inside Israel.

In terms of the army's independence in expelling or evicting Arab communities, November 1948 marked a watershed. The Lebanese border expulsion–eviction operation was ordered by OC Northern Front, probably after receiving clearance from Ben-Gurion. It was not weighed or debated in advance by any civilian political body. Thereafter, the IDF almost never acted alone and independently; it sought and had to obtain approval and decision from the supreme civilian authorities, be it the full Cabinet or one or more of the various ministerial and inter-departmental executive committees. The IDF's opinions and needs, which defined in great measure Israel's security requirements, continued to carry great weight in the decision-making councils. But they were not always decisive and the army ceased to act alone.

The army wanted Arab-free strips along all the frontiers. It failed to achieve such a strip on the Lebanese border (Rihaniya, Jish, Hurfeish, Tarshiha and Mi'ilya remained) as it was to fail – even more decisively – along the armistice line with Jordan west of the Triangle. With respect to the Arab villages in the Samarian foothills and in Wadi 'Ara, ceded to Israel in summer 1949, international political considerations overwhelmed the security arguments. Given the state of Israeli–United Nations and Israeli–United States relations against the backdrop of the Lausanne talks, Israel's leaders found that they could not allow themselves the luxury of causing the type of friction a new wave of expulsions would have generated. The American warnings on this score had been repeated and explicit. The fact that talks were proceeding intermittently with King Abdullah and that Tel Aviv still hoped for a breakthrough towards peace with the Hashemite kingdom no doubt also influenced the decision-making.

In this sense, the very success of the intimidation operation at Faluja and Iraq al Manshiya in early March, which precipitated the flight of the 3,000 or so villagers, proved counter-productive. It put the Arabs, the United Nations and the United States on their guard against a repeat performance along the border with the Triangle.

But where politics did not interfere, the army's desire for Arab-clear borders prompted by security considerations was generally decisive. Arab villagers along the border meant problems in terms of espionage and infiltration in both directions. When the villages were semi-abandoned, as was generally the case, it meant a continuous return and resettlement of Arab inhabitants in the empty houses, thus consolidating the Arab presence in the area and ultimately increasing the number of Arabs in the country. To this was added the interest of the Jewish agricultural and settlement bodies in more lands and sites for Jewish settlement and cultivation and the interest of the various relevant government ministries (health, finance, minorities) to be rid of the burden of economically unviable, desolate, semi-abandoned villages. These interests generally dovetailed.

The period November 1948 – March 1949 saw also the gradual shift of emphasis from expulsion out of the country to eviction from one site to another inside the country: what could be done during hostilities became increasingly more difficult to engineer in the following months of truce and armistice. There was still a desire to see Arabs leave the country and occasionally this was achieved (as at Faluja and Al Majdal), albeit through persuasion, selective intimidation, psychological pressure and financial inducement. The "expulsion" of the Baqa al Gharbiya refugees was a classic of the genre, with the order being channelled through the local *mukhtar*. But generally, political circumstances ruled out expulsion. Eviction and transfer of communities from one site to another was seen as more palatable and more easily achieved.

The evictions in Eastern and Upper Galilee in 1949 were designed to reduce the number of Arab villages (as was the case, for example, at Kafr 'Inan and Farradiya). Political, demographic, agricultural and economic considerations rather than military needs seem to have been decisive. The presence of Arabs in a half-empty village, given the circumstances, meant that the village would probably soon fill out with returnees. Completely depopulating the village and then levelling it or filling the houses with

Jewish settlers meant that infiltrators would have that many less sites to return to. In complementary fashion, filling out semi-empty villages (as happened at Tur'an, Ar Reina and Sha'b) with the evicted population of other villages meant that the host villages would be "full up" and unable to accommodate many infiltrees.

The border clearing operations carried out between November 1948 and 1951 were primarily motivated by security considerations but the country's political leaders were not unmindful of their "beneficial" effect in keeping static or reducing the number of Israel's Arabs. It is extremely difficult to accurately estimate the numbers of expellees and evictees in these operations. Excluding the Negev bedouin, it is probable that the number in these operations kicked out of, or persuaded to leave, the country was not far off 10,000; many hundreds more were evicted and transferred to other villages. If one includes the northern Negev bedouins, the total may have been 20,000–30,000. In addition, hundreds of illegal infiltrees during this period were rounded up and pushed across the borders.

Chapter 9

Solving the refugee problem, December 1948 – September 1949

The Palestine Conciliation Commission and Lausanne I: stalemate

International efforts to solve the refugee problem at the end of 1948 and during the first half of 1949 proceeded along two crisscrossing tracks – the activities of the United Nations agencies, primarily the Palestine Conciliation Commission (PCC), and the activities of the Great Powers, meaning, primarily, the United States. Both sets of efforts were guided in large measure by Bernadotte's testament, the interim report of mid-September 1948, and the "doctrinal" postulate that the right of the refugee's return to his home and land was absolute and should be recognised by all the parties concerned. This postulate was enshrined two months after Bernadotte's death in United Nations General Assembly Resolution 194 (III), passed on 11 December 1948. The resolution stated that "the refugees wishing to return to their homes and live at peace with their neighbours should be permitted to do so at the earliest practicable date." The PCC, set up by that resolution, was instructed to facilitate the repatriation of those wishing to return.

The absolute nature of the return provision was immediately and almost universally qualified by the appreciation that Israel would not allow a mass return and that many of the refugees, in any case, might not want to return to live under Jewish rule. It was understood by the powers, and by Bernadotte himself already from late summer 1948, that the bulk of the refugees would not be repatriated. The solution to the refugee problem, therefore, would have to rest mainly on organised resettlement in Arab-held areas and countries.

The decision in principle, not to allow a return, taken in Tel Aviv in the summer of 1948, hardened into an iron resolve during the following months. Israel, beside arguing strategic necessity by claiming that returning refugees would constitute a Fifth Column, pointed un-abashedly to the changed physical realities on the ground. In presenting the case for resettlement of the refugees in the Arab states rather than repatriation, two top Israeli officials, Michael Comay and Zalman Lifshitz, in March 1949 wrote: "During the war and the Arab exodus, the basis of their economic life crumbled away. Moveable property . . . has disappeared. Livestock has been slaughtered or sold. Thousands of town and village dwellings have been destroyed in the course of the fighting or in order to deny their use to enemy forces . . . And of those which remain habitable, most are serving as temporary homes for [Jewish] immigrants."[1]

Foreign Ministry Director General Eytan shortly afterwards wrote in the same vein to Claude de Boisanger, the French chairman of the PCC: "The war that was fought in Palestine was bitter and destructive, and it would be doing the refugees a disservice to let them persist in the belief that if they returned, they would find their homes or shops or fields intact. In certain cases, it would be difficult for them even to identify the sites upon which their villages once stood." Eytan added that masses of Jewish immigrants had poured into the country and their absorption "might have been impossible altogether if the houses abandoned by the Arabs had not stood empty. As it was, the government took advantage of this vacant accommodation . . . Generally, it can be said that any Arab house that survived the impact of the war . . . now shelters a Jewish family. There can be no return to the status quo ante."[2]

But the Arab states refused to absorb the refugees. Over the second half of 1948, the Arabs united in thrusting the refugee problem to the top of the agenda. They demanded repatriation of the dispossessed and linked all progress towards a resolution of the conflict to Israeli agreement to a return. United Nations and United States efforts to organise Israeli–Arab peace talks were dashed on the rocks of Arab insistence on, and Israeli resistance to, a refugee return. Arab policy on this score was bolstered by a genuine economic inability to properly absorb hundreds of thousands of refugees and by fear of the refugees as a major potential subversive element *vis-à-vis* their own regimes. The western governments, fed by alarmed diplomats in the field and fired by global Cold War concerns, concurred in the view that the masses of disgruntled refugees were potential tools of Communism and posed a threat to the pro-western Arab host governments.

The Arab states appeared to be in a no-lose situation. Israeli refusal to take back the refugees, leaving them in misery, would turn world opinion and perhaps western governments against the Jewish State on humanitarian grounds. Israeli agreement to take back all or many of the refugees would result in the political and possibly military destabilisation of the Jewish State, as Israel's leaders appreciated. The refugees had become for the Arab states a "political weapon against the Jews."[3]

For Tel Aviv, in complementary fashion, the refugees constituted a political weapon in so far as they were seen as a means of prising peace and recognition out of a hostile Arab world. As the months passed and the prospects of peace grew increasingly remote, Israel hesitantly and rather ungenerously brandished the refugees as a carrot in the multilateral negotiations. Israel, indeed, had little else, save hard-won territory, to offer the Arabs in exchange for peace. Tel Aviv would accept back a small number of refugees if the Arabs agreed to direct negotiations leading to peace with the Jewish State.

It is against this backdrop of policy and calculation that the two-track efforts of the United Nations and United States in the first half of 1949 to solve the Middle East conflict in general and the Palestinian refugee problem in particular must be seen.

The 11 December 1948 United Nations General Assembly resolution asserted the "right" of the refugees to return; Bernadotte had insisted on it; the Arabs would agree to nothing less; and the western powers, including the United States, supported the resolution.

But could Israel be persuaded to accede to a return? Western diplomats in the Middle East on the whole thought not. William Burdett, the United States Consul-General in Jerusalem, saw the promulgation of the Absentees Property Ordinance in Tel Aviv in December 1948 as effectively a rejoinder to the United Nations resolution. "Together with settlement of new Jewish immigrants . . . new Ordinance considered further indication PGI [i.e., Provisional Government of Israel] intends not rpt not permit return sizeable number Arab refugees." Burdett warned that this would solve Israel's Arab minority problem but would also "perpetuate refugee problem."[4] Sir Rafael Cilento, the Director of the United Nations Refugee Relief Project, told British officials the same thing. Israel was unwilling to take back most or a large number of the refugees; resettlement in the Arab countries was the only realistic option.[5] The United States representative in Jidda, Saudi Arabia, agreed, albeit reasoning somewhat differently: "There can be no question of returning large numbers of Arabs to Israeli territory. It is inevitable that they would be treated as second-class citizens . . . A new large dissident minority in a Near Eastern state is certainly not something to be sought after." J. Rives Childs thought that resettlement of the refugees "principally in Iraq and possibly Syria" would be the best solution.[6]

But the Arab states refused to absorb the exiles. The impasse pushed the United States and the PCC towards a solution based on Arab agreement to absorb, with western aid, most of the refugees coupled with Israeli agreement to the repatriation of the remaining several hundred thousand.

256

From the first, and accurately conveying official Israeli opinion, both Ambassador James McDonald and Burdett thought Israeli agreement to such massive repatriation unlikely, if not inconceivable. Burdett doubted, given Israel's major economic problems, whether Tel Aviv would even agree to pay the refugees substantial compensation. Politically, security in the region would best be served by resettlement of the refugees in the Arab countries, principally in the Arab-held parts of Palestine and in Transjordan. "Since the U.S. has supported the establishment of a Jewish State, it should insist on a homogeneous one which will have the best possible chance of stability. Return of the refugees would create a continuing 'minority problem' and form a constant temptation both for uprisings and intervention by neighbouring Arab states," wrote Burdett. But he acknowledged that, in the absence of organised, systematic absorption and resettlement in the Arab countries, the refugees represented a subversive "opportunity" on which the USSR "may capitalize."[7]

Mark Ethridge, the Southern Baptist appointed by Truman to the PCC, quickly understood that the developing impasse over the refugees was lethal to any possibility of peace in the Middle East. Ethridge thought Shertok's attitude – that the refugees were "essentially unassimilable" in Israel and should all be resettled in the Arab states – "inhuman." Ethridge said that Israel's views in this context were "similar to those which I heard Hitler express in Germany in 1933. It [*sic*] might be described as anti-Semitism toward the Arabs." At the same time, he believed that "it might be wise in long run to resettle greater portion Arab refugees in neighbouring Arab states."[8]

Ethridge, like everyone attuned to the Arab stand, realised that the refugee problem was the "immediate key to peace negotiations if not to peace" itself. The Arab states were united around the proposition that a start to the solution of the refugee problem must precede meaningful negotiations for a settlement. The Arabs, Ethridge felt, had to reduce their demand for complete and absolute repatriation and Israel had to abandon its opposition to any meaningful repatriation. Both sides were treating the refugees "as [a] political pawn." By the end of February 1949, Ethridge felt that there was need of "a generous Israeli gesture" – that is, a statement agreeing to a return of a large number of refugees and an immediate start to repatriation. This would break the "Arab psychosis" and enable movement towards a compromise. Ethridge asked the State Department to "encourage" Israel to make the gesture and the Arabs to respond favourably. The idea of a redemptive Israeli "gesture" as the key to peace was to characterise all Ethridge's work on the PCC during the frustrating weeks ahead.

The lack of such a gesture had "prejudiced whole cause of peaceful

257

settlement," Ethridge wrote in March. He dismissed as "rubbish" Shertok's insistence that Israel could not make such a gesture or specify the number of refugees it might be willing to take back.

On 14 March, Shertok wrote Ethridge that while the main solution to the refugee problem must rest on resettlement in the Arab countries, Israel might, under certain circumstances, admit a "certain proportion," though this would depend on the "kind of peace" that emerged. But Ethridge sought a precise and public Israeli commitment. Six weeks of PCC efforts had failed to elicit any concessions. Ethridge pressed Washington to "urge" Tel Aviv to make the required "gesture."⁹

Sharett (Shertok) put it bluntly at a meeting with Acheson in Washington on 22 March: the Israeli government "could not possibly make such a commitment" before negotiations began and, in any case, "it was out of the question to consider the possibility of repatriation of any substantial numbers of the refugees."¹⁰

What to do about the refugees had been debated within the United States administration since late summer 1948. The establishment and peregrinations of the PCC had in a sense taken the pressure off Washington. The PCC had to be given a chance; parallel American activities might jeopardise the Commission's prospects of success. And perhaps the PCC might achieve something before Washington was forced into arm-twisting in Tel Aviv and/or in the Arab states. But Israeli and Arab inflexibility, the PCC's lack of success and Ethridge's constant importunings (often in letters to his friend, President Harry Truman), by the end of March caused a change of tone and approach in Washington, especially in contacts with Israel. Ambassador McDonald's "soft" line was temporarily abandoned.

The joint communication on 29 March from Ethridge and George McGhee, Special Assistant to Acheson, appears to have been decisive with Truman and Acheson. Sent after a meeting of Arab leaders in Beirut on the refugee problem, the letter reflected the growing desperation felt by American policy-makers. Ethridge and McGhee forcefully argued that without "maximum possible repatriation," there was no hope of Arab absorption of a substantial number of refugees. Resettlement in the Arab countries would be a long and arduous process, contrary to the wishes of the refugees themselves and of the Arab host countries, would lay the seeds of future economic and political difficulties and would provide "lasting monuments [to] UN and US failure." Repatriation, on the other hand, could be accomplished quickly and far more cheaply. However, taking account of Israel's military, political and economic objections to total repatriation, the two officials concluded that Israel must be pressed to repatriate at least "250,000" refugees, from the areas conquered by the IDF outside the Jewish State Partition borders. The rest of the refugees, it was implied, should be resettled in the Arab countries.[11]

Washington was fired into action. McDonald "informally" pressed that Israel agree to take back the 250,000 originally from the conquered areas.[12]

On 5 April, Acheson and Sharett met in New York. Acheson performed with unwonted bluntness, deploying the "big gun" of presidential displeasure. Truman, he said, was greatly concerned about the plight of the refugees, who numbered some "800,000." "While it can be understood that repatriation of all of these refugees is not a practical solution, nevertheless we anticipate that a considerable number must be repatriated if a solution is to be found. The president is particularly anxious that an impasse not develop on this subject, with one side refusing to negotiate for a final settlement until a solution is found for refugees and the other side refusing to take steps to solve the refugee question until there is a final settlement." The President, said Acheson, felt the time was ripe for an Israeli gesture – a statement of readiness to allow back "say a fourth of the refugees" (i.e., those from the conquered areas). Such a gesture would "make it possible for the president to continue his strong and warm support for Israel and efforts being made by its government to establish its new political and economic structure on a firm basis." The threat was clear.

Sharett responded reflexively, questioning the refugee numbers offered by Acheson, rejecting the distinction between 1947 Partition boundaries and those carved out by the IDF, and rejecting a mass refugee return as a threat to Israel's homogeneity.[13]

The PCC–American pressure slowly wore down Israeli obduracy. An early sign of this appeared in Shertok's contacts over February–March 1949 with the second Transfer Committee (Weitz, Danin and Lifshitz), appointed by Ben-Gurion at the end of August 1948 to plan the refugees' organised resettlement in the Arab states. On 11 February, Shertok informed the Committee that he had told the PCC that Israel would not allow a return. Israel, he agreed, had to persuade American and Arab public opinion that there could and would be no return. A month later, however, while asking the Committee for a more detailed proposal on the possibilities of funding and resettling the refugees in Arab countries, Sharett requested that the three prepare "an absolutely secret plan for the event that the Cabinet feels itself compelled to agree to a return of part of the refugees to Israel. This plan must determine the maximal dimensions of the return . . . the method of selecting the returnees and . . . the areas and villages that can be resettled [by the returnees]." A plan was apparently prepared.[14]

Ben-Gurion himself hinted at a new-fangled flexibility at his meeting with the PCC in Tel Aviv on 7 April. (At that meeting the Israeli Prime Minister denied "emphatically that Israel had expelled the Arabs . . . The State of Israel expelled nobody and will never do it," he said. PCC chairman de Boisanger seemed to agree, noting that "no Arab maintained [before the PCC] that he had been expelled from the country. The refugees said they had fled from fear, because of the preparations for war, as thousands fled from France in 1940." Ben-Gurion thanked de Boisanger for "admitting" that the Yishuv had not expelled the Arabs.)[15]

Vague hints at a possible, ultimate readiness to repatriate some refugees served the practical purpose of parrying PCC–American pressure or deferring for a time still greater pressures to agree to a still greater return. But the Yishuv's desire to take back refugees had in no way increased; if it depended on Tel Aviv, there would be no returnees whatever.

Meanwhile, the PCC was affected by growing gloom. In late March and early April, de Boisanger, Ethridge and Yalcin, the Turkish PCC representative, concluded that their Middle East shuttle was fruitless. Yalcin, "disgruntled" chiefly with the United States, explained it this way: "Nobody was strong enough or sufficiently determined to deter the Jews from doing anything they wanted to do . . . [U.S.] diplomatists and officials seemed [not] to have the courage to tell the truth about the Jews unless they were within sight of retirement." Yalcin added that before joining the PCC, he had "always had a soft spot for the Jews . . . a universally oppressed people." Now, according to his British inter-locutor, he was "definitely anti-Semitic."[16]

The PCC took two steps to try to break the logjam: it set up a Technical Committee on Refugees to work out "measures . . . for the implementation of the provisions of the [11 December 1948 United Nations General Assembly] resolution," meaning to find out how many refugees there were, how many wished to be repatriated and how many to stay in Arab countries, and how these could be economically "rehabilitated"; and called an international conference at Lausanne where, under PCC chairmanship, the parties could discuss the whole range of issues – refugees, Jerusalem, borders, recognition – and hammer out a compre-hensive peace settlement.[17] The PCC, after months of fruitless labour, reasoned that nothing could be lost by a conference and that it might manœuvre Arab and Jew towards compromise, neither party wishing to lay itself open to a charge of torpedoing the gathering. Ethridge demanded complementary and forceful American pressure on Israel.

Israel's policy-makers met to define the country's positions at Lausanne. The meetings were attended by Ben-Gurion, Sharett, Yadin, Eytan (who was to head the delegation to Lausanne), members of the Transfer Committee, and other senior officials, including Sasson, who was to be Eytan's second in command at the conference. The refugee problem received scant attention, few of the participants anticipating that the Arab delegations intended to thrust it immediately to the top of the agenda. When Shiloah, director of the Foreign Ministry's Political Division, commented: "We have still almost not touched upon the question of the refugees," no one took him up and the discussion on border problems continued. Only Leo Kohn, Sharett's Political Adviser, who was not a participant at the meetings, predicted at the time that the Arabs would categorically demand that the refugees receive top billing. Kohn advised that the delegation stress the security threat which a mass return would pose and cited the Sudeten problem as a telling and useful comparison: "Now that the exodus of the Arabs from our country has taken place, what moral right have those who fully endorsed the expulsion of the Sudeten Germans from Czechoslovakia to demand that we re-admit these Arabs?"[18]

Yadin and, implicitly, Ben-Gurion rejected compromise on repatriation. Yadin lumped together the issues of "the refugees and the [state's final] borders." "My opinion is that we must say, with all cruelty: The refugee problem is no concern of the Land of Israel . . . We must say openly: If they [i.e., the Arabs] want war – let them continue [pressing us] on the refugee problem . . . It can be explained to them that the refugees in their countries bring them only benefit."

Ben-Gurion spoke obliquely. He stressed that Israel's primary concern and need at the moment was the absorption of new Jewish immigrants: "This comprehends all the historical needs of the state." Immigrants and their absorption were the key to Israel's security. The implication in context was that repatriation would preclude absorption of immigrants.

Lifshitz and Comay described their recent meeting with Ethridge. Lifshitz said that Ethridge believed that Israel had expelled the Arabs. Ethridge had told the two Israelis of his encounter with a column of some 200 refugees just pushed by Israel across the Lebanese border and warned against repetition of such expulsions. Ethridge called for Israel to repatriate 250,000. Comay said Israel had enough Arabs ("130,000"). Ethridge concluded that "Israel does not intend to take back one refugee more than she is forced to."

Ethridge was incensed by the denials of Ben-Gurion (on 7 April) and Comay of all Israeli responsibility for the creation of the refugee problem, as he put it, "in face of Jaffa, Deir Yassin, Haifa and all reports that come to us from refugee organisations that new refugees are being created every day by repression and terrorism." Ethridge added that Arab propaganda was ineffective as compared with the Israeli public relations machine and said that had the Arabs a "tenth of the genius at it, they would rouse public opinion to where it would engulf Israel in a wave of indignation."

The upshot of the consultative meetings in Tel Aviv was a reiteration of the traditional line – no substantial repatriation, no "gesture" and no statement on the number of returnees Israel might be willing to take back within the framework of a settlement.[19]

The lack of movement in the Israeli position was brought home to Ethridge at a meeting with Ben-Gurion in Tiberias (which, in his cable, Ethridge called "Siberias") on 18 April. Ben-Gurion treated Ethridge to an extended analysis of British misdemeanours in the Middle East since 1917 and to a lecture on how the United States "should declare its second independence of [the] British Foreign Office." On the refugees, Ben-Gurion gave not an inch. He made no mention of a possible Israeli "gesture." Resettlement in the Arab countries was the "only logical answer," he said. Israel "cannot and will not accept return Arab refugees to Israeli territory," both on grounds of security and economics. Israel, said Ben-Gurion, would compensate the refugee *fellahin* for their land, would provide advice on resettlement in the Arab countries and would allow back a few refugees within the family reunion scheme.

The meeting appropriately crowned the months of fruitless PCC shuttling. Ethridge rushed off a cable to Acheson asking to be relieved of his post. The PCC could not solve the refugee problem, he wrote; only American pressure could facilitate a solution. He did not look to the prospective meeting at Lausanne with great hope.[20]

Ethridge's resignation threat elicited a reaffirmation of the American position favouring substantial repatriation and a plea by the Secretary of State and the President that he soldier on, at least for a while longer. Acheson wrote that the United States Government "is not disposed to change policy because of Israeli intransigence"; Truman wrote that he was "rather disgruntled with the manner in which the Jews are approaching the refugee problem." Truman and Acheson both personally pressed Israeli officials at the end of April for a softening of the Israeli stance.[21] Ethridge agreed to stay on, probably hoping that at Lausanne the United States at last would bring its full weight to bear on Israel.

On the eve of the convocation of the conference, Acheson instructed his missions in the Arab world to press for greater flexibility all around. Washington asked London to make similar representations to the Arab governments. Acheson reiterated American support for the "principle of repatriation" alongside the need to obtain Arab agreement to "resettlement [of] those not desiring repatriation."[22]

The delegations gathered at Lausanne at the end of April. But the PCC's effort to bring the parties to formal face-to-face negotiations failed (though Arabs and Jews met often for informal discussions). The refugees represented the major, initial and insuperable sticking point.

The Arab delegations arrived united in the demand that Israel declare acceptance of the principle of repatriation before they would agree to negotiate on peace. Eytan, in response, mouthed only a pious plea for the refugees' "permanent settlement and rehabilitation." The Israeli delegation, he said, had "come prepared to tackle [the refugee problem] with sincerity and above all in the spirit of realism." "Realism" meant no repatriation.

Privately, however, Eytan acknowledged that Israel's opening positions were inadequate. He wrote Sharett: "I think the time has come for us to realize that mere words will not carry us much further towards peace . . . A statement such as that which I issued [at the press conference] this afternoon is interpreted by everyone as yet another attempt by us to shirk the real issues." Israel, in Ethridge's view, "had grown arrogant" on military and politcal successes, and was "unwilling to [meaningfully] negotiate." Ethridge was pessimistic, believing that Ben-Gurion alone determined policy and Ben-Gurion's attitude was "negative . . . towards the [PCC], [to Ethridge] himself, to the negotiations, [and] to the various problems which had to be solved."[23]

The PCC, the delegations and the Great Power representatives got down to work. The Commission met this or that delegation; then met with the other side, conveying the first delegation's views. Then the second delegation's responses would be submitted to the first delegation, and so on. Behind the scenes, PCC members and Great Power representatives met privately to cajole, blandish or pressure members of the Arab and Israeli delegations. Occasionally, Sasson would meet privately (often in Paris) with this or that Arab official. Eytan earlier had candidly described Sasson's prospective role at the conference: he and Shiloah had opposed Sasson's appointment as head of delegation. Rather, "we see his role as that of an ideal liaison officer between our delegation and the Arabs, making contacts, speaking soft words into Arab ears, formulating difficult matters in a way which may make it easier for the Arabs to swallow them, etc. etc."[24]

Through the spring and summer, Israel and Transjordan conducted a parallel, direct peace negotiation. Sharett met King Abdullah on 5 May 1949. They discussed borders, recognition, access for Transjordan to the Mediterranean and refugees. Amman linked the refugee and territorial questions: the more occupied territory Israel would be willing to cede to Transjordan, the more refugees Transjordan would be willing to absorb and resettle. Abdullah was primarily interested in Lydda and Ramle, but

Israel was unwilling to cede territory. Indeed, it sought further land (Tulkarm and Qalqilya). Nothing came of the talks though, in Tel Aviv's view, the Transjordanians were "most anxious" to make peace.[25]

At the same time, Sasson held talks informally at Lausanne with the Palestinian refugee delegation, headed by Mohammad Nimr al Hawari, the Jaffa lawyer who had commanded the *Najjada*. Hawari proposed that Israel agree to the repatriation of 400,000, who would live in peace with Israel and act as a "peace bridge" between Israel and the Arab states. On the other hand, if the masses of refugees continued to live stateless and impoverished along Israel's borders, they would cause the Jewish State nothing but trouble. This – not a return – was precisely what the Mufti and Abdullah wanted, argued Hawari. The Arab states did not want the refugees and would not assimilate them. Nothing came of these talks. Hawari returned to Ramallah, "desperate and depressed."[26]

No progress was achieved in May. The impasse hardened. The Arabs demanded Israeli agreement to the principle of full repatriation and a start to actual repatriation before substantive peace talks began. Israel insisted that resettlement of the refugees in the Arab states was the inevitable core of a solution and that Israel might agree to an indeterminate but small measure of repatriation only within the framework of a final peace settlement. Israel refused to throw out numbers. Eytan described the situation as "one vast vicious circle." Only the introduction of some "entirely new element" could offer an exit.[27]

Whether by Israeli design or by American misunderstanding and wishful thinking (or – as is probable – by an admixture of the two), while things at Lausanne were at a standstill, Israeli diplomats in the United States strongly signalled a far more moderate line by Tel Aviv. Abba Eban, Israel's representative to the United Nations, on 5 May told the United Nations Ad Hoc Political Committee at Lake Success that Israel "does not reject" the principle of repatriation.[28]

Eagerly awaiting such a sign of flexibility from Tel Aviv on this cardinal issue, United States policy-makers jumped for joy. Acheson took Eban to mean that Israel had formally accepted the principle of repatriation, and cabled as much to all and sundry.[29] Eliahu Elath, the Israeli Ambassador to Washington, provided further grounds for optimism by telling the Americans that Israel feels that "both repatriation and resettlement are required for solution of problem." However, Israel refused to talk numbers. Acheson believed that Israel would be more specific only after it was assured that the Arabs would integrate the remainder of the refugees and that "outside" financial assistance for such resettlement would be forthcoming.[30]

Of course, Israel had not accepted the principle of repatriation, whatever its emissaries were hinting or were understood to have said. But for weeks thereafter, American policy-makers referred to Israel's acceptance of the principle of repatriation. Israeli officials, such as Eban, found this amusing – and advantageous to Israel.[31]

But this was only a temporary semi-comic interlude. In truth, apart from fleeting moments of self-delusion, American policy-makers understood that Israel remained dead set against repatriation, and that this was a major obstacle to progress at Lausanne. Hence, at the end of May, Truman intervened personally, sending a forceful, minatory message to Ben-Gurion, conveying "grave" American concern. Washington, to no avail, had repeatedly asked Israel to accept "the principle of substantial repatriation and the immediate beginnings of repatriation on a reasonable scale . . . The U.S. Government," wrote Truman, "does not . . . regard the present attitude of the Israeli government as being consistent with the principles upon which U.S. support [of Israel] has been based." Israel's stand endangered the prospects of solving the conflict: its attitude "must inevitably lead to a rupture in [the Lausanne] conversations."[32]

American and PCC pressures on Israel increased as the prospect of any sort of settlement dimmed. Ethridge's resignation accurately reflected the situation and his personal sense of frustration. The PCC and Ethridge, as the Israelis saw it, were obsessed with "one point, and one point only" – Israel's refusal to accept the principle of repatriation. Eytan described Ethridge as a "fundamentally decent, fair-minded person, the best type of Southern liberal." But he felt that he had been "snubbed" in Tel Aviv and regarded the Israelis as dishonest, unethical and legalistic. He was returning to the United States "thoroughly disgruntled," an attitude Eytan expected Ethridge to pass on to Truman. Ethridge had regarded Israel's bland response of 8 June to Truman's message of 29 May as "impertinent," "a declaration of intellectual warfare against the U.S." Ethridge, according to Eytan, had remained "fair-minded enough" to see that the Arabs were being "unrealistic" over repatriation. But, to achieve "immediate peace," Israel had to agree to repatriate 200,000 refugees and to give the Arabs "part of the Southern Negev," Ethridge felt, according to Eytan.[33]

At the end of June, the Lausanne talks were recessed for three weeks, the PCC aiming to allow the two sides to utilise the break to contemplate the logjam and the prospect of failure, and to come up with concessions on the refugee and territorial issues.

Through June and early July, the policy-makers in Tel Aviv agonised over the problem, understanding that continued, blanket stonewalling would inevitably lead to the collapse of the conference, with Israel possibly figuring as chief culprit. The refugee problem "seems in many ways to have become now the central problem of our foreign affairs,'' wrote Teddy Kollek, one of Ben-Gurion's aides. (He was in London, trying, among other things, to interest British businessmen, including Sir Marcus Sieff, in financing development projects in the Middle East that could employ Palestinian refugees.) Kollek urged Tel Aviv to take "positive action," by which he may have meant that Israel should agree to a limited measure of repatriation.[34] The problem was to find a concession or "gesture" whose implementation could cause Israel least damage while sufficing to relieve or reduce American and PCC pressure on the Jewish State and to transfer the ball to the Arab court. The solution adopted was the "100,000 offer."

The Gaza Plan interlude

But before Israel made the "100,000 offer," another possible solution surfaced, which was intermittently to magnetise diplomatic effort for months. Given the realities of mid-1949, the "Gaza Plan" was a mirage, but it riveted the attention of policy-makers in Washington and, to a far lesser extent, in Tel Aviv and London, and held out the promise of a miraculous deliverance.

Simply and initially, the plan was that the Gaza Strip – the small strip of coastal Palestine south of Tel Aviv occupied by the Egyptian army since May 1948 – should be transferred to Israeli sovereignty along with its relatively large local and refugee populations. While gaining a strategic piece of real estate, Israel would thus be considered to have done its bit for refugee repatriation. In most American and British readings of the plan, the refugees in the Strip, after the transfer, were to be allowed to return to their cities and villages of origin. In a revised version, Israel, in addition to absorbing the Strip's refugee and local populations, was expected to give either Egypt or Transjordan (or both) territorial compensation for the Strip, probably in the southern Negev region. Discussion of the plan – even after real hope of its implementation had vanished – continued through the summer, playing a counterpoint to the American and PCC's main efforts to induce Israel to agree to a substantial "front door" repatriation and the Arab states to agree to planned refugee resettlement in the Arab countries.

In Operation Horev, between 22 December 1948 and 6 January 1949, the IDF had attempted to destroy the Egyptian army in the Strip and to conquer the area. The operation, which had involved a deep thrust into Sinai by IDF armoured columns, was only partially successful. An internationally-imposed cease-fire, on 7 January, halted the IDF onslaught in mid-stride. The Egyptian forces managed (barely) to hold onto most of the Strip. With the IDF withdrawal from Sinai back to the international frontier, under Great Power pressure, mainly by the British, the Egyptians re-established their lines of communications and supply with the Strip, and it remained in Egyptian hands.

But the position of the extended, semi-beleaguered Egyptian army remained highly uncomfortable during the following months. And, international relief efforts notwithstanding, the Strip's 200,000–250,000 refugees, whom Egypt did not want to absorb and Israel refused to take back, constituted a giant burden for the Egyptian authorities. Was holding onto the Strip worth the candle?

By March, according to Israeli officials, the Egyptians thought not. Sasson, who was in constant touch with the Egyptians in Paris, believed that Egypt wanted to evacuate the Strip. Sharett feared that Egypt would try to transfer the Strip into Transjordanian hands. Mapai Knesset Member David Hocohen suggested that it would be worth Israel's while to take over the area, even if it meant enlarging Israel's Arab minority. Sharett, while mindful of the price, thought that Israel would gain a strategic piece of real estate and "could portray the absorption of 100,000 refugees as a major contribution . . . to the solution of the refugee problem as a whole and to free itself once and for all of UN pressure in this regard."[35]

The idea was formally debated in the consultative meetings in April in preparation for the Lausanne talks. On 12 April, Sasson said that there were in the Strip altogether some "140,000" Arabs; the mooted figure of 240,000 was an exaggeration. Yadin said that an Israeli take-over of the Strip under present conditions would be a "catastrophe." There were three possibilities, he said: turning the Strip into some form of autonomous Egyptian–Israeli protectorate, which he considered "the ideal solution"; incorporation of the Strip in Israel; or "that the Arabs in the area will go somewhere else and we will receive the territory."[36]

No decision was taken. Ethridge, reporting from Jerusalem on 13 April, thought that Israel would not take the Strip – which, he said, contained 230,000 refugees and 100,000 locals – if it meant absorbing its entire population. But, as Ethridge learned a few days later, Ben-Gurion quite clearly favoured Israeli absorption of the Strip, with (and despite) its population. Ben-Gurion even seems to have suggested that the Gaza refugees would be allowed to return to their original villages.[37]

The idea of the Gaza Plan meshed with the peace plan then being secretly negotiated with Abdullah. Abdullah stressed Transjordan's need for an outlet to the sea via Gaza or Acre. The transfer by Egypt – unfriendly to Transjordan – of the Strip to Israel could facilitate the conclusion of a deal which included access to the Mediterranean for

Transjordan through Gaza, though there was a school of thought in Tel Aviv that opposed "conspiring" with Abdullah against Egypt.[38]

Matters were clarified somewhat on 22 April at the last consultative meeting before Lausanne. Sasson, eager to conclude a deal with Abdullah, backed the transfer of the Strip to Transjordan. Ben-Gurion cautioned against rushing into a decision, but Shiloah rejoined that the matter would surely soon be raised in the talks at Lausanne with the Egyptians and the Transjordanians. Ben-Gurion responded that if the Strip was transferred to Israel, "we would not refuse [it], and then of course we would take it with all its inhabitants. We will not expel them." But Shiloah, unlike Sasson, was worried that Egypt might agree to transfer Gaza to Transjordan in a deal against which Israel would be powerless. Shiloah opposed such a transfer because it would "sever" the southern Negev from the rest of Israel. Sharett argued that the war had made the Yishuv's leaders think too much in terms of territory and too little in terms of population: "We are drunk with victory [and] territorial conquests." He opposed having to "swallow 150,000" Arabs and argued against both Israeli incorporation of and joint Israeli–Egyptian condominium over the Strip. The moment Israel became responsible, the Strip's refugees would press to be allowed to return to their original homes. Lifshitz, of the Transfer Committee, also opposed Israeli incorporation of the Strip though he wanted to annex Qalqilya and Tulkarm, which had "only 20,000 Arabs." Like Shiloah, Sharett opposed the take-over of the Strip by Transjordan.[39]

Ethridge was enthusiastic about the Gaza idea, which he began calling a "plan." He probably saw it as a "back door" method of achieving a measure of repatriation and of getting the Lausanne peace ball rolling. Ethridge told Eytan that "he was sure the Egyptians did not want to keep it and he personally was in favour of giving it to Israel . . . [if] the refugees went with it. He felt that by accepting those refugees, estimated at 150–200,000, [Israel] would be making [its] contribution towards the solution of the refugee problem."[40]

But were the Egyptians amenable? An initial indication was provided in early May. Egypt would rather give the Strip to Israel than to Transjordan. But it was more likely, a Transjordanian representative at Lausanne said, that Egypt would hold onto the Strip "and give it to nobody."[41]

A cable on 2 May from Eytan to Tel Aviv brought matters to a head. The Cabinet met the next day and decided that "if the incorporation of the Gaza district into Israel with all its population is proposed, our response will be positive." Sharett had argued against the proposal, saying that Israel had not "matured sufficiently to absorb three hundred thousand

Arabs." But Ben-Gurion, mobilising geo-political and strategic arguments, brought the majority of the ministers around. In the vote, Sharett abstained.[42] On 20 May, after informing Ethridge that Israel would "demand" the Strip but would not press the demand "if Egypt said no," Israel proposed to the PCC that it be given the Strip and said it "would be prepared to accept . . . all Arabs at present located in the Gaza area, whether inhabitants or refugees, as citizens of Israel." Israel committed itself to their "resettlement and rehabilitation," and reiterated the proposal on 29 and 31 May.[43]

Israel felt that by accepting the Gaza local population and refugees, as well as a handful of refugees under the family reunion scheme, it would have had an Arab minority more or less equal in number to the Arab minority it would have had under the 1947 United Nations Partition scheme and it "would have discharged its full obligation" towards solving the refugee problem. "The proposal is an earnest of the great lengths to which the Government of Israel is prepared to go in helping to solve the problem that is central to all our discussions," Eytan wrote to de Boisanger. Israel linked acceptance of Gaza and its refugees to large-scale international aid to cover the entailed costs.[44]

But from Washington's perspective, which took account of projected Arab sensibilities, the plan could not be so simple as mere Israeli incorporation of the Strip. While the United States regarded the refugee problem and its potential solution as the "overriding factor in determining eventual disposition Gaza Strip," Washington was prepared to approve the Strip's incorporation only if achieved with full Egyptian consent "and provided [that] territorial compensation [is] made to Egypt . . . if Egypt desires such compensation." Washington added that Israel would have to provide iron-clad assurances and guarantees that the Gaza locals and refugees would enjoy full rights and protection; the fear was of a repeat "Faluja." There was also chariness in Washington about footing a Gaza refugees' resettlement bill.

The feeling of the United States Embassy in Cairo was that the Egyptian Government "might well be willing [to] cede [the] Gaza Strip" if Israel "assumed refugee burden" and that Arab League Secretary Azzam Pasha was similarly minded. But the Egyptians, the Embassy felt, would probably "reserve final decision" on the cession until formal peace negotiations took place, using Gaza as a "bargaining point."[45]

Ethridge correctly gauged the Israeli position. He thought that the plan was Israel's only real and, possibly, last significant offer: "If she cannot have Gaza Strip, she will take only small number refugees." Only the Gaza Plan, Ethridge believed, held out the promise of Israel accepting a substantial number of repatriates.[46]

The Israeli Government had given only scant publicity to its decision to incorporate the Strip with its population. The Cabinet feared a strong public reaction against the plan, especially from the Right. The plan had been approved only reluctantly and under the mistaken belief that the Strip contained substantially fewer than 200,000–250,000 refugees.[47] The lack of a positive Egyptian response after 20 May had further eaten away at any enthusiasm in Tel Aviv for the plan.

The official Israeli cageyness about Israel's acceptance of the plan stretched to covering the plan's origin, which was to become the focus of a minor, and somewhat bizarre, diplomatic scuffle. The scuffle was unwittingly provoked by Ambassador McDonald who, on 31 May, quoting an Israeli Foreign Ministry official, cabled that the plan had been first "suggested" by Ethridge to Eytan. However, a few days later, Eban said that it had been Egypt's Mohammed Abd al-Mun'im Mustafa, head of delegation at the armistice talks, who "had first raised question of Israel taking over Gaza Strip," in Rhodes, in late February. Only subsequently, on 30 April at Lausanne, had Ethridge made the suggestion to Eytan. Meanwhile, in Tel Aviv, according to British Ambassador Sir Knox Helm, the Israeli Government denied initiating any formal Gaza proposal, saying that the PCC had "put forward" the proposal. The Egyptians also denied that they had first suggested the idea.

Ethridge was also unwilling to shoulder the burdens of paternity. "It is clear from the record," he wrote, that it had been Ben-Gurion at their meeting in Tiberias on 18 April, who had first proposed the kernel of the Gaza Plan. (Sharett subsequently disclaimed that the plan had been conceived at Tiberias.) Through June, Ethridge went out of his way to repudiate authorship. He believed that Eytan's publication of the official Israeli proposal on 20 May had for the present "torpedoed" any possibility of progress in the matter.[48]

The dispute about the origin of the plan was not motivated by a penchant for accuracy so much as by political calculation. Egypt, having just lost a war with Israel, could not appear eager or willing to voluntarily cede a further chunk of Palestine to the Jewish State and to help the Jews get off the hook of total refugee repatriation. Israel, for reasons of internal unity and diplomacy, could neither appear as the fount of the idea nor over-eager to lay its hands on the Strip, lest its eagerness cause the Egyptians to think again. Moreover, Israeli conception of, or eagerness about, the plan implied that Israel was willing and able to absorb some 200,000–250,000 refugees. If the plan fell through, American and United Nations pressure for an Israeli gesture of repatriation would be renewed, no doubt citing Israel's eagerness and expressed ability to take in a large proportion of the refugees. (This, indeed, happened.) Ethridge apparently did not want to be seen as the author of a plan that promised to enlarge the State of Israel. By early June, in addition to denying authorship, Ethridge began linking any cession by Egypt of the Strip to territorial compensation by Israel.[49] Ethridge's reluctance to be identified with the plan grew as Egyptian opposition to it crystallised and as its prospects of success dimmed. No one wanted to be identified with a non-starter.

The American linkage of an Egyptian cession of the Strip to territorial compensation in the Negev (possibly at Eilat) by Israel was not manifest in the early multilateral contacts on the matter. Its appearance in late May/early June probably owed much to the seeming Egyptian disinterest in the original proposal and, possibly, also to British signals favouring Israeli–Egyptian "reciprocity," stemming from an imperial interest in obtaining a land-bridge between the British-ruled Suez Canal and Transjordan, where British troops were stationed (in Aqaba) and which was linked by defence treaty to London.[50] The United States concurred with the British strategic view that it was in the West's interests to maintain a territorially continuous Arab world, with a land-bridge across the Negev between Egypt and Transjordan.

From the start, Cairo opposed the Gaza Plan: in the circumstances, it implied a separate peace with Israel. "Not only would Egypt not give up the Gaza district but would firmly demand the southern Negev," the Egyptian head of delegation at Lausanne, Abd al-Mun'im Mustafa, told Sasson on 1 June.[51] "The Egyptian Government," Cairo told Washington a few days later, "regarded the proposal as 'cheap barter.' [The Egyptian ambassador to Washington] characterised the offer as that of exchanging human lives for territory." Or, as Arab representatives put it to a British official at Lausanne, "it is wrong to bargain territory against refugees," and that if the Israelis wanted the Strip, they should compensate the Arabs in kind (that is, with territory).[52]

Egypt's lack of enthusiasm did not kill the plan, if only because it was the only thing on the market in May and June. Taking stock of the Egyptian response, Ben-Gurion agreed, on 6 June, to Israel making territorial compensation for the Strip, with a similarly sized strip of Israeli territory in the northwestern Negev, along the border with Egypt. But Ben-Gurion "doubted whether this proposal would win the Arabs' heart."

When Eytan put it to Abd al-Mun'im Mustafa a few days later, the Egyptian "didn't think much of the idea." "And I don't think the Egyptian Government will. Why should Egypt give up the fertile Gaza belt in return for a wilderness somewhere between Rafa and Auja?" reasoned Eytan.[53] But the United States still felt that the plan was "perhaps key that would unlock whole problem." It sought to engineer a formal, face-to-face Israeli–Egyptian peace negotiation, in which the Gaza Plan in some form would figure as a major element. Israel agreed, proposing New York as the venue,[54] but Egypt demurred. Washington appealed to Britain to help persuade Egypt to negotiate.[55]

Eban was appointed to lead the projected talks with the Egyptians, on American soil. He said a successful outcome would "break back of refugee problem," which all saw as the scourge and nemesis of Lausanne, but he acknowledged that Egypt might face serious internal and inter-Arab problems if it agreed to cede territory to Israel. He apparently saw the United States playing some sort of mediating role but Acheson firmly rejected the idea.[56]

Washington, explaining Egyptian tardiness in taking up the Plan, said that Israel had handled the matter clumsily, "always [stressing] . . . the territorial rather than the refugee aspect, which, of course, made it harder for the Egyptian negotiators to accept." Eban agreed.[57]

The introduction by the United States of the idea of Israeli territorial "compensation" for the Strip was largely conceived to offset the "barter" image of the original proposal. The Americans pushed the compensation theme to such an extent that the Egyptians believed, or pretended to believe, that the United States would not allow Egypt to withdraw from the Strip without compensation. Mainstream Israeli thinking held that agreement to absorb several hundred thousand more Arabs was a sufficient quid pro quo for the Strip though it was willing to compensate Egypt with a chunk of barren Negev land if that was what Egyptian pride (and peace) demanded.[58]

In July, during the recess in the Lausanne talks, the Eastern Department of the Foreign Office, at the behest of Bevin, formulated a revised plan for an overall Middle East settlement in which the Gaza Plan figured as a prominent element, including the idea of compensation. Britain thought a breakthrough over Gaza essential if Lausanne was to succeed. The plan "formalised" the American position: Israel would get the Strip if it compensated "the Arabs" with territory and if "safeguards" were instituted concerning Israel's future treatment of the Gaza refugees, including allowing them to return to their original homes.

Britain meshed in the plan the original Israeli core with other ideas for a territorial–political solution then floating around at Lausanne. The thrust of the British plan was to assure the interests of its Hashemite client state rather than of Egypt: "If the . . . compensation . . . were to be in the form of the award to Jordan or Jordan and Egypt of part or whole of the Southern Negev, thus providing a land bridge between Egypt and Jordan," Israel must receive freedom of access to the Red Sea. The Arabs, similarly, must receive access to the Mediterranean through "Gaza and Haifa." "If another solution were adopted for the Southern Negev, there should nonetheless be guaranteed freedom of communication and access across it between Egypt and Jordan." The plan also called for incorporation into Jordan of the Arab Legion-held areas of eastern Palestine, partition of Jerusalem with international supervision of the Holy Places, the sharing by Israel and the Arab states of the waters of the Jordan and Yarmuk rivers and the establishment of a free port at Haifa, through which Iraqi oil could be exported.[59]

Acheson agreed to the bulk of the British proposal. The State Department understood that territorial "land communication" between Jordan and Egypt was of major importance to the Arab states and agreed both to the partition of Jerusalem and the desirability of the incorporation of "Arab [eastern] Palestine in Jordan." (Ethridge, incidentally, had long stressed that for the Arabs, the provision of a land-bridge between Egypt and Transjordan was a major political point, not merely "a satisfaction of strategic concepts." The Arab world needed territorial continuity; a "wedge" in the form of a completely Jewish-held Negev would make for "eternal friction" in the region.) Washington understood that the establishment of a land corridor between Jordan and Egypt was also a major British interest. Washington concurred that the Gaza Plan, more than anything else, held out hope of major achievement at Lausanne. As McGhee put it: Israeli incorporation of the Strip and its "230,000 refugees" is "the most important of all the things to be aimed at. It was more important even than the exact nature of the territorial settlement [between Israel and the Arab states]." If Israel and Egypt agreed, "the Arabs might be brought to resettle the remainder of the refugees."[60]

Sir John Troutbeck, head of the British Middle East Office in Cairo, had only one – major – objection to the evolving joint Anglo–American stand: the territorial compensation must be made to Egypt, not Jordan. "We should bear in mind [Egyptian] susceptibilities which, though childish, are nonetheless real . . . The Gaza Strip . . . does represent for the Egyptians the only asset they have got out of the campaign . . . They would not regard it as compensation to see the southern Negeb go to Jordan."[61]

What had started as a limited Israeli initiative had become a comprehensive, joint Anglo–American *démarche*. The two western powers separately but simultaneously approached the Egyptian government with the proposal. The American chargé d'affaires, Jefferson Patterson, felt that if "suitable" territorial compensation were offered, "the Egyptians might be able to get away with it." The Egyptian forces in the Strip, he said, were "rather jittery" and felt strategically exposed and isolated, and "this might dispose them to get rid of the strip against territorial compensation." And Cairo did not want the refugees.

But the Egyptians took an obstreperous tack. The Egyptian Prime

Minister, while complaining of the refugee burden, reacted "with some bitterness to the U.S. proposal for cession of the Gaza Strip to Israel."[62] At Lausanne, the Egyptians said they "could not discuss Gaza proposal. Showed complete indifference fate Gaza refugees who were international and Jewish responsibility." In Cairo, the Egyptians denounced the plan as a "forerunner of Israeli aggression against Gaza and Arabs expressed surprise U.S. should 'lend itself' to such schemes." The Egyptians questioned America's impartiality and Patterson gained the impression that if the United States continued "to play up merits of Gaza Plan, which are invisible to Arab eyes, Egypt may begin regard U.S. as accomplice of Israeli aggression." Egypt officially rejected the plan on 29 July. The Egyptian Foreign Ministry contended that the plan could serve only the interests of Israel, which was "making use" of the refugee question to extend its boundaries. The Egyptians ignored the offer of territorial compensation and asserted the refugees' right to repatriation.[63]

By July, Israel was having deep second thoughts about the plan, and not only because of the compensation element. Officially, Tel Aviv remained willing to go through with the plan, as initially conceived – incorporation in "exchange" for agreement to absorb the Strip's population. But over the months, the sceptics in Tel Aviv had gained the upper hand. Israel had agreed to the territory–population trade-off, explained Sharett, in the belief that the Strip contained "150–180,000 Arabs." But this "assumption . . . turned out to be incorrect." Israel now believed there were some 211,000 refugees and 65,000 locals in the Strip; it could not absorb such a total. Also, Israel feared that other refugees, now in Lebanon, Syria and Transjordan, would move to the Strip before its incorporation in the hope of using it as a springboard from which to return to their homes. Israel, he said, must specify the maximum number of Arabs it was willing to take back with the Strip; otherwise, in practice, the commitment would be open-ended. In early August, Sharett, Ben-Gurion, Kaplan and Lifshitz met and decided on a "200,000" ceiling. Israeli diplomats were instructed to "mention" in conversation that Israel would not take back "an unlimited number" of Gaza refugees.[64]

As to territorial compensation, Sharett instructed his diplomats to "vigorously" reject the idea. But he added: "If things reach a practical stage and it appears necessary to abandon the completely rejectionist stance, it would be possible to discuss border corrections/changes in the northern Negev, both in the east and in the west, that is, in favour of both Transjordan and Egypt, but on no account [will we be willing to discuss] any concession [i.e., cession] in the southern part of the Negev, including Eilat." (Eytan, incidentally, objected to this. He argued in favour of a cession in the southern Negev, if it brought peace with Egypt, and dismissed Eilat's strategic importance.) Sharett thought that Israel might have to decide whether to agree to take the full "300,000" Arabs in Gaza in "exchange" for the Strip but without making any territorial compensation, or to agree to take part of the Strip's population *and* to make territorial compensation in return for the Strip. In the end, thought Sharett, perhaps the Gaza status quo was best left as it was.[65]

American and Israeli officials discussed the plan through July. But for all practical purposes, the plan had died with the Egyptian veto. The rest was mere shadow-boxing. During the following weeks, the Americans occasionally hinted at the plan in meetings with Egyptian officials, but Egyptian opposition remained unwavering. The Gaza Plan had died.[66]

The PCC and Lausanne II: the "100,000 Offer" and the collapse of the talks

At a meeting between Ethridge and Eytan in Lausanne at the end of May, Eytan had reaffirmed Israel's readiness to incorporate the Gaza Strip and absorb its population. Ethridge had responded that what the PCC lacked was clarification of how many refugees Israel would be willing to take back "if she did not get Gaza Strip."[67]

Since autumn 1948, Israel had intermittently indicated in private conversations that it might agree to take back a substantial number of refugees within the context of a final peace settlement and on condition that the Arab states committed themselves to absorbing and resettling in their territory the bulk of the Palestinian refugees. What was needed, felt the United States and the PCC, was a public and firm Israeli declaration of intent regarding repatriation which would specify the number of refugees the Jewish State would be ready to take back coupled, if possible, with an immediate start to repatriation. The Americans and the PCC felt that such a "gesture" might soften the Arabs and, perhaps, induce a matching Arab commitment to absorb the bulk of the refugees.

Through May, the United States pressed Israel to make the "gesture." State Department officials, such as McGhee, took heart from the occasional report that the Israeli leaders were seriously considering a substantial repatriation and that a plan had been, or was being drawn up to repatriate as many as "300,000 or 350,000 refugees." Ambassador McDonald believed that "intensive consideration was being . . . given . . . in Tel Aviv to the repatriation of a large number of Arab refugees." But Burdett and Ethridge, who suspected McDonald of pro-Zionist sympathies, were not so sure, and believed that Tel Aviv would resist any repatriation as hard as possible.[68]

The Lausanne talks dragged on unpromisingly through June as the bright hope of the Gaza Plan rapidly faded. The Americans stepped up their demand for an Israeli "gesture," Israel's readiness to incorporate the Strip, indeed, being cited in support of this demand. "U.S. Government greatly disturbed over present Israeli attitude refugee question . . . This attitude . . . difficult [to] reconcile with Gaza Strip proposal, which represents firm admission on part [of] Israel [of] its ability [to] assume responsibility 230,000 refugees plus 80,000 normal residents area." If Israel was able and willing to absorb the 300,000 Arabs of Gaza, how could it argue inability and unwillingness to take in a smaller number outside the context of the Gaza Plan?[69]

Ethridge, retiring from the fray, primarily blamed Israel for the Lausanne impasse. Tel Aviv was "steadfastly" refusing to make concessions. Ethridge took a high moral tone: "Israel was a state created upon an ethical concept and should rest upon an ethical base. Her attitude toward refugees is morally reprehensible and politically short-sighted. She has no security that does not rest in friendliness with her neighbours." He felt, in summation, that "there never has been a time in the life of the [Palestine Conciliation] Commission when a generous and far-sighted attitude on the part of the Jews would not have unlocked peace."[70]

Israel's position, according to Israeli diplomats in the United States, was also affecting American public opinion, until then solidly pro-Israel. The Israel Consul General in New York, Arthur Lourie, transmitted a copy of a letter from American journalist Drew Pearson, which Lourie said "expressed . . . anxieties . . . characteristic of a large section of American opinion on whose support we have hitherto been able to count." Pearson had written that "in preventing Arab refugees from returning to their native land, the Jews may be subject to the same kind of criticism for which I and others have criticised intolerant Gentiles . . . Now we have a situation in which the Jews have done to others what Hitler, in a sense, did to them!"[71] Eban on 22 June assessed that the impasse was leading to a major rupture in Israeli–American relations: "We face crisis not comparable previous occasions. Careful attempt being made alienate President from us nearer success than ever before, owing humanitarian aspect refugee situation and his firm belief gesture our part is necessary condition persuade Arabs [to agree to] resettlement and Congress vote funds. We may have face choice between some compromise principle non-return before peace and far-reaching rift USA."[72]

Sasson's assessment of the situation in Lausanne did not differ greatly from Ethridge's. In mid-June, the Israeli wrote that he was sorry he had come. The city was beautiful, the climate temperate, the hotel luxurious. But the delegation had come to make peace and, after two months, had advanced "not one step" towards this goal. Moreover, he wrote, "there is no chance of such progress in the future even if we decide to sit in Lausanne for several more months . . . The Lausanne talks are fruitless and are destined to fail."

Sasson explained – and his order of priorities is worth noting – that: "Firstly, the Jews believe that it is possible to achieve peace without [paying] any price, maximal or minimal. They want to achieve (a) Arab surrender of all the areas occupied today by Israel, (b) Arab agreement to absorb all the refugees in the neighbouring [Arab] states, (c) Arab agreement to rectification of the present frontiers in the centre, south and Jerusalem area in favour of Israel only . . . etc., etc."

The refugees, wrote Sasson, had become "a scapegoat. No one pays attention to them, no one listens to their demands, explanations and suggestions. But . . . all use their problem for purposes which have almost no connection to the aspirations of the refugees themselves." For example, while all the Arab states demanded the refugees' repatriation, in practice none of the Arab states, "save Lebanon," was interested in this. Transjordan and Syria wanted to hold on to their refugees in order to receive international relief aid. The Egyptians wanted the refugee problem to remain in order to destabilise Transjordan and Israel.

Nor was Israel concerned about the refugees, wrote Sasson. Israel was "determined not to accept them back . . . come hell or high water." Sasson himself believed that, in essence, this attitude was correct but thought that Israel should demonstrate flexibility and statesmanship by favourably considering a proposal brought to him by the refugees' representatives at Lausanne, which called for Israeli annexation of the Gaza Strip and the area now known as the "West Bank" while granting these territories local autonomy and while absorbing in Israel proper some 100,000 refugees. Sasson felt that such a plan could achieve for Israel the complete withdrawal from Palestine of the Arab armies and the "complete resolution of the Palestine question," and possibly also hasten peace between Israel and the Arab states.[73]

The intense American and PCC pressure on Israel over the early summer bore minor fruit in the form of the family reunion programme, announced by Sharett in the Knesset on 15 June. Israel would "consider favourably" requests by Israeli Arab citizens to allow back "their wives and young children" – meaning "sons below the age of 15 and unmarried daughters." Israel proposed that special posts be set up on the frontiers with Egypt, Transjordan and Lebanon (no armistice agreement had yet been signed with Syria) through which the reunions could be accomplished.

Israeli officials widely described and trumpeted the scheme as a "broad measure easing the lot of Arab families disrupted as a result of the war."

But, in fact, the scheme eased the lot of only a handful of families. During the following months, according to Israel Foreign Ministry figures, 1,329 requests were received pertaining to 3,957 refugees. Tel Aviv issued 3,113 entry permits. By 20 September 1951, a total of 1,965 refugees had made use of the permits and returned to Israeli territory.[74]

If meant as a sop to the United States and the PCC and as a means of neutralising western pressure for repatriation, the family reunion scheme was not a major success.[75] The United States and the PCC wanted a grand "gesture," not a trickle. The acting United States representative at Lausanne, Raymond Hare, on 23 June delivered a strong "verbal" communication "from the U.S. Government" to Eytan, expressing Washington's "disappointment" in the lack of Israeli compliance with the United Nations' 11 December 1948 repatriation resolution. "USA emphatic that responsibility for refugee solution rests squarely on Israel and Arabs, and nowhere else . . . Israel causing delay in refugee solution."[76] The United States wanted a "gesture."

The "seeds" of such a gesture had long been hibernating in the soil of Tel Aviv. Already in August 1948, Sasson had recommended to Sharett that Israel consider allowing a return of "40–50,000" refugees and to start repatriating them "immediately." (He said he sought to neutralise the expected pressure on Israel at the impending meeting of the United Nations General Assembly in Paris.)[77] In mid-April 1949, with America demanding that Israel agree to repatriate 250,000, Sasson implied that Israel could perhaps take back "150,000."[78]

Until summer 1949, Sasson's advice had been consistently rejected. But by late June, the cumulative pressure by the United States and the PCC was proving irresistible. Sharett enjoined Ben-Gurion to agree to publicly declare that Israel would accept "25,000" refugees in the family reunion scheme. Moreover, Sharett informed Eban on 25 June, "am weighing whether [to] urge Government [to] agree should add 50,000 as further maximum contribution without Gaza . . . Will this pacify U.S. turn scales our favour?"[79]

On 5 July, Sharett proposed to the Cabinet that Israel publicly declare its readiness to absorb "100,000" refugees in exchange for peace. This number, said Sharett, would include the "25,000" refugees who had already returned to the country illegally and some "10,000" who would return within the family reunion scheme. Most of the ministers supported Sharett, but Ben-Gurion objected, arguing that the number would not mollify Washington or satisfy the Arabs. He also argued on security grounds against reabsorbing so large a number of Arabs. Sharett, who did not want to push through a major decision opposed by the Prime Minister, then proposed, by way of compromise, that the Cabinet, as a first step, authorise him to sound out the Americans as to whether an Israeli announcement of readiness to take back 100,000 would indeed reduce or neutralise Washington's pressure on Tel Aviv. The ministers agreed, and Sharett was empowered to make the 100,000 offer if, indeed, the feelers to Washington resulted in an encouraging response.[80]

The Israeli leadership had concluded that there must be some "give" if Israeli–American relations were not to be strained to the breaking point. Sharett later explained the Cabinet's vote thus: "The attempt to resurrect the Lausanne Conference is necessary also because of the urgent need to ease the tension which has been created between us and the United States. This tension has surfaced especially [over] the refugee problem, whose non-solution serves as an obstacle in the whole [Lausanne] negotiation."[81]

During the following days, the State Department and White House were indirectly, and then directly, sounded out on the American response to a prospective Israeli announcement of readiness to take back "100,000" refugees. The United States was first informed on 15 July of Israel's decision in principle to let back a specific number of refugees. Ambassador McDonald had already heard that the Cabinet "was toying with the idea of an offer of 100,000."[82]

On 27 July, Sharett told the Transfer Committee of the Cabinet's decision. He asked the Committee to produce a plan for absorbing and resettling these refugees in Israel. Weitz and Danin argued against the decision, calling it a "catastrophe." Lifshitz backed Sharett. Sharett then said that if the Committee studied the matter and ruled that there was no way Israel could absorb the refugees, "then the Cabinet would [just] have to accept this view." Weitz, Danin and Lifshitz then decided to accept the task but on condition that the Cabinet agreed to decide nothing without first considering their views.[83]

The initial Israeli feelers about the "100,000 offer" met with a mixed reception in Washington. Eban's impression on 8 July was that the "100,000" announcement "would have very deep impression," to judge from a talk with McGhee and Hare. But Andrew Cordier, a senior aide to the United Nations Secretary General, reported to the Israelis that the Americans regarded the "figure [as] as too low."[84] Acheson on 26 July reiterated the American demand that Israel absorb some 250,000 refugees – bringing Israel's Arab population up to 400,000, or roughly the number of Arabs who would have lived in the Jewish State under the 1947 United Nations Partition Plan.[85]

But President Truman's reaction proved decisive. John Hilldring, a Truman aide, reported to the Israelis after a conversation with the President on 18 July that Truman was "extremely pleased . . . thinks 100,000 offer may break deadlock."[86]

The United States was officially informed on 28 July of Israel's readiness to take back 100,000 refugees after there was an overall refugee resettlement plan and after there was "evidence" of "real progress" towards a peace settlement. Elath said on 28 July that Israel had taken the decision in order "to demonstrate [its] cooperation with the U.S." and to contribute its share to a solution of the refugee problem, and "in spite of the fact that Israeli security and economic experts had considered the proposed decision as disastrous." Elath said the figure included "infiltrees" already back in Israel as well as those returning through the family reunion scheme. Sharett, informing McDonald, stressed that 100,000 was the limit, bringing Israel's Arab minority "far beyond margin of safety by all known security standards."[87]

The State Department did not immediately react to the "100,000 offer." Acheson waited to see how the Arabs would react. The Arabs, as anticipated, immediately rejected the offer. But, unofficially, some Arab officials at Lausanne hinted at willingness to accept less than full repatriation. Israel, they said, should take back "340,000" refugees from the conquered territories (outside the Partition borders), and repatriate another "100,000" inside 1947-Israel. The Arab states, with international aid, would then absorb the remaining "410,000."[88]

The publication of the "100,000 offer" caused a major political explosion in Tel Aviv. There was enormous opposition to it within Mapai. Hapoel Hamizrahi, the General Zionists and Herut all vigorously opposed the offer. "The Progressives were silent, and the press interpreted their silence as a silent protest . . . Mapam's acknowledgement in weak language of the justice of the act . . . was buried and blurred completely in the wave of rage in which the government was swept for surrendering to 'imperialist pressure,' " Sharett reported.

Eban felt that the offer "represents a very considerable effort in advance of public opinion in [Israel]." Acheson's view was similar: "Israel . . . has allowed public opinion to develop . . . to such an extent that it is almost impossible for [the] Israeli Government to make substantial concessions re refugees and territory."[89]

A major debate on the matter took place in Mapai on 28 July. The party's Knesset faction chairman, Meir Grabovsky (Argov), put the case against the offer succinctly: "No one wanted . . . and anticipated that the Arabs would leave," he said. But events produced a "more or less homogeneous [Jewish] state, and now to double the number of Arabs without any certain recompense . . . [should be seen] as one of the fatal mistakes destroying the security of the state . . . We will face a Fifth Column." Israel would have a minority problem like that "in the Balkans."

Sharett called Grabovsky's attack "illogical." Grabovsky had supported the incorporation of the Gaza Strip with its population; how could he now oppose absorbing "65–70,000" refugees? The figure contained Sharett's second point: the "100,000 offer" was not what it seemed. Israel intended to deduct from the figure the "illegal" infiltrees and the "legal" returnees (family reunions and special deals, such as with the Eilabun and Kafr Bir'im villagers). There were some 25,000 infiltrees and thousands more of special-case returnees, according to Sharett – hence, "65–70,000."

But Sharett's main defence was historical. In the beginning, he said, referring to spring 1948

there was among us an assumption that the uprooting of these Arabs was temporary . . . , and it was [accepted as] natural that the Arab would return to his village . . .

When the Foreign Ministry began speaking publicly against a return . . . it was first of all trying to consolidate [Israeli] public opinion against such a return . . . As time passed the public understood . . . that . . . there would be a catastrophe if there was a return . . . and this policy [against a return] crystallized. It produced decisive results . . . If now they speak seriously in England and the U.S. of resettlement [of the refugees] in other countries – it is a [result] of this absolute emphasis . . . on our part.

But now the Lausanne cart was in the mud and Israel was being asked to help pull it out: the "100,000 offer" was the upshot.[90]

The internal Mapai debate continued on 1 August (just before the Knesset plenum debated the offer). Opposition was bitter. As Knesset Member Assaf Vilkomitz (Ami) put it, "there will be too large an Arab minority." Knesset Member Shlomo Lavi (Levkovich) called the offer "a grave mistake." Knesset Member Eliahu Carmeli (Lulu) said bringing back the refugees would create "not a Fifth but a First Column. I am not willing to take back even one Arab, not even one *goy* [i.e., non-Jew]. I want the Jewish state to be wholly Jewish." Moshe Dayan's father, Knesset Member Shmuel Dayan, another Mapai old-timer, opposed any return, "even in exchange for peace. What will this formal peace give us?" Knesset Member Ze'ev Herring argued that allowing back "100,000" would generate further pressure and waves of returnees.

Sharett, stung by the lack of backbench support, told Carmeli that he "envied" his willingness to live "in isolation not only from the Orient [i.e., within the Middle East] but also from the whole world." Sharett stressed that questions of peace, world public opinion, and relations with other countries were important, and that the "100,000 offer" served an important function in these contexts. "Comrade Carmeli knows only one thing, that [the] Arabs are a terrible people and that we must uproot them."

Sharett then announced that while there would be no Knesset vote on the "100,000 offer," the Government "should be interested in being attacked in the Knesset on this question . . . It is important that the uneasiness of the Mapai members in this matter be expressed." Sharett's thinking was clear: the more widespread and vicious the attacks on the Government, the easier it would be for Israel to "sell" to the United States and the PCC the offer as final and "the limit of possible concession." And, indeed, Sharett instructed his diplomats in this vein: to play up as much as possible how difficult it had been for the Cabinet to decide on the offer and how bitterly the Government had been attacked over it. Clearly, 100,000 was the absolute ceiling.[91]

In the noisy Knesset plenum debate that followed, Sharett assured the Knesset Members that the offer would not be binding on Israel except as part of a general peace settlement.

"It must be [made] clear to Paul Porter [Ethridge's replacement as United States representative on the PCC] that anything further cannot be dreamed of . . . Explain to Porter," Sharett cabled the new head of the Israeli delegation to Lausanne Reuven Shiloah on 2 August, "that our proposal generated grave opposition internally, including in Mapai, and we only with difficulty in a five-hour debate succeeded in calming the storm in the faction . . . Any further concession will destroy the Government's standing." Sharett added that if the Arabs failed to "latch onto" the Israeli offer immediately, pressure would surface, which the Cabinet could not withstand, to withdraw it. The proposal was being made on a "take it or leave it" basis. Sharett suggested that the United States counsel the Arabs to take it. He repeatedly referred to the mood of Israeli public opinion.[92]

Sharett believed that the storm over the offer had "slightly undermined" his personal political standing but that it had helped to "sell" the proposal abroad. In any case, he tended to believe that the Lausanne talks would collapse, in which event the "100,000 offer" would never have to be implemented.[93]

The Arab rejection of the "100,000 offer" did not greatly displease Israel. In general, Israel's leaders were not unhappy with the no-war, no-peace situation. Ben-Gurion in mid-July quoted Eban as thinking: "He sees no need to run after peace. An armistice is sufficient for us, if we run after peace – the Arabs will demand of us a price – [in the coin of] borders [i.e., border rectifications] or refugees or both. We will [i.e., can afford to] wait a few years." While ascribing this approach to Eban, Ben-Gurion was probably conveying his own thinking as well.[94]

This was also how Acheson assessed Israeli thinking: "Israel prefers . . . status quo . . . Objectives [of Tel Aviv Government] appear to be (1) Absorption of almost all Arab refugees by Arab states and (2) de facto recognition of armistic lines as boundaries."[95]

Israel formally presented its proposal to the PCC to take back

"100,000" refugees on 3 August, making this conditional on "retaining all present territory" and on freedom to resettle all the returnees wherever it saw fit. The PCC, considering the offer "unsatisfactory," informally transmitted it to the Arab delegations. The Arabs reacted as expected. One Arab diplomat told Porter the offer was a "mere propaganda scheme and Jews either at your feet or [your] throat." The offer was rejected as "less than token." The Arabs maintained that there were "1,000,000" refugees and that "Jews cannot oppose return large number refugees on economic ground while encouraging mass immigration [into Israel] of Jews." But Transjordan and Syria, making a concession, informed the PCC that they would be able to absorb "such refugees as might not return to their homes." Egypt and Lebanon, more vaguely, said that they could absorb "numbers of refugees."

Burdett, like the Arabs at Lausanne, immediately dismissed the proposal, along with the family reunion scheme, as a "sham" designed to frustrate American and United Nations efforts to get Israel to agree to more substantial repatriation. He believed that "in large part" the Knesset debate and the press campaign against the "100,000 offer" were geared to foreign consumption. The American Embassy in Tel Aviv, on the other hand, stressed the "genuineness" of the internal opposition to the offer. It explained: "Conditioned by a long build-up in the Hebrew press, in the Knesset and by Government leaders themselves, which had as its theme the utter undesirability of taking back any Arab refugees whatsoever, the people of this country were hardly prepared for a reversal in policy." No Israeli, "from Prime Minister down wishes see single Arab brought back if can possibly be avoided."[96]

The United States did not think that the Israeli offer "provide[d] suitable basis for contributing to solution of Arab refugee question." The offer was "not satisfactory," Acheson wrote.[97]

But Israel was immovable; 100,000 was the ceiling. By mid-August all the participants understood that Lausanne had failed. Even Shiloah was "worried [and] tense." Sharett reassured him that the Israeli offer had "vastly improved" Israel's "tactical position vis-a-vis UN and Arabs." But Shiloah, like Eytan and Sasson before him, knew that Lausanne was getting nowhere. The Arab rejection of the Gaza Plan and of the "100,000 offer" and Israel's rejection of complete repatriation and withdrawal to the Partition Plan borders left, in Acheson's phrase, "no real basis for conciliation." By the end of August it was all over. The participants raised their hands, having achieved nothing, and indefinitely suspended the "conference"; the delegations returned home in September. The PCC continued to churn out reports on the Palestine refugee problem into the 1950s.[98]

But meanwhile, in August 1949, the PCC and the United States made one last more or less co-ordinated effort. Politics had clearly failed. So they tried an indirect approach, economics. The upshot was Washington's McGhee Plan and the PCC's Economic Survey Mission. Both were geared to finding an economic solution to the refugee problem. The American policy-makers focused on a grand economic development scheme for the Middle East, a regional Marshall Plan, which would bring the Arab states into the American orbit against the backdrop of the Cold War, push these states forward economically and, possibly, politically and, incidentally, solve the refugee problem by well-funded, organised resettlement in the Arab states. The scheme was known as the McGhee Plan.

Meanwhile, the Technical Committee on Refugees, created by the PCC on 14 June 1949 to report on the scope and nature of the refugee problem, on 20 August submitted its findings. The Committee found that there were "711,000" bona fide Palestine refugees, and that the higher number of international relief recipients (totalling close to one million) was a result of "duplication of ration cards" and the inclusion "of persons who, although not displaced, are destitute." It recommended that a thorough census be conducted. The Committee found that an "overwhelming" number of refugees wished to return to their homes but that the Israelis were blocking repatriation. The Committee opined that "the clock cannot be turned back," especially in view of the increase of the Yishuv by "50 per cent" since the Palestinian exodus; immigrants were pouring into Israel at the rate of "800 a day." The Committee surveyed employment possibilities and mooted regional development projects of benefit to the refugees.[99]

Even before the Technical Committee's report was in, the PCC and the United States set in motion the creation of the Economic Survey Mission (ESM), whose focus was regional development projects that could employ the refugees. The ESM, headed by Gordon Clapp, was formally set up on 23 August, as (like the Technical Committee) a subsidiary body of the PCC under the General Assembly resolution of 11 December 1948. The United States understood that the projects' funding would be mainly American and the underlying assumption was a solution based on resettlement in the Arab countries rather than repatriation.[100] The ESM, based in Beirut, began touring the region in mid-September and presented an interim report to the PCC and General Assembly in December.

The ESM was only one of a number of economic and diplomatic devices which were invented over 1949–56 to keep the refugee problem alive and on the international agenda. Like those of the Technical Committee before it, its findings and recommendations had no effect on anything.

The refugees had been, and remained, a political problem; economic amelioration had to be preceded by political settlement.

The status quo and Arab and Israeli policies hardened and calcified as time passed. The mass influx of Jewish immigrants into Israel steadily obviated any possibility of mass refugee repatriation. Only the destruction of the Jewish State and the death or expulsion of its population could have made physically possible a refugee return. From the Arab side, resettlement in the Arab countries remained through the years a clear possibility, though one requiring a vast amount of Western capital. But the Arab states objected to such resettlement for mainly political reasons. They regarded repatriation as the "just" solution and, incidentally, as one that could help undermine the Jewish State, to whose continued existence they all objected. The Arab states were also eager to be rid of the refugee burden for internal reasons, fearing the refugees' potential as a restive Fifth Column. Meanwhile, while Israel blocked repatriation, the refugee presence and misery served as a useful political weapon against Israel.

In retrospect, it appeared that at Lausanne was lost the best and perhaps only chance for a solution of the refugee problem, if not for the achievement of a comprehensive Middle East peace settlement. But the basic incompatibility of the initial starting positions and the unwillingness of the two sides to move, and to move quickly, towards a compromise – born of Arab rejectionism and a deep feeling of humiliation, and of Israeli drunkenness with victory and physical needs determined by the Jewish refugee influx – doomed the "conference" from the start. American pressures on both sides, lacking a sharp, determined cutting edge, failed to budge sufficiently either Jew or Arab. The "100,000 offer" was a classic of too little, too late. The Gaza Plan, given the just-ended territorial expansion of the Jewish State and Egyptian–Transjordanian rivalries, was a non-starter; Egypt alone may have agreed to it, but not as part of an Arab coalition generally guided by its most extreme constituents (the key to Arab political group psychology).

So Lausanne ended on 12 September without result, setting the seal on the refugee problem. It was probably the last chance of peacefully resolving the Middle East conflict.

Conclusion

The Palestinian refugee problem was born of war, not by design, Jewish or Arab. It was largely a by-product of Arab and Jewish fears and of the protracted, bitter fighting that characterised the first Israeli–Arab war; in smaller part, it was the deliberate creation of Jewish and Arab military commanders and politicians.

The creation of the problem was almost inevitable, given the geographical intermixing of the Arab and Jewish populations, the history of Arab–Jewish hostility over 1917–47, the resistance on both sides to a binational state, the outbreak and prolongation of the war for Israel's birth and survival, the major structural weaknesses of Palestinian Arab society, the depth of Arab animosity towards the Yishuv and Arab fears of falling under Jewish rule, and the Yishuv's fears of what would happen should the Arabs win and what would be the fate of a Jewish State born with a very large, potentially or actively hostile Arab minority.

The Palestinian Arab exodus began in December 1947 – March 1948, with the departure of many of the country's upper and middle class families, especially from Haifa and Jaffa, towns destined to be in, or at the mercy of, the Jewish-State-to-be, and from Jewish-dominated districts of western Jerusalem. Flight proved infectious. Household followed household, neighbour followed neighbour, street, street and neighbourhood, neighbourhood (as, later, village was to follow neighbouring village). The prosperous and educated feared death or injury in the ever-spreading hostilities, the anarchy that attended the gradual withdrawal of the British administration and security forces, the brigandage and intimidation of the Arab militias and irregulars and, more vaguely but generally, the unknown, probably dark future that awaited them under Jewish or, indeed, Husayni rule. Some of these considerations, as well as a variety of direct and indirect military pressures, also caused during these months the almost complete evacuation of the Arab rural communities of the Coastal Plain, which was predominantly Jewish and which was to be the core of the Jewish State.

Most of the upper and middle class families, who moved from Jaffa,

Haifa, Jerusalem, Ramle, Acre and Tiberias to Nablus, Amman, Beirut, Gaza and Cairo, probably thought their exile would be temporary. These families had the financial wherewithal to tide them over; many had wealthy relatives and accommodation outside the country. The urban masses and the *fellahin*, however, had nowhere to go, certainly not in comfort. For them, flight meant instant destitution; it was not a course readily adopted. But the daily spectacle of abandonment by their "betters," the middle and upper classes, with its concomitant progressive closure of businesses, schools, law offices and medical clinics, and abandonment of civil service and municipal posts, led to a steady attrition of morale, a cumulative sapping of faith and trust in the world around them: their leaders were going or had gone; the British were packing. They had been left "alone" to face the Zionist enemy.

Daily, week in, week out, over December 1947, January, February and March 1948, there were clashes along the "seams" between the two communities in the mixed towns, ambushes in the fields and on the roads, sniping, machinegun fire, bomb attacks and occasional mortaring. Problems of movement and communication, unemployment and food distribution intensified, especially in the towns, as the hostilities drew out.

There is probably no accounting for the mass exodus that followed without understanding the prevalence and depth of the general sense of collapse, of "falling apart," that permeated Arab Palestine, especially the towns, by April 1948. In many places, it would take very little to induce the inhabitants to pack up and flee.

Come the Haganah (and IZL–LHI) offensives of April–May, the cumulative effect of the fears, deprivations, abandonment and depredations of the previous months, in both towns and villages, overcame the natural, basic reluctance to abandon home and property and go into exile. As Palestinian military power was swiftly and dramatically demolished and the Haganah demonstrated almost unchallenged superiority in successive conquests, Arab morale cracked, giving way to general, blind, panic or a "psychosis of flight,"[1] as one IDF intelligence report put it.

Towns fell first – Tiberias, Haifa, Jaffa, Beisan, Safad – and their populations fled. The panic then affected the surrounding rural hinterlands: after Haifa, came the flight from Balad ash Sheikh and Hawassa; after Jaffa, Salama, Al Kheiriya and Yazur; after Safad, Dhahiriya Tahta, Sammu'i and Meirun. For decades the villagers had looked to the towns for leadership; they followed the townspeople into exile.

If Jewish attack directly and indirectly triggered most of the Arab exodus up to June 1948, a small but significant proportion of that flight was due to direct Jewish expulsion orders issued after the conquest of a site and to Jewish psychological warfare ploys ("whispering propaganda") designed to intimidate inhabitants into leaving. More than a dozen villages were ordered by the Haganah to evacuate during April–June. The expulsions were usually from areas considered strategically vital and in conformity with Plan D, which called for clear main lines of communications and border areas. As well, it was standard Haganah and IDF practice to round up and expel the remaining villagers (usually old people, widows, cripples) from sites already evacuated by most of their inhabitants, mainly because the occupying force wanted to avoid having to leave behind a garrison.

Moreover, for military and political reasons, Arab local commanders and the AHC issued orders to evacuate close to two dozen villages during this period, as well as more general orders to local National Committees and villages to remove their womenfolk and children to safer areas. This included the Arab Legion order of 13 May for the temporary evacuation of villages north and east of Jerusalem for strategic reasons – to clear the prospective battle area. Military reasons also underlay the orders issued in the various localities to evacuate women and children. Arab irregulars' commanders later in May intimidated villagers into leaving seven sites in the Lower Galilee, apparently because they feared the villagers would acquiesce in Israeli rule.

In April–May, and indeed, again in October, the "atrocity factor" played a major role in certain areas of the country in encouraging flight. Arab villagers and townspeople, prompted by the fear that the Jews, if victorious, would do to them what, in the reverse circumstances, victorious Arab fighters would have done (and did, occasionally, as in the Etzion Bloc in May) to defeated Jews, took to their heels.[2] The actual atrocities committed by the Jewish forces (primarily at Deir Yassin) reinforced such fears considerably, especially when amplified and magnified loudly and persistently in the Arab media, particularly by AHC spokesmen, for weeks thereafter.

To what extent was the Arab exodus up to June a product of Yishuv or Arab policy? The answer is as complex as was the situation on the ground. Up to the beginning of April 1948, there was no Yishuv plan or policy to expel the Arab inhabitants of Palestine, either from the area destined for Jewish statehood or those lying outside it. The Haganah adopted a forceful retaliatory strategy against suspected bases of Arab irregular bands which triggered a certain amount of flight. But it was not a strategy designed to precipitate civilian flight.

The prospect and need to prepare for the invasion gave birth to Plan D, prepared in early March. It gave the Haganah brigade and battalion-level commanders *carte blanche* to completely clear vital areas; it allowed the expulsion of hostile or potentially hostile Arab villages. Many villages were bases for bands of irregulars; most villages had armed militias and could serve as bases for hostile bands. During April and May, the local Haganah units, sometimes with specific instruction from the Haganah General Staff, carried out elements of Plan D, each interpreting and implementing the plan in his area as he saw fit and in relation to the prevailing local circumstances. In general, the commanders saw fit to completely clear the vital roads and border areas of Arab communities – Allon in Eastern Galilee, Carmel around Haifa and Western Galilee, Avidan in the south. Most of the villagers fled before or during the fighting. Those who stayed put were almost invariably expelled.

There was never, during April–June, any political or General Staff decision to expel "the Arabs" from the Jewish State's areas. There was no "plan" or policy decision. The matter was never discussed in the supreme, political, decision-making bodies, but it was understood by all concerned that, militarily, in the struggle to survive, the fewer Arabs remaining behind and along the front lines, the better and, politically, the fewer Arabs remaining in the Jewish State, the better. At each level of command and execution, Haganah officers in those April–June days when the fate of the State hung in the balance, simply "understood" what the military and political exigencies of survival required. Even most Mapam officers – ideologically committed to coexistence with the Arabs – failed to "adhere" to the party line: conditions in the field, tactically and strategically, gave precedence to immediate survival-mindedness over the long-term desirability of coexistence.

The Arab leadership inside and outside Palestine probably helped precipitate the exodus in the sense that it was disunited, had decided on no fixed, uniform policy *vis-à-vis* the civilian evacuation and gave the Palestinians no consistent, hard-and-fast guidelines and instructions about how to act and what to do, especially during the crucial month of April. The records are incomplete, but they show overwhelming confusion and disparate purpose, "policy" changing from week to week and area to area. No guiding hand or central control is evident.

During the first months, the flight of the middle and upper classes from the towns provoked little Arab interest, except at the affected, local level: the rich families arrived in Nablus, Amman, Beirut, in a trickle and were not needy. It seemed to be merely a repeat of the similar exodus of 1936–9. The Husaynis were probably happy that many of these wealthy, Opposition-linked families were leaving. No Arab government closed its borders or otherwise tried to stem the exodus. The AHC, its members already dispersed around the Arab world, issued no blanket condemnation of the flight though, according to IDF intelligence, it tried during these early months to halt the flow out of Palestine, specially of army-age males.[3] At the local level, some of the National Committees (in Haifa, Jerusalem, for example) and local irregulars' commanders tried to fight the exodus, even setting up people's courts to try offenders and threatening confiscation of the property of the departees. However, enforcement seems to have been weak and haphazard; the measures proved largely unavailing. The irregulars often had an interest in encouraging flight as money was to be made out of it.

As to April and the start of the main exodus, I have found no evidence to show that the AHC issued blanket instructions, by radio or otherwise, to Palestine's Arabs to flee. However, AHC and Husayni supporters in certain areas may have ordered or encouraged flight out of various calculations and may have done so, on occasion, in the belief that they were doing what the AHC wanted or would have wanted them to do. Haifa affords illustration of this. While it is unlikely that Husayni or the AHC from outside Palestine instructed the Haifa Arab leadership of 22 April to opt for evacuation rather than surrender, Husayni's local supporters, led by Sheikh Murad, did so. The lack of AHC and Husayni orders, appeals or broadcasts *against* the departure during the following week-long Haifa exodus indicates that Husayni and the AHC did not dissent from their supporters' decision. Silence was consent. The absence of clear, public instructions and broadcasts for or against the Haifa exodus over 23–30 April is supremely instructive concerning the ambivalence of Husayni and the AHC at this stage towards the exodus.

The Arab states, apart from appealing to the British to halt the Haganah offensives and charging that the Haganah was expelling Palestine's Arabs, seem to have taken weeks to digest and understand what was happening. They did not appeal to the Palestinian masses to leave, but neither, in April, did they demand that the Palestinians stay put. Perhaps the politicians in Damascus, Cairo and Amman, like Husayni, understood that they would need a good reason to justify armed intervention in Palestine on the morrow of the British departure – and the mass exodus, presented as a planned Zionist expulsion, afforded such a reason.

But the dimensions and burden of the problem created by the exodus, falling necessarily and initially upon the shoulders of the host countries, quickly persuaded the Arab states – primarily Transjordan – that it were best to halt the flood tide. The AHC, too, was apparently shocked by the ease and completeness of the uprooting of the Arabs from Palestine. Hence the spate of appeals in early May by Transjordan, the AHC and various Arab leaders to the Arabs of Palestine to stay put or, if already in exile, to return to their homes. But the appeals, given the war conditions along the fronts, had little effect: the refugees, who had just left an active or potential combat zone, were hardly minded to return to it, and especially not on the eve of the expected pan-Arab invasion. Besides, in most areas the Haganah physically barred a return. Later, the Arab invasion of 15 May made any thought of a refugee return impracticable. And the invasion substantially increased the readiness of Haganah commanders to clear border areas of Arab communities.

Already in April–May, on the local and national levels, the Yishuv's military and political leaders began to contemplate the problem of a refugee return: should they be allowed back? The approach of the First Truce in early June raised the problem as one of the major political and strategic issues to be faced by the new State. The Arab states, on the local level on each front and in international forums, had begun pressing for Israel to allow the refugees back. And the United Nations' Mediator for Palestine, Bernadotte, had vigorously taken up the cause.

However, politically and militarily it was clear to most "Israelis" that a return would be disastrous. Militarily – and the war, all understood, was far from over – it would mean the introduction of a large, potential Fifth Column; politically, it would mean the reintroduction of a large, disruptive, Arab minority. The military commanders argued against a return; so did political common sense. Both were reinforced by strident anti-return lobbying by Jewish settlements around the country.

The mainstream national leaders, led by Ben-Gurion, had to confront the issue within two problematic political contexts – the international context of future Israeli–Arab relations, Israeli–United Nations relations and Israeli–United States relations, and the local political context of a coalition government, in which the Mapam ministers advocated future Jewish–Arab coexistence and a return of "peace-minded" refugees after the war. Hence the Cabinet consensus of 16 June was that there would be no return during the war and that the matter could be reconsidered after the hostilities. This left Israel's diplomats with room for manœuvre and was sufficiently flexible to allow Mapam to stay in the government, leaving national unity intact.

On the practical level, from the spring of 1948, a series of developments on the ground growingly precluded any possibility of a future refugee return. The developments were an admixture of incidental, "natural" processes and steps specifically designed to assure the impossibility of a return, which included the gradual destruction of the abandoned Arab villages, the destruction or cultivation and long-term take-over of Arab fields, the establishment of new settlements on Arab lands and the settlement of Jewish immigrants in abandoned Arab villages and urban neighbourhoods.

The second half of the war, between the end of the First Truce (8 July) and the signing of the Israeli–Arab armistice agreements in the spring and summer of 1949, was characterised by short, sharp Israeli offensives interspersed with periods of cease-fire. In these offensives, the IDF beat the Transjordanian and Egyptian armies and the ALA in the Galilee, and conquered large parts of the territory earmarked in 1947 by the United Nations for a Palestine Arab state. During and after these battles in July, October and December 1948 – January 1949, something like 300,000 more Palestinians became refugees.

Again, there was no Cabinet or IDF General Staff-level decision to expel. Indeed, the July fighting (the "Ten Days") was preceded by an explicit IDF General Staff order to all units and corps to avoid destruction of Arab villages and expulsion of Arab communities without prior authorisation by the Defence Minister. That order was issued as a result of the cumulative political pressure during the summer by the Mapam ministers and Shitrit on Ben-Gurion.

But from July onwards, there was a growing readiness in the IDF units to expel. This was at least partly due to the political feeling, encouraged by the mass exodus from Jewish-held areas to date, that an almost completely Jewish State was a realistic possibility. There were also powerful vengeful urges at play – revenge for Jewish losses and punishment for having forced upon the Yishuv and its able-bodied young men the protracted, bitter battle. Generally, all that was needed in each successive newly-conquered area, was a little nudging.

The tendency of IDF units to expel Arab civilians increased just as the pressures on the remaining Arabs by leaders inside and outside Palestine to stay put grew and just as their motivation to stay put increased. During the summer, the Arab governments intermittently tried to bar the entry of new refugees into their territory. The Palestinians were encouraged to stay put in Palestine or to return to their homes. At the same time, those Palestinians still in their villages, hearing of the misery that was the lot of their exiled brethren and despairing of salvation and reconquest of Palestine by the Arab armies, generally preferred to stay put, even though facing the prospect of Israeli rule. Staying put was to be preferred to flight. Arab resistance to flight in the second half of 1948 was far greater than in the pre-July days. Hence, there was much less "spontaneous" flight: villagers tended either to stay put or to leave under duress.

Ben-Gurion clearly wanted as few Arabs as possible to remain in the Jewish State. He hoped to see them flee. He said as much to his colleagues and aides in meetings in August, September and October. But no expulsion policy was ever enunciated and Ben-Gurion always refrained from issuing clear or written expulsion orders; he preferred that his generals "understand" what he wanted done. He wished to avoid going down in history as the "great expeller" and he did not want the Israeli government to be implicated in a morally questionable policy. And he sought to preserve national unity in wartime.

But while there was no "expulsion policy," the July and October offensives were characterised by far more expulsions and, indeed, brutality towards Arab civilians than the first half of the war. Yet events varied from place to place. In July, Ben-Gurion approved the largest expulsion of the war, from Lydda and Ramle, but, at the same time, IDF Northern Front, with Ben-Gurion's agreement if not at his behest, left Nazareth's population, which was mostly Christian, in place; the "Christian factor" was allowed to determine policy. And, in the centre of the country, three Arab villages – Al Fureidis and Khirbet Jisr az Zarka (along the Haifa–Tel Aviv road), and Abu Ghosh (near Jerusalem) – were allowed to stay.

Again, the IDF offensives of October in the Galilee and the south were marked by ambivalence concerning the troops' attitude to the overrun civilian population. In the south, where Allon was in command, almost no Arab civilians remained anywhere. Allon tended to expel and let his subordinates know what he wanted. In the north, where Carmel was in charge, the picture was varied. Many Upper Galilee Arabs, overrun in Operation Hiram, did not flee, contrary to Ben-Gurion's expectations. This was probably due in part to the fact that before October, the villagers had hardly been touched by the war or its privations. The varied religious make-up of the population contributed to the mixed picture. The IDF generally related far more benignly to Christians and Druse than to Muslims. Most Christian and Druse villagers stayed put and were allowed to do so. Many of the Muslim villagers fled; others were expelled. But many other Muslim villagers – in Deir Hanna, Arraba, Sakhnin, Majd al Kurum – stayed put, and were allowed to stay. Much depended on specific local factors.

During the following months, with the Cabinet in Tel Aviv probably convinced that Israeli–Arab enmity would remain a central feature of the Middle East for many years, the IDF was authorised to clear Arab communities from Israel's long, winding and highly penetrable borders to a depth of 5–15 kilometres. One of the aims was to prevent infiltration of refugees back to their homes. The IDF was also afraid of sabotage and spying. Early November saw a wave of IDF expulsions or transfers of villagers inland along the northern border. Some villagers, ordered out, were "saved" by last-minute intervention by Israeli politicians. The following months and years saw other border areas cleared or partially cleared of Arab inhabitants.

In examining the causes of the Arab exodus from Palestine over 1947–9, accurate quantification is impossible. I have tried to show that the exodus occurred in stages and that causation was multi-layered: a Haifa merchant did not leave only because of the weeks or months of sniping and bombings; or because business was getting bad; or because of intimidation and extortion by irregulars; or because he feared the collapse of law and order when the British left; or because he feared for his prospects and livelihood under Jewish rule. He left because of the accumulation of all these factors.

The situation was somewhat more clearcut in the countryside. But there, too, multiple causation often applied. Take Qaluniya, near Jerusalem. There were months of hostilities in the area, intermittent shortages of supplies, severance of communications with Jerusalem, lack of leadership or clear instruction about what to do or expect, rumours of impending Jewish attack, Jewish attacks on neighbouring villages and reports of Jewish atrocities, and, finally, a Jewish attack on Qaluniya itself (after most of the inhabitants had left). Again, evacuation was the end-product of a cumulative process.

Even in the case of a Haganah or IDF expulsion order, the actual departure was often the result of a process rather than of that one act. Take Lydda, largely untouched by battle before July 1948. During the first months of the war, there was unemployment and skyrocketing prices, and the burden of armed irregulars. In April, thousands of refugees from Jaffa and its hinterland arrived in the town, camping out in courtyards and on the town's periphery. They brought demoralisation and sickness. Some wealthy families left. There was uncertainty about Abdullah's commitment to the town's defence. In June, there was a feeling that Lydda's "turn" was imminent. Then came the attack, with bombings and shelling, Arab Legion pull-out, collapse of resistance, sniping, massacre – and expulsion orders.

What happened in Palestine/Israel over 1947–9 was so complex and varied, the situation radically changing from date to date and place to place, that a single-cause explanation of the exodus from most sites is untenable. At most, one can say that certain causes were important in certain areas at certain times, with a general shift in the spring of 1948 from precedence of cumulative internal Arab factors – lack of leadership, economic problems, breakdown of law and order, to a primacy of external, compulsive causes – Haganah/IDF attacks and expulsions, fear of Jewish attacks and atrocities, lack of help from the Arab world and AHC and a feeling of impotence and abandonment, orders from Arab institutions and commanders to leave. In general, in most cases the final and decisive precipitant to flight was Haganah, IZL, LHI or IDF attack or the inhabitants' fear of such attack.

During the second half of 1948, international concern mounted with regard to the refugee problem. Concern translated into pressures. These pressures, launched by Bernadotte and the Arab states in the summer of 1948, increased as the months passed, as the number of refugees swelled and as their plight became physically more acute. The problem moved to the forefront of every treatment of the Middle East conflict and the Arabs made their agreement to a settlement with Israel contingent on a solution of the refugee problem by repatriation.

From the summer of 1948, Bernadotte, and from the autumn, the United States, pressed Israel to agree to a substantial measure of repatriation as part of a comprehensive solution to the refugee problem and to the general conflict. In December 1948, the United Nations General Assembly upheld the refugees' "right of return." But, as the abandoned villages fell into decrepitude or were bulldozed or settled, and as more Jewish immigrants poured into the country and were accommodated in abandoned Arab houses, the physical possibility of substantial repatriation grew more remote. Allowing back Arab refugees, Israel argued, would commensurately reduce Israel's ability to absorb Jewish refugees from Europe and the Middle East. Time worked against a repatriation of the Arab refugees. Bernadotte and the United States wanted Israel to make a "gesture" in the coin of repatriation, to get the efforts for a comprehensive settlement off the ground. In the spring of 1949, the thinking about a "gesture" matured into the United States' demand that Israel agree to take back 250,000, with the remaining refugees to be resettled in the neighbouring Arab countries. America threatened and cajoled, but never with sufficient force or conviction to persuade Tel Aviv to relent.

In the spring, in a final major effort, the United Nations and United States engineered the Lausanne Peace Conference. Weeks and months of haggling over agenda and secondary problems led nowhere. The Arabs made all progress contingent on Israeli agreement to mass repatriation. Under American pressure, Tel Aviv reluctantly agreed in July to take back 65,000–70,000 refugees (the "100,000 offer") as part of a comprehensive peace settlement. But by summer 1949, public and party political opinion in Israel – in part, due to government propaganda – had so hardened against a return that even this minimal offer was greeted by a storm of public protest and howls within Mapai. In any case, the sincerity of the Israeli offer was never tested: the Arabs rejected it out of hand. The United States, too, regarded it as acutely insufficient, as too little, too late.

The insufficiency of the "100,000 offer," the Arab states' growing rejectionism, their unwillingness to accept and concede defeat and their inability to publicly agree to absorb and resettle most of the refugees if Israel agreed to repatriation of the rest, the expiry of the "Gaza Plan," and

America's unwillingness or inability to apply persuasive pressures on Israel and the Arab states to compromise – all meant that the Arab–Israeli impasse would remain and that Palestine's exiled Arabs would remain refugees, to be utilised during the following years by the Arab states as a powerful political and propaganda pawn against Israel. The memory or vicarious memory of 1948 and the subsequent decades of humiliation and deprivation in the refugee camps would ultimately turn generations of Palestinians into potential or active terrorists and the "Palestinian problem" into one of the world's most intractable.

The number of Palestinian refugees

Over the years, a minor point of dispute between Israel and the Arab states has been the number of Palestinian Arabs who became refugees during and as a result of the 1948 war. Arab spokesmen from 1949 onwards spoke of a total of 900,000 or one million refugees. Israeli spokesmen, in public usually referred to "about 520,000."[1] The United Nations Economic Survey Mission and the United Nations Relief and Works Agency for Palestine Refugees in the Near East (UNRWA) put the figure at 726,000.[2]

Other estimates ranged between the Israeli and Arab figures. For example, the British, in February 1949, thought that there were 810,000, of whom 210,000 were in the Gaza Strip, 320,000 in Transjordanian-held Palestine and 280,000 in Lebanon, Syria and Transjordan proper.[3]

The Director General of the Israel Foreign Ministry, Eytan, in a private letter in late 1950 referred to the UNRWA registration in 1949 of 726,000 as "meticulous" and thought that "the real number was close to 800,000."[4] But officially, Israel stuck to the low figure of 520,000–530,000. The reason was simple: "if people . . . became accustomed to the large figure and we are eventually obliged to accept the return of the refugees, we may find it difficult, when faced with hordes of claimants, to convince the world that not all of these formerly lived in Israeli territory . . . It would, in any event, seem desirable to minimize the numbers . . . than otherwise."[5]

Israel sincerely believed that the Arab (and United Nations) figures were "inflated." This inflation, Sharett thought, stemmed from the inclusion of refugees from border areas outside Israeli territory and the inclusion of "destitute people" who had preferred to jump onto the bandwagon of United Nations relief rather than stay at home impoverished. The refugees themselves tended to exaggerate their numbers (for example, by not registering deaths) in order to obtain more rations.[6]

In August 1948, Sharett (Shertok) instructed his officials to obtain expert help in arriving at the real number of the refugees. The officials responded that the statisticians were "at a loss" about how to work out the numbers and had themselves turned to the Foreign Ministry for figures.[7]

In mid-1949, Sharett asked Israel's Central Bureau of Statistics for an official estimate. On 2 June, the Bureau's Dr H. Meyuzam responded that "the number of refugees was about 577,000." The Bureau reached this figure by the following route: according to British Mandate estimates, the total number of non-Jewish inhabitants in the areas which became the Jewish State was 722,000 (including western Jerusalem). This included a 6% exaggeration. Hence, the real number was probably 679,000. There were about 102,000 Arabs left in Israel – hence 577,000 had become refugees.[8] (It was on this basis that the Israel Foreign Ministry reached the 520,000–530,000 total, arguing that about 30,000–40,000 refugees, who had infiltrated back into Israel since the November 1948 census that showed 102,000 Arabs in Israel, should be lopped off the 577,000 figure.)

But Meyuzam had qualified his estimate by saying that in estimating the number of Arabs in Mandate Palestine areas that were to become Israel (679,000), he had not taken into account "illegal" Arab immigrants resident in Palestine or the bedouin concentrations in the Negev, either left in place or in exile.

These points (among others) were taken up in a British analysis in September 1949. The Foreign Office concluded that the number of refugees was "between 600,000 and 760,000." This rather inconclusive conclusion, co-opting the extremities of the Foreign Office Research Department's estimate (600,000) and the PCC Technical Committee's "maximum number" (766,000), was based on the following criticisms of the official Israeli estimate: it took no account of natural increase among the Palestine Arabs since 31 December 1947 (which was offset only in part by war casualties); it was incorrect in deducting 6% from the Mandate total of about "725,000"; it ignored the figure of "95,000" for the bedouins, many of whom had become refugees. The thrust of the figures in the British analysis was that there were 711,000 bona fide Palestine Arab refugees.[9]

Both Meyuzam and the British understood that there was no way accurately to assess the true number of Arab illegals living in Palestine when the war broke out. There was no way accurately to estimate the net difference between births and deaths in Arab Palestine during the war. And Meyuzam rightly implied that accurately assessing the number of bedouin who had become refugees was impossible.

Because of these factors, it is impossible to arrive at a definite, persuasive estimate. My predilection would be to opt for the loose, but probably not inaccurate, contemporary British formula, that of "between 600,000 and 760,000" refugees.

Biographical notes

Allon (Paicovitch), Yigal (1918–80) b. Kfar Tavor, Palestine. Commander of the Palmah 1945–8. OC Operation Yiftah (April–May 1948), OC Operation Dani (July 1948) and OC Operation Yoav (October 1948). OC Southern Front September 1948–9. Minister of Labour 1961–8, Deputy Prime Minister, Foreign Minister 1974–7.

Abdullah, Ibn Husayn (1882–1951) b. Mecca. Emir (1921–46) and King (1946–51) of Transjordan.

Ben-Gurion (Gruen), David (1886–1973) b. Poland. Settled in Palestine 1906. Secretary-General of the Histadrut 1920–35. Chairman of the Jewish Agency 1935–May 1948. Leader of Mapai. Prime Minister and Minister of Defence of the State of Israel 1948–54, Prime Minister and Minister of Defence 1955–63.

Carmel (Zalizky), Moshe (1911–) b. Minsk Mazowiecki, Poland. Settled in Palestine 1924. Member of Kibbutz Na'an. OC Haganah Haifa District 1947. OC Carmeli Brigade April–May 1948. OC Northern Front (Operation Dekel and Operation Hiram) July 1948–1950. Editor *Lamerhav* (Ahdut Ha'avodah's daily) 1960–5, Minister of Transport 1955–6, 1965–9.

Cohen, Aharon (1910–80) b. Bessarabia. Settled in Palestine 1937. Member of Kibbutz Sha'ar Ha'amakim. Director of Arab Department, Mapam and member of Mapam Political Committee, 1948–9.

Cunningham, General Sir Alan Gordon (1887–?) b. Dublin. GOC 8th Army 1941, last British High Commissioner in Palestine 1945–May 1948.

Danin, Ezra (1903–85) b. Jaffa. Senior officer of Haganah Intelligence Service (*Shai*) 1936–48. Official of Arab Division, Political Department,

Jewish Agency 1940–8. Member of Arab Affairs Committee of the National Institutions 1940s. Member of first and second Transfer Committees and Senior Adviser on Arab Affairs to the Foreign Ministry 1948–9. Intelligence officer and orange-grower.

Eshkol (Shkolnik), Levi (1895–1969) b. Russia. Haganah Treasurer in 1940s. Deputy Minister of Defence 1948. Director Jewish Agency Land Settlement Department September 1948–June 1963. Minister of Finance 1952–63. Prime Minister 1963–9.

Eytan (Ettinghausen), Walter (1910–) b. Munich. Settled in Palestine 1946. Director General, Israel Foreign Ministry 1948–59. First head of Israel Delegation at Lausanne 1949. Israel Ambassador to France 1959–70.

Galili, Israel (1910–86) b. Ukraine. Settled in Palestine 1914. Founder-member of Kibbutz Na'an, Ahdut Ha'avodah leader. Head of the Haganah National Staff 1946–May 1948. Mapam leader 1948–54. Cabinet Minister (Labour Party) (without portfolio, information) 1966–77.

Hazan, Ya'acov (1899–) b. Poland. Member of Kibbutz Mishmar Ha'emek. Leader of Kibbutz Artzi and Mapam, 1948–9. Knesset Member 1949–74.

al Husayni, 'Abd al Qadir (1907–48) b. Jerusalem. Leader of Arab irregulars band, Jerusalem District 1936–9. Head of *al Jihad al Muqqadis* (Holy War) irregulars band 1947–8. Killed in April 1948 in battle for Al Qastal.

al Husayni, Hajj Muhammad Amin (1895–1974) b. Jerusalem. President and ("Grand") Mufti of Supreme Muslim Council 1921–37. President AHC 1936–7. Worked for Nazi Germany 1942–5. President AHC 1946–8 and political leader of Palestine Arabs 1947–9.

al Husayni, Jamal (1893?–1982) b. Jerusalem. Member of AHC 1936–7. Representative of AHC to United Nations 1947–8.

Ibrahim, Rashid Hajj (?–?) Chairman of Haifa Arab National Committee 1947–8.

Kaplan, Eliezer (1891–1952) b. Russia. Settled in Palestine 1923.

Treasurer of the Jewish Agency 1933–48. Finance Minister (Mapai) May 1948–52.

al Khatib, Haj Mohammed Nimr (?–?) Preacher, leader of the Muslim Brotherhood in Palestine. Member of Haifa Arab National Committee 1947–early 1948.

Khalidi, Dr Husayn Fakhri (1894–1962) b. Jerusalem. Mayor of Jerusalem 1934–7. Founded Reform Party 1935. Member of AHC 1936–7, 1945–8. Only AHC member to stay in Palestine in 1948. Jordanian Cabinet Minister 1950s.

Machnes, Gad (1893–1954) b. Petah Tikva, Palestine. Leading orange-grower. Director General, Minority Affairs Ministry, 1948–9.

Marriott, Cyril Herbert Alfred (1897–?) British Consular Service Officer. Consul General, Haifa, May 1948–August 1949.

Myerson (Meir), Golda (1898–1975) b. Kiev, Russia. Director of Jewish Agency Political Department (in Jerusalem 1948), Mapai Knesset Member, Minister of Labour 1949–56, Foreign Minister, Prime Minister 1969–74.

Rabin, Yitzhak (1922–) b. Jerusalem. Deputy Commander of the Palmah 1947–8. OC Harel Brigade April–June 1948. OC operations Operation Dani July 1948. OC operations Southern Front September 1948–March 1949. IDF Chief of Staff 1964–8. Prime Minister 1974–7. Minister of Defence 1984–

Sasson, Elias (Eliahu) (1902–78) b. Damascus. Settled in Palestine 1927. Director Arab Division of Political Department, Jewish Agency 1933–48. Director Foreign Ministry Middle East Affairs Department 1948–50. Member of first Transfer Committee 1948. Diplomat (Ambassador to Italy, Switzerland) 1950–61. Minister of Posts 1961, Minister of Police 1966–9.

Sharett (Shertok), Moshe (1894–1965) b. Ukraine. Settled in Palestine 1906. Director of the Jewish Agency's Political Department 1933–May 1948. Foreign Minister (Mapai) May 1948–1954. Prime Minister 1954–5. Foreign Minister 1955–6. Chairman of Jewish Agency 1960–5.

Shiloah (Zaslani), Reuven (1909–59) b. Jerusalem. Haganah Intelligence Service officer. Official of Arab Division of Political Department, Jewish Agency. Director Political Division, Foreign Ministry 1948–9. Second head of Israel Delegation, Lausanne, 1949. Founder of the *Mossad* intelligence agency. Diplomat.

Shimoni, Ya'acov (1915–) b. Berlin. Settled in Palestine 1935. Official of Arab Division, Political Department, Jewish Agency 1941–8. Deputy Director and Acting Director of Foreign Ministry Middle East Affairs Department May 1948–1949.

Shitrit, Bechor Shalom (1895–1967) b. Tiberias. Mandate police officer. Judge 1935. Chief Magistrate Lydda District 1945–8. Minister of Minority Affairs and Police May 1948–April 1949.

Tamimi, Rafiq (1890–1957) b. Nablus. School headmaster in Jaffa. Member of Arab Higher Committee 1947–8. Head of Jaffa Arab National Committee.

Weitz, Yosef (1890–1972) b. Poland. Settled in Palestine 1908. Director of Jewish National Fund Lands Department/Development Division 1932–67. Member of Arab Affairs Committee of National Institutions 1940s. JNF Representative on the Committee of Directorates of the National Institutions 1940s. Chairman of first and second Transfer Committees 1948–9. Chairman Negev Committee 1948. Member of JNF Directorate 1950–67.

Yadin (Sukenik), Yigael (1917–85) b. Jerusalem. OC Operations Haganah 1944 and 1947–May 1948. OC Operations IDF June 1948–1949. IDF Chief of Staff 1949–52. Professor of Archaeology Hebrew University, Jerusalem 1963–77. Deputy Prime Minister 1977–81.

Zisling, Aharon (1901–64) b. Russia. Settled in Palestine 1904. Member of Kibbutz Ein Harod. Ahdut Ha'avodah leader. Minister of Agriculture (Mapam) 1948–9.

Notes

1 Background

1 The following portrait of Palestinian Arab society in 1947 is based mainly on Ya'acov Shimoni, *Arviyei Eretz Yisrael* (The Arabs of Palestine); Yehoshua Porath, *The Emergence of the Palestinian–Arab National Movement 1918–1929* and *The Palestinian Arab National Movement 1929–1939*; and Rony Gabbay, *A Political Study of the Arab–Jewish Conflict: The Arab Refugee Problem (a Case Study)*.

2 Gabbay, *Political Study*, p. 6; and Shimoni, *Arviyei*, passim.

3 In 1931, only some 10% of Palestine's Muslim population were literate (Porath, *Emergence*, p. 20), and presumably almost all of these hailed from the urban upper and middle classes. However, the Mandate administration vastly expanded the school system and illiteracy was substantially reduced. In 1941 the British estimated that illiteracy in the Arab community stood at 73%, (Shimoni, *Arviyei*, p. 389).

4 Porath, *Emergence*, p. 287.

5 A fuller list is in Shimoni, *Arviyei*, pp. 211–39.

6 Porath, *Palestinian Arab*, pp. 162–273. Rosemary Sayigh, *Palestinians: From Peasants to Revolutionaries*, pp. 47–51 mistakenly says that none of the 1936 military leaders were from the elite families. There were a few, including 'Abd al Qadir al Husayni.

7 Shimoni, *Arviyei*, p. 338, footnotes 5 and 6, gives a partial list of the family affiliations. The Husaynis had the fealty of the Dajanis and 'Abu Labans (Jaffa), the Suranis (Gaza), the Hasunahs (Lydda), the Tamimis and Anabtawis (Nablus), the Abadins, Arafas and Khatibs (Hebron), the Tabaris (Tiberias), and the Nakhawis (Safad); and the Nashashibis had the loyalty of the Tawqans, Masris and Shak'ahs (Nablus), the Dajanis (Jerusalem), the Karazuns and Huneidis (Lydda), the 'Amrs and Tahabubs (Hebron), the Hanuns (Tulkarm) and the Fahums (Nazareth). Among the more prominent "neutral" families through the late 1930s and 1940s were the Shawas (Gaza), the Nusseibehs (Jerusalem) and the 'Abushis (Jenin).

8 Porath, *Palestinian Arab*, passim.

9 See, for example, DBG-YH I, pp. 64 and 66, entries for 22 December 1947; statements by Danin and Sasson at the meeting of the Yishuv's senior Arab affairs policy-makers and advisers, "Protocol of the Meeting on Shem [Arab]

Affairs, 1–2 January 1948," Israel Galili Papers Yad Tabenkin, Ef'al, Israel; and DBG-YH I, pp. 253–4, entry for 19 February 1948.

10 Shimoni, *Arviyei*, p. 205 and footnotes 12 and 13. The Palestinian pound during the mandate was equivalent to the pound sterling.

11 Porath, *Palestinian Arab*, p. 76.

12 Shimoni, *Arviyei*, pp. 376–7.

13 Nafez Nazzal, *The Palestinian Exodus from Galilee, 1948*, pp. 30–1, 34, 39–40 and 46. These figures were gleaned from memories decades after the events and are probably none too accurate. But, taken as a whole, they probably give a good idea of the reality.

14 *STH*, III, part 2, p. 1362.

15 CZA s25-3300, "*Helekh Ru'ah Arviyei Eretz Yisrael*" (The Feeling Among Palestine's Arabs), 29 October 1947, by "Pir'im," a Haganah intelligence agent. This view was endorsed by officials of the Arab Division of the Political Department of the Jewish Agency.

16 CZA s25-3300, "A Conversation with Za'fer Dajani, chairman of the Jaffa Chamber of Commerce," 26 November 1947, by "A.L."

17 Meir Pa'il, *Min Ha'Haganah Letzva Haganah* (From the Haganah to the Defence Army), pp. 279–80.

18 *Ibid.* p. 241.

19 *Ibid.* p. 285. To this should be added the combined maximum strength in 1948 of 2,000–3,000 members of the *Irgun Z'vai Leumi* (IZL, the National Military Organisation) and the *Lohamei Herut Yisrael* (LHI or "Stern Gang", the Freedom Fighters of Israel), the two dissident, terrorist organisations. Militarily, these two organisations were largely insignificant in the battles against the Arabs in the months before their disbandment and co-option in June into the IDF.

20 *Ibid.* p. 285.

21 DBG-YH I, p. 63, entry for 22 December 1947.

22 DBG-YH I, p. 169, entry for 21 January 1948.

23 CP III/1/3, High Commissioner to Secretary of State, Weekly Intelligence Report, 3 January 1948.

24 CZA s25-3300 "Conversation with Jerusalem lawyer Fa'iz Haddad," 24 November 1947, by "A.L."

25 CZA s25-3300 "Conversation with Za'far Dajani, chairman of the Jaffa Chamber of Commerce," 26 November 1947, by "A.L."

26 PRO FO371-68366 E458/11/65g, G.J.C.C. Jenkins, British Embassy Cairo, for attention of HM Ambassador, 30 December 1947.

27 CZA 28, protocol of the meeting of the Jewish Agency Executive, statement by D. Ben-Gurion, 7 June 1938. Ben-Gurion made similar statements through 1937–8. See Shabtai Teveth, *Ben-Gurion and the Palestine Arabs*, p. 188.

28 Teveth, *Ben-Gurion* p. 27.

29 *Ibid.*, p. 181, quoting Ben-Gurion's diary entry for 12 July 1937.

30 *Ibid.*, p. 189, quoting a letter from D. Ben-Gurion to A. Ben-Gurion, 5 October 1937.

31 CZA 28, protocols of the meeting of the Jewish Agency Executive, 7 June 1938.
32 CZA 28, protocols of the Jewish Agency Executive meeting of 9 June 1938.
33 CZA 28, protocols of the joint meeting of the Jewish Agency Executive and the Political Committee of the Zionist Actions Committee, 12 June 1938.
34 Yosef Weitz *Yomani Ve'igrotai Labanim* (My Diary and Letters to the Children), (henceforward Weitz, *Diary*), Vol. II, p. 181, entry for 20 December 1940.
35 CZA A246–7 (A246 are the manuscript notebooks of Yosef Weitz's diary), p. 1126, entry for 18 March 1941; and CZA A246–8, p. 1337, entry for 31 May 1942.
36 ISA FM2444/19, excerpts from "The Jewish Plan for Palestine," Jewish Agency.
37 CZA 45/1, protocol of the Jewish Agency Executive meeting of 2 November 1947.
38 DBG-YH I, pp. 22–3, statement by Ben-Gurion at the meeting of the Mapai Centre, 3 December 1947.

2 The first-wave

1 DBG-YH I, pp. 37–8, entry for 11 December 1947.
2 Israel State Archives/Central Zionist Archives, *Political and Diplomatic Documents*, December 1947 – May 1948, ed. Gedalia Yogev (henceforward referred to as Documents), p. 60 Ben-Gurion (Tel Aviv) to Moshe Shertok (New York), 14 December 1947; and LPA 23 aleph 48, protocols of the meeting of the Mapai Centre (*merkaz mapai*), statement by Ben-Gurion, 8 January 1948.
3 Documents, p. 145, Sasson to Abdullah, 11 January 1948.
4 DBG-YH I, p. 12, entry for 1 December 1947.
5 Histadrut Archive, protocols of the meeting of the Histadrut Executive Committee (*ha'va'ad ha'poel shel ha'Histadrut*), statement by Israel Galili, 10 December 1947. The complex and changing patterns of command in and over the Haganah in 1947 are described, albeit somewhat obscurely and clumsily, in Pa'il, *Min Ha'Haganah* p. 67 ff.
6 Histadrut Archive, protocols of the meeting of the Histadrut Executive Committee, statements by Galili and Hazan, 10 December 1947; *STH*, III, part 2, p. 1415; and DBG-YH I, p. 28, entry for 9 December 1947.
7 DBG-YH I, p. 58, entry for 19 December 1947.
8 DBG Archives, protocols of the Meeting of the Defence Committee, 18 December 1947.
9 DBG Archives, report: "The Murder of the Eleven in [Sidrat] Abu Suweirih (near Gan-Yavne)," *Tene* (Haganah Intelligence Service), 11 January 1948.
10 The text of "Plan May" is in *STH*, III, part 3, pp. 1939–43.
11 CP 11/3/147, "Weekly Intelligence Appreciation," High Commissioner to Secretary of State, 13 December 1947; and CP 11/3/148, High Commissioner

to Secretary of State, 15 December 1947. In DBG-YH I, p. 61, there is a list
of Haganah, IZL and LHI operations up to 20 December 1947.

12 Israel Galili Papers (Ef'al, Israel), "Protocol of the Meeting on Arab Affairs,
1–2 January 1948"; and DBG-YH I, p. 97, entry for 25 December 1947.
Khisas was a tale of Haganah inefficiency and trigger-happiness. An Arab
had killed a Jew in a months'-old vendetta. The local Palmah commander
believed that the crime had been "political" and decided to retaliate. Local
Haganah Intelligence Service officers and civil leaders appealed against the
intended operation, which was also to have included attacks on nearby Al
Khalisa and two other villages, and obtained a postponement from the
Haganah General Staff. But the local commanders, who (according to Danin)
wanted to "keep up [their troops'] morale," asked for and obtained permission from Palmah OC Allon, and attacked Khisas on 18 December. The
General Staff in Tel Aviv subsequently denied advance knowledge of the
operation. The attacking troops mistakenly blew up a house with civilians in
it. See CZA S25-3569, Danin to Sasson, 23 December 1947; *STH*, III, part 2,
p. 1415 and p. 1798; and *Sefer Hapalmah* (The Book of the Palmah), II, pp.
123–4.

13 LPA 23 aleph 48, protocol of the meeting of the Mapai Centre, statement by
Ben-Gurion, 8 January 1948.

14 Israel Galili Papers, "Protocol of the Meeting on Arab Affairs, 1–2 January
1948," for a protracted discussion on the possible infliction of civilian
casualties; and *STH*, III, part 2, p. 1379.

15 Israel Galili Papers, "Protocol of the Meeting on Arab Affairs, 1–2 January
1948".

16 CZA S25-3569, Danin to Sasson, 23 December 1947; CZA S25-4066, "*Mipi
Kafri* (from a villager)," the Arab Division of the Jewish Agency Political
Department, 27 January 1948; and DBG-YH I, p. 163, entry for 19 January
1948.

17 LPA 23/48, protocol of the meeting of the Mapai Centre, statement by Ben-
Gurion, 8 January 1948.

18 HHA 66.90 (1), protocol of the meeting of the Mapam Political Committee,
statement by Israel Galili, 5 February 1948.

19 Jewish National Fund files, 501–4, "The Negev These Days," a memorandum by Yosef Weitz, undated but most probably from the end of March
1948.

20 DBG-YH I, pp. 253–5, entry for 19 February, for the discussion between
Ben-Gurion and his Arab affairs advisers. Note especially Danin's state-
ment. The point was well made by Aharon Cohen, head of Mapam's Arab
Department, who tried to persuade the party leadership to influence Ben-
Gurion to modify Haganah tactics so that the retaliatory strikes hit only
"guilty" communities. See HHA-ACP, 10.95.11 (21), Cohen to Leib (Lova)
Levite and Ya'acov (Koba) Riftin, 13 March 1948.

21 LPA 23/48, protocol of the meeting of the Mapai Centre, statement by Ben-
Gurion, 8 January 1948; and LPA 24/48, protocol of the meeting of the
Mapai Secretariat, 20 March 1948.

22 CZA S25-8915, "Meeting of Jews and Arabs in Shomron (Samaria)," 5 September 1947, unsigned.

23 LA 235 IV, 2092, circular of the Settlement Block Committee of Shomron (Samaria), 1 November 1947.

24 LA 235 IV, 2092, circular of the Settlement Block Committee of Shomron, 4 January 1948.

25 LA 235 IV, 2093, circular of the Hefer Valley Regional Council, 24 December 1947; and CZA S25-7089, circular of the Settlement Block Committee of Shomron, 4 January 1948.

26 CZA S25-3569, Danin to Sasson, 23 December 1947.

27 CZA S25-9189, text of the poster-circular, 21 January 1948.

28 HHA-ACP 10.95.11 (4), a report by Aharon Haim Cohen, 11 February 1948.

29 *STH*, III, part 2, p. 1393.

30 KMA-PA 100/MemVavDalet/3 – 74, Haganah Intelligence Service Information (*yediot tene*), 5 March 1948.

31 KMA-PA 109/heh – 242, Haganah Intelligence Service Information, 27 February 1948, relating to 15 February 1948.

32 KMA-PA 109/heh – 190, Haganah Intelligence Service Information, 6 February 1948.

33 *STH*, III, part 2, p. 1375; DBG-YH I, p. 291, entry for 10 March 1948; and interview with Yehoshua Palmon, 1984.

34 KMA-PA 100/MemVavDalet/3 – 154, Haganah Intelligence Service Information, 9 May 1948.

35 PRO CO537-3853, "Fortnightly Report for the Period Ended the 15th January 1948," Galilee District Commissioner, 19 January 1948.

36 HHA-ACP 10.95.11 (4), protocol of the meeting of the Histadrut Arab Worker's Department, 26 March 1948; and CZA S25-2968, protocol of the meeting of the Histadrut Arab Worker's Department, 30 March 1948.

37 CZA S25-426, protocol of the meeting of the Jewish Agency Political Department, 25 March 1948.

38 PRO WO275-79, "Report No. 57 for the Week Ending 10 December 1947," 317 Field Security (FS) Section, 6th Airborne Division; and WO275-52, 6th Airborne Division Logbook, entry for 4 December 1947.

39 CZA S25-3569, "Report on the Situation in the Country," Danin to Sasson, 23 December 1947. Danin reported that Jewish refugees from Arab parts of Haifa, "apparently under [IZL or LHI] guidance, had attacked Arab civilians whose houses were located between Jewish houses . . ., took them from their homes roughly, with curses and blows, and sent them to their rioting [Arab] brothers." Quoting Arab sentiments, Danin wrote: "If you [Jews] behave this way at the start [of hostilities], how will you act when you have the power?" See also JEM LXXI/2, S. P. Emery (Haifa) to the Bishop of Jerusalem, 13 December 1947.

40 DBG-YH I, p. 177, entry for 22 January 1948.

41 *Be'einei Oyev, Shelosha Pirsumim Arvi'im al Milhemet Hakomemiut* (In Enemy Eyes, three Arab publications on the War of Independence), p. 12. The book is a collection of lengthy excerpts from three Arab memoirs of the

1948 war, translated into Hebrew by Captain S. Sabag. This quote is taken from Nimr al Khatib's *Min Athar al Nakba* (In the Wake of the Catastrophe).

42 DBG-YH I, p. 114, entry for 5 January 1948.

43 DBG-YH I, p. 177, entry for 22 January 1948.

44 Zadok Eshel, *Ma'arachot Hahaganah Be'Haifa* (The Haganah Battles in Haifa), p. 326.

45 DBG-YH I, p. 177, entry for 22 January 1948; and PRO co537-3853, "Report for the Period 16–31 January 1948," Haifa District Commissioner, 3 February 1948.

46 CZA s25-3569, "Haddad" to "Adina" (i.e., Sasson), 17 January 1948; and DBG-YH I, pp. 171 and 177, entries for 22 January 1948.

47 ISA FM2568/4, "*Yediot Mipi Hanagid Letene*" (information from the "Nagid" – the codename of an Arab informant – to Haganah Intelligence), 9 February 1948.

48 PRO co537-3853, "Report for the Period 16–31 January 1948," Haifa District Commissioner, 3 February 1948.

49 CZA s25-3993, a report on meeting with Arab leaders in the Rotary Club by Uriel Friedland, 22 January 1948.

50 PRO wo275-64, "Fortnightly Intelligence Newsletter," for 28 January–11 February 1948, Palestine Military headquarters, 13 February 1948; Eshel, *Ma'arachot*, p. 327; PRO co537-3853, "Report for the Period 16–29 February 1948," Haifa district commissioner, 5 March 1948; DBG-YH I p. 290, entry for 10 March 1948; and DBG-YH I p. 326, entry for 30 March 1948.

51 *Be'einei Oyev*, p. 18.

52 *Be'einei Oyev*, pp. 12, 17–18, 20.

53 HHA-ACP 10.95.10 (6), Krischer (Haifa) to the Arab Department, Mapam, 10 February 1948.

54 HHA-ACP 10.95.10 (6), "Bulletin No. 2 (Information About Developments in the Arab Camp – from Our Special Sources)," 1 March 1948.

55 The Haifa National Committee communiqués – nos. 1–10 and no. 12 – are reprinted verbatim, in Hebrew, in *Be'einei Oyev* pp. 55–66. No. 11, of 18 March 1948, which dealt with the funeral arrangements for al Huneiti, was for some reason omitted. Walid Khalidi, in "The Fall of Haifa," *Middle East Forum*, XXXV, 10, (December 1959), 22–32, argues that the National Committee strenuously and continuously struggled to halt the emigration from Arab Haifa. This is not borne out by the available evidence.

56 Eshel, *Ma'arachot*, p. 342.

57 CZA s25-7719, Zaslani (Shiloah), Jerusalem, to Shertok, Washington, 13 December 1947.

58 KMA-PA 101 – 45, 46, 47 and 50, Haganah Intelligence Service reconnaissance reports for 2, 5 and 6 December 1947; and PRO wo275–52, Divisional Logbook, 6th Airborne Division, entry for 3 December 1947.

59 CZA s25-4066, report from "Hapoel Ha'aravi" (the codename of an Arab informant) to the Arab Division, Jewish Agency Political Department, 2 February 1948.

60 JI IZL Papers, kaf-4, 8/9, transcripts of tapped telephone conversations from Jaffa, 4–15 January 1948.
61 CZA S25-3569, "Peh" to Sasson, 18 January 1948.
62 DBG-YH I, p. 35, entry for 10 December 1947; and CZA S25-4011, "The Situation in Jaffa," by "Arye," 11 December 1947, sent by Shiloah to Sasson, 12 December 1947.
63 CZA S25-9046, "In the Arab Camp," written by the Arab Division of the Jewish Agency Political Department, 14 December 1948; and CZA S25-3569, "Peh" to Sasson, 18 January 1948.
64 DBG-YH I, p. 121, entry for 7 January 1948; and *Documents*, p. 333, Ben-Gurion to Shertok (New York), 12 February 1948. This cable, incidentally, was passed on to the UK Delegation to the United Nations by Shertok, who presumably thought it placed the Arabs in a bad light. See PRO FO371-68367 E2260/11/65, UK Delegation (New York) to Foreign Office, 16 February 1948.
65 Galili Papers, "Protocol of the Meeting on Arab Affairs, 1–2 January 1948," pp. 38, 40, etc.
66 *Be'einei Oyev*, pp. 32–3.
67 CZA S25-9046, "In the Arab Camp," the Arab Division of the Jewish Agency Political Department, 14 December 1947.
68 DBG-YH I, p. 29, entry for 9 December 1947.
69 Galili Papers, "Protocol of the Meeting on Arab Affairs, 1–2 January 1948"; and DBG-YH I, p. 104, entry for 2 January 1948. See also DBG Archives, "Ben Avi" (Ya'akobson) to "Amitai" (Ben-Gurion), 4 January 1948 a memorandum entitled "Siege of Jaffa."
70 DBG-YH I, pp. 184–5, entry for 25 January 1948.
71 Galili Papers, "Protocol of the Meeting on Arab Affairs, 1–2 January 1948," pp. 12–23. Events in Romema and Lifta were described at the 1–2 January meeting by Sasson, who was critical of the Haganah role. See also Ya'acov Banai, *Hayalim Almonim, Sefer Mivtze'ei Lehi* (Unknown Soldiers, the Book of LHI Operations) pp. 636–7, 639, 640; PRO WO275-64, "Fortnightly Intelligence Newsletter," British Military headquarters, Palestine, 16 January 1948; PRO CO537-3855, "CID Summary of Events," 17 January 1948 (covering 16 January); and *STH*, III, part 2, pp. 1393 and 1545.
72 DBG-YH I, p. 118, entry for 6 January 1948.
73 CP III/1/9, High Commissioner to Secretary of State, 7 January 1948; CP V/1, "Notes of an Interview with Mr Ben-Gurion," by the High Commissioner, 6 January 1948; and CP V/4, Ben-Gurion to Cunningham, 8 January 1948.
74 CZA S25-4013, "Summary of Information about Hotel Semiramis . . . in Qatamon," the Arab Division of the Jewish Agency Political Department, 8 January 1948.
75 DBG-YH I, p. 141, entry for 12 January 1948.
76 From the diary of Khalil Sakakini, *That's the Way I Am, World*, extracts of which were published in *The Jerusalem Post* on 25 March 1986 and 1 April 1986. The Haganah had no "heavy artillery" in Jerusalem.

77 See *The Jerusalem Post Magazine*, 28 March 1986, interview with Anwar Nusseibeh, for a hint of this.

78 DBG-YH I, p. 165, entry for 20 January 1948.

79 David Ben-Gurion, *Behilahem Yisrael*, p. 68–9, giving the text of Ben-Gurion's speech at the meeting of the Mapai Council, 7 February 1948. A slightly abridged form of the speech is in DBG-YH I, pp. 208–12.

80 *STH*, III, part 2, p.1395; and David Shaltiel, *Yerushalayim Tashah* (Jerusalem 1948), p. 85.

81 PRO WO275-64, "Fortnightly Intelligence Newsletter," British Military headquarters, Palestine, 27 February 1948.

82 The foregoing is largely based on HHA-ACP 10.95.13 (1), "The Emigration of the Arabs of Palestine in the Period 1/12/1947–1/6/1948," IDF Intelligence Department, 30 June 1948. The expulsion of 'Arab Abu Kishk by the IZL is described in JI IZL Papers, kaf–4, 7/7, "Testimony of Arye Bachar," interviewed on 24 July 1957.

83 HHA 66.10, protocol of the meeting of the Mapam Political Committee, statement by Galili, 5 February 1948; KMA-PA 107 – 105, 105 aleph, 85, 84, 82; HHA-ACP 10.95.11 (21), Cohen to Levite and Riftin, 13 March 1948; Gershon Rivlin and Zvi Sinai (eds.), *Hativat Alexandroni Bemilhemet Hakomemiut* (The Alexandroni Brigade in the War of Independence), p. 220.

84 HHA-ACP 10.95.13 (1), "The Emigration of the Arabs of Palestine in the Period 1/12/1947–1/6/1948," IDF Intelligence Department, 30 June 1948.

85 See, for example, DBG-YH I, p. 279, entry for 4 March 1948, for what happened in Sheikh Muwannis at this time.

86 See, for example, *Hativat Alexandroni*, pp. 148–9, for the case of Biyar 'Adas, southeast of Kfar Sava, in early March.

87 CZA A202–217, Avraham Granott Papers, Weitz to Granovsky, 31 March 1948.

88 *Ibid.*

89 Weitz, *Diary* III, p. 223, entry for 11 January 1948.

90 Weitz, *Diary* III, pp. 239–40, entry for 20 February 1948. Weitz was referring to the transfer schemes of the 1930s, which envisaged a completely Jewish Beit Shean (Beisan) Valley.

91 Interview with Eliezer Be'eri, of Kibbutz Hazore'a, April 1984; and Weitz, *Diary* III, pp. 256–7, entry for 26 March 1948.

92 Weitz, *Diary* III, pp. 256–7, entry for 26 March 1948. See Benny Morris, "Yosef Weitz and the Transfer Committees, 1948–49," p. 522–61, for fuller treatment.

93 Weitz, *Diary* III, p. 260, p.261, entries for 31 March and 2 April 1948.

94 Weitz, *Diary* III, pp. 256–7, entry for 26 March 1948. The bulk of the inhabitants of Qumiya left on 26 March, apparently out of fear of Jewish attack and out of a sense of vulnerability as well as economic pressures. They were not ordered to leave by their Jewish neighbours, but there may have been "friendly advice" to this effect. The dozen or so Arab males who subsequently stayed behind to guard the village property were apparently ordered to leave. See, for the mass evacuation from Qumiya, Aharon Yanai,

Toldot Ein Harod (The History of Ein Harod), published privately by Kibbutz Ein Harod (Ihud), Israel, 1971, part I, p. 281. At Tira, in the lower Galilee, was evacuated finally on 15 April after receiving "friendly advice" from the Haganah – according to HHA-ACP 10.95.13 (1), "The Emigration of the Arabs of Palestine in the Period 1/12/1947–1/6/1948," IDF Intelligence Department, 30 June 1948.

95 KMA-PA 109/gimel – 106, 110, Palmah headquarters daily reports for 13 and 17 March 1948; PRO wo61-301, 1st Battalion Irish Guards, Quarterly Historical Report, "Diary," entry for 13 March 1948; PRO co537-3856, "CID Summary of Events," 13 March 1948; and DBG-YH I, p. 298, entry for 14 March 1948.

96 CZA s25-3569, "On Occurrences in the Negev," 22 March 1948 (signed "'RA,' 7 March 1948").

97 Figure cited in Gabbay, *Political Study*, p. 66.

98 Gabbay, *Political Study*, p. 92; and Yoram Nimrod, *"Hamahapach"* (The Change) in *Al Hamishmar* (*Hotam*), 5 April 1985.

99 CZA s25-3999, "Information on the Arab Military Preparations," the Arab Division, Jewish Agency Political Department, 9 January 1948.

100 PRO wo275-64, "Fortnightly Intelligence Newsletter," British Military headquarters Palestine, 30 January 1948.

101 Letter from E. N. Koussa to the *Jewish Observer and Middle East Review* of 1 September 1959, quoted in Michael Assaf, *Toldot Hit'orerut Ha'aravim Be'eretz Yisrael U'brihatam* (The History of the Arab Awakening in Palestine and their Flight), pp. 331–2.

102 DBG Archives, "Elkana" (a senior Haganah Intelligence Service officer) to "Amitai" (Ben-Gurion), 19 February 1948.

103 ISA FM2568/4, "Information from the 'Naggid'" (a report from an intelligence agent codenamed the "Naggid"), 9 February 1948; and ISA FM2570/11, Tahsin Kamal, the Defence and Security Department of the National Committee, Jerusalem, to the local neighbourhood committees, 22 April 1948.

104 Quoted in Gabbay, *Political Study*, p. 66.

105 HHA-ACP 10.95.13 (1), "The Emigration of the Arabs of Palestine during the Period 1 December 1947–1 June 1948," IDF Intelligence Department, 30 June 1948.

3 The second wave

1 The general guidelines section of Plan D is reproduced in *STH*, III, book 3, pp.1955–9. A summary of the general guidelines section and of the detailed outline of missions for the brigades is contained in Pa'il, *Min Ha'haganah*, pp. 308–13. Yosef Avidar, "Tochnit Dalet (Plan D)" in *Safra Veseifa*, No. 2 (June 1978), pp. 37–48, examines various aspects of the plan.

2 Weitz, *Diary* III, p. 272, entries for 22 April 1948 and 23 April 1948.

3 DBG Archives, "Summary of a Meeting with 'Amitai' [Ben-Gurion], 6 May 1948," in which "Ikar" (Gad Machnes) and "Goi" participated.

4 See *Be'einei Oyev, passim*; Nazzal, *Palestinian Exodus, passim.*
5 See *Be'einei Oyev, passim.*
6 Ben-Gurion, *Behilahem Yisrael* pp. 87–8, Ben-Gurion's speech to the Zionist Actions Committee, 6 April 1948.
7 ISA FM2570/11, Tahsin Kamal, the Defence and Security Department, the National Committee, Jerusalem, to the secretaries of the neighbourhood committees, 22 April 1948.
8 KMA-PA 100/MemVavDalet/3 – 150, "Haganah Intelligence Service Information," 6 May 1948.
9 KMA-PA 109 gimel/167, Daily Report, Palmah headquarters to Haganah General Staff, 3 May 1948.
10 CZA A246–13, p. 2373, entry for 4 May 1948.
11 HHA-ACP 10.95.13 (1), "The Emigration of the Arabs of Palestine in the Period 1/12/1947–1/6/1948," IDF Intelligence Department, 30 June 1948.
12 The former Prime Minister of Syria, Khalid al Azm, in his memoirs, *Mudhakkirat Khalid al Azm*, (Beirut, Dar al-Muttahida Lil-Nashr, 1973), vol. I, p. 386, after the war, wrote: "We have brought destruction upon 1 million Arab refugees by calling upon them and pleading with them repeatedly to leave their lands and homes and factories." (I am grateful to Gideon Weigert of Jerusalem for this reference.) I have found no contemporary evidence of such blanket, official "calls," by the Syrian government or the other Arab governments, to Palestine's Arabs to leave. Certainly, I have found no evidence that the Palestinians or any substantial group among them left after and *because* they heard such "calls" or orders from outside Arab leaders. The only, minor exceptions to this are the traces in the Palmah records of orders, apparently by Syrian officials, to some of the Arab inhabitants of Eastern Galilee to leave a few days prior to, and in preparation for, the invasion of 15 May. These orders affected at most several thousand Palestinians and "dovetailed" with Haganah efforts to expel this population. These orders and events are referred to in the treatment of Operation Yiftah below. It is possible that it was to these orders that Azm was referring. Or perhaps Azm's memory failed him. Or perhaps he inserted the passage only in order to make some point within the context of inter-Arab polemics (as, for example, to let the Palestinians themselves "off the hook" by blaming the outside Arab leaders for the exodus).
13 CZA S25-8918, text of broadcast by Kol Hamagen Ha'ivri (Haganah Radio), Jerusalem in English, on 27 April 1948; and KMA-PA 100/MemVavDalet/2 – 142, Haganah Intelligence Service Information, 28 April 1948.
14 Weitz, *Diary* III, p. 273, entry for 26 April 1948.
15 KMA-PA 100/MemVavDalet/3 – 146, Haganah Intelligence Service Information, 5 May 1948.
16 CZA S25-8918, text of broadcast of Kol Hamagen Ha'ivri (Haganah Radio), Jerusalem, 5 May 1948; and CZA S25-9045, "Information about the Arabs of Palestine (According to Arab Radio Transmissions, 6–7 May 1948)."
17 KMA-PA 100/MemVavDalet/3 – 154, Haganah Intelligence Service Infor-

mation, 9 May 1948; and DBG Archives, "Daily Monitoring Report No. 28," 6 May 1948.

18 CZA S25-8918, text of broadcast by Kol Hamagen Ha'ivri (Haganah Radio), 6 May 1948.

19 KMA-PA 100/MemVavDalet/3 – 150, Haganah Intelligence Service Information, 6 May 1948.

20 HHA-ACP 10.95.10 (4), "Our Arab Policy in the Middle of the War," Aharon Cohen, 10 May 1948; HHA-ACP 10.95.11 (8), "In Face of the Arab Evacuation," Aharon Cohen, Summer 1948; KMA-PA 100/MemVavDalet/ 3 – 158, Haganah Intelligence Service Information, 13 May 1948; CZA S25-9045, "Information about the Arabs of Palestine (from Arab broadcasts, 10–11 May)" and "Information about the Arabs of Palestine (from Arab Broadcasts over 14–15 May)"; and KMA-PA 100/MemVavDalet/3, Haganah Intelligence Service Information, 13 May 1948.

21 CZA S25-9047, "Arab Broadcasts" 6–7 June 1948; KMA-PA 100/ MemVavDalet/1 – 5, "In the Arab Public," 26 May 1948; and LA 235 IV, 2251 bet, S. Zagorsky to A. Hartzfeld, 2 June 1948, on Arab pressures on the exiled inhabitants of the Beit Shean Valley to return.

22 For example, see KMA-PA 100/MemVavDalet/1 – 9, "In the Arab Public," 11 June 1948, regarding the Syrians and the Hula Valley Arabs; or *Ilan Va'shelah, Derekh Hakravot shel Hativat Golani* (Tree and Sword, the Route and Battle of the Golani Brigade), p. 228, on the Arabs of Lubiya.

23 DBG-YH I, p. 227, entry for 10 February 1948.

24 See Nazzal, *Palestinian Exodus*, pp. 28–9.

25 Tiberias Municipal Archive, Interview with Moshe Tzahar (Weiss), head of the Defence Committee of Tiberias's Jews in 1948, on 18 January 1982, by M. Hildsheimer and Yael Avital.

26 PRO WO275-54, Divisional Logbook, 6th Airborne Division, entry for 12 April 1948; and Nazzal, *Palestinian Exodus*, p. 29, who misdates the Nasir ad Din attack 10 April. The AHC charged that the Jews had committed atrocities in the village and dated the attack 14 April. See PRO CO733-487/2, AHC memorandum on Jewish atrocities, 26 July 1948.

27 Tiberias Municipal Archive, "Written Testimony of Daniel Khidra, a resident of Tiberias," undated.

28 Nazzal, *Palestinian Exodus*, pp. 29–30.

29 *Ibid.*; and Tiberias Municipal Archive, Interview with Tzahar.

30 Tiberias Municipal Archive, Interview with Tzahar; PRO WO275-54, Divisional Logbook, 6th Airborne Division, entry for 18 April 1948; and KMA-PA 109/gimel – 145, "Daily Report (addition)," 3rd Battalion, 18 April 1948.

31 Tiberias Municipal Archive, an untitled proclamation or poster, signed "the Presidium of the Community Committee, the Temporary Situation Committee," (written by Moshe Tzahar), dated 19 April 1948.

32 CP III/4/23, Secretary of State (New York) to Cunningham (Jerusalem), 24 April 1948; and *Ilan Va'shelah*, p. 9.

33 JEM LXXII/1, letter to the editor from E. N. Koussa, *The Palestine Post*, 6 February 1949. Koussa is alone in asserting that the British coerced the Tiberias Arabs to leave their homes.

34. It is not clear exactly which notables left Tiberias and when. However, IDF Intelligence Department, in "The Emigration of the Arabs of Palestine in the Period 1/12/1947–1/6/1948," succinctly explains the causes of the Tiberias exodus thus: "Our operations [i.e., military assault]. Lack of leaders on the spot. The rich fled earlier." See HHA-ACP 10.95.13 (1). Gabbay, *Political Study*, pp. 93–4, states that the flight of the al Tabaris and other notables on 18 April was "followed blindly by the [town's Arab] middle and poor classes".

35 CP v/4/102, "Report by GOC North Sector Major General H. C. Stockwell CB, CBE, DSO, Leading Up to, and After, the Arab–Jewish Clashes in Haifa on 21–22 April 1948," (henceforward referred to as Stockwell Report), 24 April 1948. See also PRO FO371-68505, Cyril Marriott (Haifa) to Foreign Secretary Bevin, 26 April 1948, a 17-page "letter" that in the main reproduces verbatim the Stockwell Report, though adds some interesting personal impressions of the Jewish and Arab protagonists (henceforward referred to as Marriott Report). For Cunningham's views, see CP III/4/15, High Commissioner (Jerusalem) to Secretary of State (London), 23 April 1948. The Stockwell and Marriott reports are the best descriptions, from the British perspective, of what happened in Haifa. See also Sir Henry Gurney, *Palestine Postscript*, a typewritten unpublished record, in diary form, of the last days of the Mandate (in St Antony's College, Middle East Centre Archives), pp. 73–4, which concurs with the Stockwell–Marriott view of what precipitated the Haganah offensive in Haifa. Gurney, then Chief Secretary of the Palestine Government and no friend to the Zionist cause, wrote: "It became clear today that the Jewish offensive at Haifa was staged as a direct consequence of four days' continuous Arab attacks. The Arabs have played right into [Jewish] hands."

36 Pa'il, *Min Ha'haganah*, pp. 310–11.

37 CP v/4/102, Stockwell Report.

38 *Be'einei Oyev*, p. 21.

39 The text of Stockwell's statement to the heads of the two communities is in PRO WO275-62, NorthSec [i.e., GOC North Sector] to 1st Guards Brigade, CRAFORCE [i.e., the British force in Eastern Galilee], etc., 18:45 hours, 21 April 1948.

40 Eshel, *Ma'arachot*, pp. 347–9; and Moshe Carmel, *Ma'arachot Tzafon* (Northern Battles), pp. 86–7.

41 Carmel, *Ma'arachot Tzafon*, p. 104; Eshel, *Ma'arachot*, p. 375; and *The Times* (London), p. 4, 22 April 1948. Two months later IDF intelligence cited the contribution of the Carmeli Brigade's psychological warfare to the conquest of Haifa – see HHA-ACP 10.95.13 (1), "The Emigration of the Arabs of Palestine during the Period 1/12/1947–1/6/1948," 30 June 1948.

42 Eshel, *Ma'arachot*, p. 356.

43 PRO SO275-79, "257 and 317 Field Security Section Weekly Report No. 2 for Week Ending 21 April 1948."

44 CP V/4/102, Stockwell Report.

45 Khalidi, "The Fall of Haifa," argued that the departure of the Haifa Arab militia chiefs did not affect general Arab morale and remained unknown to the townspeople. This is highly improbable and contrary to all logic. News of their successive departures would have raced down the chain of command, sideways to the Haifa Arab political leaders, and downwards to the community at large. Indeed, Nafa'a's departure was already known to the Haganah and broadcast by *Kol Hahaganah* in Arabic on 22 April: "Why did . . . Yunis Nafa'a take his family with him to Beirut? Do you know that he has rented a flat there and is now living in a hotel as a normal visitor would do?" ran the broadcast. See Eshel, *Ma'arachot*, p. 375.

46 PRO WO275-79, "257 and 317 Field Security Section Weekly Report No. 3 for the Week Ending 28 April 1948".

47 CP III/4/71, High Commissioner (Jerusalem) to Secretary of State, 26 April 1948. Creech-Jones was in New York at this time; cables from and to Jerusalem had to be rerouted through London.

48 PRO WO275-64, "Fortnightly Intelligence Newsletter No. 67," Military headquarters Palestine, 6 May 1948. Stockwell and Marriott, in their reports, called the flight of the two Arab militia leaders "significant" in explaining the swift Arab collapse. Khalidi, "The Fall of Haifa," explains that Azzadin merely wanted to report on the situation (and, presumably, plead for reinforcements) in person in Damascus; had left before the shooting started; and was "guilty of miscalculation" rather than cowardice. In fact, however, it appears that Azzadin left the city at about 13:00 hours, 21 April, *after* the shooting had started and when it was (or at least should have been) clear to all that the decisive battle had begun.

49 NA Record Group 84, Haifa Consulate, Classified Records 1948, 800 – Political Affairs, Lippincott (Haifa) to Secretary of State, 23 April 1948 (two cables).

50 CP V/4/102, Stockwell Report; PRO FO371-68505, Marriott Report; and Carmel, *Ma'arachot Tzafon*, pp. 104–5. Through the negotiations, the Haganah was to refer to "surrender terms" while the British and the Arabs referred to "truce terms." All three meant the same thing, and knew that they meant the same thing.

51 Khalidi, "The Fall of Haifa," fails to mention that the remaining National Committee members and other gathered Arab notables, who then constituted themselves into the "Haifa Arab Emergency Committee," asked Stockwell to arrange a truce. Arab casualties, all told, during the two days of fighting, according to British sources, were some 100 dead and another 100 wounded (see CP V/4/102, Stockwell Report). They may have been higher, perhaps reaching 200–300 dead irregulars and civilians. But this can hardly be considered a high toll for a decisive battle for a populated city. Nor is there any evidence that a "massacre" took place in the town.

52 Khalidi, "The Fall of Haifa," *passim.*

53 CP v/4/102, Stockwell Report.

54 Assaf, *Toldot*, pp. 331–2, text of letter from Elias Koussa in the *Jewish Observer and Middle East Review* of 1 September 1959; and Khalidi, "The Fall of Haifa."

55 CP v/4/102, Stockwell Report, reproduces both the original Haganah terms and the Stockwell-amended terms.

56 Carmel, *Ma'arachot Tzafon*, pp. 105–6.

57 CP v/4/102, Stockwell Report; and PRO F0371-68505, Marriott Report.

58 CP v/4/102, Stockwell Report; PRO F0371-68505, Marriott Report; and PRO F0371-68544, Marriott (Haifa) to Foreign Office, 23 April 1948, in which Marriott spoke of "the moderation of Jews after victory."

59 CP v/4/102, Stockwell Report; PRO F0371-68505, Marriott Report; and CZA S25-10.584, "Report by Harry Beilin on the Conquest of Haifa," 25 April 1948. Beilin's is the only major contemporary Jewish report on the fall of Arab Haifa and conforms in all essentials with Stockwell's and Marriott's reports.

60 CZA S25-10.584, "Report by Harry Beilin on the Conquest of Haifa," 25 April 1948; and Carmel, *Ma'arachot Tzafon*, p. 107.

61 Carmel, *Ma'arachot Tzafon*, p. 107.

62 ISA FM2401/11, Salomon (Haifa) to the Political Department, Foreign Ministry (Tel Aviv), 1 April 1949. Salomon recalled that Makleff also appealed to the Arabs to stay put, but this is not supported by any other source and is implicitly contradicted by Carmel.

63 Carmel, *Ma'arachot Tzafon*, p. 107. The earliest version of the "AHC orders" explanation of the Arab evacuation of Haifa is contained in the announcement on 23 April of the Jewish Agency spokesman that the exodus had "been carried out deliberately by the Arabs to besmirch the Jews, to influence the Arab governments to send more help and to clear the ground for an attack by regular Arab forces later." The statement is quoted in *The Times* (London), 24 April 1948. *The Times* correspondent, incidentally, disagreed, commenting that "the simplest, most human explanation is that the Arabs have fled out of pure disorder."

64 Documents, p. 670, Sasson to Shertok, 23 April 1948.

65 It is worth noting that in their subsequent reports, neither Stockwell nor Marriott even as much as hinted that the Arab delegates at the Town Hall meeting, in opting for evacuation, had been acting under instructions from Damascus or the AHC. IDF Intelligence Department, in its analysis of 30 June 1948 of the exodus, attributed the flight from Haifa to the Haganah conquest of the city, and made no allusion to, or mention of, any orders from outside to the community to flee. See HHA-ACP 10.95.13 (1), "The Emigration of the Arabs of Palestine in the Period 1/12/1947–1/6/1948."

66 Khalidi, "The Fall of Haifa," duly noted Murad's absence but failed to explain, or offer a conjecture about, its possible significance.

67 ISA FM2401/11, Salomon (Haifa) to the Political Department, Foreign Ministry (Tel Aviv), 1 April 1949.

68 NA Record Group 84, Haifa Consulate, Classified Records 1948, 800 – Political Affairs, Lippincott (Haifa) to Secretary of State, 25 April 1948; and NA Record Group 84, Haifa Consulate, Classified Records 1948, 800 – Political Affairs, Lippincott (Haifa) to Secretary of State, 26 April 1948.

69 CP III/4/52, High Commissioner (Jerusalem) to Secretary of State, 25 April 1948; PRO WO275-54, 6th Airborne Division Logbook, entry for 4 May 1948; and PRO CO537-3875, "Extract from ME Daily Sitrep No. 147," Headquarters Middle East to certain British Cabinet Ministers, 4 May 1948.

70 *Be'einei Oyev*, pp. 23–24; Eshel, pp. 369–70; and Khalidi, op. cit.

71 Eshel, *Ma'arachot* p. 365.

72 PRO WO261-297, "Sitrep No. 10," 1st Battalion Coldstream Guards, 16:30 hours, 22 April 1948.

73 Carmel, *Ma'arachot Tzafon*, p. 107. Following the exodus from Haifa, both Arab and left-wing Jewish leaders "blamed" the British for the evacuation. The Arab states, the AHC and Arab Haifa community leaders all charged that Stockwell's precipitate withdrawal of troops from the Arab–Jewish front lines, his prevention of the entry of Arab reinforcements and his non-interference against the Haganah had "forced" the Arabs to flee the city. Aharon Cohen, the director of Mapam's Arab Department, went further, charging that "it was the English who had advised the Arabs to leave [Haifa]." He also said that the British during the battle had sowed panic among the Arabs "and while the Haganah people were calming the Arabs . . . the British . . . advised them 'to flee to the port, where the British army would protect them.'" He also noted the "alacrity" with which the British provided the evacuees with transport. See HHA-ACP 10.95.10 (4), "Our Arab Policy in the Midst of the War," by Aharon Cohen, 10 May 1948; and HHA-ACP 10.95.10 (4), Cohen (Kibbutz Sha'ar Ha'amakim) to Prof. Ernst Simon (Jerusalem), 25 April 1948. I have found no other evidence to support the thrust of this contention. But it is more than possible that the British troops guarding the port area in the morning and afternoon of 22 April, in view of the Haganah fire on the downtown areas, let the Arabs outside the gates understand that, should they enter the port compound, they would be safe from Haganah fire. This may have been the source of the rumour that the British would protect Arabs who reached the port, which caught hold among the frightened Arabs in the Suq and Old City areas and did much to precipitate the initial flight to the docks.

74 PRO WO261-297, "Battalion Sitrep No. 18," Tactical HQ, 1st Battalion Coldstream Guards, 26 April 1948; and PRO WO275-79, "257 and 317 Field Security Section Weekly Report No. 3, for Week Ending 28 April 1948."

75 PRO WO275-79, "257 and 317 FS Section Weekly Report No. 3, for Week Ending 28 April 1948."

76 PRO WO261-297, "Battalion Sitrep No. 20," 1st Battalion Coldstream Guards, 29 April 1948; NA Record Group 84, Haifa Consulate, Classified Records 1948, 800 – Political Affairs, Lippincott (Haifa) to Secretary of State, 26 April 1948; and NA Record Group 84, Haifa Consulate, Classified Records 1948, 800 – Political Affairs, Lippincott (Haifa) to Secretary of State, 29 April 1948.

77 CZA S25-10.584, "Report by Harry Beilin on the Conquest of Haifa," 25 April 1948.

78 Quoted in Eshel, *Ma'arachot*, pp. 376–7.

79 NA Record Group 84, Haifa Consulate, Classified Records 1948, 800 – Political Affairs, Lippincott (Haifa) to Secretary of State, 29 April 1948; and *The Times* (London), 26 April 1948, report datelined Haifa, 25 April 1948.

80 PRO WO275-79, "257 and 317 FS Section Weekly Report No. 4, for Week Ending 5 May 1948"; CP III/4/52, High Commissioner (Jerusalem) to Secretary of State, 25 April 1948; PRO WO261-297, "Sitrep," 1st Battalion Coldstream Guards, 23 April 1948; and PRO WO261-297, "Sitrep No. 18," 1st Battalion Coldstream Guards, 26 April 1948. The Haganah command in Haifa never issued orders to its road-blocks to stop the outflow of refugees. But the road-blocks, which searched for hidden arms, hidden "Nazis" and irregulars, apparently held up the exodus at certain points. The Arabs on a number of occasions complained to the British that the road-blocks were hampering the exodus.

81 PRO WO261-297, "Battalion Sitrep No. 18," 1st Battalion Coldstream Guards, 25 April 1948; and PRO FO371–68505, Marriott Report. Marriott also hinted that, at a meeting with the Arab Emergency Committee on 25 April, mainstream Jewish local leaders may have used "threats" designed to promote evacuation. But he quickly qualified this by adding that "the Arabs [subsequently] came to impress on General Stockwell that their evacuation is purely voluntary."

82 HHA 66.90 (1), protocols of the meeting of Mapam Political Committee, statement by P. Alonim, 26 May 1948.

83 HMA 1374, "Protocol of the Meeting of 25 April 1948."

84 Eshel, *Ma'arachot*, p. 379.

85 HMA 1374, "Protocol of the Meeting of 23 April 1948."

86 HMA 1374, "Protocol of the Meeting of 25 April 1948."

87 HMA 1374, Haifa Arab Emergency Committee (Victor Khayyat, Farid Sa'ad, Elias Koussa, George Mu'ammar and Anis Nasr) to GOC North Sector, Palestine, 25 April 1948.

88 HHA-ACP 10.95.10 (4), Cohen (Kibbutz Sha'ar Ha'amakim) to the Secretariat of the Mapam Centre (Tel Aviv), 28 April 1948.

89 ISA AM20 aleph, "The Situation in Haifa Two Weeks after the Conquest of the Arab Part of the City by the Haganah," Israel Communist Party, 10 May 1948, and Zisling to the Cabinet, 20 May 1948. Zisling urged an investigation of the charges contained in the report.

90 PRO WO261-297, "Battalion Sitrep No. 19," 1st Battalion Coldstream Guards, 27 April 1948. The unit reported that its soldiers that day had picked up a leaflet signed by "Chief of Haganah," in Arabic, saying: "All those who have left the Wadi Nisnas and Wadi Salib areas must return to their homes immediately, open their shops and start work. We will ensure that they are safe."

91 CZA A246–13, pp. 2364–5, entries for 22–24 April 1948.

92 PRO WO275-54, 6th Airborne Division Logbook, entry for 22 April 1948.

93 PRO wo275-54, 6th Airborne Division Logbook, entry for 24 April 1948; PRO wo275-66, 6th Airborne Division, North Sector Sitrep, 24 April 1948; PRO wo275-79, "257 and 317 FS Section, Weekly Report for Week Ending 28 April 1948"; and HHA-ACP 10.95.1013 (1), "The Emigration of the Arabs of Palestine During the Period 1/12/1947–1/6/1948," IDF Intelligence Department, 30 June 1948. 257 and 317 Field Security Section reported that the Arabs had evacuated the village after Haganah "intimidation." On the other hand, Aharon Cohen asserted on 10 May that the villagers of Balad ash Sheikh and its much smaller satellites, Hawassa and Yajur, had, in fact, evacuated their homes "on British advice" and "contrary to Haganah advice" (see HHA-ACP 10.95.10 (4), "Our Arab Policy in the Midst of the War," by Aharon Cohen, 10 May 1948). No other source speaks of the villagers evacuating "contrary to Haganah advice." Cohen's assertion, made over a fortnight after the events, seems suspect; that the Haganah, in the circumstances, would have advised the villagers not to evacuate runs contrary to logic. But it is quite possible that the British officers on the scene, on the morning of 24 April, thought that an Arab evacuation of the villages – modelled on the continuing exodus from Haifa – was the best solution to the problem and most likely made this clear to the Arab villagers. Probably there was at this point a dovetailing of British, Haganah and Arab views – all parties concerned, for different reasons, being keen on a speedy Arab evacuation.

94 PRO wo275-66, 6th Airborne Division, North Sector Sitrep, 26 April 1948; PRO wo275-54, 6th Airborne Division Logbook, entries for 25 and 26 April 1948; and PRO wo275-62, North Sector to MILPAL, 1st Guards Brigade, etc., 5 May 1948.

95 PRO wo261-297, "Battalion Sitrep No. 18," 1st Battalion Coldstream Guards, 26 April 1948; and PRO fo371-68507, C. Marriott (Haifa) to Foreign Office, 10 May 1948.

96 PRO wo261-297, "Battalion Sitrep No. 20," 1st Battalion Coldstream Guards, 29 April 1948.

97 DBG-YH I, p. 387, speech at meeting of People's Council, 4 May 1948.

98 Gurney, *Palestine Postscript*, p. 84.

99 *STH*, III, part 2, pp.1474–5.

100 *Be'einei Oyev*, pp. 33–4.

101 JI IZL Papers, kaf–4, 8/1, "*Kibush Yaffo*" (the Conquest of Jaffa), a 46-page report by Begin, written sometime in May or June, 1948, p. 24. It is one of the best descriptions of the battle from the IZL side.

102 Haim Lazar, *Kibush Yaffo* (The Conquest of Jaffa), pp. 124, 126.

103 CP 111/5/43, High Commissioner (Jerusalem) to Secretary of State, 3 May 1948. Nimr al Katib, in *Be'einei Oyev*, pp. 33–4, says that in two days, "2,000" mortar bombs fell on the city.

104 Quoted in Gabbay, *Political Study*, p. 90.

105 JI IZL Papers, kaf-8, 8/8, "Summary of the Interrogations of the Manshiya PoWs from 28 April 1948."

106 JI IZL Papers, kaf-4, 8/1, "*Kibush Yaffo*," Begin, p. 25.

107 Gurney, *Palestine Postscript*, p. 84.

108 CP III/4/71, High Commissioner (Jerusalem) to Secretary of State, 26 April 1948.

109 PRO CO537-3875, War Office to PS to Prime Minister, PS Foreign Secretary, etc., "Extract from Middle East Special Situation Report 29 April 1948," 29 April 1948.

110 ISA FM2451/13, Shertok speech to the United Nations General Assembly, undated but probably on 27 April 1948. A year later, on the basis of talks with Jaffa, Ramle and Lydda refugees in the Gaza Strip, representatives of the Quaker refugee relief agency, the American Friends Service Committee, told an American intelligence officer that some of the refugees at least were saying that they had "fled against their wills because their leaders told them they must do so or be considered traitors, and if they fled they could return in a few months." See NA Record Group 84, Tel Aviv Embassy, Classified Records 1949, 571 – Palestine Refugee Relief, "Intelligence Report," by Col. B. C. Anirus, 1 May 1949. However, I have found no other evidence from Haganah, British or Arab sources corroborating this explanation of why Jaffa's population fled. It is possible that some of the militia officers in the town did recommend or order inhabitants to leave with them; but there is no evidence of a general order to this effect, from inside the embattled city, or from the AHC or Arab institutions outside the city, ever having been issued.

111 Lazar, *Kibush Yaffo*, p. 138

112 JI IZL Papers, kaf–4, 8/1, "Pe'ulat Hakibush" (the Conquest Operation), an unsigned, undated, four-page, IZL military report on the battle; and kaf 4, 8/1, "Kibush Yaffo," Begin, *passim.*

113 For the Arab attacks on Britain concerning Haifa, see CP III/3/136, Secretary of State to High Commissioner (Jerusalem), 22 April 1948; CP III4/6, Secretary of State to High Commissioner, 23 April 1948; CP III/4/7, Secretary of State to High Commissioner, 23 April 1948; CP III4/23, Secretary of State to High Commissioner, 23 April 1948; PRO WO275-79, "257 and 317 FS Section Weekly Report No. 3, for Week Ending 28 April 1948," for Haifa Arab feelings of having been "betrayed" by the British; and PRO WO275-64, "Fortnightly Intelligence Newsletter No. 67 Issued by HQ British Troops Palestine," 6 May 1948, quoting an Iraqi Cabinet Minister as saying that Britain "has purposely engineered Jewish domination in Haifa as an integral part of its programme for Palestine."

114 PRO CO537-3875, War Office to PS of Prime Minister, PS of Foreign Secretary, etc., "Extract from Middle East Special Situation Report 29 April 1948," 29 April 1948.

115 Montgomery of Alamein, *Memoirs* (Collins, London, 1958), pp. 473–4.

116 PRO CAB 127-341, "Note of a Meeting Held at 10 Downing Street at 5.15 p.m. on Friday 7th May 1948," 7 May 1948.

117 *Ibid.*; and Montgomery, *Memoirs*, p. 474; and minutes attached to PRO FO371-68544 E5102/4/31G.

118 PRO CO537-3870, minute by W. A. C. Mathieson, 4 May 1948. Cunningham had in fact acted before receiving word or orders from Bevin, as he made clear in an angry telegram sent on 30 April. See PRO CO537-3870, Cunningham to Secretary of State, etc., 30 April 1948.

119 *STH*, III, part 2, p. 1552; and Montgomery, *Memoirs*, p. 473.

120 JI IZL Papers, kaf 4, 8/1, "*Kibush Yaffo*"; and Lazar, *Kibush Yaffo*, p. 138.

121 *Hativat Alexandroni*, pp. 177, 180; CZA s25-8918, Kol Hamagen Ha'ivri (The Voice of the Hebrew Defender), English broadcast, 30 April 1948; and DBG-YH III, p. 377, entry for 30 April 1948.

122 Lazar, *Kibush Yaffo, passim*.

123 *STH*, III, part 2, pp. 1553, 1574–5.

124 CP III/5/26, High Commissioner (Jerusalem) to Secretary of State, 1 May 1948; and *Hativat Alexandroni*, p. 27.

125 CP III/5/43, High Commissioner (Jerusalem) to Secretary of State, 3 May 1948.

126 *Be'einei Oyev*, p. 34.

127 CP III/5/92, High Commissioner (Jerusalem) to Secretary of State, 5 May 1948; and Gurney, *Palestine Postscript*, p. 94.

128 The text of the agreement is in ISA FM2564/5.

129 DBG-YH II, p. 438, entry for 18 May 1948.

130 KMA-PA 170 – 44, "Sasha" (Allon) to Yadin, "Hillel" (Galili), 22 April 1948.

131 Operation Yiftah is described by Allon in *Sefer Hapalmah* II, pp. 276–333. The following pages focus on the conquest of Safad and the exodus of its Arab population. The conquest of rural Eastern Galilee is dealt with later.

132 Nazzal, *Palestinian Exodus*, pp. 35–6.

133 Netiva Ben-Yehuda, *Miba'ad La'avutot* (Through the Binding Ropes), (Jerusalem, Domino Press, 1985), pp. 243–8. Nazzal, *Palestinian Exodus*, p. 36, quotes refugees from 'Ein az Zeitun who, in interviews conducted in the early 1970s, implied that the captives had been killed. Ben-Yehuda graphically describes the prelude to, and aftermath of, the slaughter of the 70, which she did not witness. Kelman's company commanders all refused to carry out the massacre or to allow their men to carry it out. The battalion OC in the end had to use two "broken" men, who did not belong to the fighting formations and who claimed that they had suffered at Arab hands earlier in the war, to do the killing. Afterwards, Kelman assigned Ben-Yehuda to untie the hands of the dead as a Red Cross visit to the area was expected. Several villagers apparently were shot in 'Ein az Zeitun on 1 May by the Palmah troops. The massacre of the POWs and possibly these deaths in the village were the source of the AHC's inaccurate charge, lodged with the United Nations on 26 July 1948, that after the conquest of 'Ein az Zeitun, the Jewish troops had "herded women and children into [the village] mosque and blew it up." See PRO co733-487/2, "AHC memorandum on Jewish Atrocities."

134 *Sefer Hapalmah* II, p. 304; and Nazzal, *Palestinian Exodus*, pp. 36–7.

135 *Sefer Hapalmah* II, pp. 279, 304.

136 Nazzal, *Palestinian Exodus*, p. 40; and *Sefer Hapalmah* II, p. 324.

137 CZA s25-8918, Kol Hamagen Ha'ivri (the Voice of the Hebrew Guard), broadcast, in English, on 2 May 1948; KMA-PA 109/gimel – 167, Palmah headquarters to Haganah General Staff, 3 May 1948; and PRO wo275-64, "Fortnightly Intelligence Newsletter No. 67 issued by HQ British Troops in Palestine (for the period . . . 19 April – 3 May 1948)," 6 May 1948.

138 *Sefer Hapalmah* II, pp. 283–4.
139 CP III/5/102, HM Minister, Damascus, to High Commissioner (Jerusalem), 5 May 1948.
140 PRO FO371-68548, Broadmead (Damascus) to Foreign Office, 6 May 1948.
141 CP III/5/119, Secretary of State for Colonies to High Commissioner (Jerusalem), 6 May 1948.
142 KMA 2 aleph/20, *Beineinu* (Among Us), a Palmah bulletin, No. 14, 13 May 1948; Nazzal, *Palestinian Exodus*, pp. 43–5; and KMA-PA 109/gimel–177, "Daily Report," Palmah headquarters to Haganah General Staff, 10 May 1948.
143 Netiva Ben-Yehuda, *Miba'ad La'avutot*, pp. 292–3.
144 *Sefer Hapalmah* II, p. 285.
145 Nazzal, *Palestinian Exodus*, pp. 16, 41; and *Be'einei Oyev*, p. 37.
146 *Sefer Hapalmah* II p. 285; and Nazzal, *Palestinian Exodus*, p. 41, footnotes 55, 56.
147 ISA MAM310/33, "A Meeting in Safad," 29 July 1948, attended by Minority Affairs Minister Bechor Shitrit, Machnes, Hanuki, and others; and DBG-YH II, p. 494, entry for 7 June 1948.
148 HMA 1374, Avraham Ye'eli, chairman of the Arab Affairs Committee, Haifa, to the mayor of Haifa, 11 June 1948; ISA FM2402/29, Foreign Ministry to the IDF General Staff, 11 July 1948; ISA FM2464/10, Harkabi to IDF OC Operations, 18 August 1948; and HMA 1374, Moshe Yitah, director of the Minority Affairs Ministry office in Haifa, to the mayor of Haifa, 9 August 1948.
149 Weitz, *Diary* III, p. 340, Weitz to Ben-Gurion, 11 September 1948; and PRO FO371-75198 E5810, Marriott (Haifa) to Foreign Secretary, 23 April 1949.
150 CZA A246-13, p. 2373, entry for 4 May 1948.
151 Nazzal, *Palestinian Exodus*, p. 48.
152 *Ilan Vashelah*, pp. 144–6; and Nazzal, *Palestinian Exodus*, p. 49.
153 KMA *Tsror Michtavim* (A Batch of Letters – an internal bulletin of the Kibbutz Me'uhad), "*Be'Beit Shean Hakevusha*" (In Occupied Beit Shean) by "Tektz," 2 July 1948; and CZA A246-13, p. 2385, entry for 12 May 1948.
154 *Ilan Vashelah* p. 146; and Nazzal, *Palestinian Exodus*, p. 49.
155 ISA FM2564/18, Bechor Shitrit to the Defence Minister, the Foreign Minister, 16 September 1948; and KMA *Tsror Michtavim*, "*Be'Beit Shean Hakevusha*" by "Tektz," 2 July 1948.
156 *Ilan Vashelah*, p. 146; and HHA-ACP 10.95.13 (1), "The Emigration of the Arabs of Palestine During the Period 1/12/1947–1/6/1948," IDF Intelligence Department, 30 June 1948.
157 KMA-PA 100/MemVavDalet/2 – 102, "Haganah Intelligence Service Information," 28 April 1948.
158 HHA-ACP 10.95.13 (1), "The Emigration of the Arabs of Palestine During the Period 1/12/1947–1/6/1948," IDF Intelligence Department, 30 June 1948; and Eshel, *Hativat Carmeli*, p. 177.
159 Carmel, pp. 151–3; Eshel, *Hativat Carmeli*, p. 176, quotes from the letter by

the Acre resident; PRO W0261-297, "Battalion Sitrep No. 18," 1st Battalion Coldstream Guards, 26 April 1948; and PRO F0371-68507, C. Marriott (Haifa) to Foreign Office 10 May 1948.

160 PRO W0275-79, "257 and 317 FS Section Weekly Report No. 3 for Week Ending 28 April 1948."

161 CP II/5, High Commissioner to Secretary of State, 5 May 1948; CP III/5/92, High Commissioner (Jerusalem) to Secretary of State, 5 May 1948; PRO W0261-297, North Sector Sitrep, 5 May 1948; and PRO C0537-3875, "Extract from Middle East Daily Situation Report No. 153," 7 May 1948. Nimr al Khatib, in *Be'einei Oyev* p. 41, also remarks on the lack of food in Acre before the town fell, caused by Jewish interdiction of Arab traffic to Acre in retaliation for Arab harassment of Jewish traffic in Western Galilee.

162 HHA-ACP 10.95.13 (1), "The Emigration of the Arabs of Palestine During the Period 1/12/1947–1/6/1948," IDF Intelligence Department, 30 June 1948.

163 *Be'einei Oyev* pp. 41–2.

164 In relating the story of the conquest of Acre, I have largely followed Carmel, *Ma'arachot Tzafon*, pp. 151–62.

165 ISA MAM307/10, Shimoni to Shitrit, 13 July 1948.

166 ISA MAM307/10, Minority Affairs Minister to Shimoni, 19 July 1948.

167 ISA MAM307/10, Kaplan to Shitrit, 20 July 1948.

168 Weitz *Diary* III, pp. 275–6, entry for 2 May 1948.

169 KMA-PA 130 – 1, Nahshon Forces headquarters to battalions, etc., ? April 1948.

170 *Sefer Hapalmah* II, p. 189.

171 KMA-PA 130 – 5, 6, unsigned, handwritten report on "The Conquest of Al Qastal, 3 April 1948."

172 KMA-PA 130 – 64-6, "Report on the Reinforcing Al Qastal," 7 April 1948.

173 KMA-PA 130 – 8, "The Reconquest of Al Qastal," 9 April 1948. The battle for Al Qastal was to have a strong impact on Palestinian Arab morale. On 7–8 April, on the periphery of the village, a Jewish sentry unwittingly shot dead 'Abdel Qadir al Husayni.

174 KMA-PA 130 – 10, "Report on the Capture of Qaluniya"; and CP III/3/91, High Commissioner to Secretary of State, 17 April 1948.

175 A basic account of what happened in Deir Yassin was published by Uri Milstein in *Ha'aretz* on 30 August 1968; and the "feel" of the episode is conveyed in Larry Collins and Dominique Lapierre, *O Jerusalem* (Great Britain, History Book Club, 1972) pp. 272–82. A confused early account is to be found in the JI IZL Papers, kaf-4, 9/33, "Testimony of Yehoshua Gorodenchik (Elimelech)"; and the official IZL account is in Manachem Begin, *The Revolt*, pp. 162–5. The later "official" IZL account, which says most of the Arab dead were hit during the fighting rather than in a massacre after it, is in David Niv, *Ma'arachot Ha'irgun Hatz'va'i Ha'leumi* (Battles of the IZL) VI, pp. 78–94.

176 CP III/3/91, High Commissioner to Secretary of State, 17 April 1948; CP III/4/48, High Commissioner to Kirkbride (Amman), 25 April 1948; and NA

Record Group 84, Jerusalem Consulate, Classified Records 1948, 800 – Syria, US Legation, Damascus, to Secretary of State, 3 May 1948.

177 JI, IZL Papers, kaf–4, 4/13, "Announcement on the Deir Yassin Episode," c. 12 April 1948; and kaf–4, 8/13, broadcast of "Kol Zion Halohemet" (the voice of fighting Zion), 14 April 1948.

178 Begin, *The Revolt*, p. 164

179 KMA-PA 100/MemVavDalet/3 – 126, "Haganah Intelligence Service Information," 14 April 1948.

180 PRO wo275-64, "Fortnightly Intelligence Newsletter, 21 April 1948," British Military headquarters Palestine; and Gabbay, *Political Study*, pp. 89–90, note the effects of the news of Deir Yassin on the other villages in the Jerusalem corridor.

181 DBG-YH I, p. 378, entry for 1 May 1948.

182 HHA-ACP 10.95.11 (8), "In Face of the Arab Evacuation," Aharon Cohen, 20 May 1948; HHA 66.90 (1), protocol of the meeting of the Mapam Political Committee, statement by Ya'Acov Hazan, 26 May 1948; and HHA 66.90 (1), protocol of the meeting of the Mapam Political Committee, statement by Aharon Cohen, 15 June 1948.

183 HHA-ACP 10.95.13 (1), "The Emigration of the Arabs of Palestine During the Period 1/12/1947–1/6/1948," 30 June 1948.

184 PRO wo275-48, "Report on the Negotiations over the Mishmar Ha'emeq Fighting by Lt. Colonel C. A. Peel, Commanding 3rd The King's Own Hussars," 12 April 1948.

185 PRO wo275-54, 6th Airborne Division Logbook, entry for 7 April 1948; and PRO wo275-48, "Report on the Negotiations over the Mishmar Ha'emeq fighting by Lt. Colonel C. A. Peel, Commanding 3rd The King's Own Hussars," 12 April 1948.

186 Mishmar Ha'emek Archive 3.64/24, "Mishmar Ha'emek sits next to the road from Haifa to Jenin," an unsigned report on the battle, probably written just after its conclusion, by Yehuda (Lovka) Ivzori, the Haganah area commander (*ma'az*).

187 LPA 23 aleph/48, protocol of the meeting of the Mapai Centre, statement by Ben-Gurion, 24 July 1948. It is not clear whether a special delegation came from the kibbutz to see Ben-Gurion or whether the delegation comprised Mapam leaders Ya'acov Hazan and Mordechai Bentov (both members of Mishmar Ha'emek), who together with Ben-Gurion, attended the meeting of the Zionist Actions Committee in Tel Aviv over 6–12 April. The two kibbutzniks on 8 April, according to the participants, made moving statements about the battle at the meeting (see CZA s5-322, protocols of the meeting of the Zionist Actions Committee, 8 April 1948). Binyamin Arnon, a Mishmar Ha'emek member and Haganah deputy area commander, interviewed in May 1985, recalled that Meir Amit, a Haganah company commander engaged in the battle, had told him that his battalion had been ordered to expel the Arabs from the area.

188 Ihud Hakkibutzim Archive (Kibbutz Hulda) 111/2, *Igeret Gimel*, Circular

No. 3, 17 September 1948; and CZA s5-323, protocol of the meeting of the Zionist Actions Committee, 23 August 1948.

189 For the raids on, and the destruction of, the villages around Mishmar Ha'emek, see *Sefer Hapalmah* II, pp. 201–2; Mishmar Ha'emek Archive, 20, "Diary of the Battle for Mishmar Ha'emek"; PRO co537-3856, "CID Summary of Events," 15 April 1948 (Appendix B, Haifa Area); KMA-PA 109 gimel – 138, Daily Report 12 April 1948, Palmah headquarters to Haganah General Staff; KMA-PA 109 gimel – 146, Daily Report 19 April 1948, Palmah headquarters to Haganah General Staff; KMA-PA 120/1/aleph – 23, 24, 25, 26, Yiftah Brigade Logbook; and PRO wo275-54, 6th Airborne Division Logbook, entry for 17 April 1948.

190 KMA-PA 100/MemVavDalet/3 – 145, Haganah Intelligence Service Information, 3 May 1948.

191 Weitz, *Diary* III, p. 271, entry for 21 April 1948.

192 JI IZL Papers, kaf-4, 7/8, "Testimony of Moshe Nesher (Wagner)," an IZL officer. Niv, *Ma'arachot Ha'irgun* VI, pp. 131–2, writes that the As Sindiyana inhabitants "were allowed to leave eastwards."

193 HHA-ACP 10.95.13 (1), "The Emigration of the Arabs of Palestine During the Period 1/12/1947–1/6/1948," IDF Intelligence Department, 30 June 1948.

194 HHA-ACP 10.95.13 (1), "The Emigration of the Arabs of Palestine During the Period 1/12/1947–1/6/1948," IDF Intelligence Department, 30 June 1948; interview on 10 November 1985 with Aharon Braverman (Bar-On) in Ein Hahoresh; *Hativat Alexandroni* p. 104; DBG Archives (Sdeh Boqer), "Summary of the Meeting of Arab Affairs Advisers in Netanya, 9 May 1948"; and KMA-AZP 8/8 aleph/11, Z. Lurie to Ben-Gurion, 3 August 1948.

195 DBG Archives, "Summary of the Meeting of Arab Affairs Advisers in Netanya, 9 May 1948."

196 *Hativat Alexandroni*, pp. 29, 206; and HHA-ACP 10.95.13 (1), "The Emigration of the Arabs of Palestine During the Period 1/12/1947–1/6/1948," IDF Intelligence Department, 30 June 1948.

197 *Hativat Alexandroni* pp. 31–2, and 220 ff.

198 ISA mam302/48, Shitrit to Ben-Gurion, 31 May 1948.

199 HHA-ACP 10.95.10 (4), report on a meeting held on 17 June 1948 between Aharon Cohen, head of Mapam's Arab Department and "Yosef" (Kibbutz Ma'anit), Haganah district OC Yitzhak Shemi (Kibbutz Ein Shemer), Haim Kafri and Aharon Braverman (Kibbutz Ein Hahoresh); and ISA mam307/48, "On the Visit to Al Fureidis and the Ratification of the Agreement with the Agricultural Committee of Binyamina," Moshe Erem, 2 August 1948.

200 DBG Archives, "Summary of the Meeting of the Arab Affairs Advisers in Netanya, 9 May 1948"; and HHA-ACP 10.95.13 (1), "The Emigration of the Arabs of Palestine During the Period 1/12/1947–1/6/1948," IDF Intelligence Department, 30 June 1948.

201 KMA-PA 170 – 44, "Sasha" (Allon) to Yadin and "Hillel" (Galili), 22 April 1948.

202 *Ibid.*

203 HHA 5.18 (2) "Operation Yiftah for the Liberation of the Galilee," by Yosef Ulitzky, IDF Press, 1948 (?); KMA-PA 109/gimel – 167, Palmah head-quarters to Haganah General Staff, Daily Report, 3 May 1948; and KMA-PA 109/gimel – 174, Palmah headquarters Daily Report, 8 May 1948, for Arab orders to the villagers of Hunin to quit their homes by 14 May.

204 HHA 5.18 (2) "Operation Yiftah for the Liberation of the Galilee," Yosef Ulitzky. In its daily report for 2 May, (KMA-PA 109/gimel – 165) Palmah headquarters explained the mortaring as designed "to end the harassment of [Jewish traffic] on the Rosh Pinna–Ayelet Hashahar road ... Mass flight from the villages began and the firing was stopped." The text of the Palmah daily report is also in KMA 2 aleph/20, *Beineinu* (a Palmah bulletin), No. 13, 9 May 1948.

205 KMA-PA 109/gimel – 168, 169, Palmah headquarters to Haganah General Staff, Daily Report, 4 May 1948; KMA 2 aleph/20, *Beineinu*, No. 13, 9 May 1948; and HHA 5.18 (2) "Operation Yiftah for the Liberation of the Galilee," Yosef Ulitzky.

206 PRO FO371-68371 E685/11/65, Broadmead (Damascus) to Foreign Office, 4 May 1948.

207 *Sefer Hapalmah* II p. 281.

208 *Sefer Hapalmah* II p. 286; KMA 2 aleph/20, *Beineinu*, No. 15, 20 May 1948; and KMA-PA 109/gimel – 183, Daily Report, Palmah headquarters to Haganah General Staff, 15 May 1948.

209 KMA-PA 109/gimel – 1–4, a report on the Haganah deployment in the Galilee during the first half of May, unsigned and undated.

210 There is an apparent contradiction here between Allon's account in *Sefer Hapalmah* II and the IDF Intelligence Department analysis: Allon's account implies that the whispering campaign worked instantly and before the 15 May Arab invasion whereas the intelligence report, in detailed fashion, brackets the flight due to psychological warfare between 19 and 25 May. My predilection would be to go with the dates offered in the contemporary document. It is possible that the whispering campaign was indeed initiated by Allon between 11 and 15 May, but took effect only several days later.

211 HHA-ACP 10.95.13 (1), "The Emigration of the Arabs of Palestine During the Period 1/12/1947–1/6/1948," IDF Intelligence Department, 30 June 1948. See also Nazzal, *Palestinian Exodus*, pp. 42–3, 46–8, for treatment of the Arab exodus from Dhahiriya and Al Khalisa.

212 Eshel, *Hativat Carmeli*, p. 166; and Nazzal, *Palestinian Exodus*, pp. 52–4. There is a general description of Operation Ben-Ami by its commander, in Carmel, *Ma'arachot Tzafon*, pp. 120–47.

213 Eshel, *Hativat Carmeli*, p. 167; and Nazzal, *Palestinian Exodus*, pp. 55–7.

214 Eshel, *Hativat Carmeli*, pp. 168–9; Nazzal, *Palestinian Exodus*, pp. 57–9; ISA FM2401/21 aleph, "Protocol of the Meeting of the Ministerial Committee for Abandoned Property," 31 December 1948; and ISA MAM302/93, "Notes on a Tour of the Village of Al Mazra'a," by the Nahariya District officer, M. Vandor (?), undated.

215 Eshel, *Hativat Carmeli*, pp. 172–3; and Nazzal, *Palestinian Exodus*, pp. 59–63.

216 KMA-PA 100/MemVavDalet/3 – 154, "Haganah Intelligence Service Information," 9 May 1948; PRO C0737-48712, "Arab Higher Committee Memorandum on Jewish Atrocities," 26 July 1948; and HHA-ACP 10.95.13 (1), "The Emigration of the Arabs of Palestine During the Period 1/12/1947–1/6/1948," IDF Intelligence Department, 30 June 1948.

217 Eshel, *Hativat Carmeli*, p. 173; Nazzal, *Palestinian Exodus*, pp. 63–4; and *Piskei Din shel Beit Hamishpat Hagavohah Letzedek* (Judgements of the Israel High Court of Justice), Vol. IX, p. 692. Some of the villagers returned several months later to the village and were expelled by the IDF for the second and last time in January 1950.

218 Eshel, *Hativat Carmeli* p. 173; Weitz *Diary* III, p. 290, entry for 22 May 1948; and LPA, protocol of the meeting on 1 June 1948 of the Mapai Bureau (*lishka*), statement by M. Yaffe on impressions from a visit to Western Galilee.

219 Avrahon Eilon (ed.), *Hativat Givati Bemilhemet Hakomemiut* (The Givati Brigade in the War of Independence), p. 485.

220 *Hativat Givati*, pp. 523–4; HHA 66.90 (1), protocol of the meeting of Mapam's Political Committee, 15 June 1948; and HHA 10.18, statement by M. Erem in meeting of Mapam defence activists, 26 July 1948.

221 *Hativat Givati*, pp. 525–6; and HHA-ACP 10.95.13 (1), "The Emigration of the Arabs of Palestine During the Period 1/12/1947–1/6/1948," IDF Intelligence Department, 30 June 1948. It appears that initially the villagers were allowed to stay. But when the Egyptian army reached the area of near-by Isdud, Avidan apparently decided that he could not allow such a concentration of Arabs immediately behind his front lines.

222 *Hativat Givati*, pp. 527–8.

223 DBG-YH I, p. 411, entry for 12 May 1948.

224 *Hativat Givati*, p. 460; and HHA-ACP 10.95.13 (1), "The Emigration of the Arabs of Palestine During the Period 1/12/1947–1/6/1948," IDF Intelligence Department, 30 June 1948.

225 *Hativat Givati*, pp. 543 ff.; HHA-ACP 10.95.10 (4), (a man identified by Aharon Cohen only as) "S.K." to the editors of *Al Hamishmar*, undated but almost certainly from early June 1948. "S.K." explained that he was writing the letter not for publication, as it could harm the war effort, but to get Mapam's leaders to do something. The Haganah, he charged, was acting hypocritically and immorally, and turning friendly Arabs into lasting enemies. See also KMA-AZP 9.9.1, statement by Zisling at the Cabinet meeting of 20 June 1948; and LA 235 IV, 2251 aleph, Kvutzat Schiller to the Agricultural Centre, 23 August 1948.

226 For a description of the capture of Yibna, see JI IZL Papers, kaf-4, 7/12, "Testimony of Yosef Zekzer ('Yeshurun')," a company commander in the 8th Battalion, Givati Brigade; and HHA-ACP 10.95.13 (1), "The Emigration of the Arabs of Palestine During the Period 1/12/1947–1/6/1948," IDF Intelligence Department, 30 June 1948.

227 HHA-ACP 10.95.13 (1), "The Emigration of the Arabs of Palestine During the Period 1/12/1947–1/6/1948," IDF Intelligence Department, 30 June 1948.

228 KMA-PA 109/gimel – 205, "Daily Report," Palmah headquarters to Haganah General Staff, 28 May 1948; KMA-PA 105–123, "Sergei" (Nahum Sarig, OC Negev Brigade) to Palmah headquarters, 28 May 1948; and ISA FM2564/9, the *mukhtars* of the kibbutzim Dorot, Nir-Am and Ruhama, Arye Farda, Ya'acov Gavri and Eliezer Frisch, to the Prime Minister and Defence Minister, 4 August 1948.

229 PRO WO275-52, 6th Airborne Division, Division Log Book of Events, entry for 15 December 1947; KMA-PA 105/122, "Oded" to Palmah headquarters, 1 June 1948; and ISA FM2564/9, the *mukhtars* of the kibbutzim Dorot, Nir-Am and Ruhama – Arye Farda, Ya'acov Gavri and Eliezer Frisch – to the Prime Minister and Defence Minister, 4 August 1948. The *mukhtars* had complained of the treatment meted out to the friendly villagers by the IDF. Ben-Gurion (DBG Archives, Ben-Gurion to the *mukhtars* of Dorot, Nir-Am and Ruhama, 29 August 1948) responded that he had sent a copy of their letter to the Negev Brigade headquarters "and I hope that the HQ will pay attention to what you say, and will avoid such unjust and unjustified actions in the future, and will set right these things insofar as possible with respect to the past." But Ben-Gurion avoided a specific condemnation of the IDF for the expulsion and refrained from instructing the IDF to allow the Huj villagers to return or to safeguard their property.

230 HHA 68.90 (1), protocol of the meeting of the Mapam Centre, 11 May 1948.

4 Deciding against a return of the refugees

1 See for example Weitz, *Diary* III, p. 257, entry for 26 March 1948, describing Yosef Weitz's meeting with local leaders from the Beit Shean and Jezreel valleys, in which a consensus emerged against allowing an Arab return to the region. An earlier, somewhat different treatment of the theme covered in this chapter is Benny Morris, "The Crystallization of Israeli Policy Against a Return of the Arab Refugees: April–December, 1948".

2 CZA 45/2, protocols of the meeting of the Jewish Agency Executive, statement by Golda Myerson, 6 May 1948.

3 LPA 48/23 aleph, protocol of the meeting of the Mapai Centre, statement by Golda Myerson, 11 May 1948.

4 DBG-YH I, p. 382, entry for 1 May 1948; and Ben-Gurion, *Behilahem Yisrael*, pp. 68–9, text of speech by Ben-Gurion on 7 February 1948 at meeting of Mapai Council. Indeed, there is evidence that on his visit to Haifa on 1 May 1948, Ben-Gurion went further. Hearing that Abba Khoushi was trying to persuade Arabs in the city to stay, Ben-Gurion is said to have remarked: "Doesn't he have anything more important to do?" This anecdote, based on interviews with Danin, Yosef Vashitz and Palmon, is in Yoram Nimrod, "Patterns of Israeli–Arab Relations: The Formative Years, 1947–1950," p. 268, an unpublished Ph.D. thesis, Hebrew University of Jerusalem, 1985.

5 Documents p. 674, Shertok to Zaslani (Shiloah), 25 April 1948.

6 See HHA-ACP, 10.95.10 (4), "Our Arab Policy During the War," by Aharon Cohen, 10 May 1948; and NA Record Group 84, US Consulate General, Jerusalem, Classified Records 1948, 800 – Political Affairs, a translation of "A Call from His Majesty King Abdullah to the Arab People of Palestine on Behalf of the Arab League," as carried in *An Nasr*, an Amman daily, 5 May 1948.

7 ISA MAM303/41, protocol of the meeting in Haifa, 6 June 1948.

8 Yosef Weitz Papers (Institute for the Study of Settlement, Rehovot), Danin to Weitz, 18 May 1948. A full examination of the history of the Transfer Committees and of the activities of Weitz is in Benny Morris, "Yosef Weitz and the Transfer Committees, 1948–49."

9 ISA FM2564/20, memorandum entitled "[Talk] with Yosef Weitz," in pencil, by hand, 28 May 1948, signed M(oshe) S(hertok).

10 Weitz, *Diary* III, p. 294, entry for 30 May 1948.

11 ISA FM2564/19, memorandum entitled "Retroactive Transfer, A Scheme for the Solution of the Arab Question in the State of Israel," undated but certainly from the first days of June 1948, signed "Y. Weitz, E. Sasson, E. Danin"; CZA, A246-13, p. 2411, entry for 5 June 1948 (which is Weitz's diary entry on the meeting); and DBG-YH II, p. 487, entry for 5 June 1948 (Ben-Gurion's diary entry on the meeting).

12 ISA FM2564/19, Weitz to Ben-Gurion, 6 June 1948 (also dated "Year One to the Freedom of Israel").

13 ISA FM2444/19, Shertok to Eytan, 6 June 1948.

14 ISA FM2345/10, Kaddar to Cabinet Secretary Ze'ev Sharef, 3 June 1948; and ISA AM aleph 19 aleph, report on a visit of the Committee for Abandoned Property to Safad, 5 July 1948.

15 Weitz, *Diary* III, p. 297, entry for 3 June 1948.

16 ISA AM5 kof, Vizhensky to Zisling, 3 June 1948; and LPA, protocol of the meeting of the Mapai Secretariat, statement by Shertok, 13 June 1948.

17 LA 235 IV, 2251 bet, Zagorsky to Hartzfeld, 2 June 1948.

18 ISA FM2426/9, the Director, IDF Intelligence Department, to Shiloah, 16 June 1948.

19 ISA FM2444/19, Yadin to Shertok, 14 August 1948.

20 ISA FM2570/6, *Batziburiut Ha'aravit* (In the Arab Public), a daily intelligence sheet produced by the Foreign Ministry Middle East Department's Research Section, 11 June 1948.

21 DBG-YH II, p. 477, entry for 1 June 1948.

22 For example, see HHA-ACP 10.95.10 (5), "Levi" (IDF OC Jezreel Valley District) to area commanders, 9 June 1948.

23 Israel State Archives, *Documents on the Foreign Policy of the State of Israel, May–September 1948*, Vol. I, ed. Yehoshua Freundlich, (henceforward referred to as *Documents I*), p. 163, Shertok (Tel Aviv) to Goldmann (London), 15 June 1948.

24 David Ben-Gurion, *Medinat Yisrael Hamehudeshet* (The Resurgent State of Israel), Vol. I, p. 167. Abridged versions of this speech, omitting Ben-

Gurion's views about also barring a refugee return after the war, are to be found in DBG-YH II, p. 524, entry for 16 June 1948, and in Ben-Gurion, *Behilahem Yisrael*, pp. 130–1.

25 Ben-Gurion, *Medinat Yisrael Hamehudeshet* pp. 164–5.

26 ISA FM2466/2, "Meetings: M. Shertok–Count Bernadotte and Assistants, Tel Aviv, 17 and 18 June 1948," memorandum by Walter Eytan.

27 HHA-ACP 10.95.11 (1), "Our Policy Toward the Arabs During the War" (decisions of the Mapam Political Committee of 15 June 1948), issued by the Secretariat of the Mapam Centre, 23 June 1948.

28 HHA, "Kibbutz Artzi Movement Fact-Sheet" No. 274/43, 8 August 1948, containing Meir Ya'ari's speech ("If You Go to War") delivered on 14 June 1948 at a Kibbutz Artzi seminar to members being inducted into the IDF.

29 *Documents I*, p. 234, Bernadotte (Rhodes) to Shertok (Tel Aviv), 27 June 1948, letter and "Appendix and Suggestions Presented by the Mediator on Palestine."

30 *Documents I*, pp. 262–4, Shertok to Bernadotte, 5 July 1948.

31 *Documents I*, p. 353 and footnote 2, Michael Comay (New York) to Shertok (Tel Aviv), 19 July 1948.

32 ISA FM2329/20, Shertok (Tel Aviv) to Comay (New York), 22 July 1948.

33 ISA FM2444/19, Kohn to Shertok, 22 July 1948.

34 *Documents I*, pp. 409–14, memorandum on "Meeting: M. Shertok–Count Bernadotte and Assistants, Tel Aviv, 26 July 1948," unsigned, probably by Eytan.

35 ISA FM2563/21, "Details of a Conversation with Archbishop Georgius Hakim on Saturday, 26 June 1948," by Ya'acov Salomon; and ISA FM2563/21, Shitrit to Ben-Gurion, 6 July 1948, a report on the conversation with Hakim of 27 June 1948.

36 ISA FM2564/5, for the text of the 13 May 1948 Jaffa–Haganah surrender agreement. Because of this surrender agreement and its repercussions, Danin urged that the IDF stop signing surrender agreements with conquered Arab communities. (See ISA FM2564/5, Danin to Shertok, 28 July 1948).

37 ISA FM2566/15, Jaffa Emergency Committee to Haganah HQ, Tel Aviv District, 26 June 1948.

38 ISA FM2566/15, Chisik to Shitrit, 27 June 1948.

39 ISA FM2566/15, Shitrit to Ben-Gurion and Shertok, 30 June 1948.

40 ISA MAM307/49, Kaddar to Shitrit, 5 July 1948.

41 ISA FM2566/15, Palmon to Shertok, 6 July 1948.

42 ISA FM2566/15, Shimoni to Shertok, 7 July 1948, "Comments on the Attached Memorandum by Yehoshua Palmon, in Answer to a Letter by Mr Shitrit on the Jaffa [Emergency] Committee Regarding the Return of Jaffa's Arab Residents."

43 ISA FM2566/15, Shimoni to Palmon and Shiloah, 12 July 1948, quoting Shertok's minuted reaction to Palmon's letter.

44 KMA-PA 141–419, Rabin, Operation Dani headquarters to the Harel, Yiftah, Kiryati and 8th brigades, 19 July 1948; and KMA-PA 141–250, Allon to the Kiryati, 8th, Yiftah and Harel brigades, 19 July 1948.

45 ISA FM2444/19, "Note from the Mediator to be Submitted to the Consideration of the Provisional Government of Israel, on the Subject of Arab Refugees," by Count Foke Bernadotte, 28 July 1948.

46 ISA FM2444/19, "Lines for a Reply to Mediator on Return of Refugees," Leo Kohn, undated.

47 *Documents I*, pp. 415–16, "Note on Walter Eytan's Memorandum," Leo Kohn, 27 July 1948.

48 *Documents I*, pp. 441–4, Shertok to Bernadotte, 1 August 1948.

49 *Documents I*, pp. 465–87, a protocol of "Meeting: M. Shertok and Members of the Staff of the Ministry for Foreign Affairs with Count Bernadotte and His Associates," Tel Aviv, 5 August 1948.

50 ISA FM2444/19, Kohn to Shertok, 5 August 1948.

51 NA 501 BB. Palestine/7-3048, New York (Ross) to Secretary of State, 30 July 1948.

52 NA Record Group 84, US Consulate General Jerusalem, Classified Records 1948, 800 – Refugees, MacDonald to Secretary of State, 27 July 1948.

53 NA Record Group 84, Haifa Consulate, Classified Records 1948, 800 – Political Affairs, Patterson to Secretary of State, 29 July 1948.

54 LPA 48/23 aleph, protocol of the meeting of the Mapai Centre, statement by Ben-Gurion, 24 July 1948. Ben-Gurion's statement was revealing about his attitude to the Palestine Arabs, especially in the light of their behaviour and flight during the war. "Meanwhile," he said, "[a return] is out of the question until we sit together beside a [peace conference] table ... and they will respect us to the degree that we respect them and I doubt whether they deserve respect as we do. Because, nonetheless, we did not flee en masse. [And] so far no Arab Einstein has arisen and [they] have not created what we have built in this country and [they] have not fought as we are fighting ... We are dealing here with a collective murderer."

55 ISA FM2425/1, "Meeting: D. Horowitz–J. Reedman, Tel Aviv, 8 August 1948," by David Horowitz, the Director General of the Israel Finance Ministry.

56 *Documents I*, pp. 501–6, "Meeting: M. Shertok–Count Bernadotte, Jerusalem, 10 August 1948."

57 NA 501 BB. Palestine/8-548, Patterson (Cairo) to Secretary of State, 5 August 1948.

58 ISA FM2451/13, precis of a letter from Sasson (Paris) to Shertok (Tel Aviv), 13 August 1948.

59 See ISA FM3749/1, Shimoni (Tel Aviv) to Sasson (Paris), 16 September 1948; ISA FM3549/1, Sasson (Paris) to Danin (Tel Aviv), 29 November 1948; and Weitz, *Diary* III, p. 365, entry for 14 December 1948. Shimoni, in the letter of 16 September, incidentally, informed Sasson that Sharett (Shertok) had instructed his officials, without Cabinet sanction, to say that Israel would be willing to discuss a partial return of the refugees if the Arab states would begin to settle the bulk of the refugees in their territory.

60 ISA FM2570/11, Shimoni (Tel Aviv) to Sasson (Paris), 19 August 1948.

61 There are four contemporaneous sources for the 18 August meeting. Shimoni

(in ISA FM2444/19) wrote the "Precis of Things Said at a Meeting in the Office of the Prime Minister about the Problem of the Arab Refugees and their Return, 18 August 1948," an abbreviated 4-page record of the discussion that omits Shertok's, Ben-Gurion's and Lifshitz's opening remarks. Both Ben-Gurion and Weitz wrote diary entries about the meeting – see DBH-YH II, pp. 652–4, entry for 18 August 1948, and Weitz, *Diary* III, p. 331, entry for 18 August 1948. And ISA FM2570/11, Shimoni (Tel Aviv) to Sasson (Paris), 19 August 1948.

62 ISA FM2570/11, Shimoni (Tel Aviv) to Sasson (Paris), 19 August 1948.
63 ISA FM2444/19, "Precis of Things Said . . . 18 August 1948."
64 ISA FM2570/11, Danin (Tel Aviv) to Sasson (Paris), 22 September 1948.
65 Weitz, *Diary* III, p. 331, entry for 18 August 1948.
66 For further details, see Benny Morris "Yosef Weitz and the Transfer Committees, 1948–49."
67 *Documents I*, p. 369, Shertok (Tel Aviv) to Weizmann (Montreux), 20 July – 22 August 1948.
68 *Documents I*, pp. 549–51, Epstein (Washington) to Shertok, 24 August 1948.
69 DBG-YH III, p. 657, entry for 20 August 1948.
70 *Documents I*, pp. 570–1, "Statement Delivered by James McDonald at a Meeting with M. Shertok, Tel Aviv, 6 September 1948."
71 DBG-YH III, p. 675, entry for 8 September 1948.
72 *Documents I*, pp. 585–6, Shertok to the Members of the Provisional Government, 10 September 1948, "Instructions to the Israeli Delegation to the UN General Assembly," and p. 586, n. 4; ISA FM3749/1, Shimoni (Tel Aviv) to Sasson (Paris), 16 September 1948; and ISA FM2451/13, address by Shertok at meeting of the Provisional Council of State, 27 September 1948.
73 ISA FM2527/9, for parts of the "Progress Report of the UN Mediator on Palestine," 16 September 1948.
74 *Documents I*, pp. 626–7, "Statement by the Spokesman of the Government of Israel," Tel Aviv, 23 September 1948.
75 ISA FM2564/13, "Protocol of the Meeting of the Ministerial Committee for Abandoned Property," statement by Gad Machnes, Tel Aviv, 27 August 1948. See also ISA FM2564/18, Shitrit to Ben-Gurion and Shertok, 16 August 1948; Shimoni to the Foreign Ministry Political Division, 21 September 1948; and Shitrit to the Foreign Ministry Middle East Affairs Department, 26 September 1948.
76 ISA FM2564/18, Shimoni to Foreign Ministry Political Division, 21 September 1948.
77 ISA FM2564/18, Shitrit to the Foreign Ministry Middle East Affairs Department, 26 September 1948.
78 Even Chaim Weizmann, traditionally a softliner, agreed, or had been brought around to agreeing, with Yosef Weitz's inflexible opposition to a return. See Weitz, *Diary* III, p. 363, entry for 9 December 1948.
79 *Documents I*, pp. 641–2, "Note on Discussions of M. Comay with Bunche, Reedman and Mohn – Haifa, 23–24 September 1948," by M. Comay, sent to

the Israel delegation to the United Nations General Assembly, Paris, on 27 September 1948.

5 Blocking a return

1 *STH*, III, part 2, pp. 1333, 1334–6.

2 KMA-PA 103 – 16, "Instructions on Planning Initiated Actions," Haganah General Staff/Operations, signed "Yadin", 18 January 1948.

3 KMA-PA 109 – 123–126, operational order and operational report from the attack on Salama, 3 January 1948.

4 KMA-PA 109/gimel – 106, Palmah headquarters daily report to Haganah General Staff, 13 March 1948; KMA-PA 109/gimel – 110, Palmah headquarters daily report to Haganah General Staff, 17 March 1948; PRO co537-3856, "CID Summary of Events," 13 March 1948; and PRO wo261-301, 1st Battalion Irish Guards Quarterly Historical Report, "Diary," entry for 13 March 1948.

5 DBG-YH I, pp. 253–5, entry for 19 February 1948.

6 *STH*, III, part 3, p. 1957.

7 KMA-PA 130 – 10, "Report on the capture of al Qaluniya"; KMA-PA 109/gimel – 149, 150, Palmah headquarters daily report to Haganah General Staff for 21 April 1948; DBG-YH I, p. 361, entry for 21 April 1948; PRO, wo275-54, 6th Division Logbook, 20 April 1948; KMA-PA 130 – 76, OC "D" Company to 1st Battalion OC, "Report – Shu'fat," 26 April 1948 and KMA-PA 109/gimel – 155, Palmah headquarters daily report to Haganah General Staff, 23 April 1948; DBG-YH I, p. 366, entry for 23 April 1948; KMA-PA 131 – 13, Harel Brigade Communications Logbook, 11 May 1948; KMA-PA 130 – 45, "Report No. 3" to Palmah headquarters, [11 May 1948].

8 PRO co537-3856, "CID Summary of Events," 15 April 1948 (Appendix B, Haifa Area); KMA-PA 120/1/aleph – 23–26, Yiftah Brigade Logbook; and PRO, wo275-54, 6th Airborne Division Logbook, 17 April 1948.

9 KMA-PA 109/gimel – 146, Palmah headquarters daily report for 19 April 1948 to Haganah General Staff. Other abandoned Arab villages were demolished in training exercises elsewhere. Golani Brigade troops near Menahamiya, in the Jordan Valley, in early May put a village to the torch after training in it for the attack on Samakh in early May. See *Ilan Va'shelah*, p. 120.

10 KMA-PA 107 – 186, Palmah headquarters to "Haggai," 19 April 1948.

11 KMA 2 aleph/20, *Beineinu*, No. 13, 9 May 1948, quoting the Operation Yiftah Logbook.

12 HHA-ACP, 10.95.10 (4), handwritten notes, dated 6 May 1948.

13 HHA-ACP, 10.95.10 (4) "Our Arab Policy in the Midst of the War," Aharon Cohen, 10 May 1948.

14 See Benny Morris, "Yosef Weitz and the Transfer Committees, 1948–9."

15 Yosef Weitz Papers, the Institute for the Study of Settlement, Rehovot, Danin to Weitz, 18 May 1948.

16 CZA A246-13, p. 2410, entry for 4 June 1948). On 10 June the JNF directorate formally voted IL10,000 for Weitz's use "to cover eviction expenses." See Weitz, *Diary* III, p. 301, entry for 10 June 1948.

17 ISA FM2564/19, "Retroactive Transfer, a Scheme for the Solution of the Arab Question in the State of Israel," undated (from early June), by Weitz, Danin and Sasson.

18 CZA A246-13, p. 2411, entry for 5 June 1948. Ben-Gurion's diary entry on the meeting – in DBG-YH II, p. 487, 5 June 1948 – is less forthcoming.

19 ISA FM2564/19, Weitz to Ben-Gurion, 6 June 1948.

20 CZA A246-13, p. 2412, entry for 7 June 1948.

21 CZA A246-13, p. 2415, entry for 10 June 1948; ISA MAM307 gimel/33, Shitrit to Ben-Gurion, 23 June 1948 (for a report on Berger's activities); and LA 235 IV, 2060 aleph, Bobritzky to (Jewish Agency) Settlement Department, 21 June 1948, for Bobritzky's report, listing the villages to be destroyed and those suitable for Jewish settlement.

22 Weitz, *Diary* III, p. 301, entry for 13 June 1948.

23 CZA A246-13, p. 2418, entry for 14 June 1948.

24 Weitz, *Diary* III, p. 303, entry for 15 June 1948.

25 DBG-YH II, pp. 523–4, entry for 16 June 1948.

26 CZA A246-13, p. 2425, entry for 25 June 1948.

27 Weitz, *Diary* III, p. 310, entry for 1 July 1948.

28 KMA-AZP 9/9/1, agendas of the meeting of the Provisional Government of Israel, 16, 20, 23, 27 and 30 June 1948.

29 KMA-AZP 9/9/3, Zisling's statement at the meeting of the Cabinet, 16 June 1948; and ISA FM2401/21 aleph, Zisling to Ben-Gurion, 16 June 1948. The destruction of Beisan apparently truly worried Ben-Gurion. He cabled Golani Brigade headquarters: "Ask Avraham Yoffe [the responsible battalion OC] is it true that he burned the town of Beit Shean in whole or in part, and on whose instructions did he do this?" See DBG Archives, Minister of Defence to Golani, ? 18 June 1948.

30 KMA-AZP 9/9/1, "Decisions of the Provisional Government Meeting," 20 June 1948. After the meeting, Ben-Gurion asked the IDF for information about "circumstances of" the destruction of Al Qubeiba and Zarnuqa. IDF OC Operations Yadin replied that he would have to look into it. Whether he did so, and what were the results, is unknown. See DBG Archives, David Ben-Gurion to Yigael Sukenik (Yadin), 23 June 1948, and Sukenik to David Ben-Gurion, 23 June 1948.

31 ISA AM gimel/19/aleph, Gvirtz to Shitrit, 23 June 1948; and ISA AM gimel/19/aleph, "Report for the Month of June," by Yitzhak Gvirtz, undated but copy received in the Agriculture Ministry on 7 July 1948.

32 KMA-AZP 9/9/3, Zisling's statement at the Cabinet meeting of 4 July 1948.

33 Weitz, *Dairy* III, p. 309, entry for 28 June 1948 and p. 310 entry for 1 July 1948.

34 KMA-AZP 9/9/1, IDF General Staff (Zvi Ayalon) to OCs brigades, battalions, districts, corps, the military police and branches, 6 July 1948.

35 ISA MAM304/76, Zvi Lurie to the Prime Minister and Minority Affairs

Minister, 13 July 1948; KMA-AZP 8/8 aleph/11, Lurie to Mordechai Bentov, Zisling, Berl Repetor, B. Nir, 26 July 1948; HHA 10.18, Protocol of Meeting of Mapam Defence Activists, 26 July 1948, statement by Moshe Erem; and KMA-AZP 8/8 aleph/11, Lurie to Ben-Gurion, 3 August 1948.

36 KMA-AZP 9/9/3, Zisling's statement at the Cabinet meeting of 14 July 1948; and KMA-AZP 9/9/1, "Decisions of the Provisional Government," 14 July 1948.

37 ISA FM2401/21 aleph, Protocol of the Meeting of the Ministerial Committee for Abandoned Property, 26 July 1948.

38 KMA-AZP 9/9/4, Ben-Gurion to Zisling, 13 September 1948, and Zisling to Ben-Gurion, 15 September 1948.

39 DBG-YH III, p. 778, entry for 27 October 1948.

40 DBG-YH III, pp. 652–4, entry for 18 August 1948. Compare to Weitz diary entry on the meeting – in Weitz, *Diary* III, p. 331 – and Shimoni's official abridged protocol of the meeting – in ISA FM2444/19. Ben-Gurion exercised "censorship" as he made his diary entries, which were in part written during meetings.

41 HHA 11.18, "Letter to the Mobilised No. 3," the Secretariat of the Actions Committee of the Kibbutz Artzi, 25 August 1948.

42 HHA 66.90 (1), protocol of the meeting of the Political Committee of Mapam, 19 August 1948.

43 KMA-PA 141–46, "Lifshitz"/Dani headquarters to OC Engineers, Sappers (Yiftah Brigade), 10 July 1948; and KMA-PA 141 – 54, "Lifshitz"/Dani headquarters to OC Engineers 8th Brigade, 10 July 1948.

44 KMA-PA 142 – 37, Yiftah Brigade headquarters to Dani headquarters, undated, probably 10 July 1948.

45 KMA-PA 141 – 102, "Lifshitz"/Dani headquarters to Yiftah Brigade Forward headquarters, 11 July 1948. It is worth noting that not all sites ordered destroyed were in fact completely or even partially destroyed in any operation. Often, the unit ordered to carry out such demolition lacked manpower or explosives. Occasionally, units reported that they had blown up a village when they had managed only to destroy a few houses.

46 Jewish National Fund files, 501–4, report on the period 11 August 1948 to 11 September 1948, diary by Israel Libertovsky, an official of Mekorot, the national water company.

47 Jewish National Fund files, 501–4, report on the period 14 September 1948 to 12 October 1948, diary by Israel Libertovsky; and KMA-PA 120/1/bet – 39, 42, Palmah headquarters daily reports to IDF General Staff for 1 and 4 October 1948.

48 HHA-ACP 10.95.10 (4), Sha'ar Ha'amakim to the Defence Minister and Minister of Finance, 4 August 1948; HHA-ACP 10.95.10 (5), Sha'ar Ha'amakim to Golani Brigade headquarters, Jezreel Valley, 8 August 1948; and HHA 66.90 (1), protocols of the meeting of the Mapam Politcal Committee, statements by Meir Ya'ari and Aharon Cohen, 19 August 1948.

49 KMA-AZP 9/9/1, "Decisions of the Provisional Government," 8 August 1948.

50 HHA-ACP 10.95.10 (6), Major Elisha Sulz, Military Governor of Nazareth, to Sha'ar Ha'amakim, 14 October 1948; and HHA-ACP 10.95.10 (6), Gad Machnes to Sha'ar Ha'amakim, 22 October 1948.

51 ISA FM2564/9, Arye Farda (Dorot), Yaakov Gavri (Nir-Am) and Eliezer Frish (Ruhama) to the Prime Minister and Defence Minister, 4 August 1948.

52 ISA FM2570/11, Avira to Danin, 29 July 1948, and Danin to Avira, 16 August 1948.

53 HHA-ACP 10.95.39 (2), Erem to Shitrit, October, 1948.

54 For example, Marshak's statement in HHA 10.18, protocol of a meeting of Mapam defence officers and officials, 26 July 1948.

55 HHA, Meir Ya'ari Papers 7.95.3 – bet (2), Prag to Meir Ya'ari, 27 July 1948.

56 KMA-AZP 8/8 aleph/11, Peterzil to Zisling, Bentov and Erem, 2 August 1948.

57 HHA-ACP 10.95.10 (6), Salem Horowitz (?) to (probably) Aharon Cohen or the Political Committee of Mapam, September 1948.

58 HHA-ACP 10.95.10 (5), Peterzil to Erem, Bentov, Hazan and Zisling, 10 August 1948, quoting an extract of a letter, undated, from Faivel Cohen of Ma'ayan Baruch to himself.

59 CZA A246-14, p. 2530, entry for 23 November 1948.

60 Weitz, *Diary* III, p. 367, entry for 18 December 1948. Weitz's reference to "revenge" related to his son, Yehiam, a Palmah officer, who had died during a Palmah raid in 1946 on the Az Zib bridge, killed by Az Zib villagers.

61 ISA FM2401/21 aleph, Protocol of the Meeting of the Ministerial Committee for Abandoned Property, 5 November 1948.

62 I have not dealt here at all with the destruction carried out by the IDF in the empty Arab urban neighbourhoods of Jaffa (Manshiya), Haifa, Beersheba and Tiberias (the Old City) in 1948–9. It was mostly carried out with an eye to urban development and public health, not for political or military reasons. For the destruction of Tiberias' Old City, see correspondence in ISA PMO5525 gimel. For demolitions in Haifa, see DBG-YH II, p. 522, entry for 16 June 1948 and p. 570, entry for 30 June 1948, and correspondence in ISA MAM298/82 and HMA 556.

63 Ben-Gurion, *Behilahem Yisrael*, p. 71.

64 Weitz, *Diary* III, p. 232, entries for 3 and 4 February 1948.

65 Weitz, *Diary* III, p. 235, entry for 10 February 1948.

66 PRO CO537-3857, "CID Summary of Events (of 21 March 1948)," 23 March 1948. For a fuller treatment of this subject, see Benny Morris "The Battle for the Harvest of 1948."

67 Weitz, *Diary* III, Appendix 1, p. 377, Negev Committee to Sarig, 4 May 1948.

68 LA 235 IV, 2251 bet, "Things Said at a Meeting of the Settlements Block Committee in Tel Aviv, 26 May 1948," the Arab (later Minority) Affairs Ministry; and ISA MAM303/41, "Report of the Arab Property Department at the End of May 1948," unsigned but almost certainly by Gvirtz.

69 ISA AM aleph/19/aleph, "Summary of the Meeting with the Arab Property Committee in the Tel Hai [Galilee panhandle] district, 5 June 1948." For the

allocation of Arab fields and their cultivation around Hadera, see LA 235 IV, 2082/aleph, "Circular [No. 11]," Samaria Settlements Block Committee, 24 May 1948.

70 LA 235 IV, 2251 bet, Gvirtz to Ma'ayan Zvi, 3 June 1948.

71 For example, see LA 235 IV, 2251 bet, Z. Stein (Tsur) and V. Wilder, the Agriculture Centre, to Kibbutz Ramat Hakovesh and Kibbutz Mishmar Hasharon, 19 May 1948.

72 ISA AM aleph/19/gimel (part 1), "Report [of the Arab Property Department] for the Month of June 1948," by Y. Gvirtz, received at the Agriculture Ministry on 7 July 1948.

73 Treated more fully in Benny Morris, "The Battle for the Harvest of 1948."

74 LA 235 IV, 2251 bet, Weitz to Machnes, 2 May 1948.

75 LA 235 IV, 2179, Kibbutz Sde Nehemia to Hartzfeld, 18 May 1948. The neighbouring Kibbutz Manara made a similar request for the lands of Qadas, "suitable for winter crops" (implying an interest in more than ephemeral cultivation) – see LA 235 IV, 2251 bet, Haim Gvati to members of the committee responsible for Arab property in Upper Galilee, 2 June 1948.

76 LA 235 IV, 2251 bet, Tel Mond Settlements Block Committee to Agricultural Centre, 25 July 1948; "Mishmeret" to Agricultural Centre, 29 July 1948; Kibbutz Neve-Yam to Agricultural Centre, 3 August 1948; and Kibbutz Ein Harod to the Agricultural Centre, 10 August 1948; LA 235 IV, 2251/aleph, Kvutzat Schiller to the Agricultural Centre, 23 August 1948; LA 235 IV, 2251/bet, Kibbutz Genossar to the Agricultural Centre, 8 August 1948, and Nahalal and Kishon Regional Council to (?), 8 August 1948; and LA 235 IV, 2088, Nahalal and Kishon Regional Council to the settlement department of the Agricultural Centre, 8 August 1948.

77 ISA AM gimel/19/aleph (part 1), 2185/gimel, Gvirtz to the finance minister, 29 June 1948, and "Report [of the Arab (Abandoned) Property Department] for the Month of June 1948."

78 ISA FM2401/21 aleph, "Protocol of the Meeting of the Ministerial Committee for Abandoned Property, 13 July 1948"; and ISA, FM2401/21 bet, memorandum by Zalman Lifshitz "The Legal Settlement of Absentees Property for Purposes of Settlement, Housing and Economic Reconstruction," 18 March 1949.

79 ISA AM gimel/19/aleph (part 1), 2185/gimel, "Cabinet Announcement – Emergency Regulations . . .," 26 November 1948; and ISA FM2401/21 bet, "Legal Settlement . . .," 18 March 1949.

80 ISA FM2401/21 bet, "Legal Settlement . . .," 18 March 1949; Lifshitz to the Prime Minister, Foreign Minister, etc., 30 March 1949, and "Summary of A Meeting Held on 1 May 1949 in the Prime Minister's Office."

81 Weitz, *Diary* III, p. 288, entry for 20 May 1948.

82 CZA KKL10, protocol of the meeting of the JNF directorate, 7 July 1948; ISA, AM bet/19/aleph, 2185/gimel, JNF to the Provisional Government of Israel, 28 July 1948; ISA AM gimel/19/aleph (part 1), Weitz to David Shafrir, the Custodian for Abandoned Property, 28 July 1948; ISA AM gimel/19/aleph (part 1), 2185/gimel, JNF (Weitz) to Minister of Agriculture, 29 August 1948

and A. Z[isling] to the JNF, 14 October 1948; and CZA A246-13, pp. 2464–5, entry for 17 August 1948.

83 ISA AM bet/19/aleph, 2185/gimel, A. Hirsh, deputy Director General of the Agriculture Ministry, to the Organisation of Cooperative Settlements, 8 August 1948, and the Organisation of Cooperative Settlements to A. Hirsh, 11 August 1948.

84 Mishmar Ha'emek Archive, 3.64/5, Mishmar Ha'emek to Carmeli (of Kibbutz Genigar), a member of the Committee for the Distribution of Abandoned Fields in the Jezreel Valley, 9 August 1948.

85 For example, see LA 235 IV, 2251 bet, Gvirtz to the Committee for the Displaced Population and the Reconstruction of the Settlements, 7 July 1948, for a rejection of Kibbutz Negba's compensation claims.

86 For examples of the settlements' leasing requests and the inter-departmental handling of them, see ISA AM gimel/19/aleph (part 1), 2185/gimel, Creative Cooperative Farmers Association Yoqne'am Ltd., to the Government of Israel, [*sic*] Agriculture Department, 6 August 1948; Kibbutz Sha'ar Hagolan to the Ministry of Agriculture, 16 August 1948; A. Schechter, Agriculture Ministry, to the Custodian for Abandoned Property, 19 August 1948; Z. Tsur (Stein), the Agricultural Centre, to A. Hanuki, the Agriculture Ministry, 22 November 1948 (referring to receipt of letter of 1 August from Kibbutz Beit Keshet); Southern Sharon (Settlements) Block (Committee) to the Agriculture Ministry, 26 August 1948; and ISA AM gimel/19/aleph (part 3), Shomron Jewish Settlements Block Committee to Ministry of Agriculture and the Custodian for Abandoned Property, 1 September 1948.

87 ISA AM aleph/19/gimel (part 1), A Hanuki to the Minister of Agriculture, 10 October 1948.

88 ISA AM aleph/19/gimel (part 1), Berger to Haim Halperin, Director General of the Ministry of Agriculture, 29 October 1948, and Hanuki to Berger, 8 November 1948.

89 ISA AM aleph/19/gimel (part 2), Migdal to Hanuki, 12 December 1948, and Reuven Aloni, Ministry of Agriculture, to Migdal, 21 December 1948; and ISA AM aleph/19/gimel (part 3), Ministry of Agriculture to Migdal, 21 July 1949.

90 ISA AM aleph/19/gimel (part 2), Shmuel Zimmerman, the Moshava Sejera Council, to the Ministry of Agriculture, Abandoned Lands Department, undated, received at the Ministry on 16 December 1948, and Aloni, the Ministry of Agriculture, to Moshav Sharona, 17 December 1948.

91 ISA AM aleph/19/gimel (part 1), Gruenbaum to the ministers of Finance and Agriculture, 9 November 1948; and ISA AM aleph/19/gimel (part 3), Hanuki to Tel Mond Settlements Block Committee, 14 November 1948, and Hanuki to the Even-Yehuda Council, 2 June 1949.

92 For a typical wrangle over land between two kibbutzim, Ma'abarot and Mishmar Hasharon (in the Coastal Plain), see LA 235 IV, 1695, Mishmar Hasharon to the Settlement Department, Agricultural Centre, 25 July 1948; ISA AM aleph/19/gimel (part 2), Mishmar Hasharon to Hakal, 25 November 1948, and Hanuki to Mishmar Hasharon, 13 December 1948; and ISA AM

aleph/19/gimel (part 3), the Hefer Valley Regional Council to A. Lebovsky, the Ministry of Agriculture, 7 December 1948.

93 ISA AM210/11, Agriculture Ministry to the Prime Minister, 22 March 1949.

94 DBG-YH III, p. 892, entry for 21 December 1948.

95 Weitz, *Diary* IV, p. 9, entry for 28 January 1949; and CZA KKL10, protocols of the meeting of the JNF Directorate, 8 March 1949, statement by Weitz.

96 ISA AM29/7, protocols of the meetings of the Committee for Agricultural and Settlement Development, 12 and 26 July 1949 and appended statistics – "Estimate of the Sown Area of the State," "The Areas of Irrigated Fields in the Jewish (Agricultural) Economy" and "Summary of Area of Abandoned Land Leased by the Agriculture Ministry."

97 ISA AM29/7, "To Settle New Land," by Yosef Weitz, 1949.

98 See for example ISA AM aleph/19/gimel (part 3), the Settlement Department, the Jewish Agency, to the Northern District (office), received at the Agriculture Ministry on 3 July 1949.

99 For the 53, see ISA AM kof/5, "List of the New Settlements from the Start of the Hostilities in the Country," unsigned, dated 16 March 1949. DBG-YH III, pp. 778–89, lists the 32 established between the start of hostilities and 27 October 1948. Dr Charles Kamen, in his monograph *Aharei Ha'ason: Ha'ochlosiah Ha'aravit Bemedinat Yisrael 1948–1950* (After the Catastrophe: the Arab Population in the State of Israel 1948–50), in *Mahbarot Lemehkar u'Lebikoret*, No. 10, pp. 38–9, states that 109 settlements were set up between October 1948 and August 1949.

100 Ben-Gurion, *Behilahem Yisrael*, pp. 70–1, text of Ben-Gurion's speech to Mapai Council, 7 February 1948.

101 LPA 24/48, protocol of the meeting of the Mapai Secretariat, 20 March 1948.

102 LPA 24/48, protocol of the joint meeting of the Mapai Secretariat, the secretariat of the Ihud Hakevutzot kibbutz movement and the Mapai faction in the Zionist Actions Committee, 4 April 1948.

103 Ben-Gurion, *Behilahem Yisrael*, pp. 86–7 and 92, Ben-Gurion's speech before the Zionist Actions Committee, 6 April 1948.

104 Weitz, *Diary* III, p. 260, entry for 31 March 1948.

105 Yosef Weitz Papers, the Institute for the Study of Settlement, Rehovot, Galili to Weitz, 13 April 1948. Most of the sites named had not yet been abandoned by their Arab inhabitants.

106 Weitz, *Diary* III, pp. 271–2, entry for 22 April 1948 and p. 268, entries for 17 and 18 April 1948.

107 Weitz, *Diary* III, pp. 256–7, entry for 26 March 1948. Two new settlements, Sheluhot and Reshafim, were established in the valley ten weeks later, on 10 June 1948, on the lands of Al Ashrafiya. Kibbutz Ramot-Menashe was founded on the lands of Daliyat ar Ruha on 31 July 1948.

108 HHA, *Yoman Hamazkirut*, Hakibbutz Ha'artzi, 28 June 1948, a record of the deliberations of the secretariat of the Kibbutz Artzi on 18 April.

109 CZA A246-13, p. 2372, entry for 3 May 1948.

110 CZA A246-13, p. 2372, entry for 3 May 1948.

111 DBG-YH I, p. 398, entry for 7 May 1948; Weitz, *Diary* III, pp. 280–1, entry

for 9 May 1948; and LPA 23 aleph/48, protocol of the meeting of the Mapai Centre, 12 May 1948.

112 ISA, Finance Ministry papers 10/1/9, Haim Gvati, "Socialist Agriculture and the Mass Immigration," in *Molad*, I, No. 2–3, (May–June 1948), 103–7.

113 HHA 66.90 (1), protocol of the meeting of the Mapam Political Committee, 26 May 1948.

114 ISA AM kof/5, "A list of the New Settlements from the Start of Hostilities in the Country."

115 The settlements were Habonim (later called Kibbutz Kfar Hanassi) at Mansurat al Kheit, on the Jordan River (2 July 1948), Yesodot, southeast of 'Aqir (on 6 July 1948), Kibbutz Regavim, at Buteimat (on 6 July 1948), Hagilboa-Zeraim, near the Harod spring, in the Jezreel Valley (on 20 July 1948) and Kibbutz Ramot-Menashe, between Daliyat ar Ruha and Sabbarin (on 31 July).

116 Weitz, *Diary* III, pp. 318–19, entry for 21 July 1948.

117 Weitz, *Diary* III, p. 319, entry for 23 July 1948; and DBG-YH II, p. 618, entry for 23 July 1948.

118 KMA-AZP 8/4 aleph, "Proposal for New Settlements by the Agricultural Settlements Committee of the National Institutions . . .," 28 July 1948; KMA-AZP 8/4 aleph, Settlement Officer, General Staff/Operations to the Defence Minister, 6 August 1948; and LPA 23 aleph/48, protocol of the meeting of the Mapai Centre, Hartzfeld statement, 9 August 1948.

119 CZA KKL 10, protocol of the meeting of the JNF directorate, 16 August 1948.

120 HHA 68.9 (1), protocols of the meeting of the Mapam Centre, 15–16 July 1948; and HHA 10.18, protocol of meeting of Mapam defence activists, 26 July 1948, statement by Haim Kafri.

121 HHA 66.90 (1), protocol of the meeting of the Political Committee of Mapam, 19 August 1948.

122 ISA AM kof/5, the Settlement Committee of the National Institutions (Weitz, Horin, Hartzfeld) to the Minister of Defence, 20 August 1948; and ISA FM2564/13, "Protocol of the Meeting of the Ministerial Committee for Abandoned Property," 20 August 1948; "Protocol of the Meeting of the Ministerial Committee for Abandoned Property," 27 August 1948; and Weitz, *Diary* III, p. 334, entry for 23 August 1948.

123 ISA AM kof/5, "Report for September 1948," by Y. Eshel, Settlement Officer, IDF General Staff, to Defence Minister, IDF Chief of Staff, Minister of Agriculture, General Staff/Operations, etc., 8 October 1948.

124 HHA 5.10.5 (2), protocol of the meeting of the Actions Committee of the Kibbutz Artzi, 4 November 1948.

125 HHA, *Yediot Hakkibutz Ha'artzi*, No. 278 (1), January 1949, "Report from the meeting of the Kibbutz Artzi-Hashomer Hatzair Council," Nahariya, 10–12 December 1948.

126 CZA A246-14, p. 2540, entry for 4 December 1948; Weitz, *Diary* III, p. 401, protocol of the meeting of the Committee of Directorates of the National Institutions, 11 December 1948; and CZA A246-14, p. 2558, entry for 24 December 1948.

127 Weitz, *Diary* III, p. 366, entry for 18 December 1948, and p. 369, entry for 19 December 1948.

128 KMA-AZP 4, aleph/8, memorandum by Ra'anan Weitz to the Ministerial Committee for Abandoned Property, 30 November 1948. A handful of non-collective settlements were also established in the last months of 1948.

129 CZA KKL 10, protocol of the meeting of the JNF directorate, 7 December 1948; and Weitz, *Diary* III, p. 364, entry for 10 December 1948, and p. 360, entry for 3 December 1948.

130 DBG-YH III, p. 969, entry for 10 February 1949.

131 CZA S53-526/dalet, "Information of the Immigration Department," Jewish Agency Immigration Department, 18 February 1948.

132 DBG-YH I, p. 197, entry for 31 January 1948. New immigrants were not yet arriving in Palestine, still under British Mandate rule, so Ben-Gurion was then probably thinking of using Jerusalemites for this purpose. But the nature of the policy, which was to be implemented when the immigrants began to pour in a few months later, was clear: to fill with Jews abandoned houses, districts and towns in order to prevent an Arab return and reoccupation, and, at the same time, to ease the Yishuv's housing problem.

133 Yosef Weitz Papers, the Institute for Settlement Research, Rehovot, Danin to Weitz, 18 May 1948.

134 ISA FM2564/19, "Retroactive Transfer, A Scheme for the Solution of the Arab Question in the State of Israel," by Weitz, Danin, Sasson, undated.

135 See, for instance, Weitz, *Diary* III, pp. 301–2, entries for 13 and 15 June 1948.

136 LPA 24/48, protocol of the meeting of the Mapai Secretariat, 5 July 1948.

137 For more on the concentration of Haifa's Arabs, see Benny Morris, "The Concentration of the Arabs of Haifa, July 1948," in *Middle East Journal*, forthcoming.

138 LPA 23 aleph/48, protocol of the meeting of the Mapai Centre, 9 August 1948; and Weitz, *Diary* III, p. 346, entry for 11 September 1948.

139 DBG-YH II, p. 622, entry for 25 July 1948; ISA MAM306/76, "Weekly Report No. 2, 5 August 1948 – 12 August 1948," by M. Laniado, 13 August 1948, and "Weekly report No. 3, 13 August 1948 – 20 August 1948," by M. Laniado, 20 August 1948; and ISA MAM308/9, "[Protocol of the] First Meeting of the Committee Next to the Military Government, 29 August 1948."

140 ISA MAM1322/2, Moshe Yitah to the Military Commander, Haifa, 31 August 1948; DBG-YH II, p. 684, entry for 13 September 1948; ISA PMO5440, David Shafrir, Custodian for Absentees Property, to the Prime Minister, 24 March 1949; and ISA AM210/05, "Report on the Activities Until 31 March 1949," by David Shafrir, Custodian for Absentees Property, 18 April 1949.

141 DBG-YH II, p. 662, entry for 26 August 1948.

142 CZA 46/1, protocol of the meeting of the Jewish Agency Executive, 20 October 1948.

143 ISA FM2401/21 aleph, protocol of the meeting of the Ministerial Committee for Abandoned Property, 5 November 1948.

144 ISA FM2564/11, protocol of the meeting of the Military Government Committee, 16 November 1948.

145 ISA FM2401/21 aleph, "Decisions of the Meeting of the Six Ministers for Arab Affairs, 5 December 1948," and protocol of the meeting of the Ministerial Committee for Abandoned Property, 17 December 1948.

146 ISA FM2564/11, protocol of the meeting of the Military Government Committee, 9 September 1948; and ISA FM2564/13, protocol of the meeting of the Ministerial Committee for Abandoned Property, 10 September 1948.

147 DBG-YH II, p. 701, entry for 18 September, and III, p. 839, entry for 22 November 1948.

148 ISA FM2401/21 aleph, "Decisions of the Meeting of Six Ministers for Arab Affairs, 2 December 1948"; and Weitz, *Diary* III, p. 363, entry for 8 December 1948.

149 DBG-YH III, p. 897, entry for 23 December 1948; and Weitz, *Diary* IV, p. 14, entry for 23 February 1948.

150 DBG-YH III, p. 897 entry for 23 December 1948; ISA AM aleph/19/gimel, (part 3), and A. Shechter, Agriculture Ministry, to A. Bergman, the Military Governor's office, Jerusalem, 20 December 1948.

151 ISA FM2431/2, Dayan to Eytan, the Foreign Ministry, 15 March 1949.

152 ISA FM2431/4, A. Bergman, head of Jerusalem District, to the Foreign Ministry, 25 May 1949.

153 ISA PM05559/gimel, Buber, Simon, W. D. Senator (a former member of the Jewish Agency Executive and official in the administration of the Hebrew University of Jerusalem) and H. Y. Roth, (a professor of philosophy and former Rector of the Hebrew University), to Ben-Gurion, 6 June 1949; and Tom Segev, *1949 Ha'yisraelim Harishonim* (1949 The First Israelis), pp. 100–3. Eventually, part of Deir Yassin became a mental hospital.

154 ISA FM2564/11, protocol of the meeting of the Military Government Committee, 23 September 1948.

155 DBG-YH III, p. 799, entry for 6 November 1948.

156 KMA-AZP 4, aleph/8, "Proposal for a Plan to Settle *Olim* in Upper Galilee (In Outline)," by Yosef Weitz, 21 December 1948.

157 DBG-YH III, p. 897, entry for 23 December 1948.

158 HHA, *Yediot Hakkibutz Ha'artzi-Hashomer Hatzair*, No. 278 (1), January 1949, "Report from the meeting of the Kibbutz Artzi-Hashomer Hatzair Council," Nahariya, 10–12 December 1948.

159 ISA FM2401/21 aleph, protocol of the meeting of the Ministerial Committee for Abandoned Property, 31 December 1948.

160 DBG-YH III, p. 926, entry for 4 January 1949; and KMA-AZP 9/9/1, "Decisions of the Provisional Government," 9 January 1949.

161 Weitz, *Diary* IV, p. 4, entry for 13 January 1949; p. 5, Weitz to "Rema" (his wife), 15 January 1949; p. 15, entry for 2 March 1949; and p. 16, Weitz to "Rema," 7 March 1948.

162 ISA AM aleph/19/gimel, Gvirtz, Agricultural Workers Organisation, to the

Ministry of Agriculture, 26 June 1949; the Ministry of Agriculture to the Custodian for Absentees Property, 5 July 1949; the Custodian for Absentees Property to the Ministry of Agriculture, 17 July 1949; Aloni, the Ministry of Agriculture, to the Custodian for Absentees Property, 24 July 1949; Aloni to the Jewish Agency Settlement Department, 24 July 1949; and A. Bobritzky, Jewish Agency Settlement Department, to Aloni, 24 July 1949.

163 Weitz, *Diary* IV, p. 36, entry for 24 June 1949.
164 ISA, Finance Ministry Papers 10/1/9, "A Consultation About Immigration Absorption (in the [Mapai] party)," 22 April 1949.
165 ISA FM2401/19, "Report of the Committee Probing the Problems of the Military Government and its Future," by General E. Avner, 3 May 1949.
166 ISA PMO5559/gimel, Settlement Department, Jewish Agency, to Gershon Zack, Prime Minister's bureau, 27 May 1949.

6 The third wave

1 KMA-AZP 9/9/1, Ayalon to brigade, battalion, district and corps OCs, the Military Police, and the branch staffs, 6 July 1948.
2 Eshel, *Hativat Carmeli* p. 210; and Nazzal, *Palestinian Exodus*, pp. 71–4.
3 Carmel, *Ma'arachot Tzafon*, pp. 199–200.
4 *Ibid.*, pp. 202–3.
5 Nazzal, *Palestinian Exodus*, pp. 74–7; and HHA 10.18, statement by Moshe Erem at the Meeting of Mapam defence activists, 26 July 1948. Erem, highly critical of what he regarded as the IDF's expulsion policy elsewhere, said that what had happened in Nazareth and Saffuriya – where not one person had been expelled – had left him bewildered.
6 Kamen, *Aharei Ha'ason*, p. 48. About 1,200 refugees from Al Mujeidil were in Nazareth at the end of July 1948.
7 ISA FM2570/11, Avira to Danin, 29 July 1948. The word "expelled" (*gurshu*) was often used rather loosely by Israelis in 1948. It was quite often assumed by non-witnesses that a given community had been expelled when in fact it had left before Israeli forces arrived. The desire to see the Arabs leave often triggered the assumption that commanders – who it was presumed shared this desire – had had to act overtly and directly to obtain this result, when this had not been the case. But if denial of the right to return to villagers immediately after the conquest of their homes by the IDF was a form of "expulsion," then a great many villagers – who had waited near their villages for the battle to die down before trying to return home – can be considered "expellees."
8 DBG-YH II, p. 591, for the text of Ben-Gurion to Yadin and Northern Front headquarters, 15 July 1948
9 Eshel, *Hativat Carmeli*, p. 218; and *Ilan Va'Shelah*, pp. 275 and 23.
10 DBG-YH II, p. 598, entry for 17 July 1948.
11 DBG-YH II, p. 598, entry for 18 July 1948. The episode places Ben-Gurion in an "anti-expulsion" light. I have found rather vague confirmation of it in the assertion three months later by Nazareth's Military Governor, Major Elisha Sulz, that Ben-Gurion had given an order "prohibiting expelling inhabitants

from the town." See ISA FM2564/11, "Report on the Activities of the Military Government in Nazareth and [the Surrounding] District for the Three Months 17 July – 17 October 1948," undated, by Sulz. Michael Bar-Zohar, *Ben-Gurion*, (3 vols., Tel Aviv, Am Oved, 1977), vol. II, pp. 775–6, however, says that Lt Colonel Makleff, Northern Front's OC Operations, told him in an interview that on a visit to Nazareth a few days after its conquest, Ben-Gurion asked in surprise: "Why [are there] so many Arabs [here]? Why did you not expel them?" Both stories could be true.

12 ISA JM5756 gimel/4820, Shitrit to all members of the Cabinet, "Report of the Visit of the Minority Affairs Minister in Nazareth on 19 July 1948," 23 July 1948; and ISA FM2564/11, "Report on the Activities of the Military Government in Nazareth and [its Surrounding] District for the Three Months 17 July – 17 October 1948," undated, by Major Sulz. The exact number of local inhabitants who fled from Nazareth is uncertain. H. Werfel, of the Religious Affairs Ministry, and Yehoshafat Harkabi, Shertok's aide-de-camp, who visited the city on 17 July, reported that "a considerable number of Moslems had fled northwards." See ISA MAM308/44, "Report on a Visit to Nazareth on 17 July 1948," 18 July 1948, by Werfel and Harkabi, to the Minority Affairs Minister, Eytan and Shiloah. One American diplomat serving in the north put the number of local inhabitants who fled Nazareth at "approximately 500" – in NA Record Group 84, Haifa Consulate, Classified Records 800 – Political Affairs (General), Randolph Roberts, US vice-consul, Haifa, to Secretary of State, 30 July 1948. But a more reasonable estimate of the number of refugees from Nazareth would be about 4,000–5,000, based on the probable local population figure of 17,000 in early 1948 and a 17,000 figure (comprising local inhabitants plus some 4,500 refugees from elsewhere) towards the end of 1948. These figures are cited in Kamen, *Aharei Ha'ason*, pp. 47–8. Nazzal, *Palestinian Exodus*, pp. 78–80, briefly describes the fall of Nazareth and gives the testimony of a Nazareth doctor who, panicked by the fall of Saffuriya, first tried to flee the city on 15 July but was turned back by the ALA.

13 Nazzal, *Palestinian Exodus* pp. 80–6; and *Toldot Milhemet Hakomemiut*, p. 251.

14 DBG-YH II, p. 468, entry for 30 May 1948; and Elhanan Orren, *Baderekh el Ha'ir, Mivtza Dani* (On the Road to the City, Operation Dani), pp. 66–7, and p. 299, footnotes 29–30. Orren's book, written under constraints of IDF censorship, is extremely terse and selective in describing the exodus from Lydda and Ramle. For greater detail about the exodus from the two towns, see Benny Morris, "Operation Dani and the Exodus from Lydda and Ramle."

15 KMA-PA 100/MOD/3 – 171, "Intelligence Service Information," 31 May 1948; and KMA-PA 141 – 535, "Summary of Information on the Enemy Towards the End of the Truce in the Ramle–Lydda Front and Environs," Kiryati Brigade Intelligence Officer, 28 June 1948.

16 CZA S25-4066, for reports from "The Arab Labourer," the code name of an Arab agent working for the Arab Division of the Jewish Agency Political Department. On 18 January and 2 February, he reported on the employment and food situation in Ramle. And KMA-PA 141 – 535, "Summary of

Information on the Enemy Towards the end of the Truce in the Ramle–Lydda Front and Environs," Kiryati Brigade Intelligence Officer, 28 June 1948.

17 KMA-PA 141 – 60, 498, Operation Dani headquarters to IDF General Staff/ Operations, 10 July 1948; KMA-PA 141 – 66, Operation Dani headquarters to IDF General Staff/Operations, 10 July 1948; KMA-PA 141 – 67, Operation Dani headquarters to Yiftah Brigade headquarters, 19 July 1948; and KMA-PA 142 – 1, "Malka" to "Tziporen," 10 July 1948. Orren, *Baderekh*, p. 93, says Operation Dani headquarters through the bombings sought "to bring about a collapse of civilian morale."

18 KMA-PA 120 – 91, Yiftah Brigade Intelligence Officer to Operation Dani headquarters, 11 July 1948; KMA-PA 141 – 105, Operation Dani head-quarters to IDF General Staff/Operations, 11 July 1948; and KMA-PA 141 – 109, Operation Dani headquarters to IDF General Staff/Operations, 11 July 1948.

19 KMA-PA 120 – 92, "Daily Report," Yiftah Brigade Intelligence Officer, 12 July 1948; and KMA-PA 141 – 360, "Yigal [Allon]" to Yiftah Brigade headquarters, undated; and Orren, *Baderekh*, p. 108.

20 See *Sefer Hapalmah* II, p. 717, for the Yiftah soldiers' sense of vulnerability in Lydda on 11–12 July. The two alternatives are given in *Sefer Hapalmah* II, p. 571 and KMA-PA 142 – 163, "Comprehensive Report of the Activities of the Third Battalion from 9 July until 18 July," 3rd Battalion Intelligence Officer, 19 July 1948.

21 Orren, *Baderekh*, p. 110.

22 Yeruham Cohen, *Le'or Hayom U'bamachshah* (During the Day and the Night), (Tel Aviv, Amikam, 1969), p. 160.

23 *Sefer Hapalmah* II, p. 565; and KMA-PA 142 – 163, "Comprehensive Report of the Activities of the 3rd Battalion from 9 July until 18 July," 3rd Battalion Intelligence Officer, 19 July 1948. Subsequent Arab estimates of the Arab death toll in Lydda were higher. Orren, *Baderekh*, p. 110, quotes Aref al Aref as writing that 400 townspeople were killed. Nimr al Khatib, in *Be'einei Oyev*, p. 36, wrote that the townspeople had "revolted" and 1,700 of them had been killed. Nimr al Khatib was interested in glorifying the resistance of the Lydda townspeople to their conquerors. The Israeli figure, while a general estimate, was given in contemporary military dispatches and had no political or propagandistic intent or purpose. In any case, it is not far off Aref al Aref's.

24 *Sefer Hapalmah* II, pp. 810 and 885.

25 "Avi-Yiftah" (Shmarya Guttman), *"Lod Yotzet Lagolah* (Lydda goes into Exile)," *Mibifnim*, XIII, No. 3 (November 1948).

26 Michael Bar-Zohar, *Ben-Gurion*, vol. II, p. 775. Bar-Zohar cites an interview with Rabin as his source. Arieh Itzchaki, *Latrun, Hama'aracha al Haderekh Leyerushalayim* (Latrun, the Battle for the Road to Jerusalem), Vol. II, p. 394, says that Ben-Gurion did not say "Expel them" but only made a gesture meaning "expel them." Itzchaki, who was director of the archive at IDF General Staff/History Branch, adds that "Allon and Rabin then . . . decided that it was crucial to expel the inhabitants."

27 KMA-PA 141 – 143, Operation Dani headquarters to Yiftah Brigade head-

quarters, 8th Brigade headquarters, 13:30 hours, 12 July 1948. A coded (and undated) version of this order is in KMA-PA 142 – 18. Orren, *Baderekh*, makes no mention of this order.

28 Orren, *Baderekh*, p. 124.

29 ISA FM2564/10, "A Report of the Minister's Visit to Ramle on 12 July 1948," written by Shitrit on 13 July and sent to the Prime Minister and other senior Cabinet ministers on 14 July 1948.

30 ISA FM2564/10, Foreign Minister to Minority Affairs Minister, 13 July 1948. The essence of Shertok's letter was appended by Shitrit to his report of 13 July on his visit to Ramle.

31 KMA-PA 142 – 3, General Staff/Operations to Operation Dani headquarters 23:30 hours, 12 July 1948. See also Orren, *Baderekh*, p. 124.

32 See Guttman, *"Lod Yotzet Lagolah"*, *Mibifnim*, XIII, No. 3 (November 1948). Guttman's memoir is the only evidence I have found relating to this "negotiation." *Mibifnim* was a publication of the Kibbutz Me'uhad, to which Guttman's kibbutz, Na'an, belonged. The Kibbutz Meuhad's kibbutzim were the mainstay of the Palmah, including the 3rd Battalion. Guttman, no doubt, imposed self-censorship (and the editor may, in addition, have imposed external censorship) on his account, both because of party political considerations and considerations of national interest. The account, while valuable, is autobiographical and impressionistic.

33 KMA-PA 141 – 516, Operation Dani headquarters to General Staff/ Operations, 13 July 1948; KMA-PA 141 – 597, Operation Dani headquarters to Yiftah, Kiryati and 8th brigades, 13 July 1948; and KMA-PA 142 – 133, Operation Dani headquarters to Kiryati Brigade, 13 July 1948.

34 KMA-PA 141 – 173, Operation Dani headquarters to Yiftah Brigade headquarters, 13 July 1948.

35 HHA-ACP 10.95.10 (6), Aharon Cohen to Yigal Allon, 12 October 1948, and Allon to Cohen, 31 October 1948; JEM LXXXII/1, Winifred A. Coate (Amman) to "Mabel," 30 July 1948; and KMA-AZP 9/9/3, text of Zisling's statement at the Cabinet meeting of 21 July 1948.

36 See Guttman, *"Lod Yotzet Lagolah"*, *Mibifnim*, XIII, No. 3 (November 1948).

37 KMA *Tsaror Michtavim*, a Kibbutz Meuhad publication, 5 August 1948.

38 *Sefer Hapalmah* II, p. 718; *Be'einei Oyev*, p. 36; and Sir John Glubb, *A Soldier with the Arabs*, p. 162.

39 KMA-PA 142 – 51, untitled, undated, printed report on Operation Dani, signed "Yigal." The signature and the content indicate authorship by Allon, and soon after the operation.

40 DBG-YH II, p. 589, entry for 15 July 1948.

41 HHA 5.20.5 (4), protocols of the meeting of the Kibbutz Artzi Council, 10–12 December 1948, speech by Ya'ari, 12 December 1948.

42 The capture of Suba and Khirbet Deir 'Amr is sketchily described in *Sefer Hapalmah* II, pp. 580–1.

43 Major Avraham Eilon (ed.), *Hativat Givati Mul Hapolesh Hamitzri* (The Givati Brigade Opposite the Egyptian invader), pp. 226–8 and 254.

44 ISA FM2427/1, statements by Naif Halif, headmaster of the school at Jaba, and

Muhammad Zayada, a teacher at the Jaba school, and Majid Haj Salah and Ali Muhammad Hanuti, elders of Ijzim, made on 30 July 1948, probably to IDF interrogators; ISA FM2427/1, Israel Ginsburg, OC POWs Department, Central POW Camp No. 1, to IDF General Staff, Operations, 15 September 1948; ISA FM2427/1, "Statement by POW No. 10004, Ibrahim al Mahdi, of Ijzim," 17 September 1948; ISA FM2427/1, Harkabi to Shertok, 17 September 1948; and ISA FM2426/12, Shertok to Acting Mediator Ralph Bunche, 28 September 1948. A brief IDF account of the battle is in *Toldot Milhemet Hakomemiut*, pp. 252–4.

45 ISA FM2426/11, Eytan to Paul Mohn, Political Adviser to the Chief of Staff, United Nations headquarters Observer Group, Haifa, 8 September 1948; NA 501 BB. Palestine/8-248, Kuniholm (Beirut) to Secretary of State, 2 August 1948, and message from Bernadotte to Azzam Pasha, 29 July 1948.

46 ISA FM2426/11, Count Bernadotte to Shertok, 9 September 1948, enclosing a copy of the 8 September United Nations report, signed by General W. E. Riley, acting chairman of the Central Truce Supervision Board.

47 ISA FM2426/12, Shertok to Bunche, 28 September 1948; and ISA FM2426/13, Bunche to Shertok, 14 November 1948.

48 *Hativat Givati mul Hapolesh Hamitzri*, pp. 364–8.

49 Jewish National Fund files 501–4, "The Events of 11 August – 11 September 1948," from the diary of Israel Livertovsky, of the Mekorot water company, 15 September 1948; and *Hativat Hanegev Bama'arachah* (The Negev Brigade during the War), p. 83.

50 KMA-PA 120/1/bet – 36, "Daily Report for 27–28 September 1948," 1st Battalion Intelligence Officer, 28 September 1948; KMA-PA 120/1/bet – 34, "Daily Report for 24 September 1948," by 1st Battalion Intelligence Officer, 25 September 1948; KMA-PA 120 – 21, Yiftah Brigade headquarters/Operations to 1st Battalion, 30 September 1948; Jewish National Fund files 501–4, "Events of 14 September–12 October 1948," from the diary of Israel Livertovsky; KMA-PA 120/1/bet – 39, "Daily Report for 1 October 1948," 1st Battalion Intelligence Offier, undated; KMA-PA 120/1/bet – 42, "Daily Report for 4 October 1948," 1st Battalion Intelligence Officer, undated; and KMA-PA 120/3/bet – 71, "Police actions of our [3rd Battalion] armoured column in cooperation with an armoured column of the First Battalion over 1–3 October 1948."

51 ISA FM2564/10, Shimoni to the (Foreign Ministry) Political Department, 10 October 1948; and ISA FM2564/9, Arye Farda (Dorot), Ya'acov Gavri (Nir-Am) and Eliezer Frisch (Ruhama) to the Prime Minister, 4 August 1948.

7 The fourth wave

1 DBG-YH III, pp. 788–9, entry for 31 October 1948; and CZA A246-14, p. 2512, entry for 31 October 1948.

2 HHA 66.90 (1), protocol of the meeting of the Political Committee of Mapam, 21 October 1948.

3 Protocol of the Israel Cabinet meeting of 26 September 1948; ISA FM2570/11,

Danin to Sasson (Paris), 24 October 1948; and DBG-YH III, p. 759, entry for 21 October 1948.

4 DBG-YH III, pp. 788–9, entry for 31 October 1948.

5 ISA FM2564/10, Shimoni to the management of Peltours, 26 October 1948; and CZA A246-14, p. 2511, entry for 29 October 1948, and p. 2512, entry for 31 October 1948.

6 PRO FO371-68690 E14041/11366/31, acting consul-general Beaumont (Jerusalem) to Foreign Office, 30 October 1948; *Sefer Hapalmah* II, p. 646; and *Sefer Hapalmah* II, p. 656, "In the Hebron Hills" by "Aviva R."

7 Weitz, *Diary* III, p. 348, entry for 25 October 1948; and *Hativat Hanegev Bama'aracha*, pp. 166–7.

8 Weitz, *Diary* III, p. 348, entry for 25 October 1948; ISA FM2401/21 aleph, "Protocol of the Meeting of the Ministerial Committee for Abandoned Property," 5 November 1948; DBG-YH III, p. 780, entry for 27 October 1948; and HHA-ACP 10.95.10 (6), notes (handwritten, by Aharon Cohen) from the meeting of the Political Committee of Mapam, 11 November 1948.

9 KMA-PA 109/daleth – 132, "Intelligence Daily Report No. 18," Intelligence Officer, Yiftah Brigade, 2 November 1948; "Intelligence Summary No. 41 for 29 October 1948," Intelligence Officer, Southern Front headquarters, 30 October 1948; "An Estimate Summary of Enemy Forces Around Bethlehem," Intelligence Officer, 4th Battalion, 29 November 1948; "Intelligence Summary No. 43 for 31 October 1948," Intelligence Officer, Southern Front headquarters, 1 November 1948; PRO FO371-68689 E13642/11366/31, Kirkbride (Amman) to Foreign Office, 21 October 1948; and PRO CAB21-1922, Kirkbride (Amman) to Foreign Office, 25 October 1948.

10 DBG-YH III, p. 807, entry for 10 November 1948; KMA-AZP 6/6/4, Kaplan to Pra'i, 8 November 1948.

11 KMA-PA 124 – 77, Allon to Sadeh, 3 November 1948.

12 HHA-ACP 10.95.10 (6), notes (handwritten, by Aharon Cohen) from the meeting of the Political Committee of Mapam, 11 November 1948; and HHA 66.90 (1), protocol of the meeting of the Political Committee of Mapam, 11 November 1948.

13 *The Times* (London), 6 November 1948, a report from Paris, dated 5 November.

14 NA Record Group 84, US Consulate General Jerusalem, Classified Records 800 – Palestine, Burdett (Jerusalem) to Secretary of State, 16 November 1948.

15 ISA FM2401/21 aleph, "Protocol of the Meeting of the Ministerial Committee for Abandoned Property," 5 November 1948; and Weitz, *Diary* III, p. 349, entry for 29 October 1948.

16 KMA-PA 109/daleth – 129, "Daily Intelligence Report No. 17," Intelligence Officer, Yiftah Brigade, 28 October 1948.

17 KMA-PA 109/daleth – 132, "Daily Intelligence Report No. 18," Intelligence Officer, Yiftah Brigade, 2 November 1948.

18 HHA-ACP 10.95.10 (6), notes (handwritten, by Aharon Cohen) from the meeting of the Political Committee of Mapam, 11 November 1948.

19 NA 501 BB. Palestine/11-1648, Patterson (Cairo) to Secretary of State, 16 November 1948.

20 DBG-YH III, pp. 788–9, entry for 31 October 1948; ISA FM2401/21 aleph, "Protocol of the Meeting of the Ministerial Committee for Abandoned Property," 5 November 1948; and NA 501 BB. Palestine/11-448, Keeley (Damascus) to Secretary of State, 4 November 1948.

21 Weitz, *Diary* III, p. 353, entry for 6 November.

22 Elias Shoufani, "The Fall of a Village," p. 113.

23 ISA MAM302/114, "Villages that Surrendered and [Villages that] Conquered [after Resistance] Outside the State of Israel," 17 November 1948. The list does not include any of the villages – all Muslim – from which the population fled before the IDF arrived or some of the Muslim villages which did not surrender and from which the remaining inhabitants were expelled (such as Saliha and Sa'sa). Nor does it include some of the Christian and Druse villages that surrendered (such as Kafr Bir'im, Iqrit, Hurfeish, etc.). But it gives an idea about the inter-relationship between surrender and staying put, and resistance and depopulation in Operation Hiram.

24 ISA FM2570/11, Shimoni to Sasson (Paris), 12 November 1948.

25 ISA FM186/17, Shimoni to Eytan, "On Problems of Policy in the Galilee and on the Northern Border and on the Link between the Foreign Ministry and the Army Staff," 18 November 1948.

26 Nazzal, *Palestinian Exodus*, pp. 32–3; and ISA MAM299/78, M. Yitah, Minority Affairs Ministry office, Haifa, to the Minority Affairs Ministry, 16 May 1949.

27 Nazzal, *Palestinian Exodus*, pp. 89–90.

28 *Ibid.*, pp. 91–2.

29 See Shoufani, "The Fall of a Village," p. 121.

30 Nazzal, *Palestinian Exodus*, pp. 96–7; and *Toldot Milhemet Hakomemiut*, pp. 323, 324.

31 ISA FM2564/10, Faraj Diab Surur, the *mukhtar* of Eilabun, Father Yukha Daud Almualim and other priests of the village, to the Minority Affairs Minister, 21 January 1949.

32 ISA FM2563/22, Extraits d'une lettre de S. B. le Patriarche à S.E. Mgr Hakim, 8 November 1948; ISA FM2563/22, Hakim to Tuvia Arazi, Israel Embassy, Paris, 12 November 1948; ISA FM2564/18, Father Basilius Laham (Nazareth) to the Military Governor, Nazareth, 15 November 1948; ISA FM2564/10, six Eilabun notables to the Minority Affairs Minister, 25 January 1949; and ISA MAM302/80, six Eilabun notables to the Interior Minister, 21 January 1949.

33 ISA MAM302/80, the Minority Affairs Minister to Sulz, 28 November 1948; ISA MAM302/80, Sulz to Shitrit, 12 December 1948; ISA FM2564/18, Sulz to Headquarters Military Government, 30 December 1948; ISA FM2564/18, Yadin to the Foreign Ministry, 7 December 1948; and ISA FM2564/18, Shimoni to Yadin, 10 December 1948.

34 ISA MAM302/80, Zisling to the Prime Minister, the Minority Affairs Minister, the Interior Minister and the Justice Minister, 4 February 1949; and ISA MAM302/80, Shitrit to Ben-Gurion, 8 February 1949.

35 ISA MAM302/80, Minister of Police to Defence Minister, 18 April 1949; and ISA MAM302/80, Major Ezra Omer, adjutant to the Chief of Staff, to OC Northern Front, 23 May 1949.

36 ISA FM2563/22, "Mr Palmon's Commitment in the Name of the Government [of the State of Israel]," 10 June 1949.

37 HHA-ACP 10.95.10 (6), (handwritten notes by Aharon Cohen) from the meeting of the Political Committee of Mapam, 11 November 1948. At the meeting, Eliezer Bauer (Be'eri) of Kibbutz Hazorea, an aide of Labour Minister Bentov, described the IDF excesses in the Galilee as "Nazi acts." Galili's "review" of the IDF excesses in operations Hiram and Yoav was not exhaustive, and its detail was not recorded in the official protocol. Nazzal, *Palestinian Exodus*, p. 93–5, describes what happened in Safsaf. Many of the villagers fled in May 1948, under the impact of the fall of Arab Safad. Some or all later returned after ALA units garrisoned the village. The village was bombed on 29 October. Some villagers fled. Some died in the subsequent battle for the village. The IDF entered the village on 30 October. According to Nazzal's witnesses, the soldiers then raped four village women and blind-folded and executed "about 70" men. "The soldiers [then] took their bodies and threw them on the cement covering of the village's spring." Soldiers who subsequently reached the village assured the inhabitants who had remained that no harm would come to them and that those who had fled could return in safety to their homes. But the villagers had no faith in these assurances and fled to Lebanon. Nazzal's account of what happened at Safsaf in the main tallies with Galili's account, as jotted down by Aharon Cohen. But accounts of what happened at Sa'sa vary. Nazzal, *Palestinian Exodus*, pp. 95–6, quotes a witness as recalling that the villagers fled to Lebanon without a fight, after hearing of the fall of Safsaf and after the withdrawal of the local ALA garrison. Shoufani supports this. Galili spoke of killings and expulsion. Carmel, interviewed in early 1985, recalled that, soon after Sa'sa's capture, he had seen evidence of killings in the village. This is the only reference I have found to an atrocity at Saliha. Perhaps Galili (or Cohen) had confused the name of the village and was referring to the atrocity that had taken place in the Lebanese village of Hule, in which 34 villagers were murdered by IDF troops.

38 See Sayigh, *Palestinians*, p. 92.

39 Carmel, *Ma'arachot Tzafon*, pp. 275–6.

40 KMA-AZP 9/9/1, "Decisions of the Provisional Government," 7 November 1948; HHA 66.90 (1), protocol of the meeting of the Political Committee of Mapam, 11 November 1948; and DBG-YH III, p. 809, entry for 10 November 1948.

41 HHA 66.90 (10), protocol of the meeting of the Political Committee of Mapam, 11 November 1948; and HHA-ACP 10/95.10 (6), handwritten notes by Aharon Cohen from the meeting of the Political Committee of Mapam, 11 November 1948.

42 DBG-YH III, p. 820, entry for 12 November 1948; KMA-AZP 9/9/1, "Decisions of the Provisional Government," 14 November 1948; KMA-AZP 9/9/1, "Decisions of the Provisional Government," 17 November 1948; KMA-AZP 9/9/3, transcript of Zisling's statements in the Cabinet meeting of 17 November 1948; and DBG-YH III, p. 832, entry for 19 November 1948.

43 DBG Archives, DBG to the Attorney General, Ya'acov Schapira, 19 November 1948.

44 DBG-YH III, p. 835, entry for 21 November 1948. The diaries, pp. 835–6, reprint the text of the poem as well as the letter to Alterman, which compared the power of the poem's stanzas to that of an IDF armoured column.

45 KMA-AZP 9/9/1, "Decisions of the Provisional Government," 5 December 1948. The existence and findings of the Schapira probe have remained a well-kept state secret. The Schapira report is in ISA JM25/1/0 – but remains classified and closed to historians by order of the Israel State Archivist, a Special Ministerial Committee (consisting of Yitzhak Rabin, Moshe Arens and Avraham Sharir) and Israel's High Court of Justice.

46 DBG-YH III, p. 896, entry for 23 December 1948; and KMA-PA 34 – 3 aleph, "A Special Appendix to Operation Orders Operation Horev," by Yigal Allon, 17 December 1948. Weitz, incidentally, got wind of Ben-Gurion's anti-expulsion order to Avner concerning the Gaza Strip "refugee population" and sent Ben-Gurion a note questioning the decision. See CZA A246-14, pp. 2560–1, entries for 30–31 December 1948; and Yosef Weitz Papers, Weitz to Ben-Gurion 31 December 1948.

47 An exception, perhaps, should be made of villages, such as Mi'ilya, that had fields in Jewish-occupied areas. See Shoufani, "The Fall of a Village," pp. 116–18.

8 Clearing the borders

1 Segev, *1949, Ha'yisraelim*, p. 73; and ISA FM186/17, Shimoni to Eytan, "On Problems of Policy," 18 November 1948.

2 ISA FM186/17, Shimoni to Eytan, "On Problems of Policy," 18 November 1948.

3 DBG-YH III, p. 828, entry for 16 November 1948.

4 DBG-YH III, pp. 832–3, entry for 19 November 1948.

5 ISA FM2564/9, Shitrit to Ben-Gurion, 2 December 1948; and ISA MAM302/12, a report on Shitrit's visit on 20 November to Jish.

6 KMA-AZP 9/9/1, "Decisions of the Meeting of the Provisional Government," 24 November 1948; ISA FM2564/9, Shitrit to Ben-Gurion, 2 December 1948; and private information.

7 ISA MAM302/73, Weekly Report for week 25–30 November 1948, by Minority Affairs Ministry office, Safad; and ISA FM2564/9, Shitrit to Ben-Gurion 2 December 1948. Ben-Zvi in late 1949 wrote that all the Bir'im refugees at Rmaich were taken to Jish but that some 250–300 had returned to Rmaich because no housing was found for them in Jish. See ISA FM2570/1, Ben-Zvi to Ben-Gurion, 14 October 1949.

8 ISA FM2564/18, General Avner, to the Middle East Affairs Department, Foreign Ministry, 18 March 1949; ISA AM gimel/19/aleph (part 2), Major Rehav'am Amir, Military Governor of Western Galilee, to A. Hanuki, Agriculture Ministry, 13 December 1948; ISA AM gimel/19/aleph (part 2), the

mukhtar of Iqrit (at Ar Rama) to the Prime Minister, 19 June 1949; ISA AM gimel/19/aleph (part 2), Palmon to the Custodian of Absentees Property, 29 June 1949; ISA AM gimel/19/aleph (part 2), Aloni to Palmon, 5 July 1949; and ISA FM2563/22, "A Summary of a Conversation with the Bishop Hakim, 26 October 1949," by Dr Y. P. Cohen, 8 November 1949.

9 CZA KKL10, protocol of the Meeting of the JNF Directorate, 7 December 1948; Weitz, *Diary* III, p. 364, entry for 10 December 1948, p. 401, "Protocol of the Meeting of the Committee of Directorates of the National Institutions," 11 December 1948, and p. 399, "Protocol of the Meeting of the Committee of Directorates of the National Institutions," 10 December 1948; and ISA FM2401/21 aleph, Protocol of the Meeting of the Ministerial Committee for Abandoned Property, 17 December 1949; and Weitz, *Diary* IV, p. 4, entry for 2 January 1949.

10 ISA FM2401/21 aleph, Protocol of the Meeting of the Ministerial Committee for Abandoned Property, 31 December 1948.

11 ISA MAM1319/42, Yitah (Haifa) to Shitrit, 18 January 1949, Yitah to Major Rehav'am Amir, the Military Governor of Western Galilee, 18 January 1949, and Shitrit to Yitah, undated.

12 NA Record Group 84, Haifa Consulate, Classified Records, 350 – Political Affairs, 1949, "Report of an Interview with Representatives of the American Friends Service Committee," Thomas S. Bloodworth Jr., US vice-consul, Haifa, to Secretary of State, 7 June 1949, with enclosure: "Report on Evacuation of Residents from the Town of Tarshiha," by Charles Freeman (of the AFSC), 25 March 1949; and ISA FM2444/19, an unsigned complaint about expulsion of Palestinians from Shafa 'Amr, Tarshiha and Mi'ilya to the Foreign Ministry, 25 January 1949. The expellees complained that the troops had robbed them before pushing them across the border near Nablus. According to Minority Affairs Ministry official Giora Zeid, the 25 persons expelled from Mi'ilya were "suspected of . . . passing information to the enemy." See ISA MAM1319/40, Yitah (Haifa) to T. Ashbal, Secretary of the Minority Affairs Ministry, Tel Aviv, 14 March 1949.

13 ISA MAM1322/22, "Protocol of the Seventh Meeting of the Committee for Transferring Arabs from Place to Place," 21 January 1949; and ISA MAM1322/22, "Protocol of the Tenth Meeting of the Committee for Transferring Arabs," 20 March 1949. The inter-departmental committee, set up in November 1948, was chaired by Shitrit.

14 NA Record Group 84, Haifa Consulate, Classified Records 350 – Political Affairs, 1949, "Developments in Israeli Controlled Arab Sections of Galilee," Thomas S. Bloodworth Jr., US vice-consul, Haifa, to Secretary of State, 10 June 1949; and ISA FM2563/22, "A Report on the Visit of Archbishop Hakim to Tarshiha," undated, unsigned.

15 ISA MAM1322/22, "Protocol of the Third Meeting of the Committee for Transferring Arabs," 15 December 1948; ISA MAM297/59, a five-page proposal entitled "Transfer of Arab Population," unsigned and undated, possibly by Yosef Weitz and probably from December 1948; and ISA MAM308/38, Sulz to the Headquarters Military Government, 11 January 1949.

16 ISA MAM307 gimel/41, a report on a tour of Arab villages in the Galilee by a representative of the Muslim Department, Ministry of Religious Affairs, 15–17 December 1948; Kamen, *Aharei Ha'ason*, p. 32; ISA MAM302/97, Minority Affairs Ministry office, Nazareth, to Shitrit, 13 January 1949; DBG-YH III, p. 897, entry for 23 December 1948; ISA MAM1322/22, "Protocol of the First Meeting of the Committee for Transferring Arabs," 30 November 1948; ISA AM gimel/19/aleph (part 2), A. Hanuki to the directors of the Anglo-Palestine Bank, 23 February 1949 and A. Hanuki to the directors of the Anglo-Palestine Bank, 17 February 1949; and ISA AM aleph/19/aleph, "List of the Lands Leased for Cultivation for 1949/50 until 31 October 1949," Ministry of Agriculture.

17 See Kamen, *Aharei Ha'ason*, p. 32.

18 ISA FM2401/19, "Report of the Committee Probing the Problems of the Military Government and Its Future," 3 May 1949.

19 *Ha'aretz*, 7 August 1949; and ISA JM5667 gimel/25, "In the Name of the Oppressed," Sheikh Attiya Jawwad, to the Justice Minister, 9 June 1949.

20 ISA MAM302/99, director of IDF Intelligence Service 1 to the Minority Affairs Ministry, 28 January 1949; Kamen, *Aharei Ha'ason*, pp. 32–3; NA Record Group 84, Tel Aviv Embassy, Dec. #571, Classified Records 1949, Richard Ford (chargé d'affaires) to Secretary of State, 11 August 1949; *Ha'aretz*, 7 August 1949; ISA FM2570/1, Ben-Zvi to Ben-Gurion, 14 October 1949; and ISA AM591, "Protocol of a Meeting Regarding the Resettlement of the Arabs of Khisas, Qeitiya and Halahala," 5 October 1949.

21 ISA FM2402/29, Eytan to Sharett (New York), 4 December 1949.

22 Israel State Archives, *Documents On the Foreign Policy of Israel, Armistice Negotiations with the Arab States, December 1948 – July 1949*, vol. III, ed. Yemima Rosenthal, (henceforward *Documents III*), p. 725.

23 See, for example, ISA FM2433/4, Moshe Belhorn, Tiberias District headquarters Israel Police, to IDF, 5 August 1949.

24 ISA AM591, "Report on the Activities of the Authority [for the Resettlement of Arab Refugees inside Israel] Until the End of December, 1949," 5 January 1950, by A. Hanuki; ISA FM2433/5, Lt. Colonel Shaul Ramati to IDF Deputy Chief of Staff General Mordechai Makleff, 8 March 1951; ISA FM2433/5, Ramati to Makleff, Shiloah, etc., 1 April 1951; ISA FM2433/7, Middle East Affairs Department, Foreign Ministry, to Shiloah, 26 April 1951; ISA FM2433/6, unsigned, undated report, probably by IDF Intelligence Branch from April 1951; ISA FM2433/7, Middle East Affairs Department, Foreign Ministry, to Reuven Shiloah, 26 April 1951; and ISA FM2433/7, Colonel Bennett L. de Ridder, Acting chief of staff, United Nations Truce Supervision Organisation, to United Nations Secretary General Trygve Lie, 17 April 1951; ISA FM2434/4, Lt. Colonel Arye Shalev, IDF Staff Officer for Mixed Armistice Commissions, to IDF OC Operations, etc., 27 August 1953; and ISA FM2434/6, Captain Shlomo Reichman, Israel–Syria Mixed Armistice Commission, to IDF Staff Officer for Mixed Armistice Commissions, IDF Intelligence Branch, etc., 14 December 1954. See also E. L. M. Burns, *Between Arab and Israeli*, London, George Harrap, 1962, pp. 115–18.

25 *Documents III*, p. 257, Eytan (Rhodes) to Sharett, 20 February 1949; and *Ibid.*, p. 257, footnote 143/1.

26 *Ibid.*, pp. 702–3.
27 NA Record Group 84, Haifa Consulate, Classified Records 350 – Political Affairs 1949, Bloodworth, vice-consul, Haifa, to Secretary of State, 7 June 1949; ISA FM2431/1, Bunche to Shiloah, 4 March 1949; and ISA FM2477/3, Department for International Institutions, Foreign Ministry, to the Director General (Eytan), 13 March 1949. The Arab media alleged (wrongly) that "Men, women and children have been murdered in Faluja by the Jews" – the sort of wildly inaccurate charge that led western governments in 1948 to discount almost all reports from Arab sources about Israeli atrocities. See "All Palestine Government, Ministry of Foreign Affairs," 19 March 1949, in PRO FO371-75455.
28 ISA FM2431/1, Yadin to Shiloah (Rhodes), 4 March 1949.
29 ISA FM2425/7, Sharett to Dori, 6 March 1949.
30 Weitz, *Diary* III, pp. 343–4, entry for 22 September 1948 and p. 344, entry for 26 September 1948; DBG-YH III, p. 721, entry for 26 September 1948, and p. 931, entry for 6 January 1949; Weitz, *Diary* IV, p. 15, entry for 28 February 1949; and ISA MAM297/60, Y. Berdichevsky to Gad Machnes, 3 March 1949.
31 ISA FM2426/5, "Report of the HQ of [IDF] Southern Front on the Evacuation of the Villagers of Faluja to the Hebron Hills," by Major Amos Horev, 1 June 1949.
32 ISA FM2451/13, report on the meeting between Ben-Gurion and the PCC, 7 April 1949; NA Record Group 84, Tel Aviv Embassy, Classified Records 1949, 350 – Israel, McDonald to Secretary of State, 11 April 1949; NA Record Group 84, Tel Aviv Embassy, General Records 1949, 321.9 – Israel–Transjordan, McDonald to Secretary of State, 12 April 1949; NA Record Group 84, Tel Aviv Embassy, Classifed Records, McDonald to Secretary of State, 2 May 1949; and LPA 2-11/1/1, protocol of the Meeting of the Mapai Knesset Faction and Secretariat, statement by Sharett, 28 July 1949.
33 ISA FM2564/10, Shimoni to the Political Department, Foreign Ministry, 14 October 1948; and ISA FM2570/11, Shimoni to Sasson (Paris), 2 November 1948.
34 ISA FM2570/11, Shimoni to Sasson (Paris) 2 November 1948.
35 ISA MAM297/60, Berdichevsky to Machnes, 4 November 1948; and ISA MAM297/60, "Report of the Meeting with Beduin Sheikhs, 2 November 1948," by Michael Hanegbi, 5 November 1948.
36 CZA A246-14, p.2526, entry for 18 November 1948; DBG-YH III, p. 832, entry for 19 November; Weitz Papers, Weitz to Ben-Gurion, 19 November 1948; and ISA FM2570/11, Shimoni to Sasson (Paris), 23 November 1948.
37 DBG-YH III, pp. 844–5, entry for 25 November 1948; and Weitz, *Diary* III, p. 357, entry for 25 November 1948.
38 Weitz, *Diary* III, p. 359, entry for 30 November 1948; Weitz, *Diary* IV, p. 9, entry for 28 January 1949; and ISA MAM297/60, Berdichevsky to the Minority Affairs Ministry, 20 February 1949.
39 PRO FO371-75354 E14040/1017/31, Sir A. Cadogan (New York) to Foreign Office, 21 November 1949; PRO FO371-75354 E14040/1017/31, Foreign Office to UK Delegation to United Nations, 26 November 1949; PRO FO371-

75355, Sir Hugh Dow (Jerusalem) to Foreign Office, 24 November 1949; PRO
FO371-75355 E14136/1017/31, Kirkbride (Amman) to Foreign Office, 24
November 1949; and PRO FO371-75355, Knox Helm (Tel Aviv) to Foreign
Office, 24 November 1949.

40 ISA FM2402/12, "Information for the Israeli Missions Abroad: General
Riley's Statement on Expulsion of Beduins [and] Israel's Reaction," 22
September 1950.

41 ISA MAM1322/22, "Protocol of the Ninth Meeting of the Committee for
Transferring [Arabs]," 25 February 1949; and CZA A246-14, pp. 2584-5,
entry for 23 February 1949.

42 ISA FM2402/29, Zalman Lef (Lifshitz) to the Finance Minister, 15 June 1950;
ISA FM2402/12, "Information for the Israeli Missions Abroad: General
Riley's Statement on Expulsion of Beduins [and] Israel's Reaction," Israel
Foreign Ministry, 22 September 1950; Gabbay, *Political Study*, p. 294; and
Kamen, *Aharei Ha'ason*, p. 32.

43 NA 501 BB. Palestine/3-2349, Stabler (Amman) to Secretary of State, 23
March 1949; *Documents III*, pp. 468-74, Eytan to Sharett (New York), 23-24
March 1949; PRO FO371-75386 E3844/1095/31, Pirie Gordon to Foreign
Office, 24 March 1949; and PRO FO371-75386 E3824/1095/31, FO to UK
Embassy, Washington, 24 March 1949.

44 NA 501 BB. Palestine/3-2349, Stabler (Amman) to Secretary of State, 23
March 1949; *Documents III*, p. 473; PRO FO371-75386 E3824/1095/31, Pirie
Gordon to Foreign Office, 23 March 1949; and PRO FO371-75386 E3844/
1095/31, Pirie Gordon to Foreign Office, 24 March 1949.

45 PRO FO371-75424 E4458/1821/31, Dow to Foreign Office, 4 April 1949.

46 NA Record Group 84, Tel Aviv Embassy, General Records 1949, 321.9 –
Israel–Transjordan, Acheson to US Embassy, Tel Aviv, 4 April 1949; ISA
FM2431/4, "Secret: Intelligence Report," 19 April 1949, probably by Major
Yehoshafat Harkabi, Sharett's military aide; and NA Record Group 84, Tel
Aviv Embassy, General Records 1949, 321.9 – Israel–Transjordan, Mc-
Donald to Secretary of State, 12 April 1949.

47 NA Record Group 84, Tel Aviv Embassy, Classified Records 1949, 350 –
Israel, McDonald to Secretary of State, 26 April 1949.

48 LPA 2, 11/1/6, Sharett statement at "Meeting of the Secretariat of the [Mapai
Knesset] faction with our Cabinet Members," 26 April 1949.

49 LPA 2, 11/1/1, "Protocol of the Meeting of the Faction and the Secretariat,"
28 July 1949.

50 *Ibid.*

51 ISA FM2431/7, Captain Arye Friedlander (Shalev) to IDF Military Intelligence Branch (*Shin Mem 9*), 5 August 1949. The Transjordanians argued that
"the Mukhtar was a spokesman for the Israeli Government." The Israelis
concerned, including Sharett and Dayan, in internal correspondence almost
invariably referred to the 1,200–1,500 as "expellees" (*megorashim*). It is
probable that the *mukhtar* had been "advised" by the Israelis to order the
refugees to leave.

52 ISA FM2431/4, "Details About the Exodus of the 1344 Refugees who had

Lived in and around Baqa al Gharbiya," unsigned (possibly by Palmon, the Arab Affairs Adviser at the Prime Minister's Office), undated; ISA FM2431/4, Dayan to the Foreign Minister, 3 July 1949; and ISA FM2431/4, Dayan to the Minister of Defence, the IDF Chief of Staff, 30 June 1949.

53 ISA FM2431/7, "Special Committee Meeting Held at Mandelbaum Gate – 1100 hrs 10 August 1949," Ramati to IDF Intelligence Branch; and NA 501. BB. Palestine/8-1549, Burdett (Jerusalem) to Secretary of State, 15 August 1949.

54 ISA FM2431/7, Dayan to the Foreign Minister, Palmon, etc., 11 August 1949; and ISA FM2431/7, Friedlander to Dayan, 26 August 1949.

55 NA Record Group 84, Tel Aviv Embassy, Classified Records 1949, 321.9 – Israel, Burdett (Jerusalem) to Secretary of State, 17 September 1949.

56 ISA MAM307/44, A. Bergman, the Interior Ministry, to "the Government Committee for Settling Dispossessed Arabs," 16 March 1949; ISA MAM307 gimel/44, the Interior Ministry official in charge of the Jerusalem District to the Government Committee for the settlement of Arab refugees (inside Israel), 22 March 1949; Weitz, *Diary* IV, p. 69, entry for 14 January 1950; ISA AM2166 gimal/642, "Report on the Health Situation in the Village of Zakariya, 14 February 1950"; and ISA FM2402/11, Palmon to the British Commonwealth Department, Foreign Ministry, 18 October 1950.

9 Solving the refugee problem

1 ISA FM2431/13 "The Arab Refugee Problem," Michael Comay and Zalman Lifshitz, 16 March 1949.

2 ISA FM2447/2, Eytan to de Boisanger (Lausanne), 25 May 1949. De Boisanger reportedly months earlier had independently arrived at the same position. See PRO FO371-75346 E39/1017/31, H. Beeley to H. Ashley Clarke (Paris), 4 January 1949.

3 NA 501 BB. Palestine/3-2849, Mark Ethridge (Beirut), the American member of the PCC, to Secretary of State, 29 March 1949.

4 NA Record Group 84, Jerusalem Consulate, Classified Records 1948, 800 – Israel, Burdett to Secretary of State, 23 December 1948.

5 PRO FO371-75417 E263/1821/31, minute by C. Waterlow on "Resettlement of Arab Refugees," 5 January 1949 and minute on it by F. B. A. Rundall, 11 January 1949.

6 NA 501 BB. Palestine/1-2149, American Legation, Jidda to Secretary of State, 21 January 1949.

7 NA 501 BB. Palestine/2-549, Burdett to Secretary of State, 5 February 1949, and NA 501 BB. Palestine/2-949, Burdett to Secretary of State, 9 February 1949. Burdett was no friend of the Zionist enterprise and was highly critical of Israeli policies (often clashing over them with McDonald).

8 NA 501 BB. Palestine/2-849, Burdett to Secretary of State, 8 February 1949, and NA 501 BB. Palestine/2-849, Ethridge to Secretary of State, 8 February 1949.

9 NA 501 BB. Palestine/2-2849, Ethridge to Acheson, 28 February 1949; NA 501 BB. Palestine/3-2949, Ethridge (Beirut) to Secretary of State, 29 March

1949; NA 501 BB. Palestine/3-1449, Ethridge (Jerusalem) to Secretary of State, 14 March 1949; NA 501 BB. Palestine/3-1449, Ethridge (Jerusalem) to Dean Rusk (Washington), 14 March 1948; and NA 501 BB. Palestine/3-1649, Satherthwaite, Director of Office of Near Eastern and African Affairs, State Department, to Secretary of State, 16 March 1949.

10 NA 501 BB. Palestine/3-2249, "Memorandum of Conversation," 22 March 1949.

11 NA 501 BB. Palestine/3-2949, Ethridge and McGhee (Beirut) to Secretary of State, 29 March 1949.

12 ISA FM2447/3, "Protocol of A Consultative Meeting Concerning the Peace Negotiations with the Arab States, 12 April 1949."

13 NA 501 BB. Palestine/4-549, "Memorandum of Conversation," 5 April 1949, New York.

14 Weitz, *Diary* IV, p. 11, entry for 11 February 1949; and ISA FM2444/19, Shertok to Weitz, Lifshitz and Danin, 14 March 1949.

15 ISA FM2451/13, "Meeting of the PCC and Ben-Gurion," 7 April 1949; and ISA FM2447/1, "The Meeting of the Conciliation Commission with Ben-Gurion," 7 April 1949.

16 PRO FO371-75349 E4281/1017/31, Houstoun Boswall (Beirut) to Foreign Office, 1 April 1949.

17 ISA FM2444/19, PCC communiqué, Beirut, 5 April 1949.

18 ISA FM2447/3, "Protocol of Consultative Meeting in Advance of Lausanne," 19 April 1949; and ISA FM2444/19, "Note on the Arab Refugee Problem," Leo Kohn to Gershon Hirsh and Sharett, 24 April 1949.

19 ISA FM2447/3, "Protocol of Consultative Meeting in Advance of Lausanne," 19 April 1949.

20 NA 501 BB. Palestine/4-1949, Ethridge (Jerusalem) to Acheson, 19 April 1949, and NA 501 BB. Palestine/4-2049, Ethridge (Jerusalem) to Secretary of State, 20 April 1949.

21 NA 501 BB. Palestine/4-2049, Acheson to Ethridge, 20 April 1949, and NA 501 BB. Palestine/4-2949, Truman to Ethridge, 29 April 1949.

22 NA 501 BB. Palestine/4-2949, Acheson to Certain American Diplomatic and Consular Officers, 29 April 1949.

23 ISA FM2447/7, memorandum on Walter Eytan press conference at Lausanne, 30 April 1949; ISA FM2447/6, Eytan to Sharett, 30 April 1949; and ISA FM2447/6, Hirsh to Sharett, 1 May 1949.

24 ISA FM2447/2, Eytan (Tel Aviv) to Sharett (New York), 10 April 1949.

25 ISA FM2451/13, "Sharett-Abdullah Conversation, 5 May 1949"; Israel State Archives, *Documents on the Foreign Policy of Israel, May–December 1949* Vol. IV, ed. by Yemima Rosenthal, (henceforward *Documents IV*), pp. 33–7, "Meeting: M. Sharett–King Abdullah (Shuneh, 5 May 1949)," a memorandum, 9 May 1949, by Moshe Sharett; and ISA FM2447/1, Eytan to Sharett, 21 June 1949.

26 ISA FM2444/19, "Extract from a Letter by Mohammad Nimr al Hawari to ..." undated; and ISA FM2447/13, Sasson (Lausanne) to Sharett, 17 August 1949.

27 ISA FM2447/6, Eytan (Lausanne) to Sharett, 9 May 1949.

28 ISA FM2444/19, "Mr A. Eban's Statement on the Arab Refugee Question Before the Ad Hoc Political Committee at Lake Success on 5th May 1949 in Connection with Application of Israel for Admission to Membership in the United Nations."

29 NA 501 BB. Palestine/5-1649, Acheson to US Legation, Amman, 16 May 1949.

30 NA 501 BB, Palestine/5-1949, Acheson to Ethridge, 19 May 1949.

31 ISA FM2444/19, Eban (New York) to Eytan (Lausanne), 24 June 1949.

32 ISA FM2451/13, Truman to Ben-Gurion, 29 May 1949.

33 ISA FM2447/6, Eytan (Lausanne) to Sharett, 13 June 1949; ISA FM2447/6, Eytan to Eban (New York), 9 June 1949; ISA FM2414/26 aleph, Gideon Rafael to Eban, 22 June 1949; and ISA FM2447/2, Eytan to Sharett, 13 June 1949.

34 ISA FM2444/19, Kollek to Sharett, 10 June 1949.

35 ISA FM174/2 aleph, Sharett to Eytan, 15 March 1949.

36 ISA FM2447/3, "Protocol of A Consultation at the Prime Minister's Office on the Arab Refugee Problem, 12 April 1949."

37 NA 501 BB. Palestine/4-1349, Ethridge to Acheson, 13 April 1949, and NA 501 BB. Palestine/4-2049, Ethridge to Acheson, 20 April 1949; and ISA FM2447/6, Eytan (Lausanne) to Sharett, 30 April 1949.

38 ISA FM2447/3, "Protocol of a Consultative Meeting Concerning Peace Negotiations with the Arab States, 19 April 1949."

39 ISA FM2447/3, "Protocol of A Consultative Meeting Concerning Peace Negotiations with the Arab States (Lausanne), 22 April 1949."

40 ISA FM2447/6, Eytan (Lausanne) to Sharett, 30 April 1949. In contacts with Israelis, Ethridge's estimate of the number of refugees in the Strip tended to be on the low side, the better to sell the plan to Tel Aviv. The usual American estimate at this time was 225,000.

41 NA 501 BB. Palestine/5-949, Ethridge to Acheson, 9 May 1949.

42 *Documents IV*, p. 10, "Editorial Note."

43 NA 501 BB. Palestine/5-2049, Ethridge to Secretary of State, 20 May 1949, and NA 501 BB. Palestine/5-3149, McDonald to Secretary of State, 31 May 1949; ISA FM2447/2, "Memorandum transmitted by the PCC to the Arab delegations summarizing proposals made by Israel on May 20," 23 May 1949; ISA FM2447/1, Eytan to de Boisanger, 29 May 1949; and ISA FM2447/2, Eytan to de Boisanger, 31 May 1949.

44 NA 501 BB. Palestine/5-2849, Ethridge to Secretary of State, 28 May 1949; and *Documents IV*, pp. 74–5, W. Eytan (Lausanne) to C. de Boisanger, 29 May 1949.

45 NA 501 BB. Palestine/5-2849, Acting Secretary of State James Webb to US Delegation, Lausanne, 28 May 1949; and *Documents IV*, pp. 72–3, G. Rafael (New York) to M. Sharett, 27 May 1949. Rafael wrote: "[State] Department (my guess [Dean] Rusk) doubts sincerity our offer accept Gaza refugees, believes that after annexation Strip [Israel] will have [the refugees] leave like Faluja Pocket inhabitants."

46 NA 501 BB. Palestine/6-249, Ethridge to Secretary of State, 2 June 1949.

47 NA Record Group 84, Tel Aviv Embassy, Classified Records 1949, 321.9 –
    Israel–Transjordan, Burdett (Jerusalem) to Secretary of State, 16 June 1949,
    reporting on a conversation with Dayan, then Military Governor of
    Jerusalem. The head of the opposition Revisionist camp, Menachem Begin,
    was also unenthusiastic about the plan. See NA Record Group 84, Tel Aviv
    Embassy, Classified Records 1949, 321.9 – Israel, "Memorandum of Con-
    versation" between Ambassador McDonald, First Secretary Knox and
    Begin, in Tel Aviv, 14 June 1949.
48 NA 501 BB. Palestine/5-3149, McDonald (Tel Aviv) to Secretary of State, 31
    May 1949; NA 501 BB. Palestine/6-2349, McDonald to Secretary of State, 23
    June 1949; NA 501 BB. Palestine/6-149, Ross (US Delegation to United
    Nations) to Secretary of State, 1 June 1949; NA 501 BB. Palestine/6-149,
    Webb to Ethridge, 1 June 1949; NA 501 BB. Palestine/6-1049, Ross to
    Secretary of State, 10 June 1949; PRO FO371-75350 E6832/1017/31, Helm
    (Tel Aviv) to Foreign Office, 2 June 1949; NA 501 BB. Palestine/6-249,
    Ethridge to Secretary of State, 2 June 1949; NA 501 BB. Palestine/6-1249,
    Ethridge (Paris) to Secretary of State, 12 June 1949; NA 501 BB. Palestine/6-
    2249, "Memorandum of Conversation" between Webb, Ethridge, Eban,
    Shiloah and others, in Washington, on 17 June 1949; NA 501 BB. Palestine/6-
    2249, McDonald (Tel Aviv) to Secretary of State, 22 June 1949; and PRO
    FO371-75350 E7011/1017/31, Sir O. Franks (Washington) to Foreign Office,
    6 June 1949.
49 NA 501 BB. Palestine/6-1249, Ethridge (Paris) to Secretary of State, 12 June
    1949.
50 For the British interest in the Gaza Strip's future, see H. Beeley memoran-
    dum of 9 July 1949, in PRO FO371-75350 E8393/1017/3. A dominant school
    of thought in the Foreign Office explained Israel's acceptance of the Gaza
    Plan as motivated by the Israeli need for cheap Arab labour: Israel, contrary
    to its public protestations, argued the British officials, wanted the return of a
    substantial number of refugees. The British Ambassador to Tel Aviv, Knox
    Helm, wrote on 10 June 1949: "My objective reasoning leads me to the
    conclusion that the Israelis never wanted the Arabs to leave and that, in spite
    of their propaganda, they wish in their innermost hearts that they had them or
    many of them back . . . The Arabs provided cheap and good labour . . . the
    Jews, in spite of all their publicity, do not take to farming . . . Thus Israel
    seems to me to need the Arabs. But it would want them as the tillers of the soil,
    the hewers of wood and the drawers of water." William Strang, the
    Permanent Under-Secretary of State, in a minute on 7 July, endorsed Helm's
    conclusions: "The Israelis' offer to accept the refugees in the Gaza area must,
    as you say, reflect a feeling on the part of Israel that she can make some use of
    these Arabs. It seemed at the time unlikely that the Gaza Strip in itself would
    be worth the price of looking after the refugees if they were to be a complete
    burden." See Helm (Tel Aviv) to Michael Wright (Foreign Office), 10 June
    1949, and William Strang minute of 7 July 1949, in PRO FO371-75429 E7465/
    1821/31. Even Hugh Dow, the British Consul General in Jerusalem, agreed,
    though he took issue with Helm about what had happened in 1948. He wrote

to Wright that "it cannot be sustained that 'the Israelis never wanted the Arabs to leave.' . . . The immediate advantages to the Jews of the Arab migration are patent enough. It offered an unexpected solution to the security problem . . . it gave them new lands for Jewish settlement; it offered a great alleviation of the housing problem created by the influx of new immigrants" and so on. But Dow then agreed with Helm that the Jewish leadership now – mid-1949 – was having second thoughts and saw that the "wholesale expulsion of the Arabs was great mistake . . . Helm's remarks about the poverty of Jewish agriculture are illuminating." Dow agreed that the Jews now wanted a substantial return of refugees to place the Jewish economy "on a sound basis" of cheap labour. See PRO FO371-75432 E8231, Dow to Wright, 27 June 1949.

51 *Documents IV*, p. 86, E. Sasson (Lausanne) to M. Sharett, 1 June 1949.

52 NA 501 BB. Palestine/6-1049, "Memorandum of Conversation" between Acting Secretary of State James Webb and other American officials and Egyptian Ambassador to Washington Kamil Abdul Rahim, Washington, 10 June 1949; and PRO FO371-75350 E8393/1017/31, memorandum by Michael Wright on his talk on 1 July 1949, at Lausanne, with Ray Hare, the acting US representative to the PCC, 1 July 1949.

53 *Documents IV*, pp. 186-7, W. Eytan (Lausanne) to M. Sharett, 30 June 1949, and p. 187 footnote 3.

54 *Documents IV*, p. 204, A. Eban (New York) to M. Sharett, 4 July 1949, and p. 204 footnote 1.

55 NA 501 BB. Palestine/6-2249, McDonald (Tel Aviv) to Secretary of State, 22 June 1949; NA 501 BB. Palestine/6-2549, Acheson to US Embassy, Tel Aviv, 25 June 1949; NA Record Group 84, Tel Aviv Embassy, Classified Records 1949, 321.9 – Israel–Egypt, Acheson to US Embassy, Tel Aviv, 2 July 1949.

56 NA 501 BB. Palestine/7-649, W. Austin, US representative to the United Nations, to Secretary of State, 6 July 1949; and NA 501 BB. Palestine/7-649, Acheson to US Delegation to United Nations, 6 July 1949.

57 PRO FO371-75350 E8707, British Embassy, Washington DC, to Eastern Department, Foreign Office, 12 July 1949; and NA 501 BB. Palestine/7-749, "Memorandum of Conversation," (Eban, McGhee and Hare), Washington DC, 7 July 1949.

58 ISA FM3749/2, Sasson (Lausanne) to Ziama Zeligson (Shmuel Divon) (Tel Aviv), 16 June 1949; and ISA FM2447/6, Eytan to Sharett, 30 July 1949.

59 PRO FO371-75350 E8393/1017/31, "Suggested Basis for a New Approach by the Conciliation Commission to the Parties on their Resumption of Work on the 18th of July," Eastern Department, Foreign Office, 9 July 1949.

60 NA 501 BB. Palestine/7-1349, Acheson to US Embassy, London, 13 July 1949; PRO FO371-75350 E8636/1017/31, Hoyer Millar, UK Embassy, Washington DC, to Foreign Office, 14 July 1949; and NA 501 BB. Palestine/6-1249, Ethridge (Lausanne) to Secretary of State, 12 June 1949.

61 PRO FO371-75350 E8636/1017/31, Foreign Office to UK Embassy, Washington, 16 July 1949; and PRO FO371-75350 E8704/1017/31, Sir J. Troutbeck (BMEO Cairo) to Foreign Office, 16 July 1949.

62 PRO FO371-75351 E9059/1017/31, A. Mayall, UK Embassy, Cairo, to G.L. Clutton, African Department, Foreign Office, 19 July 1949.

63 NA Record Group 84, Tel Aviv Embassy, Classified Records 1949, 321.9 – Israel–Egypt, Acheson to US Embassy, Tel Aviv, 19 July 1949; NA 501 BB. Palestine/7-2049, Rockwell (Lausanne) to Secretary of State, 20 July 1949; NA Record Group 84, Tel Aviv Embassy, Classified Records, 1949, 321.9 – Israel–Egypt, Acheson to US Embassy, Tel Aviv, 22 July 1949; and NA Record Group 84, Tel Aviv Embassy, Classified Records 1949, 321.9 – Israel–Egypt, Acheson to US Embassy, Tel Aviv, 29 July 1949.

64 ISA FM2447/1, M. Sharett to E. Sasson (Lausanne), 21 August 1949.

65 ISA FM2447/2, "Guidelines for the Missions (briefing No. 3) the Foreign Minister's Briefing to the Delegation to Lausanne," 25 July 1949; ISA FM2447/5, Sharett to Shiloah and Sasson (Lausanne), 7 August 1949; Weitz, *Diary* IV, p. 42, entry for 27 July 1949; LPA 2-11/1/1, Sharett's statement at meeting of Mapai Secretariat and parliamentary faction, 28 July 1949; ISA FM2447/6, Eytan to Sharett, 30 July 1949; and NA 501 BB. Palestine/7-2849, "Memorandum of Conversation," (Elath, McGhee, Rusk, etc.), Washington DC, 28 July 1949.

66 NA 501 BB. Palestine/8-149, Acheson to US Embassy, Tel Aviv, 1 August 1949; NA 501 BB. Palestine/8-149, Acheson to US Embassy, London, 1 August 1949; and NA 501 BB. Palestine/9-1949, Patterson (Cairo) to Secretary of State, 19 September 1949.

67 NA 501 BB. Palestine/5-2849, Ethridge to Secretary of State, 28 May 1949.

68 NA Record Group 84, Tel Aviv Embassy, Classified Records 1949, 321.9 – Israel–Transjordan, Burdett (Jerusalem) to Secretary of State, 16 June 1949; NA Record Group 84, Tel Aviv Embassy, Dec. #571, Classified Records, 1949, McDonald to Secretary of State, 31 May 1949; NA 501 BB. Palestine/5-2449, McGhee (Washington) to McDonald, 24 May 1949; NA 501 BB. Palestine/6-249, Ethridge (Lausanne) to Secretary of State, 2 June 1949; and NA 501 BB. Palestine/7-1349, McDonald to Secretary of State, 13 July 1949. See also PRO FO371-75436 E9822/1821/31, British Legation, Tel Aviv, to Eastern Department, Foreign Office, 5 August 1949, for a report on alleged Israeli preparations to take back refugees.

69 NA 501 BB. Palestine/6-1449, Acting Secretary of State Webb to US Delegation, Lausanne, 14 June 1949; and NA 501 BB. Palestine/6-1549, Ethridge to Rusk, 15 June 1949.

70 NA 501 BB. Palestine/6-1249, Ethridge (Lausanne) to Secretary of State, 12 June 1949; and NA 501 BB. Palestine/6-1549, Ethridge to Dean Rusk, 15 June 1949.

71 ISA FM2444/19, Arthur Lourie (New York) to Esther Herlitz (Tel Aviv), 6 July 1949.

72 *Documents IV*, p. 150, A. Eban (New York) to M. Sharett, 22 June 1949.

73 ISA FM3749/2, E. Sasson (Lausanne) to Z. Zeligson, 16 June 1949.

74 ISA FM2451/17, "Press Release No. 1" by the Information Services of the Government of Israel Foreign Press Division, 7 July 1949; and ISA FM2451/17, "An Extract from Information to the Israeli Missions Abroad," undated.

75 See, for example, PRO F0371-75350 E8707/1821/31, UK Embassy, Washington, to Eastern Department, Foreign Office, 12 July 1949.

76 *Documents IV*, pp. 154–5, W. Eytan (Lausanne) to M. Sharett, 23 June 1949.

77 ISA FM2451/13, a précis of a letter from Sasson (Paris) to Shertok (Tel Aviv), 13 August 1948.

78 ISA FM2447/3, "Protocols of the Consultative Meeting in Advance of the Lausanne Conference, Tel Aviv," 12 April 1949.

79 *Documents IV*, p. 176, M. Sharett to A. Eban (New York), 25 June 1949.

80 *Documents IV*, p. 206, "Editorial Note," and p. 207, M. Sharett to A. Eban (New York), 6 July 1949.

81 ISA FM2444/19, "Guidelines to the Missions Abroad, Briefing No. 3, the Foreign Minister's Briefing to the Lausanne Delegation," 25 July 1949.

82 NA Record Group 84, Tel Aviv Embassy, Classified Records 1949, 321.9 – Palestine Conciliation Commission, McDonald to Secretary of State, 20 July 1949. See also PRO F0371-75425 E5343/1821/31, Marriott (Haifa) to Foreign Office, 28 April 1949; and PRO F0371-75434 E9296/1821/31, Colin Crowe, UK Embassy, Tel Aviv, to B. A. B. Burrows, Eastern Department, Foreign Office, 19 July 1949, for President Weizmann's reference already in April to a return of "100,000." Perhaps it was thought that the number would have nostalgic appeal for President Truman, who in 1946 had demanded that Britain let into Palestine "100,000" World War II Jewish refugees; it was also a round, tidy number, not too small to be dismissible as insignificant.

83 Weitz, *Diary* IV, p. 42, entry for 27 July 1949.

84 *Documents IV*, pp. 211–12, A. Eban (New York) to M. Sharett, 8 July 1949, and p. 218, A. Lourie and G. Rafael (New York) to M. Sharett, 12 July 1949.

85 NA 501 BB. Palestine/7-2649, Acheson to US Delegation, Lausanne, 26 July 1949.

86 *Documents IV*, p. 227, A. Lourie (New York) to M. Sharett, 19 July 1949, and p. 257, A. Eban (New York) to M. Sharett, 27 July 1949.

87 NA 501 BB. Palestine/7-2849, "Memorandum of Conversation," (Elath, Rusk, McGhee, etc.), Washington DC, 28 July 1949; NA 501 BB. Palestine/7-2849, Porter (Lausanne) to Secretary of State, 28 July 1949; and NA 501 BB. Palestine/7-2849, McDonald (Tel Aviv) to Secretary of State, 28 July 1949.

88 ISA FM2447/1, Shiloah (Lausanne) to Sharett, 10 August 1949.

89 ISA FM2412/26, Sharett to M. Eliash, Israel Minister to London, 10 August 1949; ISA FM1444/19, Eban (New York) to Elath (Washington), 26 July 1949; and NA 501 BB. Palestine/8-149, Acheson to US diplomatic posts, 1 August 1949.

90 LPA 2-11/1/1, Protocol of the meeting of the party Knesset Faction and the Secretariat, 28 July 1949.

91 ISA FM2451/13, text of Sharett's speech in the Knesset, 1 August 1949; and LPA 2-11/1/1, Protocols of the Special Meeting of the Mapai Secretariat and Knesset Faction, 1 August 1949.

92 ISA FM2451/13, Sharett to Shiloah (Lausanne), 2 August 1949; and ISA FM2412/26, Sharett to Eliash (London), 10 August 1949.

93 ISA FM2412/26, Sharett to Eliash (London) 10 August 1949; and ISA

FM2447/5, Sharett to Shiloah and Sasson (Lausanne), 7 August 1949.

94 ISA FM2412/26, Sharett to Eliash (London), 10 August 1949; ISA FM2447/5, Sharett to Shiloah and Sasson (Lausanne), 7 August 1949; and DBG-YH III, p. 993, entry for 14 July 1949.

95 NA 501 BB. Palestine/8-149, Acheson to United States diplomatic posts, 1 August 1949.

96 ISA FM2447/4, "United Nations Conciliation Commission for Palestine: Fourth Progress Report to the Secretary General of the United Nations," 15 September 1949; NA 501 BB. Palestine/8-349, Porter (Lausanne) to Secretary of State, 3 August 1949; NA 501 BB. Palestine/8-549, Porter (Lausanne) to Secretary of State, 5 August 1949; NA 501 BB. Palestine/8-1649, Rockwell (Lausanne) to Secretary of State, 16 August 1949; NA Record Group 84, Tel Aviv Embassy, Classified Records 1949, 571 – Palestine Refugee Relief, Burdett (Jerusalem) to Secretary of State, 4 August 1949; NA Record Group 84, Tel Aviv Embassy, Classified Records 1949, 321.9 – Israel, Burdett (Jerusalem) to Secretary of State, 12 August 1949; NA Records Group 84, Tel Aviv Embassy, Classified Records 1949, 321.9 – Israel, Richard Ford (chargé d'affaires, Tel Aviv) to Secretary of State, 9 August 1949; NA Record Group 84, Tel Aviv Embassy, Classified Records, Dec. #571, 1949, Ford (Tel Aviv) to Secretary of State, 11 August 1949; and NA 501 BB. Palestine/8-1949, Ford (Tel Aviv) to Secretary of State, 19 August 1949.

97 NA Record Group 84, Tel Aviv Embassy, Classified Records 1949, 321.9 – Israel, Porter (Lausanne) to Secretary of State, 3 August 1949 and Acheson to Porter (Lausanne), 9 August 1949; NA 501 BB. Palestine/8-1149, Acheson to US Delegation, Lausanne, 11 August 1949; and NA 501 BB. Palestine/8-1849, "Memorandum of Conversation," with Elath, McGhee and Wilkins among the participants, in Washington on 18 August 1949.

98 ISA FM2451/13, Sharett to Shiloah (Lausanne), 10 August 1949; and NA Record Group 84, Tel Aviv Embassy, Classified Records 1949, 321.9 – Israel, Acheson to US Embassy, Tel Aviv, 16 August 1949.

99 ISA FM2444/19, "Terms of Reference of the Technical Committee on Refugees," 14 June 1949; and ISA FM2447/4, "Report of the Technical Committee on Refugees to the Conciliation Commission," 20 August 1949.

100 ISA FM2447/5, "Report of Conversation Between Abe Feinberg and Paul Porter," 18 August 1949, by A[rthur] L[ourie]; ISA FM2447/4, "Terms of Reference of the Economic Survey Mission," 1 September 1949; and ISA FM2447/4, "United Nations Conciliation Commission for Palestine: Fourth Progress Report to the Secretary General of the United Nations," 15 September 1949.

Conclusion

1 HHA-ACP 10.95.13 (1), "The Emigration of the Arabs of Palestine in the period 1.12.1947–1.6.1948," IDF Intelligence Department, 30 June 1948.

2 Aharon Cohen, no enemy of the Arabs, in this regard at the time quoted two observations. An English sergeant told an American newsman on the day of

Jaffa's surrender: "The Arabs were frightened to death when they imagined to themselves that the Jews would do to them half of what they would have done to the Jews were the situation reversed"; and an educated Haifa Arab said, according to Cohen: "The Arabs always thought that they [themselves] were a primitive, wild and uncivilized people, capable of anything while the Jews [they thought] were a civilized people, able to restrain their impulses; but in face of the Deir Yassin atrocity, [the Arabs] began to think that this was not exactly the picture. And because at that time [April] the Jews were winning the military struggle, the flight began," in HHA-ACP 10.95.11 (8), "Nochah Hapinui ha'Aravi" (In face of the Arab evacuation), by Aharon Cohen, written in late May and published in *Ahdut Ha'avodah* in June, 1948.

3 HHA-ACP 10.95.13 (1), "The Emigration of the Arabs of Palestine in the Period 1.12.1947–1.6.1948," IDF Intelligence Department, 30 June 1948.

Appendix I

1 For example, ISA FM2451/13, Comay to the PCC Technical Committee on Refugees, 24 July 1949; and ISA FM2444/19, Sharett to Elath (Washington), 31 July 1949.

2 Gabbay, *Political Study*, p. 175. Gabbay himself (p. 177) estimated that the total number was 710,000.

3 PRO FO371-75419 E2297/1821/31, McNeil response to question on 16 February 1949 by Brigadier Rayner.

4 CZA A340/24, Eytan to Daniel Sirkis (*Hatzofe*), 10 November 1950.

5 ISA FM2564/22, Arthur Lourie to Eytan, 11 August 1948.

6 ISA FM2444/19, Sharett to Elath (Washington), 31 July 1949.

7 ISA FM2564/22, Shimoni to Eytan, 25 August 1948 (with minute by Shertok), and Shimoni to Shertok, 2 September 1948.

8 ISA FM2444/19, Dr H. Meyuzam, to Asher Goren, the Political Department of the Foreign Ministry, 2 June 1949.

9 PRO FO371-75436 E10083/1821/31, Foreign Office to UK Delegation to the United Nations (New York), 2 September 1949.

Bibliography

Primary sources

David Ben-Gurion Archives (DBG Archives), Sdeh Boqer, Israel

Central Zionist Archives (CZA) Jerusalem, Israel – papers of the Political Department of the Jewish Agency, protocols of the meetings of the Jewish Agency Executive and of the Jewish National Fund Directorate, Eliezer Granovsky Papers, manuscript notebooks of Yosef Weitz diary, etc.

Sir Alan Cunningham Papers (CP) – (Middle East Centre Archives, St Antony's College, Oxford)

Hashomer Hatzair Archives (HHA) – (Givat Haviva, Israel) papers of the Kibbutz Artzi, Mapam (Political Committee, Mapam Centre protocols), Aharon Cohen Papers (HHA-ACP), Meir Ya'ari Papers, etc.

Histadrut Archive (Va'ad Hapoel Building, Tel Aviv)

Archive of Ihud Hakibbutzim Vehakvutsot (Kibbutz Hulda)

Israel State Archives (ISA) Jerusalem – state papers of the Agriculture Ministry (AM), Foreign Ministry (FM), Justice Ministry (JM), Minority Affairs Ministry (MAM), Prime Minister's Office (PMO)

Jabotinsky Institute (JI) Tel Aviv – papers of the IZL, LHI, Revisionist Movement and Herut Party

Jerusalem and East Mission Papers (JEM) – (Middle East Centre Archives, St Antony's College, Oxford)

Kibbutz Meuhad Archives (KMA) – (Efal, Israel) papers of the Kibbutz Meuhad (protocols of meetings of the movement and Ahdut Ha'avodah institutions), Aharon Zisling Papers (KMA-AZP), Palmah Archive (KMA-PA)

Labour Archives (LA) – (Histadrut – Lavon Institute, Tel Aviv)

Labour Party Archives (LPA) – (Beit Berl, Israel)

National Archives (NA) – (Washington DC) State Department Papers

Public Record Office (PRO) – (London) papers of the Cabinet Office (CAB), Colonial Office (CO), Foreign Office (FO) and War Office (WO)

Yosef Weitz Papers (at the Institute for Settlement Research, Rehovot)

Individual kibbutz archives – Mishmar Ha'emek, Ma'anit, etc.

Municipal archives in Israel – Haifa (HMA), Tiberias

Bibliography

Interviews

Yigael Yadin, Yitzhak Ben-Aharon, Yehoshua Palmon, Ya'acov Shimoni, Moshe Carmel, Eliezer Be'eri (Bauer), Binyamin Arnon, Aharon Bar-Am (Brawerman)

Published primary sources

Begin, Menachem, *Bamahteret, Ketavim* (In the Underground, Writings and Documents), 4 vols., Tel Aviv, Hadar, 1959

Ben-Gurion, David, *Behilahem Yisrael* (As Israel Fought), Tel Aviv, Mapai Press, 1952

   Medinat Yisrael Hamehudeshet (The Resurgent State of Israel), 2 vols; Tel Aviv, Am Oved, 1969

   Yoman Hamilhama, 1948–1949 (DBG-YH) (The War Diary, 1948–1949), 3 vols., ed. by Gershon Rivlin and Elhannan Orren, Tel Aviv Israel Defence Ministry Press, 1982

Israel State Archives/Central Zionist Archives, *Te'udot Mediniot Ve'diplomatiyot, December 1947–May 1948* (Political and Diplomatic Documents, December 1947–May 1948), ed. by Gedalia Yogev, Jerusalem, Israel Government Press, 1980

Israel State Archives, *Te'udot Lemediniut Hahutz shel Medinat Yisrael, 14 May–30 September 1948* (Documents on the Foreign Policy of the State of Israel, May–September 1948), Vol. I, ed. by Yehoshua Freundlich, Jerusalem, Israel Government Press, 1981

Israel State Archives, *Te'udot Lemediniut Hahutz shel Medinat Yisrael, October 1948–April 1949* (Documents on the Foreign Policy of the State of Israel, October 1948–April 1949), Vol. II, ed. by Yehoshua Freundlich, Jerusalem, Israel Government Press, 1984

Israel State Archives, *Te'udot Lemediniut Hahutz shel Medinat Yisrael, Sihot Shvitat-Haneshek im Medinot Arav, December 1948–July 1949* (Documents on the Foreign Policy of the State of Israel, Armistice Negotiations with the Arab States, December 1948–July 1949), Vol. III, ed. by Yemima Rosenthal, Jerusalem, Israel Government Press, 1983

Israel State Archives, *Te'udot Lemediniut Hahutz shel Medinat Yisrael, May–December 1949* (Documents on the Foreign Policy of Israel, May–December 1949), Vol. IV, ed. by Yemima Rosenthal, Jerusalem, Israel Government Press, 1986

Weitz, Yosef, *Yomani Ve'igrotai Labanim* (My Diary and Letters to the Children), Vols. III and IV, Tel Aviv, Massada, 1965

Secondary works

Assaf, Michael, *Toldot Hit'orerut Ha'aravim Be'eretz Yisrael U'brihatam* (The History of the Awakening of the Arabs in Palestine and Their Flight), Tel Aviv, Tarbut Vehinuch, 1967

366

Avidar, Yosef, "Tochnit Dalet (Plan D)", in *Sifra Veseifa* No. 2, June 1978

Banai (Mazal), Ya'acov, *Hayalim Almonim, Sefer Mivtze'ei Lehi* (Unknown Soldiers, the Book of LHI Operations), Tel Aviv, Hug Yedidim, 1958

Be'einei Oyev, Shelosha Pirsumim Arvi'im al Milhemet Hakomemiut (In Enemy Eyes, three Arab publications on the War of Independence), Israel Defence Forces, General Staff/History Branch, Tel Aviv, IDF Press – Ma'arachot, 1954. The book, translated into Hebrew by Captain S. Sabag, is composed of lengthy excerpts from Mohammed Nimr al Khatib, *Min Athar al Nakba*, Camel Ismail al Sharif, *Al Ihwan al Muslemin fi Harb Falastin* and Mohammed Ghussan, *Ma'arak Bab al Wad*

Begin, Menachem, *The Revolt*, London, W.H. Allen 1964

Bentov, Mordechai, *Yamim Mesaprim* (Days Tell), Tel Aviv, Sifriyat Hapoalim, 1984

Carmel, Moshe, *Ma'arachot Tzafon* (Northern Battles), Tel Aviv, IDF Press– Ma'arachot, 1949

Carta's Atlas of Palestine From Zionism to Statehood ed. by Jehuda Wallach, Jerusalem, Carta, 1972, 1974

Carta's Historical Atlas of Israel, The First Years 1948–1961 ed. by Jehuda Wallach and Moshe Lissak, Jerusalem, Carta, 1978

Cohen, Aharon, *Yisrael Ve'ha'olam Ha'aravi* (Israel and the Arab World), Tel Aviv, Sifriyat Hapoalim, 1964

Eshel, Zadok, *Hativat Carmeli Bemilhemet Hakomemiut* (The Carmeli Brigade in the War of Independence), Tel Aviv, Ma'arachot – IDF Press, 1973

Ma'arachot Hahaganah Be'Haifa (The Haganah Battles in Haifa), Tel Aviv, Ministry of Defence Press, 1978

Gabbay, Rony, *A Political Study of the Arab–Jewish Conflict: The Arab Refugee Problem (a Case Study)*, Geneva, Librairie E. Droz, and Paris, Librairie Minard, 1959

Glubb, Sir John, *A Soldier with the Arabs*, London, Hodder and Stoughton, 1957

Hativat Hanegev Bama'arachah (The Negev Brigade during the War), Tel Aviv, IDF Press–Ma'arachot, c.1950

Hativat Givati Bemilhemet Hakomemiut (The Givati Brigade in the War of Independence) ed. and compiled by Avraham Eilon, IDF Press – Ma'arachot, 1959

Hativat Givati mul Hapolesh Hamitzri (The Givati Brigade Opposite the Egyptian Invader), ed. by Major Avraham Eilon, Tel Aviv, IDF Press – Ma'arachot, 1963.

Hativat Alexandroni Bemilhemet Hakomemiut (The Alexandroni Brigade in the War of Independence) ed. by Gershon Rivlin and Zvi Sinai, Tel Aviv, IDF Press – Ma'arachot, 1964

Ilan Va'shelah, Derekh Hakravot shel Hativat Golani (Tree and Sword, the Route of Battle of the Golani Brigade) ed. and compiled by Binyamin Etzioni, Tel Aviv, IDF Press – Ma'arachot, c.1951

Israel Defence Forces, General Staff History Branch, *Toldot Milhemet Hako-memiut* (History of the War of Independence), Tel Aviv, IDF Press – Ma'arachot, 1959

Itzchaki, Arieh, *Latrun, Hama'aracha al Haderekh Leyerushalayim* (Latrun, the Battle for the Road to Jerusalem), 2 vols., Jerusalem, Cana, 1982

Kamen, Charles, *"Aharei Ha'ason: Ha'aravim Be'medinat Yisrael, 1948–1950"* ("After the Catastrophe: the Arabs in the State of Israel"), in *Mahbarot Lemehkar U'lebikoret* (Notebooks on Research and Criticism) No. 10, 1985

Kimche, Jon and David, *Both Sides of the Hill*, London, Secker and Warburg, 1960

Lazar (Litai), Haim, *Kibush Yaffo* (The Conquest of Jaffa), Tel Aviv, Shelah, 1951

Lorch, Netanel, *The Edge of the Sword, Israel's War of Independence, 1947–1949*, revised ed., Jerusalem, Massada Press, 1968

Mishmar Ha'emek Ba'ma'aracha (Mishmar Ha'emek in the War), Tel Aviv, Sifriyat Poalim, 1950

Morris, Benny, "The Crystallization of Israeli Policy Against a Return of the Arab Refugees: April–December 1948," *Studies In Zionism*, 6, 1 (Spring 1985), 85–118

"The Causes and Character of the Arab Exodus from Palestine: The Israel Defence Forces Intelligence Branch Analysis of June 1948," *Middle Eastern Studies*, 22, 1 (January 1986), 5–19

"Yosef Weitz and the Transfer Committees, 1948–49," *Middle Eastern Studies*, 22, 4 (October 1986), 522–61

"The Harvest of 1948 and the Creation of the Palestinian Refugee Problem," *The Middle East Journal*, 40, 4 (Autumn 1986), 671–85

"Operation Dani and the Palestinian Exodus from Lydda and Ramle in 1948," *The Middle East Journal*, 40, 1 (Winter 1986), 82–109

"The Initial Absorption of the Palestinian Refugees in the Arab Host Countries, 1948–1949", forthcoming in *Refugees in the Age of Total War: Europe and the Middle East*, London.

Nazzal, Nafez, *The Palestinian Exodus from Galilee, 1948*, Beirut, The Institute for Palestine Studies, 1978

Niv, David, *Ma'arachot Ha'irgun Hatz'va'i Ha'leumi* (Battles of the IZL), 6 vols., Tel Aviv, Klausner Institute, 1980

Orren, Elhannan, *Baderekh el Ha'ir, Mivtza Dani* (On the Road to the City, Operation Dani), Tel Aviv, IDF Press – Ma'arachot, 1976

Pa'il, Meir, *Min Ha'Haganah Letzva Haganah* (From the Haganah to the Israel Defence Forces), Tel Aviv, Zmora, Bitan, Modan, 1979

Peretz, Don, *Israel and the Palestine Arabs*, Washington DC, The Middle East Institute, 1958

Porath, Yehoshua, *The Emergence of the Palestinian–Arab National Movement 1918–1929*, London, Frank Cass, 1974

The Palestinian Arab National Movement 1929–1939, London, Frank Cass, 1977

Sayigh, Rosemary, *Palestinians: From Peasants to Revolutionaries*, London, Zed Press, 1979

Sefer Toldot Hahaganah (The History of the Haganah), 3 vols. sub-divided into eight books, ed. by Shaul Avigur, Yitzhak Ben-Zvi, Elazar Galili, Yehuda Slutzky, Ben-Zion Dinur and Gershon Rivlin, Tel Aviv, Am Oved, 1954–73.

Sefer Hapalmah (The Book of the Palmah), 2 vols., ed. and compiled by Zerubavel
    Gilad together with Mati Megged, Tel Aviv, Kibbutz Meuhad Press, 1956
Segev, Tom, *1949 Ha'yisraelim Harishonim* (1949, The First Israelis), Jerusalem,
    Domino 1984
Shaltiel, David, *Yerushalayim Tashah* (Jerusalem 1948), Tel Aviv, Defence
    Ministry Press, 1981
Shimoni, Ya'acov, *Arviyei Eretz Yisrael* (The Arabs of Palestine), Tel Aviv, Am
    Oved, 1947
Shoufani, Elias, "The Fall of a Village," *Journal of Palestine Studies*, 1, 4 (1972),
    108–21
Teveth, Shabtai, *Ben-Gurion and the Palestine Arabs*, Oxford, Oxford University
    Press, 1985.

Index